PUBLIC HISTORY:
An Introduction

edited by
Barbara J. Howe
Emory L. Kemp
West Virginia University

ROBERT E. KRIEGER PUBLISHING COMPANY
MALABAR, FLORIDA
1986

Original Edition 1986

Printed and Published by
ROBERT E. KRIEGER PUBLISHING COMPANY, INC.
KRIEGER DRIVE
MALABAR, FL 32950

Printed in the United States of America

Library of Congress Cataloging-in-Publication Data
Main entry under title:

Public History

1. Public history—Addresses, essays, lectures.
2. History—Vocational guidance—Addresses, essays,
lectures. I. Howe, Barbara J. II. Kemp, Emory Leland.
D16.163.P83 1986   902.3′73   85-23665
ISBN 0-89874-881-X

10   9   8   7   6   5   4   3   2

CONTENTS

ACKNOWLEDGEMENTS

We were cautioned that involving more than thirty authors in producing the first book on public history could be a difficult endeavor. We are happy to report that the team approach has worked very well and resulted in a collection of essays which simply could not have been produced by a single author. In a very real sense it is the essayists' book and we wish to acknowledge their contributions. Their staunch support of the enterprise has been most welcome. We are very grateful to many who have served as advisers throughout the project and thus have done more than write one of the essays. Particularly, we would like to thank Heather Huyck for all her assistance in compiling the list of authors.

Our colleague, John Luchok, the university editor of the West Virginia University Office of Publications, has served as our copy editor and we are most grateful for the cheerful and professional manner in which he handled this assignment. Many memoranda have been sent addressed to "Pat, Page, and Mike" with the request that they review yet another batch of essays. Their reviews were most helpful to us and we believe to the authors. This was certainly an act of supererogation on the part of dedicated public historians and we are greatly indebted to our consulting editors Patricia Mooney Melvin, Associate Professor of History and Director of the Public History Program, University of Arkansas at Little Rock; Page Putnam Miller, Executive Director, National Coordinating Committee for the Promotion of History; and Michael Scardaville, Associate Professor of History and Director of the Public History Program, University of South Carolina.

In the wake of modern computer technology the entire text of the book was entered on floppy discs only to reappear in the form of letter quality prints. This work was handled with aplomb by Jean Losh, Jina Secreto, and Mike Brantmeyer. We would also like to thank Cyndee Harrington and Lilly Moody of the West Virginia University Department of History and Chris Tarabrella of the College of Arts and Sciences Dean's Office who provided cheerful assistance throughout the process of teaching us how to use the computers. Cathy Pack, Dolores Fleming, and all the work-study students in the Department of History provided valuable assistance in clearing up last minute details.

It has been a joy to work with Mary Roberts of Robert E. Krieger Publishing Company, Inc. She has given enthusiastic support throughout the project and we value her counsel. It is extraordinary to have a publisher who will contract to publish a book on the basis of a prospectus, outline, and a couple of professional resumes only. We are, thus, most grateful for this vote of confidence.

Finally, a special thanks to Janet Kemp who, in one way or another, was involved in all aspects of this book and made significant contributions to our efforts, especially when we were trying to meet deadlines. We have come, perhaps unfairly, to rely on her for all our joint ventures.

INTRODUCTION

To many, history as a discipline is central to a liberal education because it preserves a memory of civilization from ancient times and interprets who and what we are as a society. The past, however, is not history but rather provides the data with which history can be written, and thus, the historian is not just an antiquarian or chronicler of past events, but an interpreter of the past. Therefore, the validity of any history rests upon the historian's ability to evaluate evidence from the past and put it in a comprehensible narrative. These insights are obtained by digging around in archives, libraries, reading letters and other manuscript material, and occasionally seeking information from artifacts and monuments of the past. Although one is seldom given the opportunity to see historians at work, their activities can be fascinating intellectual enterprises as they raise challenging questions, test hypotheses, proceed along an interesting trail only to find it is a dead end, and test historical points which may seem to be in conflict with each other. Because few understand what historians do as professionals, it is little wonder that many believe that historians just assemble facts in chronological order and then expect them to speak for themselves. In *Public History: An Introduction* the reader will obtain not only a picture of what public historians do for a living in a wide range of positions, but how they go about investigating their source material and writing history.

Historians are, however, more than just chroniclers or mere evaluators of historic facts, because they maintain a literary tradition which cherishes narrative history written with elegance and free from jargon. In the past, this tradition emphasized the great themes in political and diplomatic history. Recently, however, historians have paid increasing attention to social history and to specialized fields such as the history of science and women's history, as well as to the area of public history where the tradition continues.

Being firmly rooted in academia, traditional historians also have a major commitment to teaching in addition to writing history. This involves educating future generations of historians as well as sharing the importance of the past in the light of the present with legions of students as part of their liberal education. Thus, historically conscious members of the public have been educated through lectures, seminars, and courses at universities and colleges as well as reading published histories in books and journal articles.

For decades, a select number of historians have made careers outside academia in a variety of positions which demanded the skills of a historian in research and writing and, perhaps most important of all, the insights and attitudes historians could bring to bear on subjects with a historical dimension. These careers included professional positions in libraries, museums, historical societies, government service, and increasingly with private corporations. Heretofore those employed in positions serving the public directly were relatively small in number and widely

1

dispersed. They hardly constituted a new movement within history that required the development of a national organization, offering of specialized courses on "applied" history or indeed the name *public history*. The situation has, however, changed markedly in the past few years. Many new positions outside academia have been established which require the services of historians. These opportunities have accelerated at just the time when the rapid expansion in higher education had become a faded memory. As a result faculty positions were in short supply, with attendant decreases in enrollments because history students sensed that there were few career opportunities in academia. The new nonacademic positions included not only the more traditional occupations mentioned above, but entirely new opportunities in fields such as historic preservation. Thus, conditions were right for those employed in public history to seek a common identity.

The term *public history* defies precise definition and has been used to mean applied as well as professional or even entrepreneurial history. Nevertheless, the movement has spawned a national organization and the establishment of a growing number of programs and courses devoted to the subject. These programs and courses have appeared in the context of history departments where they offered bright prospects of increasing sagging enrollments, while at the same time causing consternation amongst many historians about the "nature of the beast" and whether indeed it is even "history."

While other branches of history have their own introductory literature, there has been no succinct source that students, faculty members, guidance counsellors, or those interested in the field can consult to learn about public history and the wealth of opportunities open to them. *Public History: An Introduction* is expected to fill this need. It is intended for graduate and advanced undergraduate students in public history programs where it can be used in an introductory course and for those interested in exploring this new field through self-study. The book also focuses on the concerns of professionally educated historians and the means of imparting a sense of history to the various public bodies which they serve.

Unlike teaching and research in the traditional fields of history, public history by its very nature is a multidisciplinary activity, demanding a team approach to projects which have well-defined and often limited objectives. The program of the Historic American Engineering Record provides a good example of the team approach to recording historic sites. In the course of three summers, a team of historians, architects, and engineers recorded the most significant engineering and industrial sites in West Virginia. Although not called public historians, this is precisely the role the project historians were playing on the recording team. We have used this team approach with our students on a wide variety of projects as well as in the classroom. It is the same approach we have used in producing this, the first text on public history.

The field is wide-ranging and consists of a complex web of interrelated activities carried on by professionals representing many disciplines.

Thus, we were convinced that the best approach to use in producing an introductory book in this new field was to invite selected experts to prepare essays on topics which constitute the field at the moment. Space did not permit us to include every permutation of public history, as, for example, we have excluded "traditional" fields for history majors such as journalism, law, and foreign service careers. Nor have we included documentary film making, although certainly historians often have a vital role in that activity. Each essay emphasizes the ways in which a historian's education and perspective on problems relate to his or her work in public history. The essays are not, therefore, just a recording of one's daily routine, but are intended to include a broad perspective on the range of activities involved in each professional position.

These essays present a number of important projects in public history around the country as case studies, and they focus on the issues which we and the team of authors feel are most important. Thus, the book does not claim to be definitive, but rather to be a comprehensive view of the field and to give insights into opportunities for those contemplating careers in the field.

Each aspect of the field, such as historic preservation, archival management, museology, or editing, has its own rich literature, but this wealth of information has not previously been distilled for classroom purposes into one volume. In addition, there are still no satisfactory introductory texts on some aspects of public history, and little historiographical material for public historians on such subjects as techniques of site recording (for instance, what are the primary sources that make up the history of a site one is recording through the use of drawings, photographs, etc.?).

Public History: An Introduction, like Caesar's Gaul, or a well-crafted sermon, is divided into three parts. Part I consists of an essay by Leslie H. Fishel, jr., in which he defines the field of public history and its relationship to traditional history as practiced in academia. If this book were a conference, Fishel's essay would be the keynote address. It raises serious issues about public history and its relationship to the discipline of history which the reader should keep in mind while reading the other essays in the book. It is hoped that this essay will also lead to a lively debate on the role public history plays as a distinct part of a well-established discipline. In quite a different vein, Gerald George's essay is really a situation comedy with a serious message. It relates the perils enthusiastic converts to public history may very well face on their first attempts to bring the "gospel of public history" to a public not always receptive to new ideas.

In order to impart to the reader an idea of the rich variety of activities which constitute the practice of public history, a series of essays by various specialists form Part II of the book. Each of the essayists describes the relationship of his or her subject to the field of public history and the range of activities a historian may expect to discover in working in the subject area. The subjects include archival management; oral history; editing public records, letters, and manuscripts; editing contemporary journals and books; and the role of historians in libraries. Also in Part II are essays on historic preservation and industrial archeology, which have come to constitute a broader range of opportunities for public historians, especially since federal involvement in historic preservation grew after the passage of the 1966 National Historic Preservation Act. The final essay in this section deals with historic site interpretation, an area that historians may too often criticize as inadequate or naive without being aware of the opportunities and constraints placed on those trying to convey complex ideas to visitors at historic sites.

The practice of public history is explored in Part III in a series of essays dealing with historians working in local, state, and federal museums and in an analogous way with historical and learned societies at the local, state, and national levels. A set of essays examines the role of historians in government, both in civilian and military agencies. Because of their long-term commitment and the level of involvement, two essays have been prepared on the public historian in the National Park Service, a federal agency. The third part concludes with a pair of essays on public history and public policy and with two essays on the historian in the world of business. One of these deals with the role of the public historian in a large corporation and the other with a small firm specializing in public history.

The concluding section is intended to be more than just a summary of the essays, but rather to provide the reader with guidance for further information in the field through a bibliographic essay by Ted J. Ligibel on utilizing library resources, together with a specially prepared directory of resources and organizations for those public historians engaged in research and writing. Thus, the material included in the appendices has been provided to make the book a reference work or source book on public history as well as an introductory overview.

It seems apparent from the foregoing essays that public history has now reached a level of development in the United States that makes it a serious factor to be considered in curriculum development in history departments across the nation. Recent surveys indicate that there are now more than seventy-five institutions offering programs or courses, and the movement appears to be spreading. In addition, there is a growing constituency of people who are attracted to public history and could profit from extramural short courses, workshops, and seminars. Thus, the idea for a book on public history was born in response to a strongly felt need. We hope that this collection of essays will help to advance the professional and public aspects of the time-honored discipline of history.

PART I:
AN OVERVIEW OF
PUBLIC HISTORY

INTRODUCTION

Public history as a new field of endeavor for historians has now reached a level of development in the United States where a detailed discussion of just what is meant by the term "public history" and its relationship to the more general and traditional term "history" is in order. This is a difficult but necessary assignment which is presented here with the felicity and vision of one who has served with distinction as both a traditional and a public historian.

The birth of a new field within an academic institution is nearly always accompanied by labor pains affecting both mother and child. The birth of public history as a defined, vigorous, unconventional activity for historians is no exception. Leslie H. Fishel, jr., skillfully weaves his essay around the rise and present flourishing state of public history and its relationship to academic historians. While not raising the strident voice of a revolutionary, he does not gloss over the sources of current tensions which have developed. Thus, this essay is crucial in a debate on the meaning and future of public history.

Such important issues as whether this reformation movement constitutes a new professionalism within the discipline of history and hence will remain safely within the folds of traditional history departments or whether the present zeal will result in the formation of separate public history programs need to be given serious consideration. It is just these issues which are succinctly presented in this keynote paper. It sets the context into which the other seemingly disparate essays can be viewed as a developing sense of the breadth and depth of public history.

Like John Bunyan's *Pilgrim's Progress*, Gerald George's essay might well be described as "delivered under the similitude of a dream." It is a cautionary tale of a latter-day Christian entering Vanity Fair. In George's tale the hero meets entrenched tradition and those representing the power structure of the local community in the form of prominent families in his attempt to implement more enlightened policies and purposes in a community museum. It would be presumptuous to compare the holy writ with this collection of essays, but one wonders if the hero of public history might not have benefited greatly from having a copy of this book during his progress through the world of public history. The tale is thought-provoking not only for recently minted public historians but for all who attempt to bring a balanced view of history to the public.

Leslie H. Fishel, jr., received his A.B. from Oberlin College and his A.M. and Ph.D. from Harvard University. He served as director of the State Historical Society of Wisconsin from 1959 to 1969 before becoming president of Heidelberg College in Tiffin, Ohio. He left Heidelberg in 1980 to become director of the Rutherford B. Hayes Presidential Center. He co-edited three editions of The Black American: A Documentary History *with Benjamin Quarles and has published in scholarly journals. Fishel has served as a member of the Governing Council of the American Association for State and Local History, as a member of the Council of the National Endowment for the Humanities, and as a member of the Board of Trustees of the Ohio Historical Society, in addition to his work with local historical societies and museums in Ohio. He is an Adjunct Professor of History at Bowling Green State University, teaching courses in historical agency administration.*

PUBLIC HISTORY AND THE ACADEMY

Leslie H. Fishel, jr.

Public history is an old-timer. It goes back at least to the mid-nineteenth century and the fortitude and foresight of Lyman C. Draper, the first secretary of the State Historical Society of Wisconsin, and his successor, Reuben Gold Thwaites. Draper recognized the value of a wide range of historical resources, although he never could bring himself to use them. He merely collected them, by stealth or strategem, and created a scholars' gold mine. Thwaites was a full-time historical society director, a founder of the Mississippi Valley Historical Society (predecessor to the Organization of American Historians), and editor of such monumental works as *Jesuit Relations* and *Early Western Travels*. Both men were highly respected as historians.[1]

But changes came, as changes do. Later archivists, editors, and museum curators did not earn the status accorded to the earlier giants. In the late 1950s and early 1960s, as academic opportunities narrowed in the face of expanding numbers of graduate students, historians moved into other areas and gave substance to the idea that history and the historians' skills were functional outside as well as inside the classroom and library carrel. Later on, someone called it public history and Professor Robert Kelley of the University of California at Santa Barbara popularized the phrase. At long last, the old-timer began to put on new clothes.

In a very real sense, public history was part of the upheaval which struck all of higher education in the last two decades. Its increasing stature added to the confusion of the late 1960s and 1970s, decades which watched history enrollments drop and history departments shrink. Like the New Englanders who populate Sam Bass Warner's book, *Province of Reason*, historians today, including public historians, find themselves "bewildered about how to adapt to a rapidly-changing world."[2] This book is about how public historians have gone about adapting.

Steeped in a tradition which, some say, goes back to the reportorial skills of Thucydides and the deft insights of Tacitus, among others, historians since World War II have tended to be scrupulously fair in interpreting the past, but less certain about accepting in the profession qualified men and women who labored outside of departmental or campus boundaries. The reasons for this bifurcated approach are complex; whatever its causes, few can doubt its existence. The historical profession had become an almost private academic preserve, suffering from its own parochialism. Until public history was rounded into describable shape, there was no large category into which to fit those who did not wish to teach—the fallout, if you will, from the halls of ivy. In ignoring those who wandered into, say, archival work or a museum job, the academic historians protested that they were only protecting their profession, confounding, perhaps, the trappings of scholarship with the substance of understanding the past.[3]

The profession which the academic historians had tried to protect has a long tradition but a short history. Granting the skills of Greek and Roman prototypes, they were unlike proud professionals who stalk the lobbies and crowd the reception rooms at historical conventions. Certification by degree, a badge worn blatantly by some and quietly by many, is even more recent than the modern beginnings of the historians' craft. Today's historians, properly certified, most frequently delve into limited chronological, geographical, or situational segments, usually with enviable skill, while a century ago giants like George Bancroft and John Bach McMaster were magisterial proponents of the sweep of history. They and their contemporaries did not adapt the monographic approach so characteristic of good historical writing in this century. Neither James Ford Rhodes nor Henry Adams had to depend upon history for a livelihood, yet in producing compelling narratives, each wrote with a bias not acceptable in today's professional world. Adams, though, was a transitional figure; before he turned his back on historical investigation, he had successfully adopted major elements of modern research techniques.

Like other disciplines in the humanities and social sciences, history began to take shape in the late nineteenth century as the graduate schools at Johns Hopkins, Harvard, and Michigan, to name some leaders, introduced rigor and method into their graduate programs. From then on, the course was not smooth, but traceable. H. B. Adams of Johns Hopkins was among the first to use the seminar, insisting on more intensive scholarly explorations. James Harvey Robinson moved the discipline away from its preoccupation with political events with the publication of his groundbreaking book, *The New History* (1912). Although Charles A. Beard left an academic post, he has been accepted into the profession by the traditionalists as an influential innovator who persisted in coming to grips with economic motivation. Beard's contribution opened all kinds of doors in this century, giving historians from a wide spectrum of economic perspectives an acceptable platform from which to introduce their interpretations. Contemporary scholars like William Appleman Williams are free to question broadly held beliefs from new points of view because of older historians like Beard.[4]

One scholar who followed Beard chronologically set off in a different direction. Merle Curti points out that the field to which he has dedicated his distinguished career, intellectual history, did not have a usable name when he began to probe its dimensions. He drew from subjects within and without the then-traditional orbit of historical scholarship, using material from literature and sociology, as he stretched to measure the ideas which ordinary people embraced.[5] Arthur M. Schlesinger, Sr., to whom Curti pays tribute, carved out an area which he called "social" or "social and intellectual" history. It gained acceptance, albeit reluctantly, primarily because it was a nurturing ground for excursions into all kinds of hitherto undetected historical phenomena. The history of science, as historians view it, is one example, while others include black history, urban history, and women's history.

That is not to say that Schlesinger created these fields; they grew from his conviction that history envelops those currents in life which touch the lives of ordinary folk. A man of pervasive influence and wide-ranging interests, he attracted able young scholars whom he encouraged to branch out, to break new ground. Early in his career, he had published a book of essays, *New Viewpoints in American History*. Thirty years later he would joke about how his colleagues teasingly referred to the book as Few Newpoints in American History. Along with John Allen Krout and Carl Russell Fish, among others, Schlesinger planted seeds in the name of social history which matured as new areas of concentration and study.[6]

The scholars initially attracted to social history came from the major graduate programs, and they began to stake their claim as urbanists, historians of science, historians of sports, and so on. In addition to using standard historical research techniques, they were more apt to dip into obscure government reports, raw census data, little-known newspapers, remote periodicals, and other then-esoteric sources. They supported themselves as traditional members of the profession, teaching undergraduates in survey courses and upperclass students in seminars. Some moved into and became movers of graduate programs. Over time, as new tools surfaced, like cliometrics, social historians had probed a multitude of subject areas, some of large dimension, but some a small slice of life, Melba-toast thin and spread with vitamin-rich detail. Macro and micro history evolved in part from social history's broadening menu.

This fragmentation, however productive it was for scholarship, almost created the demise of social history. In the last decade a group of young scholars have begun to collect the pieces, define different approaches, and identify their interest as the "new social history." To some it might seem a proper projection of the old social history, but to its proponents, the links between its various content areas (labor, women, blacks, health, etc.) are stronger and more all-inclusive. It emphasizes process rather than detail, stresses "ordinary people," acknowledges new influences like European scholarship and the social sciences and probes more deeply exotic and still-unconventional sources. Although it derides as "pots and pans" history the older version of social history from which it sprang, it has many of the same characteristics. It, too, will no doubt spawn a host of new perspectives in fresh water, providing food for thought and research for future generations.[7]

What meaning does this evolution have for public history? Simply this: that public history is even now a loose confederation of content areas and occupational interests. As the field matures, the underlying concept may diminish, much as social history faded before the current generation attempted its revitalization. Public historians, like some social historians, may prefer to be known by their specialties: archivists, professional researchers, corporate historians, curators, and so on. There are some indications that the older specialties now embraced by the public history label are discomforted, if not disquieted by the attachment. Is public history shatterable? Will it peak and valley like social history? Will it survive more than two generations of historical titans, as social history faded after Schlesinger, Krout, and Fish and their students or, to cite another area, as frontier history has barely outlasted giants like Frederick Jackson Turner, Frederick Merk, and Ray A. Billington? Even those who claim perfect hindsight cannot assert clairvoyance on these questions, but for serious-minded public historians, who value a close relationship with tradition-minded academic historians, these questions deserve pondering.[8]

Public historians begin with an assumption which underlies the conception and production of this book: that public history is alive, well, and growing. To put it in more sedate terms, public history is viable as a respectable field of study, a useful field for a career, and a peer field which yields no quarter to teaching and research historians. There is a sound reason for this assumption, clearly implied in some of the essays which follow: that the study and practice of public history begins with a thorough knowledge of the art and craft of the historian. Public history requires as much immersion in and awareness of historical phenomena and methodology as any other kind of serious history. The major difference between a public historian and a teaching or research historian is neither knowledge nor awareness. It is delivery. The public historian delivers the fruits of his or her research, study, field work, interpretations, categorizations, calculations, and measurements in substantially different ways and locations from the more traditional historian. The means of delivery must be learned and the skills of delivery honed. Here, almost at a career's beginning, the dissimilarities pop up. It is the difference of delivery which has created resistance on the part of the academic historians just as it is that difference which has given public historians so wide a range of potential activity.

This same wide range of potential activity might be considered a weakness. Because public history covers so broad a span of study areas and career opportunities, it almost defies definition.[9] If we were to define it negatively—historians who do not teach—we are not defining but pointing up a distinction. If we change the name and call it "applied history," as some applicators are wont to do, we are merely substituting one ambiguity for another. Like social history, public history as a phrase lacks focus and clarity. Merely to say "Let's give public history focus and clarity" is simplistic. The various definitions which have been offered are generally cumbersome and circuitous, but public historians must keep trying to delineate their field in a way that creates greater understanding of it. The following statement might serve as a stepping stone toward that end: "Public history is the adaptation and application of the historian's skills and outlook for the benefit of private and public enterprises."

Hammering out an acceptable definition of public history is not a one-person task. It may be that usage over time will provide the understanding at which a short-term definition can only hint, but the process should continue. Public history requires identification, a tag, if you will, which is both magnet and exposition. The tag has to say first that public history is the study of history as an art with some scientific qualities. It must say further that this study includes some but not necessarily all of the specific skills historians develop in order to undertake research, writing, editing, document management, artifact interpretation, statistical analysis, evidence selection, policy development, and generalization. This means that those who call themselves public historians need to be trained as historians, with specialization in content fields, just like their academic brothers and sisters. Whether these fields are in a traditional mode or a ground-breaking area is of less consequence than the fact that public history students learn to dig and dissect, detail and describe, delineate and disseminate, like all good historians should.

One technique adopted by public historians on appropriate occasions—the team approach for investigation and interpretation—exemplifies the mix of the traditional and the innovative. For projects in historic preservation and public policy, for investigations within corporate structures, and for a variety of other issues, public historians have found value in seeking data and framing conclusions in concert with others. The traditionalists have a precedent for this in historical editing projects, which early on brought scholars together to prepare manuscript collections for publication, but in general, academic historians work by themselves. The public historians, taking a cue from editors and other disciplines, have emphasized the cooperating group, a practice which might become more acceptable to all historians.[10]

In one sense, this example of a mix of the traditional and innovative in "doing" history responds to those who, though tempted to enter the public history field, have doubts about why public historians like, say, a historical museum curator or an archival administrator, require the educational trappings of a historian. The reason is plain; whether working in a group or singly, public historians like a museum curator or archivist will face historical data such as documents and artifacts, shape them into useable or comprehensive form, serve those who need to interpret the data and assist, often in anonymous ways, in making historical relationships with and for those who use and view the data. One can make similar assertions about the responsibilities of almost all public historians; they must learn the historian's craft because that is the unique talent they bring to their position. The historical perspective, that special view of relationships which one must work to acquire, is the quintessence of public history and differentiates public historians from service professionals in every other segment of society.

Doubters might wonder about those who miss out on the apprenticeship and still try to pass as historians. They qualify more readily as dabblers, those who dip into history without fully understanding its dimensions. Some time ago the National Register of Historic Places undertook to write biographical sketches of the people who were responsible for major historical landmarks. The initial draft of the essay on President Rutherford B. Hayes was filled with errors and called him "an avid" historian, with a good library. The truth is that Hayes had a fine library and was an avid reader, but he was not, and never claimed to be, a historian. His historical interests were sporadic, and he neither thought nor wrote nor studied as a historian. Like the author of the draft, he was a dabbler.[11]

Dabblers are not historians any more than are undergraduates or graduate students who just take copious notes on sterling lectures. This may be their first step toward becoming historians, but they are only beginning the journey. Those who look to public history for career commitments must go beyond first steps or remain as dabblers. Public historians are baptized with training, not birthed like Athena.

"The historian," Philip D. Jordan noted two decades ago, "is a quester." Lecturing before a public history audience at the Historical Society of Michigan, he warned that the historian is "doomed to failure" if he or she proceeds on the quest "without preparation," and he went on to describe the basics:

> . . . a thorough grounding not only in languages and the liberal arts but also in the biological sciences. . . . Logic, grammar, philosophy, government, literature—all these are an imperative. Anthropology, sociology, and psychology are equally necessary.

And later,

> The wide world is every historian's backyard—the world of literature, of music, of art, of philosophy, of ethics, of culture. . . . If the historian does

not thrill to poetry, to magnificent drama, to polished essays, to goodness and truth and beauty in all their forms, he is, despite his academic degrees, no accomplished member of the guild.[12]

Hyperbole, surely, or possibly empty rhetoric for one who will spend time writing corporate history, backgrounding urban planning designs for a sewage plant, or processing manuscripts. Perhaps, but the real historian, public or otherwise, strives to be just such a person—a quester, grounded in the essentials which separate the human species from other animals.

The opportunities to prepare oneself for Jordan's quest, with a public history emphasis, are myriad. A few undergraduate programs exist, but the real explosion has developed in graduate schools. Those who have surveyed the field report that most programs include one or more of four offerings: business and public policy analysis, archival studies, historic preservation, and museology.[13] These tracks usually combine with historiographic and historical research seminars along with some content courses to give depth and perspective to the career-oriented experiences. Career options are so numerous that it is tempting for students to aim narrowly and give short shrift to history in favor of hands-on exercises. This is a judgment error which may penalize students at a later career level. Like adults who wished they had practiced the piano, instead of faking it, students may well rue what they passed by in graduate school.

It has been the tradition among historians to label their specialties in terms of content, so that an academic department had among its Americanists a colonialist, a Civil War and Reconstruction historian, a historian of American Indians, and so on. More recently, cliometricians, who depend more heavily on statistical analysis, and comparative historians, who seek answers in the comparability of cultures, have surfaced in academe, but rarely, until public historians came along, were historians hired in academic departments because of occupational skills. Archivists, museum curators, preservationists, editors, and the extensive range of career opportunities available to public historians have little currency among academic historians, who have tended to regard those careers as peripheral, and the professionals who chose those careers as other than historians.[14]

Karl Compton, science educator and an esteemed president of the Massachusetts Institute of Technology, once claimed for science "a valuable part in education because it creates knowledge, disciplines the mind, and has great utility."[15] Historians can claim with Compton that history is a valuable part of education for the first two reasons, but what of utility? Traditional historians have rarely confronted the issue of utility; they have dismissed it from their vocabulary as irrelevant or commercial. Yet public history provides that "great utility" which Compton claimed for science and which is already firmly embedded in many other areas in the humanities and social sciences.

Most of the major disciplines have long since staked out a practical segment and incorporated it more or less willingly into their family of acceptable subsidiaries. Among the social sciences, utility endows sociology, psychology, economics, and even political science with dimensions that have stimulated more intense scholarly explorations and even pushed practitioners into national spotlights. In the humanities, a variety of disciplines embrace utilitarian phases. Literature scholars deal with writing; philosophers have moved toward the resolution of concrete problems; foreign language instructors teach students to overcome language barriers; religion professors serve churches and denominations. Only history has hung back from pragmatic involvement with the outside world, other than training more historians.

Service is a connecting rod to all or most of these practical subdivisions of scholarly disciplines; each one serves a component of society in concrete ways. Back in 1958, William B. Hesseltine and Donald R. McNeil edited a book which they called *In Search of Clio*.[16] The essays described the various ways in which Clio was sought and, incidentally, society was served. The book highlighted manuscript collections, the WPA historical records survey, public archives, "mechanical aids," editing, and even historic restorations. This is public history in its infancy, but there is a twist in the title. Public historians "in search of Clio," they implied, would find and serve her almost invariably on college and university campuses. Even today, a generation later, many public historians practice their craft in the service of academic historians; their function is to be useful to the traditionalists.

Now there is more. Public history has moved beyond the limited concepts of three decades ago. Public historians today, as the authors who follow ably demonstrate, serve in a rainbow spectrum of activities as diverse as industrial archeology, corporate history, tourist attractions, consulting firms, government offices, and policy studies for the public and private sectors. It is nevertheless still true that to be useful, these public historians are performing a service. Those who write sponsored history serve the sponsor; those who manage tourist attractions must keep the public coming; those who consult have their clients' needs foremost in mind. None of these pressures and the postures which they shape are discreditable. It is only that they are new to the profession and new to the academic historian.

For the latter, it will not be easy to accept as peers historians who neither produce monographs or narratives nor teach in a classroom. Not only is public history strange enough to stimulate latent xenophobia in some professorial ranks, but the mere threat of a possible invasion could set off shock waves. Karl J. Weintraub, T. E. Donnelly Distinguished Service Professor of History and a former Graduate Dean at the University of Chicago, recently noted the tendency of historians to protect their turf: "Is it serious or merely funny to see how much passion historians invest in the expansion and defense of such subdisciplinary territories as intellectual history or social history or quantitative history?"[17] In spite of the bulwarks which might be thrown up to circumscribe public history programs, the early evidence suggests that acceptance will come, that public history will flourish as an integral component of the discipline. There will be the obdurate and the die-hards who will, they say, never allow public historians to cross the line, but in time, these, too, will pass away.

Currently, however, there is some measurable tension between some academic and public historians wherever these professionals meet—in organization, convention, workshop, or informal gathering, but the arena in which the pulls and tugs are most apparent is the history department itself. When departmental resources have to be stretched to cover additional faculty members, when course loads are redistributed to allow public historians time for field work, when other than tradition- alists are considered for vacancies, battle lines are often drawn, though the battle itself may peter out, or confine itself to minor skirmishes.

In a still more sensitive area, faculty historians and university admin- istrators will be under added pressure as faculty members who are public historians challenge traditional promotion and tenure require- ments. Even at a time in which colleges and universities are constrained to review and possibly change these rules, the manner in which public historians prove they are worthy of a permanent appointment differs from the more traditional modes, to the degree that even the revised requirements may not apply. Teaching techniques are less formal, research is often a group project, nonmonographic and/or for a partic- ular sponsor. Service, usually a less heavily weighted general faculty requirement, is a strong suit for public historians who work with community and regional groups which do not have high visibility or standing in academic circles.[18]

While resistance among academics is measurable, there are now some countervailing forces which appear to be growing in strength and acceptance with every passing year. The Organization of American Historians (OAH) has begun publication of a semiannual column titled "Perspectives on Public History" in its quarterly newsletter. In another effort, the OAH and the National Council on Public History have scheduled their annual meetings in the same city and at a time when both meetings overlap by a day or so, giving members of each organi- zation the chance to attend sessions, stroll the lobbies, and interact. The American Historical Association (AHA) offers a public history prize and has made it possible for public historians to be elected to responsible positions in the organization. Many historical organizations support the National Coordinating Committee for the Promotion of History, a national lobby group which watches over the interest of history in the rarefied atmosphere of the nation's capital.

The hurdles facing public history are far from insurmountable. The advantages of carving out a public history speciality, of welcoming new historians to a vibrant and fulfilling career are not lost on departmental chairs, deans, and academic vice-presidents. For those colleges and universities which need the good will of neighbors and the financial support of regional friends, the opportunity to stretch one more helping hand into the community is too good to reject.

The benefits of a public history program in an academic department spread 360 degrees. Since public history is a service and the professionals who practice it work with, or for, a wide variety of organizations in the public and private sectors, in profit and nonprofit corporations, what they do touches the many rather than the few in any given location or on a national scale. I know a public historian who so turned on a community that a group of citizens spearheaded a movement to restore its downtown historic buildings, which spruced up the town and gave it a dignified, inviting look. She brought credit to the college where she taught and increased cultural awareness to the community.[19]

Another historian has in the course of his career transformed a large research library into a major force for scholarship and the general public, serving its city and the nation. The recent Archivist of the United States in less than five years successfully led the fight to make the National Archives and Record Center an independent federal agency, comparable to the Library of Congress and the Smithsonian Institution, thereby giving it a fuller measure of control over its staff, its budget, and its programs and making it more sensitive to the needs of its users.[20]

Public historians serve, and their service counts. That is the message of this book. You will not find public historians saying they count more or less than their colleagues in library carrels and the classroom. They will only affirm that, because public history is important, even crucial at times, public historians count.

NOTES

1. William B. Hesseltine, *Pioneer Mission: The Story of Lyman Copeland Draper* (Madison, Wis.: State Historical Society of Wisconsin, 1954), esp. chs. 3 and 8; and Clifford L. Lord and Carl Ubbelohde, *Clio's Servant: The State Historical Society of Wisconsin, 1846–1954* (Madison, Wis.: State Historical Society of Wisconsin, 1967), chs. 6–10.
2. The quotation is from a brief review of Warner's book by Nancy Ramsey in the *New York Times Book Review*, 4 November 1984, 25.
3. Dianne Martin, "History Goes Public," *History News* 34 (May 1979): 121–22.
4. Oscar Handlin, *Truth in History* (Cambridge, Mass.: The Belknap Press of Harvard University, 1979), ch. 3; and Bradford Perkins, "The Tragedy of American Diplomacy: Twenty-five Years After," *Reviews in American History* 12 (March 1984): 1–18.
5. Merle Curti, "The Evolution of American Intellectual History," *OAH Newsletter* (May 1984): 8–10.
6. Arthur M. Schlesinger, Jr., "Introduction," and Arthur M. Schlesinger, [Sr.], "History," in Schlesinger, [Sr.], *Nothing Stands Still* (Cambridge, Mass.: The Belknap Press of Harvard University, 1969), 1–17, 19–46. The reference to *New Viewpoints* is a personal recollection.
7. The status of social history is somewhat controversial today. A recent, and ardent defense, from which this paragraph is drawn, can be found in Peter N. Stearns's essay, "The New Social History: An Overview," in James B. Gardner and George Rollie Adams, eds., *Ordinary People and Everyday Life* (Nashville: American Association for State and Local History, 1983), 3–21. Doubters like myself believe that specialists such as those who contributed to

the Gardner-Adams book are more accurately labeled by their speciality (urbanists, agricultural historians, or historians of women, blacks, etc.). The umbrella term, "new social history," appears to be an ex post facto attempt at integration with little independent meaning. I question, too, the wisdom of Stearns's condescending dismissal of the "older" social history, as if the earlier practitioners were amateurs. This is not only gauche, but a rejection of the very historic continuity which Sterns and his colleagues seek to document. This is apposite here because "public history" is also an umbrella term, not yet fully accepted even by some groups which are presumably included in it. The aggressive stance of the new social historians, and the dust which they have kicked up in so standing, is worthy of public historians' attention.

8. In her report for 1984–85, Joan Hoff-Wilson, an active scholar and the executive secretary of the Organization of American Historians, expressed concern over the "fragmentation within the profession represented by the formation of new, small historical societies since 1960." There are, she stated, more than seventy such historical associations whose total membership exceeds that of the OAH and the American Historical Association combined. "This fragmentation," she points out, "reflects healthy, committed scholarship and professional interest, but not unified activity. Pluralism rather than unity has characterized the last twenty years of professional development within the field of history" (Joan Hoff-Wilson, "The Plight of a Mom and Pop Operation," *OAH Newsletter* 13 [May 1985]: 2).

9. In a "Perspectives on Public History" column, Brit Allan Storey confronts without resolving the identification issue (Brit Allan Storey, "Who and What are Public Historians?" *OAH Newsletter* 12 [May 1984]: 22–23).

10. Dianne Martin, "History Goes Public," 125; and Suellen Hoy, "Opportunities in Applied History: State and Local Government," reprinted in "Widening the Scope of the Profession," (Papers and a Commentary at a Meeting of the Southern Historical Association, November 9, 1978 and sponsored by the National Coordinating Committee for the Promotion of History, n.p., n.d.), n.p.

11. National Register of Historic Places 1983 Inventory draft, Item 7, p. 2, Director's Files, Rutherford B. Hayes Presidential Center.

12. Philip D. Jordan, *The World of the Historian* (The Burton Lecture, Lansing, Mich.: Historical Society of Michigan, 1963), 3.

13. *Humanities in the South: Newsletter of the Southern Humanities Conference*, No. 59 (Spring 1984): 2.

14. Suellen Hoy, "Opportunities in Applied History," n.p.

15. Karl T. Compton, *A Scientist Speaks: Excerpts from Addresses . . . 1930–1949 . . .* (Cambridge, Mass.: Undergraduates Association, MIT, 1955), 42.

16. William B. Hesseltine and Donald R. McNeil, *In Search of Clio* (Madison, Wis.: State Historical Society of Wisconsin, 1958).

17. Karl Weintraub, "Recovering the Humanities," *Humanities* 5 (October 1984): 3.

18. *Humanities in the South . . .* , 3; and Kendricks A. Clement, "Promotion and Tenure Criteria for Faculty in Applied History," *The Public Historian* 6 (Spring 1984): 51–61. David A. Johnson and C. Raymond Starr provide commentaries to this article, *Ibid.*, 61–65.

19. The public historian referred to is Barbara Howe, an editor of this volume. She performed her magic in her four years as a faculty member at Heidelberg College in Tiffin, Ohio, while she was, simultaneously, the regional historic preservation officer.

20. For the last two decades, Lawrence W. Towner has been president of the Newberry Library in Chicago. His accomplishments merited a laudatory article in the *Sunday Magazine* of the *Chicago Tribune* on January 13, 1985. Towner, originally a colonialist, studied under Ray Billington at Northwestern. In 1980, Robert M. Warner moved to Washington, D.C., from his post as Director of the Bentley Library at the University of Michigan to become Archivist of the United States. Before he left in April 1985 to return to Ann Arbor as Dean of the University of Michigan Library School, the Congress and the White House had responded positively to his efforts, and those of historians and historical organizations, to free the National Archives from its unhealthy status as a General Services Administration agency. On April 1, 1985, the National Archives and Records Administration opened its doors as an independent government agency.

Gerald W. George is director of the American Association for State and Local History. He received his B.A. degree from the University of Wichita and did graduate work in history at Yale University, receiving his M.A. in 1962. He taught briefly in an extension program for Bethany College, Lindsborg, Kansas, and then entered newspaper work as a reporter for the Salina, Kansas, Journal. In 1964 he became a staff writer for The National Observer.

In 1967 he joined the Woodrow Wilson National Fellowship Foundation in Princeton, New Jersey, as editorial associate to write a history of the organization's first twenty-five years. Completing that assignment in 1968, he became special assistant to the chairman of the National Endowment for the Humanities, in Washington, D.C.

In 1971 he left the endowment to work as a free-lance writer, based first in Washington and then in the Netherlands. He returned to the United States in 1973 to join the staff of the American Association for State and Local History as managing editor of a book series, "The States and the Nation," consisting of a volume on the history of every state and the District of Columbia, which AASLH co-published with W. W. Norton and Company of New York. He became the association's director in 1978. He has addressed meetings of numerous historical organizations, and his articles have appeared in books, journals, and magazines as well as in newspapers.

THE PERILS OF "PUBLIC" HISTORY: AN IMAGINARY EXCURSION INTO THE REAL WORLD

Gerald George

A sudden flash of lightning and a burst of smoke erupt in one corner of a dark, dank room near the campus of a contemporary American university—it could be any. A poverty-striken history graduate student, who has been head-down on his arms on his desk in deep despair, looks up. To his amazement, there, sitting in his one good chair, is a ghostly looking old gentleman in a wig and other accoutrements of the eighteenth century. The old gentleman is grinning and says:

"What's the matter, young friend? Why the gloom?"

The young man, to whom let us give the highly improbable but historically significant name of Eddie Gibbon, cannot help but exclaim:

"Who—who are you?"

"I?" says the spectre. "I am the Reverend Jeremy Belknap. I was founder of the Massachusetts Historical Society, the nation's first. And I come to you from the past with a message that I think may help. But first, describe for me yourself the affliction from which I see you suffering."

Well, young Gibbon was historian enough to know that the Massachusetts Historical Society is the repository for one of our most valued collections of papers of the great Patriots and Founding Fathers of the United States—the Adamses, Thomas Jefferson and so on. What he did not know was that old Jeremy, author of an early history of New Hampshire, was one of the seven founders of that society back in the first presidential term of George Washington. They had formed the society to save documents associated with the dramatic creation of so wonderful a new nation.

"Speak up," Belknap now encourages.

"Well, sir," says Eddie, "I am about to get my graduate degree in history at last. But I've realized that I'm not cut out to be a teacher. On the other hand, I'm a good historian and love history and don't want just to go back home to my father's bathtub business. But what else can I do?"

"Ah!" says the spectre. "It is well that I have come, then, because you're overlooking a vast range of opportunities for serious historians. Consider what is happening in the country at large, my friend! In just the past two or three decades, public interest in history has grown phenomenally. Genealogy has become one of the most popular of hobbies, aided now by sophisticated professionals. Every racial and ethnic group now seems to have some kind of organization to document and study its history. Institutions and businesses are increasingly developing archives to care for theirs. Tax incentives have spurred the preservation of historic buildings. State and federal governments have joined patriotic organizations in interpreting more historic sites. And almost every community now has a historical society or museum. Fifty percent of them have been founded just since 1960 and more are created every day. In fact, the American Association for State and Local History publishes a *Directory* that lists more than 6,000 of them.

"Son, that is your destiny. Go out and run a local historical society or museum."

"Hey, great," Eddie agrees. "I'll do it."

"Wonderful," says Belknap. "Of course, after you finish your history Ph.D. you'll also need to get an M.B.A. so that you'll understand financial management, accounting, personnel administration, and all the other business matters that contemporary museum and historical agency directors have to be expert at. Also, a law degree will be handy in the litigious atmosphere that surrounds contemporary museums. And naturally you'll want special courses in archival science, art and artifact conservation, exhibit design, visitor evaluation, computerized collections control, and other basics that every modern historical agency or museum director needs."

"Naturally," says Eddie. "I'll get on it right away."

"Good," Belknap replies. But a crafty look has come into his ancient eyes as he adds: "You may wonder why I am telling you all this?"

"Why, to help me have a career in history, I thought," Eddie speculates in surprise.

"Yes, my boy," says Belknap, "but more than that. You see I'm not too keen about a lot of things I'm seeing as I float around these days looking over modern historical societies of the kind I founded. I want you not only to train to enter the field. I want you also, when you enter, to reform it."

"And how am I to do that, sir?" Eddie says.

"You'll figure it out," says Belknap, "if you simply remember this. The statement of purpose for the society I founded was to 'elucidate the . . . history of America from the earliest times to the present day. . . .' Let that be your motto, my boy, and all else will follow from it."

Then—poof!—in a cloud of smoke and a flash of lightning before the amazed Eddie Gibbon's eyes, the old eighteenth century gentleman unceremoniously disappears.

Well, ten or fifteen years later, Eddie Gibbon has added the desired training to his history degree and is ready for work in the field. He fails to land a job at the Smithsonian, his first choice. But a director is wanted for the Hickory City Historical Society and Museum, in Tennessee, in fact, not far from the headquarters of the American Association for State and Local History. The starting pay sounds pretty good for this field—$10,000 a year and Sunday mornings off—so Eddie applies. In light of his excellent training, the board boosts the salary to $11,000 and hires him. At last he has an institution upon which to impose his will, in response to the mandate that old Jeremy gave him.

He comes to the museum on his first day. It is in a former post-office building, made of solid limestone, with great steps leading up to the front door. Eddie picks his way carefully through the school groups of third-graders who happen to be visiting at that moment, uses the shoe scraper at the top of the steps to get their bubblegum off, and notes the inscription that somebody has chiseled into the stone above the entry. It says—"When a society or civilization perishes, one condition may always be found. They forgot where they came from." It is attributed to Carl Sandburg.

Inside, Eddie is immediately attracted to a great glass case in the central hall. What should he find within it but one of George Washington's wigs. George Washington left it in the town, a sign or "label" says, when George Washington slept there, on a quick social tour of settlements in Tennessee late in his career. The wig reposes on a flag that once flew over Fort Hickory. And all around the room on the walls are portraits of the patriots—Washington, Patrick Henry, Jefferson, Lafayette, Andrew Jackson, General Eisenhower, and the town's current congressional representative.

On either side of the central hall, Eddie finds two great galleries. One is called Hall of the Pioneers. In it are portraits of the town's male founders in coonskin caps and buckskin jackets. Ancient long rifles and powder horns are mounted in magnificent displays, along with Indian arrowheads, tomahawks, and moccasins. Old engravings are used with labels to explain how the town came into being, who founded it, what perils they endured, what Indians they evacuated, and when it was that the settlement finally became established and secure.

Eddie finds all this local history very interesting. Then he proceeds back across the central hall, with another quick glance at Washington's wig.

The great gallery on the other side, he discovers, is a period room. It exhibits the furnishings and adornments of the sitting parlor and bedroom of one of the town's tycoons in the Victorian era. Dark wallpaper, horsehair sofas, leather-bound books, fabulous bedpans, beautiful toys—a wonderful collection well displayed. After feasting on its visual delights for half an hour, Eddie proceeds back to the wig exhibit, gazes once again toward the Hall of the Pioneers as well as the Victorian Period Gallery and sighs:

"So this is history!"

But not quite. Because he then notices, out on the front lawn, something that was obscured, when he came in, by having so many children climbing on it. It is a Civil War cannon. Of course. Eddie knew some central facet of the city's history remained to be contemplated, and there it is—green and grim, with a metallic plaque explaining its importance as a memorial to those Hickory City citizens who fell in the fateful War of Northern Aggression.

Now then, none of what he is seeing surprises Eddie Gibbon, who knows that it all is quite typical. For only about one American historical organization out of five has any kind of collection pertaining to the Colonial era, 1607–1776. About half have some collection related to the period of national formation and consolidation, from the Constitution through the Civil War. Almost three-fourths have collections illustrating the Gilded Age from the Civil War's end to the start of the twentieth century, which in the West was the Settlement Era. For the twentieth century, the figure falls back around 50 percent.

Yes, patriots and pioneers, settlement and Civil War and vast collections of Victorian antiques. Eddie Gibbon ponders all this and then slowly mounts to his director's office in the rafters to lay his long-range plans. At the top he writes:

"Our purpose is to elucidate the history of Hickory City from the earliest times to the present day. . . . "

A few days later, the president of the society happens to be driving past the museum on his way to the bank when he sees workmen up on a scaffolding with a lot of dust. He parks, and finds Director Gibbon out front observing their progress.

"What's going on, Eddie?" he says.

"Oh," says Eddie, "I am having them chisel out that old Sandburg quotation about perishing if we don't remember our beginnings. Too limiting an emphasis," he says.

"Really?" says the president. "But it had such morally uplifting effects on the kids around here. Scared the hell out of them. Made them pay attention when the teacher talked. What are you putting up there instead?"

"Change over time," Eddie replies. "History is the study of change over time. All time."

"You don't say," the president says. "Well, you're the expert I guess. But it sounds awfully boring to me."

Several more days later, the wife of the president of the historical society mounts the stairs to the museum with a couple of out-of-town visitors in tow. "We have some very rare items," she is explaining. Suddenly, she stops dead in her tracks. She points to where the glass case in the center hall stands. It is empty. She screams—"Washington's wig— the wig is gone!"

Recovering, she runs quickly up the stairs to the loft containing the director's office, and breathlessly, fearfully asks:

"What has happened to Washington's wig?"

"Oh," Eddie Gibbon responds, helping her into a chair. "I sent it up to Sotheby's in New York to sell at auction. It doesn't have much to do with Hickory City, and it might just fetch a nice pot of cash for us to finance a new exhibit in the central hall, using all our wonderful photographs and artifacts that show changes in lifestyles here over the years, such as what people wore in different eras, what kind of social groups they formed, how they entertained themselves, what different ethnic groups appeared and how they changed the composition of the community and what each contributed to our cultural heritage, and—"

"What?" the astonished woman says. "Sell the wig? The rarest, most significant artifact we have—our town's one tie to the great George Washington? To be replaced by pictures of Chinese restaurant operators and baseball games and Baptist conventions and labor unions and the Kiwanis Club? You must be out of your mind."

"You'll like it," Eddie says reassuringly. "You know, I've discovered that this town had a lot of Slavic immigrants in it, which is rare for a town in Tennessee, and they gained political influence after helping develop the coal mines near town that early in this century led to great growth of the city."

"Slavic miners?" the desperate woman wails. "I want George Washington's wig!"

Well, she finally calms down enough to go home to think over all this. But the next week, when both she and her husband return, they find a tremendous transformation in the Hall of the Pioneers. Everything is being taken down, and there is Eddie Gibbon, supervising the work.

"What now?" they both exclaim.

"Oh, hi," says Eddie. "I hope you don't mind. We need space in here for more than just the town's founding. You see, in the Pioneer period, this place was not much different from Knoxville. I'm trying to de-emphasize that a little to make room for more significant later developments such as—"

"De-emphasize the town's founding?!" the society's president exclaims. "Son, we founded this society to celebrate the struggle to establish this place. We're talking pioneers, son. We're talking about trekking through the wilderness, fighting off Indians, enduring adversity to bring about the American dream, giving posterity an eternal object lesson about faith, hope, hard work, and unwavering determination. We're talking my great-grandfather here!"

"I know, I know," Eddie says. "We'll keep his portrait and the long rifle and Indian stuff right over in the corner there, with a label about conflicting claims to the land and how Indians' values and those of the settlers differed. But we've also got room to trace the town's development with all the wonderful artifacts I found out in the museum's storage shed—there's a milking stool and some unusual barbed wire and an old buggy and a Model-T and tools from several eras and a bank teller's table and photographs of early industries. And by the way, if you'd make the society a gift of your old Studebaker and some of that paraphernalia you recently discarded when you modernized your plant, and also let me go up in your attic for a few days, I bet we could bring the story of urbanization and industrialization right up through the twentieth century and—"

The society's president and his wife both look aghast.

"Attics?" they exclaim. "Industrialization? Urbanization? Studebakers? This is supposed to be a history museum. Who cares about plant equipment? We see enough of that as it is. What we want is the real past, son—pioneers, adventure, victory over adversity!"

"Oh well," says Eddie, "perhaps you'll like my plans better for renovating the Victorian Period Gallery. Just step over here—"

"On no!" the president and his wife exclaim as they see great clouds of dust around scurrying workmen in the Victorian Gallery as well. "What are you doing with our beautiful antiques?"

"It's going to be fascinating," Eddie says. "I'm creating exhibits that compare and contrast artifacts of everyday life from era to era. For example, we'll keep the mannequin showing this small-waisted Victorian female finery, of course, but also, this dress from the 1920s will show how flappers liberated women from the constrictions of the corset—yet not entirely from all restricting apparel, such as these spiky high heels from the 1970s, for example, that continue to keep women confined and—"

"That does it!" the society's president says. "High heels from the 1970s in a history museum! I am calling a meeting of the board immediately!"

It is a dark chilly night soon thereafter when all the members of the society's board gather on folding chairs around a table next to the empty glass case in the museum's central hall.

"Young man," the society's president begins, "there are some things about your plans we must say to you."

"Very good, sir," Eddie says, "but first, let me explain what some of the rest of the plans are. I have noticed an unfortunate thing about our collections here. We have a wonderful, huge collection of political campaign buttons—very colorful and fun—because one of you thought campaign buttons were interesting and collected them and then gave them to the museum. But the old voting booths and polling-place equipment burned up in the last county courthouse fire, and the actual election records for several decades got pitched out as no longer needed by the county clerk, so it's hard to document much about politics in the history of Hickory City, except from three or four of the campaign buttons that have pictures of local candidates on them.

"We've got serious gaps in trying to account for previous centuries, or even the first half of this one because our collections represent chiefly the whims of what was interesting to private collectors, such as yourselves, or what managed to survive somehow the caprice of fortune. If we are to bequeath a continuous historical record of our community to future generations—an accurate account of all that continuously shaped it—we must incorporate in our plan a policy for collecting more systematically, at least in the here and now. For history never stops and never holds still."

Eddie does not notice that there is a lot of fidgeting going on around the table. But what he does see is a momentary image of old Jeremy Belknap floating around the ceiling, urging him on. He continues:

"Obviously we can't keep everything. We don't have space and couldn't afford indiscriminate collecting anyway. So I have begun to work on standards of historical significance or influence to guide us, so that we can keep things that are representative as well as rare, influential in the story of the city as well as curiously interesting, valuable for educating our great grandchildren as well as for intrinsic worth.

"Additionally," he goes on, "we will want to collect two different kinds of things in our own time—artifacts to be conserved for *permanent* collections of *original* things, and artifacts to be collected *temporarily* for documentation. For educational exhibiting is just part of the potential value of local museum work in the future. Museums are also places for the study of artifacts. And what we don't save permanently for its special historical value, we can collect long enough to photograph, to catalogue, to describe, to document, to understand, to keep a permanent *record* of."

"Son," the society president suddenly breaks in, "is this some fantasy about the role of museums that you've just made up?"

"Oh far from it, sir," Eddie Gibbon replies. "This is the sort of thing that museums are actually doing in Sweden. They've collaborated there on something called SAMDOK. That is an abbreviation of the Swedish words for 'contemporary documentation'. They've formed groups to look at different kinds of economic activity in the twentieth century, such as construction, textiles, food, metals, communications, trade, services, public administration and homes, meaning domestic life. They are carrying out research on artifacts in each of those areas of life, documenting different kinds and the varieties among them, and also parcelling out responsibilities among different museums for collecting contemporary artifacts of different kinds.

"You see, I think we could do something like that here, too. There is no necessity for us here in Hickory City to duplicate collections at the Tennessee State Museum or the Pink Palace Museum in Memphis or the

East Tennessee Historical Society. We can concentrate on elements of the state's history that are particularly important in our region. And we can start working now to see that each museum in the twenty-first century will be covering some special part of the state's total history, so that Tennesseans have access to it all. Not just claims to fame. Not just why are we unique and different from Knoxville. But where have we stood within evolving historical relationships? What give and take has our home had with the world?"

But in his enthusiasm, Eddie has not noticed that the society's president has surreptitiously slipped away into the Hall of the Pioneers, that he is there removing the old frontier rifle from the little exhibit in the corner, that he is pouring powder into it from the powder horn, that he is arming it with a ball from the exhibit as well, and that he is steathily moving back towards the central hall with the thing in hand. Eddie is saying:

"Just one more thing. Once we have set up historical standards for artifact collecting, then parcelled out responsibilities for it among museums, and prepared ourselves to keep only some artifacts and document others with careful research and study, we will recognize the needs for surveys in our communities too. Surveys of artifacts available or needed for study and preservation."

The society's president peers around the corner of the Hall of the Pioneers, a gleam of anticipation in his eye. Eddie goes on:

"We have already begun this reasonably well in this country with historic preservation of buildings. We have created the National Register of Historic Places, with guidelines for assessing historical significance. We have created a historic preservation office in every state to survey buildings throughout the state to identify those that are most historically and architecturally significant. To a lesser extent, we have also begun doing that with historical records. The National Historical Publications and Records Commission in particular has financed records surveys in several states now, as well as some local and regional surveys. All I am proposing is to do more assessing and surveying of structures, sites, records, and historical artifacts too, including what we will need from our own time."

And then—a warwhoop suddenly fills the room from the throat of the society's president. He emerges from behind the hallway door. He takes aim at Eddie with the long rifle, and—"bam!"—an old lead bullet parts Eddie's hair and lodges in the ceiling just above his head. And from the ceiling there comes the most mysterious sound, as if something was wounded there. Alas, poor Jeremy.

As Eddie cowers from his narrow escape, the board president shouts out: "Let the spirit of our ancestors live again! It's time to take up arms as our pioneer predecessors did to claim our rightful heritage and drive out all this nonsense about history that you are inflicting on us. We like history precisely because it isn't the present. History is inspiration, shining example, the great and glorious, the rare and beautiful. Where are you going to find any of that today? Out—out—before I make history, in the form of this old flintlock rifle, repeat itself!"

Well, Eddie could take a hint, and soon was gone.

The story concludes much later in the twenty-first century.

A docent is conducting a special tour through the Hickory City Museum for a group of your grandchildren. "On your left," she says, "is the Hall of the Pioneers, where you will learn of the first settlement of our city. On the right is the Victorian Period Room, where you will see spectacular examples of the decorative arts from an earlier age. And there, in this central hall, we commemorate the last great historical event in Hickory City, which is known as the Battle of the Historical Society, back in 1985. There, in the ceiling, you can still see a bullet-hole made in that battle; the bullet itself is in this glass case here, which once housed a wig of George Washington's, the loss of which stirred our local citizens to defend themselves against further desecrations of their heritage. In terms of extraordinary occurrences, our history ended then. Subsequently we have had only happenings."

The moral of the story?

There are no captive audiences off-campus.

Mr. George's views in this article are personal, rather than those of the American Association for State and Local History.

PART II:
VARIETIES OF
PUBLIC HISTORY

INTRODUCTION

Without considering all of the positions currently held by public historians, the essays collected in Part II present convincing evidence of the rich diversity of careers pursued by professional historians. It is equally apparent that there is a strong interdisciplinary current associated with most of the positions held by historians outside educational institutions. In the burgeoning field of public history, interdisciplinary work conducted by teams of professionals has become so common that it can be said to be a hallmark of the field.

Amongst the great diversity of public history positions there emerges an essential unity. The unifying factor is history. Regardless of what else a public historian does, the career is that of a historian. Without this core of the practice of history, one must define public history as "any old job" in which historians can be gainfully employed. Such a definition is so diffuse and vague that it loses all credence and does a great disservice to a vital field seeking to establish the historical nature of work done by public historians in a wide variety of positions.

In reading these essays the reader will also quickly realize that in nearly every case the public historian will find it necessary to develop, through education and/or experience, special skills not usually associated with a historian's role as scholar and teacher. It is analogous to Rudyard Kipling's description of the British Royal Marine as being soldier and sailor, too. Thus, public historians must become the Royal Marines of the history world.

Libraries and archives are often thought of as institutions providing challenging and appropriate careers for historians. Indeed, historians have long been employed in such positions and their association with libraries and archives predates the idea of "public history." While recognizing that there is a long and fruitful tradition of historians working in libraries and archives as both researchers and employees, perhaps most historians would be hard pressed to describe in detail what archivists and librarians do on a day-by-day basis and where there are opportunities for employment. The essay by Fredric Miller addresses the hiatus between the activities of academic historians and those public historians working in libraries and archives who are responsible for the management of records; in so doing, he presents a penetrating analysis of one of the cornerstones of public history. Carolyn Colwell's essay is really a sequel to Miller's in that it deals with a closely related career for public historians in libraries. Both essays give perspectives on careers which have long included historians.

With the advent of the wire and later tape recorder, oral history projects have flourished and provided important primary data for social and political historians as well as for historians of technology and the new breed of archeologists concerned with our industrial past. Indeed, oral histories have been used by historians of every stripe concerned with the late nineteenth and twentieth centuries. Producing quality oral histories is much more subtle and complex, however, than just letting octogenarians ramble on about the "good old days" in front of a microphone.

Producing oral histories of national political leaders is a challenging and rewarding activity which has been carried out with aplomb by Donald A. Ritchie of the U.S. Senate Historical Office. Not only does his case study provide the rationale and methodology for producing an accurate oral history which emphasizes the salient points of the informant's life, but it could easily persuade public historians "to go and do likewise." Much has been written on the correct ways to produce oral histories and those interested in trying their hand at oral history will find his selected bibliography on the subject a useful starting place.

Editing public records, journals, books, and letters has been a longstanding interest of generations of historians. In fact, editing has been a "stock in trade" for historians and does not constitute a new endeavor devised by public historians. However, it increasingly has become the responsibility of those who identify themselves as public historians. Brent Tarter of the Virginia State Library gives a fascinating account of the editing and publishing of colonial minute books of Norfolk, Virginia, while also providing a brief history of the editing of public documents. All of the decisions regarding how to present and interpret the minute books are described in sufficient detail for the reader to understand the process of editing public records in general.

Many historians are familiar with the published letters and papers of famous political leaders of the country such as George Washington, Thomas Jefferson, the Adams family, and Abraham Lincoln. There are also edited works of Thomas A. Edison and Joseph Henry in the history of science and technology, to name just a few of the prominent people who have had their papers edited and published. Although not as well known, Albert Gallatin, Jefferson's Secretary of the Treasury and a strong proponent of the internal improvement movement in America, is the subject of a current editing project. Barbara Oberg is the editor of the Gallatin papers; she writes about her role as a historian in the editing process and, in a larger sense, about the entire editing process in which she says:

> Editing documents that were not intended for general perusal or publication presents some different problems from editing public documents, and public historians ought to know the skills necessary for producing a good volume of correspondence. This essay will introduce the student to the history of editing correspondence in this country and to its evolution from a private, family venture into a public profession. . . .
> . . . As a person trained relatively traditionally in the historian's craft and as one who made a transition some eight years ago from the practice of

writing conventional intellectual history to that of constructing historical editions, I am particularly aware that even for the trained historian there are additional skills required for turning primary source materials into well-edited letters.

Editing also implies serving as an editor for a university press, large commercial publishing house, specialized publishing firm, business concern, or government agency. Rather than dealing directly with historical documents such as letters and journals, the historian in the publishing business deals with manuscripts prepared by authors for publishing in contemporary journals and in books. Scott L. Bills succinctly relates how editors trained as historians address all aspects of turning a manuscript into a published work. In describing the responsibilities of an editor, Bills states:

> Editing for a publisher of any kind is rigorous: the job requires an abiding but practical perfectionism; a well-developed sense of nuance; a solid knowledge of grammar and usage; a thoughtful and consistent attention to detail; a tolerant, tactful, ego-minimal attitude toward the work to be done; and probably a stubborn, inexorable love of the printed word. Many of these characteristics are nurtured in graduate programs in history; however, technical expertise and familiarity with the process of publishing may also be job requirements.

Here is a clear description of the contention that public historians, like the Royal Marine, must be "soldiers and sailors too."

Historic preservation, historic site interpretation, and both historical and industrial archeology are comparatively new disciplines for public historians to enter. Recording, preserving, and interpreting the tangible remains of our past in many cases require a historian to serve as part of an interdisciplinary team. Historic preservation as an activity involving professionals can be conveniently dated with the Williamsburg projects in the 1920s, but its real growth has occurred during the past two or three decades during which the movement's focus has been greatly enlarged to include not only the stately houses of prominent Americans such as Mount Vernon, but the preservation of a wide variety of structures representing all segments of society. Thus, historic districts of workers' houses and the industries in which they work have been preserved both on an individual basis and, increasingly, as historic districts. With the passage of the Tax Reform Act of 1976 and subsequent legislation, the adaptive reuse of historic properties has become an attractive investment proposition for developers and a new field of endeavor for public historians.

Barbara J. Howe has a longstanding commitment to and experience in historic preservation. In two essays she explores the role of historians in historic preservation and presents a convincing argument for the interdisciplinary team approach to preserving and interpreting historic sites. Historic preservation seminars, internships, short courses, and classes are noteworthy features of many public history programs or are specialized options in schools of architecture; in a few cases they constitute a self-contained program.

As a measure of its coming of age, there are now federal programs which support and regulate historic preservation activities. The federal presence is also felt at the state level through federal support of State Historic Preservation Offices and state programs. The federal government also provides major funding for the National Trust for Historic Preservation. To understand the historic preservation movement in America, it is necessary to be familiar with this federal involvement. Thus, Beth Grosvenor's essay serves as a history of the development of an increasingly important aspect of public history, as an introduction to federal preservation programs and regulations, and as reference for those engaged in preservation projects.

The federal government's stewardship of land for conservation and recreation purposes is symbolized by Smokey the Bear. The public, one suspects, is most familiar with the conservation of natural resources in the national park system. This stewardship of land on behalf of the public also extends to the USDA Forest Service, the U.S. Army Corps of Engineers, and other federal agencies. The idea of conservation has been extended so that federal agencies are not just concerned with conserving *natural* resources but are equally responsible for the management of *cultural* resources, especially sites involving historic properties or significant archeological remains. In her essay Janet G. Brashler, an archeologist with the USDA Forest Service, succinctly defines cultural resources management:

> Cultural resources management may be defined as a philosophy, legal framework, and decision-making process which guides treatment of historic and prehistoric properties on federal lands or lands affected by federally funded or licensed activities. Another phrase with similar meaning, federal historic presrvation, is less consistent with the orientation of most federal land managing agencies whose primary philosophy is conservation-oriented instead of strictly preservation-oriented. A conservation orientation relies on management strategies of differential allocation— some resources are used or consumed, some discarded, some preserved intact, and some are renewed. While these practices can occur in preservation-oriented organizations, the emphasis tends to be on "preserving" or "saving" resources rather than "using" resources.

This definition undergirds a case study of a historic property in the Monongahela National Forest which, in turn, illustrates the approach used to resolve questions of preservation, historic significance, and interpretation in the face of a special interest group seeking "full" restoration of a property of questionable historic value.

Both classical archeology and history share many common concerns, and each has been enriched by the other. A comparative newcomer to the field is industrial archeology which seeks to record, interpret, and in selected cases preserve extant structures, machines, and manufacturing processes which are tangible reminders of the origins and development of the Industrial Revolution.

In his essay Emory L. Kemp establishes the relationship of industrial archeology to the more widely recognized and broader field of archeology. It is through the techniques and methodology employed by industrial archeologists that the role of the historian emerges as an essential and often leading member of a team recording an industrial site. Industrial archeology has provided primary source material, which could not be obtained by any other means, for historians of technology concerned with the development of technology in the context of social history.

Many have visited historic sites across the country and participated in guided tours, museum exhibits, and other forms of interpretation intended to provide the visitor with some sense of the history and significance of the site. In the Middle Atlantic states Civil War battlefields have been perennial favorites with the public and especially with brigades of Civil War buffs.

In the craft of historical writing the skilled historian defines, classifies, and evaluates a myriad of historical evidence into an understandable narrative. The same is true in providing a sound and accurate interpretation of a historical site. The development of dioramas, brochures, exhibits, and interpretive panels is all part of the job of historians associated with historical sites. The Antietam Battlefield provides a fascinating case study of the preparation necessary by historians for a succesful site interpretation. With his firsthand knowledge of all facets of such an enterprise, Lige Benton Miller, Jr., gives an insider's view of the complexities and challenges in historic site interpretation.

From these essays emerges a picture of the rich varieties of positions held by public historians and unique insights into what each type of career requires of a public historian. The picture that emerges is of a developing profession united in bringing a sense of history to the public with integrity and competence in the best tradition of historical scholarship, creative presentation, and competent management.

Fredric Miller received a B.A. in Social Sciences from the State University of New York-Binghamton in 1967 and both the Ph.D. in History (1972) and M.S. in Library Science (1973) from the University of Wisconsin-Madison. He has been Curator of the Urban Archives Center of Temple University since 1973 and Adjunct Associate Professor of History since 1978. He is the co-author of Still Philadelphia: A Photographic History, 1890–1940 *(Philadelphia: Temple University Press, 1983) and the author of articles on archival administration, black migration to Philadelphia, and British social policy in the 1930s.*

ARCHIVES AND HISTORICAL MANUSCRIPTS

Fredric Miller

Then Darius the king issued an official document and they conducted an investigation into the archives of the treasuries deposited there at Babylon, and a roll was found in the fortress of Ecbatana in the province of Media with the following written on it—Memorandum: In the first year of Cyrus the king, Cyrus the king issued an official document. About the house of God at Jerusalem: Let the house where sacrifices are offered be reconstructed and its foundations retained. . . .

Ezra 6: 1–3

But fortunate too the man who is friends with the country gods. . . . He spares not a glance for the iron rigour of law, the municipal racket, the public records.

Virgil, Geogrics, ii (493, 500–02)

Both the importance of historical records and their unhappy public image clearly date back thousands of years. Civilization often is identified with writing, and the earliest writing was in fact record keeping. As Virgil noted in his hymn of praise to the rural life, the Tabularia—the archives—were connected intimately to the ordered life of cities and public administration. For him—as for others who have followed—they symbolized some of the routine and regimented aspects of urban society. Yet many of his fellow Romans used archives readily in the writing of history and the administration of government, much as Darius had used his archives to retrieve that memorandum for the grateful Hebrews four centuries before.[1]

Such ambivalent attitudes toward archives and archivists have dominated the relationship between the historical and archival professions.
Since the late nineteenth century, the reliance of historical research on
primary sources, the increasing identification of "professional historian"
with "history professor," and the fluctuating job market for historians
have combined to produce a variety of patterns in the United States.
Archivists are regarded by academic historians sometimes as colleagues,
sometimes as assistants, and sometimes as unrelated professionals. Much
of the uncertainty is based on incomprehension. To understand the
archival profession as part of the larger world of historical work, it is
necessary to understand what archives are and what archivists do—
subjects which have recently not been part of the training of most
historians.

ARCHIVES AND MANUSCRIPT COLLECTIONS

Unfortunately, the use of the word *archives* in the English language
adds to the confusion. To begin with, it can mean an actual building, an
agency, or a collection of historical documents. Strictly speaking, archives as historical documents are "the noncurrent records of an
organization or institution preserved because of their continuing value"
by that organization or institution.[2] They are in effect those of its files
which are of historic interest. In direct contrast to deliberate intellectual
creations like books, "archives were not drawn up in the interest or for
the information of Posterity."[3] They derive instead from some kind of
ongoing activity.

Archivists are responsible for determining which records deserve to
be retained permanently, and for ensuring that they are then preserved
and made available for use. But of course there are many records—
ranging from the old files of a YMCA to the personal papers of a long
dead Congressman—which are not maintained by their creators but are
instead held by such institutions as university libraries, historical societies, and private research centers, which may each have the papers and
records of hundreds of individuals and organizations. Technically such
materials held outside of their original custody are called manuscript
collections. The professionals who work with them are often called
manuscript curators, though to add to the confusion the generic term
archivist can also include them, and hundreds of manuscript curators are
members of the Society of American Archivists. Some people are both
archivist and curator, being responsible for the archives of their own
institution while also collecting related records and personal papers.

In terms of modern historical materials, archives and manuscript
collections have many similarities. "Most recent private records have the
organizational quality of public records and are therefore archival in
character."[4] Archivists and manuscript curators have the same kinds of
duties, and both tend to become experts in the subjects documented by
their collections. Since manuscript curators are responsible for records
coming from different sources, they are in one sense "a kind of multiple

archivist."[5] Adding to the complexity of the field is the development of new types or formats of historical materials. Thus, some archivists specialize in a kind of record, such as photographs, maps, or machine-readable records, just as many others specialize in more traditional historical themes.

The relationship of archives and manuscripts to the writing of history lends itself to a multitude of images, some flattering, others less so. Archives have customarily been described as the primary resources of history. Historians "mine" archives and manuscript collections, which are often stored in conditions which justify the metaphor. For those of a more scientific bent, collections of primary materials are the laboratories of the historical profession, the places where the raw data is kept and the experiments performed. Even those historians who rarely venture outside the secondary literature usually think of archives as in some way the foundation of historical research. As Philip Brooks pointed out, "the scholar is wholly dependent upon the archivist not only for the preservation, the condition and the order of the documents, but also for their identification."[6]

Yet archives and manuscript repositories are far more than the preserve of the lonely scholar. They might instead be thought of as the original public history programs, established to serve the direct needs of institutions, in the case of archives, or citizens interested in the past, in the case of manuscript collections and historical societies. It is crucial to recognize that the vast majority of the users of these materials are not professional historians, just as the people who create original records and personal papers are not historians. But it is equally true that in the end archives and historical manuscripts are about history. Individuals come to them to find out about something in the past, whether as part of their work or for purely personal reasons. In a fundamental sense, "the primary purpose of archives is cultural, and it is the research value of documentation that invests this essentially cultural purpose with substance and significance."[7] The archivist is thus the quintessential public historian, interacting first with a variety of people to identify historical materials, and then making it possible for others to put those materials to different uses.

Such a field is naturally diffuse.[8] And the nature of American social and political institutions reinforces that tendency, for it is institutional settings that define the work of archivists and manuscript curators. Most archivists in the strict definition of the word work in the comparatively straightforward area of public records. Here there is a clear geographic structure of repositories from the National Archives, through the fifty state archives, to those relatively scarce cities and counties fortunate enough to have professional archivists on their staffs. With some variations and exceptions, these archivists work primarily on the records generated by the government which employs them.

The National Archives and Records Administration, established in 1934, dwarfs all other archival repositories in size and importance. Now an independent agency of the government, like the Library of Congress and the Smithsonian Institution, it employs hundreds of professional archivists and has custody over about 1.4 million cubic feet of records. The staff of the National Archives is responsible for determining which files produced by each agency of the federal government are worthy of permanent retention. In addition, the archives runs the nine presidential libraries which contain the papers of the presidents since Herbert Hoover, as well as many of their associates. While the National Archives has pioneered in some aspects of archival administration, its complex bureaucracy and the sheer mountain of paper with which it deals make it very atypical.[9]

In contrast, the state archives range from long-established, highly active institutions to small operations in obscure agencies. Despite the fact that the first state archives was established as early as 1901 in Alabama, a national overview reveals a very uneven pattern of support.[10] Nevertheless, the diversity of state archives and their large but manageable size has ensured that some have always been in the forefront of archival experimentation. Current activities in such states as New York, Illinois, Texas, Kentucky, Alabama, and Wisconsin continue that tradition.

Not all archivists work for governments. Private institutional archives form the other major type of archival repository. All kinds of agencies, societies, and organizations maintain their own archives. Among the most common in the United States are those of colleges and universities, churches and other religious organizations, and corporations. Archives are also maintained by some labor unions, hospitals, social service organizations, and scientific groups. In sharp contrast to the government repositories, private institutional archives are often very small operations, with only one or two full-time professional archivists.

The world of manuscript repositories in many ways parallels this archival system, though there are significant differences. Because they go out into society to acquire from many different sources both personal papers and organizational records—"fugitive archives" in a sense—the lines of division between manuscript repositories are not as neat as they are for archives. Collecting policies overlap considerably. So there is no one institution like the National Archives, though the Library of Congress comes closest. The library's Manuscript Division, which was created in 1897, contains the papers of twenty-three presidents and the records of such national organizations as the NAACP. Of course other institutions have collected on a national scale, such as major universities like Harvard, Texas, and Indiana; libraries like the New York Public and the Newberry in Chicago; and research establishments like the Hoover Institution.

Most manuscript repositories are far more focused than these by geographic area or subject concentration, though in either case they can and do acquire collections of national importance. Manuscript collections with a geographic orientation are commonly found in public libraries, and many have recently been established at universities. But the most prominent are in the state and local historical societies, which already numbered over 200 in the United States by 1900, and nearly 1,500 in 1944.[11] They range from such large and professionally run institutions as the Massachusetts Historical Society (founded in 1791), to county repositories and even town or neighborhood societies, which are often open only a few hours a week and staffed by volunteers. Historical societies tend to include libraries, museums, and educational programs, as well as manuscript collections.[12] Some double as genealogical societies, while others serve as the official public archives, as in Wisconsin.

Very different are subject-oriented manuscript collections, generally found in either academic settings or independent research institutions. Paralleling private institutional archives, in virtually every area of American life, they have collected personal papers and the records of defunct organizations or organizations unable to support their own archivist.[13] For example, labor records are collected by Cornell, Wayne State, Georgia State, and Pennsylvania State universities and the State Historical Society of Wisconsin, among others, while the Baker Library at Harvard and the Hagley Museum in Delaware are prominent collectors of business records.[14] Many religious denominations and ethnic groups have historical societies or university collections devoted to their development. Larger repositories often specialize in a number of subjects. The State Historical Society of Wisconsin, for example, has important groups of collections on contemporary social action and mass communications, as well as on labor. With private libraries like the Morgan in New York, the Clements in Michigan, and the Huntington in California, which specialize in rare and valuable items, added to the mixture, the rich complexity of the manuscripts world is evident.

RESPONSIBILITIES OF ARCHIVISTS AND CURATORS

Archivists and manuscripts curators clearly work on a wide variety of subjects, with various types of records and in many different settings, all depending on the specific mission of the repository. Yet whatever that mission, archivists and curators share a broad range of professional responsibilities. The degree to which any individual is involved with one or all of them varies according to the size and organization of different repositories. But there is an essential core common to the work of all those responsible for historical records.

To put it succinctly, that core is the charge to preserve historically valuable materials and make them available for use. Everything else is an expansion of that deceptively simple assignment. It is important to remember this essential goal, because its implementation involves a great deal of detailed and often technical work, whose basic justification must always be kept in mind. Similarly, archivists and curators learn to adapt policies and procedures to both the nature and the content of their holdings. Archival work holds its interest only by avoiding a divorce between content and technique. Thus, the daily work of most professionals usually has a direct relationship to what their collections document.

The most fundamental set of tasks involves acquiring materials for the repository. "Adapting the aphorism that 'each generation rewrites history', it may be said that each generation collects records anew, not replacing what is already in hand, but enriching the accretion."[15] To that end, archivists have to ensure that the "life cycle of records" in their organization culminates in the retention of historically important materials in the archives. Manuscript curators have to decide what areas and/or subjects they are willing and able to document. Archival decisions are often related to records management programs, which regulate the creation and destruction of internal paperwork, usually with a view toward efficiency rather than history.[16] Manuscript repositories in contrast have to establish collecting policies, not unlike libraries. They look at their institutional mission and decide which of the thousands of potential collections of papers and records in the outside world they should even attempt to acquire. The transfer of organizational records can sometimes involve manuscript repositories in records management, but the operations of most repositories remain comparatively isolated from the creation of materials they hold.

Deciding what should be kept is still a long way from putting record cartons on the shelves. Both archives and manuscript repositories often conduct surveys to locate and identify potential acquisitions. An in-house survey is an obvious prelude to a sensible records management and archives program. For manuscript curators, general surveys of the potential donors in a field may help define a collecting policy. A more detailed survey of a possible acquisition can precede one of their most challenging tasks—obtaining an agreement for the transfer of records or personal papers.[17] Unlike archivists, manuscript curators must persuade organizations and individuals to physically part with their property— whether by deed, will, deposit, gift, or some other agreement. An elaborate negotiation is often involved, and diplomatic skills are not the least of the requirements for many manuscript positions. A whole range of donor relationships and conditions of access can be discussed, and the discussions can go on for years before the material appears in the repository. While an archivist confronting a bureaucrat reluctant to part with "his" files might disagree, the process of establishing and implementing a collecting policy clearly distinguishes the world of manuscripts from that of archives.

Having been offered a set of records or successfully concluded a negotiation, one crucial task still lies ahead in the area of acquisitions— that of determining precisely which materials should be accepted into the respository. This process is called appraisal. Here the archivists' task is probably the more challenging. They may face tens of thousands of cubic feet of files, while manuscript collections rarely exceed a few hundred feet. As early as 1904, the first guide to federal archives noted that "the mere mass of these records of the government is well-nigh appalling," and the problem has gotten far worse in the ensuing decades.[18] The National Archives saves less than 5 percent of the paper produced by the federal government, and a similar standard applies to many other public and corporate archives.

The decision-making process involves many complex considerations, of which value to historical scholarship is only one. To a large extent, appraisal is informed guesswork. "Recognizing that associating records with future use was a prophetic act, Philip Bauer concluded that 'prophecy is the essence of archival evaluation'."[19] Inactive records may have permanent value for the continued operation for the organization which created them—as a reference to past policies and procedures; for financial accounting; for legal requirements; for public relations programs; or for some other administrative purpose. Key files, such as minutes, are often saved as the basis of the corporate memory, without any thought of outside users. In the rather unique phraseology of the eminent British archivist Sir Hilary Jenkinson, the "Golden Rule of Archive-Making" is to ensure that records are in "such a state of completeness and order that, supposing (an administrator) and his staff to be by some accident totally obliterated, a successor totally ignorant of the work of the office would be able to take it up and carry it on with the least possible inconvenience and delay simply on the strength of a study of the Office files."[20] In contrast to such considerations of "evidential value," saving records for their research potential involves an informed evaluation of the kind of information they contain, the nature of the activity they document, and how they might be useful to the research community. The archivist or curator must also assess how information is contained in the records—to what extent the collection can be made usable for research.

Whatever the arguments for saving records, whether for internal or external use or both, their value has to then be weighed against the mission and the resources of the respository. All records have some potential use to someone, which is often made clear to the archivist shortly after they are destroyed. But appraisal is the very difficult task of balancing that value against other factors, and often making the irreversible decision not to retain original records. One of the most important principles of appraisal is that not all old records are by definition archival; not all original documents deserve to be saved. As Leonard Rapport noted after many years in this field, "Appraisal is at best an inexact science, perhaps more an art; and a conscientious appraiser, particularly an imaginative one with an awareness of research trends and interests, is apt to know nights of troubled soul searching."[21]

Most archival and manuscript work begins when appraisal ends. Records have to be arranged, described, stored, and occasionally restored, before they can be used. These are detailed, labor intensive internal operations, a good deal of which can be done by nonprofessional staff under the general supervision of the archivist or curator. The first manual on such archival operations, published by three Dutch archivists in 1898, opens with the forthright declaration that "This is a tedious and meticulous book. The reader is warned."[22] The admonition applies most directly to the arranging and describing of materials, known as "processing." This is somewhat analagous to physical classification and book cataloging as done in a library.

There are, however, major differences. Both archivists and manuscript curators keep their holdings together by creator rather than by subject—the principle of "provenance." They arrange the materials by organizational structure or personal activity, and within that structure by type of filing group, such as memoranda, correspondence, diaries, ledgers, and so forth. The filing groups themselves—known to archivists as "series"—are kept in the same order as they were during their active life, where this was not purely idiosyncratic. This is known as the principle of "original order." Both provenance and original order are based upon the concept that, in Theodore Schellenberg's words, "records have a collective rather than a unitary significance. All records arising from a particular activity have a cohesive character and are part of one another. . . . Their subject content is only incidental to accomplishing an action."[23] Finally, the main method of describing collections to others is not the catalog card but the inventory. Inventories can be many pages in length and customarily include an organizational history or personal biography, an essay on the major components of the collection, and a list of the different file units, sometimes down to the folder level. Archivists and curators thus think in terms of a folder containing a year of correspondence within the "outgoing correspondence" series of someone's papers or office files. They think in terms of a document's place within an organically unified whole, rather than in terms of an individual book or article, as is the case with most library work.[24]

The arrangement of records and the preparation of inventories are the bases for other internal operations. As records are arranged, those in need of repair, restoration, or special storage (such as photographs) can be separated. Preservation is a vital operation in all repositories, whether or not they can afford specialized staff, space, and equipment.[25] Basic descriptive work also generates further activity. Many respositories produce published guides based on their inventories and report their holdings as described in the inventories to national data bases. These external "finding aids" are complemented by internal aids which supplement the inventories, such as special lists, card catalogs, and computerized indexes. Because manuscript repositories have many different collections with no organizational relationship to each other, it is especially important that they have some overall system to help provide users with access to information spread throughout their holdings.

COLLECTION USERS

Use is the ultimate justification for all the work outlined above. Archivists and curators have to be service-oriented rather than research-oriented. For those with traditional historical training, this can be a difficult assignment. The very knowledge and training which enables them to assist researchers can also tempt them to view the collections as researchers. Many do in fact use their own collections. But their primary goal has to be enabling others to use them. The tension can be aggravated by the depth of knowledge which archivists and curators acquire about their holdings. Inventories, guides, and catalogs never provide the kind of detailed familiarity that comes from working on the materials. Library systems are designed to send people directly to books and articles. In contrast, because of what Richard Lytle has termed a "creator-oriented" approach, archival and manuscript systems lead researchers to the archivist for assistance.[26] "The archivist is assumed to be a subject specialist who introduces the user to relevant records through the finding aids, and continues to mediate between the user and the archival system throughout the user's research."[27]

People come to archives and manuscript repositories for a variety of reasons. In many repositories, especially historical societies and public archives, the majority of users are genealogists. Most users of collections at colleges and universities are students or scholars. Institutional archives may rely on internal use in support of ongoing programs. In all repositories, professional historians are a distinct minority, while use by such people as lawyers and homeowners interested in historic preservation is increasing. Archivists and curators have to establish policies and procedures for access to and use of their materials which take the nature of their users into consideration. In addition, to maintain and increase both use and consequent institutional support, many repositories engage in public programs. These can include in-house or traveling exhibits, instructional sessions, and media presentations.[28] Based on a widespread popular interest in history, they bring people into what are usually regarded as dusty, antiquated, and yet exclusive institutions to try to break down the barrier between the interest in history and the aversion to historical collections.

That same barrier exists for many professional historians, though in somewhat different form. While far from reluctant to use collections, they are usually unfamiliar with the application of historical skills in archival work. As users, they naturally have little interest in internal operations, and the most efficient repositories are those which bring researchers and materials together with the minimal amount of intervention from the archivist. So it is not difficult to see a respository in terms of stacks of boxes and an overwhelming amount of clerical detail. Yet the skills and knowledge of the historical profession are central to archival operations. Archivists and curators have to understand how research is conducted and how to evaluate historical evidence. They must be able to analyze large collections of documents, to determine what about them is significant, and to write about them in clear prose. In most cases, they must be knowledgable about the subjects which their collections document and the trends in research on those subjects. These historical skills are especially important in such key functions as acquisitions, appraisal, description, use, and public programs. It is no accident that graduate historical training has always been considered essential for the administrators of major archival programs. For, in practice, "the archivist's use of history is as obvious as the historical researcher's use of archives."[29]

This symbiotic relationship is evident in a number of recent projects and publications. Perhaps the most interesting in the basic area of acquisitions was the work of the Joint Committee on the Archives of Science and Technology (JCAST). The committee was created in 1978 as a cooperative venture of the History of Science Society, the Society of American Archivists, the Society for the History of Technology, and the Association of Records Managers and Administrators. Its members spent five years analyzing the documentation of post-World War II American science and technology. Both the nature of research and development and the extremely complex structure of the scientific establishment itself pose unique difficulties for historians and archivists. Experiments produce huge amounts of data, the overwhelming mass of which cannot and should not be saved. Yet somehow the process of discovery—as opposed to merely the published results—has to be preserved. Much of that work of discovery takes place in industrial settings or private research institutes, where security is of far greater concern than history. Even if corporations and institutes saved their records, there would remain the problem of personal notes and papers, where many would argue that the real history of innovation can be found. And for all these records there is a wide variety of potential repositories, from specialized archival centers to the university archives which solicit the papers of prominent graduates. The JCAST group made recommendations for action and research in all these areas and more in their final report.[30] Whatever its ultimate impact, by the time it was published in 1983, centers for the history of information processing, electrical engineering, physics, and chemistry were already in existence.

TYPES OF RECORDS

While archivists try to acquire the records of technology, they also have to deal with records made possible by technology—computerized or machine-readable records. In public agencies and large corporations, such records are increasingly used to document routine transactions such as cases and interoffice communication. A major effort is required to convince administrators that records are records whether they are on a paper base or a magnetized plastic base. Such an effort was made in Wisconsin between 1979 and 1981, when a survey of state agency files conducted jontly by the State Historical Society and the university's Data Library resulted in a program to apply archival principles to machine-readable records. The final report of the project analyzes the records produced by several key finance and service agencies and emphasizes the urgency of the problem.[31] Unless archivists and historians can establish some control over the generation of such records early in their life cycle, there may be little usable social and economic documentation left for the future.

As some archivists struggle to identify records in unfamiliar fields like

science or unfamiliar formats like computer tapes, many others still fight
the mountain of paper. The most prominent recent field of battle was at
the Federal Bureau of Investigation. After a complicated series of court
cases in the 1970s, the National Archives and the FBI were ordered to
prepare a retention and disposition plan for the bureau's case files,
which the FBI had wanted to destroy. The resultant FBI Appraisal
Project staff found themselves facing 25 million files in fifty-nine field
offices as well as Washington. There were 214 different case classifications. Working with historians and FBI personnel, the staff evaluated
each classification by examining nearly 18,000 files in detail and preparing a statistical profile for each classification. Historians contributed a list
of 4,000 exceptional cases to be saved, while sampling percentages and
procedures were developed for each classification. Statistical criteria of
research significance were developed, the most reliable of which turned
out to be the thickness of the folder. The "fat file" test of historical
significance, first revealed in a study of Massachusetts court records, was
thus reconfirmed. In the end, the staff recommended the retention of
some fifty thousand cubic feet of files, or one-sixth of the original total.[32]

GUIDES AND INVENTORIES

Archivists and curators use one set of historical skills and knowledge
in acquisitions and appraisal. They use other skills in descriptive work.
Guides and inventories are the major vehicles for them to write about
their collections. In such publications "the archivist has the opportunity
and the obligation to analyze in some detail the content and the potential
use of the records as well as (their) function and composition."[33] By their
nature such writings are not usually best sellers, and their prose is rarely
scintillating. But they can and sometimes do rise above the level of
bureaucratic recitations. Both the organizational history or personal
biography and the analysis of holdings, which precede the box lists in
standard inventories, should be viewed as a legitimate form of critical
historical writing. Similarly, the indices and appendices which often
conclude inventories may involve considerable research and analysis of
the collection. The inventories to record groups at the National Archives, though not known for their innovative style, are widely available
examples of these customarily in-house documents and illustrate the
kind of historical writing involved in archival description.

Institutional guides are intended for wider public distribution. Since
they often list almost all of a respository's holdings in a very summary
way, they offer only limited opportunities for creative writing. One
partial exception is the *Guide to the Swarthmore College Peace Collection*.
Each collection entry is a capsule history or biography, and many offer
evaluations of the collection.[34] A different publication from a very
different institution is the *Guide to the Hoover Institution Archives*, which
relies on a detailed index, taking up one-third of the 420-page volume,
and very short collection entries.[35]

Perhaps more challenging than the preparation of an institutional guide is the preparation of a guide to collections on a particular subject held by repositories around the country. The recent model in this area is the massive *Women's History Sources: A Guide to Archives and Manuscript Collections in the United States*, published in 1979. The product of four years of work by a team of archivists and historians based at the University of Minnesota's Social Welfare History Archives, the guide describes 18,026 collections in 1,558 institutions. It is arranged geographically and supplemented by a separate index volume. Using both a mail survey of 11,000 repositories and a team of twenty field workers, the survey staff did everything from working out a definition of "women's collections" to occasionally processing a collection in order to find out what it contained. The success of the survey project resulted in a guide which has lived up to its promise to mark "the beginning of a new era of research into women's lives."[36]

ARCHIVISTS AND THEIR PUBLICS

Historians and archivists collaborate on projects like the Women's History Sources survey because of their common interest in use. But not all interactions over use are so friendly. The interest of archivists and curators in long-term preservation, their reluctance to open unprocessed collections, and their need to respect the wishes of donors and depositors can conflict directly with the desire of researchers for access to documents. The basic issues were dealt with in 1976 at a conference on access to the papers of recent public figures sponsored by the Organization of American Historians–American Historical Association–Society of American Archivists Committee on Historians and Archivists. This conference at New Harmony, Indiana, did not entirely live up to the name of its location, as major disagreements arose on a variety of issues. The topics included such sensitive matters as the length of restrictions on records, archivists' responsibilities as advocates for history in relation to donors, the validity of privacy restrictions, the nature of "national security" files, the disposition of congressional and judicial papers, and the operation of the Freedom of Information Act. These are among the most difficult ethical issues faced by archivists. As the final report noted, "Perhaps the most persuasive theme of the discussions was the special character of the demands for access made by historians of the contemporary era."[37] Here historians of earlier periods allied with archivists in arguing that extreme demands could lead to the destruction of records rather than their preservation. But there was something of an adversarial climate at New Harmony, with a recognition that "the twin goals of preservation and use of historical sources are not always easily reconciled."[38]

Archivists and curators usually interact with the public in the much less controversial area of historical public programming. Historical resources form the basis for a wide variety of programs, many of which go well beyond the traditional in-house exhibit. The Vanishing Georgia project begun in 1975 is an excellent example of a project which both raised historical consciousness and saved valuable records. Using a mobile laboratory, a team of archivists traveled throughout the state copying photographs in the hands of individuals and institutions.[39] As with so many old photographs, the content could only be explained by the owners. In a sense, the project was not only photographic history, but oral history. The Minnesota Historical Society has also been active in public programming, with a somewhat different approach. Drawing upon its own resources, the society has created multimedia History Research Units for distribution throughout the state. A unit on the Ojibwe people included thirty-five small booklets for classroom use, eight filmstrips, and a variety of charts, diagrams, and posters.[40] The society has also offered mini-classes in such subjects as graphic resources, church records, and genealogical research.

One well-known program which involved many different kinds of public history activities was the New York State Historians-in-Residence Program. Many of its local projects involved either utilizing existing archival and manuscript resources, as in Minnesota, or helping people to uncover hidden resources in their own communities, as in Georgia. The program had a "philosophical commitment to the democratization of scholarship and learning."[41] It thus viewed historical materials in an active sense, as resources which should be brought to people, rather than passively remaining in the proverbial dark stacks.

ARCHIVISTS AS ADMINISTRATORS

Such programs bring the archivists out of those stacks as well. Though their major concern is the core of activities comprising the acquisition, processing, preservation, and use of materials, archivists and curators have a variety of other roles and relationships. The most universal are as both administrators and employees within an organization. Except for the National Archives, archives and manuscript collections are always within some larger operation, whether a department of education supervising a state archives, a historical society which contains a manuscript section, or a university library with a department of special collections. Throughout the United States, "manuscript repositories are parts of a great variety of administrative structure but . . . none exists as an administrative unit unto itself."[42] Since the numbers of people using their resources are always smaller than those visiting the museums or libraries which generally form the other parts of the organization, archivists and curators have to be able to justify the long-term value of their work to their superiors and contribute to the work of their colleagues in related cultural programs.

At the same time, archivists and curators have their own internal managerial responsibilities. Because most archives and manuscript collections are relatively small, administrative arrangements tend not to be elaborate. However, in contrast to academic historians, archivists and curators generally work a thirty-five to forty-hour week within an organized hierarchy. Few repositories are run collegially. In larger operations, the professional staff may be organized functionally or by type and subject of records, with a few senior archivists responsible for overall policy and administration. But most professional archivists and curators, even in entry-level positions, have some staff of their own, which might consist of paraprofessionals, clerks, student assistants, and/or volunteers. Archivists have to not only plan and organize their work but also supervise it as it proceeds. So in dealing with people on all administrative levels, archivists and curators develop and employ the same kinds of common sense skills in human relations found necessary in all modern organizations.

Other administrative responsibilities are similarly removed from typical academic concerns. Many archivists and curators, especially in smaller operations, also have some responsibilities for physical planning, security, public relations, and budgeting. Perhaps their most important administrative task is fund raising, since repositories are chronically short of money. Internal support can sometimes be increased by participation in such ongoing activities as a commemorative history or a research project. A more regular flow of funds can come from an endowment campaign or the establishment of a "Friends" group, both activities drawing on people with a special interest in the respository's holdings. In addition, there are a variety of external funding sources. Preparing grant proposals for submission to these sources is a challenging task, drawing upon the archivist's skill in conceptualizing needs, developing work plans and budgets, and presenting the proposal in clear but persuasive prose.

National and local private foundations sometimes support archival or manuscripts projects, but the archivist has to know the interests and requirements of the foundation being approached. Many are limited both in geography and scope, though local foundations are often responsive to local historical needs. The federal government has been a more reliable source of funding for the profession as a whole. The primary purpose of both the Access Section of the Reference Works Program (formerly the Research Resources Program) of the National Endowment for the Humanities and the Records Program of the National Historical Publications and Records Commission is to support archives and manuscript repositories. Together they have funded hundreds of projects. Both agencies insist on sound internal funding before they approve proposals. Looking ahead, one NEH administrator predicted that "increasingly, federal funds will be seen as only one of several sources of support, with additional monies to come from the institution itself and from private sources."[43] Archivists and curators thus have to sustain basic support even as they seek outside grants for special projects.

THE ARCHIVISTS' NETWORK

That sometimes delicate balancing act emphasizes the network of professional relationships within which archivists and curators operate.

Financial and administrative arrangements often link them with records managers and/or librarians. Archives in the narrow sense of in-house repositories are especially close to records management operations. In fact, records management as a separate field grew out of the archival profession in the 1940s as a result of the New Deal–World War II government paper explosion. Records managers were thus naturally oriented toward rapid disposal. The field expanded rapidly since it offered government and business a bottom line saving in space and office efficiency. By 1955 records managers had their own organization and soon developed their own training system. They are now essential to all large public and private bureaucracies and are often found well placed in the organization charts. But in their rise they have generally left behind history as well as archivists. As early as 1951, the Archivist of the United States explained that "management outlook and experience are essential to the records management specialist if he is to develop as a member of the management team. . . . "[44] In some respects, the records manager's orientation underlines the essential ties between archivists and the historical profession. In relation to the records manager—usually the only other professional in an organization who is primarily concerned with records—the archivist inevitably becomes the advocate for history.

Relations between the archival profession and librarianship are also close and complex. The former is sometimes described as a cross between historical study and librarianship, for "archives and libraries exist as cultural institutions for a common purpose, to collect, maintain, and make available the written and graphic record of man's intellect and experience."[45] The comparison is especially apt for manuscript collections, which like libraries develop collecting policies, have elaborate descriptive systems, and are justified on intellectual rather than administrative grounds. But innovative library practices such as automated information retrieval and overall collection management are increasingly useful to archives as well.

However, the administrative placement of archives and manuscript collections within libraries raises serious difficulties, even while providing materials a safe haven. Libraries are oriented toward the acquisition and handling of widely used books and periodicals, and "any library responsive to its clientele will place funding emphasis on the services most in demand."[46] Archives and manuscripts are often found in special collections departments removed from the central work of the library. Library administrators have in addition become increasingly preoccupied with automation and management, minimizing their involvement with specialized research materials. Similarly, graduate training in librarianship is now oriented toward the "information sciences" rather than specific bibliographic knowledge, a development which has exacerbated the issues both of the placement of archives in libraries and the role of library education in archival training.

THE ARCHIVIST'S EDUCATION

The latter issue remains alive because agreement has never been reached on an educational system for archivists and manuscript curators. Traditionally, graduate work in history was combined with post-appointment on-the-job training or attendance at the short institute conducted by the National Archives. By the early 1970s, graduate courses in archival management had been developed by individual archivists at a number of universities. The common core of their programs was codified as the guidelines for education adopted by the Society of American Archivists (SAA) in 1977.[47] These mandate an introductory course on theory and operations, an internship of at least 140 hours providing professional preparation, and an independent research project—in practice, three courses completed in a year of study. The courses should be taught at accredited universities by archivists. The society refrained from trying to enforce the guidelines, and while most programs accommodate them, there remains little standardization in archival education.

The SAA guidelines notably failed to state within what larger graduate program the courses were to be offered. Some are in history departments, some in library schools, and others in both. Advocates of historical training argue the need for subject expertise and a knowledge of the research process. The SAA guidelines state clearly that "training in research methods and experience in conducting original research are essential if the archivist is to fully discharge his or her professional responsibilities."[48] Supporters of librarianship note the archivists' need for administrative and technical skills, and a service orientation. Further, they claim that the guidelines "fail to integrate archival education into the larger field of information sciences."[49] The ideal combination may well be history and some elements of information sciences. While the debate continues, changes are taking place. Regardless of department, education according to the SAA Guidelines is becoming the professional norm. From now on, "archival institutions administered by well-trained and experienced archivists will insist that new employees also be well-trained and educated."[50]

Archival education does not necessarily lead to a standard entry-level position. Most people do begin by doing a good deal of processing and basic reference work, but in small operations they may do much else besides. Many beginning positions are specialized grant projects and can lead to permanent specialized positions in larger repositories. In such repositories, there is a career ladder of increasing administrative and policy responsibility, as in the library or museum fields. Administration of an archival or manuscript program can lead to higher level of overall historical agency administration. But most archivists and manuscript curators seem to find the absence of large-scale organization an attraction of their work, with its consequent closeness to historical materials and their users.

That almost intimate scale of work is reflected in the profession's structure. The Society of American Archivists, headquartered in Chicago, has about two thousand members and publishes the journal of record, the *American Archivist*. In addition, through its publications program, workshops, placement service, lobbying efforts, national convention, and other activities, the SAA offers the full range of professional services. Regional and state archival organizations have flourished since the early 1970s, and these less elaborate groups "have largely supplanted the SAA as the vehicle by which younger archivists gain much needed organizational experience and professional maturity."[51] Recently even more informal archival groups have formed in most major metropolitan areas. The fairly complete coverage of the profession geographically and its small size—with only about four thousand members in all organizations in 1982—means that few people are long unaware of major new trends and developments in the field.

NEW CHALLENGES AND OPPORTUNITIES

In the 1980s those trends and developments range from the automation of internal operations to the increase in university trained archivists. Automation is perhaps the most ubiquitous and certainly the most discussed. Archives and manuscript collections were traditionally idiosyncratic, with no common holdings or purchasing procedures to justify standardization on the library model. Each repository had its own forms and system of finding aids. Until some uniformity was achieved, there could be no automated information sharing between institutions, though individual repositories could automate such operations as the internal preparation and updating of inventories. By the early 1980s, basic rules and formats for the cataloging and summary description of archives and manuscript collections had finally been developed through cooperation between the SAA, the Library of Congress, and the Research Libraries Group. This breakthrough is making possible the gradual emergence of a computerized, searchable national data base encompassing descriptions of the holdings of many different repositories. In addition, the automating of descriptions and related information about individual collections will lead many repositories to use computers and data bases for internal housekeeping, assistance to researchers, and better overall archival planning. For the future, "systems that combine records management and information management functions will soon be the sine qua non of modern archives."[52]

The holdings of archives are changing as well as their internal operations. The rise of social history as a field of study in the past twenty years has had a great impact on the profession. Both the subjects of and the sources for new collections have begun to change. Archivists and, more directly, manuscript curators have become conscious of the need to document the experiences of the majority of the people in our society and the processes which affected their lives. Thus, repositories have collected vigorously in such areas as women's history, black history, labor history, and urban history. They began to approach neighborhood organizations and community activists in addition to the traditional civic leaders and prominent families. Nevertheless, most collections still come from a fairly narrow spectrum, and "the most crucial problem" remains "the lack of representative documentation for the entire range of socioeconomic classes."[53] In addition to altering the contents of repositories, social history has also demanded a rethinking of archival practices. The need to study everyday life translates in archival terms into an argument for retaining large numbers of typical records or cases, rather than focusing on the exceptional. Further, social history requires the retrieval of thematic information which cuts across organizational lines, while records are arranged organizationally according to the principle of provenance. Fortunately, the automation of finding aids may well make it "possible to satisfy both the archivist's need to preserve original order and the researcher's desire for subject access."[54]

Social history and the computer also combine in the troublesome area of machine-readable records, which now contain so much of our socioeconomic documentation. As more "files" are retained in a computerized format, archivists are faced with an increasingly fundamental challenge. Unless the problems of obsolescence and incompatibility affecting both hardware and software are solved, it is hard to see how repositories can deal with these records.[55] And yet computerized information storage is a possible solution to two major problems confronting all repositories—the continuing paper explosion and the long-term deterioration of paper. While microfilming and mass deacidification are fairly effective short-term responses, the basic issues remain. In addition to computer storage, a better technological response may be laser-encoded optical disks. By the late 1980s, these could hold up to 54,000 pages or images on a 12-inch diameter record; be assembled in searchable juke box systems of a thousand or more; and provide a permanent storage medium for such diverse records as paper, photographs, and machine readable data. This technology has the potential for causing a true archival revolution.

Archivists and manuscript curators have responded in several ways to changes in operations, research interests, and record formats. In the words of F. Gerald Ham, "technology and society push us into a more activist role in managing the archival record," inevitably leading archivists into what he has called the "post-custodial era."[56] Drawing upon the experience of libraries, they have begun to think in terms of repository-wide collection management, which can include budget and cost analysis of each operation and collection, reappraisal and deaccessioning, and cooperation among repositories in acquisitions, processing, and preservation. As a result of financial restrictions, they have become more active in promoting the values of historical materials and working with allied professions. Closely related is a more systematic approach to discovering who users are, what they need, and why they use materials—an attempt "to think of archives as client-centered, not materials-centered."[57]

All of these activities have called forth a new type of archivist. Graduate training in the administration of archives and historical manuscripts is becoming essential. The growth of professional education has been as much a trend of the past two decades as automation. As archivists and curators increasingly find themselves in such environments as corporations and universities, legitimate credentials become both necessary and justifiable—necessary because in practical terms, "Society deserves professional value for its money, and requires from us a recognizable badge";[58] but justifiable as well, because of the increasing complexity and sophistication of the field. The archival profession is the oldest of the applied historical sciences. Yet it is also the one most closely related to the far newer information sciences. The challenge facing today's archivists and manuscript curators is to draw upon these two traditions while retaining their unique focus on our society's documentary heritage.[59]

NOTES

1. The two references to archives are cited in Ernst Posner, *Archives in the Ancient World* (Cambridge, Mass.: Harvard University Press, 1972), 126, 160. The translations are from *The Anchor Bible*, trans. Jacob Meyers (Garden City, NY: Doubleday, 1965) and Virgil, *Georgics*, trans. C. Day Lewis (New York: Oxford University Press, 1947).
2. Frank B. Evans et al., "A Basic Glossary for Archivists, Manuscript Curators and Records Managers," *American Archivist* 37 (1974): 417.
3. Hilary Jenkinson, *A Manual of Archival Administration*, rev. ed. (London: Percy Lund, Humphries & Co., 1937), 11.
4. Theodore R. Schellenberg, *The Management of Archives* (New York: Columbia University Press, 1965), 65.
5. Lester J. Cappon, "Historical Manuscripts as Archives: Some Definitions and Their Application," *American Archivist* 19 (1956): 103.
6. Philip C. Brooks, *Research in Archives: The Use of Unpublished Primary Sources* (Chicago: University of Chicago Press, 1969), 42.
7. William Joyce, "Archivists and Research Use," *American Archivist* 47 (1984): 125.
8. See National Archives and Records Service, *Directory of Archives and Manuscript Repositories in the United States* (Washington, D.C.: National Archives and Records Service, 1978); and O. Lawrence Burnette, *Beneath the Footnote: A Guide to the Use and Preservation of American Historical Sources* (Madison, Wis.: State Historical Society of Wisconsin, 1969).
9. See Donald R. McCoy, *The National Archives: America's Ministry of Documents, 1934–1968* (Chapel Hill: University of North Carolina Press, 1978); and H. G. Jones, *The Records of A Nation: Their Management, Preservation, and Use* (New York: Athenaeum Press, 1969).
10. See Lisa Weber, ed., *Documenting America: Assessing the Condition of Historical Records in the States* (Atlanta: National Association of State Archivists and Records Administrators, 1984); and Ernst Posner, *American State Archives* (Chicago: University of Chicago Press, 1964).
11. Schellenberg, *Management of Archives*, 21.
12. See American Association for State Local History, *Directory of Historical Societies and Agencies*, 12th ed. (Nashville: American Association for State and Local History, 1982).
13. See Linda Henry, "Collecting Policies of Special-Subject Repositories," *American Archivist* 43 (1980): 57–63.

14. A good overview of one field is the special archives issue of *Labor History* 23 (Fall 1982).
15. Lester J. Cappon, "The Archivist as Collector," *American Archivist* 39 (1976): 429.
16. See for example David Hyslop and Irene Place, *Records Management* (Reston, Va.: Reston Publishing, 1982); Violet Thomas and Dexter Schubert, *Records Management: Systems and Administration*, (Silver Spring, Md.: Association for Information and Image Management, 1983); and Mina Johnson and Norman Kallaus, *Records Management* (Cincinnati: Southwestern Publishing, 1982).
17. See John Fleckner, *Archives and Manuscripts: Surveys* (Chicago: Society of American Archivists, 1977).
18. Quoted in Brooks, *Research in Archives*, 94.
19. Maynard Brichford, *Archives and Manuscripts: Appraisal and Accessioning* (Chicago: Society of American Archivists, 1977), 7.
20. Jenkinson, *Manual*, 153.
21. Leonard Rapport, "No Grandfather Clause: Reapparaising Accessioned Records," *American Archivist* 44 (1981): 149.
22. S. A. Muller, J. A. Feith, and R. Fruin, *Manual for the Arrangement and Description of Archives*, 2nd ed., trans. Arthur Leavitt (New York: H. W. Wilson Co., 1968), 9.
23. Schellenberg, *Management of Archives*, 67.
24. See David B. Gracy II, *Archives and Manuscripts: Arrangement and Description* (Chicago: Society of American Archivists, 1977); and Karen T. Lynch and Helen W. Slotkin, *Processing Manual for the Institute Archives and Special Collections* (Cambridge, Mass: MIT Libraries, 1981).
25. See Mary Lynn Ritzenthaler, *Archives and Manuscripts: Conservation* (Chicago: Society of American Archivists, 1983).
26. Richard H. Lytle, "Intellectual Access to Archives: I. Provenance and Content Indexing Methods of Subject Retrieval," *American Archivist* 43 (1980): 71.
27. Mary Jo Pugh, "The Illusion of Omniscience: Subject Access and the Reference Archivist," *American Archivist* 45 (1982): 36.
28. See Ann E. Pederson and Gail Farr Casterline, *Archives and Manuscripts: Public Programs* (Chicago: Society of American Archivists, 1982).
29. Brichford, *Appraisal and Accessioning*, 13.
30. Clark Elliott, ed., *Understanding Progress as Process: Documentation of the History of Post-War Science and Technology in the United States* (Chicago: Society of American Archivists, 1983).
31. *Archival Preservation of Machine-Readable Records: The Final Report of the Wisconsin Survey of Machine-Readable Public Records* (Madison, Wis.: State Historical Society of Wisconsin, 1981).
32. *Appraisal of the Records of the Federal Bureau of Investigation: A Report to the Hon. Harold H. Greene, United States District Court for the District of Columbia* (Washington, D.C.: National Archives and Records Service, 1981).
33. Pugh, "The Illusion of Omniscience," 42.
34. *Guide to the Swarthmore College Peace Collection* (Swarthmore, Penn., 1981).
35. Charles G. Palm and Dale Reed, *Guide to the Hoover Institution Archives* (Stanford: Stanford University Press, 1980).
36. Andrea Hinding, ed., *Women's History Sources: A Guide to Archives and Manuscript Collections in the United States* (New York: R. R. Bowker Co., 1979).
37. Alonzo L. Hamby and Edward Weldon, eds, *Access to the Papers of Public*

Figures: The New Harmony Conference (Bloomington, Ind.: Organization of American Historians, 1977).

38. Ibid., 8.
39. See *Vanishing Georgia: Photographs from the Vanishing Georgia Collection, Georgia Department of Archives and History* (Athens, Ga: University of Georgia Press, 1982).
40. Vickie Sand, "History Resource Units from the Minnesota Historical Society," *American Archivist* 41 (1978): 163–168.
41. G. David Brumberg, "The Case for Reunion: Academic Historians, Public Historical Agencies and the New York Historians-in-Residence Program," *Public Historian* 4 (Spring 1982): 89.
42. Kenneth Duckett, *Modern Manuscripts: A Practical Manual for their Management, Care and Use* (Nashville: American Association for State and Local History, 1975), 25.
43. Margaret Child, "Federal Funds for Archives: A View from NEH," *American Archivist* 45 (1982): 470.
44. Wayne Grover quoted in Frank B. Evans, "Archivists and Records Managers: Variations on a Theme," *American Archivist* 30 (1967): 51.
45. Robert L. Clark, Jr., ed., *Archive-Library Relations* (New York: R. R. Bowker Co., 1967), xii.
46. Ibid., 155.
47. Society of American Archivists, *Education Directory* (Chicago: Society of American Archivists, 1983), 2–3.
48. Ibid., 2.
49. Nancy E. Peace and Nancy Fisher Chudacoff, "Archivists and Librarians: A Common Mission, A Common Education," *American Archivist* 42 (October 1979): 457.
50. Frank Burke, "Archival Cooperation," *American Archivist* 46 (Summer 1983): 302.
51. Patrick Quinn, "Regional Archival Organizations and the Society of American Archivists," *American Archivist* 46 (1983): 437.
52. W. Theodore Durr, "Some Thoughts and Designs about Archives and Automation, 1984," *American Archivist* 47 (1984): 272. See also Lawrence J. McCrank, ed., *Automating the Archives: Issues and Problems in Computer Applications* (White Plains, N.Y.: Knowledge Industry Publications, 1981).
53. Henry, "Collecting Policies of Special-Subject Repositories," 59. See also Fredric Miller, "Social History and Archival Practice," *American Archivist* 44 (1981): 113–124.
54. Durr, "Some Thoughts and Designs," 272.
55. See Carolyn Geda and Francis X. Blouin, Jr., eds., *Archivists and Machine-Readable Records* (Chicago: Society of American Archivists, 1980).
56. F. Gerald Ham, "Archival Strategies for the Post-Custodial Era," *American Archivist* 44 (1981): 209.
57. Elsie Freeman, "In the Eye of the Beholder: Archives Administration from the User's Point of View," *American Archivist* 47 (1984): 112.
58. Hugh Taylor, "The Discipline of History and the Education of the Archivist," *American Archivist* 40 (1977): 397.
59. For a related essay, on business archives, see Philip F. Mooney's "The Practice of History in Corporate America: Business Archives in the United States" elsewhere in this book.

Donald A. Ritchie is Associate Historian in the Senate Historical Office. He graduated from the City College of New York and received his Ph.D. in History from the University of Maryland. Among his publications are James M. Landis: Dean of the Regulators *(Cambridge, Mass.: Harvard University Press, 1980) and a high school textbook,* Heritage of Freedom: History of the United States *(New York: Scribner, 1985). He chaired the American Historical Association's committee on Congressional Fellowships, the Oral History Association's publications committee, and the Society for History in the Federal Government's subcommittee on oral history. A past president of Oral History in the Mid-Atlantic Region (OHMAR), in 1984 he received OHMAR's Forrest C. Pogue award for significant contributions to the field of oral history. In 1985, after completing a term on its council, he was elected vice president/president-elect of the Oral History Association.*

THE ORAL HISTORY/PUBLIC HISTORY CONNECTION

Donald A. Ritchie

Public historians, because they are still creating and refining their craft as they practice it, have found the tape-recorded, transcribed interview an infinitely adoptable and usable tool. Whether in government agencies, museums, corporations, labor unions, documentary film-making, or folk festivals, oral history provides a means of collecting information and developing new perspectives about individuals and institutions. It also creates a record in a vernacular form that can be easily transmitted to the popular audience that public historians try to reach.

My own contact with both public history and oral history happened more by chance than by careful career planning. I entered graduate school in history in the 1960s, excited by the prospects of researching, writing, and teaching, and emerged in the 1970s to find precious few academic positions available. But I had the opportunity to develop some skills not traditionally included in a graduate education, which were unexpectedly handy when making the transition to public history. For one, I participated in a historical editing program at the University of Maryland that involved an editing seminar, work on several editorial projects, and editing a graduate student journal, *The Maryland Historian*. My introduction to oral history was considerably less systematic.

While researching for a doctoral dissertation on the career of James M. Landis, who held posts in the New Deal, Fair Deal, and New Frontier,

I came across a portion of an interview, among his papers in the Library of Congress. The transcript, numbered pages 670–716, was not identified, but was obviously part of an interview conducted with Landis shortly before his death in 1964. Naturally, I wanted to find the first 669 pages. On the advice of Martha Ross, who taught an oral history course at Maryland, I contacted the Columbia Oral History Research Office. The complete interview was part of Columbia's collection, but remained unlisted because its use was restricted. With the Landis family's permission, I gained access to the transcript. It was a magnificent find for a biographer: the subject's life in his own words. Even relatively well-known facts and incidents took on a new immediacy when presented in the first-person; and the direct quotations made for a more authoritative narrative.[1]

The oral history also opened new doors and provided unexpected information. The best example of this was Landis's description of a trip he made to the Soviet Union in 1924, after graduating from the Harvard Law School. Many prominent American reformers of that era traveled to Moscow to observe the experimental new society, and Landis especially wanted to see the Soviet legal system at work. In his interview he gave a vivid account of the trip, and the disillusionment it caused seemed to bolster his belief in liberal rather than radical solutions. But no other biographical account supported the oral history's version of that trip, nor had any of his family ever heard him mention the trip. An article written about Landis in a 1934 issue of *Fortune* magazine reported that during the summer of 1924 he had "toured Cornwall and Devon on bicycle."[2] By then, Landis had become a prominent New Dealer and founder of the Securities and Exchange Commission, and admission of a trip to the Soviet Union in his youth might have been politically embarrassing. Or could Landis, then at a low point in his career, have embellished his life story to impress his young interviewer? I was skeptical enough of oral sources to wonder how much faith to place in this 700-page transcript, and hesitated to cite its information without verification.

In the interview, Landis mentioned that to help pay for the trip he had written a few articles for the *Baltimore Sun*. A search through the *Sun's* index uncovered two articles published under his byline in the fall of 1924. In addition to supporting his Soviet story, the articles served as a testament to Landis's phenomenal memory—which had served him so well in his legal career. The articles closely paralleled the anecdotes he told and the people and events he described in his interview forty years later. I knew his manuscript collection well enough to be sure that he did not have clippings of the articles to refresh his memory. My confidence in oral testimony increased significantly, and every other case I tested against documentary evidence further substantiated the interview's reliability.

Like other professional men, Landis rarely talked about his private life. Except for references to his parents and childhood, he devoted the interview exclusively to his years as a lawyer, dean of the Harvard Law

School, and government official. He made almost no mention of his two marriages, his children, or the income tax delinquency that eventually sent him to jail. As a biographer, I needed to know more. I began to conduct my own interviews with his widow and children, friends and colleagues, and even his psychiatrist. As a graduate student with limited resources, I did not tape record these interviews, but simply took notes. Of the more than twenty interviews I conducted, I recorded only the last, with the former attorney general who had supervised Landis's tax case.

Despite making nearly every mistake in the oral history manuals, I learned a great deal from the interviews that I could not have gotten from Landis's letters or from published accounts. The variety of people I talked with presented vastly different perspectives on his life. Some admired him and patterned their lives after his; others had still not forgiven him his trespasses. Each interview provided some new information, explained some vague or incomplete reference in his papers, or led to additional documentation still in private hands. The interviews also gave me the opportunity to meet some fascinating individuals who had lived the events I was trying to recreate. These experiences won me to oral history.

Oral history also helped make me a "public historian." When the Senate Historical Office advertised a new position, it called for a specialist in twentieth-century political history with a familiarity of Washington-area research facilities and some expertise in editing and oral history. My background seemed tailored for the job, and luckily I got the position. A political historian could not ask for a more stimulating place to work.

THE SENATE HISTORICAL OFFICE
ORAL HISTORY PROGRAM

The Senate Historical Office performs a diversity of tasks, including the preparation of bibliographies and other reference material.[3] It assists Senate committees in the management and preservation of their records, and helped establish the first systematic access rule for Senate records at the National Archives.[4] The office advises senators on appropriate repositories for their office files, which are considered personal papers. The staff answers reference questions from senators' offices, the press, scholarly researchers, and the general public. It occasionally drafts speeches and prepares reports for historical celebrations. My specific projects include editing for publication the previously closed executive session transcripts of the Senate Foreign Relations Committee, and conducting an oral history program with retired members of the Senate staff.[5]

In designing an oral history program, the Senate Historical Office followed an observation which the British sociologist Beatrice Webb made: "The mind of the subordinate in any organization will yield richer deposits of fact than the mind of the principal." It was not because subordinates were less guarded when they gave interviews, Webb argued, but because they were more involved in the day-to-day activities of the organization, more aware of its changing character, and less likely to "serve up dead generalizations."[6]

Rather than interviewing United States senators, we decided to interview the long-time staff of the Senate. Senators leave behind a massive paper trail, and are more likely to be interviewed by oral history programs at universities and historical societies, often as a supplement to their manuscript collections. Prime examples are the George Aiken oral history project at the University of Vermont and the John Stennis collection at Mississippi State University. The Senate Historical Office keeps track of such independent projects and has listed them in its *Guide to Research Collections of Former United States Senators, 1789–1982*.[7]

We believed we could make the greatest contribution by interviewing those who observed the Senate from behind the scenes and who survived in their positions largely because of their "passion for anonymity." As an agency of the Senate, we were Senate staff too and could establish rapport with retired staff members, including those unaccustomed to speaking for attribution. We also had access to records still closed for general research, which helped in preparing for the interviews. Most importantly, we wanted to record the institutional history of the Senate as well as its political history, and these were the staff members who had witnessed and contributed to the Senate's growth and development over the past half century. We were mindful of missed opportunities. In 1956, for example, the Senate halted debate one day to pay tribute to five staff members, still employed, who had each worked for the Senate over sixty years. They included the first superintendent of the press gallery, the first official parliamentarian, and the chief reporter of debates—a man whose uncle had been appointed a Senate reporter by John C. Calhoun. Within a short time, all of these octogenarians had died, and none had left a collection of personal papers or reminiscences. An enormous amount of institutional memory died with them.

The Senate oral history program focused on a later generation of staff members, many of whom came to the Senate after the enactment of the Legislative Reorganization Act of 1946, which established a nonpartisan, professional staff. When Francis Wilcox became the first chief of staff of the Senate Foreign Relations Committee in 1947, he found that the committee's staff consisted of one full-time and two part-time employees. Wilcox appointed four foreign policy specialists. In recent years, the committee's staff has exceeded sixty people. We interviewed Wilcox and two of his successors, Carl Marcy and Pat Holt, who served continuously as chiefs of staff of the Foreign Relations Committee from 1947 through 1977.[8]

Other interviewees included Ruth Watt, who in 1947 joined the staff of the Truman Committee, or Special Committee to Investigate the National Defense Program. When the special committee became the Permanent Subcommittee on Investigations, she continued as its chief clerk and held the post until her retirement in 1979. During those years she worked for such diverse chairmen as Joseph McCarthy, John McClellan, and Henry Jackson. Another interviewee, Stewart McClure, served for many years as chief clerk of the Labor and Education Committee, where he contributed to the conception and passage of the National Defense Education Act. Darrell St. Claire, who started his career on the Senate staff during the "First Hundred Days" of the New Deal, served as secretary to the Democratic patronage committee and later played an instrumental role in converting the staff from patronage to professional status. Floyd Riddick watched the proceedings from his vantage as parliamentarian; Francis Attig recorded the debates as an official reporter; and Leonard Ballard offered the unique insights of an inspector on the Capitol police force.[9]

These staff members arrived in the Senate when it resembled a small town, before it grew into a large urban complex. At the end of World War II there were less than a thousand Senate staff members; they operated out of one office building; they dined in the same cafeteria; they knew all of their counterparts by name; and they were able to facilitate the passage of legislation through their many personal contacts. Senators tended to be more austere, answerable only to God and their constituents, but approachable when a staff member had an interesting idea. In the decades that followed, the staff swelled to over seven thousand; they are divided among three office buildings and a variety of annexes; they eat in a multitude of restaurants; and they are hard pressed to know everyone working for their own senator or committee, let alone those from other offices. Senators have abandoned their cutaway coats and are less austere, but have also become more enveloped in layers of protective staff, busier with committee work and out-of-town travel, and less approachable than in the past. This transformation of life on Capitol Hill emerges from the collective reminiscenses of the staff we interviewed.

Although the interviews concentrate on each individual's years with the Senate, they follow a full life-review, biographical scheme of questioning. The interviews open with a discussion of the person's family, schooling, childhood, and path taken to the Senate. They trace an individual's movement from one senator's office to another, or from one committee to the next, and ask the interviewees to make comparisons between the different members with whom they have associated. Francis Wilcox, for example, described how Arthur Vandenberg, as chairman of the Foreign Relations Committee, would stop by Wilcox's office in the mornings, light a cigar, put his feet up on the desk, and engage in a discussion of the substantive issues of foreign policy. By contrast, Wilcox found the next chairman, Tom Connally, less interested in substantive issues than in the political side of the debate. Wilcox then measured Vandenberg and Connally against Alexander Wiley, who as chairman simply did not understand the substantive issues of foreign policy. Carl Marcy and Pat Holt revealed how Senate Majority Leader Lyndon Johnson maneuvered the ninety-one-year-old Theodore Francis Green to step aside voluntarily as chairman of the Foreign Relations Committee in favor of J. William Fulbright.[10] Marcy and Holt further narrate the painful break between Fulbright and Johnson in the 1960s, and the gradual independence of the committee from presidential domination of foreign policy.

Since each interviewee's experiences are different, we construct questions to fit each person, rather than use a standard questionnaire. However, certain questions, dealing with institutional developments, are repeated in every interview. Information from one interview invariably helps in preparation for the next, giving a coherency to the whole series. We anticipate that these oral histories will give researchers a participant's eye-view of the Senate's part in the legislative process and national affairs. Most of the interviews have been opened immediately for research, and restrictions on personally and politically sensitive material were held to a minimum. Copies of the interviews are deposited in the Manuscript Division of the Library of Congress and the Legislative Records Division of the National Archives, and are available on microfiche through Scholarly Resources, Inc.

Along with other archival oral history collections, the Senate Historical Office has been concerned that its interviews will genuinely be of use to future researchers. An oral historian serves as surrogate for researchers who will not have the opportunity to question participants in the events they are studying. In my own experience, James Landis had died eight years before I began my study of his life. That made me dependent on the questions the Columbia interviewer, Neil Gold, chose to ask. Gold had a background in law, did thorough research, was interested enough in the subject to pursue many different lines of inquiry, and established a good rapport with Landis (who had a reputation for intolerance of those he considered intellectually inferior). Most importantly, Gold listened to what Landis said, caught unexpected remarks—such as the reference to the Soviet trip—and followed up on them. Although certainly well prepared, he never hesitated to ask "Why was that?" or to admit he was unaware of something and ask Landis to explain his remarks. Of course, there were frustrating moments in the interview when the subject changed before its completion, an opportunity was missed, or an area was left untouched. A biographer hungers for minute detail, and an archival oral historian has an obligation to conduct interviews as broadly and as deeply as possible, keeping in mind all of the areas in which the interviewee was involved, and the types of questions that historians and biographers will likely want answered.

ORAL HISTORY IN THE FEDERAL GOVERNMENT

The Senate Hisorical Office is one of more than twenty federal agencies currently conducting oral history programs. Oral history has extensive roots in the federal government, beginning in World War II when Lt. Col. S. L. A. Marshall, a former journalist, sent army historians out to interview soldiers immediately after a battle.[11] In 1983 the Society for History in the Federal Government conducted a survey to determine the scope and nature of federal oral history. In addition to the more familiar collections at presidential libraries, the society found oral history programs in every branch of the military, the Joint Chiefs of Staff, and the Department of Defense; in the departments of State, Labor, Energy, and Commerce; in many of the intelligence agencies; in most of the museums within the Smithsonian Institution; in the National Aeronautics and Space Administration; in the National Science Foundation and the National Library of Medicine; and in the Social Security Administration. By far the largest number of programs were those sponsored by the ten regional offices of the National Park Service, encompassing an estimated 150 separate oral history projects.[12] The size of these collections ranged from a few hours of interviews with a handful of people to those that count their interviews in the thousands. The Marine Corps Historical Center at the Washington Navy Yard, for instance, houses 6,424 Vietnam War debriefings and 425 in-depth interviews transcribed into more than 30,000 pages.[13]

These statistics show how entrenched oral history has become in public history, as practiced in the federal government. The expansion of oral history programs reflects federal historians' uneasiness over the written documentation of modern government. Written records have become so voluminous that they can obstruct rather than promote historical research. They can be unrevealing, impersonal, and computer-generated. They can be inadequate, because so many significant interactions are never recorded on paper. They can be unclear or misleading—sometimes deliberately so. Ernest May, in his presidential address to the Society of Historians of American Foreign Relations, called for a better understanding of government documentation, and urged historians to learn the language of the bureaucracy, who the key players were, and what the documents were covering up. "But mostly," May said, "we have to ask questions of the humans who worked within these large organizations."[14] That is precisely where oral history enters the picture.

A few federal agencies conduct interviews solely for internal use: to prepare official histories; to preserve the collective memory of the institution; to untangle bureaucratic mazes; and in some cases to create a substitute for records that no longer exist. But most federal oral history projects recognize that they are creating additional resources that will someday become available to outside researchers. That places additional burdens on the interviewers. In its "Principles and Standards for Federal Historical Programs," the Society for History in the Federal Government has urged that: "To the extent practicable, oral interviews should encompass the potential interest of other researchers and not just the immediate needs of the interviewer."[15]

WHO IS AN ORAL HISTORIAN?

Oral history, largely as a result of the efforts of the Oral History Association, stands in advance of public history in its search for self-definition. The Wingspread Conference in 1979 prepared and promulgated evaluation guidelines for oral history projects, and workshop sessions of the national, state, and regional oral history associations have promoted standards for conducting and processing interviews.[16] However, methodological differences continue to exist. For years, oral historians argued over "elitist" versus "nonelitist" interviewing—whether to concentrate on the prominent or the rank and file—but that issue seems to have been resolved with a consensus that all types of interviewees are legitimate, and that the most useful projects are those which cast their nets the widest.[17] Other disagreements concern the interviewers. "Scratch an oral historian and you are just as likely to find a folklorist, sociologist, economist, someone from the field of communications, medicine, government, business, literature, entertainment, and so the list goes on," wrote Waddy Moore, a former president of the Oral History Association. But Herbert T. Hoover, director of the oral history center at the University of South Dakota, responded that: "These are not oral historians!" Hoover contended that "the person who conducts interviews should possess credentials that reflect advanced training in the particular field of history under study. . . . "[18]

Not all oral history transcripts support the assertion that graduate training in history is the prime ingredient in making a good interviewer. Critical to the interviewing process is a familiarity with the interviewee's particular field, and the best interviewer might well be a fellow practitioner in that field. Proper training in oral history techniques and self-awareness of the interviewer's role are essential, as is the interviewer's ability to persuade people to speak freely and frankly, and to move the discussion beyond hearsay and superficial responses. Political scientists are often adept at interviewing politicians. While historians as interviewers tend to structure their questions in a biographical and chronological format, political scientists pursue more institutional issues, such as seniority, agenda-setting, and log-rolling.[19] Oral historians have also admired and learned from the work of Lynwood Montell, a folklorist; Sidney Mintz, an anthropologist; and Eliot Wigginton, a high school English teacher who launched the *Foxfire* series.[20]

In fact, a fundamental strength of the oral history movement is its interdisciplinary nature. Historians may collect and interpret oral evidence differently from specialists in other fields, but can still benefit considerably from interviews conducted by well-trained, well-prepared specialists outside of history. Recognizing that the interviewer is more than a neutral figure, and can shape the interview by the line of questioning, future researchers will have good reason to be curious about the interviewers as well as the interviewees. Those involved in oral history projects have a responsibility to provide information on the training and background of each of their interviewers.

The controversy over who is an oral historian illustrates the lingering suspicions that many historians feel toward oral history. Some of this suspicion results from the different approaches to interviewing of individual researchers and archival oral historians. Individual researchers conduct interviews to generate source material for their own writings. They generally lack the time and resources to compile full-scale life reviews, and confine their interviews to those portions of an individual's life that apply to their topic. They have absorbed themselves in their research and know exactly what questions they want answered. Often archival oral histories disappoint them by failing to ask those specific questions, by not probing more deeply, by accepting testimony uncritically, or by only interviewing individuals favorable to their subject. Archival oral historians have different purposes, primarily to collect interviews for permanent preservation and general use. Although they may lack the individual researcher's specificity, they often compensate by concentrating on particular research areas or types of interviewees.

If their goal is to produce convincing, verifiable oral evidence, both individual researchers and archival oral historians need to bridge their differences. By not depositing their interviews, whether notes, tapes, or transcripts, where others can examine them, individual interviewers are creating masses of unverifiable information. Readers are forced to accept footnotes to "personal interview with the author" as acts of faith. Such journalistic devices as the use of confidential and otherwise unnamed sources undermine the credibility of scholarly studies. One author acknowledged that the two hundred interviews he conducted constituted "a major source of information for this book," but cited only one by name.[21] Blanket anonymity serves only to deprive other researchers of any means of determining how these sources shaped the book's interpretation, and how accurately the author used the material these interviews provided. Some individual interviewers deposit their interviews in archives after completing their projects. While this practice preserves the tapes and transcripts for future use, it puts the archives in the passive role of accepting material without any control over its standards of collection.

A better arrangement would result if individual researchers who planned extensive interviews would associate themselves with oral history archives at the beginning of their projects. The archives designated as the ultimate repository for the interviews can be so noted in any resulting publication. In return for gaining additions to their collections, the archives might provide assistance in the form of equipment, appropriate deeds of gift, and transcribing services. Through such cooperation, granting agencies might also have more assurance of tangible results from the oral history projects they fund. Some public history offices, generally archival in nature, have already established mechanisms for bridging this gap through their use of contract interviewers and through research grants that help fund interviews which the agencies will later acquire.[22]

PUBLIC HISTORIANS AND ORAL HISTORIANS

Not all public historians are oral historians, or vice versa, but a special bond exists between them. Those public historians involved in oral history seem to have adopted a broader view of public history. Among oral historians there is a sense that having gathered information from the public they have a responsibility for sharing the product with the community. Recent years have seen a profusion of oral history-based documentaries, slide-tape presentations, and theatrical dramatizations aimed at popular audiences. At its Harpers Ferry headquarters, the National Park Service operates a studio to transform interviews and other material collected at national parks and historic sites into documentary films to be shown to visitors to those sites. The stage production of *Baltimore Voices* drew its script from interviews collected by the Baltimore Neighborhood Heritage Project. The Southwest Library Association ran a series of workshops to train local public librarians in oral history, both to build local history collections and to prepare public exhibitions for their libraries.[23]

Had I been pressed to define public history when I first went to work for the Senate, I might have described it simply as the activities of a historian in a public agency, outside of a university. As a result of my experiences with oral history and dealings with oral historians, I now agree with those who do not limit the definition of public history to one's place of employment.[24] More important to the definition is the audience the historian seeks to reach. A public historian aims for a public audience, which might include the officials of the agency, corporation, or union which employs the historian, or the press—which often uses public historians as sources in writing for its own audience—or the library-using, documentary-watching, museum-going public. Other professional historians, for whom the bulk of historical literature is intended, represent only a small portion of the public historian's audience.

But reaching a popular or nonprofessional audience cannot be the sole criteria for public history. Some standards must be applied. Just as oral historians express concern over the uncertain methods of popularizers in their field, public historians have to disassociate themselves from the undocumented, romanticized, and quasi-historical presentations that often lure the public. Increased peer review is essential for improving standards of public history. Historical journals should review documentaries, museum exhibits, and other public historical performances, and subject them to the same scrutiny they do historical monographs. Historians who participate in public history projects deserve professional recognition for their accomplishments. Poor work needs to be identified and analyzed. Reviews of this nature have appeared all too sporadically.[25]

If public history is defined as an organized effort to bring accurate, meaningful history to a public audience, then oral history is a natural tool for obtaining that goal. Both are immensely satisfying forms of professional occupation, as I have found from direct participation. It seems only fitting to conclude with one of the Senate Historical Office's oral history interviews, with whose sentiments I wholeheartedly concur. A retired Senate staff member observed: "If you have a sense of theatre and enjoy the incredible number of scenes that are available to you at any day, this is an absolutely fabulous place to enjoy yourself, in your own committee or in other committees, or on the floor. It's a great scene, a great show, and I loved every minute of it—in fact, even the parts I didn't love. In the long run, it was a wonderful place to work."[26]

NOTES

1. "The Reminiscences of James M. Landis," Columbia Oral History Research Office, Columbia University; and Donald A. Ritchie, *James M. Landis: Dean of the Regulators* (Cambridge, Mass.: Harvard University Press, 1980).
2. "The Reminiscences of James M. Landis," 98–110; and "The Legend of Landis," *Fortune*, August 1934, 47.
3. See Richard Allan Baker, "Documenting the History of the United States Senate," *Government Publications Review* 10 (1983): 415–26.
4. U.S. Congress, *Relating to Public Access to Senate Records at the National Archives*, S. Rept. 96–1042, S. Res. 474, 96th Cong., 2nd. sess., 1 December 1980.
5. U.S. Congress, *Executive Sessions of the Senate Foreign Relations Committee (Historical Series)* (Washington: Government Printing Office, 1976–). Volumes begin with closed hearings held in 1947 and proceed chronologically.
6. Paul Thompson, *The Voice of the Past: Oral History* (New York: Oxford University Press, 1978), 158–59.
7. U.S. Senate, Senate Document 97-41, 97th Cong., 2nd session, 1983. See # 4.
8. "Francis O. Wilcox, Chief of Staff, Foreign Relations Committee, 1947–1955," Senate Historical Office Oral History Interviews, 1984; "Carl M. Marcy, Chief of Staff, Senate Foreign Relations Committee, 1955–1973," Senate Historical Office Oral History Interviews, 1983; and "Pat M. Holt, Chief of Staff, Senate Foreign Relations Committee, 1973–1977," Senate Historical Office Oral History Interviews, 1980.
9. "Ruth Young Watt, Chief Clerk, Permanent Subcommittee on Investigation," Senate Historical Office Oral History Interviews, 1979; "Stewart E. McClure, Chief Clerk, Senate Committee on Labor, Education, and Public Welfare," Senate Historical Office Oral History Interviews, 1982–83; "Darrell St. Clair, Assistant Secretary of the Senate," Senate Historical Office Oral History Interviews, 1976–78; "Floyd M. Riddick: Senate Parliamentarian," Senate Historical Office Oral History Interviews, 1978–79; "Francis J. Attig, Reporter of Senate Debates," Senate Historical Office Oral History Interview, 1978; and "Leonard H. Ballard, Inspector, United States Capitol Police, 1947–1984," Senate Historical Office Oral History Interviews, 1983–1984.
10. Donald A. Ritchie, "Making Fulbright Chairman: Or How the 'Johnson Treatment' Nearly Backfired," *Society for Historians of American Foreign Relations Newsletter* 15 (September 1984): 21–28.
11. Robert K. Wright, Jr., "Clio in Combat: The Evolution of the Military History Detachment," *The Army Historian* 6 (Winter 1985): 3.
12. The National Park Service, through its Harpers Ferry Center, has prepared

a guide to coordinate its many oral history projects. See Blair Hubbard, Heather Huyck, and David Nathanson, "Collecting, Using and Preserving Oral History in the National Park Service," 1984.

13. "Oral History Survey," *The Federalist: Newsletter of the Society for History in the Federal Government* 4 (September 1983): 1, 8.

14. Ernest R. May, "Writing Contemporary International History," *Diplomatic History* 8 (Spring 1984): 109–111.

15. "Principles and Standards for Federal Historical Programs," *The Federalist* 6 (March 1985): insert.

16. *Oral History Evaluations Guidelines* (Denton, Tex.: Oral History Association, 1980); also contains the "Goals and Guidelines of the Oral History Association." In addition to the national Oral History Association, a series of regional organizations have also developed, including the New England Association of Oral History, Oral History in the Mid-Atlantic Region (OHMAR), the Southwest Oral History Association, and the Northwest Oral History Association. Each holds regular workshops and publishes a newsletter. Kentucky and Pennsylvania have state-funded oral history commissions, and eleven other states have oral history associations, roundtables, and interest groups which meet regularly to share information.

17. Alice M. Hoffman, "Who Are the Elite and What Is a Nonelitist?" *Oral History Review* 4 (1976): 1–5.

18. Herbert T. Hoover, "Oral History in the United States," in *The Past Before Us: Contemporary Historical Writing in the United States*, ed. Michael Kammen (Ithaca: Cornell University Press, 1980), 401.

19. The Former Members of Congress oral history project utilized a variety of interviewers, including historians and political scientists, allowing for a comparison of interviewing styles. See Donald A. Ritchie, "Beyond the *Congressional Record*: Congress and Oral History," *The Maryland Historian* 13 (Fall/Winter 1982): 10–11.

20. See articles by Montell, Mintz, Wigginton, and others in David K. Dunaway and Willa K. Baum, eds., *Oral History: An Interdisciplinary Anthology* (Nashville: American Association for State and Local History, 1984).

21. Robert A. Pastor, *Congress and the Politics of U.S. Foreign Economic Policy, 1929–1976* (Berkeley: University of California Press, 1982), 355.

22. Most notably the U.S. Army Corps of Engineers and the U.S. Department of Energy.

23. "Urban Oral History Dramatized," and "SWLA Public Programing Completed," *Oral History Association Newsletter* 15 (Summer 1981): 1, 4, 6, 7.

24. Brit Allen Storey, "Who and What Are Public Historians?" *Organization of American Historians Newsletter* (May 1984): 22–23; Daniel J. Walkowitz, "On Public History . . . " *Organization of American Historians Newsletter* (August 1984): 11; and Enid H. Douglass, "Oral History and Public History," *Oral History Review* 8 (1980): 15.

25. Barbara Melosh makes this point in "Museum Exhibits: Breaking the Silence," *Organization of American Historians Newsletter* 13 (May 1985): 23.

26. "Stewart E. McClure," 281–82.

SUGGESTED READING

Two handy reference volumes are available for public historians interested in oral history. David F. Trask and Robert W. Pomeroy III, eds., *The Craft of Public History: An Annotated Select Bibliography* (Westport,

Conn.: Greenwood Press, 1983), includes a sixty-five-page section on oral history, edited by Enid H. Douglass. Broken down into nineteen units, this section provides annotated entries covering the major books and articles in the field. A useful companion volume is David K. Dunaway and Willa K. Baum, eds., *Oral History: An Interdisciplinary Anthology* (Nashville: American Association for State and Local History in Cooperation with the Oral History Association, 1984), which includes the text and notes of thirty-seven articles on interpreting, designing, and applying oral history.

Oral history manuals are essential for serious projects, and public historians may find most useful William W. Moss, *Oral History Program Manual* (New York: Praeger, 1974), which is drawn from the author's experiences directing the oral history program at the John F. Kennedy Presidential Library. Other helpful manuals include Willa K. Baum, *Oral History for the Local Historical Society* (Nashville: American Association for State and Local History, 1971); Cullom Davis, Kathryn Black, and Kay McLean, *Oral History: From Tape to Type* (Chicago: American Library Association, 1977); and Brad Jolley, *Videotaping Local History* (Nashville: American Association for State and Local History, 1982).

Less a manual than a methodological evaluation, Paul Thompson, *The Voice of the Past: Oral History* (New York: Oxford University Press, 1978) should be required reading for all oral historians.

Brent Tarter was an editor for the Virginia Independence Bicentennial Commission from 1974 to 1982 and edited, with Robert L. Scribner, Revolutionary Virginia, The Road to Independence: A Documentary Record, *vols. 3–7 (Charlottesville, Va.: University Press of Virginia for the Virginia Independence Bicentennial Commission, 1977–1983). He has also edited* The Order Book and Related Papers of the Common Hall of the Borough of Norfolk, Virginia, 1736–1798 *(Richmond, Va.: Virginia State Library, 1979). Since 1982 he has been a member of the Publications Branch staff of the Virginia State Library and is an editor of the* Dictionary of Virginia Biography.

EDITING PUBLIC RECORDS

Brent Tarter

Long before different job descriptions suggested a distinction between students of history who teach and students of history who do other things, and now are called public historians, there were editors of public documents. They might even be called the first public historians in the United States. Along with those early writers who celebrated the colonial and revolutionary heritage, the men, they were all men then, who published public documents were the pioneers of the American historical profession. Through the publication of the basic texts of political and institutional history, they helped lay the foundation for modern historical scholarship. The nineteenth-century editors, who began their careers as antiquarians, archivists, lawyers, or librarians, discovered and made available the primary documents of political history. This democratized the study of history by bringing the sources to those without the private means to travel and burrow for months in mounds of unorganized manuscripts. This in turn made it possible for graduate schools, beginning in the 1890s, to promote relatively inexpensive historical research in primary sources. It is eloquent testimony to the fundamental importance of these publications that even in this day of methodological innovation, notes continue to bristle with citations to century-old editions of public documents.[1]

Editors of public documents work with the papers created and accumulated by public agencies. These are mainly documents of political history, such as legislative journals, statutes, judicial records, correspondence of governors and presidents, or diplomatic records and military dispatches; but editors have also published government reports and other documents, such as municipal government and census records, that contain the basic data of the social historian. Governments did not always accumulate and distribute information in such great quantities as they do now. In 1790 Congressman James Madison proposed to use the federal census to gather information about the country's population and commerce to enable Congress to legislate more wisely. The Senate rejected the proposal, leading Madison to grumble that the senators regarded the generation of information as "a waste of trouble and supplying materials for idle people to make a book."[2] But it is not idle business to make books containing useful information. Retrieval of the documents that governments did accumulate is an important scholarly undertaking and an essential part of the historian's discovery and explanation of the past.

HISTORICAL EDITING

The first serious editor of public records in the United States was Ebenezer Hazard, who began collecting documents before the American Revolution.[3] In 1791 he sent Secretary of State Thomas Jefferson two large volumes of copy for his *Historical Collections; Consisting of the State Papers . . . Intended as Materials for an History of the United States.* Jefferson read some of the documents (he called them "curious monuments of the infancy of our country") and returned the collection to Hazard with congratulations and encouragement to continue. Jefferson's words to Hazard have become one of the rationales for the editing of public records:

> Time and accident are committing daily havoc on the originals deposited in our public offices. The late war has done the work of centuries in this business. The lost cannot be recovered; but let us save what remains: not by vaults and locks which fence them from the public eye and use, in consigning them to the waste of time, but by such a multiplication of copies, as shall place them beyond the reach of accident.[4]

Hazard was a freelance editor, a gentleman amateur who used his own funds to finance his research and who depended upon sales receipts to cover the costs of publication. His venture was a financial failure, and since his time the Department of State, the National Archives, the Library of Congress, the state historical societies, and the states' archives and libraries have become the midwives in the delivery of primary sources to the public. Ready availability as well as preservation are important goals for the editors of public documents. In addition to historians, the reading audience includes teachers, journalists, legislators, jurists, and curious citizens.

Among some of the more enduring and well known of the early publications are William Waller Hening, ed., *The Statutes at Large; Being a Collection of All the Laws of Virginia, From the First Session of the Legislature, in the Year 1619*, 13 vols. (Richmond: Samuel Pleasants, Jr.; Printer to the Commonwealth; New York: R. W. G. Bartow; Philadelphia: William Brown, 1809–23); Edmund B. O'Callaghan and B. Fernough, eds., *Documents Relative to the Colonial History of the State of New York*, 15 vols.

(Albany, N.Y.: Weed, Parsons & Co., 1856–83); the 130 vols. of the *Pennsylvania Colonial Records* and nine series of *Pennsylvania Archives* published by the office of the secretary of state of Pennsylvania between 1838 and 1935;[5] Peter Force's *American Archives*, eight vols. in two series (Washington, D.C.: M. St. Clair Clarke & Peter Force, 1837–53); William L. Saunders and Walter Clark, eds., *The Colonial [State] Records of North Carolina*, 26 vols. and general index (Raleigh: P. M. Hale; Raleigh: Josephus Daniels; Winston: M. I. and J. C. Stewart; Goldsboro: Nash Bros.; Charlotte: Observer Printing House, Inc., 1886–1914); Worthington C. Ford et al., eds., *Journals of the Continental Congress, 1774–1789*, 39 vols. (Washington, D.C.: Government Printing Office, 1904–37);[6] the Department of State's continuing *Foreign Relations of the United States* begun in 1861 and now including more than 260 vols. (Washington, D.C.: Government Printing Office, 1861–); and the War Department's mammoth and indispensable *The War of the Rebellion: A Compilation of the Official Records of the Union and Confederate Armies*, 70 vols. in 128 parts, with general index and atlas (Washington, D.C.: Government Printing Office, 1881–1901).[7]

Publication of the sources of political and institutional history continues. Some of the larger such editorial projects are the *Documentary History of the Supreme Court*, being prepared under the auspices of the United States Supreme Court Historical Society; the *Documentary History of the First Federal Congress*, being edited at the George Washington University; a new edition of *Letters of Delegates to Congress, 1774–1789*, being published by the Library of Congress; a comprehensive *Documentary History of the Ratification of the Constitution*, being prepared at the University of Wisconsin; a *Documentary History of the First Federal Elections*, also being prepared at the University of Wisconsin; the large and useful *Naval Documents of the American Revolution* and its companion set, the *Naval Documents of the War of 1812*, both being prepared by the United States Navy Historical Office; and *Freedom: A Documentary History of Emancipation, 1861–1867*, an innovative publication based upon a variety of public documents and the first large editorial enterprise to draw upon the rich archives of the Freedman's Bureau.[8] Many states maintain active publication programs,[9] and several agencies of the federal government regularly issue volumes of public documents of historical interest.[10]

Publication of the official papers of public persons also has been a function of government agencies, libraries, and historical societies. The editing of a public officer's official correspondence is not essentially different from editing the letters and papers of any other person. What Barbara Oberg has written about editing personal papers in the following essay applies to the editing of a public official's letters; and in fact the publication of the papers of such persons as Thomas Jefferson, Benjamin Franklin, and Woodrow Wilson involves both private and public documents. Since the establishment in 1950 of the National Historical Publications Commission (now the National Historical Publications and Records Commission—NHPRC in the patois of the editorial business), much of the editing and publishing of personal papers has migrated into the universities, but the publication of many sorts of public documents remains a thriving enterprise, still largely in the branches of the federal government and the historical agencies of the various states. There the editors, who are now called public historians, still perform those essential tasks of preservation and multiplication that Jefferson applauded.

DECIDING WHAT TO EDIT

A personal example may illustrate what editors do and point out some of the characteristics of the work. In the mid-1970s, when I was one of the editors of a documentary series on the American Revolution in Virginia, I had several occasions to consult a microfilm copy of the journal of the town council of Norfolk, Virginia, a document known as the order book of the common hall. I discovered that this was the only such municipal record surviving from Virginia's colonial period. In fact, no other southern colonial municipal government journal was in print, giving this document a potentially wide importance. It appeared to be complete and spanned the period between incorporation in 1736 and the autumn of 1798. The only other incorporated Virginia city before the revolution was Williamsburg, and its records are lost; thus, the surviving Norfolk record remains the only one that offers an opportunity to make a careful examination of the evolution of urban government in a rural colony. I thought that useful things might be learned by preparing an edited text of the order book. At the very least, this would make the document easier to evaluate, because the handwriting of one of the long-tenured clerks is difficult to decipher.

I discussed my ideas with the clerk of the city, in whose office I inspected the original document, and with several experts in Virginia colonial history, as well as with the director of publications at the Virginia State Library, who expressed an interest in publishing the edited text if in fact it proved to be an informative document. The nature of the documents is always one of the first things to consider, because some subjects are more effectively treated in essay form than as documentary collections, and some interesting individual documents might not add much to the sum total of knowledge. This municipal government record, however, is unique. It contains different kinds of information from any other local government records from the period. That argued in favor of publication.

I then read everything I could find about Norfolk, including newspapers and manuscripts, during the period covered by the record. In doing this, I found the texts of some municipal ordinances that were not transcribed into the order book, records of meetings held during the revolution when the order book was hidden for safekeeping on a country plantation, texts of public letters mentioned but not recorded in the order book, and texts or summaries of petitions from the common hall to the General Assembly. Moreover, I learned by reading all the statutes relating to Norfolk that the assembly altered provisions of the city charter several times, changed the relationship between the city and neighboring county government, and expanded the discretion and authority of the municipal government.

I soon reached four conclusions: (1) although I could examine the records and write an essay about municipal government in eighteenth-century Virginia, the order book was of sufficient intrinsic value to be useful in and of itself; (2) publication of it would increase our understanding of the development of urban government in eighteenth-century Virginia; (3) it was sufficiently different from all other surviving public records of the period that it should be useful to persons studying other Virginia towns, incorporated or not, and perhaps southern urban history generally; and (4) the order book should be supplemented with the text of the charter, all the relevant statutes, and the letters, petitions, and newspaper accounts of actions not included in the basic document. In this augmented form, the order book would have a scholarly value as an edited text.[11]

PREPARING THE TEXT

This much understood, the Virginia State Library agreed to publish the order book and related documents as part of its continuing program of printing significant public documents from Virginia's history. The state library supplied me with a photocopy of the entire text of the order book, and for several weeks I sat at my primitive old typewriter evenings and weekends transcribing the document. I then made another trip to Norfolk to check unclear passages against the original. I also prepared transcripts of all the related documents I had found.[12] This, alas, was before the days of affordable word processors, even before I knew about these marvelous instruments that are capable of vastly simplifying and expediting the creation of an accurate text. Editors can now save a great deal of valuable time, which, in the long run, can also be a saving of much money, in the preparation of their edited texts. This also reduces the need for retyping and repeated proofreading, which in turn reduces the opportunities to introduce errors.

While preparing the transcriptions I had to make some important editorial decisions because the texts of several important documents do not exist in their original form. The selection of the copy-text, the copy from which the transcription is to be made, is one of the most important and occasionally difficult decisions an editor has to make.[13] If you edit the wrong thing you may sabotage your own work.

For instance, the royal governors occasionally sent to England manuscript copies of letters that had passed between the governors and the common hall, and somebody caused some of the letters to be printed in the colonial newspapers. The original signed letter from the common hall to the governor or from the governor to the common hall would certainly be the most authentic text, but none of the originals exists. Therefore, which of the remaining copies would most closely approximate the original? I knew enough about colonial printers to suspect that compositors probably altered the spelling and punctuation to conform the text to the editorial rules employed in the printing house; and indeed, when more than one newspaper published a letter, the punctuation and spelling and sometimes the wording contained variants. Alteration of the text appeared to be more likely in the newspaper versions than in the manuscript copies, so I used the manuscript copies, when they existed, as my copy-texts.

After I had made choices for copy-texts and carefully transcribed all the available documents, I returned to Norfolk to pursue a rumor that the clerk had a large quantity of nineteenth-century records stored in the old city hall. Might he have some eighteenth-century documents as well? Sure enough, in some old steel cabinets in a dusty basement room I found several dozen municipal ordinances adopted in the 1790s. The clerk enabled me to make photocopies of the fragile, oversize documents, which I then transcribed. Documentary editing requires a comprehensive collection of all potentially relevant documents. They may not all ultimately be printed or even used, but incomplete research at this stage will produce serious problems later.

EDITING THE DOCUMENTS

I now had to decide what to do with a sizeable batch of supplementary documents. I decided to insert them into the text of the order book in their proper chronological places so that the published volume would present one continuous record of the actions of the municipal government. The charter, statutes, letters, petitions, and ordinances could have been printed as appendices, leaving the uninterrupted order book in its original state. That would have had the advantage of lumping the charter and statutes together for ready comparison and of placing all the ordinances together in one handy place. I believed, however, that the chief value of publishing the records was in exhibiting the development of the city government, and this could best be demonstrated by interpolating the documents into the text of the order book. Editors must often choose between two or more justifiable editorial options. The important thing is to choose the one that best suits the purpose of the publication and keeps the focus clearly upon the needs of the users.

Another choice appeared when the transcription was completed. How much annotation should I do?[14] I rejected the notion of writing identifications of all the persons mentioned in the records or even of all the members of the common hall. The emphasis was upon the institutional development and operations of the municipal government, not upon the officers as persons; and although a prosopographer could certainly throw illuminating light upon municipal politics by tracking down information about all the members, that was not what I was doing.[15] I therefore opted for light annotation to explain only those few things that could not be easily understood by reading the documents themselves. I also decided to let a comprehensive index do the work of cross-referencing the common hall's actions upon various subjects, but I wrote a chapter-length introduction describing the most important developments in municipal governance in order to spotlight those features of the records that most warranted attention.

SEEING THE DOCUMENTS THROUGH THE PRESS

These decisions taken and the typing done, I turned the typescript over to the Virginia State Library. The publisher and copy editor, with whom I had discussed each of the editorial decisions as they arose, carefully examined all my editorial apparatus, queried some of my readings of text, suggested removing some notes, and suggested adding some others. A final check of the typescript against all the manuscripts preceded the setting of type, and another close reading of the galleys and manuscripts preceded the production of page proofs. When page proofs arrived, I spent three or four hours a night and eight or ten hours each Saturday and Sunday for about a month indexing all the names and subjects in the entire volume. This was pen and index card work, too! Lucky the prosperous or well-connected editor who these days can enlist the aid of a computer in preparing the index.

This last drudgery is of the highest importance. It is an unusual person who reads all the way through a volume of public records. Researchers look things up in them, and they must be able to find everything they need. A badly indexed document is not much better than an unindexed one. Subject indexing, perhaps the most difficult aspect of indexing most books, is essential, but in this instance my most perplexing problem was how to treat persons with the same names. The records contain, among other complications, three men named Samuel Boush and three named Thomas Newton, two of each with Jr. occasionally appended. To distinguish these persons from one another, I included their dates as part of the primary index entry. I also separated within each index entry the references to service as councilman, alderman, mayor, recorder, city sergeant, and the like to enable the users to locate the exact information they sought. Foremost in my mind at each stage of the preparation of the index was the convenience of the users, who might be interested in problems of municipal governance, taxation, politics, public health, or genealogy.

We also located some maps and a few illustrations to embellish the work and help point out some salient features of the records. The city clerk produced from his desk drawer the original silver seal of the city, the receipt of which is mentioned in the order book, and we included an illustration of that remarkable relic upon the title page. Finally, about two years after the initial decision to edit, the published volume came from the bindery bearing the cumbersome but informative title, *The Order Book and Related Papers of the Common Hall of the Borough of Norfolk, Virginia, 1736–1798.* I opened the book at random, which happened to be to page 27 in the introduction, and instantly spotted an uncorrected printer's error, which is to say, one of my own proofreading errors. Fortunately, none of the document texts has been found faulty. The

volume was well received and, although not of earth-shaking importance, should be useful to students of Norfolk's history, eighteenth-
century Virginia institutional history, and southern urban history.

EDITING IS SCHOLARSHIP

That is what editors of public documents do, either as employees of
libraries or government agencies or as independent scholars. The basic
research skills and ability to evaluate evidence are precisely those most
useful to any historian doing any primary research. The technical
process of converting a document text into published form requires an
extra amount of patience and close application to minute details. This is
essential because the users of the volumes will rely upon the editor's
precision and will treat the published text with the same reverence they
would treat the original primary source itself.[16]

Although much of what editors do is exacting and even laborious,
much is also creative and stimulating to the critical faculties. The editing
of public documents often poses distinctive scholarly puzzles. Some of
these arise because the papers may have an unknown or a corporate
authorship. The journal of a legislative body, for instance, contains the
collective judgment of its members, only some few of whom may have
taken an active part in forming that judgment into the language with
which the body expresses itself. It may not always be possible or even
important to know which legislators contributed what during the evolution of the language, but an editor has the responsibility to discover as
much detail as possible about the steps taken in the development of the
language in order to know what to do in those cases in which the basic
documents may be incomplete or contain variant texts.[17]

Editors develop a special intimacy with the documents. The process of
editing requires repeated close readings of the manuscripts, collation of
texts, and minute inspection of related documents. The result is often a
better understanding of what the documents have to say about the past.
This, besides the preservation and multiplication of copies, gives documentary editors the opportunity to make contributions to understanding at the same time they make the historical evidence more readily
available. This is one particularly rewarding aspect of documentary
editing.

EDITORS AS HISTORIANS

Editors shoulder a number of important responsibilities. The late
William M. E. Rachal, longtime editor of the *Virginia Magazine of History
and Biography* and one of the editors of the *Papers of James Madison*, once
quipped that an editor must have the mind of a scholar and the soul of
a clerk. What he meant was that a good editor, in addition to being a
good historian, must also have the temperament to be patient and
painstaking with all the minute details of editorial craftsmanship.
Editing requires constant close attention to detail in the production of

accurate texts; but editing is more than just the galley slavery of checking proofs against manuscripts. All the tools of historical scholarship must be brought into play. If an editor stumbles at any one of several key steps in the editorial process, the utility of the publication will be compromised. Those who consult the edition will unknowingly carry its biases or limitations into whatever scholarship is based in whole or in part upon the edited text. (Editorial imperfections are not always evident to the users. The occasional printer's or proofreader's error is about the most conspicuous though least significant such imperfection.)

No editor, however diligent in searching for documents, meticulous in transcription, erudite in annotation, or imaginative in indexing will be a good editor without first being a skillful historian. One must know the needs of the scholarly community to know what will be useful. One must know the archival resources to know what might best be brought to light and comprehensively edited. One must master the subtleties of the time and subject matter being edited. And one must be clear and concise in exposition so that the editorial apparatus is helpful to the users, not intrusive or misleading. The qualifications for a good editor are the same as those for a good historian. Editors require special patience, perhaps, but they are not a different breed of scholar. In addition, as with other historians both inside and outside the academic community, editors may often have to develop skills in grantsmanship, fund raising, and administrative management to enable them to perform the labor intensive tasks of editing.

HISTORIANS AS EDITORS

The number of historians who make their livings editing public documents is relatively small compared with the number of historians who teach. In spite of a recent trend toward the isolation of some editors into discreet editorial projects of large size,[18] much of the editing that currently takes place is still done on small projects by editors employed in state library or historical society publishing programs or by historians for whom editing is one of several scholarly pursuits.

As Barbara Oberg has suggested, historians do not often set out early in their careers specifically to become editors, although several history departments offer courses in documentary editing as part of professional training programs, and several will accept edited texts in fulfillment of thesis or dissertation requirements.[19] It is more common for the practicing historian to become an editor as one of the things to be done during a varied career in scholarship. The result is that editing is usually learned on the job; and, indeed, the best way to learn how to edit is as the colleague of an experienced editor.[20]

There is no cookbook method for editing documents. The nature of the documents and the purpose of publication will dictate the answers to such questions as what to edit, whether to modernize or regularize spelling and punctuation, and how much annotation to do. The first edition of the *Harvard Guide to American History*, published in 1954, contains general guidelines for determining how much of what kind of editing to do and stresses that consistency and accuracy are the highest priorities, criteria repeated in the revised edition published in 1974.[21] In his how-to-do-it manual, *Historical Editing*, Bulletins of the National Archives, Number 7 (1952), Clarence E. Carter argued for a bare minimum of annotation and explanatory apparatus, leaving the reader to decide upon the meaning of the text. In contrast, Julian P. Boyd led the way into a more erudite editing in 1950 when he published the first volume of the textually sophisticated and extensively annotated *Papers of Thomas Jefferson*.[22] But because each batch of documents requires its own special presentation and will dictate its own style of explication and annotation, the editor must decide in each case what editorial interventions to make in the text and how much commentary is required to elucidate the documents. This is to be a central theme of Mary-Jo Kline's *Guide to Documentary Editing in the United States*, currently being completed under the auspices of the Association for Documentary Editing.

WHERE TO LEARN MORE ABOUT
DOCUMENTARY EDITING

The literature cited in the notes to this essay and in Barbara Oberg's essay on editing personal correspondence provides ample commentaries on the development of historical editing as a scholarly enterprise and references to informative articles on questions of document selection, transcription, annotation, and fund raising. Suellen Hoy and Jeffrey J. Crow, *Historical Editing: A Guide for Departments of History* (Bloomington, Ind.: Organization of American Historians, 1984) is a useful general overview, and it contains a short bibliography and a section on editing professional journals. Two longer bibliographies are Ross W. Beales, Jr., "Documentary Editing: A Bibliography," *Newsletter of the Association for Documentary Editing* 2 (December 1980): 10–16; and Suellen Hoy, "Historical Editing," in *The Craft of Public History: An Annotated Select Bibliography*, ed. David F. Trask and Robert W. Pomeroy III (Westport, Conn.: Greenwood Press, 1983), 171–227. The Association for Documentary Editing, a national professional organization of editors who work with a wide variety of textual materials, has published a quarterly journal since 1979: the *Newsletter of the Association for Documentary Editing*, renamed *Documentary Editing* in 1984. Among other features, it contains several articles on the use of computers and word processors in the editing and indexing of texts.

The Association for Documentary Editing also maintains a job placement file. As of this writing, the file is kept by David W. Hirst, Associate Editor, Papers of Woodrow Wilson, Firestone Library, Princeton University, Princeton, New Jersey 08544.

The NHPRC has sponsored an annual two-week summer Institute for Historical Editing since 1971; and when tight budgets permit, the NHPRC has funded a few one-year internships with established documentary editing projects. For information, write to the

National Historical Publications and Records Commission, National Archives, Washington, D.C. 20408.

NOTES

1. Some useful reviews of the history of documentary editing are: Worthington Chauncey Ford, "The Editorial Function in United States History," *American Historical Review* 23 (1918): 273–86; Clarence E. Carter, "The United States and Documentary Historical Publication," *Mississippi Valley Historical Review* 25 (1938): 3–24; Julian P. Boyd, "Some Animadversions on Being Struck by Lightning," *Daedalus* 86 (1955): 49–56; George H. Callcott, "Antiquarianism and Documents in the Age of Literary History," *American Archivist* 21 (1958): 17–29; Lester J. Cappon, "The Historian as Editor," in *In Support of Clio: Essays in Memory of Herbert A. Kellar*, ed. William B. Hesseltine and Donald R. McNeil (Madison, Wis.: State Historical Society of Wisconsin, 1958), 173–93; Lyman H. Butterfield, "Historical Editing in the United States: The Recent Past," American Antiquarian Society *Proceedings*, 72, part 2 (1962): 283–308; Philip M. Hammer, "' . . . authentic Documents tending to elucidate our History,'" *American Archivist* 25 (1962): 3–13; H. G. Jones, "The Publication of Documentary Sources, 1934–1968" in *The Records of a Nation: Their Management, Preservation, and Use* (New York: Athenaeum Press, 1969); and Lester J. Cappon, "American Historical Editors before Jared Sparks: 'they will plant a forest . . . ,'" *William and Mary Quarterly*, 3d series, 30 (1973): 375–400.
2. James Madison to Thomas Jefferson, 14 February 1790, in William T. Hutchinson, William M. E. Rachal et al., eds., *The Papers of James Madison*, vol. 13 (Chicago: University of Chicago Press; and Charlottesville: University Press of Virginia, 1962–): 41.
3. Fred Shelley, "Ebenezer Hazard: America's First Historical Editor," *William and Mary Quarterly*, 3d series, 12 (1955): 44–73.
4. Thomas Jefferson to Ebenezer Hazard, 18 February 1791, in Julian P. Boyd et al., eds., *Papers of Thomas Jefferson*, vol. 19 (Princeton, N.J.: Princeton University Press, 1950): 287. The case for editing is most thoroughly developed in Lester J. Cappon, "A Rationale for Historical Editing Past and Present," *William and Mary Quarterly*, 3d series, 23 (1966): 56–75.
5. The son of Ebenezer Hazard began the Pennsylvania project. See Roland M. Baumann, "Samuel Hazard: Editor and Archivist for the Keystone State," *Pennsylvania Magazine of History and Biography* 107 (1983): 195–216.
6. For an excellent account of this editor's career, see Lyman H. Butterfield, "Worthington Chauncey Ford, Editor," Massachusetts Historical Society *Proceedings* 83 (1971): 46–82.
7. Dallas D. Irvine, "The Genesis of the *Official Records*," *Mississippi Valley Historical Review* 24 (1937): 221–29.
8. For a thought-provoking discussion of this unconventional series, see LaWanda Cox, "From Great White Men to Blacks Emerging from Bondage, with Innovations in Documentary Editing," *Reviews in American History* 12 (1984): 31–39.
9. See, for example, Jack P. Greene, "The Publication of the Official Records of the Southern Colonies, A Review Article," *William and Mary Quarterly*, 3d series, 14 (1957): 268–80; Michael G. Kammen, "Colonial Court Records and the Study of Early American History: A Bibliographical Review," *American Historical Review* 70 (1965): 732–39; Charles Gehring, "New York's

Dutch Records: A Historiographical Note," *New York History* 56 (1975): 347–54; and Michael E. Stevens, "Documentary Editing in the Southeastern State Archives," *Documentary Editing* (formerly the *Newsletter of the Association for Documentary Editing*) 7 (June 1985): 8–13.

By way of example, these are the major public documents that the Virginia State Library has published in this century: John Pendleton Kennedy and H. R. McIlwaine, eds., *Journals of the House of Burgesses of Virginia*, 13 vols. (1905–15); H. R. McIlwaine, ed., *Legislative Journals of the Council of Colonial Virginia*, 3 vols. (1918–19); H. R. McIlwaine, ed., *Minutes of the Council and General Court of Colonial Virginia* (1924); H. R. McIlwaine et al., eds., *Executive Journals of the Council of Colonial Virginia*, 6 vols. (1925–66); H. R. McIlwaine, ed., *Official Letters of the Governors of the State of Virginia*, 3 vols. covering the years 1776–83 (1926–29); H. R. McIlwaine et al., eds., *Journals of the Council of the State of Virginia*, 5 vols. covering the years 1776–91 (1931–82); Wilmer L. Hall et al., eds., *Journals of the Senate of Virginia* for the sessions of 1792, 1793, 1794, 1795, 1796, 1797–98, 1798–99, and 1802–03 (1949–77); George H. Reese, ed., *Proceedings of the Virginia State Convention of 1861*, 4 vols. (1965) and its companion set, *Journals and Papers of the Virginia State Convention of 1861*, 3 vols. (1966); Waverly K. Winfree, ed., *The Laws of Virginia: Being a Supplement to Hening's "The Statutes at Large," 1700–1750* (1971); James I. Robertson, Jr., ed., *Proceedings of the Advisory Council of the State of Virginia, April 21–June 19, 1861* (1977); Brent Tarter, ed., *The Order Book and Related Papers of the Common Hall of the Borough of Norfolk Virginia, 1736–1798* (1979); George H. Reese, ed., *Proceedings in the Court of Vice-Admiralty of Virginia, 1698–1775* (1983); and Walter Minchinton, Celia King, and Peter Waite, eds., *Virginia Slave-Trade Statistics, 1698–1775* (1984).

The library has also published four small volumes of Revolutionary War documents: H. R. McIlwaine, ed., *Proceedings of the Committees of Safety of Cumberland and Isle of Wight Counties, Virginia, 1775–1776* (1919); H. R. McIlwaine, ed., *Proceedings of the Committees of Safety of Caroline and Southampton Counties, Virginia, 1774–1776* (1929); Richard B. Harwell, ed., *The Committees of Safety of Westmoreland and Fincastle: Proceedings of the County Committees, 1774–1776* (1956); and Lee A. Wallace, Jr., ed., *The Orderly Book of Captain Benjamin Taliaferro, 2d Virginia Detachment, Charleston, South Carolina, 1780* (1980).

It has published Landon C. Bell, ed., *Charles Parish, York County, Virginia: History and Registers, Births 1648–1789, Deaths, 1665–1787* (1932); and half a dozen sets of colonial parish records edited by C. G. Chamberlayne: *The Vestry Book of Petsworth Parish, Gloucester County, Virginia, 1677–1793* (1933); *The Vestry Book of Stratton Major Parish, King and Queen County, Virginia, 1729–1783* (1933); *The Vestry Book of Blisland (Blissland) Parish, New Kent and James City Counties, Virginia, 1721–1786* (1935); *The Vestry Book and Register of St. Peter's Parish, New Kent and James City Counties, Virginia, 1684–1786* (1937); *The Vestry Book of St. Paul's Parish, Hanover County, Virginia, 1706–1786* (1940); and *The Vestry Book of the Upper Parish of Nansemond County, Virginia, 1743–1793* (1949).

At present the Virginia State Library has in preparation Warren M. Billings's edition of the letters of Francis Howard, baron Howard of Effingham, who was governor of Virginia from 1683–92; and George H. Reese and John C. Van Horne's edition of the notoriously difficult-to-read letter book of James Abercromby, who was Virginia's agent in London during the two decades prior to the American Revolution.

10. Three thoughtful analyses of the present state of documentary editing are Fredrika J. Teute, "Views in Review: A Historiographical Perspective on Historical Editing," *American Archivist* 43 (1980): 43–56; Richard H. Kohn and George M. Curtis III, "The Government, the Historical Profession, and Historical Editing: A Review," *Reviews in American History* 10 (1980): 145–55; and John Y. Simon, "Editors and Critics," *Newsletter of the Association for Documentary Editing* 3 (December 1981): 1–4.

11. Some manuscripts impose logical limits upon themselves by the nature of their contents, but others, particularly collections of material gathered from more than one basic source, pose additional problems of selectivity. For some comments on the problems and pitfalls, see Louis Galambos, "The Eisenhower Papers: Editing Modern Public Documents," *Documentary Editing* 6 (June 1984): 5–7; Lorraine M. Lees and Sandra Gioia Treadway, "Review Essay: A Future for Our Diplomatic Past? A Critical Appraisal of the *Foreign Relations* Series," *Journal of American History* 70 (1983): 621–29; and John Y. Simon, "The Canons of Selection," *Documentary Editing* 6 (December 1984): 8–12.

12. A large literature exists concerning the transcription of documents, the rendering of abbreviations, punctuation, obsolete spellings, and the like. The most important are Clarence E. Carter, "The Territorial Papers of the United States: A Review and a Commentary," *Mississippi Valley Historical Review* 42 (1955): 510–24; Clarence E. Carter, *Historical Editing*, Bulletins of the National Archives, Number 7 (1952); and G. Thomas Tanselle, "Literary Editing" in *Literary & Historical Editing*, ed. George L. Vogt and John Bush Jones (Lawrence, Kans.: University of Kansas Press, 1981), 35–56.

   For a comprehensive and somewhat controversial review of the transcription practices of some of the major recent historical editors, see Tanselle's classic "The Editing of Historical Documents," *Studies in Bibliography* 31 (1978): 1–56, which prompted a stimulating discussion at the 1980 meeting of the Association for Documentary Editing in Williamsburg, Virginia, for part of which see Don L. Cook, "The Short Happy Thesis of G. Thomas Tanselle" and Robert J. Taylor, "Editorial Practices—An Historian's View," *Newsletter of the Association for Documentary Editing* 3 (February 1981): 1–8.

13. An even larger and more esoteric literature, largely the production of the editors of literary texts, exists on the fine points of selecting copy-texts. The starting point is W. W. Greg, "The Rationale of Copy-Text," *Studies in Bibliography* 3 (1950–51): 21–36, reprinted in J. C. Maxwell, ed., *The Collected Works of Sir Walter Greg* (Oxford, Eng.: Oxford University Press, 1966), 374–91; with these essential commentaries: G. Thomas Tanselle, "Greg's Theory of Copy-Text and the Editing of American Literature," *Studies in Bibliography* 28 (1975): 167–229; and Fredson Bowers, "Greg's 'Rationale of Copy-Text' Revisited," ibid., 31 (1978): 90–161.

14. No body of theoretical work on annotation exists, but for a survey of recent practices, see Charles T. Cullen, "Principles of Annotation in Editing Historical Documents; or, How to Avoid Breaking the Butterfly on the Wheel of Scholarship," in Vogt and Jones, ed., *Literary & Historical Editing*, 81–95.

15. One reviewer, though, thought that was exactly what I should have been doing. See Donald R. Lenon in *North Carolina Historical Review* 56 (1979): 420–21.

16. In the mid-1940s a volume of fake documents created a sensation in the historical profession and resulted in the publication of an inquiry that

brilliantly presents the criteria for evaluating edited texts. See Arthur Pierce Middleton and Douglas Adair, "The Mystery of the Horn Papers," *William and Mary Quarterly*, 3d series, 4 (1947): 409–45.

17. I described this technique at greater length in "Ideas Competent to the Fact; or Some Musings on Eclectic Texts of Some Sorts of Public Documents," (Paper delivered at the annual convention of the Association for Documentary Editing, Baltimore, Maryland, 8 October 1983).

18. For an assessment of the implications of this trend (with which I do not entirely agree), see Charles T. Cullen's 1983 presidential address to the Association for Documentary Editing, "Some Reflections on the Soft Money Generation," *Newsletter of the Association for Documentary Editing* 5 (December 1983): 1–4.

19. Thomas E. Jeffrey, "The Education of Editors: Current Status and Future Prospects," *Documentary Editing* 7 (March 1985): 12–17.

20. For interesting and pertinent comments by one of the masters of literary textual editing, see Fredson Bowers, "The Education of Editors," *Newsletter of the Association for Documentary Editing* 2 (December 1980): 1–4. See also Warren M. Billings, "Cardinal Principles, Historical and Archival," ibid., 2 (February 1980): 15–16.

21. Oscar Handlin et al., *The Harvard Guide to American History* (Cambridge, Mass.: Harvard University Press, 1954), 95–104; Frank Freidel, *The Harvard Guide to American History*, 2d ed., vol. 1 (Cambridge, Mass.: Harvard University Press, 1974): 27–36.

22. Boyd, "Editorial Method," *Papers of Thomas Jefferson*, 1: xxv–xxxviii.

Barbara Oberg received a B.A. in History from Wellesley College and an M.A. and Ph.D. from the University of California at Santa Barbara. She has completed a two-volume selected edition of the correspondence of David Hartley. Formerly associate editor of Philip Mazzei: The Comprehensive Microform of His Papers, *she is now editor of the Papers of Albert Gallatin at Baruch College of The City University of New York. She is a member of the editorial board of* Journal of the Early Republic *and on the executive committee of the Society for Textual Scholarship.*

HISTORICAL EDITING: CORRESPONDENCE

Barbara Oberg

When we think of correspondence, it is probably private communication which first comes to mind. As a result, editing letters as a field of public history may seem at first glance less obviously within the scope and interests of the public historian than is the editing of public documents. But there is, of course, the correspondence of public figures and public institutions, as well as the family letters of a wider public. Correspondence of both a public and private nature presents a rich field that can be mined. The letters of public figures often shed light on critical issues of official policy in which the public historian is interested, and the well-trained historian must know what to do with them. But since the term "public history" also embraces the presentation of history to the public, not the professors, its practitioners must know how to edit private correspondence as well. The letters of private individuals as they turn up in attics, local historical societies, and family collections ought to be attended to by those public historians who speak to a public, a nonacademic, a general audience.

Editing documents that were not intended for general perusal or publication presents some different problems from editing public documents, and public historians ought to know the skills necessary for producing a good volume of correspondence. This essay will introduce the student to the history of editing correspondence in this country and to its evolution from a private, family venture into a public profession. It does not attempt to offer a uniform body of rules for editing correspondence. Learning how to carry on all the editorial tasks requires substantial reading, and the student is urged to make use of the bibliographic references following this chapter and the essay on "Editing Public Records" by Brent Tarter.

The essay also recounts the experiences of one individual's development into an editor of correspondence. As a person trained relatively traditionally in the historian's craft and as one who made a transition some eight years ago from the practice of writing conventional intellectual history to that of constructing historical editions, I am particularly aware that even for the trained historian there are additional skills required for turning primary source materials into well-edited letters. I would like to see all students of history taught to recognize the importance of using correspondence as primary source materials, and one way that students can get a sense of that importance is by becoming acquainted with some basic techniques of editing.

In the spring of 1975, while I was doing historical research at the Berkshire County Record Office in Reading, England, I began my conversion from primarily monographic-historian to editor-historian. I was there because I wanted to find out more about the family background of the eighteenth-century English philosopher, David Hartley (1705–1757), on whom I had written my dissertation in intellectual history at the University of California, Santa Barbara. Poring over the Hartley-Russell family folders of deeds, wills, receipts, account books, and correspondence which comprised the history of a family tracing its roots back to Henry St. John, Viscount Bolingbroke, I finally made the connection that the son of my philosopher-physician David Hartley was the David Hartley (1732–1813) who had been a loyal supporter of the American rebels during the American War for Independence. On September 3, 1783, he was the British signer of the Treaty of Paris, the counterpart of our Benjamin Franklin, John Adams, and John Jay. Naturally he was not as well known to us as our own diplomats. Nor, as it turned out, was he well known to his own countrymen.

I came to Reading a traditional research scholar, but when I left a few months later I was on the road to redefining myself as an editor as well. I came to search for the genesis of the elder Hartley's extreme materialistic philosophy, but jumping ahead a generation from the father's early eighteenth-century collection of papers (essays on the best methods for dissolving kidney stones, prescriptions for his patients, letters to chemists), I found very different materials—a significant collection of American-related political letters.

Along with drafts of Hartley's speeches for the House of Commons, there were drafts of his son David's letters to Benjamin Franklin, crudely written petitions from American prisoners protesting their captivity in deplorable conditions at England's Mill Prison, and extensive correspondence from Hartley's constituents at the northern English port of Hull. These letters from his constituents told of the concrete impact of the American war on their trade; some of them urged him to speed the conclusion of the war, and others asked him to resign from Parliament. Many of the letters were simply gathered in uncatalogued bundles, and clearly few had been extensively used. I felt that I had discovered a secret treasure of documents which were a part of American history relatively unknown to Americans.[1]

As I sifted through the letters, I knew that they formed a piece of Anglo-American history of the late eighteenth century and that they deserved to be preserved as such. Handling the manuscripts was exciting; it felt like "doing" history in a significantly different way from what I knew. While I had worked with primary sources before—with both printed editions of correspondence and collections of public documents—there was something unique about these materials. They were letters and they were manuscripts. They shed light on the revolution and on at least one British politician's long-term efforts to arrive at a commercial arrangement between Great Britain and America. That they were historical evidence was clear. But that recognition was not particularly special, because in general one of the excitements of writing history is discovering new evidence or unexpectedly seeing old evidence in a new way.

What was not necessarily clear was the best way to bring together and organize the material or the best format for putting it before the potential public audience of historical readers. I was confronted with a methodological decision. A full-length biography, a biographical essay, or a monograph on the British opposition to the prosecution of the American war were all possible choices and would all make extensive use of the new materials which I had come upon. Biographies are "good reads," and the most successful, accurate, and enduring ones are based upon primary sources objectively and scrupulously used. But for some reason it gradually occurred to me that I could begin work not on a biography of Hartley, but on an edition of his letters. As I read the original manuscripts, the notion of a biographical or critical piece written *about* them seemed a step removed from the immediacy of the history I held in my hands. A narrative piece would move the reader farther away from, not closer to, the materials. Why write about letters when the letters could speak about themselves? In that realization was my initiation into the world of the editing of historical documents.

Unlike public documents, which may be of concern primarily to the writer of political, legislative, or institutional history, surviving correspondence, whether public or private, is a source not only for historians but for writers from a number of fields. Letters are the way in which we communicate with each other in writing when the thought conveyed is worth preserving. Written correspondence ranges from the long handwritten epistles of the eighteenth century, to the typed inter-office memos of today. The latter record the exchange of thoughts between two people working in the same office or on the same committee. In either case, the documentary editor is responsible for translating that handwritten or typed document into a printed, accurate representation of the text.

For the purpose of this essay on the editing of correspondence, I assume that the correspondence has a concrete, physical existence, and that it survives in some tangible, visually recognizable form: holograph, typescript, or hard copy from a computer or word processing system. Future editors of correspondence will have additional forms and mechanics to deal with as they strive to define the nature and limits of correspondence, but at the present we are speaking of a written document which passes between two or more individuals. As the technology continues to change and leaves us with magnetic tape, floppy disks, or messages exchanged via computer-linked networks like Bitnet, we will have to become increasingly inventive in the search for an error-free way to edit the "written word." But even technological changes will not reverse or radically alter the problems editors of correspondence have encountered in historical editing. For now, historical editors must face the traditional issues outlined here; and in the future, although their materials may take a different shape, their methods and goals will remain remarkably constant. The significant questions, tools, and purposes will remain the same, and if public historians learn the proper way to approach the selection, transcription, and annotation of a letter now, their training will not become outmoded.

The possibilities for the epistolary form of communication are endless. A letter is an integral piece of writing and stands on its own; it need not be part of a larger work, although other letters which surround it can help elucidate it. Letters can be long or short, intimate or formal, personal or impersonal, confidential or public, broad or narrow in subject matter, and literate and articulate or semiliterate and unpolished. And naturally the categories are not rigidly separated, but rather overlap. When Ulysses S. Grant, for example, wrote the following letter to his wife Julia, the information conveyed to historians was public and private, formal and intimate, impersonal and personal.

> City Point Va. Oct 26 1864
>
> Dear Julia,
> To-morrow a great battle will probably be fought. At all events I have made all the arrangements for one and unless I conclude through the day to change my programme it will take place. I do not like to predict results therefore will say nothing about what I expect to accomplish. The cake you sent by Mr. Smith come to hand but the other you speak of having sent by Express has not.[2]

This is a personal letter from Grant to his wife in Burlington, New Jersey, rather than a military report to an official. But as an insight into the general's military maneuvers it may be of value to historians of public papers. The detail of the cake which Julia Grant's cousin, William W. Smith, carried to General Grant is of interest to social historians in its depiction of army life, domestic life, and the connection between the two. Distinctions between public and private blur in this letter, as they very frequently do in the correspondence of public figures.

The forms for letters are various but what defines the document as a letter (rather than a diary, journal, or essay, for example) is its direction to another individual or individuals. It was intended to be seen by someone. The subject matter is infinitely diverse, whether we move from one historical era to another or whether we consider letters within the same time period and cultural context. An oft-repeated occasion for correspondence is this scenario. The wife writes to her husband who is fighting in a distant war and in conveying to him the details of life at home, the documentary record which she leaves behind for the future historical editor is a personal record of her thoughts on their forced separation, the growth of the young children which the husband is missing by his absence, and the management of the household which occupies her efforts. But in addition to this, her letter stands as a broader comment on the impact of the war upon the society at home (from reports in the newspapers or the observations she exchanges with other women and tradespeople, for example), and as a record of the wartime economy reflected in the scarcity and high cost of goods in the stores. It may also stand perhaps as a reflection of the political attitudes which the civilians display toward the conduct of the war.

Abigail Adams offers us an illustration of a well-known figure in American history who was frequently separated from her husband, John Adams. She remained home in Massachusetts during the months that he spent sitting with the Continental Congress in Philadelphia before the signing of the Declaration of Independence, and she continued to reside there while he undertook a mission to negotiate a loan in Amsterdam and then proceeded to Paris to negotiate the peace. Her letters are a blend of national and local news and of family reports and political gossip. His too are filled with political gossip, with requests for news of his family, and with solid political information.

The record of the thoughts of two prominent, introspective yet articulate, public figures provides us with a matchless portrait of what went on in the minds of two persons from that particular region and social class in the late eighteenth century.[3] The historian pays attention to that correspondence for what it reveals of wife and husband corresponding, what it narrates of the era, and what it demonstrates of broader issues. Where else are we to glean the insights and details of social, economic, and political life if not from the letters which pass between people who know one another well enough to reveal thoughts and observations openly? Abigail and John Adams are a classic couple whose correspondence preserved for posterity an unsurpassed record of the American revolutionary and early national period.

Public historians and historical editors will care about what John and Abigail Adams wrote to each other because they are famous. But they also care about what other less well-known wives and husbands wrote to each other. A nation is made up of its citizens as individuals, and each has a unique history of his or her own. The history of the whole cannot be complete without the correspondence of the others. Across the country local historical societies and private manuscript collections contain similar, lesser and partial to be sure, recordings. The Madison Historical Society in Madison, New Jersey, for example, received a gift in 1984 of letters exchanged in the middle of the nineteenth century between Auguste du Rest Blanchet and his wife, Sarah Henriques Blanchet. Most of the letters are from Sarah to Auguste while he was in Kentucky attending to large tracts of lands he inherited there. Like many of her contemporaries, she cared not for the wilderness and remained "at home," sometimes in Madison and sometimes in Brooklyn. The letters are an account of how she managed, what she paid for goods and labor, and how little cash she had. They serve as an economic mini-history of the period, as they tell of what it meant to keep the farm producing:

> Madison, Wednesday night,
> April 14 [1854]
>
> I have been compelled to hire a horse to plough with, from Mr Burnes. I think Le'o said he charges five shillings a day, the horse will be wanted about two days and a half I shall have to pay it when they get through, they began this morning, I shall have to buy oats as well, I thought it was best to do so, than not to have the work done.[4]

Not only do the letters narrate the story of this family, but they must typify the situation in which many American couples found themselves during a period of westward expansion and widely scattered landholdings. The collection and publication of the letters allows us to reconstruct American history.

In his essay on editing public records, Brent Tarter outlined a history of the development of American historical editing. As Ebenezer Hazard, Thomas Jefferson, and others of their contemporaries realized, the collection and preservation of the nation's documentary heritage was a significant task. They were a generation conscious of their own history. They saw their revolutionary aspiration, musings, and achievements as unique and they wanted to record them. It was not simply that they were a generation conscious of their own history, but also in some cases that they wanted to ensure the correct cast was given to the historical record. Jefferson, Adams, and Franklin wanted the record of American achievements preserved. Each also wanted to preserve the "true" and proper interpretation of his own role in it. Adams, for example, feared that the history of the revolution would be "one continued Lye from one end to the other!" He predicted that Benjamin Franklin would convey the message of his own importance and that "the essense of the whole will be *that Dr. Franklins electrical Rod, smote the Earth and out sprung General Washington.*"[5] No room there for John Adams, and surely he could not tolerate that. Out of these desires of our Founding Fathers and out of the efforts of their progeny to carry out these wishes, came the first national efforts to edit private correspondence of public figures for a public audience. William Temple Franklin, who had acted as his grandfather's secretary, set out to preserve Benjamin Franklin's thoughts for posterity. In the preface to *The Memoirs of Benjamin Franklin*, William Temple contended that the volume would record Franklin's "social epistolary correspondence, philosophical, political, and moral letters and essays, and his diplomatic transactions as agent at London and minister plenipotentiary at Versailles."[6] This was the public, alleged aim. But beneath it was the personal motive: defense of the family name.

One way to write the nation's history is to use the institutional records which Tarter describes. Another way is through the collection, editing, and printing of the correspondence of the individuals who played prominent roles in creating the national history. The nineteenth-century institutional records like the *Pennsylvania Colonial Records* and Peter Force's *American Archives* had a parallel in early editions of the writings of the nation's founding fathers.[7] The early efforts to publish correspondence of the founding fathers were frequently undertaken by younger generations of the same family. Hence, we have William Temple Franklin's two-volume edition of his grandfather's letters and Charles Francis Adams's ten volumes of John Adams's letters and writings.

Charles Francis Adams wrote a number of works which were both the nation's history and his family's history: *Correspondence Between John Adams and Mercy Warren, Familiar Letters of John Adams and His Wife, Abigail Adams,* and *The Works of John Adams.* In 1840, he discovered and published a collection of letters exchanged between Abigail Adams and her husband during the revolution. Charles Francis found the letters of his grandparents interesting and thought "they might possibly interest others also, especially the growing generations not familiar with the history of the persons and events connected with the great struggle."[8] In 1875, with the centennial celebration of American independence impending, Adams sought to reproduce and supplement his original work with newly discovered letters. The editions of letters of his ancestors, then, were both a personal and a public testimony for this Adams; he celebrated the dignity and merits of his own past as he celebrated the nation's history.

The family member as editor of correspondence from the nation's early statesmen was a key fact of the nineteenth-century editorial profession.[9] In Charles Francis Adams's preface to his 1875 collection were even rudiments of an editorial method. In his 1840 work he separated John's letters from Abigail's, designating a volume for each. By 1875 he deemed it

> ... more judicious to collect them together and arrange them in the precise order of their respective dates, to the end that the references to events or sentiments constantly made on the one side or the other may be more readily gathered and understood.[10]

He was acting as more than just an amateur editor who sought to save a bit of his family's history. By setting forth in his preface a rationale for putting the volume together in a chronological framework with John's and Abigail's contributions interspersed rather than segregated or compartmentalized, he was performing editorial tasks: he made selections from the material and he imposed an order on the material.

The practice of this generation of historian-editors was, at least in one prominent case, carried to later generations. Later in the nineteenth century, Henry Adams continued the tradition of Charles Francis, with the variation that although he was indirectly commenting upon a period of history in which his forebears had been active and eminent, he was actually preparing an edition of a nonfamily member. Henry Adams, history professor at Harvard, editor of the *North American Review*, and essayist, set out to make a statement about American politics, the democratic process, and the fate of the brilliant individual in an imperfect society. The work is a revealing statement about Adams himself, which R. P. Blackmur has argued, "so well struck the theme of Adams' whole career that it can be bracketed with Adams' own autobiography and be called 'The Education of Albert Gallatin.'"[11]

It is Henry Adams's conception of Albert Gallatin that has shaped and dominated our knowledge of Thomas Jefferson's Secretary of the Treasury, for the little writing produced about him since relies heavily upon Adams's work. In a period of just under three years (1877–1880), Adams produced two volumes of selected correspondence, one volume of published pamphlets, and a single-volume biography, *The Life*. This classic Gallatin edition is, ironically, everything we would tell a modern documentary editor not to do. The principle of selection is flawed, the transcription policies do not render an accurate text, and like many editions of the late nineteenth and early twentieth century, there is no annotation. But at the same time it is a monument to its generation of editors. From its conception and initial execution, the work was interpretive. The very principle of selection led to a distinct and subjective portrait of Gallatin, of his life and career, and of his place in the American political and economic system; but Adams said nothing of the editorial method or what principles he would use to select only a very few of the thousands of documents available to him.

Adams ignored almost entirely the early period of Gallatin's life—his life in Geneva, his stay in Maine and Massachusetts, and his entrance into state and national politics in Pennsylvania. Of all the letters included in Volume I, only two predate 1801, the year in which Gallatin assumed the office of Secretary of the Treasury in Jefferson's first cabinet. In actuality Adams began his edition of Gallatin's political correspondence only when he began to approve of Gallatin's behavior. It is not simply that Adams concentrated on the national period of Gallatin's life, but that he did not understand or condone Gallatin's early enthusiasm for Rousseau, his decision to leave Geneva rather than reform the Genevan political system with which he was dissatisfied, or his preference for an unsettled life on the American frontier. Of Gallatin's decision to emigrate to America, Adams simply noted in the *Life* that "the act was not a wise one,"[12] and then he eliminated that period of Gallatin's life from the edition of correspondence.

What is amazing is not that Adams's edition has lasted and that it has served us well, but that it is an outright subjective presentation and interpretation of Gallatin and his place in American history. There is not a single comment on what the author deems as Gallatin's "undesirable" period of life. Just as Edward Gibbon's *Decline and Fall of the Roman Empire* tells us as much or more about eighteenth-century England and about Gibbon's intellectual and emotional biases than it does about the fall of Rome, so too does Adams's historical writing and the edition of Gallatin's correspondence in particular reveal Henry Adams as much as it does Albert Gallatin. Adams chose to edit Gallatin because of his profound sense of identification with him. Gallatin was the ideal American statesman, and Adams wrote that his work on Gallatin was a labor of love.[13]

Modern editors may undertake their work as a labor of love, but they also use guidelines and rules designed to ensure that they produce texts as accurate and unbiased as possible. The rules of research a twentieth-century editor follows are a series of guidelines which also bind a responsible conventional narrative or quantitative historian: do not ignore or mishandle evidence; give the reader a precise, accurate, *as perfect-as-possible* account of the materials (the editorial text); leave the tracks by which others can retrace your steps if they have any doubts (the source notes and footnotes which give others a pathway into your conclusions). The principal steps to the creation of a good edition of correspondence are choice of subject, selection of letters, establishment of an error-free text, provision of a methodological statement, and historical annotation of the letters included.

The steps for editing correspondence are like those for editing public documents, with perhaps a few variations. Choice of subject is the obvious first step, although for the public historian this choice may be a moot point. If he or she is employed by a public agency, historic site, or corporation, the choice may be predetermined. It is useful, still, to say something about possible subjects for an edition of correspondence, because the field of possibility is markedly broader than it was a generation ago. In 1971 Jesse Lemisch attacked the publications program of the National Historical Publications Commission for being narrowly confined to support for publishing the writings of the "Great White Men."[14] Since then, whether in response to particular criticisms like this, or as a reflection of the broadening needs of historians seeking to study minorities, women, socialists, artists, businesspeople, or social organizations, the field for editorial subjects has grown much larger. Students of history and the historical profession as a whole have been well served by this opening up of the field.

Having chosen a subject, the editor must define a principle for selection and a rationale of transcription, for these decisions are at the core of the editorial task. Both decisions require familiarity with the materials to be edited and a sophisticated understanding of textual methods. The decision on what percentage of extant documents to select is one that is probably made by the editor and the publisher or sponsor of the work. Even though the editor believes in the uniqueness and significance of each document found, the comprehensive letterpress edition is simply not feasible.[15] In most cases multivolume editions of correspondence are out of the question, and so the editor faces the task of constructing a partial record of the extant correspondence in front of him. Unlike the tack the family editor may have taken in eliminating the unfavorable letter, the contemporary editor must strive to present as accurate and faithful a representation as can be created from the surviving sources. The better command the editor has over the source materials before him and the wider general historical knowledge he possesses, the more competently the task of selection will be effected. Judicious use of abstracts of the letters, significant quotations from them, and reference to their contents in footnotes will alleviate what the editor may at first see as the obligation to include everything.

The textual methods chosen for an edition must be designed to suit the manuscript materials that will provide source texts for the volumes undertaken. Historical editors, as Tarter notes, have moved closer to the methods of the literary editors in the production of a more literal rendering of every fact of a manuscript, but there is no one method which works for everything. The peculiarities of the source texts determine the method chosen. Literal or expanded, printed facsimile, clear text or inclusive are all reliable methods of transcription when used knowledgeably.[16]

Tarter has quipped that the editor must have the mind of a historian and the soul of a clerk. It might be said with equal validity that, when making any decision which will affect the shape of the edition, "When in doubt, do it the hard way." The editorial profession is not one which can be carried on in a half-hearted or casual manner. Editing correspondence takes both the knowledge of the historical period surrounding the letters and a command of particular editorial techniques. It is the successful union of the two that produces the memorable edition.

NOTES

1. One American historian, George H. Guttridge, had made use of some of them for a monograph, *David Hartley, M.P.: An Advocate of Reconciliation, 1774–1783*, vol. 14 of *University of California Publications in History* (Berkeley, Calif., 1926). A microfilm of portions of the letters and a rudimentary calendar had been prepared by E. P. Microfilm Limited, East Ardsley, Yorkshire, England. But the letters were still little used and had not been edited.
2. Ulysses S. Grant to Julia Dent Grant, 26 October 1864, in *The Papers of Ulysses S. Grant*, ed. John Y. Simon, vol. 12 (Carbondale: Southern Illinois University Press, 1984), 350–51.
3. See Charles Francis Adams, ed., *Familiar Letters of John Adams and His Wife Abigail Adams, During the Revolution* (New York: Hurd and Houghton, 1876), and, of course, the multivolume edition of *The Adams Papers*, initially under the direction of Lyman H. Butterfield and sponsored by the Massachusetts Historical Society. The first volume appeared in 1961.
4. Blanchett Papers, Manuscript Collection, Madison Historical Society, Madison, N.J. Letter quoted with the kind permission of the society. Larisa Van Kirk, intern at the society, brought this collection to my attention.
5. John Adams to Benjamin Rush, 4 April 1790, in *Letters of Benjamin Rush*, ed. Lyman H. Butterfield, vol. 2 (Princeton, N.J.: Princeton University Press, 1951), 1207.
6. Benjamin Franklin, *Memoirs of Benjamin Franklin*, ed. William Temple Franklin (Philadelphia: McCarty & Davis, 1824), i.
7. See, for example, Charles Francis Adams, *The Works of John Adams*, 10 vols. (Boston: Little Brown & Co., 1850–56); Gaillard Hunt, ed., *The Writings of*

James Madison, 9 vols. (New York: 1900–10); Francis Wharton, ed., *The Revolutionary Diplomatic Correspondence of the United States* (Washington, D.C., 1887); and Charles Lee, ed., *The Lee Papers*, 4 vols. (New York, 1872–75).

8. Charles Francis Adams, *The Works of John Adams*, iii.

9. The practice is also much wider than this. Often possessing the manuscripts, at least to start with, a family descendent is a likely candidate for the first post as editor. Elizabeth Cady Stanton's children, for example, published an edition of her diary and letters in 1922, twenty years following her death: Theodore Stanton and Harriet Stanton Blatch, ed., *Elizabeth Cady Stanton as Revealed in Her Letters, Diary and Reminiscences* (New York, 1922). This work exhibited the flaws most family editions have had: lack of objectivity and misleading selectivity. Patricia G. Holland, the present editor of the papers, noted that only a fraction of the extant letters was included and "those that were received revision to the point of gross distortion" (Patricia G. Holland, "The Papers of Elizabeth Cady Stanton and Susan B. Anthony: Reconstructing the Record," *Documentary Editing* 6 [June 1984]: 9).

10. Charles Francis Adams, *Familiar Letters of John Adams and His Wife Abigail Adams During the Revolution* (New York: Hurd and Houghton, 1876), iv.

11. R. P. Blackmur, *Henry Adams* (New York and London: Harcourt Brace Jovanovich, 1980), 10.

12. Henry Adams, *The Life of Albert Gallatin* (Philadelphia: J. B. Lippincott & Co., 1879), 18.

13. Portions of this paragraph appeared in "Interpretation in Editing: The Gallatin Papers," *Newsletter of the Association for Documentary Editing* 4 (May 1982): 7–8.

14. Jesse Lemisch, "The American Revolution Bicentennial and the Papers of Great White Men: A Preliminary Critique of Current Documentary Publication Programs and Some Alternative Proposals," *AHA Newsletter* 9 (1971): 7–21.

15. The editions simply cost too much for publishers to undertake. Even the editions of major statesmen like Franklin or Jefferson do not publish each and every bit of correspondence. Editors of twentieth-century figures like Dwight D. Eisenhower, George C. Marshall, or Thomas Edison could not begin to compile anything like comprehensive editions.

16. See Note 10 in Brent Tarter's essay "Editing Public Records" for reference to the large literature on the transcription of documents.

Scott L. Bills is former assistant editor for the Kent State University Press, where his responsibilities included copyediting and production for scholarly journals, bibliographical works, and monographs. He is editor of the book, Kent State/May 4: Echoes Through a Decade *(1982), and has recently contributed an article, "The World Deployed: U.S. and Soviet Military Intervention and Proxy Wars in the Third World Since 1945," to the volume* East-West Rivalry in the Third World *(1986), edited by Robert W. Clawson. Dr. Bills is currently assistant professor of history at Stephen F. Austin State University.*

HISTORIANS IN PUBLISHING: A CAREER AS EDITOR?

Scott L. Bills

Any discussion of desirable nonacademic careers for historians should include the array of editorial positions available in the publishing world: a landscape inhabited by such diverse entities as business conglomerates; traditional commercial publishing houses; small independent presses, often specialized in topic or ideology; and scholarly presses sponsored and subsidized by universities. Within this group, character is defined, of course, by size and income and further by the frontier between commercial and scholarly publishing. This boundary line, though not always so distinct as it might seem, concerns the role of the marketplace in routine decision making regarding the range, topics, and style of book manuscripts to be sought and possibly accepted for publication. For the academic press, affiliated with a university community and governed to a greater or lesser degree by a board of faculty members, publishing decisions ideally and often in fact reflect not potential profits but instead an evaluation of a manuscript's originality and quality of scholarship. As Marsh Jeanneret has written:

> The scholarly press's function is to produce works which in the main may not be published elsewhere. It must be able to investigate which of such manuscripts are likely to be most valuable to the scholars for whom they have been written, it must prepare them for publication and produce them in appropriate editions and runs, and it has the further duty of ensuring that they are brought to the attention of potential users throughout the academic world and catalogued and distributed through the most efficient channels there are.[1]

Commercial presses, certainly the major houses, do not share a set of views and goals which provide for the regular and timely publication of scholarly research, and this has been well known for some time. Hence, it is likely that for master's and doctoral-level historians seeking jobs in publishing, the overall objectives of the university press will offer a more familiar and amenable work environment. On the other hand, some commercial publishers cater essentially to an academic market, and, as well, those commercial houses with textbook and reference divisions might offer useful employment opportunities.[2]

Editing for a publisher of any kind is rigorous: the job requires an abiding but practical perfectionism; a well-developed sense of nuance; a solid knowledge of grammar and usage; a thoughtful and consistent attention to detail; a tolerant, tactful, ego-minimal attitude toward the work to be done; and probably a stubborn, inexorable love of the printed word. Many of these characteristics are nurtured in graduate programs in history; however, technical expertise and familiarity with the process of publishing may also be job requirements. This latter need has been addressed by the growth in publishing-oriented coursework, often as part of the expanding scope of public history programs, and in the scheduling of special institutes within academia providing practical experience in editorial work.[3]

Editing is also many-faceted, which enhances its appeal for historians in search of meaningful nonacademic careers. Editing tasks are most commonly differentiated by echelons of responsibility: manuscript evaluation and acquisition, suggestions for substantive text revision, line-by-line analysis, and the nuts-and-bolts work of correcting grammar and punctuation and checking the format and accuracy of notes and bibliographies. This hierarchy might be expressed by such titles as acquisitions editor, managing editor, line editor, and copy editor, respectively. However, in practice, and inevitably, the positions overlap and combine in various ways dependent upon the size of the press and the scope of its publishing activities. An editorial position at a small scholarly press, for example, could well include nearly all of the above responsibilities. Therefore, I will use the broad term "manuscript editor" in the following discussion to collapse categories somewhat and to indicate the frequent convergence of the substantive and the more technical blue-pencil editing—more often in small presses, more rarely in large publishing houses.[4]

Clearly, trained historians have talents which find ready expression in the demands of editorial work; further, publishing can offer both an amiable and a productive environment for academics and, more generally, for many college graduates with a liberal arts background.

MANUSCRIPT EDITING AND PRODUCTION

Since an editing position with any publisher is unlikely to offer immediate opportunities to work with familiar materials, the transition from academic to manuscript editor will require a shift of professional interests, hitherto founded on a special topic area, to something else: to a process of book preparation and production which encompasses numerous fields of inquiry, likewise demands constant mental precision, and operates according to a timetable determined by contractual obligation, marketing concerns, and other business considerations. The publisher must seek, for instance, to maintain a balanced "list": the creative grouping of books scheduled to appear as a unit, usually in the spring and fall but also sometimes in the summer and winter. The components and characteristics you would likely encounter as a participant in this editing/production process are described below.

Readers' reports. A university press's acceptance of a manuscript for publication will be based largely upon favorable readers' reports, perhaps two of them: evaluations of the author's work by scholars in the appropriate field. List considerations and other market-related judgments will also play a role, even here. More to the point for editors, even favorable reports will generally recommend manuscript revisions, sometimes substantial ones, regarding such items as organization, sources, and historiography. Less often will the reports dwell on stylistic matters, though lack of clarity in expression and textual redundancy are frequent complaints.

As a manuscript editor, you will need to familiarize yourself with the pertinent readers' reports; there may also be suggestions for changes in the manuscript from the press director or an acquisitions editor. It may be that the typescript, when you receive it, has already been considerably rewritten; nevertheless, it is important to judge whether or not the author has made substantive changes—if sought—in tune with the readers' evaluation. Or instead have there been minor, cosmetic alterations? Revising a manuscript is difficult and time-consuming, and it should not be surprising that an author who has spent four or five years researching and writing upon a topic, perhaps with little encouragement, is inclined to minimize final changes once the book is accepted for publication. And certainly, slavish adherence to readers' reports is neither wise nor necessary. But if, for example, the manuscript was accepted with the condition that specific kinds of revisions be made, the manuscript editor must evaluate the author's response.

Manuscript editing and markup. Despite the increasing use of word processors by both authors and publishers, most editing is still done with blue pencil or some time-honored variant thereof. Page-by-page editing of a manuscript is critically important to ensure accuracy, conciseness, consistency, and proper grammar. For a book-length typescript, it is no small task to make certain that the author has been consistent in capitalization, hyphenation, spelling, and citation style. As you read and edit the manuscript, it will be necessary to maintain a list of both queries and possible or likely errors, sometimes a long list; otherwise, you will find yourself endlessly paging backward in search of the sentence that did not lowercase "senator" or the one that italicized "vis-à-vis" (Should "senator" be lowercased? Should "vis-à-vis" be in italics? See below regarding style guides.)

Copyediting symbols can be easily learned; the system is standardized.

Nonetheless, editing a long manuscript can be both tedious and frustrating if you do not find the topic very appealing. Or possibly at three o'clock in the afternoon the topic is fine, but the writing seems hopelessly jumbled, the thesis progressively more confused. Still, you must not seek to impose or graft on your own writing style but instead work with the author's: to polish, to limit ambiguity, to hone expression.

It is important to keep multiple copies of everything at each stage of the editing/production process, from the initial manuscript editing through the final proofs. Regular use of a photocopier will protect everyone: the author, the editor, and the publisher's schedule. An author may complain, for example, that certain revisions were made without permission: can you provide a copy of the various versions of the edited typescript to reassure him/her? In practice, it is not unusual for an author to overlook small alterations or to interweave separate drafts. Also, a piece of writing will look different once it is in print, when paragraphs, and hence ideas, are physically much closer on a page—and when any repetitive phrasing becomes painfully obvious. And there are other reasons for the extra copies: a manuscript may be lost in the mail, or at least long delayed; a typesetter's establishment has been known to burn down, with all manuscripts and proofs destroyed. The list could go on.

The shift by a few presses to the use of word processors has eliminated, for them, the need to work with the original typescript. Instead, the contents of the manuscript are transferred onto a storage disk, and the editing is done on the monitor screen—producing a clean copy with revisions incorporated, a new text. This method initially made it difficult for authors to discover the full extent of editors' revisions; however, improvements in software have addressed this issue. Duplicate disks should be made of all essential materials.

The edited manuscript must then be sent to the author for his/her examination of and response to all queries and suggested alterations. When it has been returned and after appropriate adjustments have been made (see "Relations with authors" below), the editor may be responsible for doing the "markup" for the typesetter; a shortened notation on the manuscript pages indicating the typeface and type size to be used and where—carefully noting, for instance, such changes as the reduced type size and different spacing for extracts (block quotes). The markup must provide a precise guide for the typesetting and placement of chapter title, subheadings, figure captions, running heads, folios (page numbers), and so forth. If your job entails responsibility for journal copyediting and production, as it well might at a scholarly press, the markup will include additional variables such as the updating of volume and issue number, copyright date, editorial board membership, manuscript submission guidelines, and cover art. A good rule for preparing a markup is that an editor cannot supply too much information to the typesetter.

As a further editorial concern, journals generally have a fixed length per issue, meaning that the amount of available space is predetermined. An editor will be asked to indicate how much manuscript material is needed to fit this prescribed limit, which is accomplished through a "castoff": the application of a formula revealing what amount of print space will be filled by typescript pages. The use of advertising copy and possibly the inclusion of a flexible book review section provide the easiest means to tinker with journal issues and fit them snugly between the covers.

Style guides. The means to work toward accuracy and consistency in expression is the style guide, of which there are several. Many presses rely on a single guide for the so-called house style; however, there are always exceptions made, especially for a highly specialized scholarly study. A journals copy editor might be required routinely to follow different style systems, reflecting different practices in such academic fields as history, literary criticism, archeology, and so on.

The most commonly used guide is *The Chicago Manual of Style* (1984), now in its thirteenth edition.[5] It is the most comprehensive compilation of rules for punctuation, footnoting, and bibliographic form as well as such critical details, for editors, as word division, abbreviations, italicization, capitalization, hyphenation, the use of quotation marks, inclusive numbers, and many more. This manual also includes very useful sections on organizaing and editing tables and on indexing.

Another frequently used guide is the *MLA Handbook for Writers of Research Papers* (2d ed., 1984). And by necessity, editors regularly consult dictionaries of all kinds, encyclopedias, atlases, and other reference books.

Relations with authors. The editor-author relationship requires a genuine spirit of reciprocity. It demands tact and flexibility from both ends; however, you will soon recognize that it is an unequal relationship and appropriately so. The author will generally have the final word on all suggested text revisions beyond simple matters of house style; it is his/her article or book, and the work will be reviewed essentially on that basis. Still, the manuscript editor's role is a vital one, as Miller Williams has observed: " . . . The very critic a writer needs before a work sees print is one who can represent, not other writers, but the literate and objective reader who is not a professional author."[6] This may be less true for highly specialized works; but even so, clarity, readability, and cohesiveness remain of central importance. In point of fact, reviewers often take note of careless editing and poor design characteristics in books.

Undoubtedly, there will be some problems. There are authors, mostly inexperienced ones, who believe that the job of an editor and publisher is essentially to reproduce a manuscript without alteration; they view a press as a transmission device for already-perfect prose. Some authors will mistake an editor's suggestions for attempts to rewrite and distort the meaning of their work. And in truth, it *is* easy to alter the nuance of an author's thought without realizing it, since you cannot be, as an editor, a specialist in all the diverse topics that come across your desk.

Therefore, you must always remember that your role is to assist the author, never to coerce. Most confrontations with authors, whether seen to be substantive or more technical in scope, will be later regretted for obstructing the establishment of a creative and productive dialogue. Unnecessary editor-author conflict or tension does not serve the publisher or the publishing process.

Proofing. In one sense at least, this is probably the simplest stage of editing/production procedures: the manuscript has been set into type. The decision to have a book typescript or a group of journal articles set first in galley rather than page proofs will have to do with the condition of the manuscript (i.e., is it heavily edited?) and with the production timetable. Either way, the task of proofing remains the same: to pore over the print for mistakes in spelling, word order, punctuation, spacing, and so on.

Proofreading may be left to the author or may be free-lanced, but it is often the responsibility of the copy editor. As such, proofing offers an excellent opportunity to discover how meticulous you were or were not in correcting errors in the original typescript and providing clear instructions to the typesetter. As you read through the proofs, each mistake should be labeled PE (printer's error) or AA (author's—or your—alteration). The author will also read a set of proofs and offer his/her own corrections and perhaps seek to make a few final changes in the text. Typesetting is expensive, and the author is expected to pay for all changes over 10 percent resulting from AAs; the final bill will clearly display this additional cost. Here again, the ability to pay attention to the smallest detail, to seek perfection—and to do so simultaneously and consistently with several projects in different stages of production—is a major requirement of editing.

Typically, the process of checking for typographical errors is done by listening to a reading, by a copyholder, of the edited manuscript pages: the reader indicates all capital letters, punctuation marks, oddly spelled words, italics, and special spacing. Having such readers tape-record the edited manuscript is an effective alternative which allows for more flexibility in proofing, especially in terms of scheduling. After this initial proofreading has been completed, there should also be a "read for sense": best done by a staff member other than yourself. This entails a careful reading of the proofs to identify any content or typesetting problems which escaped previous scrutiny. Such things as a sentence fragment or a nonsensical phrase will occasionally appear, undetected in word-for-word proofing, usually the result of a heavily revised manuscript page. The author's proofreading is important to discover any errors in fact or sense that might not be questioned by in-house editors.

Certain kinds of articles and books make extensive use of tables, formulas, equations, or illustrations, and these also have to be checked in the proof stage. The use of illustrations, either photographs (called "halftones") or drawings, requires another editorial skill; if you work with such materials it is necessary to indicate the desired placement of the art in the text and to compute by what percent the size of the illustrations must be reduced or increased to fit the printed page. Ensuring the clear reproduction of halftones is also necessary.

Timetables. The editing/production process must proceed in an orderly fashion. An editor, for instance, might be working simultaneously on several journal issues, two or more books, and a bibliographical study— all in different stages of completion. The components of your timetable typically will consist of the following: the manuscript editing; the author's review of and response to your work; the typesetting; the initial correction of proofs; possibly several reviews of the corrected proofs; the transfer of the "boards" or "mechanicals" (the actual paste-up of the type) from the typesetter to the printer, if composition and printing are not in the same plant; the printing and binding; and the shipment of finished copies. Journals then have to be mailed to subscribers, while books are sent to a distributor. Hence, planning for editing and production work has to allow several months' lead time.

The above list could be lengthened or greatly shortened. A book with many illustrations or complex technical symbols and equations will likely be longer in production than a book without them. On the other hand, the increasing use of "camera ready" copy from authors eliminates the work of the manuscript editor as well as the typesetter; given the rising costs of publishing, this method has become a realistic and acceptable alternative for topics with a limited readership. Further, the increased use of word processors not only has begun to redefine traditional editing practices but also, through telecommunication, can simplify author-publisher arrangements and allow publishers to do their own typesetting. However, the application of more sophisticated technology does not mean that the basic skills and talents required of the manuscript editor have changed dramatically; rather, it is the environment in which those skills are used that has started to change.

Undeniably there is a tedium to editing, which certainly is not a regimen of daily joyous discovery, fresh insight, and new experience. Not all projects are interesting, and much of the work is repetitious: the manuscripts and proofs come and go, heroic blue-pencil deeds can be overshadowed by a tide of mundanities. But the job remains a vital element of publishing. Perfect books cannot, realistically, be produced; however, exceedingly imperfect ones, those with errors that have nothing to do with the author's thesis and organization, may impugn content and style, denigrate the editorial process, and harm the publisher's reputation.

Copyediting, with its narrow focus on mechanics, is the position where such repetition and tedium is most pronounced. It is, thus, a good entry level job but not so attractive as a career choice. But the broader scope of upper-echelon editing, for either a scholarly or a commercial press, presents the opportunity to translate basic skills into a position of greater responsibility, including involvement in manuscript acquisition, marketing strategies, and long-range publishing goals.

THE HISTORIAN AS EDITOR

While the professional historian brings to editing various important skills, as already indicated, it is likewise true that editing offers the historian valuable experience. Whether an editing position is taken as part of a short-term transition period between graduation and teaching or as part of a long-term career option, the work will provide a stimulating learning environment. The scholarly press is an especially congenial atmosphere for academics, one which does not replicate the university calendar but nonetheless moves to the same rhythm and is part of the same community. Indeed, for many, a career in publishing may prove preferable to a position in a traditional academic department. The latter does not offer the stability that it once did. Teaching positions in history in particular remain scarce, and the current generation of scholars, with Ph.D. in hand, must often accept one-year or two-year appointments, at the bottom of the pay scale, which can necessitate a too-frequent relocation that disrupts family life and significantly reduces research opportunities.

Editing is not perfect either. Salaries could be higher, and, especially for copyediting, the pay is very low and will remain so. Certainly, it will be only a determined historian who, after years of academic training, takes a low-paying, entry-level position with a large press and/or does free-lance editing work to live hand-to-mouth while building a resume. And, of course, as Jack Miles has pointed out, there is no such thing as a "University of Elysium Press" wherein publishing fulfills all our noblest aspirations and eschews the material world.[7] Nevertheless, editing/publishing is a learned profession which requires special technical and interpersonal skills and carries through the very necessary and meaningful task of producing the printed word. As Morris Philipson has noted: "There is a very special aesthetic and psychological satisfaction in participating in, contributing to, the birth of a book. . . . It can engage the mind and character of a person who would make the most of a liberal education and a gentle persuasion while doing a minimum of damage to himself or herself and the world he or she wants to enhance."[8]

For those who begin or resume a teaching career, experience as an editor can provide a valuable means to enhance professional performance. To start with, you will have acquired a better knowledge of the technical aspects of editing and a more realistic appreciation of the components of the publishing process. The demands of an editor and the requirements of house style, for example, now stem from understood sources. The importance of deadlines and cost considerations is clear. In addition, your ability to make helpful suggestions to your publisher and to distinguish more effectively between warranted and unwarranted editorial intervention will be improved. Most simply, you will have learned to speak a new language of sorts, one that can serve a very practical purpose.

Secondly, as might be expected, editing experience will improve your own writing. The change will be not only a better sense of where and how to sharpen and polish style or structure, but also a heightened ability to view your work objectively—critical for the task of effective revision. Editors appreciate an author with an eye for concise, nontrite, and lively expression, delighting in the discovery of a fellow student of usage who will strive convincingly for internal consistency through the myriad details of manuscript preparation.

Thirdly, work as an editor will strengthen your ability to conceptualize lengthy writing tasks, either monographs or more comprehensive histories. The regimen of the manuscript editor—looking through readers' reports, watching authors rethink organizational themes, advising on textual matters—teaches indispensable lessons regarding, for instance, the qualitative difference between a good doctoral dissertation and a good book manuscript. What is publishable and what is not? In part, experience as an editor provides the answer. What is a meaningful professional life? Work as an editor, in publishing, may provide that answer for you.

NOTES

I would like to thank Linda L. Kucan, Laura L. Nagy, and Jeanne M. West, editors all, for their valuable assistance in the preparation of this essay. Responsibility for the final draft is, of course, my own.

1. Marsh Jeanneret, "God and Mammon: The University as Publisher," *Scholarly Publishing* 15 (April 1984): 203. This article also discusses the effects of increased commercialization upon university presses over the past two decades. The author notes: "It was not widely enough appreciated that the commercial model was essentially wrong for scholarly publishing. Instead the presses were invited to strive for as much commercial impact as possible by everyone to whom they were beholden. . . . The trouble was that the volume of scholarly publishing that university presses could undertake depended too often on how much successful commercial publishing they could turn out at the same time." Jeanneret concludes, however, that growing commercialization has not led academic presses to abandon their original scholarly mission (p. 198). See also Jack Miles, "Intellectual Freedom and the University Press," *Scholarly Publishing* 15 (July 1984): 291–99, who observes: "What makes university publishing different from commercial publishing is that, by and large, in commercial publishing, those employees who are more concerned with books as ideas report to those who are more concerned with books as products. In university publishing, to a surprising extent, the reverse obtains: those who are more concerned with books as products report, whether they like it or not, to those who are more concerned with books as ideas" (p. 292).

2. A key reference book for listings of book publishers in the United States and Canada, including addresses and phone numbers and the names of important personnel, is the annual issue of *Literary Market Place* (New York: R. R. Bowker Company). Also included is information on book packagers, em-

ployment agencies specializing in the publishing marketplace, and a variety of academic courses dealing with the book trade. Scholarly presses are listed in the *LMP*, but an alternate source of information is the Association of American Univerity Presses (AAUP), which sponsors workshops, has annual meetings, and publishes a quarterly newsletter called *The Exchange*; the AAUP has over eighty member presses. The journal *Scholarly Publishing* and the trade magazine *Publishers Weekly* regularly feature useful articles and essays about aspects of academic and commercial publishing. See also Caryn James, "14,000 Small Presses: Something More Than the Sum of Their Parts," *New York Times Book Review*, 23 December 1984, 3–4.

3. See *LMP 1985*, 322–23, for listings of such courses; often cited in this context as an especially successful program is the Radcliffe Publishing Procedures Course—see, for instance, Judith Appelbaum, "Paperback Talk: Launching People Into Publishing," *New York Times Book Review*, 11 September 1983, 55–56. See also Beth Luey, "Teaching for Nonacademic Careers," *The Public Historian* 4 (Spring 1982): 43–56.

4. The best brief explanation of manuscript editing can be found in *The Chicago Manual of Style*, 13th ed. (Chicago: University of Chicago Press, 1982); see, especially, chap. 2. As well as having become the basic style book for all manner of editing questions, this manual includes a section titled "Production and Printing" and contains a helpful glossary of terms. See also Karen Judd, *Copyediting: A Practical Guide* (Los Altos, Calif.: William Kaufmann, Inc., 1982). For categories of editing, see *The Chicago Manual*, 50–51; Norman S. Fiering, "Editing the Historian's First Book," *The Maryland Historian* 7 (Spring 1976): 65–69; and J. G. Bell, "On Being an Uncompromising Editor," *Scholarly Publishing* 14 (February 1983): 155–61. Bell analyses the editorial process in terms of four categories: " . . . acquisitions (including appraisal), substantive editing, language editing, and mechanical editing" (p. 155). See also "The Decline of Editing," *Time*, 1 September 1980, 70–72, and Nancy Evans, "Line Editors: The Rigorous Pursuit of Perfection," *Publishers Weekly*, 15 October 1979, 24–31. The latter includes interviews with editors from commercial presses.

5. See Catharine Seybold, "A Brief History of *The Chicago Manual of Style*," *Scholarly Publishing* 14 (February 1983): 163–77, and also note 4 above.

6. Miller Williams, "The Writer and the Editor," *Scholarly Publishing* 14 (February 1983): 150.

7. Miles, "Intellectual Freedom and the University Press," 294.

8. Morris Philipson, "Publishing as a Profession," *Scholarly Publishing* 6 (April 1975): 227–28.

Carolyn Colwell has been an assistant reference librarian at Georgetown University Library since 1976. Prior to that she was a reference and government documents librarian at the State University of New York Albany. She has an M.A. in History from the University of Wisconsin-Milwaukee and an M.L.S. from Catholic University of America.

ACADEMIC LIBRARIES AND HISTORIANS

Carolyn Colwell

Many types of libraries offer career opportunities for individuals with training in history. Some obvious examples are local history collections of large public libraries or historical society libraries. Another type, which this essay will discuss, is academic libraries, that is, libraries that serve a college or university. Although most professional positions in academic libraries require a master's degree in library or information science, some, particularly those in special collections departments and archives, do not. Among the professional positions in college and university libraries that historians might consider are those of subject bibliographer, archivist, manuscript curator, and reference librarian.

SUBJECT SPECIALISTS

Many university libraries have professional positions for subject specialists.[1] These positions vary both in title and responsibilities. Individuals in these positions, usually called bibliographers or subject specialists, are responsible for the development of the library's collection in a specific field or fields. Some large libraries have a subject bibliographer just for history. Other libraries have bibliographers who are responsible for broader areas, perhaps the social sciences including history. The subject specialist works closely with the teaching faculty in the appropriate department or departments to identify and acquire materials for the library. The position requires familiarity with historical literature as well as the university's history curriculum.

The bibliographer must see that the library acquires basic materials in the fields of history taught at the university. In addition the individual in this position must understand the different types of library materials required to support graduate work in a subject and monitor the library's acquisitions to be certain that items needed for graduate level research are being acquired. Knowledge of the significant publishers, both U.S. and foreign, in the field is necessary to ensure that the appropriate books are acquired. Depending on what areas of history are emphasized at the institution, bibliographers may need special foreign language skills to enable them to monitor foreign publications. Although many academic libraries have standing order or approval plans, someone with knowledge in the subject must set up and monitor these plans to assure that the appropriate titles are being received. Bibliographers also need to be aware of new periodical publications in their field. In history, especially, many large and expensive collections of primary source materials are now usually available in microfilm. Since no library can afford to acquire all such sets, the bibliographer must identify these sets and work with the teaching faculty in deciding which collections to acquire.

While development of the library collection is usually the primary role of the subject bibliographer, several other activities may be involved as well. Subject specialists may provide bibliographic instruction to students and faculty. Bibliographic instruction takes many forms, from orientation tours for new students to semester-long courses on the use of the library. For the subject specialist, most bibliographic instruction would consist of one- or two-hour sessions on the use of the library as it relates to a specific subject and, often, a specific assignment. Bibliographic instruction for undergraduates might involve taking one class session to teach students the use of particular reference sources for doing research in history. Typically, the librarian would present an appropriate search strategy or procedure to follow in focusing on and researching a manageable topic. Overview sources, specialized dictionaries and encyclopedias, bibliographies, and periodical indexes would be discussed. Use of these materials would be explained, often through hands-on use if the class is small enough to permit such an approach. The subject specialist would work closely with the faculty member teaching the course to make certain that the instruction is appropriate to the level of the students and the required assignment.

A history bibliographer also would provide library instruction to graduate students in history. This could take many forms, including instruction to a class, similar to that discussed for undergraduates, but at a more advanced level. It might also involve orientation sessions for new students which discussed the services available to graduate students and the research materials available in the library in their field. Individual research conferences for master's or Ph.D. candidates starting to research a thesis or dissertation is another type of bibliographic instruction. Such a research conference would include showing the graduate student the important sources in the library for researching the topic and would also include discussing how to locate manuscript collections, books, and periodicals not held by the library.

Subject bibliographers also often provide reference assistance to library patrons both in their field of expertise and in other areas. The activities of the reference librarian will be discussed elsewhere in this essay. Faculty liaison is another part of the bibliographer's job. It includes the collection development and instruction aspects mentioned above, as well as assistance to faculty members in dealing with other areas of the library, such as the interlibrary loan or reserves sections.

Bibliographers may meet with new faculty members to explain the services and facilities of the library that are available to faculty. Clearly the bibliographer must have an understanding of what teaching faculty do and what their library needs are both as teachers and as researchers.

The subject bibliographer's position normally requires a master's degree in library science (M.L.S.) and at least a master's or Ph.D. degree in the subject speciality. The history subject bibliographer must work well with people, have a clear understanding of what teaching faculty do, and be familiar with the historical literature and publishers in the field.

REFERENCE LIBRARIANS

Academic libraries hire reference librarians to assist students and faculty in the use of the library. The relationship between training in history and the activities performed by a reference librarian are not as direct as for history subject bibliographers, archivists, or manuscript curators. However, it is a professional position in a library in which one can make use of the skills acquired through training as a historian. Reference librarians assist students in using the library in a variety of ways. They locate specific pieces of information, direct scholars to the most appropriate sources for doing research on a topic, and instruct students in the use of these sources. Clearly training in history would help a librarian assisting a scholar in doing research in history. However, librarians deal with a variety of subjects. Library science courses teach the various sources for specific subject areas. All reference positions require a degree in library science. The reference librarian not only needs to know the sources, but must be able to analyze the information the scholar needs. It is this area of reference work where the skills of the historian in research and analysis are useful.

Another aspect of reference work where training in history can be useful is computerized literature searching. Since the mid 1970s, it has been possible to search by computer a number of bibliographic databases.[2] Most academic libraries now offer this service to their patrons, and the searches are usually done by reference librarians. While a certain protocol must be learned to do a search, the greatest skill required is that of analyzing the subject of the search and choosing the best vocabulary and search strategy to be used. The skills acquired by the historian in analyzing and defining a research topic are useful to the searcher.

The historian's skills are useful in other aspects of reference work. Reference librarians are actively involved in bibliographic instruction, discussed above. In addition, college and university reference librarians prepare guides for research. These guides are typically a few pages in length and present a strategy for approaching a certain subject, such as American history. The guides list and explain the use of materials for researching the topic. Again the research skills of the historian are of use in preparing such guides. Many academic libraries have government document collections consisting of U.S. and, often, foreign and international government publications. These collections are often part of the reference department and are another area where both the skills and knowledge of the historian can be useful. Reference librarian positions always require a master's in library or information science. Often they require a subject master's as well. Some libraries try to hire reference librarians from a variety of academic backgrounds. Thus, a librarian with a master's degree in history might use his or her skills as a historian in all aspects of the job as well as specialized knowledge of the subject in compiling guides, doing computer searches, and providing bibliographic instruction specifically in history.

SPECIAL COLLECTIONS

Many college and nearly all university libraries have a special collections section or division. A variety of materials are housed in special collections, including rare books, manuscripts, and archives. Special collections sections, especially in the areas of archives and manuscripts, offer employment for historians. The activities of archivists are discussed in Fredric Miller's essay "Archives and Historical Manuscripts" elsewhere in this book. However, it is important to mention here since college and university libraries employ a significant number of archivists. Indeed, the largest group of archivists as defined by type of employer are college and university archivists.[3] A 1979 survey of college and university archives indicated that nine out of ten are located in the library.[4] Clearly academic libraries are an area that one interested in archival work might consider.

Special collections areas also usually include manuscripts. Manuscript curator positions often require training as a historian. The need for historians is apparent when one considers that " . . . almost all requests in manuscripts [in academic library special collections] relate to historical and related research."[5] Manuscripts are also discussed in Fredric Miller's essay but are mentioned here since academic libraries often employ manuscript curators.

Unlike subject bibliographer and reference positions which virtually always require a master's in library science, positions in special collections do not usually require that degree. Only 35 percent of college and university archivists have a master's in library science.[6] Positions in academic library collections vary both in job requirements and activities performed. A small library might have one professional in special collections who works with archives, manuscripts, and rare books as well. Large institutions might have many professionals, some of whom may be responsible for a specific manuscript or archival collection within the special collections section.

For many years, individuals with history degrees have used their skills in academic libraries, usually after acquiring an M.L.S. to teach them the intricacies of library work. Without the assistance provided by these history-conscious librarians, few other historians would be able to pursue their research interests so efficiently and effectively.

NOTES

1. For a discussion of the role of the subject bibliographer, see Thomas J. Michalak, "Library Services to the Graduate Community," *College and Research Libraries* 37 (1976): 257–65; and Dennis W. Dickinson, "Subject Specialists in Academic Libraries," in *New Horizons for Academic Libraries*, ed. Robert Stueart and Richard D. Johnson (New York: K. G. Saur, 1979), 438–44.
2. For a discussion of the historian and the production of bibliographic databases, see Joyce Duncan Falk, "The Historian Enters the Electronic Age," *The Public Historian*, 4 (Spring 1982): 35–42.
3. Nicholas C. Burckel and J. Frank Cook, "A Profile of College and University Archivists in the United States," *American Archivist* 45 (1982): 410.
4. Ibid., 424.
5. Clifton H. Jones, "Remarks on the Integration of Special Collection," *College & Research Libraries* 45 (1984): 439.
6. Burckel, "A Profile of College and University Archives," 41.

Barbara J. Howe received her B.A. in History from the University of Cincinnati, her M.A. from the University of Wisconsin-Milwaukee, and her Ph.D. from Temple University, where she studied American and English history. She became interested in historic preservation when working with the Spring Garden Civic Association in Philadelphia as a volunteer in the early 1970s and, after completing her Ph.D. in 1976, she worked as a Regional Preservation Officer for the Ohio Historic Preservation Office from 1976 to 1980. Based at Heidelberg College in Tiffin, Ohio, she was responsible for most of the activities of the State Historic Preservation Office for a seven-county area and worked with students interested in historic preservation. She helped organize and served as an adviser to the Tiffin Historic Trust and was a member of the downtown revitalization committee.

Howe moved to West Virginia University in 1980 to direct the new public history option. Since then, she has worked on preservation contracts with the West Virginia Historic Preservation Unit, U.S. Department of Agriculture Forest Service, and U.S. Army Corps of Engineers. She helped organize and served as the first president of the Preservation Alliance of West Virginia, Inc., and has served as an adviser for numerous grants from the Humanities Foundation of West Virginia (HFWV). Many of the HFWV grants have provided opportunities for her students to be active in local history efforts around the state.

In Morgantown, she serves on the Morgantown Bicentennial Commission and on the Riverfront Development Task Force. She was also one of the founding members of the Friendship Hill Association, to support the Friendship Hill National Historic Site.

She is active in the National Council on Public History (NCPH), having completed terms as a board member and as secretary, and now serves as its first executive secretary. She has served as a consultant on the development of public history programs at other universities and edited Teaching Public History Newsletter *for NCPH.*

Currently, she is working on a book for the American Association for State and Local History on researching the history of housing and is co-authoring, with Emory L. Kemp, a book on industrial archeology in West Virginia.

THE HISTORIAN IN HISTORIC PRESERVATION: AN INTRODUCTION

Barbara J. Howe

As long as history plays a part in historic preservation, there is a role for historians in historic preservation, particularly in the all-important area of preservation education. Historians—as staff members, board members, or volunteers for nonprofit organizations, as staff members for State Historic Preservation Offices, as employees or owners of preservation-related firms—now play an important role in developing and implementing the programs or projects for these organizations and businesses, but, as in any aspect of historic preservation, historians must be able to work in an interdisciplinary world.

Historians have not always been active in preservation. In his *Preservation Comes of Age*, Charles B. Hosmer, Jr. notes that "the profession of architecture was already history-minded in the 1920s" but that "historians merely paid lip service to the idea that buildings could be classed as documents. They were probably more poorly prepared for participation in the Williamsburg restoration than any other major professional group."[1] This began to change in the next decade as historians became involved in the increasingly active federal historic preservation programs growing out of the New Deal and an expanded role for the National Park Service in the administration of historic sites.[2] Historians interested in historic preservation long were considered "second-class" citizens by those in the ivy-covered tower, and many of these individuals who were uncomfortable in the American Historical Association because of their interest in local history or historic preservation transformed the AHA's Conference of State and Local Historical Societies into the American Association for State and Local History in 1940. While not primarily a preservation organization, this nonprofit group gave a home to historians and others interested in the field and remains a very vital organization.[3]

Education in history generally provides a good preparation for a career in historic preservation. Looking back on their education, historians active in historic preservation organizations were generally favorable toward their apprenticeship in the discipline, citing the common strengths of training in writing, research, and analysis as the most useful skills learned. Historians tend to downplay the value of these skills and to forget that a history education helps them, for example, "to present convincing arguments for preservation and to evaluate preservation priorities in an historical context." History conveys the "social, intellectual, human perspective—also historical—of values and trends." Historic preservation involves developing a context for saving a site, and here the historian's skills are obviously valuable and critical. Douglas Stern, of the Jefferson County [Kentucky] Office of Historic Preservation and Archives, noted that history provided a valuable context "in two ways: first, historians typically have a healthy perspective towards events and towards change in general; and, second, an historian's education prizes the ability to communicate." History provides, therefore, "a perspective beyond *just* the built environment" and helps historians in dealing with "anecdotal" local history that often needs careful analysis to understand accurately.[4]

Historic preservation and cultural resources management are relatively new aspects of public history. Both have exploded in growth since the National Historic Preservation Act of 1966, but historic preservation activities have been part of America's efforts to study and save its past since the early nineteenth century. This series of essays explores various aspects of historic preservation from the point of view of the federal programs in preservation (Beth Grosvenor's "Federal Programs in Historic Preservation" and cultural resources management (Janet Brashler's "Managing the Past in a Natural Resources Management Agency") as well as the interdisciplinary nature of historic preservation (Barbara Howe's "Historic Preservation: An Interdisciplinary Field"). This introductory essay, then, attempts to define preservation terms and techniques and explore areas in which historians can be involved in preservation, particularly in educational and research efforts and through the work of nonprofit organizations. It should provide a basis for the more specialized essays to follow. For regardless of the cause or project, historians need to be familiar with the basic techniques of historic preservation and to know how their skills fit this endeavor.

DEFINITIONS

First, preservationists routinely use a number of terms, sometimes too loosely, to define their work. Therefore, it is important at the outset to agree on the definitions which will be used throughout these essays. *Historic preservation* as a term is usually used to include any of a broad number of activities that relate to "doing something" with old buildings or structures, such as bridges. This is often meant to encompass any of the more specialized terms defined below, as well as the educational and legal activities that may accompany efforts to protect sites. *Cultural resources management* is most frequently used in federal agencies to describe the numerous procedures used to manage buildings, structures, districts, sites, objects, or documents significant in American history, architecture, archeology, or culture. Management, in this sense, can include any of the procedures defined below, as well as sophisticated surveys to locate archeological sites, inspection procedures to locate potential maintenance problems, routine or cyclic maintenance, site planning to locate the best places for parking lots and restrooms at parks, and computerized inventories of museum objects, buildings, or archeological sites. *Stabilization* is defined "as the act or process of applying measures designed to reestablish a weather-resistant enclosure and the structural stability of an unsafe or deteriorated property while maintaining the essential form as it exists at present." *Preservation* is defined "as the act or process of applying measures to sustain the existing form, integrity, and material of a building or structure, and the existing form and vegetative cover of a site. It may include initial stabilization work, where necessary, as well as ongoing maintenance of the historic building materials." *Rehabilitation* is "the act or process of returning a property to a state of utility through repair or alteration which makes possible an efficient contemporary use while preserving those portions or features of the property which are significant to its historical, architectural, and cultural values." *Reconstruction*, the lowest step on the preservation canonization ladder, is "the act or process of reproducing by new construction the exact form and detail of a vanished building, structure, or object, or a part thereof, as it appeared at a specific period of time." *Restoration*, the highest step on the ladder, is "the act or process of accurately recovering the form and details of a property and its setting as it appeared at a particular period of time by means of the removal of later work or by the replacement of missing earlier work."[5]

DETERMINING THE OPTIONS

But which of these is the right course of action? That depends solely on the purpose of the building, site, district, object, or structure that you are working with and the resources available to you. This is why survey and planning procedures are so important in historic preservation. In fact, planning has become the basis of historic preservation, and historians need to be involved in determining the historical significance of buildings to be included in state or local surveys, nominated to the National Register of Historic Places, protected by easements or land-mark status, etc. If money, time, and expertise are unlimited, if you have the best of all possible worlds, you can afford to do endless research and spend untold hours discussing the solutions for the use of your client's building. Since that luxury is rarely available, owners and professional advisors, including historians, will soon need to make some decisions about a course of action for the structure, building, or historic district. This usually involves defining an acceptable adaptive reuse for a building—do we still need a 1900 factory building to continue to make widgets or should it become a "spaghetti factory" restaurant, complete with widgets on the walls to remind us of its past?

If you are interested in general educational programs, an overview of the neighborhood's history, plus detailed research on the landmark structures, may be satisfactory. There may be no need to determine important interior features if people using your publication will not be allowed to see them or if owners are concerned about valuable stained glass windows being stolen if everyone knows about these treasures.

Education provided through such publications can be an excellent first step in preservation. Owners reading about the significance of their buildings may decide to "do something" with their structures, for example.

Documentation can also lead to a wide range of educational programs, including media presentations, books, and tours. Thoughtful, concise writing, explaining the development of a neighborhood on a brochure, can be far more taxing than an article or term paper of fifteen to twenty pages on the same subject—what *really* is critical to tell people and how do you write it in such a way that the average reader will understand it?

Owners obviously have a wide range of options for their properties. Downtown merchants may want to fix up the outside storefront to participate in a downtown revitalization plan while thoroughly modernizing the interior to meet modern health and safety codes or merchandizing needs. In this case, the historian will be most interested in finding old photographs of the streetscape to share with the architect or contractor. Large photographs of the store's original interior, if they can be found, may be used as part of the interior design scheme. Owners wishing to "do something" with historic houses may want to restore as much as possible of the original fabric, inside and out, and even buy reproduction kitchen and bathroom fixtures to match the date of the house. At this point, it is necessary, as it is for the storefront, to choose a date for the restoration work—additions after that time need to be removed, appropriate paint schemes need to be replicated through paint analysis or reference to the published paint catalogs now available.[6] If anything is going to be removed during this process, it should be documented through photographs or drawings before removal to provide a record for the future, for those additions were a part of the growth of the house.

Owners interested in the rehabilitation tax credits need to follow the guidelines of the Economic Recovery Tax Act of 1981 and the Department of the Interior, getting their plans approved as they work by the State Historic Preservation Office and the appropriate regional office of the National Park Service. Existing conditions must be well documented along with future plans for each part of the building. If an old hotel is being converted to office space, can original significant interior spaces be maintained or restored, with alternate methods of fire escape provided to allow keeping the grand staircase? Can original woodwork be kept? Can old small hotel rooms be redesigned to meet modern larger office space requirements? What economical use can be made of the building in the first place and is it significant enough to list on the National Register of Historic Places, individually or in a district, to qualify for the tax incentives?

Few buildings really qualify for restoration in the purest sense of the word. Most buildings that are truly restored are public buildings such as museums, house museums, and other "shrines" that are not lived and worked in daily. Restoration can be extraordinarily expensive, especially since problems with historic buildings are not always visible until one is well into the project. How can you incorporate modern services, including electricity and air conditioning/humidity control, into the building without being obvious? Climate control here is more important for the building than the visitor. To what period should the building be restored if it has had a long and distinguished history? In the case of West Virginia Independence Hall in Wheeling, choosing a restoration date was easy because the building was the site of the meetings that led to the creation of the State of West Virginia in 1863; there were also numerous documents in the National Archives to use as a basis for the restoration since the building was a custom house and federal courthouse. Fortuitously, *Harper's Weekly* featured the courtroom, where the deliberations took place, in an 1861 drawing to accompany a story on the statehood movement. The gas lights still provide the only illumination in the courtroom, the cast iron doors and shutters have been recast, and the lobby chandeliers have been reproduced, an elevator installed to allow handicapped staff and visitors access to the third-floor historic courtroom, and a fire escape stairway added at one end of the building. Use is also limited by the fact that the structure is not sound enough to withstand large crowds in some of the rooms. Extensive historical research, including detailed searches through the various Wheeling newspapers, led to the information needed to restore the building and develop an interpretive program—for what is the purpose of having a shrine if no one knows what it celebrates?

RESEARCH

Historians are as well qualified as any professional to determine the best future for a building because they have the best access to the historical record. A good researcher, working with a good creative historical architect or engineer, can unravel many a mystery in preservation. Historians can do even more unraveling if they learn to "read" buildings and structures as carefully as traditional historical sources.

Research in historic preservation, hereinafter taken to include all the variations noted above, can start with the traditional written record or the object itself. Feeling more comfortable with words than with nails, historians probably peruse the documents first, combing city directories, maps, deeds, tax records, county and city histories, building permits, insurance company records, and other sources for any possible clue to the date of construction of the building and its various uses and alterations. The business and professional directories in the city directories, like telephone book "yellow pages," are also valuable sources and can include ads for products made or sold in buildings you are researching. City and county histories can provide detailed biographical or genealogical sketches for families prominent enough to be included—or who paid to be listed. Wading through all the superlatives used to describe these city fathers (women are rarely included) can provide a wealth of information on the individual's public life. Diaries, journals, letters, or other personal papers may be available

Figure 1. Research materials for house historians include Sanborn insurance maps, topographical maps, local histories, city directories, and local preservation guides. *Photograph courtesy of Emory L. Kemp.*

from people who lived in or owned the house or commercial building you are working with. Are there ledger books showing expenses on the building, for example?

Cities that kept building permits have collected a valuable set of records; early records may be uneven in the information provided, unindexed or, like the ones in Morgantown, West Virginia, scattered through the city manager's reports to City Council each week. Cities also have used insurance maps and may have some stuck away in the engineer's office, perhaps along with more modern aerial photos of the city that have been transformed into blueprints for use in planning purposes. If the city government has been actively using federal funds for many years, it likely has collected its own historic preservation file, documenting buildings and sites that were affected by proposed federally funded programs, from Community Development Block Grant housing rehabilitation programs to major riverfront or down-town revitalization schemes. Usually a basic knowledge of building technology will be sufficient for the initial phase of your research; knowing, for example, that buildings can have brick bearing walls, wood frames, and walls with a brick veneer will help you understand the terminology used.

Next, it is important to go to the courthouse and master a basic legal vocabulary to understand the deeds, wills, fiduciary and estate records, and tax records one is likely to find there. Deeds record the name of the grantor (sellor) and grantee (buyer), date of the transaction and date it was recorded, selling price, and description of the property sold. These may or may not contain a specific reference to a building on the property, but if you are lucky, you will run into a deed referring to a boundary line through a party wall or an elaborate set of building restrictions and specifications, setting out in detail the dimensions of the house to be built, materials to be used, and restrictions on the use of the property. Before zoning was common, developers controlled the quality of their subdivisions by including in the deeds prohibitions against the use of the property for a distillery, tannery, or other "obnoxious purposes." Much of the city of Morgantown, West Virginia, for example, was developed in the early twentieth century under these restrictions. Unfortunately, it was also developed under restrictions that limited the sale of housing to members of the Caucasian race or, in one 1920s suburban development, to the native-born or aliens who had been naturalized for at least ten years. Historians encountering these types of restrictions can begin to set a scene for the neighborhood in which a historic house was built and place the house in a better context. For example, if all the houses on the street are two stories high and equally set back from the street line, this may have been dictated in the deeds. Thus, an addition that would spoil that historic scale of the streetscape should be discouraged, even though the original restrictions have been superseded by modern zoning ordinances.

In addition to deeds and tax records, which can indicate when a building was erected or substantially altered by changes in the value of taxes paid, courthouses can tell us a great deal about the people who owned or lived in the house. Birth, death, and marriage records are the obvious sources, but wills and all the paperwork accompanying them also are stored in courthouses. If you are lucky, the owners of the house you are researching will have died without a will and left a large household of furniture to be divided up among a number of squabbling potential heirs who initiated interminable legal action to settle the estate, leaving a long paper trail behind to track the disposition of each piece of furniture and a lengthy inventory—the first step toward refurnishing the house, if your goal is to make it a house museum, period room, or just your own home. Wills can be very explicit in the distribution of the deceased's possessions, or the writer can simply say, "I bequeath everything I own to my beloved husband," without even naming him.

Having exhausted the written records available, the historian may start to feel a bit uneasy about the next steps in the research process needed to "do something" with a historic house. Here the researcher turns to photographs, lithographs, atlases, "bird's-eye" views, paintings, insurance maps, postcards, blueprints, and other visual sources to locate the building and detect any changes over the years. Sanborn and other insurance company maps were made for thousands of towns and cities across the United States in the nineteenth and twentieth centuries and are excellent sources of information for basic floor plans, construction materials, alterations over the years (additions and subtractions of porches, outbuildings, stone or brick veneer are depicted) and, often, old street numbering schemes that then make it feasible to use city directories to locate occupants and their occupations.[7] Undated, unidentified photographs are a bane to the preservation researcher, but they can often be "read," like documents, by noting period clothing and cars, other buildings whose dates of construction are known, and advertising signs in store windows for particular businesses that can be dated from a city directory. Companies like Hardesty's produced county atlases in the late nineteenth century, although owners who showed off their buildings in the lithographs could have embellished their property in the illustration. "Bird's-eye" views are available for cities as large as Baltimore in the nineteenth century and as small as Morgantown (under 1,000 people). These often attempted to show every building in the town and have proven to be very accurate, even to the point of showing the number of windows and the roof types. Postcards abound for towns from the early twentieth century. Tiffin, Ohio, which had no cards of the downtown or residential areas in the late 1970s, had dozens of views surviving in the files of private collectors or the local historical society museum from the turn of the century. These showed the expected courthouse and major downtown buildings but, also, the parks, residential streets, schools, and churches.

Talking to long-time residents of the house or neighborhood can also yield valuable information. As historians become increasingly comfortable with oral history, they can learn to ask the right questions about alterations to the building, neighborhood change, introduction of utilities, lifestyle of the residents, products of local industries, and more, fitting this into the picture developed through written and visual evidence.

Finally, if you are lucky, you will find the architect's floor plans, elevations, and cross sections for the building to help you interpret the structure. Since most private homes were not custom-designed by an architect, these will be rare. However, we are beginning to learn that many homes of the early twentieth century came from catalogs of companies like Sears, Roebuck and Montgomery Ward. Thus, if your house was likely to have been built between about 1905 and 1930, try to track down long-time residents or old catalogs to see if you can locate the house there. The owners may have purchased the plans from the company or the whole house in kit form, with furnishings, lumber, and nails arriving by rail.[8]

A thorough inspection of the house, inside and out, is the next step. If old photographs showed a porch, can you see the scar or "ghost" left from its removal on the brick wall? Do the photos show wood siding, but you now see metal siding? Have windows or doors been blocked in? Are those foundation blocks rough-cut stone or cast concrete block? If they are all uniform in size and texture and the house dates from the early twentieth century, they are undoubtedly rough cast concrete blocks. Have additions been added that can be identified by breaks in the brick pattern, wood siding, or foundation stone? Does something simply not "look right"? Buildings, if scrutinized as closely as photographs or documents, are intelligible to the historian, even on first viewing.

Next, go inside and examine the interior for more frequent changes. People may restore the outside of a building while refusing to accommodate 1920s plumbing in the bathroom or vintage appliances in the kitchen. Are there scars on the floor showing where walls were removed or stairs moved? Were closets added? Was woodwork painted (or stripped of its original graining)? Check window frames to see if there are screw holes indicating the former presence of interior shutters. Dating such alterations, inside and out, can be very difficult unless the current owner or long-time residents can help, or unless tax assessors' records give notice of remodellings. Sometimes, however, craftspeople signed and dated the wall before papering or carved their names in the woodwork. In turn, help future researchers by asking craftspeople working with you to date alterations they make.

While inspecting your building, it is wise to document the structure through photographs. Black and white 35mm or 4 x 5 view camera photos can be of archival quality (color fades) and provide a good record of the house at that date, making it easier for future researchers to know what was done and when. Perspective-corrected photographs are best. Documentation can also be in the form of floor plans, elevations, and cross sections that you prepare while recording the house. Architects, draftsmen, interior designers, and landscape architects can provide assistance in this phase of the work, although historians can certainly learn to use a scale and t-square well enough to do this work themselves.

Finally, the most sophisticated method of recording available today is close-range photogrammetry in which a camera takes a pair of photographs (at one time or in two settings) which are then projected onto a computer screen and printed out. Through "computer graphics," one can "remove" porches that may be additions, "add" a wing here or there, "straighten" a sagging roof line, etc., producing drawings showing the building exactly as it is today, including every nail hole and broken piece of siding, and variations on how it could look when restored. While expensive in terms of equipment, this is a much faster procedure than drawing everything by hand and is much more accurate; elevations and floor plans done by hand, for example, use symbols to represent siding instead of drawing in every board in detail. For a more complete discussion of this process, and of the importance of site recording in general, see Emory L. Kemp's essay entitled "A Perspective on Our Industrial Past Through Industrial Archeology" elsewhere in this book. Kemp's essay includes illustrations showing the stages of drawings done with close-range photogrammetry.

Once the building is recorded, only half the battle may be over. Documentation such as that described above could lead the historian to try to provide additional protection for the building by placing it on a local landmarks list or a local or state historic properties inventory or nominating it to the National Register of Historic Places. Beth Grosvenor's essay, "Federal Programs in Historic Preservation," explains this program further. The goal may be to create a historic district protected by local legislation or zoning codes for historic districts, and the historians can then find themselves in front of a zoning commission or city council meeting arguing for the historic significance of a building or neighborhood—or arguing that a building someone wants listed has *no* historical significance. Historic districts are only as strong as the residents of the city will allow them to be. Some historic district commissions review paint schemes and delay demolitions, while others are merely advisory. In addition, properties may be covered by easements on the exterior, interior, or open space around the building; the easement is held by a nonprofit organization and is a restriction that runs with the deed so that the current or future owners may not harm the protected parts of the building or open space around the building.

Thus, the historian's ability to do research and analyze the results are critical to his or her success in historic preservation careers. Documentary research in legal records, local history sources, and catalogs of suppliers is the first critical step to a succcessful historic preservation project. The historian is best able to determine the historical significance of a building and fit it into a pattern of area development—is this a new type of building or one of hundreds built at the same time? Can the endless claims of "first," "oldest," "only surviving unaltered," "biggest," and "best example" be documented and how significant is it if they can be documented? A knowledge of architectural history is a vital supplement to the historian's skills in historic preservation, and there are many guides available to introduce you to architectural history that are easy to use.[9]

IMPLEMENTATION AND EDUCATION

After mastering the basics of historic preservation, where can one find a place to use them? All State Historic Preservation Offices hire historians, as each office is required by law to have a historian on staff. Also, historians develop their own history businesses, which can concentrate on historic preservation issues, as shown in Ruth Ann Overbeck's essay, "History as a Business." Others work for architectural firms or real estate developers. Historians also work for nonprofit organizations at the state, local, or national level, and it is at this last category that I want to look more closely.

The historic preservation movement in the United States has relied heavily on volunteer citizen involvement. From the founding of the Mount Vernon Ladies Association in 1856 to preserve the home of

George Washington to the 1949 organization of National Trust for Historic Preservation (the national nonprofit historic preservation association) to the widespread proliferation of state-wide and local nonprofit groups today, preservation has been successful in large part because of this citizen involvement. Historic preservation has definitely moved away from the lonely efforts of the traditional "little old ladies in tennis shoes" to the rather sophisticated efforts of large state-wide nonprofit groups and multi-million-dollar real estate corporations.

The 1982 (twelfth edition) of the American Association for State and Local History's *Directory of Historical Societies and Agencies* listed a total of 5,865 entries for the United States and Canada. It included "historic preservation" as a separate program category for the first time, and a total of over 800 organizations identified themselves as primarily interested in preservation/restoration.[10] Organizations listed in the preservation/restoration category vary in size, including the Mystic Seaport Museum, founded in 1929 and listing 16,100 members, plus a staff of 250 full-time and 100 part-time employees and 300 volunteers. Mystic Seaport's program includes a library, manuscript collections, museum, junior history program, oral history program, educational programs, books, newsletters, and pamphlets. While preservation/restoration has the longest list of organizations of all the special interest groups, it is not complete. Most of us would consider the Colonial Williamsburg Foundation as a natural organization for this category, since it has had an enormous influence on the preservation movement in this country, but it is not shown in this index. The Colonial Williamsburg Foundation was founded in 1926 and, in 1982, had 2,886 full-time and 877 part-time employees, including historians. A library, archives, manuscripts collection, museum, historic sites preservation, oral history, and education programs make up the agenda for the foundation.[11]

Other major organizations that operate historic sites, either recreated or consisting of buildings moved to a new site, are Plimouth Plantation and Old Sturbridge Village, both in Massachusetts. Plimouth Plantation was founded in 1947 and operates a library, museum, and educational program with 55 full-time and 110 part-time staff. Old Sturbridge Village operates a library, archives, manuscripts collection, museum, historic site, tours/pilgrimages program, oral history operation, educational programs, newsletters, pamphlets, and a historic preservation program. It employs 360 full-time and 240 part-time staff and utilizes 160 volunteers. Founded in 1946, Old Sturbridge Village now has 11,000 members.[12]

While these larger organizations may lead individuals to believe there are unlimited possibilities, it is important to remember that those staff include custodial staff, craftspeople, gift shop clerks, and visitor center staff, in addition to the historians, educators, architects, archeologists, and other professionals. Also, most historic preservation organizations are far more modest in size. The Association for the Preservation of Virginia Antiquities (APVA), dating from 1889 and one of the oldest nonprofit groups, has 6,500 members, 16 full-time staff, 22 part-time staff, and 56 volunteers to operate its library, museum, historic sites preservation, and publications programs. Its New England counterpart, the Society for the Preservation of New England Antiquities, was founded in 1910 and engages in historic sites preservation and educational programs, in addition to supporting a library and museums program. The 5,000 members utilize the services of 37 full-time staff, 25 part-time staff, and 15 volunteers. Sleepy Hollow Restorations, based in Tarrytown, New York, was founded in 1951. Like APVA, it owns historic properties, but it also has a library, manuscripts collection, museums, and educational and publishing programs. Fifty-six full-time staff and 84 part-time staff handle these programs. Don't Tear It Down (DTID), an effective historic preservation movement in Washington, D.C., is an example of local level historic preservation groups. DTID was organized in 1971 to fight the proposed demolition of the Old Post Office, which has since been converted to a successful downtown mall complex. It has 1,200 members and operates educational programs, provides newsletters or pamphlets, and is active in historic preservation, zoning, planning, lobbying, technical or neighborhood assistance, and legal action. All this is done with the support of 1 full-time staff member, 1 part-time staff person, and 10 volunteers! Don't Tear It Down changed its name to D.C. Preservation League in 1984.[13]

The professional preservation world is "young" compared to that of academia. This is undoubtedly due to the expansion of the federal role in historic preservation in the late 1960s and 1970s. Although such stalwarts as the Mount Vernon Ladies Association date from the mid-nineteenth century and the Society for the Preservation of New England Antiquities from 1910, the National Trust for Historic Preservation was only organized in 1949, and the vast majority of state-wide or local nonprofit historic preservation groups date from after the passage of the National Historic Preservation Act in 1966. Some state-wide organizations were being formed as late as the 1980s, sometimes, as in West Virginia, in response to cutbacks in federal funding for historic preservation under the Reagan administration.

Historians interested in working for preservation organizations can get involved in these groups in a variety of ways. Historic preservation courses and programs, like those in public history in general, are comparatively new, so most of the people working in nonprofit groups today probably did not get there through internships or formal graduate work in historic preservation. More often, they began as volunteers for a local or state group and moved into a paid position as they gained experience with the organization and as the organization grew in size. Others had a "general interest in historic structures and sites" activated or complemented by coursework in historic preservation. People who were generally interested in history found historic preservation to be an interesting outlet for their diverse interests, and they were attracted to the interdisciplinary nature of historic preservation. Historians generally interested in architecture are also naturally attracted to historic preservation.[14]

But more than an academic interest draws historians to historic preservation. The field offers historians an active outlet for creative energies tuned to producing a better society. Charles M. Jacobs of the Historic Landmarks Foundation of Indiana saw the diverse interests of historic preservation suited to his needs but also noted that he saw "its aims/objectives . . . as essential to society's well-being." Georgia Trust for Historic Preservation's Gregory B. Paxton turned to historic preservation as a career "because of my realization that our country's bias toward progress failed to include adequate consideration of the best of our existing buildings. The cultural and economic resources that these buildings represent have fortunately been dramatically demonstrated in recent years." For others, such as R. Eugene Harper of Charleston, West Virginia, historic preservation was a logical outgrowth of his responsibilities as a professor of history at a small college in that city; if one needs help, one calls the local college for assistance—a merger of town and gown.[15]

Nonprofit organizations can focus on many activities, through statewide organizations that sponsor publications, exhibits, lecture series, seminars for property owners and real estate developers, tours, revolving funds for the purchase and restricted sale of buildings, easement programs to protect facades and open spaces, and support for landmarks and historic district commissions. Others may be formed to save one building or support one historic district, and all efforts focus on that issue.

PRESERVATION EDUCATION

Historians in historic preservation are involved in many exciting educational opportunities through nonprofit groups. Education is at the heart of the historic preservation movement—or should be at its heart if the movement is to survive for anyone other than the developers.

Education can take many forms. Adele Weiler of the Utah Heritage Foundation "developed the enrichment programs now used in four of the largest school districts in Utah, . . . developed teacher workshops which provide the background information teachers need in their curriculum programming" and coordinates volunteers who assist in these productions. The foundation's programs "take shapes and give them names/use in the built environment. Our programs take folklore of Utah and compare it to the facts that are known." Further, "our programs present time and space concepts relative to the students." Other programs aimed at schoolchildren include the Idaho Historic Preservation Council's grade school poster contest for the national annual Historic Preservation Week in May. This idea has also been used by the Tiffin Historic Trust, a local nonprofit preservation group in Tiffin, Ohio. Students learned to look at buildings that were important in the community and, in turn, awakened the interest of their parents and adults so used to their surroundings that they no longer saw important structures that newcomers noted immediately.[16]

Opportunities to educate adults and the general public in historic

Figure 2. Brochures and books can be useful in interpreting a site's history. *Photograph courtesy of Emory L. Kemp.*

preservation are limitless. It would be safe to say that almost every historian working for a nonprofit historic preservation group has delivered a lecture, prepared a slide show (the standard teaching format in historic preservation), written a newsletter/newspaper article or letter to the editor on a preservation issue, and, probably, has worked on an exhibit, tour brochure, site interpretation plan, or book of some kind, dealing with historic preservation on at least the local level. Lectures to historical societies, boards of realtors, chambers of commerce, civic and service organizations, downtown merchants, bar associations, and other groups become routine ways of drawing on the public's basic interest in history and convincing them to act on behalf of historic preservation concerns.

While the methods may be different than most historians are educated to handle, the presentations should all be grounded in solid historical research and a context of local, regional, or national development. Lectures on the history of Chicago's Michigan Avenue or the city's theatres can presumably be used to help the public understand the development pressures that have created the current problems and opportunities for historic preservation in these parts of the city. In the same vein, tours of Philadelphia's late nineteenth-century churches concentrate on "the history and survival of the architecture amidst changing neighborhoods." Exhibits on the "History of Public Accommodations along the National Road" in Indiana, sponsored by the Historic Landmarks Foundation of Indiana, or on architectural history in West Virginia, sponsored by the Preservation Alliance of West Virginia, are temporary educational tools. Historic sites open to the public merit more permanent interpretive exhibits, such as those done by the Delaware Historical Society at its historic properties or the History Center at the Supreme Court building for Hawaii to "orient visitors to the history, processes and present functions of the State Judiciary." "Political Turf," an exhibit at the restored New York State Capitol, complements the restoration work by examining "important political issues of the era through the medium of political cartoons."[17]

One-time productions, such as exhibits, tours, and brochures, are exciting projects to work on and can have a strong impact on people's perceptions of the relevance of a historic area and the built environment in general. In addition, the results of survey and planning work can have a broader impact, as happened in Morgantown, West Virginia, when West Virginia University students set out to complete historic properties inventory forms for the early twentieth-century suburb of South Park. This wealth of material later led to a slide show Dolores Fleming and I developed on the growth of the neighborhood, which traced the history of houses there. It drew 100 people to the public library one sleety Friday evening. Encouraged by the reponse to the show, Fleming developed Morgantown's first walking tour brochure with some assistance from the county historical society and conducted tours of the neighborhood, with one attracting sixty-five people for a Sunday afternoon stroll up the hills of South Park. Hopefully, the slide show, tours, and brochure will generate enough interest to create a historic district in South Park, a historic district in which the residents have had ample opportunity to learn of the historical and architectural value of their neighborhood.

PREPARING FOR A PRESERVATION CAREER

As historic preservation seems to be turning increasingly to the needs of real estate developers interested in certifiable rehabilitation of a National Register property, I asked those responding to a survey to indicate if they felt the educational efforts played an important role in the activities of nonprofit historic preservation groups and whether historians were valuable to their organizations. Responses to these questions were mixed and may well depend in part on individual personalities. Some felt their work as historians lent credibility to their organization or felt their own credentials, including a history background, afforded "more credibility and, perhaps therefore, more effectiveness." Respondents generally agreed that nonhistorians felt the historians in their organizations were valuable in helping to make decisions, set policy, and carry out projects, but they also noted that, after awhile, a historian in historic preservation is acting largely on an accumulation of skills and experience gained from the "real world" of historic preservation work.[18]

While history can provide a solid base for work in nonprofit historic preservation organizations, most people involved in this area felt that traditionally structured history curricula were inadequate and needed to be supplemented to convey the interdisciplinary nature of historic preservation. Classes in historic preservation legislation; field classes in architectural surveys; hints on dealing with public and local officials on historic preservation; public administration; and historic geography, decorative arts, and public history were all cited as valuable additions to history courses to prepare students for work with nonprofit organizations in preservation.[19] The same skills would be necessary for someone working in a state or federal preservation program.

But the one consistent theme in the "what else do you need" category was coursework in business, including management, real estate, accounting, finance, and personnel management. Most historians working in organizations will soon move up the ladder to management of some type as an almost inevitable product of professional advancement. Whether it is overseeing interns on a project, supervising employees on an exhibit or publication, or running a large organization, historians often find themselves increasingly removed from the daily tasks of "doing history" that drew them to the first job of writing National Register nominations or compiling a slide show. This has its parallels in the academic world where history department chairpersons and administrators lose time to publish in a sea of computer forms, budget proposals, and personnel matters that must be handled.

Historians interested in careers in preservation should not shy away from the administrative challenges presented and need not switch to straight business courses to proceed, but they should not be so idealistic as to believe that pure research and writing jobs are awaiting them and that any formal program, no matter how strong, can prepare them for all the challenges and opportunities they will face as employees of preservation organizations at any level. Developing management skills, a knowledge of budgeting, and skill in working with volunteers will be valuable first steps in preparing yourself for administrative responsibilities. Also, working with a board of directors or some kind of governmental commission is important. Nonprofit groups are governed by boards of directors responsible for the direction of the organization. Government agencies have advisory boards with varying degrees of power. Attending board meetings, if possible, or talking to board members about their responsibilities can help historians used to the classroom understand the group dynamics and board/staff relationships that must be developed to have a successful group. Fund-raising expertise and public relations skills are also valuable in the world of nonprofit organizations.

When asked what advice they would give to history students interested in preservation careers, the professionals queried responded with the same concerns listed above. In addition to developing strong research, writing, and communications skills, students were encouraged to be interdisciplinary and volunteer their services to get experience. F. Bogue Wallin, executive director of the Preservation Fund of Pennsylvania, Inc., noted that "you may be hired for your skills as an historian, but your success will be directly related to your ability to translate those skills into activities and disciplines well removed from the domain of history as you know it."[20]

It would be unfair not to mention that a few respondents felt the historic preservation careers were overcrowded and the pay low, discouraging people from entering the field. Much of this negative feeling undoubtedly relates to the uncertainty of federal support for historic preservation in the 1980s and efforts to curtail, through a thorough reorganization of the federal income tax structure, the tax incentives which have provided so much impetus to historic preservation since 1976. But organizations are still forming throughout the country at the state and local levels, gathering their resources to afford staff at a time when many people have limited time to volunteer. And, as historic preservation seems to be moving more toward real estate development, maybe there is an even stronger need for good historians to work in the field. While the pay may not be terrific, there are plentiful opportunities to reach many people and be an integral part, even if only as a volunteer, of a nation-wide effort to save the best of the past for the future.

NOTES

1. Charles B. Hosmer, Jr., *Preservation Comes of Age: From Williamsburg to the National Trust, 1926–1949*, vol. 1 (Charlottesville: University of Virginia Press for the Preservation Press of the National Trust for Historic Preservation, 1981), 31; reference to John D. R. Platt, "The Historian and Historic Preservation," Paper for the American Historical Association Annual Meeting, 28 December 1963, Independence National Historical Park.
2. Hosmer, *Preservation Comes of Age*, vol. 1, 579; see, also, Beth Grosvenor, "Federal Programs in Historic Preservation" and Janet G. Brashler, "Managing the Past in a Natural Resources Management Agency" elsewhere in this book.
3. See Gerald George, "The American Association for State and Local History: The Public Historian's Home?" elsewhere in this book.
4. Historians working for nonprofit state-wide historic preservation organizations were surveyed informally during the summer of 1984 to learn why and how they got involved in historic preservation work, the history-related projects of their organizations, and the advantages of a history education for their careers. The survey yielded thirty-one responses from staffs of local landmarks councils, local historic preservation development corporations, state government historic preservation agencies, local and state-wide nonprofit groups in states across the country from Delaware to Hawaii, from Washington to Georgia. Respondents ranged in experience from two to

twenty-six years in the field, with most falling in the seven-to-ten year range. Professional careers in historic preservation are relatively new. One might expect a survey of top professionals in the archival or museum world to show a higher number of years of experience for these older aspects of the public history world. I have included the remarks of some of those who gave permission to be quoted here and have used composite data from some of the others in preparing this essay. I am deeply grateful to all those who took the time to respond. A few of those who responded indicated that their academic degrees were not in history, but I have included their remarks to show how people get interested in historic preservation and to illustrate the types of programs historic preservation organizations carry out, since historians could respond in the same way.

Specific references for this citation are to Emily J. Harris, Landmarks Preservation Council of Illinois, questionnaire response, 5 September 1984; Amy R. Hecher, Landmarks Preservation Council of Illinois, questionnaire response, 4 September 1984; Douglas Stern, Jefferson County Office of Historic Preservation and Archives, questionnaire response, 29 August 1984; David J. Zdunczyk, Temporary State Commission on the Restoration of the Capitol [of New York], questionnaire response, 1 October 1984; and R. Eugene Harper, Kanawha Valley Historical and Preservation Society, questionnaire response, 11 September 1984.

5. Maddex, Diane, ed. *The Brown Book: A Directory of Preservation Information* (Washington, D.C.: The Preservation Press, 1983), p. 53, with reference to the Secretary of the Interior's Standards.

6. See, for example, Roger Moss, *Century of Color: Exterior Decoration for American Buildings, 1820–1920* (Watkins Glen, N.Y.: American Life Foundation, 1981) or *The Old-House Journal*, a monthly magazine for those interested in rehabilitating old houses. Other books on downtown revitalization or home rehabilitation are available through libraries, local or state historic preservation organizations, the State Historic Preservation Office, or the National Trust for Historic Preservation's Preservation Press.

7. The Library of Congress has published a catalog of Sanborn Insurance maps in its collection, entitled *Fire Insurance Maps in the Library of Congress: Plans of North American Cities and Towns Produced by the Sanborn Map Comapny* (Washington, D.C.: Library of Congress, 1981). Drawings and photographs collected through the Historic American Buildings Survey are also available at the Library of Congress; these include cross-sections, floor plans, and elevations for buildings recorded.

8. Numerous nineteenth-century builders' catalogs have been reproduced and are readily available in library collections with holdings in architectural history or historic preservation. The National Trust for Historic Preservation will be publishing Katherine Cole and Ward H. Jandl's *Mail-Order Housing: Sears, Roebuck and Company Houses, 1900–1930* through its Preservation Press.

9. Basic introductions to architectural history include John J.-G. Blumenson, *Identifying American Architecture: A Pictorial Guide to Styles and Terms, 1600–1945*, rev. ed. (Nashville: American Association for State and Local History, 1981); John C. Popplier, S. Allen Chambers, Jr., and Nancy B. Schwartz, *What Style Is It? A Guide to American Architecture*, 2nd ed. (Washington, D.C.: Preservation Press of the National Trust for Historic Preservation, 1983); Mary Mix Foley, *The American House* (New York: Harper & Row, 1980); Marcus Whiffen and Frederick Koeper, *American Architecture*

(Cambridge, Mass.: MIT Press, 1981); and Virginia and Lee McAlester, *A Field Guide to American Houses* (New York: Alfred A. Knopf, 1984). For additional references see "The Arts" section of Ted Ligibel's bibliographical essay, "Utilizing Library Resources" at the end of this book. Also, check with local organizations or libraries to see if specialized guides to the architecture of your area are available.

10. Tracey Linton Craig, *Directory of Historical Societies and Agencies in the United States and Canada*, 12th ed. (Nashville: American Association for State and Local History, 1982). The list probably includes some defunct groups, as it lists those from previous directories who did not return the questionnaires this time; it also includes the major state history agencies.

11. Ibid., 35, 272.

12. Ibid., 117, 119.

13. Ibid., 270, 190, 196, 41.

14. Jenna Gaston, Idaho Historic Preservation Council, questionnaire response, 22 August 1984; Charles M. Jacobs, Historic Landmarks Foundation of Indiana/Morris-Butler House Museum, questionnarie response, 15 September 1984; Douglas Stern, questionnaire response, 29 August 1984; and Charles T. Lyle, The Historical Society of Delaware, questionnaire response, 31 August 1984.

15. Charles M. Jacobs, questionnaire response; Gregory B. Paxton, Georgia Trust for Historic Preservation, questionnaire response, 23 August 1984; and R. Eugene Harper, questionnaire response.

16. Adele Weiler, Utah Heritage Foundation, questionnaire response, 31 August 1984; and Jenna Gaston, questionnaire response.

17. Emily J. Harris, questionnaire response; A. Robert Jaeger, Philadelphia Historic Preservation Corporation, questionnaire response, 29 August 1984; Charles M. Jacobs, questionnaire response; Charles T. Lyle, questionnaire response; Jane L. Silverman, The Hawaii Judiciary, questionnaire response, 22 September 1984; and David J. Zdunczyk, questionnaire response.

18. Emily J. Harris, questionnaire response; and Douglas Stern, questionnaire response.

19. Jenna Gaston, questionnarie response; Richard P. Matthews, Washington County Museum [Portland, Oregon], questionnaire response, 30 August 1984; Gregory B. Paxton, questionnaire response; and Kirby Turner, Blue Grass Trust for Historic Preservation, questionnaire response, 27 September 1984.

20. F. Bogue Wallin, questionnaire response.

Beth Grosvenor is the senior staff historian with the National Register of Historic Places, National Park Service, U.S. Department of the Interior, Washington, D.C. 20240. In addition to serving as the National Register reviewer and liaison for preservation activities in eleven central states, her current responsibilities include preparing technical guidance on preservation issues and helping to develop and revise procedures and review questions and guidelines by which all state survey and nomination programs are evaluated. Her numerous technical publications include "How To Apply National Register Criteria to Post Offices," which discusses an appropriate approach for evaluating and documenting common institutional buildings. Earlier, she was a principal contributor to the two-volume Bicentennial Edition of The National Register of Historic Places.

Since joining the National Register in 1974, she has lectured extensively and conducted workshops on various aspects of surveying and evaluating historic resources for such organizations as the National Trust for Historic Preservation, the National Conference of State Historic Preservation Officers, the National Council on Public History, and many local and state groups. Having majored in American Studies at Mount Holyoke College and as a Smithsonian Institution/George Washington University Predoctoral Fellow, she is particularly interested in nineteenth century social and intellectual history.

FEDERAL PROGRAMS IN HISTORIC PRESERVATION

Beth Grosvenor

Historic preservation is an interdisciplinary field, as the following descriptions of various federal programs will illustrate. History is a major discipline in preservation, but it is combined with architecture, architectural history, archeology, anthropology, public administration, law, urban studies, conservation, information systems and records management, photography, planning, and other fields. Historians in preservation will benefit by combining knowledge of some of these disciplines in their own repertory of skills, although this is not essential, as they will have access to interdisciplinary knowledge through working constantly with professionals in these fields. Preservationists in government perform tasks in each of the five major preservation activities of planning, identification, evaluation, documentation, and treatment. These tasks include those traditionally viewed as "historical" and those not often associated with historians, but which nevertheless rely heavily on historians' skills: research, development of professional standards, evaluation of historical significance, assessment of the relationship of history and tangible resources, development of policy and policy statements, analysis of issues and problems, recommendations for solutions to problems, and records management. Regardless of the actual tasks or whether they involve direct performance or a review of the historical work of others, historians bring critical skills and knowledge to government preservation work. A good general knowledge of major themes in American history and of sound methods and sources of research, good analytical skills, and the ability to construct adequate and appropriate contexts for both evaluating the historic significance of resources and making management and policy decisions are essential qualifications for government historians in the field of historic preservation.

FEDERAL PRESERVATION ACTIVITIES

In the National Preservation Act of 1966 (Public Law 89-665, 16 U.S.C. 470), Congress declared that "although the major burdens of historic preservation have been borne and major efforts initiated by private agencies and individuals, and both should continue to play a vital role, it is nevertheless necessary and appropriate for the Federal Government to accelerate its historic preservation programs and activities, to give maximum encouragement to agencies and individuals undertaking preservation by private means, and to assist state and local governments and the National Trust for Historic Preservation in the United States to expand and accelerate their historic preservation programs and activities." Since then, the federal government has indeed increased its influence over the treatment of historic resources, not only by continuing its direct stewardship of a multitude of nationally significant cultural properties, but also by recognizing that all government actions have potential ramifications for the cultural environment, and by providing increased support and direction for preservation activities throughout the country.

The federal government participates in historic preservation at three levels of involvement: cultural resources management, compliance with preservation legislation, and support and coordination of a variety of government and nongovernment activities. For federal agencies that administer large areas of land or a substantial number of cultural resources, the management of these resources may constitute a significant portion of their work. Federal participation in the historic preservation movement transcends direct management of cultural resources, however, as important as these responsibilities may be. By law, all federal agencies are charged with incorporating into the fulfillment of their principal responsibilities a plan for identifying and considering appropriate treatment of historic resources. A few of these agencies, principally the National Park Service (NPS) and the Advisory Council on Historic Preservation, contain programs specifically established to provide leadership and a national focus for historic preservation activities.

The last have the greatest influence on the larger arena of preservation and will be the focus of this essay.

Historic preservation consists of the identification, evaluation, documentation, and treatment of historic resources, and the planning necessary to coordinate all other activities. The federal government and the historians it employs have an important role in each of these areas. By embodying a national commitment recognized through legislation, federal programs can set national goals and provide leadership and direction in achieving these goals. One of the chief ways in which this is done is by formulating and promoting professional standards for preservation functions and monitoring their consistent application. The government can also serve as a focus by coordinating its own activities, cooperating with those of others, and providing encouragement and support for programs and projects consistent with its goals and standards. This support takes the form both of financial incentives and of advice and guidance on technical aspects of preservation. In conducting its programs, the government compiles a wealth of information on cultural resources and preservation issues. Its lists, archives, and statistics serve as a source of information available to assist other public agencies, private organizations, and individuals plan and conduct preservation projects. Coordination efforts and compiled information also allow a unique national overview and perspective on a variety of preservation topics. The government can use this information to keep current on national and regional trends and concerns, provide a mechanism for resolving problems and making decisions in a consistent manner, and contribute technical literature useful to the field at large.

ORIGINS OF FEDERAL INVOLVEMENT

Administration of government is a dynamic process, ever adapting to changing executive and legislative mandates. The government's involvement in historic preservation has evolved according to this principle. Specific programs and regulatory procedures have come and gone, but the incorporation of an appreciation for cultural values has continually grown, and the standards for protecting these values have progressed in accordance with those of the related professional disciplines. Although it was an important milestone in the evolution of the national preservation movement, the 1966 National Historic Preservation Act did not begin, but rather strengthened, a federal commitment to our cultural environment that was initiated in the beginning of this century.

Early laws, programs, and policies established the Department of the Interior as the lead agency in protecting resources having important associations with the nation's past. The 1906 Antiquities Act (Public Law 209, 16 U.S.C. 431-330) was the first law to create a national accountability for cultural resources. This law authorized the president to designate resources on public lands as national monuments and provided some protection for prehistoric and historic properties by assigning criminal penalties for unauthorized actions that would disturb them. Certain cabinet members were entrusted with issuing permits for archeological investigations for the purposes of acquiring scientific data. The creation of the National Park Service in 1916 and the transfer of military parks and national monuments from other agencies to the Interior Department in 1933 increased Interior's custodial responsibilities.

Also in 1933, as part of its relief efforts of the Depression, and in recognition of the loss of many important American buildings, the federal government initiated the survey and recording program within NPS that grew into the current Historic American Buildings Survey. Architects, draftsmen, and photographers were hired to record outstanding examples of American architecture. By 1934, the program had already compiled 5,000 sheets of drawings and over 3,000 photographs. The program was so successful that NPS entered into an agreement with the Library of Congress and the American Institute of Architects (AIA) whereby NPS would set standards and administer the recording projects, the library would preserve the records, and AIA would provide professional guidance. This program received legislative authority through the Historic Sites Act of 1935 (Public Law 292, 16 U.S.C. 461-67).

With the passage of the Historic Sites Act of 1935, Congress declared it national policy to protect historic resources of national significance for public use. The law empowered the Secretary of the Interior to conduct surveys to identify, evaluate, document, acquire, and preserve nationally significant sites and buildings, including those not located on federal lands. In addition to authorizing the Historic American Buildings Survey, the act instituted the National Survey of Historic Sites and Buildings, which identified nationally significant properties for possible acquisition by NPS. The survey outlined important themes in American prehistory and history and conducted studies within those themes through which to evaluate the national significance of properties. These studies resulted in the creation of the Registry of National Historic Landmarks in 1960.

THE NATIONAL HISTORIC PRESERVATION ACT OF 1966

Despite the growing federal role in the recognition and protection of historic resources, this role was still essentially confined to those elements of the past related to important themes in the overall history of the nation and bypassed the historic treasures of a state's or community's individual identity. Yet, by the 1960s, the growth of other federal programs and their influence in state and local jurisdictions were conspicuous. Other factors were also exacting a heavy toll on the tangible reminders of our past. *With Heritage So Rich*, a 1966 report prepared under the auspices of the United States Conference of Mayors, chronicled the public and private threats to the nation's heritage:

highway construction, urban renewal, land values, neglect and vandalism, deterioration and demolition, scavenging for historic artifacts, remodeling of individual buildings, and institutional expansions. At the same time, there was a growing public appreciation for the "value inherent in many older structures: not that they are old, but that they contain so much of ourselves."[1] The report concluded that the pace of preservation was too slow to keep up with the results of rapid urbanization, was too limited in scope in its emphasis on individual landmarks and its relative neglect of architecture and design, and lacked a strong national focus. The movement needed to find ways to "give a sense of orientation to our society, using structures and objects of the past to establish values of time and place."[2] Recommendations included a plea for strong federal legislation to define national goals and provide leadership.

Congress responded with the passage of the National Historic Preservation Act. The act supported the principle that state and local resources, as well as national landmarks, deserved the attention of preservationists, and that "the historical and cultural foundations of the Nation should be preserved as a living part of our community life and development." Several key provisions initiated programs that still form the heart of the federal preservation effort. The act authorized the Secretary of the Interior to "expand and maintain a national register of districts, sites, buildings, structures, and objects" important to the understanding of American history and culture. It also established a grants program to aid states in preserving, acquiring, and developing properties listed in the National Register and to assist the private organization, the National Trust for Historic Preservation, to conduct its programs. The act created the Advisory Council on Historic Preservation to advise the President and Congress and to comment on federally assisted projects affecting historic properties. All federal agencies were charged with taking such properties into consideration in carrying out their programs.

The National Park Service has assumed most of the Interior Department's responsibilities for cultural resources programs. Created in 1916 to protect historic and natural parks, NPS now manages over 300 natural, historic, and recreational parks, over half of which have been established primarily because of the worth of their historic or prehistoric resources; many of the predominantly natural or recreational areas also possess cultural significance. In addition to its responsibilities to manage the cultural resources within its parks, NPS participates in all aspects of the broader field of historic preservation: planning, identification, evaluation, documentation, and treatment. Several specialized programs, discussed below, pursue NPS preservation objectives to identify and register qualified properties in the National Register of Historic Places, to assist sound stewardship of cultural resources by federal agencies, to identify and promote the preservation of nationally significant properties, to produce precise documentation for selected properties, and to cooperate with preservationists outside the federal government and provide them with information and economic incentives useful in their preservation eforts.

THE NATIONAL REGISTER OF HISTORIC PLACES

Created and refined by the National Historic Preservation Act of 1966, as amended, the National Register of Historic Places has become a keystone of the federal preservation structure and an important influence on historic preservation efforts throughout the country. The title "National Register" refers both to the federally maintained list defined by Congress as the record of properties "significant in American history, architecture, archeology, engineering, and culture"; and to the program that maintains the list. Properties listed in the Registry of National Historic Landmarks, which by 1966 numbered almost 1,200, were immediately incorporated into the National Register; newly designated landmarks, now numbering approximately 1,600, are automatically added. Also included automatically in the National Register are historic areas of the National Park System. Expansion of the list occurs primarily through nominations from other federal agencies and the states and territories. The National Register receives several thousand nominations each year, and by August 1985 had accepted for listing almost 38,000 historic properties. The actual number of resources represented by this figure is much higher, as many of these properties are historic districts, each of which contains as few as three or four, or as many as several thousand properties. Listed properties include a wide variety of districts, sites, buildings, structures, and objects, such as the Fort Worth Stockyards Historic District, the New England Glassworks Site, Victorian houses in San Francisco, U.S. Coast Guard lighthouses on the Great Lakes, and Colorado's narrow gauge locomotive Engine No. 463.

The nomination process illustrates an important partnership between the federal and state governments that is characteristic of the federal emphasis on cooperative programs. Efforts were initiated immediately after the creation of the program to build a network of federally assisted preservation programs in all states, as well as to encourage the appointment of preservation officials in all federal agencies. Federal responsibilities for locating and nominating properties within their jurisdiction that qualify for the National Register were spelled out in the National Historic Preservation Act of 1966, and reinforced by both Executive Order 11593 in 1971 and by 1980 amendments (Public Law 96-515) to the 1966 act. The vast majority of historic resources added to the National Register are privately owned, however, and are nominated by state officials. Each state governor appoints a State Historic Preservation Officer who is responsible for coordinating preservation activities in the state, including the identification and nomination of properties to the National Register. Other responsibilities of this state official, with the help of a professional staff, include: preparing a comprehensive state preservation plan; directing a state-wide survey of historic properties;

advising and assisting federal, state, and local governments in carrying out their preservation responsibilities; and developing programs to educate the public and encourage public participation in historic preservation. States receive matching federal grants to assist in carrying out these duties. There are many requirements states must meet to qualify for these funds, including a staff composed of historians, architectural historians, archeologists, and related professionals and a system for monitoring the quality of work submitted from outside their offices.

While the states conduct the actual research and surveys essential for finding, evaluating, and documenting historic properties for National Register listing, the federal government provides the critical leadership role in setting and maintaining the standards and policies that determine the contents of the list. One of the major advantages of maintaining a national list is the opportunity to provide the means for evaluating similar resources in a consistent manner according to a uniform standard. The criteria for significance that govern eligibility for listing and that incorporate historic, aesthetic, design, and scientific values are written in general language to accommodate the wide diversity of historic factors that have shaped different areas of the country. In addition to describing the qualities of significance necessary for listing, the criteria enumerate the types of physical characteristics that should remain as little altered as possible since the historic period, identify types of resources and significance that generally will not be accepted, and establish an appropriate lapse of time for an objective analysis of significance. National Register historians and other professionals review nominations to ensure that nominated properties meet National Register criteria and are properly documented.[3]

Because the concept of significance is relative, depending on a particular historical and physical context, and the criteria are intended for broad application in many contexts, National Register historians, architectural historians, and archeologists provide guidance in interpreting the criteria consistently and monitor adherence to its policies. The National Register also sets standards for written and graphic documentation for properties listed in the Register and reviews documentation submitted with nominations. The National Register maintains and regularly publishes lists of properties listed or determined eligible for listing and manages an archives of the documentation on these properties.[4] Through the review of the application of the criteria and prepared documentation, and through analysis of information in the archives, the National Register can identify issues and topics requiring specific guidance in the areas of identification, evaluation, and documentation. Topics of published guidance have included survey methodology, assessing the effects of alterations or deterioration on a property's ability to convey significance and improving photographic quality. Historians have also joined other staff professionals to develop categories of data to enter into a computerized data system. And historians will help determine patterns of data to retrieve in order to develop future technical guidance and policies.

PRESERVATION PLANNING

Listing in the National Register has greater value to the preservation community than bestowing the honor of official recognition to historically significant properties. The identification of properties and their locations, along with physical descriptions and analyses of significance, provide information useful in the planning activities of governmental bodies, private organizations, and individuals. This information can be added to social, demographic, economic, and political data available from other sources to assure that decisions are not made in ignorance of important historical values.

Planning is therefore an important aspect of an adequate preservation program of related activities: both planning to assure a compilation of information that is adequate in scope and quality and planning to assure the appropriate and full use of that information in making decisions. The National Historic Preservation Act of 1966, as amended, spells out federal responsibilities to take the value of historic resources into consideration in planning and conducting their activities. State Historic Preservation Officers must also develop and conduct comprehensive preservation plans to qualify for NPS grants for preservation activities. The Secretary of the Interior has promulgated standards and guidelines for planning in his Standards and Guidelines for Archeology and Historic Preservation.[5] This publication also includes standards and guidelines for identification, evaluation, and documentation and for historic preservation projects involving acquisition and physical treatments of properties. The National Park Service has also developed a model planning process that includes developing adequate historic contexts, evaluating properties within the appropriate contexts, developing management goals and priorities, and integrating preservation planning into broader local, state, and federal planning.

FINANCIAL ASSISTANCE FOR PRESERVATION PROJECTS

In addition to awarding grants for states to carry out their survey and planning activities, the National Historic Preservation Act authorizes grants to assist in the preservation of properties listed in the National Register. Although often criticized as being insufficient to meet the tremendous need, these latter grants for years constituted the only financial assistance offered by NPS for restoration and maintenance of historical properties. The grants also instigated the publication of valuable technical guidance from NPS on the type of preservation treatments that would least disturb the historic character and physical integrity of properties.

In recent years, NPS has rarely offered funds for the physical treatment of properties because Congress has not authorized the necessary funding. However, a series of federal tax laws has assured the existence of financial incentives to preserve historic properties. The Tax

Reform Act of 1976 (Public Law 94-455, 26 U.S.C. 191, 280B), the Revenue Act of 1978 (Public Law 95-600), and the Economic Recovery Tax Act of 1981 (Public Law 97-34) have combined investment credits and other financial benefits for rehabilitating older buildings that have had a major impact on preservation activities.[6] Between 1977 and September 1983, these incentives inspired $4.82 billion in private investment for preservation projects, a far greater amount than was available through preservation grants for restoration and rehabilitation.

The restriction of the incentives to projects for income-producing properties has resulted in the identification and recognition of the historic value of properties too neglected in previous years: commercial and industrial structures. The program has also refined survey and documentation efforts because benefits apply to properties within historic districts as well as to individually listed resources. It is now necessary to evaluate all individual resources within each historic district to determine if they contribute to the historic significance of the district as a whole since only these contributing properties qualify for the tax benefits. This requirement has had two results that demand the involvement of qualified historians in advancing the purpose of the legislation to encourage the preservation of truly significant historic structures: it has created a market for those who can provide the necessary research and evaluation to support eligibility for the program, and it has necessitated the development of much more refined and defensible standards for assessing the historic character of significant buildings. In administering the program and reviewing the significance and appropriate treatments for properties, NPS has continued to develop and disseminate guidance on aspects of historic character, standards for rehabilitation, and technical information on topics such as evaluating structural deterioration and appropriate treatments for historic storefronts and windows.[7]

NATIONAL HISTORIC LANDMARKS, HABS, AND HAER

As the legislation and programs of the past twenty years have exerted their intended influence on the preservation movement, many of the early programs have also remained important. The National Historic Landmarks program, the Historic American Buildings Survey (HABS), and archeological assistance programs remain strong components of federal preservation efforts. Historians in the National Historic Landmarks program continue to conduct research for theme studies and make on-site inspections of properties which may possess national significance within these themes. "Recreation" and "Man in Space" are currently under study. Until the late 1970s, the landmarks program published a series of books on various themes in American history, including *Signers of the Constitution*; *Lewis and Clark*; *Prospectors, Cowhands, and Sodbusters*; and *The Presidents*. Continuing to identify and document the design and construction of architecturally and historically significant structures, HABS was joined in 1969 by the Historic American Engineering Record (HAER), which concentrates on the country's engineering and industrial heritage. Both programs conduct inventory and recording surveys; provide advice and assistance to federal agencies, which often record historical structures to HABS and HAER standards if the structures must be altered or demolished; and encourage public interest in and knowledge about our built environment through publications and exhibits. Over the years, HABS and HAER have published a series of state catalogs with information on recorded properties in these states. In commemoration of its fiftieth anniversary, HABS produced, in conjunction with the Library of Congress, *Historic America: Buildings, Structures, and Sites*, a collection of essays on the HABS program and a comprehensive checklist of properties recorded by HABS over the last fifty years. Cooperative survey projects are another important aspect of the HABS/HAER programs. These projects are usually conducted by summer teams of students under professional direction and are co-sponsored by groups and institutions interested in preserving and recording historic structures. Projects have included studies of properties at local, state, and national levels of significance, but during the summer of 1984, HABS and HAER concentrated on NPS historic structures and National Historic Landmarks. These projects included a historical report and measured plans and elevations of the Boott Mill Complex in Lowell, Massachusetts, to aid future redevelopment plans, and a historical resources study in the Gates of the Arctic National Park in Alaska to inventory the park's historical architecture. Completed documentation submitted to the Library of Congress includes measured drawings, large-format photographs, and written historical data. By the end of September 1984, the library's collection contained documentation on over 18,000 structures. This documentation is used for several purposes: as a reference for the maintenance and restoration of properties, to recommend preservation strategies, and to monitor changes in fragile resources; as a lasting record for resources that will be lost; and as a resource for interpretation and education projects.

ARCHEOLOGY

Concern for endangered archeological resources was a decisive factor in the passage of the Antiquities Act, the Historic Sites Act, and subsequent legislation, including the 1960 Reservoir Salvage Act (Public Law 86-523), the Archeological and Historic Preservation Act of 1974 (Public Law 93-291, 16 U.S.C. 469a), and the Archeological Resources Protection Act of 1979 (Public Law 96-95). These laws give the Secretary of the Interior responsibility for preserving scientific, prehistoric, historic, and archeological data in all federally assisted construction projects, set forth procedures for archeological work on federal lands, and encourage cooperation among archeologists in the public and private sectors.

The National Historic Preservation Act and the National Environmental Policy Act of 1969 (Public Law 91-190, 42 U.S.C. 4321) also had a major impact on federal responsibilities for archeological resources, especially for large land-holding agencies. The National Park Services's archeological program consolidated many of the Department of the Interior's archeological responsibilities. This program functions to co-ordinate federal archeological activities by setting forth policies and procedures for federal agencies, monitoring federal data recovery efforts, overseeing the federal archeological permit program, and providing professional expertise to other agencies. Although archeology is a specialized discipline, not all archeological resources are prehistoric, and historians have much to contribute to archeological investigations for sites such as abandoned settlements, mining or other industrial complexes such as those recorded by HAER, or urban archeological projects such as those conducted in Alexandria, Virginia, and New York City.

THE ADVISORY COUNCIL ON HISTORIC PRESERVATION

Additional assistance to federal agencies is available through the Advisory Council on Historic Preservation, an independent executive agency created by the 1966 National Historic Preservation Act to advise the President, Congress, and government agencies on historic preserva-tion issues and procedures and to promote preservation education. The council also coordinates United States membership in the International Centre for the Study of the Preservation and Restoration of Cultural Property.[8] Possibly the most conspicuous of the council's responsibilities is its approximately 2,000 annual reviews of federal projects affecting significant historic properties. Legal imperatives that federal agencies incorporate an awareness of cultural resources into their activities include the requirement that they allow the Advisory Council on Historic Preservation an opportunity to comment on projects that might affect properties listed or eligible for listing in the National Register, whether those projects are directly conducted by an agency or receive federal funding, permits, or other assistance. The government need not own or control the affected properties, but only share responsibility for actions that could have an impact on their historic character. Agencies often lack qualified salaried staff to locate and document affected resources. Thus, survey contracts to identify and evaluate properties that may meet National Register criteria provide another major avenue for historians to be involved in federal preservation programs.

Once an agency has identified and evaluated properties in consulta-tion with State Historic Preservation Officer(s) and received an opinion from NPS concerning their significance, it must determine what effect the proposed project will have on the properties and report this to the council. If the effect might harm the historic properties, the agency and the council consult in an effort to agree on a way to avoid or lessen the potential damage. Some of the ways to do that are to change the project's location, modify its design, limit its scope, or include plans to preserve or restore historic properties. Not all properties can be saved, or it may be more important to complete a project as planned than to preserve an identified resource. In these cases, the agency may agree to prepare measured drawings or other documentation on the property according to HABS or HAER standards or to undertake an excavation to recover valuable archeological data. The Advisory Council on Historic Preservation has no power to dictate an agency's decision, but it reports success in reaching agreements in 98 percent of the cases it reviews.

OTHER FEDERAL AGENCIES

Many other federal agencies besides NPS and the Advisory Council on Historic Preservation operate programs that have an appreciable influence on historic resources; many of these agencies are subject to additional legal requirements for considering historic resources besides those included in legislation already mentioned. Agencies with large land-managing responsibility include the Bureau of Land Management, the Bureau of Reclamation, and the Bureau of Indian Affairs in the Department of the Interior, and the USDA Forest Service in the Department of Agriculture. The Secretary of Transportation is prohibited by law from approving projects requiring the use of land from historically significant sites unless there is no feasible and prudent alternative and the project includes planning to minimize any potential harm to the property. The Department of Defense, General Services Administration (GSA), and the U.S. Postal Service each own or manage a large number of buildings, many of which are historic. Laws require GSA to acquire properties of historic or architectural significance for federal offices whenever possible and also allow that agency to transfer surplus property free of charge to states and municipalities to serve as historic monuments or compatible uses for public benefit. The Department of Housing and Urban Development has administered a series of urban assistance grants, many of which have allowed funds to be expended for historic preservation purposes. The National Endowments for the Arts and Humanities have bestowed grants for design and conservation studies and for historic surveys.

COOPERATION

Many public and private organizations conduct preservation activities, and cooperation with these organizations is important in achieving federal preservation goals. The National Register's network of federal and state preservation officials, and the HABS and HAER summer teams demonstrate this. In addition, both NPS and state preservation programs utilize review boards of outside experts for certain aspects of their programs. The National Park Service has also collaborated with the National Trust for Historic Preservation, the Association for Preservation Technology, and others to provide training in historic preservation issues and techniques. This approach of involving as many organizations and individuals as possible has helped broaden the base of support for preservation efforts and institutionalized preservation concerns as a routine part of planning. A 1983 study on government cultural programs found that existing programs "have contributed to a new perception of the array of cultural resources and a mounting concern for the decline of communities in our society."[9]

In response to both a growing constituency and a growing mastery of preservation skills, the government has moved in the direction of decentralizing historic preservation programs and has adapted the way it monitors participants in these programs. The role of local governments in federal preservation programs has expanded as a result of tax legislation and the 1980 amendments to the National Historic Preservation Act. For example, the NPS and State Historic Preservation Offices are currently establishing a network of Certified Local Governments authorized to fulfill many of the states' historic preservation responsibilities. As of September 1985, all fifty states had approved procedures for certifying local governments, and 103 local governments had been certified. The increased involvement of these governments in preservation activities is likely to become another major area for the participation of professional historians. Both NPS and the Advisory Council on Historic Preservation have initiated procedures for evaluating the quality of preservation activities by monitoring state and federal programmatic procedures whenever possible, lessening the amount of case-by-case review. This trend increases the responsibility of historians employed by other parties in the preservation partnership by making NPS and the council more dependent on the quality of their work. It also expands opportunities for federal historians to use their analytical skills, familiarity with a variety of issues, and national perspective to influence the direction of the practice of historic preservation by participating in the formulation of national policies and professional preservation standards.[10]

> *The views expressed in this article are those of the author and not necessarily those of the National Park Service.*

NOTES

1. George Zabriskie, "Window to the Past," *With Heritage So Rich*, A Report of a Special Committee on Historic Preservation under the auspices of the United States Conference of Mayors with a grant from the Ford Foundation (New York: Random House, 1966), 58.
2. Albert Rains and Laurance G. Henderson, *With Heritage So Rich*, 207.
3. For a copy of the National Register Criteria for Evaluation, write to the National Register of Historic Places, National Park Service, Washington, D.C. 20240.
4. Annual listings are generally published in February or March in the *Federal Register*.

5. U.S. Department of the Interior, National Park Service, *Archeology and Historic Preservation: Secretary of the Interior's Standards and Guidelines, Federal Register*, Vol. 48, No. 190 (Washington, D.C.: Government Printing Office, 29 September 1982): 44716-44742.

6. Because these benefits and specific provisions are subject to change by Congress, current information should be obtained from State Historic Preservation Offices.

7. Preservation standards formerly called the "Secretary of the Interior's Standards for Rehabilitation" have been incorporated into *Archeology and Historic Preservation: Secretary of the Interior's Standards and Guidelines.* In addition, a current list of technical information may be obtained by writing to either The National Register of Historic Places or Technical Preservation Services, National Park Service, Washington, D.C. 20240. Some of these publications are cited in the "Suggested Reading" below.

8. The other principal government involvement in international preservation is in the World Heritage Convention, established to recognize and preserve natural and cultural resources that contribute to the significant heritage of the whole world. The National Park Service conducts studies and recommends U.S. properties for nomination.

9. Ormand H. Loomis, *Cultural Conservation: The Protection of Cultural Heritage in the United States*, A Study by the American Folklife Center, Library of Congress, carried out in cooperation with the National Park Service, Department of the Interior (Washington, D.C.: Government Printing Office, 1983), 25.

10. For related essays in this book on historic preservation, please see Barbara J. Howe, "The Historian in Historic Preservation: An Introduction" and "Historic Preservation: An Interdisciplinary Field" and Janet G. Brashler, "Managing the Past in a Natural Resources Management Agency." For further information on the National Park Service, please see the essay by Heather Huyck and Dwight Pitcaithley entitled "National Park Service: Historians in Interpretation, Management, and Cultural Resources Management" and Ronald W. Johnson's "History in the National Park Service: The Denver Service Center as a Case Study."

SUGGESTED READING

Sample publications from the National Register of Historic Places, Technical Preservation Services, and other government agencies include: Peter Bartis, *Folklife and Fieldwork: A Layman's Introduction to Field Techniques* (Washington, D.C.: American Folklife Center of the Library of Congress, 1979); Elizabeth Benchley, *Overview of the Prehistoric Resources of the Metropolitan St. Louis Area* (Washington, D.C.: Interagency Archeological Services, 1976); J. Henry Chambers, *Cyclical Maintenance for Historic Buildings* (Washington, D.C.: U.S. Government Printing Office, 1976); John Obed Curtis, *Moving Historic Buildings* (Washington, D.C.: Technical Preservation Services, 1979); Anne Derry et al., *Guidelines for Local Surveys: A Basis for Preservation Planning* (Washington, D.C.: U.S. Department of the Interior, 1977); Catherine Lynn Frangiamore, *Wallpapers in Historic Preservation* (Washington, D.C.: Government Printing Office, 1977); Margot Gayle, David W. Look, and John Waite, *Metals in America's Historic Buildings* (Washington, D.C.: U.S. Government

Printing Office, 1978); Beth Grosvenor, "How to Apply National Register Criteria to Post Offices," National Register of Historic Places Bulletin 13, Fall 1984; Historic American Buildings Survey/Historic American Engineering Record, *HABS/HAER Procedures Manual* (Washington, D.C.: National Park Service, 1980); "How to Apply the National Register Criteria for Evaluation," National Park Service, 1 June 1982; William J. Mayer-Oakes and Alice W. Portnoy, eds., "Scholars as Contractors," U.S. Department of the Interior Cultural Resource Management Studies, 1979; *Preservation Briefs* series of brochures on topics such as "Cleaning and Waterproof Coating of Masonry Buildings," "Repair of Historic Wooden Windows," and "Rehabilitating Historic Storefronts" (copies are available through State Historic Preservation Offices); State Plans and Grants Division, Heritage Conservation and Recreation Service, *New Directions in Rural Preservation* (Washington, D.C.: U.S. Government Printing Office, 1980); and Technical Preservation Services, "Preservation Tax Incentives Information Sheets," Preservation Assistance Division, Technical Preservation Services Branch, National Park Service.

Janet G. Brashler currently serves as forest archeologist for the Monongahela National Forest in Elkins, West Virginia, in addition to teaching part-time at Davis and Elkins College. She earned an undergraduate degree in anthropology from Northwestern University and M.A. and Ph.D. degrees from Michigan State University. Brashler has worked for the Forest Service as an archeologist for seven years, with previous assignments in Michigan and Wisconsin.

MANAGING THE PAST IN A NATURAL RESOURCES MANAGEMENT AGENCY

Janet G. Brashler

The objective of this essay is to define the philosophy and requirements of cultural resources management (CRM) in a natural resources–land managing agency and to provide a case study that illustrates the process of cultural resources management. The case study briefly documents the management of a nineteenth-century homesite in West Virginia, by the U.S. Department of Agriculture, Forest Service, Monongahela National Forest, headquartered in Elkins, West Virginia.

Since much has been written on the subject of cultural resources management policy during the recent past, this essay will only introduce the legal framework, philosophy, and history related to the management of cultural resources in an agency like the U.S. Forest Service. Details of the process and philosophy can be found elsewhere.[1] In addition, other essays in this book (see Beth Grosvenor, "Federal Programs in Historic Preservation," in particular) discuss details of cultural resources management, including the importance of history, architecture, and archeology in an agency whose primary objectives are linked to multiple resources management.

Cultural resources management may be defined as a philosophy, legal framework, and decision-making process which guides treatment of historic and prehistoric properties on federal lands or lands affected by federally funded or licensed activities. Another phrase with similar meaning, federal historic preservation, is less consistent with the orientation of most federal land managing agencies whose primary philosophy is conservation-oriented instead of strictly preservation-oriented. A conservation orientation relies on management strategies of differential allocation—some resources are used or consumed, some discarded, some preserved intact, and some are renewed. While these practices can

145

occur in preservation-oriented organizations, the emphasis tends to be on "preserving" or "saving" resources rather than "using" resources.

With roots in the nineteenth century, contemporary cultural resources management shares an early common heritage and parallel development with private sector historic preservation efforts.[2] Early historic preservation activities in the late nineteenth and early twentieth centuries were directed toward properties primarily owned by private individuals including the homesites of great men and women, and buildings important to the history of our nation. At about the same time, several programs through the Smithsonian Institution, the Department of the Interior, especially the National Park Service (NPS), and a few state governments were initiated as part of the growing conservation effort to wisely use and in some cases set aside land significant to our nation's natural and cultural heritage. Throughout most of the twentieth century, the development of federal historic preservation programs and policy was dominated by architects, anthropologists, and archeologists in the National Park Service, while private sector preservation efforts were led by historians and lay persons committed to saving and restoring specific sites such as Williamsburg, Mt. Vernon, and others in their local communities or regions.[3]

THE FEDERAL PRESERVATION SYSTEM

The following discussion introduces the laws and regulations related to the federal preservation system in general and the case study which follows in particular. While the legal framework is essentially the same for federal land managing agencies, the private sector, and federal agencies which license, permit, or fund projects, important differences do exist between these three groups. This section, therefore, highlights the important legislation and policy for land managing agencies such as the USDA Forest Service in particular. For a more detailed treatment of the legal framework and how it relates to other agencies and the private sector, see Grosvenor (this volume), King, Hickman and Berg, and Hosmer (see footnote 1).

The first major law pertaining to cultural resources on public lands was the 1906 Antiquities Act. It and the later Historic Sites Act of 1935 propelled the Department of the Interior and NPS into the major role of responsibility to "locate, record, acquire, preserve, mark, and commemorate properties of 'national significance'."[4] Other events in the 1930s which stimulated the development of conservation-oriented federal historic preservation included the development of the Historic American Buildings Survey (HABS) and extensive field-oriented archeology programs cosponsored by the Works Progress Administration (WPA) and the Smithsonian Institution.[5]

Much of the government-sponsored work between 1935 and 1960 was related to river basin salvage archeology, culminating in 1960 with passage of the Reservoir Salvage Act. During this same period, in 1949, the National Trust for Historic Preservation was formed to "receive and preserve historic sites, buildings, and objects in the public interest."[6] The trust, while chartered by the federal government, was and remains a private organization which receives federal as well as private support.

The National Historic Preservation Act of 1966 (NHPA) was the most significant statute for both private sector historic preservation and the development of federal cultural resources management. NHPA established the National Register of Historic Places as a listing of sites significant at the local, state, or national level; the Historic Preservation Fund to provide matching grants to the states; and the Advisory Council on Historic Preservation to advise the president and Congress. Section 106 of the act was of particular importance for federal agencies, because it directed them to consider the effect of undertakings on properties either on or eligible for the National Register of Historic Places. In 1980, amendments to the 1966 act were passed which reaffirmed and strengthened federal agency responsibility to cultural resources and consolidated a variety of disparate aspects of previous legislation and regulation.

Under the National Historic Preservation Act, private and federal historic preservation efforts became intertwined, but it was when several more statutes were enacted that the current complex of laws affecting federal land managing agencies were implemented. Passed in 1969, the National Environmental Policy Act (NEPA) directed federal agencies to use an interdisciplinary approach to planning and decision making and declared it the policy of the federal government to preserve our historic, cultural, and natural heritage. NEPA, however, did not provide specific instructions to federal land managers. Therefore in 1971 Executive Order 11593 was enacted which specifically directed federal agencies to develop policies and plans to preserve and maintain significant properties; to inventory, evaluate, enhance, and protect cultural resources; and until inventories and evaluations are complete, exercise caution so that significant or potentially significant sites are not inadvertently damaged or destroyed.

During the 1970s, two more significant laws were passed pertaining to the development of historic preservation and cultural resources management. In 1974, the Historical and Archeological Data Preservation Act (the Moss-Bennett bill) was passed which amended the 1960 Reservoir Salvage Act and authorized expenditure of funds by federal agencies for cultural resources inventory, recovery, analysis, and publication on all federally funded or licensed projects. This legislation and the projects differ considerably from CRM done internally within land managing agencies such as the Forest Service and the Bureau of Land Management. For example, Moss-Bennett projects include federally funded highways, waste water treatment facilities, and housing projects which are funded by appropriating up to 1 percent of the project cost for CRM activities. Another significant step in the 1970s was the employment of several hundred archeologists by federal agencies to provide technical assistance in interpreting the growing body of law and policy.

In 1976 the National Forest Management Act (NFMA) was passed. Regulations implementing NFMA required forest plans developed in response to the law to specify how cultural resources were going to be managed on each forest. Forest plans, when complete, will be comprehensive planning documents which identify standards and guidelines for management of all natural and cultural resources on a given national forest.[7]

The Archeological Resources Protection Act of 1979 (ARPA) supplemented the 1906 Antiquities Act and established criminal and civil penalties for removal of cultural resources from federal lands. ARPA was aimed at the wholesale destructive excavation of Pueblo ruins in the southwest and other sites across the United States including rock shelters, prehistoric cemeteries, and village sites.

In addition to the battery of statutes pertaining to cultural resources management, a variety of agency regulations and procedures exist which supplement the legal framework. The most important regulations for federal agencies and the private sector are found in the Code of Federal Regulations (CFR) 36 CFR 800 (1974, revised 1979) which specifies the coordinating regulations necessary for compliance with Section 106 of the National Historic Preservation Act and E.O. 11593 (Figure 1). Other regulations pertaining to the legal statutes include: 36 CFR 60, "National Register of Historic Places"; 36 CFR 61, "Criteria for Comprehensive Statewide Historic Surveys and Plans"; 36 CFR 63, "Determination of Eligibility for Inclusion in the National Register of Historic Places"; and 36 CFR 66, "Recovery of Scientific, Prehistoric, Historic, and Archaeological Data: Methods, Standards, and Reporting Requirements."

Many departments and agencies within departments have developed specific implementation policy contained in federal regulations, planning documents, manuals, and handbooks. The Department of the Interior has also developed standards for the treatment of historic structures and archeological properties. Within the Forest Service, manual direction exists at the national and regional levels, and some national forests have manual direction as well.

By 1980 the extensive and initially bewildering array of law, policy, regulation, and acronyms resulted in considerable confusion and apprehension on the part of some agency officials and members of the private sector who conduct activities under federal auspices. Three categories of concern had been raised. Perhaps the major concern among federal land managers in the Forest Service, Bureau of Land Management, and National Park Service was the realization that the survey and evaluation requirements were labor intensive, time consuming, and costly. The Forest Service alone was and is responsible for managing nearly 200 million acres of land, and survey costs can vary from 1 to 36 dollars an acre. Evaluation costs for an unknown number of sites can vary from between 1 and 25 thousand dollars per site.[8] In a period of serious concern over the size and growth of federal spending, these figures appeared staggering to agency managers.

Another source of concern to land managing agencies was the

complexity of the consultation process established by law and regulation. Some managers saw the complexity of the system and the implementation cost as constraints that could cause delays of up to several years before all necessary survey, evaluation, consultation, and mitigation could be concluded. The third major problem area was in determining just what constituted a significant site. Many managers feared that all sites were going to be significant and would have to be preserved, creating yet another perceived barrier to managing other resources such as minerals, recreation, timber, range, and wildlife.

As a result, federal land managing agencies, including the Forest Service, have focused recent efforts on several alternative approaches to the piecemeal, project-oriented survey and evaluation studies. Three approaches have been taken. First, to deal with the issue of significance and the concern over having to save everything, thematic studies of a variety of site types have been undertaken. Thematic studies require evaluation of sites in the context of other similar sites and allow for the preservation of the best sites, defined in terms suited to that theme or category. A research orientation is required by thematic studies but such studies also demand an allocation strategy which designates at least two management categories: those sites which will be preserved and those which will not. More elaborate allocation strategies have also been devised, including several categories such as preservation for future scientific research, preservation for interpretive value, as well as no further management needed. (See Dee F. Green and Fred Plog, eds. *Problem Orientation and Allocation Strategies for Prehistoric Resources on the New Mexico National Forests*). Studies of the logging industry, prehistoric lithic scatters, Forest Service fire towers and other administrative facilities, and New England farmsteads are a few examples that are currently underway.[9]

A second approach—aimed primarily at reducing cost, creating confidence in, and/or modifying existing survey and evaluation strategy—is the development of predictive or locational models of prehistoric and historic site locations.[10] Predictive models, which vary from common sense to elaborate statistically derived models, can be useful in identifying areas of high or likely site potential. When appropriately defined, developed, and tested, they can aid managers in reducing the considerable effort needed to identify sites. They cannot, however, always be sufficient to meet the requirements of the National Historic Preservation Act and associated regulations. Considerable discussion has occurred on the validity of predictive models, and, as Tainter has recently pointed out, the "debate has been somewhere on the far side of lively."[11]

Finally, efforts have also focused on development of Programmatic Memoranda of Agreement (PMOAs) among agencies, State Historic Preservation Offices (SHPOs), and the Advisory Council on Historic Preservation. MOAs differ from PMOAs in that MOAs tend to be project specific. They usually result from one of the last stages of the 36 CFR coordination requirements between agencies, SHPOs, and the advisory council (see Figure 1). PMOAs are agreements primarily

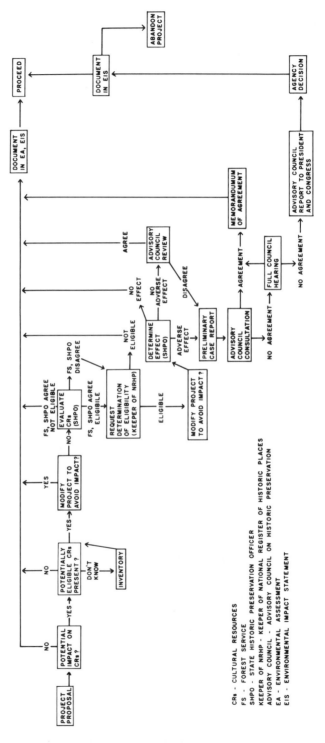

Figure 1. 36 CFR 800 Coordination Requirements.

designed to reduce the delays, uncertainty, and perceived ambiguity between major agencies and in most phases of the compliance process. Relatively simple PMOAs have streamlined the reporting and coordinating process between the Forest Service and the SHPOs. On a larger scale, some PMOAs are being or have been drafted between major agencies such as the Office of Surface Mining, the Forest Service, Bureau of Land Management, and the advisory council.[12]

A CASE STUDY FROM WEST VIRGINIA

To illustrate the previous discussion of the cultural resources management framework within a federal agency, attention will now focus on a relatively simple case study which has developed over the previous fifteen years on the Monongahela National Forest in West Virginia.

In 1969 the Monongahela National Forest acquired a tract of land at the foot of Seneca Rocks, one of the focal points of the Spruce Knob–Seneca Rocks National Recreation Area (Figure 2). Included in the purchase were several buildings formerly owned and occupied by Jacob Sites, an eighteenth-century German immigrant to the new United States, and his descendants. One building, built in the late nineteenth century after the original one burned, was moved from south of Seneca Creek to nearby private land by descendants of the family in the early 1970s. The building on the north side of Seneca Creek, however, was deemed worth only scrap value by land appraisers at the time of acquisition and was left on the lot. This was the Sites Homestead, built originally in the early nineteenth century by Jacob Sites when he first moved to Seneca Rocks.

Though dilapidated, the Sites Homestead, also mistakenly known as the Wayside Inn or Seneca Inn, was the object of considerable local oral history. The building reportedly functioned as a tavern, an inn, and a doctor's office, in addition to family residence during the nineteenth century. Confusion existed about the exact age of the building, though a single pen log cabin was built first and was later incorporated into a two- story frame dwelling. The logs were covered by the frame structure and remained relatively sound.

The apparent local importance and emerging federal policy on historic sites led the Forest Service to move cautiously. Thus, between 1970 and 1977 a number of letters were exchanged between the Forest Service and the State Historic Preservation Officer located in the West Virginia Antiquities Commission and later the West Virginia Department of Culture and History, attempting to determine the significance of the Sites Homestead. Opinions on the degree of significance varied considerably, though the building seemed to gain prominence in the opinions rendered after 1973.[13] Though unclear, the increasing prominence of the building may be attributed to the growing interest in historic preservation associated with the American Bicentennial. Meanwhile, plans to develop a visitor information center and associated recreation complex proceeded with at least two proposals for treatment

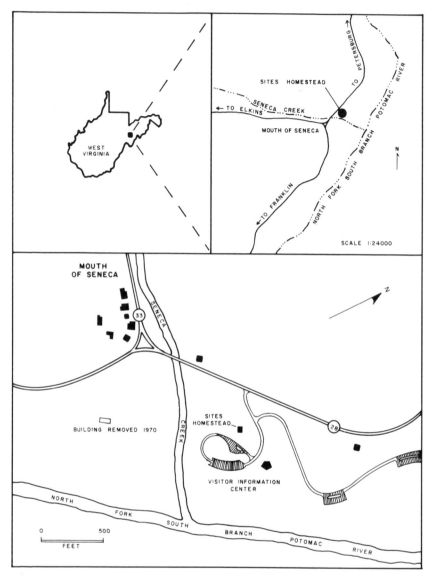

Figure 2. Sites Homestead location maps. For photographs of the Sites Homestead, see Figures 5 and 6 in Barbara Howe's essay, "Historic Preservation: An
Interdisciplinary Field," elsewhere in this book.

of the homestead: one to expand and use it as the visitor center, and the
other to remove it entirely. A new visitor center was finally built within
200 yards of the main homestead building in 1973 and was dedicated in
1978. In 1977, the Forest Service requested a Determination of Eligibility from the Keeper of the National Register of Historic Places. The
building was found eligible at the local level of significance due to

architectural characteristics, apparent local historic significance, and the potential for archeological information on regional ethnic patterns.

Once determined eligible, the Forest Service could not do anything to the homestead without working through the consultation process (Figure 1). In 1981 the Forest Service submitted a preliminary case report to the State Historic Preservation Officer and the Advisory Council on Historic Preservation which identified that the building was being adversely affected due to benign neglect.[14] Many of the interesting architectural details such as the banister and window moulding had been removed by vandals and the siding was being used for firewood. The second story was sagging and the building was becoming a serious safety hazard. The preferred alternative was to remove the structure after documentation. Early in 1982 a Memorandum of Agreement was ratified by the State Historic Preservation Officer, advisory council, and Forest Service to document and remove the above ground structure, and to preserve and interpret subsurface remains associated with the earliest part of the structure.

To accomplish the necessary documentation, the Forest Service contracted with historians at West Virginia University. The Forest Service entered into the contract using program budget funds and contracted outside the agency because relatively few historians work within the Forest Service. Such contracts differ from projects funded through the Moss-Bennett bill which pertains to federally funded projects such as highway construction. Necessary documentation for the Sites Homestead included annotated measured drawings of the building and a narrative report according to standards set by the National Park Service. In addition to the historic and architectural work, the Monongahela National Forest conducted limited archeological test excavation to determine the extent of subsurface remains in the area surrounding the structure, and to corroborate the historical research being done. The excavations were done "in house" under the supervision of the Forest Archeologist.

The work documenting the history of the structure was supervised by a professional historian. Using the general information and oral history available on the homestead as the basis for hypotheses, research focused on the ownership history of the land itself; the history of the Sites family, including genealogies, wills, tax, and census information; construction dates of the structure; documents pertaining to inns, travelers, and visitors to the area, as well as distillery licenses, Civil War records, and medical records; and other sources. The results of the research were curious.

First, while it was apparent that a member of the Sites family was indeed granted a license to operate a distillery, it was apparently for only a short one- or two-year period and could have been at the other Sites property south of Seneca Creek. Second, there could have been a doctor's office in the building during the 1870s when it appears not to have been occupied by the Sites family, but there is no specific historic document supporting the presence of doctors in the community. Third, there are absolutely no documentary references to the building ever

serving as a formal inn, tavern, or stage coach stop, though it is likely
that residents of the house would have from time to time taken in
travelers, given the building's prominent location along the road and
near Seneca Rocks. Finally, it appears that the earliest portion of the
building, a single pen log cabin, was built not earlier than 1839 when the
Mouth of Seneca community already boasted a store and several homes.
The two-story frame expansion was probably constructed in 1876,
though this assumption is based only on an increase in property taxes
that appeared in the family tax records for that year. Subsequent
modification to the interior probably occurred during the late nineteenth or early twentieth century when the building housed at least two
adults and several children.[15]

Archeological research conducted at the Sites Homestead supports
the historical data. Location of excavation units was based on an oral
history interview with Mrs. Pearl Kisamore (nee Sites) who grew up in
the homestead during the early years of the twentieth century. Time
sensitive artifacts from the Sites Homestead, particularly ceramics,
suggested occupation during the last half of the nineteenth and early
twentieth centuries.

In addition to information on site chronology, excavated materials
also provided some data regarding site function and socioeconomic
status of the Sites family. Archeological data as well as documentary and
oral history sources all suggest the site functioned primarily as a
domestic farmstead.[16] The types and quality of artifacts present at the
site were similar to patterns observed at other eighteenth and
nineteenth century dwellings, though previous research has shown it is
difficult to differentiate inns from homesteads on the basis of artifact
patterns alone.[17] The doctor's office function was also unverifiable,
possibly because a short term, turn-of-the-century doctor's office may
not be identifiable on the basis of the archeological record alone.

The archival, oral history, and archeological data taken together seem
to suggest that the Sites Homestead did indeed function as a home-
farmstead. If it functioned as an inn, it was not a formal licensed inn or
tavern, but a residence occupied by a family who took in weary travelers
occasionally.

The Sites Homestead is one of the most thoroughly researched
nineteenth-century sites in West Virginia. Archival, architectural, oral
history, and archeological research have been completed, and virtually
no concrete data emerged to support a number of the local legends and
stories about the house. The architectural quality of the building is
seriously affected by deterioration and vandalism. It seems likely that if
a Determination of Eligibility were sought from the National Register of
Historic Places today, the building would be found not eligible.

A discussion of this particular case study would be incomplete,
however, without mentioning the role of public involvement and its
effect on the fate of the Sites Homestead. Late in 1981 the Monongahela
National Forest notified the public through its annual tabloid that
archeological and historical studies of the Sites Homestead would be

undertaken during 1982. The article was read by Naomi Spencer, a Sites family descendant living in Maryland. In January she called the Forest Service and, realizing that the building was destined to be torn down after the studies were complete, began a campaign to save the structure.

In early 1983, to comply with NEPA, the Forest Service completed a draft Environmental Assessment which analyzed alternatives for the future of the homestead. The preferred alternative was to remove the structure because of the high cost to restore it and the extreme safety hazard. After the draft Environmental Assessment was issued the Forest Service received over 300 primary contacts—either letters, written statements on a form, or verbal expressions asking that the building be saved. In addition, more than 1,000 signatures were submitted on petitions. Among the contacts made between 1982 and 1983 were seven inquiries from the West Virginia Congressional delegation and one inquiry from the White House.

Concern expressed by the public led the Forest Service to adopt a decision which allowed the private sector one year to develop a proposal to save the building. To protect both the public and the agency the Forest Service specified that several conditions needed to be met, including the need for a legally incorporated entity to accomplish the work, a requirement for 50 percent of the necessary funds to be available before initiating the project, and a requirement that any work done meet the "Secretary of the Interior's Standards for Rehabilitation and Guidelines for Rehabilitating Historic Buildings."

At the time of this writing, a proposal has been received which the Forest Service has considered acceptable. The existing Memorandum of Agreement has been amended. The next step is to issue a special use permit with an incorporated organization, the "North Fork Historical and Cultural Society," to stabilize the Sites Homestead. Once issued, the society will be allowed to stabilize the Sites Homestead according to the Secretary of the Interior's standards.

The example given above involves a relatively simple case compared to many of the issues dealt with daily by many members of the preservation community in the state, federal, and private sectors. However, the Sites Homestead case does illustrate that cultural resources management functions do protect our nation's cultural heritage. It works because of a system of law and policy that requires certain steps followed before willful destruction of a site; it works because a variety of professionals participate in an interdisciplinary format to document and understand the role a site played in our nation's history; and it works because people in both the government and private sector are committed to managing our cultural heritage in a spirit of stewardship for future generations.[18]

The views expressed in this article are those of the author and not necessarily those of the USDA Forest Service.

NOTES

1. Thomas F. King, Patricia Parker Hickman, and Gary Berg, *Anthropology in Historic Preservation: Caring for Culture's Clutter* (New York: Academic Press, Inc., 1977). King, Hickman, and Berg present one of the best treatments of federal historic preservation through the late 1970s. Additional works on the subject include Michael B. Schiffer and George Gummerman, *Conservation Archaeology: A Guide for Cultural Resource Management Studies* (New York: Academic Press, Inc., 1977); C. R. McGimsey, *Public Archaeology* (New York: Seminar Press, 1972); and more recently Janet L. Friedman, "Federal Cultural Resource Management: Constraint or Opportunity," *Journal of Forestry*, 79 (March 1981): 142–45. A source not extensively used in this paper is Charles B. Hosmer, Jr., *Preservation Comes of Age: From Williamsburg to the National Trust, 1926–1949*, 2 vols. (Charlottesville: University Press of Virginia for the National Trust for Historic Preservation, 1981).
2. King, Hickman, and Berg, *Anthropology in History Preservation*, 11–18.
3. Ibid., 19–21.
4. Ibid., 23.
5. Ibid., 25.
6. Friedman, "Federal Cultural Resource Management," 145.
7. Evan I. DeBloois, *Measuring Cultural Resource Management Accomplishments* (Washington, D.C.: USDA Forest Service, 1984), 54.
8. Ibid.
9. An example of a thematic study recently published is Vernon J. Glover, *Logging Railroads of the Lincoln National Forest, New Mexico*, Report No. 4 of *United States Department of Agriculture, Forest Service, Southwestern Region Cultural Resources Management* (Albuquerque: USDA Forest Service, 1984).
10. A selection of predictive modelling and related types of reports include: Dee F. Green and Fred Plog, eds., *Problems Orientation and Allocation Strategies for Prehistoric Resources on the New Mexico National Forests*, Report No. 3 of *United States Department of Agriculture, Forest Service, Southwestern Regional Cultural Resources Management* (Albuquerque: USDA Forest Service, 1984); Linda S. Cordell and Dee F. Green, eds., *Stage 1 Site Location Modelling in the Southwestern Region*, Report No. 5, *United States Department of Agriculture Forest Service, Southwestern Region Cultural Resources Management Report* (Albuquerque: USDA Forest Service, 1984); William A. Louis, *A Culture Resource Management Study of the Hiawatha National Forest, Michigan: Phase II, The Hypothesis Tests*, No. 36, *Michigan State University Museum Archaeological Survey Records* (East Lansing, Mich.: Michigan State University, 1979); and Joseph A. Tainter, ed., "Predictive Modelling and the McKinley Mine Dilemma," *American Archaeology* 4:2 (1982): 82–113.
11. Joseph A. Tainter, "Predictive Modelling and the McKinley Mine Dilemma," 82.
12. Thomas F. King, "The OSMPMOA is Coming," *American Archaeology* 4:2 (1984): 83.
13. USDA Forest Service, Monongahela National Forest, "Preliminary Case Report on the Wayside Inn, Pendleton County, West Virginia," Report submitted to the Advisory Council on Historic Preservation, July 1981.
14. Ibid.
15. Barbara J. Howe and Emory L. Kemp, "The Sites Homestead: Architectural and Historic Recording Project of an Historic Structure Located at the Seneca Rocks Complex, Monongahela National Forest," (prepared for the

USDA Forest Service–Monongahela National Forest, in partial fulfillment of the contract number 21-00332, 1983).

16. Steven W. McBride and Kim A. McBride, "Sites Homestead Artifact Analysis" in "Archaeology and History at the Sites Homestead: A Nineteenth- Century Farmstead in West Virginia", ed. Janet G. Brashler (USDA Forest Service, Monongahela National Forest, 1983), 72.

17. Ibid.

18. For another view of this project, see Barbara J. Howe, "Historic Preservation: An Interdisciplinary Field," elsewhere in this book.

For a biographical sketch of Barbara J. Howe, see her essay, "Historic Preservation: An Introduction," elsewhere in this book.

HISTORIC PRESERVATION: AN INTERDISCIPLINARY FIELD

Barbara J. Howe

INTRODUCTION

While many aspects of public history require the historian to work with colleagues or clients in a variety of disciplines, historic preservation is perhaps the most interdisciplinary of all public history fields. Lawyers, real estate agents, bankers, art historians, architects, engineers, contractors, business people, city and regional planners, and many others are active in historic preservation for a variety of reasons—to pursue legal cases defining property rights, to buy or sell historic properties, to finance investors in downtown properties or protect the bank's investment in those areas, to study the built environment, to design and restore or renovate historic properties, to invest in or operate a business in a historic property, or to develop a master plan for development. The historian in historic preservation who does not realize the needs, expertise, and interests of these colleagues, clients, or, sometimes, competitors is likely to be ignored as a starry-eyed idealist, and history is apt to go out of historic preservation. After all, historians are not typically trained to study artifacts or buildings— almost anyone who has had a history class knows that—so what role can historians play in historic preservation?

Historians can have a leading role in the field of historic preservation, and in the broader area of cultural resources management, if they will get out of their library carrels and look around them. Most historians involved in urban history or local history research have encountered people curious to know about the history of a particular building or neighborhood in a town, or they have uncovered material in their own research related to the significance of a particular building or neighborhood. Probably, they have found this information by accident and dismissed it as useful for illustrations only. However, it occasionally leads to venturing out into the neighborhood and meeting with people interested in the current state of the buildings.

When historians leave their offices or library carrels, they are much more likely to encounter people from a variety of disciplines. That is one of the aspects of public history and historic preservation that makes it so exciting—and frustrating. It is exciting to help people discover their own past and watch them gain the skills to carry out projects without your assistance, but it can be tiring to explain constantly terms to people unfamiliar with the jargon of historic preservation or to always feel that you are "on duty" when you are around people interested in old buildings, downtown revitalization, city government, or any of the other areas that relate to historic preservation.

Initially, the historian might be asked to supply the information needed for a National Register of Historic Places nomination for a particular structure as the first step toward having it saved. This, in itself, requires a re-thinking of the traditional scholarly approach to writing, where one tries to set the stage carefully and completely, leaving out no influences or details that the reviewer might question in critiquing the manuscript. For a National Register nomination, it is important to abandon the rules of term-paper writing. Pretend the reader, a busy government official, has a few minutes to review your nomination and will stop reading at the first period or, at most, the first paragraph. There is no time to build suspense. You have checked several areas of significance and just completed a lengthy architectural description of the property. The trick to doing a good National Register nomination is to assume that the reviewer will only read that one paragraph or sentence. This, in essence, is the heart of a good journalistic style of writing and is appropriate for the historian in this case. Then write the most coherent, tight sentence(s) you can, summarizing the architectural description and areas of significance as thoroughly as you can. After making your case, for the record, you can proceed to elaborate on the history of the building or area, assuming that your reader may be totally unfamiliar with the building, its location, or the events you feel make it significant. While documenting, you are also educating, and education is one of the historian's strongest contributions to historic preservation concerns.[1]

After you have researched the history of a building, and perhaps had it listed on the National Register, you quickly learn that buildings cannot be saved unless there are uses for them. There are very few properties that the country can afford to "mothball," hoping that someone, someday, will come up with a use. The owner will be interested in insurance coverage if there is vandalism to a vacant building, the police will be watching for break-ins, the bank holding the mortgage will want to know about the security of its investment, the neighbors will likely complain about an unsightly vacant structure nearby.

Additionally, not all perceived uses are appropriate for a building, and its use will depend on whether it is to have symbolic, political, or economic value to the community or agency involved. If the value is to be symbolic, the historian may have the most influence, for there will usually have to be at least some concern for the structure's history. These can also be the trickiest cases because the historian's definition of significance and appropriate accompanying interpretation may not coincide with the public's perceived significance. If the value is strictly economic, history may be relegated to advertising purposes. If the value is political, the historian needs to be aware that all the research in the world may be considered second in importance to the needs of particular interest groups. Examining several case studies will better illustrate the value of this significance.

JACKSON'S MILL: SYMBOLIC VALUES IN HISTORIC PRESERVATION

Jackson's Mill State 4-H Camp in Weston, West Virginia, offers an interesting case study of the interdisciplinary nature of historic preservation and of the symbolic value of buildings and sites. The camp is on land that was the boyhood home of General Thomas J. "Stonewall" Jackson, a state hero even though the Confederate soldier gave his life to prevent the victory of the Union armies that guaranteed the formation of West Virginia as a Union state. Jackson lived on the farm near Weston for about twelve years, leaving to go to West Point in 1842. While at Jackson's Mill, his Uncle Cummins operated a gristmill and sash sawmill, a very common combination in rural areas. Jackson grew up in a log cabin that has long since disappeared, and the two-story white frame house that Cummins built just when Jackson left for West Point

Figure 1. Jackson's Mill Museum, Jackson's Mill State 4-H Camp, Weston, West Virginia, showing exterior of 1841 mill building in its current condition; siding and roofing are not original. *Photograph courtesy of Emory L. Kemp.*

burned in 1915, leaving only the foundation and a few photographs to document the building.

Ever since the property became a 4-H camp in the 1920s, there have been efforts to develop a historic area to commemorate the Jackson family, prominent land owners and politicians in Western Virginia, and, especially, to honor the general, one of West Virginia's favorite sons. Numerous plans and studies have been formulated and abandoned over the years, because of lack of money, the onset of the Great Depression of the 1930s, World War II, and other priorities of the camp program. The most recent of these was a study done in the early 1970s that involved recreating an extensive historic homestead area with numerous outbuildings and a reconstructed boyhood log home of Jackson, although no illustrations of this building have ever come to light. Although this plan got as far as the diorama stage, lack of funding stopped its implementation.

In the summer of 1980, West Virginia University officials appointed a new Jackson's Mill Restoration Committee. Members included the camp director, a retired newspaper editor and long-time 4-H supporter, the 4-H program leader, WVU facilities planners, and a retired extension home economist. The camp is a state-owned property administered by the Center for Extension and Continuing Education at WVU, and the committee consists almost entirely of individuals that are part of the extension network in the state, several of whom have shared the dream of "doing something" with Jackson's Mill for many years and who did not want to waste their time on plans that could not be implemented this time around. The committee's original goals were to focus on projects that would enhance the 4-H camping program and fulfil the decades-old dream. Throughout our work, then, historic preservation concerns had to be balanced with the programming already carried on at the site for its tens of thousands of visitors who come each year for events as diverse as Black Angus cattle shows, church women's conferences, extension homemakers conferences, and graduate coursework through WVU. Thus, a collection of historic buildings that could not be used was not feasible, and while the committee members were very familiar with the needs of Jackson's Mill as an extension center, none were experts in historic preservation or West Virginia history.

Emory Kemp and I became involved with the Jackson's Mill Restoration Committee as advisors in January 1981 and have been working with the committee ever since. We reviewed the earlier studies of Jackson's Mill and felt it was imperative to look very hard at the evidence available for the history of the site, concentrating on the Jacksons and their history of the land and later owners, ignoring the standard accounts of Stonewall which focused on his military career. Two students, one a historian and one a civil engineer, were hired to write a site-specific history of Jackson's Mill and to prepare an industrial archeology study of the surviving gristmill building that dated from 1841 and had been greatly altered over the years. Another history student was hired to inventory the museum in the gristmill building, which had been collecting artifacts for many years with little direction and fewer records, a serious matter since these were now state-owned artifacts and could not be disposed of as easily as those in a privately owned museum if we decided they did not fit the scope of a museum focused on sawmilling, gristmilling, and the Jackson family.

After extensive research in local and archival collections, the students found that very little documentary evidence exists about Stonewall's life at Jackson's Mill. A few inventories tell us about the family, but we would be hard-pressed to present anything that could be unique to Stonewall's boyhood at that site. And rural life in central Western Virginia at that time generally has reached the history books in sketchy fashion through oral tradition. Also, we found that the existing gristmill building has been so heavily altered over the years that it is impossible to even know for certain what type of wheel powered it in the past. Flooring, siding, foundation—everything that might provide a clue to the trained industrial archeologist has been changed. That alone would make it difficult for the committee to pursue its initial main goal—restoring the mill so that campers and adults could see how grain was ground when Stonewall was a boy there.[2]

To accompany the historical and industrial archeology work on the site, the committee hired John Nass, Jr., a historical archeologist, to conduct two digs on the site in the summers of 1981 and 1982. Using

Figure 2. Jackson's Mill Museum, showing interior of 1841 mill building in 1981; sash sawmill is at right of photograph; only original interior feature is the framing system. *Photograph courtesy of Emory L. Kemp.*

college students, 4-H campers, and community volunteers, Nass attempted to find the remains of the boyhood log cabin, the frame house, and any outbuildings or other features that might help interpret the site. Unfortunately, the site has been heavily landscaped in many areas, so much has been lost. Nass did uncover the foundations of the frame house but could not conclusively find the log cabin before the work ended. His work reinforced the feeling that the historians already shared, i.e., that it would be impossible to reconstruct the boyhood home of Stonewall Jackson in anything like an accurate fashion, even if reconstruction was an acceptable preservation technique, and we firmly believed that it was not acceptable.

We were then faced with being the "dream killers." The boyhood home could not be reconstructed, and we knew very little about what happened there, anyway. The frame house foundations were intact, but we knew nothing about the interior except that it had once been so deteriorated that one could throw baseballs through it. Reconstruction would therefore be expensive, not totally accurate and difficult to interpret—the house was built as Stonewall was leaving, he only returned twice in the final twenty years of his life, and Cummins himself left for the California Gold Rush about 1849, never to return. The existing gristmill may have had an original framing system, but Stonewall would not have recognized the rest of the building, and we were fairly certain that it never had the "romantic" New England-type overshot wheel the architect proposed in the 1970s. One hydraulic engineer said only an undershot or breast wheel would work with the present water conditions in the West Fork River. Also, the river floods regularly, the dam has been washed away over the years, and the river has changed course. Rebuilding a dam to get enough head to power any kind of water wheel would involve flooding acres and acres of farmland in the valley, farmland which the state does not own. Also, we did not feel it would be a good idea for an agriculturally oriented group like 4-H to be advocating flooding farmland.

What, then, were our alternatives? We decided that the existing gristmill building should be reorganized as a museum emphasizing gristmilling, sawmilling, and the Jackson family history only. The student hired to do the inventory was then hired again to work on plans for the museum and to design the exhibits on paper. She also recommended storing many of the artifacts—like 1920s vacuum cleaners—that did not fit the scope of the museum. A heritage arts graduate from a local college was eventually hired to translate the words and illustrations of the exhibit into models and exhibit panels. An organized museum is slowly emerging from a hodge-podge collection. Anything stored in the museum will have to be able to survive without temperature or humidity controls because there is no heating system in the wood frame mill.

A c. 1795 log cabin had been moved to the camp in the 1920s from a nearby community to symbolize Jackson's boyhood home. Sited prominently on a knoll as one enters the camp, the McWhorter Cabin has developed its own significance over the years. This, we feel, should be left and used to interpret log architecture in general, with artifacts removed to better storage conditions, as there are no temperature or humidity controls here, either. The cabin itself needs restoration work done in the form of removing the Portland cement mortar chinking and replacing it with a more appropriate mixture. Logs now infested with dry rot and powder post beetles must be replaced. A new roof of wood shakes has been installed.

In the process of planning the historic area in the 1940s, the camp had acquired the Hammer sawmill from Pendleton County, West Virginia. This excellent example of a sash sawmill had been stored in the gristmill building and poorly interpreted, with other artifacts resting on top of it where needed and no real explanation of how a saw worked. However, since it was protected so well, it has acquired great value as an artifact. We have decided to give it its own shed building, of a type it would have had originally, and to encase this in a modern building to protect it from the weather. This modern building will then allow us room to interpret the history of sawmilling in the state (lumber-related industries were among the chief industries for many years). We will explain how the mill was originally water-powered but will use an electric motor to move the blade up and down for demonstration purposes.

We have outlined vague plans for the development of the other parts of the historic area, which, by the 1970s plan, included many outbuildings, gardens, etc. These will depend on how successful the initial section is and what kind of funding is available in the future. An office/visitor center building likely will be designed to meet our needs and be built of logs salvaged from other deteriorating buildings. The archeological sites will be interpreted with wayside exhibits and a ground-level outline indicating the location of the foundations for the 1915 frame house.

Having addressed all the secondary issues, as far as the committee was concerned, we were faced with the most important question—how do we handle the dream of grinding grain at Jackson's Mill? Robert H. Blaker, who owned a family gristmill in southern West Virginia, contacted the committee and said that he would be willing to give the mill to Jackson's Mill if we would pay to have it moved. Blaker had originally dreamed of restoring the mill himself, but he no longer planned to do so, and the mill was in a vulnerable isolated setting. With the original parts dating from 1795, Blaker's Mill perfectly fit the timeframe for Jackson's Mill, where milling had begun about 1801. Most important, everything was intact in the turbine-powered mill—bolters, sifters, stones, elevators, etc., even a barrel packer that is reputed to be quite rare. The problem became how to move the mill to Jackson's Mill, and many months passed as we debated moving possibilities, tried to get permission from the West Virginia Board of Regents, which controlled the $186,000 in state funding given us through the efforts of a local legislator, and tried to find an appropriate route over the 125 mountainous miles we had to move the mill. Eventually, in 1984, we were able to hire Paul D. Marshall & Associates, an architectural firm from Charleston, West Virginia, to prepare a moving plan and began to recruit talented volunteers through the extension and 4-H network to assist with moving the mill. Trucks, cranes, and other heavy equipment were donated through the extension system's vast state-wide contacts.

By the spring of 1985, public history students at West Virginia University had prepared the new master site interpretation plan to include an exhibit on the evolving nature of historic preservation as practiced at the camp, written an interpretive brochure for the historic area, and provided the background information for interpretive panels at Blaker's Mill and Jackson's Mill. The landscape architects had revised the master site plan for locating the sawmill shed and Blaker's Mill at the camp; the WVU architect and Marshall had prepared moving specifications; the industrial archeologist was confident that the sawmill and gristmill buildings would be installed correctly; the millwright had reviewed the moving and site location plans; the camp director had organized his volunteer crew; and the move was underway. Groundbreaking for the historic area at Jackson's Mill took place April 24, 1985, promoting the theme of "Jackson's Mill—A Dream Coming True" to recognize the work of those who had contributed to this dream in various forms over the past sixty years. The dedication ceremony was scheduled for August 30 during the camp's annual Jubilee Days crafts fair that draws people from all over the state. Everything was properly recorded for future reference and publication.

THE SITES HOMESTEAD: POLITICAL VALUES IN HISTORIC PRESERVATION

Historic preservation projects with political value can involve federal agencies mandated to consider eligible properties in all their planning efforts. Federal agencies involved in cultural resources management face many competing pressures for scarce dollars—if money is spent to preserve buildings, they should have some use other than as "scene setters." Recreation facilities, historic preservation projects, road maintenance, and salaries can all compete for the same funding in an agency. Also, it is important to remember that most federal agencies needed to pay little, if any, attention to historic preservation or cultural resources management before the preservation legislation of the late 1960s and subsequent acts. Thus, historians working with these agencies, as employees or contractors, may find themselves working with contracting officers who are experts at timber sales and dam construction contracts but who have had little experience with the vagaries of restoration contracts or the needs of researchers.

Emory Kemp and I have recently been involved in several federally funded projects that included historic preservation, where the historians were responsible for documenting the sites while those with other interests were likely to be making the final decisions. In one case, we were under contract to the USDA Forest Service to research the history of the Sites Homestead at Monongahela National Forest in West Virginia which had been declared eligible for the National Register. Our

Figure 3. Blaker's Mill, near Alderson, West Virginia, exterior of mill with building in its original location. *Photograph courtesy of Emory L. Kemp.*

Figure 4. Blaker's Mill, interior showing mill stones and hopper in place. All of this type of equipment would have been in Jackson's Mill but has been lost. *Photograph courtesy of Emory L. Kemp.*

Figure 5. Sites Homestead, Seneca Rocks, West Virginia, west side of building showing Seneca Rocks in background. This is the most popular view of the building and shows it in the best condition. *Photograph courtesy of Emory L. Kemp.*

research could not verify the areas of significance identified by nonhistorians who had worked on the site over the years. Much of their work had been based on oral tradition, and the same limited evidence was listed in report after report. Starting anew, we tried unsuccessfully to verify the building's most important claim to fame, its use as a local tavern during the Civil War and later years. Nor could we confirm an early nineteenth-century construction date supposedly attached to the building. Archeological evidence confirmed our efforts—nothing that should have gone with a tavern (glass bottles, for instance) was found, and no ceramic evidence predated the late 1830s–1840s. An investigator unfamiliar with rural West Virginia vernacular architecture had once waxed eloquent about the wonderful woodwork in the building— woodwork now heavily vandalized or long since lost to campers' fires. In addition, most of the north wall of the two- story structure is gone, and the second floor is leaning precariously out toward the gap left by the missing wall. To further weaken the significance of the building, many other examples of this style of architecture are extant in the area.

This might have been an easy building to write off, and it should

Figure 6. Sites Homestead, Seneca Rocks West Virginia, south side of building showing original one-story single pen log cabin later enclosed in frame house. When this photograph was taken in 1983, the second floor north side of the building, on the west end, was completely gone. *Photograph courtesy of Emory L. Kemp.*

probably never have been declared eligible. However, one branch of the family became adamant that the building should be preserved and started a letter-writing campaign, collecting some 1,000 signatures and $300 to save the building. Janet G. Brashler's essay on "Managing the Past in a Natural Resources Management Agency" discusses this public campaign to save the building.

Our report was crucial to the Forest Service's future plans for the property, as we were the historians hired to unravel the truth about the structure, insofar as possible. If we found that it had a great deal of historical significance, the foresters, archeologists, and planners of the Forest Service would probably have had to consider spending more federal funds to preserve the building in some fashion, and many doubted it was worth that. When we found the significance was probably minimal, the Forest Service gave the family time to develop an acceptable preservation plan. This included forming a nonprofit group to handle funding and family-supported stabilization work on the building. Thus, Forest Service planners could spend their funds on projects with a higher priority while the family worked to save their homestead.

DOWNTOWN REVITALIZATION: ECONOMIC VALUES IN HISTORIC PRESERVATION

Economic values are at the root of most historic preservation projects today because of the tax incentives provided by the Economic Recovery Tax Act of 1981 and its predecessors, the Tax Reform Act of 1976 and the Revenue Act of 1978. While the Sites Homestead project was done for a federal agency, historians in historic preservation are also very likely to find themselves involved in some of the most basic preservation projects dealing with economics—downtown revitalization projects. One of the strongest impetuses for the modern historic preservation movement was the urban renewal efforts of the 1950s and 1960s that wiped out downtown businesses and neighborhoods throughout the country. Led by the National Trust for Historic Preservation's Main Street Project, now the Main Street Center, small towns across the United States have been working hard recently to revitalize their downtown commercial areas and halt the "flight to the mall," while cities like Charleston, South Carolina, long ago recognized that historic preservation makes good sense economically.

Most downtown revitalization commissions appointed to lead these efforts will probably not think to put a professional historian on the commission unless the historians come forth and identify themselves as willing to serve on these groups and to devote the time needed to these projects. The commissions are typically composed of downtown business people, city or county officials, architects, landscape architects, or contractors, and, sometimes, members of the local preservation group or general community volunteers. Some revitalization schemes have been aimed at wiping out the community's past, such as one midwest project that covered all the storefronts with pastel aluminum siding. Hopefully, this has ended, but historic preservation and downtown revitalization are by no means synonymous.

The historian, by knowing what downtown has been, can help focus the group's attention on what downtown should be in the future. The malls are not going to disappear, and people will not be stopped from getting in their cars to shop, so downtown's historic function is gone—the self-sufficient marketing center that people came to on foot or on trolley in the "good old days." Should downtown turn into boutiques? Should all efforts be made to get the hardware store to come back downtown in cramped space? Should we provide tax abatements to help downtown businesses stay in business?

Historians involved in this aspect of historic preservation usually do not have a direct economic stake in the results of this project, and that can be both good and bad. On the good side, they can see the broad picture, look at options "objectively," and study all angles. On the bad side, business people concerned about rental costs per square foot and sales volume and city officials concerned about traffic flow or votes may well feel that historians have little to contribute unless they are willing to learn about the realities of business and running a city.

I spent several years in Tiffin, Ohio, working with the downtown revitalization efforts there. Because I had seen downtown projects in other areas, had access to a network of preservationists around the state who were dealing with downtown projects, and was basically interested in urban and local history, I was accepted readily as a member of the commission. In fact, I had fewer problems than the struggling downtown businessman who had purchased a quarter block of downtown Tiffin after a major fire in a building and was trying desperately to get it restored and filled with tenants—yet always faced criticism when he voted, as a city council member, for projects that benefited the downtown area. While I contributed a National Register historic district nomination that then made owners eligible for the tax incentives accompanying register-listed properties, I learned about marketing problems, parking problems (the supposed cause of every downtown's decline), and street furniture (benches, lamps, newspaper stands, bus shelters, drinking fountains).

My goal was to keep the town from going "phony-colonial" in style. Tiffin was an early nineteenth-century town and most of its extant buildings downtown dated from its growth boom in the late nineteenth century. Triangular pediments, colonial 9/9 windows, and Williamsburg paint colors were totally inappropriate. Fortunately, an artist/draftsman in town became interested in our work and was willing to use old photographs and other information I supplied to produce his sketches for the exterior decoration of the buildings to appropriate late nineteenth-century styles. Historic preservation has to involve translating the historian's words into an artist's sketch or landscape architect's plans to be comprehensible to most people. We are a visually oriented society, and downtowns, after all, are three-dimensional objects, not research papers or scholarly articles. Downtown Tiffin is now much more attractive than it was in 1980. The streetscape work is finished, and several buildings have been repainted. However, the town and county have been plagued by high unemployment and a sluggish economy. These factors, plus a new mall on the edge of town, have produced too many empty buildings downtown.

DEVELOPING YOUR SKILLS IN PRESERVATION

Historians should be taught to think critically and to analyze carefully. They should also be able to organize their material well. These skills certainly help in handling any preservation problem—why did a particular downtown decline? can it be saved? which plan offers the best alternatives?

In addition, historians interested in preservation have to learn some of the language and skills of those they are working with. Remember the local government/civics courses and learn how your local government actually operates, so that you will know how much power the mayor really has when expressing support for a project and promising to get it passed by city council. What does state law allow a planning commission to do? Can the city establish a historic district under state enabling legislation or must some other method be used to control a historic downtown? And how much control will local property owners agree to, i.e., can you delay demolitions and regulate the use of signs or metal sidings or can you only attempt to prevent show windows from being blocked up and hideous signs erected? Find out how healthy the downtown is and what the status of industry is in the community; advocating that the city spend thousands of dollars on street paving and lights when the largest factory has just announced its closing, cutting the city's tax revenues, will be counterproductive.

Learn to read blueprints and at least learn the basics of good preservation techniques for historic buildings so that you can visualize what the blueprint represents and can be sure the contractor or architect is not advocating methods harmful to the building, such as dangerous cleaning practices. The basics, like "no sandblasting," are easily learned through publications like the Department of the Interior's "Preservation Briefs" series, available through your State Historic Preservation Office.

How does one learn these skills in a traditional history curriculum? First, learn to do research with primary materials, especially those related to local history concerns, including deeds, tax maps, photographs, city directories, etc. Students from design-oriented programs come to history classes to learn how to do research for their projects, so history students should take advantage of opportunities given in these courses to research and write. Use electives and required courses outside of history carefully. Urban geography and urban planning, art history, landscape architecture and architecture, business and economics, civil engineering, law, real estate, and many others are avenues to explore at the undergraduate or graduate level. Or audit classes after you have graduated. Continuing education courses, vocational-technical school courses, and adult education programs all usually offer elementary or advanced courses in some of these areas and are relatively inexpensive. The National Trust for Historic Preservation, Victorian Society in America, Seminar for Historical Administrators, Association for Preservation Technology, and West Dean College (England) offer a variety of short courses and seminars for beginners or advanced professionals, and scholarships may be available to qualified applicants. "Outsiders" are also welcome in some National Park Service training courses; numbers are limited, but you may learn more about these opportunities by contacting the National Park Service at the regional office addresses given in the Directory of Resources and Organizations at the back of this book.

Use class assignments effectively where possible. For example, a public history student at West Virginia University designed a walking tour of downtown Morgantown for a class project and later, during Morgantown's bicentennial, was able to revise her work and see it in print for sale to the public, through the cooperation of the local newspaper and Main Street Morgantown. She also conducted two walking tours of downtown to introduce people to the brochure.

Another student who participated in our historic buildings survey class then helped design a slide show on the neighborhood she surveyed that has been shown to many groups around town. She has also designed and written a brochure for sale to the public, and has conducted walking tours of the neighborhood.

Most important, perhaps, is to volunteer to help any group in your community remotely interested in these areas. Attend City Council meetings; talk to the director of the Chamber of Commerce, mayor and county commissioners; join civic-oriented groups like the League of Women Voters (one of the most effective groups supporting downtown revitalization efforts in Tiffin). Every group needs good volunteers, and students can learn how these groups operate while adding valuable experience to their resumes.

If you are in a university or college town, you will probably find that people are accustomed to working with students on many projects. They may not be used to meeting history students, but they will quickly learn if you point out to them that you can do research for them, write reports, help develop ideas. This will mean evening hours and commitments beyond just a semester or so—few things move quickly or fit an academic calendar—but the rewards are there to be found.

Finally, if you are going to be actively involved in historic preservation in your community, be sure that you express your support in tangible ways— make it a habit to shop downtown and patronize merchants who are fixing up their buildings. Be prepared to talk about your work or the current city plans whenever you meet someone—you may think that you are "off-duty," but it is hard to ever be "off-duty" in a preservation career, particularly in a small community or anywhere that you play a leadership role. Yes, it can be tiring but it can also be very satisfying to know your work is needed, your opinions are valued, and that you, as a historian, are considered a colleague of your co-crusaders in the cause of saving our built environment.

NOTES

1. For assistance in preparing National Register nominations, contact your State Historic Preservation Office; the staff there can supply forms and instructions for procedures used in your state.
2. For a basic introduction to industrial archeology, see Emory L. Kemp's essay, "A Perspective on Our Industrial Past Through Industrial Archeology" elsewhere in this book.

Emory L. Kemp is a public historian quite by accident, since many of his long-standing interests are now subsumed under this new banner. He is coordinator of the Program for the History of Science and Technology at West Virginia University. His formal education at the University of Illinois and the Imperial College of Science and Technology in London is in engineering. Previous to his present position he served as chairman of the Department of Civil Engineering, West Virginia University, where he was active in teaching and research in structural engineering. Before coming to West Virginia University in 1962, he was an engineer with leading consulting firms in London.

Professor Kemp's interest in the history of technology, industrial archeology, and the historic preservation of engineering works stretches over more than two decades. He is a founding member of the Society for Industrial Archeology and served as the first editor of the journal IA.

He has organized, led, and served as a consultant for industrial archeology projects around the country, including those of the Historic American Engineering Record. His special interest is the history of engineering during the Industrial Revolution with emphasis on the history of structural engineering. He was a fellow of the American Council of Learned Societies to study in Britain the Industrial Revolution and was a Regents' Fellow at the Smithsonian Institution during 1984–85, where he completed research for a book on the history of suspension bridges.

A PERSPECTIVE ON OUR INDUSTRIAL PAST THROUGH INDUSTRIAL ARCHEOLOGY

Emory L. Kemp

INTRODUCTION TO INDUSTRIAL ARCHEOLOGY

The Ironbridge Gorge Open Air Museum at Coalbrookdale, England, proudly advertises with the slogan "Where it all began in 1709." Many interested in the history of eighteenth-century Britain would recognize the dates of the great victories of the Duke of Marlborough, perhaps the birth date of John Wesley, or even the year of Sir Isaac Newton's death, but few would associate 1709 with the first successful smelting of iron with coke at Coalbrookdale in Shropshire. The interrelationship of coal, iron, and steam is essential to the understanding of early phases of the Industrial Revolution. For more than a century, since Elizabethan times,

Britain had suffered a severe shortage of timber which was then the principal fuel as well as being widely used for building and a variety of agricultural and industrial purposes. If Britain's iron industry was to expand to meet increasing demands of commerce and industry, an alternative fuel had to be found to smelt iron. Raw coal produced a very brittle iron which could not be used, but coke, the distilled product of coal, was found to be quite satisfactory to serve both as the source of heat and as a powerful reducing agent in the smelting of iron from its ore. Thus, in the minds of those at Ironbridge, the Industrial Revolution began there in 1709. Although not all historians would agree with this date or even with the event, nearly every one would agree that we live in an urban-industrial society which is markedly different than any earlier societies anywhere in the world.

Ironically, until recently, neither the men responsible for this revolution nor historians, with a few exceptions, have been concerned with the history of engineering or industry. These few notable exceptions, such as Sir Samuel Smiles, hardly constituted the rise of a subdiscipline of history. Happily, the history of technology has come of age since the Second World War and is now an established field of inquiry in history. This new concern for our industrial past has also given rise to the discipline of industrial archeology, which provides primary information for historians and essential material for those sites whose preservation is contemplated. Although this new field has not gained the respectability of either traditional history or archeology, it has attracted a truly interdisciplinary team of loyal supporters including professionals and amateurs from engineering, archeology, architecture, and especially historians. This fact in itself is significant. It provides a meaningful bridge between C. P. Snow's "two cultures."[1] Even more importantly, the future may well be shaped by our understanding of the past influence of technology on society. This understanding depends on the painstaking investigation of all phases of industry, including site investigation of intact remains. This latter activity is precisely what industrial archeology is all about.

Before attempting either to explain the origins of industrial archeology or to describe what archeologists do, it is appropriate to define the subject. R. A. Buchanan, one of Britain's leading historians of technology and of industrial archeology, has provided what is probably the most complete definition of this new branch of archeology:

> Industrial Archaeology is a field of study concerned with the investigation, surveying, recording and, in some cases, the preservation of industrial monuments. It aims, moreover, at assessing the significance of such monuments in the context of social and technological history.
>
> For the purpose of this definition 'industrial monument' should be interpreted very widely to include all sorts of relics of industrial processes and industrialization: it would take in, for example, the homes, public houses, and churches of industrial workers. 'Industrial monuments' may be of any date, although the implication of 'monument' is that they are obsolete or on the point of becoming obsolete. A Neolithic flint mine or a

Medieval harbour come within these terms of reference, although they are
normally covered by more conventional archaeology. The great bulk of the
material dates from the last two hundred years—the period of the continuing Industrial Revolution—and some of it may be very modern indeed.

The study is 'archaeological' in so far as it is related to tangible relics of
industrialization and to a careful examination of these. But unlike conventional archaeological studies, it also relies heavily upon documentary
material; of many varieties, and may thus be described as 'industrial history'
or 'industrial architecture' for parts at least of its activities. It is useful,
however, to retain the term 'archaeology' in conjunction with 'industry'
because it serves to remind its practitioners of the tangible basis of their
subject.[2]

This definition is the most comprehensive statement on industrial
archeology available and identifies the various activities which constitute
this new field as it is practiced not only in Britain but also in America and
elsewhere.

In order to see how industrial archeology fits into the larger discipline
of archeology it is well to quote J. P. M. Pannell, a mechanical engineer
who was one of the early leaders in industrial archeology in Britain:

O. G. S. Crawford, that great field archaeologist, appreciated that, as a
branch of anthropology, the subject of archaeology could not be confined
within dates or periods, but represented the study of man through the
physical remains of his past activities. If we accept this view, then industrial
archaeology becomes a subject rather than a chronological subdivision of
the main study—archaeology—and should include the archaeology of
industry in all periods of the past. As, however, archaeologists of prehistoric, classical, medieval and other periods have included industries of those
times in their studies, it has been accepted that industrial archaeology
started where the already established periods end, or at the beginning of
the Industrial Revolution.[3]

When Queen Victoria rode on the Great Western Railway from Windsor
to London, it was a symbolic seal of approval for the new technology. In
the same way Crawford not only places industrial archeology in the
context of the field but in so doing gives his seal of approval for the new
field and provides a vehicle to its acceptance in academia.

The field of classical archeology, or as some wag has said, "dirt"
archeology, in contrast to the industrial form, is also of comparatively
recent origin and yet it has won a secure place in academia. Few would
challenge its place in the social science disciplines or its close relationship
to ancient history. In fact, what we know of the ancient world is largely
the fruit of classical archeology. The earliest archeological investigations
were the handiwork of wealthy amateurs such as Heinrich Schliemann
(1822–1890) and Sir Arthur Evans (1851–1941). By the end of the
nineteenth century classical archeology had become a serious academic
discipline.

As V. Gordon Childe indicates in his introduction to archeology,
archeologists have become preeminent in the study of prehistoric man
and are thus often grouped with anthropologists rather than historians

in many universities.[4] With this emphasis on prehistoric societies some archeologists have insisted that for archeology to remain true to its origins, artifacts and monuments must be excavated. To this writer and to historic archeologists this appears to be an undue restriction on the entire field. To accept a broader view of the field, one must recognize monuments in terms of existing and often occupied buildings and other structures, relics in terms of machinery and other industrial "bits and pieces," and archival material in terms of company records, and view industrial processes as the source of primary historical data. Thus, we see that industrial archeology is closely related to historical archeology and shares many of its techniques.

Following World War II, with the loss of Empire and the need to play a new role in Europe, many in Britain sought to celebrate the nation's leading role in the Industrial Revolution by investigating and in selected cases preserving the physical remains of Britain's early industries and transportation systems. In the best British tradition industrial archeology sprang from groups of amateurs interested in specific local industries and particularly in canals and railways. The work of these local groups includes published histories and, increasingly, the preservation and restoration of industrial monuments. These activities include re-opening abandoned railway lines and restoring rolling stock, especially steam locomotives; and the restoration to operating condition of a variety of stationary steam engines used for pumping, milling, and as power sources for textile mills and factories. Perhaps the most impressive work has been and is devoted to the British canal system which had been largely abandoned by the twentieth century for commercial use. Now it appears that by the end of this century all of the primary canals, and many of the branch ones, will be functioning to provide a unique recreational resource. Since the war the British have pioneered the development of open air museums featuring historic industries as well as more traditional regional themes. Thus, we see a close connection between a nation-wide interest in Britain's role in the Industrial Revolution and the rise of industrial archeology and associated museums. Because of its local and amateur origins industrial archeology has had difficulty in establishing itself in universities, the notable exception being the joint program of the Ironbridge Gorge Museum and the University of Birmingham. With the field firmly rooted at the local level the formation of a national society was late in coming.

Industrial archeology in America was inspired by the British example but developed along quite different lines. Its development was begun at the Smithsonian Institution in Washington, D.C., by a group composed largely of professionals working in various phases of industrial archeology and often associated with government. This group formed the Society for Industrial Archeology (SIA).[5] Thus, the American development was not a "grass roots" movement and is still more national than local in its outlook and activities. The SIA has established chapters to provide an impetus to local activities. Typically, these activities include teams recording historic industrial sites, tours of regional industries, and guest speakers. The journal *IA* and the newsletter, together with the annual convention, have become hallmarks of the society. The SIA is the only national organization devoted entirely to industrial archeology and thus holds a unique position in the country. Other professional organizations have instituted industrial archeology, in a limited way, in their activities. In addition to these nonprofit professional organizations, several government programs (the most important are in the U.S. Department of the Interior) include the recording of industrial, transportation, and engineering works in their activities.

One of the government programs established under the New Deal was the Historic American Buildings Survey (HABS) of the National Park Service. In 1969 a tripartite agreement was signed by the National Park Service, the American Society of Civil Engineers, and the Library of Congress, which established the Historic American Engineering Record (HAER). This program was modeled after the HABS and was charged with recording historic engineering structures by preparing measured drawings, producing archival quality photographs, and writing histories. The results of these recording projects are lodged in a special collection in the Library of Congress. This highly professional approach to recording historic structures has secured for the United States a leading role in recording techniques of industrial archeology and indeed for historic structures in general. To celebrate the fiftieth anniversary of the founding of HABS during the Great Depression, a commemorative volume was published with a series of essays on the history of both HABS and HAER, together with a checklist of all the buildings, structures, and sites recorded by these two programs.[6] Thus, anyone interested in local industrial archeological sites should consult this checklist to determine if they have been recorded and what is available in the way of drawings, photographs, and other historical data. The entries are made under state and county headings.

With the passage of the 1966 National Historic Preservation Act, it is incumbent upon those responsible for historic properties threatened by new construction to submit a plan of how the adverse effects of changes in the site can be mitigated. Such studies are required of all projects involving federal funds. Many of these historic sites involve industrial structures and require the service of a skilled industrial archeologist. Often the mitigation agreement involves the preservation of the structure by recording it to HAER standards. If the structure is to be used adaptively, moved, or restored, then a field recording of the site and the structure represents a first step in preservation.

TECHNIQUES OF INDUSTRIAL ARCHEOLOGY

The techniques employed in industrial archeology are, perhaps, the best means of showing how historians can relate to this new discipline. The techniques discussed will also give insights into the field. Several books have been written on industrial archeology in general, or with a focus on a geographical region or on a particular industry.[7] Except for one or two British publications there is a dearth of published material on the techniques of industrial archeology.[8] This essay is not intended to fill this void but rather to give a general perspective on the techniques employed and the role of the public historian in this enterprise.

Inventories and Evaluation. Often the first step in an industrial archeological investigation is to complete an inventory on a thematic or geographical basis. One could, for example, develop an inventory of the sites of early iron furnaces in western Pennsylvania, locating the geographical coordinates of each site and noting the condition and extent of any remains, together with a brief history of each furnace. Carefully designed, detailed inventories can, therefore, provide useful information for economic and social historians as well as those interested in the history of technology. To be of optimum value an inventory should be done with the computer in mind. Unfortunately, there is no national information retrieval system established for industrial archeology, although HAER has developed a classification system which is useful for a wide range of inventories. All of their work uses this sytem. A number of inventories have been published by HAER and by other agencies, most notably those on historic bridges, which have been undertaken on a state by state basis.[9]

Historic Bridges As a Case Study. Inventories of historic bridges have served as the basis for developing evaluation and rating procedures which may serve as the model for other categories of historic industrial sites. Under the aegis of the Federal Highway Administration, state highway departments in cooperation with State Historic Preservation Offices have been urged to make inventories of their historic bridges. The survey of West Virginia's historic bridges was one of the first comprehensive state-wide surveys made and can serve as a case study of how industrial archeologists go about developing the inventory and evaluation of a large number of "monuments" or historic sites.[10]

Although the public readily accepts that an old building may have historic significance, with one or two exceptions this kind of acceptance is rarely accorded to old bridges. The notable exceptions are the famous structures such as the Brooklyn or Golden Gate bridges or the covered timber bridge which has won the hearts of legions of Americans because of its association with a romantic perception of our bucolic nineteenth-century past. Bridges are, however, important in understanding how the fabric of society is held together by transportation links. Because they represent an art form which depends on major commitments on the part of the public of its resources, these structures are an integral part of the social history of cities, states, and even the nation.

Because they represent a case of pure structure in that their only function is to carry loads, quite unlike a building, bridges represent a way to trace the development of engineering ideas in the building arts, unencumbered by architectural or other requirements which tend to influence structural form in buildings.

Bridge building is an art form in that it is a creative activity on the part of the builders, whether they be craftspeople or engineers. Conception, design, and construction are the sequences in building a bridge, while science is the handmaiden of this process. Hence, like other art forms there is not a unique solution for a given bridge site but, rather, many possibilities based upon a number of factors, some of which are clearly nontechnical.

Following the Civil War in the United States a new approach to bridge building was introduced on a wide scale, namely, the catalogue bridge produced by companies in which standardized designs were prefabricated and promoted through the use of catalogues.[11] Unlike Sears, Roebuck and Company, the catalogues were used by salesmen to promote the "wares" of fabricating companies. The clients were usually cities and counties which were represented by elected officials who were expected to select a bridge design without benefit of any technical advice and upon the urgings of bridge company representatives.

Thus, the factors influencing the type, age, and distribution of historic bridges in West Virginia include geography, settlement patterns, industry, and such human factors as the proclivities of county courts and the sales acumen of bridge company representatives. West Virginia has a great diversity of these factors, with the result that each of the state's highway districts has its own unique distribution of historic bridges.

In dealing with a large number of historic structures such as bridges, a classification or taxonomy must be established for use in historical research, environmental impact studies, or for the development of a comprehensive historic preservation plan encompassing a county or even an entire state. The need is not just to classify historic structures but to develop an information retrieval system so that various kinds of information can be readily compiled. For example, in the case of bridges, one may wish to know how many Whipple (i.e., double-intersection Pratt) trusses are extant in West Virginia (see Figure 1). Equally likely, information may be required on all bridges built before 1850, or on all extant bridges built by a particular company. It should also be possible to retrieve information on a geographical basis by cities, counties, and highway districts.

Preservationists regularly evaluate historic data in preparing nominations for the National Register of Historic Places, writing preservation plans, and in interpreting historic sites. The historian's primary concern is not in amassing data from the past, but in evaluating historic facts in order to write meaningful history. Preservationists are, however, often reluctant to use an evaluation as the basis for establishing a rating system which would identify which historic structures should be preserved, claiming that such criteria must be highly subjective and therefore of limited utility. In addition, many preservationists maintain that each structure is unique and therefore must be treated on an individual basis. These arguments are most appropriate for "high style" architecture such as Mount Vernon or Monticello. This view would also be applicable to the world's great bridges, such as the Eads Bridge of St. Louis, the Brooklyn Bridge, and the Wheeling Suspension Bridge, which are unique.

The "uniqueness" argument for each historic structure is a position that

Figure 1. Whipple truss bridge, 1887, by the Columbia Bridge Company. *Photograph courtesy of Emory L. Kemp.*

is quite inappropriate when trying to establish a historic preservation plan for bridges on a state-wide basis. In West Virginia alone there are more than 4,000 bridges potentially eligible for the National Register of Historic Places on the basis of being at least fifty years old. A rating method is essential to the development of a historic preservation plan. A comprehensive rating procedure must include the historicity, i.e., the historic significance of the bridge and site, together with an evaluation of its aesthetic qualities. The decision to preserve a given bridge must also rest on the compatibility of the bridge with modern safety requirements for strength, alignment, and clearance. While the age of a historic structure can be dealt with in a straightforward manner, evaluating its aesthetic qualities is necessarily a subjective matter, at least in part. A number of states have developed evaluation methods, shown in Tables 1 and 2, which have been taken from a report on bridge inventories and rating methods prepared for the National Transportation Research Board.

Perhaps the most difficult task is to develop and implement a plan which will preserve an appropriate number of historically significant bridges. The implications of the term "historic preservation" do not mean that every old bridge in the state is to be restored to its original pristine condition. Full restoration is not justified for many historic

Table 1. Parameters of numerical rating systems. Source: Chamberlin, William P. *Historic Bridges—Criteria for Decision Making*, National Cooperative Highway Research Program Report 101, Transportation Research Board, National Research Council (Washington, D.C., 1983), 18.

	Hawaii	Michigan[b]	N. Carolina	Ohio	Virginia	W. Virginia	Wisconsin
Limiting date	1940	1936	None	1941	1932	1933	1936
Scale range (pts.)	27	100	26	100	27	41	100
Standard (min. pts.)							
National Register eligible	19	50	15	None yet	20	26	Not used[c]
Possibly eligible	10	35	—	None yet	10	18	Not used
Applicability	All bridges	Metal trusses	Metal trusses[d]	All bridges	Metal trusses	All bridges	Metal trusses
Implementation							
National Register eligible	Not appl'd.	Not appl'd.	13	Not appl'd.	9	In progress	NA[c]
Possibly eligible	Not appl'd.	Not appl'd.	41	Not appl'd.	39	In progress	NA
Not eligible[e]	Not appl'd.	Not appl'd.	196	Not appl'd.	465	In progress	NA

[a]Current as of December 31, 1981.
[b]Proposed only.
[c]Used only to rank within bridge type categories.
[d]Exclusive of deck trusses and movable bridges.
[e]Reserved for future consideration.

Table 2. Evaluation factors in numerical rating systems stated or implied. Source: Chamberlin, William P. *Historic Bridges—Criteria for Decision Making*, (same as Table 1), 19.

Factor	H.I.	Mich.	N.C.	Ohio	Va.	W. Va.	Wis.
A. *INTRINSIC*							
1. Builder identified on bridge	x	x	x	x	x	x	x
2. Construction date identified on bridge	x	x	x	x	x	x	x
3. Patented elements	x	x	x	x	x		
4. Ornamental features	x	x	x	x	x	x	x
5. Distinctive/artistic structural details	x	x	x	x	x	x	x
6. Unusual materials	x	x	x	x	x	x	
7. Structural integrity	x	x	x	x*	x	x	x
8. Materials integrity							
9. Number of spans	x	x	x	x	x	x	x
10. Span length	x	x	x	x	x	x	x
11. Height	x						
B. *EXTRINSIC-HISTORICITY*							
1. Builder known, and significance	x	x	x	x	x	x	x
2. Construction date known, and significance	x	x	x	x	x	x	x
3. Rarity at present	x	x	x	x	x	x	
4. Typicality in its time	x	x	x		x	x	
5. Site significance	x	x	x	x	x	x	x
6. Association with events/persons	x	x	x	x	x	x	x
C. *EXTRINSIC-ENVIRONMENTAL QUALITY*							
1. Structure esthetics						x	
2. Site esthetics	x	x	x	x	x	x	x
3. Site integrity	x	x	x	x	x	x	x
4. Site accessibility	x						
5. Vantage quality	x						
D. *EXTRINSIC-PRESERVATION POTENTIAL*							
1. Condition				x			x
2. Route compatibility						x	
3. Bypass Potential				x			
4. Maintenance Difficulty				x			
E. *ENDEMIC*							
1. Local designer/builder		x					
2. Geographic distribution			x*				
3. Oldest/longest		x*				x	

*Not considered in first instance

bridges, but this does not mean a historic bridge must be replaced. It can be upgraded, in many cases, to meet modern highway requirements without compromising the historic fabric of the structure. Upgrading historic structures, especially bridges, is a specialized field requiring a great sensitivity to the historic fabric of the bridge, while at the same time satisfying the engineers' traditional concern for the safety of the public. Among the most popular means of upgrading a bridge is to replace the deck with one of similar appearance but with more strength and stiffness than the decks of early truss bridges which are usually the weakest elements. Other techniques are used for timber and concrete bridges and for other structural forms. In those cases where a historic bridge must be removed in the wake of route relocation or because it is functionally obsolete, one of the mitigating factors in an environmental impact study would be to record the structure with an appropriate set of measured drawings, photographs, and a history of the structure. This type of recording is central to the practice of industrial archeology and is discussed in more detail below.

The rating system developed for the West Virginia study has three broad categories: historicity, technological significance, and environmental quality of the bridge and its site (see Tables 1 and 2). Evolving through a series of trial methods and discussions with members of the West Virginia Department of Culture and History and the West Virginia Department of Highways, the system was further refined through presentations at a series of national, regional, and state meetings.

Applied to bridges in West Virginia, the method appears sound for identifying those of such historical merit (rating in the top 3 percent) that they are eligible for the National Register of Historic Places and also those of little historic or aesthetic merit (in the lower 88 percent), which can be replaced if required. The method also provides a basis for judgment on the level of preservation of bridges which have some historical or aesthetic qualities (ratings in the next highest level amounting to 9 percent) but do not merit individual listing on the National Register of Historic Places, although they may be included in a historic district.

If properly organized, local historical societies and other voluntary groups with historical interests can undertake inventories which can make valuable contributions to our understanding of particular industries or geographical areas. Inventories appear to be the kind of activity that can involve both amateur and professional historians/industrial archeologists in meaningful projects.

Written and Graphic Records. Like historical archeologists, but unlike prehistoric archeologists, those engaged in industrial archeology use written records. They constitute a special kind of relic. The use of the written record is "stock in trade" for traditional historians. In the case of preparing a written account of a specific site, one needs to peruse company records and accounts; public records in city, county, and state archives; newspapers; magazines; engineering journals; patent records; specifications; plans; trade catalogues; photographs; etchings; and paintings. Many of these sources will be familiar to historians involved in research and writing of local and regional histories and will not be elaborated here. One should note, however, that in public records it may be necessary to peruse the minutes of the town meeting or county commissioners' minute books regarding the need and later the approval for building a bridge or other public works. Deed records can prove fruitful sources for information on the establishment of industries as well as for right-of-way information for streets and roads. In the case of highways, every state maintains a file on each bridge in the system. In those states with county and township roads and bridges, similar records can be found at the local level. In such archives one often finds a treasure trove of material on early canals, turnpike roads, and industries. The records of the Board of Public Works and the early turnpike roads in the Virginias, held by the Virginia State Library, are a notable example of such archival holdings.[12] These sources provide important information in preparing a site history which gives details of the specific site but in the context of the technological and social history of the period.

No site should be recorded without a search for written and graphic records to establish the significance of the site and the most important artifacts one should seek. Thus, study of the written and/or graphic record can give valuable insights into industrial processes and in identifying unique features of design which are important in understanding the history of technology.

Photographs are an essential part of the graphic record of an industrial site and reveal information which cannot be easily obtained by any other method. In the first place, old photographs can provide information on the original appearance of a structure or machine, which aids considerably in historical research as well as in restoration work. The dinky steam engine and lary car charging a coke oven is a fine example of a period photograph which helps to document not only a specific site but also the early history of the coke industry in America (see Figure 2).

In the case of recording a structure for full restoration, the approach and level of documentation are quite different than simply preparing a contextual history of a site. Detailed information on all aspects of the structure are needed if an authentic restoration is to result. This means answering qustions on the correct lighting fixtures, doorknobs, cast iron shutters, and marble mantelpieces for fireplaces as an example. It is here that the work of the industrial archeologist in recording and interpreting a structure overlaps with the preservationist's activities in preparing plans, specifications, contract drawings, supervising the restoration work, and determining how the restored edifice is to be interpreted to the public. Public historians can be involved in both phases of restoration and make a major contribution to a project.

The Wheeling Custom House, under construction from 1856 to 1859, provides a fine example of the kind of information required by the public historian for a "full" restoration project carried out to the highest

Figure 2. Dinky steam engine and lary car charging coke ovens, ca. 1880. *Photograph courtesy of R. M. Vogel stereo card collection.*

standards. In the 1850s the United States Treasury Department under-took the construction of ten custom houses from New Orleans to New England. Located at ports of entry, including the inland ports of Wheeling and Chicago, these buildings served, as do our modern-day federal buildings, not only for the customs service, but also as central post offices and the location of federal courts. Because of the ever present danger of fire in American cities and factories at the time, resulting from the widespread use of timber frame and wood siding construction, it was decided to use the latest construction techniques and to erect a building that was "fireproof." These custom houses were also to be of substantial construction befitting a federal building. In order to provide a fire resistant building, cast and wrought iron were substituted for traditional interior timber framing. Brick arches supported on iron beams replaced the usual wood floors and joists so that the amount of wood in the building was reduced to floorboards, interior doors, and trim. The exterior walls were stone and all of the window frames and shutters and exterior doors were of cast iron. It was thought that even if the entire town of Wheeling burnt to the ground, the Custom House

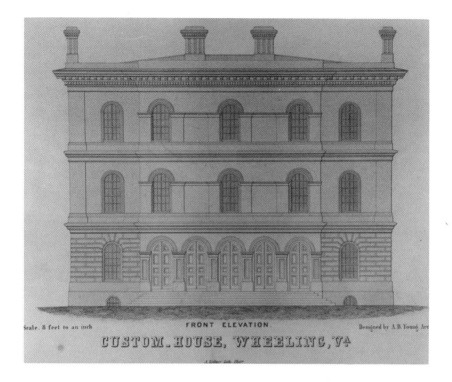

Figure 3. A. B. Young's elevation of the Wheeling Custom House, ca. 1854.
Photograph courtesy of West Virginia Independence Hall Foundation.

and its contents would survive. Thus, the Wheeling Custom House and
its sister buildings represent one of the earliest examples of the type of
construction which would lead in America to the skeletal iron framed
skyscraper.

The engineering work was under the direction of Capt. A. H.
Bowman, and A. B. Young, the first architect of the United States
Treasury, was the chief architect. Young produced a series of refined
and carefully detailed custom houses all done in what was called the
Italianate style (better known now as Renaissance Revival). An illustration prepared by Young is shown in Figure 3. Thus, the building is of
considerable historic significance from both the architectural and engineering points of view. To this significance one can add that it was the
birthplace of West Virginia in 1863. These were compelling reasons why
the building should be restored. The original set of illustrations and
drawings, together with a wealth of written material, which have
survived at the National Archives in Washington, D.C., and in collections
in Wheeling and elsewhere, have enabled a team of preservationists to
restore the building accurately. As an example, none of the original light
fixtures survived, but illustrations of them were located so that exact

Figure 4. Detail of replica gas lighting fixture, courtroom, Wheeling Custom House. *Photograph courtesy of West Virginia Independence Hall Foundation.*

replicas could be produced. A reproduction gas wall fixture mounted in the federal courtroom is an example of restoration work accurately done based upon painstaking historical research (see Figure 4).

With the advent of the tape recorder, oral histories of persons who worked in industries which are now obsolete can be invaluable in interpreting the artifacts discovered and recorded on site. A tape depository for oral histories pertaining to the careers of civil engineers has been established by the Smithsonian Institution and the American Society of Civil Engineers and another oral history series has been established by the Public Works Historical Society.[13] Oral histories of those who labored in mines and factories need to be made and those oral histories already in archives need to be made more readily available to industrial archeologists. There is a chronic problem of historical materials in archives not being readily available to industrial archeologists, preservationists, and historians of science and technology because the information they seek is seldom indexed under headings that are useful to them. A good case in point is a rich collection on the life of a leading Victorian engineer whose professional work is catalogued under the headings of those with whom he corresponded during his career.

In many cases the most important aspect of a given industrial site is the industrial process and not the buildings which housed the production. Wherever such processes have lingered beyond the period in which they flourished, cinematography (i.e., motion picture films and videotapes) has an important role to play. Grist milling, cut nail making, casting iron, sawing lumber, producing cut glass, or coking coal are all worthy subjects to be recorded on film. These latter two industries have been recorded as part of a HAER/West Virginia Survey and are available from HAER.[14]

Site Recording. The importance of actual on-site recording cannot be overemphasized. In the context of archeology in general, it is appropriate to quote V. Gordon Childe, former director of the Institute of Archaeology, University of London:

> The public, I suspect, still thinks of monuments as ivyclad ruins and isolated blocks of stone, carved or inscribed. To many, relics are single coins or flint implements, turned up in ploughing or ditching, if not personal mementoes—a button from Prince Charlie's vest, the joint of a martyr's toe, a tooth of Buddha. None of these, least of all the last group, are likely to be significant archaeological data. To have a meaning that an archaeologist can hope to decipher, an object must be found in context.[15]

Thus, the result of site recording is to generate primary sources which are the "building blocks" for the historian, or the fundamental data needed when one is contemplating full restoration, adaptive reuse of a structure, or merely the preparation of a nomination for the National Register of Historic Places. The artifacts located and the monuments measured must not only be recorded in "context" as suggested by Childe, but the industrial archeologist has to have a very clear idea of what is to be recorded and the detail of the recording necessary to achieve the goals of the project.

A series of photographs of a historic building may be sufficient for listing in the National Register but would hardly be sufficient for the preparation of contract drawings and specifications for the restoration of the same building. Even the types of photographs and measured drawings will vary depending on the intended use. Most of the measured drawings produced by HABS were intended to be illustrative and used in publications or for gallery or museum exhibitions.[16] Such an approach may fall short in providing the kind of information a historian of technology is seeking.

In order to place the archeological data gleaned from a site in proper context, the first activity on site should be the preparation of a site map to an appropriate scale if one is not available. Site maps can be prepared by using a plane table and alidade, transit, and level or aerial photographs.

Measured drawings and photographs should be viewed as complementary ways of obtaining data from a historic site. In fact, photographic techniques can be used to produce measured drawings. Under controlled conditions, discussed below, both techniques can produce graphic representations which are to scale and can be used to obtain the dimensions of an artifact or archeological monument.

Measured drawings are closely related to the more familiar architect's or engineer's plans with the notable exception that they are prepared from measurements obtained from extant structures or artifacts. The

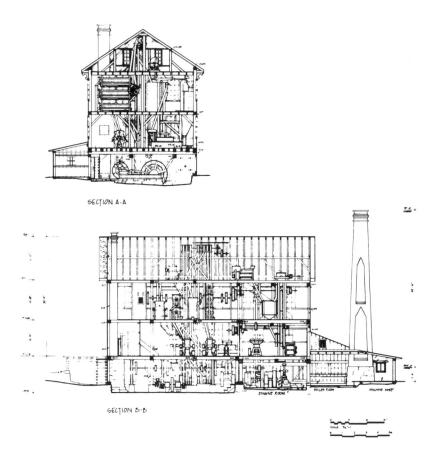

Figure 5. Historic American Engineering Record drawing of the Easton Roller Mill, ca. 1870. *Photograph courtesy of the Historic American Engineering Record/West Virginia Survey.*

traditional means of preparing measured drawings is to obtain the dimensions from the structure by hand in the form of field notes and sketches. These are then used as the data for the preparation of the measured drawings. If they are done to HAER/HABS standards, the final drawings are in Indian ink on specially produced plastic sheets sold under the trade name Mylar. For the traditional measured drawing intended for the Library of Congress, state archives or exhibition purposes, there is a strong emphasis on the aesthetic quality of the resulting drawing and a de-emphasis on dimensions and details. The longitudinal cross-sectional drawing of the Easton Roller Mill was prepared as part of the HAER/West Virginia Survey and is indicative of HAER quality drawings (see Figure 5). Measured drawings are rather like maps of a structure, showing details and dimensions in both horizontal and vertical planes. They can depict floor plans, cross sections, and details of architectural and/or engineering features which cannot be photographed. In the case of floor plans it would be necessary to remove the entire structure above the floor to be studied if a camera were to be employed to produce the plans which are routinely done based on hand measuring.

Photogrammetry has been used extensively in aerial photography to produce topographic maps, i.e., those which show contour lines to represent elevations. Thus, photogrammetry in the modern sense is a technique which measures three dimensions photographically. The underlying principles can, perhaps, be best elucidated by referring to the old-fashioned stereograph in which a pair of images can seem to produce a single three-dimensional picture when viewed through a stereograph. Thus, instead of taking one photograph of an object, two photographs are taken, either with two cameras or by one camera from two different positions, so that the resulting photographs overlap. This "stereo pair" can not only be viewed in a stereograph so that the observer can see in three dimensions, but it is possible, by knowing certain distances, to produce a map or drawing in which the three dimensions can be measured. Photogrammetry thus finds its most extensive applications in mapping. This technique can be adapted to close range work and applied to archeological artifacts. In a recent publication, Paula A. C. Spero demonstrates the versatility of the close range photogrammetry by producing measured drawings of bridges, buildings, tunnels, and canals, all the "real stuff" of industrial archeology.[17] The stereo photographs are used in a plotter to produce a map or measured drawing. Until recently this work was done by skilled operators, but it is now possible to complete finished drawings on a fully automated plotter.

A single example, while not being sufficient to illustrate the technique in detail, can provide an insight into how the method works and of its potential for recording historic sites. The Cunningham House, ca. 1830s plus later additions, is owned by the U.S. Army Corps of Engineers and is part of a historic area at the Burnsville Reservoir in central West Virginia. As part of a study of the house and the development of a site interpretation plan, measured drawings were required of all four elevations. The sequence was to photograph the house with a matched pair of cameras mounted on a range bar of known length between cameras. Targets for control dimensions were mounted on the house and stereo photographs made of the sides and ends of the house. A typical photograph of the house is shown in Figure 6a. A first run on the plotter produced preliminary drawings which were reviewed by the recording team, with corrections, alterations, and additions marked on a copy of the drawing. The preliminary results are shown in Figure 6b, complete with notes. The corrections were made so that the final finished drawings were made of the structure the way it should appear when restored. In Figure 6c the finished drawing of the front elevation is shown based on the photograph shown in Figure 6a. The photography was completed in a few hours and the rest of the work done in the

Figure 6a. Cunningham House: front elevation, photographed with a Wild C120 stereo metric camera by Hans Muessig. Recording done under contract from U.S. Army Corps of Engineers—Huntington District. *Photograph courtesy of Dennett, Muessig & Assoc. Ltd.*

office of the consultants. The results are much more accurate than hand measurements, more quickly obtained, and show both the extant structure and scale drawings of the house as it will appear after restoration. These final drawings can be used as part of the contract documents for the project as well as for permanent exhibits at the site. In addition to the drawings, the photographs are on glass plate negatives so that drawings of the Cunningham House could be made a century hence if required. Close-range photogrammetry is a powerful tool in the arsenal of the industrial archeologist and should find increasing application in site recording because it is a rapid, versatile method, and economical compared to the time-honored method of hand measurements.[18] With aerial photographs site maps can be easily prepared to any convenient scale. For small sites these photographs can be taken from portable towers or even tethered balloons.

For recording sites photographically, large format cameras are preferred. The standard is a 4-by-5-inch view camera in which the front lens can be moved vertically to correct any distortions which might occur in photographing a building. Public history students at West Virginia University are shown in Figure 7 receiving instructions on archival

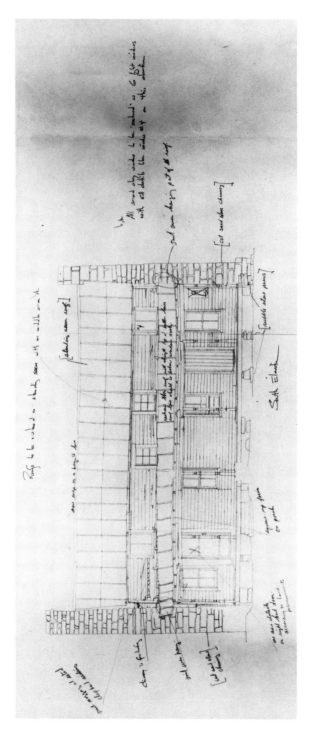

Figure 6b. Preliminary drawing of Cunningham House: front elevation, plotted on a Wild A40 autograph. *Photograph courtesy of Dennett, Muessig & Assoc. Ltd.*

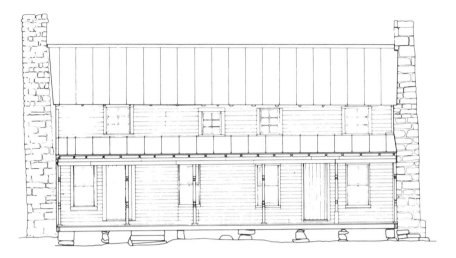

Figure 6c. Finished drawing of Cunningham House: front elevation, plotted on a Wild A40 autograph. *Photograph courtesy of Dennett, Muessig & Assoc. Ltd.*

quality photographs from William Edmund Barrett, a noted photographer of industrial structures. The camera shown is a 4-by-5-inch view camera. Barrett's skill with the equipment is shown in Figure 8, which depicts the coking of coal at Bretz, West Virginia. In connection with the West Virginia bridge study, a series of photographs were taken of those bridges of particular historic significance. The bridge in Figure 1 is an 1887 Whipple, more correctly designated a double intersection Pratt, truss by the Columbia Bridge Company and was taken with a view camera. Large format and even 35mm cameras are suitable for making measured drawings, without the capability of measuring depth, by carefully noting the position of the camera with reference to the subject and placing a control dimension on it in the form of targets or a surveyor's stadia rod. The same technique can be used to photograph details to provide dimensions for measured drawings.[19]

In the absence of large format cameras, 35mm and other popular cameras can be used. For detailed photographic coverage in connection with restoration work the 35mm format is ideal because of its versatility and ease of operation. Because color film is not stable over a long period of time, only black and white film is acceptable in most archives.

Finished Product. Thus, complete site recording involves the writing of a history of the site based upon archival research, the preparation of a site map, measured drawings, and archival photographs, and, in some cases, oral histories and motion pictures or videotapes. These constitute the finished product. Field notes, written and graphic material, and artifacts are the raw material for the recording; they are a valuable archive in themselves and should be preserved. What sites to record and the level of recording are often determined by inventories and associ-

Figure 7. William E. Barrett and public history students with a 4-by-5-inch view camera. *Photograph courtesy of William Seymour, photographer.*

ated evaluation. Preservation and historic site interpretation are closely related to the activities of industrial archeologists.

CONCLUSIONS

Many historians have chosen not to specialize in the history of technology while at the same time recognizing its pervasive influence on the history of the Western world, at least on the past two centuries. This reluctance is in part the result of a lack of readily available source material and a need to understand the technical or engineering details of the subject. Industrial archeology can enrich archival sources for the history of technology by providing archeological evidence from historic sites.

If, however, the results of site recording are to be meaningful to historians, preservationists, and those seeking to interpret historic sites and artifacts, the historian must play a central role in site recording as part of a multidisciplinary team. The historian's judgment is needed to determine the salient features which need to be recorded and how the results are to be presented to obtain optimum value for the effort

Figure 8. Coke making at Bretz, West Virginia, photographed by William E. Barrett. *Photograph courtesy of Historic American Engineering Record / West Virginia Survey.*

expended. If historians are to provide leadership in a recording team, they will have to be familiar with the methodology and techniques of recording industrial sites and industrial processes. The techniques needed in site recording have successfully been taught to public history students, who have applied these newly acquired skills to a number of research projects.

In addition to a role of leadership in site recording, the historian's traditional skills are essential to any industrial archeological recording project: in archival research, data evaluation, and the preparation of histories which are not only a detailed narrative of a specific site, but one which is in the context of the broader issue of the history of technology and appropriate social history.

NOTES

1. C. P. Snow, *The Two Cultures and a Second Look* (Cambridge, England: Cambridge University Press, 1969).
2. R. A. Buchanan's definition of industrial archeology was supplied to the

author by Robert M. Vogel, Curator of the Mechanical and Civil Engineering Collection, Smithsonian Institution.

3. J. P. M. Pannell, *Techniques of Industrial Archaeology* (Newton Abbott, England: David and Charles, 1966), 9.

4. V. Gordon Childe, *A Short Introduction to Archaeology* (New York: Collier Books, 1968, third printing).

5. Information on the Society for Industrial Archeology can be obtained by writing to Society for Industrial Archeology, Room 5020, National Museum of American History, Smithsonian Institution, Washington, D.C. 20560. See the Directory of Resources and Organizations at the end of this book for further information.

6. The Historic American Buildings Survey and the Historic American Engineering Record, *Historic America: Buildings, Structures, and Sites*, (Washington, D.C.: Library of Congress and the U.S. Government Printing Office, 1983).

7. The Society for Industrial Archeology has produced a bibliography of works in English on industrial archeology (Society for Industrial Archeology, *An Introductory Bibliography in Industrial Archeology [English Language]*, (Washington, D.C.: Society for Industrial Archeology, n.d.).

8. A limited number of introductory books have been published on the techniques employed by industrial archeologists. The works by Major and Pannell are intended for the amateur and represent the development of the field in Britain. The work by McKee and the HAER field guide are intended for use by summer recording teams. See Historic American Engineering Record, *Field Instructions* (Washington, D.C.: HAER, Heritage Conservation and Recreation Service, n.d.); Harley J. McKee, *Recording Historic Buildings*, (Washington, D.C.: Historic American Buildings Survey, U.S. Department of the Interior, Government Printing Office, 1970); J. Kenneth Major, *Fieldwork in Industrial Archaeology* (London: B. T. Batsford, Ltd., 1975); and J. P. M. Pannell, *Techniques of Industrial Archaeology*.

For further information, see, also, Emory L. Kemp and Theodore A. Sande, *Historic Preservation of Engineering Works* (New York: American Society of Civil Engineers, 1981), 70. Papers particularly related to recording engineering structures are Emory L. Kemp, "The Fundamentals of Preservation through Recording"; Joel Kobelin, "Report on the Development of Close Range Photogrammetry Educational Technician Program"; and Kathleen Hoeft, "Measured Drawings of Engineering Works."

9. A listing of all the published HAER surveys is given in Robert E. Haynes and Kenneth T. Pribanic, *A Bibliography of Historic Preservation* (Washington, D.C.: Office of Archaeology and Historic Preservation, National Park Service, 1977). Information on inventories and evaluation methods for historic bridges can be found in William P. Chamberlin, *Historic Bridges— Criteria for Decision-Making* (Washington, D.C.: Transportation Research Board, National Research Council, 1983).

10. Emory L. Kemp, *West Virginia's Historic Bridges*, (Charleston, W. Va.: West Virginia Department of Highways, 1984).

11. The various truss types can be identified by referring to T. Allan Comp and Donald Jackson, "Bridge Truss Types: A Guide to Dating and Identifying," AASLH Technical Leaflet 95, May 1977.

A discussion of bridge companies and catalogue bridges can be found in Emory L. Kemp, *West Virginia's Historic Bridges*.

12. The Virginia State Library in Richmond has published an inventory of the collections associated with the Virginia Board of Public Works. See John S.

    Salmon, *Board of Public Works Inventory* (Richmond: Virginia State Library, 1978).

13. Both the American Society of Civil Engineers and the Public Works Historical Society have developed oral history programs that feature interviews with leading engineers. Information on these programs can be obtained from the Committee on the History and Heritage of American Civil Engineering, c/o American Society of Civil Engineers, 345 East 47th Street, New York, NY 10017; and the Public Works Historical Society, 1313 East 60th Street, Chicago, IL 60637.

14. In connection with the HAER / West Virginia Survey, two films were made to record industrial processes. They are *Coke Making at Bretz, West Virginia* and *Glass Making at Seneca*. For rental and purchase information contact HAER, National Park Service, Department of the Interior, Washington, D.C.

15. V. Gordon Childe, *A Short Introduction to Archaeology*, 11.

16. Harley J. McKee, *Recording Historic Buildings*, 21–23.

17. The work by Spero gives a brief introduction to the history and fundamentals of close-range photogrammetry, which is followed by a number of examples; see Paula A. C. Spero, *The Photogrammetric Recordings of Historic Transportation Sites* (Charlottesville, Va.: Virginia Highway and Transportation Council, 1983).

18. Further information on close-range photogrammetry can be found in Perry E. Borchers, *Photogrammetric Recording of Cultural Resources* (Washington, D.C.: Technical Preservation Services Division, Office of Archaeology and Historic Preservation, National Park Service, 1977).

19. A method of photodocumentation and the preparation of working drawings for industrial archeologists and others associated with the building arts is given in: J. Henry Chambers, *Rectified Photography and Photo Drawings for Historic Preservation* (Washington, D.C.: Technical Preservation Services Division, Office of Archaeology and Historic Preservation, National Park Service, 1975).

Lige Benton Miller, Jr., is a museum exhibit planner with the U.S. National Park Service, assigned to the Harpers Ferry Center at Harpers Ferry, West Virginia. In the normal course of a year, he will visit a dozen or so sites, each in various stages of exhibit development. He has served on the initial "ice-breaking" teams, at which times ideas are discussed and themes explored, and has participated in the final design process as the finished project goes off for fabrication. He is president of a local history organization which undertook the total restoration of a tavern and hotel. He has been involved in exhibit planning and research for a decade and finds the field "ever-expanding and filled with new experiences."

HISTORY ON THE DRAWING BOARD: THE HISTORIAN AS DEVELOPER OF INTERPRETIVE MEDIA

Lige Benton Miller, Jr.

INTRODUCTION

Visitors come to historic sites to learn about the past, to track down a detail of particular interest. Those who work at these sites hope all visitors will learn at least a little history before they leave. Thus, one of the more exciting applications of the historical profession is the selection, arrangement, and presentation of material to be conveyed to the public at these sites.

The story of any public place that is visited on a regular basis is a story that in the telling becomes modified, often reflecting the interests of many, taking on a new life of its own and becoming a part of history. In the forward movement, it can carry the errors of past efforts, misplace emphasis, or fail to do justice to the deeper meaning of the site. It can echo anecdotes that have hovered about the scene for years or introduce insights and observations that enhance the overall quality of the site visitation to both the casual and scholarly visitor.

The historian interpreting a historic site must give meaning to a physical part of the past. While not being able to bring the past to life, the historian can give life to the past by making its ideas and experiences useful to the contemporary visitor. This can be a challenging objective. Several sites within the National Park Service can provide case studies to illustrate these challenges and opportunities.

Antietam National Battlefield in western Maryland, for example, presents a pleasing and pastoral image to the modern visitor. Sturdy fieldstone and wire fences enclose pastures and cornfields. Stately granite monuments border the park road and appear unexpectedly on outcroppings of limestone rock. In the distance the smoky blue line of the Blue Ridge Mountains marks the horizon. This rural landscape could be from the last century, with the Victorian monuments adding a touch of solemnity to the scene. Indeed, great care and effort have been expended to preserve the land as it was on September 17, 1862, when Union and Confederate armies fought the Battle of Antietam across these rolling Maryland hills.

The scene during the battle, however, despite the careful preservation of the landscape, was dramatically different than it is today. Soldiers and witnesses did their best to describe it. Charles Carlton Coffin, a correspondent for the *Boston Journal,* wrote of the awesome sound, "It was no longer alone the boom of the batteries, but a rattle of musketry—at first like the pattering drops upon a roof; then a roll, crash, roar, and rush, like a mighty ocean billowing upon the shore, chafing the pebbles, wave on wave, with deep and heavy explosions of the batteries, like the crashing of thunderbolts." Confederate staff officer Lt. Col. A. S. "Sandie" Pendleton recalled, "shot and shell shrieking and crashing, canister and bullets whistling and hissing most fiend-like through the air until you could almost see them. In that mile's ride I never expected to come back alive." Union Corps Commander Maj. Gen. Joseph Hooker described the battlefield, "In the time that I am writing, every stalk of corn in the northern and greater part of the field was cut as closely as could have been done with a knife and the slain lay in rows precisely as they had stood in their ranks a few moments before." Sgt. Jacob Fryberger, Company K, 51st Pennsylvania Infantry, wrote his sister that "I have seen more than I ever expected to see. I have layed on the field in front of the enemy, where the dead and wounded were laying in heaps around us."[1]

These participants in the Battle of Antietam experienced an event that is difficult for us to imagine. The most devoted student of the Civil War might stop short of claiming that knowledge and imagination can retrieve the sights and sounds of this battle from the past. The historian cannot recreate the battle. The historian, of course, also knows that the Battle of Antietam was more than blood and shrieking shells; the battle was an event of great historical consequence. At Antietam, the Union Army halted a major Confederate invasion of the North. President Abraham Lincoln, wanting to appear to act from strength rather than weakness, seized the opportunity offered by this victory and issued the Emancipation Proclamation. Great Britain decided not to side with the slave-holding power and withheld diplomatic recognition of the Confederacy.

INTERPRETING HISTORIC SITES

The visitor to Antietam Battlefield deserves an explanation of the event that occurred there, and the historian has the responsibility to provide that explanation. The historian must interpret the battle, the place of the battle in the history of the Civil War, and the meaning of the Civil War to American history. While doing this, the historian also must enable the visitor to find a personal meaning in the events at Antietam on September 17, 1862.

In this example the National Park Service is the agency responsible for preserving Antietam National Battlefield and interpreting the events and consequences of the battle to visitors. The park service has two primary methods of interpretation of historic sites—one consists of personal interpretation provided by historians and interpreters who administer the site and communicate directly with the public. Personal interpretation can be the most effective method of communicating. It is, however, limited by the number of people the site can employ. Not every visitor can be contacted.

The other method of interpreting historic sites is to present interpretive media such as films, slide shows, exhibits, and publications. The park service assumes that each visitor will have the opportunity to view these media and that this will enhance the visitor's enjoyment, appreciation, and understanding of the historic site. For the National Park Service most interpretive media are developed at its Harpers Ferry Center in Harpers Ferry, West Virginia.[2]

The development of interpretive media for Antietam followed guidelines established by a planning document called an interpretive prospectus. It is used by a team of historians, administrators, and media specialists to design interpretive themes for the historic sites and to determine the media which can best present them to the public.

At Antietam, several media are used. A twenty-five minute film shown in the visitor center presents the consequences of the battle and focuses on Lincoln's visit there shortly after the battle. Scenes of the battle are realistically shown. The cost in human life and suffering is emphasized by Lincoln's visit to a field hospital. The film presents the great significance of the battle by showing how Lincoln used the opportunity of the Union victory to issue the Emancipation Proclamation.

The museum exhibits present the physical textures of the battle and concentrate on the personal experience of war. Original artifacts, photographs, drawings, and quotations are grouped to represent the stages of the battle. "Before the Battle" is represented by weapons and equipment in good condition. Photographs show rows of soldiers ready for battle. Quotations of the soldiers reveal the emotions of the men as the inevitable battle neared. "During the Battle" has drawings of the fighting, weapons, and equipment used in the battle, a saddle with a bullet in the pommel received during the battle, and quotations from the men who fought. The "Aftermath of Battle" shows broken muskets, fragments of artillery shells, and other equipment abandoned in the dust. Photographs of the dead at Antietam—some of the most dramatic taken during the Civil War—lend a special sense of grim reality. The survivors describe the fighting in words that are hard to believe. The exhibits use words, images, and objects to create an exciting experience for the visitor. Floor-level displays of artifacts fascinate children; the rich use of first person accounts of the battle intrigues adults.

Publications and panels also help interpret the site. A brochure given to each visitor is a guide to the battlefield. It contains a synopsis of the battle, some attractive period and modern graphics, and a map of the battlefield for use on the driving tour. On this tour, outdoor panel exhibits explain with words, maps, and graphics the events of the battle that occurred at a particular location. A few of the more important sites are the Dunkard Church, the Cornfield, Bloody Lane, and Burnside Bridge. At several stops, recorded audio messages narrate a description of the battle at those points. The outdoor exhibits and the brochure are the primary means of interpreting the tactics of the battle. Books and sales publications on the battle and other aspects of the Civil War are available for purchase at the Visitor Center.

EVALUATING THE SITE

It can be argued that the Battle of Antietam is being over-interpreted by the National Park Service. Visitors might wish to experience the battlefield using their own knowledge and drawing their own conclusions about what it represents. This is a question that a historian interpreting a historic site to the public must ask. The dilemma is that individual visitors range from Civil War buffs who make the Civil War their hobby, to military historians especially interested in troop move-

Figure 1. Battle of Antietam, 1862. Alexander Gardner photographed these Confederate soldiers killed in the Battle of Antietam. *Photograph courtesy of National Park Service.*

ments and battlefield tactics, to people whose knowledge of the Civil War is limited to the notion that the Rebels fought the Yankees and the slaves were freed. Children's needs and interests differ from those of any group of adults. Interpretation for children can be a separate field of expertise.

With all of these levels of knowledge and interest, the historian must consider the extent and depth of the interpretation and the degree of difficulty that can be explained. One consideration might be the ability of the historic site to communicate on its own. Antietam is a well-preserved battlefield. There are few modern intrusions to confuse the visitor. Even with this advantage, visitors may have more difficulty envisioning what happened there than they would have at a restored colonial town like Williamsburg or a western fort like Fort Larned in Kansas. A ruin of an iron furnace or a battlefield bordered by a shopping center might require a lengthy explanation of what the site represents.

Another consideration is the technical complexity of the story to be told. Antietam is a battle that was tactically simple, and the movements of the troops covered a small area. The Battle of Gettysburg, by contrast, occurred over a three-day period with the armies gaining and losing large areas of ground. This is a more difficult battle to understand and to interpret.

The historian must also evaluate the historical significance of the event, person honored, and historic structure. What is the significance of Antietam, Mount Vernon, Independence Hall, or the U.S.S. *Constitution?* The historian should be able to place the historic site in the overall sweep of history. This may be the real and lasting value of the site to historians and the public.

RESEARCH

The historian developing a film, brochure, or exhibit for a site like Antietam begins by researching the subject. Primary and secondary sources are read and evaluated. Historians who work at the site are interviewed about their knowledge of the site and the story that is presented to their visitors. The artifact collection is evaluated. Historic photographs, prints, and paintings are located and reviewed as possible resources.

It should be mentioned that the historian developing interpretive media may not have time to do original research. This may cause some frustration, but it may not be a real problem. In the National Park Service research historians write historic resources studies on individual sites, and these represent valuable sources that provide access to research based on primary sources. If a site has not been researched adequately, interpretation should be postponed until that work is done.

DEVELOPING A THEME

Developing a theme may be the historian's most difficult, demanding, and, ultimately, rewarding task. The historian knows the subject; the visitor presumably does not. The historian must distill a theme from a mass of original and secondary source material. This theme is the underlying or unifying idea that gives meaning to the historic site or event. The historical experience thus becomes an idea—a modern idea, a contemporary idea—with power to excite and to change our knowledge of the past and awareness of the present.

Mound City National Monument in Chillicothe, Ohio, for example, preserves burial mounds originally built by prehistoric people of the Hopewellian culture. A museum displaying a collection of exquisite burial artifacts is introduced by the theme statement, "Here an ancient people buried their honored dead in their own time and way." This recognition of a common human experience is the theme carried throughout the exhibits.

CURATORIAL RESPONSIBILITIES

Artifacts are the principal resource of the exhibit planner. Exhibits work best when they display artifacts. Locating and evaluating artifacts is a primary responsibility of the historian in developing this medium of interpretation because, like photographs or maps, artifacts can convey much more information than a simple verbal description. They are tangible reminders of the past.[3]

One of the most exciting exhibit projects in the park service has been the display of the Union gunboat U.S.S. *Cairo* and the thousands of artifacts recovered with it. The *Cairo* was sunk in 1862 by a Confederate mine (then called a torpedo) and lay submerged in the Yazoo River in Mississippi until it was raised in the early 1960s. The *Cairo* went down in less than three minutes. Although all of the sailors escaped drowning, they were able only to recover a few small items. The *Cairo* became a time capsule filled with cannons, projectiles, ship's stores, and sailors' personal items, including razors, photographs of their families, eyeglasses, and mess kits. Many of the artifacts, thanks to the thick Yazoo mud, were remarkably well preserved. Displayed in the U.S.S. *Cairo* Museum at Vicksburg National Historical Park, the collection of artifacts interprets the life of the men aboard the gunboat. Outside the museum the structure of the preserved gunboat is displayed. Illustrated plaques explain the mechanical operation and military function of the ironclad steamboat.

The historian has an ethical responsibility in displaying artifacts. The conservation of the artifact should be the first consideration. The artifact must be protected from deterioration, damage, or theft. If the preservation of the artifact cannot be guaranteed by all reasonable standards, the exhibit planner should consider displaying a reproduction or not using an artifact in that place. The artifact also must be

Figure 2. U.S.S. *Cairo*. The crew of the U.S.S. *Cairo* ran out the guns for this photograph taken in Cairo, Illinois, in early 1862. *Photograph courtesy of National Park Service.*

identified accurately. If the historian does not have expertise in the type of artifact being considered for display, a specialist in that field of material culture should be consulted. The historian also must have a good intellectual reason for including an artifact in the exhibit. The artifact should support the theme the exhibit and the historic site is presenting. Antiquity and interest are not sufficient reasons for displaying an artifact in an interpretive exhibit.

In addition, some artifacts have their own special magic that can never be replaced by words or reproductions. Big Hole National Battlefield in Montana is the site of a battle between the fleeing Nez Perce and soldiers of the U.S. Army. Displayed there on loan from the West Point Museum is the coat worn by Chief Joseph when he surrendered and vowed, "From where the sun now stands I will fight no more forever."

WORKING WITH OTHER PROFESSIONALS

The historian developing interpretive media works with professionals from other fields. The best product is often the result of a cooperative effort by designers, artists, architects, film makers, and subject-matter specialists. The historian may become the coordinator of a variety of creative efforts or serve as the specialist in the area under review.

Exhibit planners work closely with designers in producing exhibits, although there is no set formula by which this is done. Sometimes the exhibit planner will take the lead in determining the theme, story line, and content of the exhibit. At other times the designer may create a visual and spatial solution to an interpretive problem. In this case the historian may follow rather than lead (with an eye out for historical accuracy, of course). The Museum of Western Expansion at Jefferson National Expansion Memorial in St. Louis is an example of a museum that was a design solution for an interpretive exhibit. Artifacts, photographs, and words are used as symbols of the American progression westward. The Lewis and Clark expedition is emphasized. The use of design symbolism seems appropriate there since the museum is housed at the base of Eero Saarinen's great arch beside the Mississippi—the arch itself being a dramatic symbol.

Historians and artists also need to work together, for art can interpret history quite effectively. For an exhibit on John Brown at Harpers Ferry National Historical Park, artist Richard Schlect produced a drawing of Harpers Ferry in 1859, the year of Brown's raid on the U.S. Armory and Arsenal. The town had changed since 1859, and visitors had difficulty understanding the events of the raid. Even "John Brown's Fort"—the fire engine house—was in a new location. A historian, exhibit planner, and exhibit designer worked with the artist to recreate the nineteenth-century town in art. A large photographic enlargement of the art work is now displayed in the John Brown Museum and is a popular part of the exhibit.

A more symbolic piece of art was produced by sculptor Lloyd Lillie for Booker T. Washington Birthplace National Monument. This living farm in rural Virginia creates the environment that Booker T. Washington knew as a child during the 1850s and early 1860s. Lillie made a full-size sculpture of the boy Booker as a "child is father of the man" symbol of the slave boy who became a national figure.

Teamwork also is essential in creating appropriate publications. Writing a manuscript is only the beginning of the process of producing a book, handbook, or brochure. The historian working in the medium of print quickly becomes aware of the requirements of graphic designers, printers, mapmakers, typesetters, and photographers. The writer also learns that the appearance and readability of a publication is critical to its effectiveness. The ability to write well is a valuable tool in developing all interpretive media. Labels for exhibits, scripts for films, and text for books must interpret the subject clearly and concisely. The effectiveness of good museum design, skillful photography, or inspired graphic layout will always be enhanced by graceful expression.[4]

In the preparation of interpretive media, the historian may call on the expertise of historians who specialize in particular fields. The National Park Service, with many battlefields and forts in its system of parks, relies heavily on military historians to advise interpreters and media specialists. Historians with a knowledge of costume and material culture acquire and identify artifacts, make historic reproductions, and provide references for art depicting historical scenes.

Figure 3. Booker T. Washington statue. The boy, Booker—a sculpture of the young Booker T. Washington by Lloyd Lillie. *Photograph courtesy of National Park Service.*

Of course, you may not always work with people skilled in your area of interest. The historian and interpreter must develop personal communication skills in presenting ideas for media development to people with no background in history or interpretation. These people may be managers, administrators, directors, trustees, and supervisors. This may cause problems and inspire solutions. It is part of the specialist/non-specialist dichotomy that exists in every job situation.

CREATING THE PRODUCT

The historian who produces publications, makes films, or plans museum exhibits will soon encounter the word "creativity." It is the necessary element in creating an interpretive product. Despite individual variations in academic background, depths of research, and characteristics of the historic site, the historian creating a product faces the same dilemma as anyone who sits at a typewriter or word processor—a blank piece of paper and the problem of filling it.

Everyone has different combinations of skills to bring to the task of creating something. Everyone possesses varying amounts of originality, imagination, insight, perception, expressiveness, and organizational skills. The trick, and the excitement of the work, is to use one's abilities to create something of value for the client and the public. This is the source of the greatest satisfaction in the job.

NOTES

1. "Antietam Scenes," in *Battles and Leaders of the Civil War Based upon "The Century War Series"*, vol. 2, ed. Robert Underwood Johnson and Clarence Clough Buel (New York: The Century Co., 1884–1888), 683; Douglas Southall Freeman, *Lee's Lieutenants* (New York, 1946), 208; General Hooker's Report in U.S. War Department, *The Official Records of the Union and Confederate Armies*, series 1, vol. 19, part 1 (Washington, D.C.: U.S. Government Printing Office, 1887), 167; and Jacob Fryberger to sister, 6 October 1862, files of the National Park Service at Antietam National Battlefield.

2. Among the publications available on historic site interpretation and exhibits are: William T. Alderson and Shirley Payne Low, *Interpretation of Historic Sites* (Nashville: American Association for State and Local History, 1976); Frederick L. Rath, Jr., and Merrilyn Rogers O'Connell, eds., *Interpretation: A Bibliography on Historical Organization Practices*, vol. 3 (Nashville: American Association for State and Local History, 1978); Jay Anderson, *Time Machines: The World of Living History* (Nashville: American Association for State and Local History, 1984); Grant W. Sharpe, ed., *Interpreting the Environment* (New York: John Wiley & Sons, Inc., 1976); and Freeman Tilden, *Interpreting Our Heritage* (Chapel Hill: The University of North Carolina Press, 1957).

3. For further information, see Thomas Schlereth, *Artifacts and the American Past* (Nashville: American Association for State and Local History, 1980); Thomas J. Schlereth, *Material Culture Studies in America* (Nashville: American Association for State and Local History, 1982); Arminta Neal, *Exhibits for the Small Museum* (Nashville: American Association for State and Local History, 1976); and Arminta Neal, *Help! For the Small Museum* (Nashville: American Association for State and Local History, 1969).

4. Examples of good interpretive writing include Aldo Leopold, *A Sand Country Almanac* (New York: Oxford University Press, 1949); Edwin Way Teale, *Autumn Across America: A Naturalist's Record of a 20,000-Mile Journey through the North American Autumn* (New York: Dodd, Mead, 1956), with companion volumes by the same publisher entitled *Journey into Summer* (1960), *North with the Spring* (1951), and *Wandering through Winter* (1965); and Willa Cather's novels, including *Death Comes to the Archbishop* and *My Antonia*. Shelby Foote and Bruce Catton are excellent writers on the American Civil War. The Time/Life series entitled *The American Wilderness* also provides excellent interpretive articles. A simple guide to good writing may be found in William Strunk, Jr., and E. B. White, *The Elements of Style* (New York: Macmillan, 1959).

PART III:
THE PRACTICE OF
PUBLIC HISTORY

INTRODUCTION

Richard Scarry enjoys an international reputation as the writer and illustrator of children's books. His followers include many adults as well as children. One of his most popular books is entitled *What Do People Do All Day?* Through a series of marvelous illustrations, Scarry manages to explain to his young readers what the butcher, baker, and candlestick maker do for a living, and, indeed, what people do in nearly every occupation one might encounter in a small town. In much the same way the essays in *Part III: The Practice of Public History* cover a wide range of positions which, taken as a group, really do answer the question "What do public historians do all day?" In the absence of a Richard Scarry mural depicting the disparate activities of public historians, the context for the essays has been provided by grouping them under appropriate headings. These categories should provide a clearer idea of the role of public historians which could not be obtained by merely reading the essays at random. It is well to reiterate that these topic headings do not represent a definitive list of the type of work public historians do, but rather they are thought to be among the most important areas at the present time and in the near future.

The first category is museums, where historians have had a long tradition of employment. Although most Americans are familiar with the Smithsonian Institution as the home of the Star Spangled Banner, the Foucault pendulum, or even the John Bull locomotive, few have any idea of the nature and scope of activities carried on in the museum, much less the role of historians in this museum. Thus, Steven Lubar's essay is a welcome addition to the collected essays since it provides a thoughtful and penetrating picture of life in the "Nation's Attic" from the perspective of one of the staff historians. The essay can also serve as a case study of what one might expect to encounter in other federal museums.

Outdoor museums have enjoyed increasing public patronage in recent years, whether they be specialized in the subjects treated, such as the Mystic Seaport Museum or a railway museum, or set in the wider context of a period village. Interpretation is really the key to the success of such museums; this, in turn, is usually the responsibility of the historian. Thus, John Durel's essay on his experience at Strawbery Banke provides the reader with a detailed understanding of the historian's role in the design and operation of an interpretive program at a historic site which serves as a museum.

There are scores of local historical society museums across the country. Many are too small to have a paid professional historian and are run by part-time volunteers. Many historians have entered the museum world on a paid full-time basis by first serving as volunteers. There are, nevertheless, a number of museums of sufficient size and financial strength to have a fulltime staff. As Douglas Dolan indicates in his essay, "The Historian in the Local Historical Museum,"

> Traditionally, historians have gravitated to local historical museums and historical agencies as places of employment that utilized their skills as researchers and historians. From the onset, though, historians have had to develop new skills to augment their academic training and enable them to communicate a sense of the past to their audiences. These audiences may range from children to senior citizens, and they may come in contact with the museum either individually or as part of an organized activity. Each audience brings along its own set of perceptions of history and time. The challenge for historians is to discover the key that will enable them to make the transition between history as an abstraction to history as a meaningful experience for each audience group.

In part, the challenge is met by organizing workshops, lectures, and school programs as well as exhibits which one usually associates with such museums. In nearly all museums the historian functions as a manager, promoter, research historian, curator, fund-raiser, and interpreter. Historians have been involved in many roles in the museum world long before the term "public history" was coined. In a similar way, historical societies have been served by historians for decades.

As far as public history is concerned, the American Association for State and Local History stands in a unique position as a leader in supporting nonacademic history projects in association with museums, archives, historical societies, and, indeed, wherever historians have been busy bringing a sense of history to the public. Gerald George, executive director of AASLH, has prepared an important and thoughtful essay on the role of AASLH in the realm of public history and in so doing gives us a very real sense of both the history of his association and the recent discussion of public history within the organization which helped to shape its objectives, while at the same time it brought new perspectives on the nature of public history. This thought-provoking essay is complete with references to AASLH publications of particular interest to public historians as well as a history of AASLH from its origin in 1940 as a separate organization (the predecessor began in 1904) to the recent debate on the possible change of name for the organization which would better define its mission. The name was not changed, but the debate raised several important issues with regard to public history. As an explanation of one leading organization in the field, this essay should be of considerable interest to public historians.

It may appear to be a giant step from the debate on the possible change of name for AASLH to historians engaged in public projects, but such a step gives some measure of the variety of opportunities and concerns of public historians. In her essay, Cynthia Little describes an innovative program called "Philadelphia Moving Past," part of the

Philadelphia Century IV celebration, which successfully brought to Philadelphians a sense of the history of their city and neighborhood areas. It was very much the case of taking social history to the people by having mobile exhibits and programs in various city neighborhoods. One of the most popular and educational projects was on house history, in which local people could begin to trace the history of their own home.

In contrast to the urban environment of "Philadelphia Moving Past," George McDaniel writes of the educational benefits and enjoyment of audiences participating in a folklife festival in the South. Using cotton farming as an example, he explains that the audience was "not offered a simplified portrait of the past, but learned about issues historians grapple with in trying to decipher America's history." He further states:

> It is this combination of education and entertainment that make festivals a unique "classroom" for the teaching of history to the general public. By working with festival producers, many of whom are professional folklorists, historians can help ensure that festivals are more than nostalgic crafts demonstrations or old-time music concerts and that discussion and interpretation of historical issues which shaped the culture are interwoven throughout the event. These issues, such as race, class, gender, politics, and economics, manifest themselves in the work and life of everyday people, and by presenting folklife within the context of these issues, the historian can inspire thoughtful consideration by the public of these issues often taught in textbooks as apart from their personal or community life.

Thus, cotton farming, a seemingly prosaic subject, was used to raise fundamental questions about local and regional history in a non-traditional "classroom setting."

From folk festivals to the federal government implies another large leap in the kinds of things "public historians do all day." It is clear, however, that the same skills and professionalism necessary to make public projects successful are necessary for historians to function with integrity and effectiveness in government positions which involve dealing with an established bureaucracy and with specific projects having well-defined objectives of which the historian's concerns as a professional may be only peripheral. In considering the variety and number of public historians employed in government, one must conclude that these historians constitute the majority of professionals in public history working for a single employer. As Martin Reuss's essay illustrates, there are an amazing variety of positions in government filled by historians. Indeed, it is quite impossible in an introductory work to present a comprehensive picture of this aspect of public history. We have, therefore, represented government service and public works history by five carefully selected essays representing local, state, and federal government, along with an essay on historians in the armed services, which is a rapidly growing cadre of both civilian and military historians. In fact, as Thomas Ofcansky points out in his essay on historians in the U.S. Air Force, the writing of military and naval history was one of the earliest tasks of government historians and has a long and distinguished record.

Much of what public historians do all day occurs at the state level where historians are involved in a wide variety of activities. The essay by Larry Tise on public history in state government is much more than a recital of such activities, but is rather a succinct history of the establishment of history and history-related programs in state government. As a result, one sees the variety of positions held by historians in state government in the context of programs which have been developed to serve state government and as a means of implementing federal programs at the state level.

If one hungers for action, involvement in decision making, and the rough and tumble of politics, while at the same time having the opportunity of exercising one's skills as a historian, then a position in local government may be attractive. In any case, Roy Lopata's essay should be of interest to all concerned with public history, since it explores professional activities which are quite foreign to most historians, especially those in academia. It also provides a suitable case study of how historians in any public history position function as part of an interdisciplinary team.

As Asa Briggs states in his book *Victorian Cities,* the cities of the Victorian era and indeed of our own day:

> The building of the cities was a characteristic Victorian achievement, impressive in scale but limited in vision, creating new opportunities but also providing massive new problems. Perhaps their outstanding feature was hidden from public view—their hidden network of pipes and drains and sewers, one of the biggest technical and social achievements of the age, a sanitary 'system' more comprehensive than the transport system. Yet their surface world was fragmented, intricate, cluttered, eclectic and noisy, the unplanned product of a private enterprise economy developing within an older traditional society.

While Briggs focused on English cities, the same comments would have held true for those in America.

The provision of this network of services is, in fact, the history of public works. Until the establishment of the Public Works Historical Society, this was a neglected aspect of the history of technology in North America. It was not that the various parts of the field had not received the attention of historians, but rather the history of public works lacked a focus. As executive secretary of the Public Works Historical Society, historian Howard Rosen brings a perspective on public history that addresses the role of historians in the activities of engineers as well as giving the reader a sense of the importance public works engineering plays in urban life.

While historians may not traditionally feel they have a role in public works history, most budding public historians probably have thought about working for the National Park Service at some time. For one reason, the rangers traditionally are very "public" as they give tours of historic sites in their gray and green uniforms. The National Park Service is often identified as the premier agency in the federal government designated as steward of our cultural and historical resources. This stewardship, which is explored in the essay by Heather Huyck and Dwight Pitcaithley, includes cultural resources management or the preservation, management, and interpretation of historic properties and artifacts held in the public trust by the federal government. Through the National Park Service's Historic American Buildings Survey which dates from the Great Depression of the 1930s to the later Historic American Engineering Record, founded in 1969, nationally significant historical, architectural, and engineering sites have been recorded and made available to the public through a special collection at the Library of Congress. Thus, in nearly every aspect of historic preservation, the National Park Service has held a leading position in an important aspect of public history.

In order to accomplish its mission on a nation-wide basis, the National Park Service has established two centers, one at Denver, Colorado, and the other at Harpers Ferry, West Virginia. These centers provide necessary professional support for the wide-ranging activities of the national park system and include historians, architects, engineers, conservators, archeologists, and audio-visual experts on their staffs. In his essay, Ronald Johnson focuses on the activities of historians at these service centers.

The argument for using historians in the development of public policy in government agencies is forcefully stated in essays by David Mock and Edward Berkowitz. Increasingly, there is an awareness that a historical dimension is important in developing public policy. Historians in these positions must guard against the real temptation that history can be used in a prophetic way to predict the future, while at the same time claiming the value of historical perspectives in developing public policy.

While helping government agencies determine public policy, public historians also work in corporate America, gathering and interpreting the records that help companies understand their own past policies. Like historians specializing in public policy, these corporate historians, and most public historians, provide products or render services of value to their particular "publics."

For example, many people were surprised that, after years of successful sales, The Coca-Cola Company changed its formula in 1985 and marketed a "new" Coke. That decision is certainly a significant event in corporate history and in a larger sense in the social history of America. In the midst of that decision, at least one researcher was using the records of The Coca-Cola Company's archives to study an earlier company marketing campaign. In his essay on the life and fortunes of a historian in the business world, Philip Mooney interprets the expectations a company like The Coca-Cola Company has for historians they employ. In addition to writing corporate history, these historians are often involved in public relations efforts, and because they are keepers of the archives, their services may be called upon in legal matters involving the company and its products. This essay provides a clear idea of what a historian may expect in the world of big business.

Historians may also be businesspeople themselves. One of the most recent phenomena in public history is the establishment of firms specializing in public history. This involves not only contract work to write histories, but also preservation of properties and historic districts; research and preparation for exhibits; public education programs, including walking tours of historic districts, lectures, short courses, and seminars; interpretation of historic sites; and cultural resources management work for government agencies. Ruth Ann Overbeck writes with zest of a historian who has founded her own firm and in the course of a decade has been involved in an amazing number of projects requiring the expertise of a historian. This essay should be required reading of any historian interested in opening his or her own firm, since it deals not only with historical matters, but also provides sound advice on how to run such a firm.

After reading this series of essays, one senses that the practice of public history is rich in its diversity while at the same time sharing a unity of purpose in bringing history to the public. It is this unity that is at the core of the recent development of public history as a professional discipline in the context of traditional history. If nothing else, these essays are very effective in answering the paraphrased question of Richard Scarry, "What do public historians do all day?"

IN MUSEUMS
AND
HISTORY ORGANIZATIONS

Steven Lubar is a historian at the National Museum of American History, Smithsonian Institution, Washington, D.C., where he is working on a book and an exhibit on the American Industrial Revolution. His research interests include the history of the management of manufacturing technology and the history of industrial work, especially in the nineteenth century. His Ph.D. is from the University of Chicago.

PUBLIC HISTORY IN A FEDERAL MUSEUM: THE SMITHSONIAN'S NATIONAL MUSEUM OF AMERICAN HISTORY

Steven Lubar

There is a vast variety of federal museums. Many are run by the park service, part of the Department of the Interior. Other departments run museums also, among them the Department of Commerce and the Treasury Department. But the foremost museums supported by the federal government are not really part of the government at all: they are the museums that make up the Smithsonian Institution. There are at present fourteen Smithsonian "bureaus," six of which employ historians or art historians: the National Museum of American History, the National Museum of American Art, the National Portrait Gallery, the National Air and Space Museum, the Hirschorn Gallery and Sculpture Garden, the Freer Gallery of Art, and the Cooper Hewitt Museum.

The original funding for the Smithsonian came from the 1838 bequest of James Smithson, an English scientist, who bequeathed to the United States government about one-half million dollars "to found at Washington, under the name of the Smithsonian Institution, an Establishment for the Increase and Diffusion of Knowledge among Men." Historians have disagreed over whether Smithson intended a research institute or a school for training skilled mechanics. Contemporaries too debated the issue, disagreeing over whether or not such a gift could legally be accepted and also over the nature of the "Establishment" Smithson had in mind. The United States Government accepted the gift, and in August 1846, the Smithsonian Institution was established. The first secretary, the scientist Joseph Henry, sent the newly founded Smithsonian on its way as a place for scientific research.

It was not until the last third of the nineteenth century that the Smithsonian began to take on some of the attributes of a museum. The Patent Office transferred its "National Cabinet of Curiosities" to the

Smithsonian in 1858. Spencer Baird, the second secretary, was a naturalist; natural history and anthropology demanded large collections. The closing of the Philadelphia Centennial Exposition in 1877 made available to the Smithsonian a host of artifacts—then of industrial and cultural interest, today of great historical value. The National Museum Building (now the Arts and Industries Building) was erected in 1881 to house these new collections. The Natural History Museum was built across the mall from the National Museum in 1910, and the Museum of American History (originally the Museum of History and Technology) in 1964. The last twenty years have seen a flowering of museums on the mall and off, as the Smithsonian has taken its mission as a national museum to heart.

This article will concentrate on the museums of the Smithsonian and, in particular, one of those museums, and one exhibit within that museum. In that exhibit, as in all of the work of the Smithsonian museums, the dual interests of research and outreach—the "increase and diffusion of knowledge" that Smithson hoped for—are present. Smithsonian exhibits, publications, and collections, like good exhibits, publications, and collections at all museums, demand a combination of research and presentation.

THE NATIONAL MUSEUM OF AMERICAN HISTORY

The National Museum of American History (NMAH) is one of the foremost museums of American history and the history of science and technology in the United States. The mission of this museum is "to illuminate, through collections, exhibitions, research, publications and educational programs, the entire history of the United States, including the external influences that have helped to shape the national character." The recently added subtitle of the museum, "Science, Technology, and Culture," indicates some of the dimensions of the museum's work.

Collections, of course, are the core of a museum. The National Museum of American History holds over sixteen million objects, representing America's social, cultural, political, military, scientific, and technological heritage. A small fraction of these objects are shown in the museum's exhibits. Some thirty exhibit halls include more than 360,000 square feet of exhibits which fall into four rough categories: the history of science and technology; American social, cultural, and political history; military history; and numismatics and philately. About six million people visit the museum each year.

The museum is undertaking at present a major overhaul of its exhibits, many of which remain largely untouched from its opening twenty years ago. One part of this "major reinstallation" is an exhibit entitled "Engines of Change: The Industrial Revolution in America." This exhibit, the first of the exhibits on the history of science and technology to be redone, is intended as an introduction to all of the exhibits on the history of technology. It will be the major focus of this essay.

Before outlining the process of undertaking this new exhibit, a brief outline of the structure and workings of the museum is essential. The annual budget for the museum (1984) is almost $10 million. The staff at NMAH presently numbers 327, of whom about 50 are curators. The curators at the National Museum of American History represent the largest concentration of historians of science and technology in the country, as well as many distinguished social, cultural, and political historians. Many of the curators have Ph.D.s in history; all are experts in their field. Curators have a multitude of responsibilities. In addition to working on exhibits, they carry out original research, build and study the museum's collections, answer the volume of inquiries that come to the museum from throughout the world, and, inevitably, help with the managerial aspects of the museum.

Supporting the curators are museum specialists and technicians. These people undertake many of the same tasks as the curators, but with direction and supervision from the curators. Specialists and technicians are responsible for the day-to-day care of the collections. Many have training in museum and material culture studies; some are trained as historians.

There are relatively few individuals at NMAH whose job title is "historian"—though many who are historians. The job title "historian" covers a wide variety of positions at the Smithsonian—people who elsewhere might be called archivists, historical editors, or even, occasionally, historians. Some of these historians—and this is how the term will be used henceforth—are hired to work on specific exhibits. Their job is to undertake, under the supervision of the curator of an exhibit, the detailed research that is needed for the exhibit. They assist with selecting objects for the show, writing the "script"—the labels that go on the wall—and working with designers to ensure that the form of the exhibit reinforces the messages contained in the labels. The exhibit historians for the major reinstallation program have been Ph.D.s or have completed all requirements for the Ph.D. except the dissertation.

The historian is one member of the team that is responsible for an exhibit. (The author of this essay is the historian for "Engines of Change.") Responsible for the conceptual outline of the exhibit is its curator. The curator of "Engines of Change" is Brooke Hindle, Senior Historian at NMAH and author of a number of books on eighteenth- and nineteenth-century American science and technology. Each exhibit has a project manager as well, to keep it on schedule and within budget; William Withuhn, Curator of Transportation and Deputy Chairman of the Department of the History of Science and Technology, has that job. An advisory committee for the exhibit consists of curators from the Division of Extractive Industries and the Division of Physical Sciences. In overall charge is the Chairman of the Department of the History of Science and Technology.

Historical content, the subject of interest here, is only one part of the work of putting on an exhibit. Curators and historians work along with personnel from other departments of the museum, people who concentrate on activities including fund-raising, exhibit design, exhibit construction, educational programs, public affairs, and performances, and so forth. There is a constant back-and-forth trading of ideas and resources between the various groups. Overseeing the entire process are the various managers of the museum.

WRITING AN EXHIBIT: THEORY AND PRACTICE

What happens to the three-quarters of a million dollars and two or three or four years that it takes to put on a major exhibit? Where does the history that eventually ends up on the wall come from? Who decides what that history should be, and how it should be presented? What decisions need to be made? What research is needed? What objects are available, or can be acquired or borrowed? How can the design of the exhibit reinforce the themes of the exhibit?

The first essential in putting together an exhibit is to determine the point of the exhibit: what should a visitor to the museum know, understand, believe, or think about after he or she has been through the exhibit that he or she didn't know, understand, believe, or think about before? A truism of museum practice holds that the average museum visitor comes away from an exhibit with four or five new facts or ideas. It is good to boil down the point of the exhibit to a few sentences. One NMAH curator deals with the problem this way: "Write the press release first, and that way you'll know what the exhibit is really about."

The content, theme, and viewpoint of an exhibit is determined in a series of meetings, memos, and informal discussions. Usually many people at the museum have both interest and expertise in the field of the exhibit; one person is responsible for the final formulation, but many offer advice. The themes of the exhibit take into account many considerations. In addition to the facts of history, anyone who puts together an exhibit must consider the resources of the museum: artifacts, time, money, and personnel.

While a small exhibit can express one person's point of view, a large exhibit usually reflects some compromise among the people interested in the subject. All history is an interpretation; whose interpretation goes "on the wall" is sometimes a matter of contention. The National Museum of American History is an important public textbook, and men and women of good will disagree over just what message should be presented.

There is nothing to be gained from detailing the various conflicting viewpoints that entered into "Engines of Change," but a look at some of the alternatives proposed for one small element of the exhibit—the title—reveals some of the considerations. Before the present title was settled on, a variety of others were proposed. One was "Industrializing America," with its dual meanings: on the one hand a connotation of an ongoing activity, and on the other a vaguely Marxist implication that someone or some group was responsible for inflicting industrialization on the United States, and that some other group opposed it. Another was "The American Industrial Revolution" but was there indeed an Industrial Revolution at all, let alone an American one? Historians disagree. Some would put the date of the Industrial Revolution in the sixteenth or seventeenth, not the nineteenth, century; others would insist that the American Industrial Revolution lasts until the 1890s. Beyond the historical considerations, there is the public relations aspect of a title: "The American Industrial Revolution" promises a dull exhibit, not easy for the public affairs people at the museum to sell.

"Engines of Change" is more exciting. It carries no specific meaning, though, and so is subtitled "The Industrial Revolution in America, 1790 to 1860." The title has its controversial aspect: it implies that the "engines"—the machines—caused the change. Some historians would reject this implication. They would argue that the people who decided to use the machines, or the economic forces that allowed their use—not the machines themselves—were more fundamentally responsible for the changes, that the title glosses the deeper structure of the course of industrialization. The title is a compromise. Just as the "facts" of history are always subject to selection and interpretation, so even the title of an exhibit has its element of controversy.

The title, though important, is only one small aspect of the exhibit. Behind it is a historical presentation of important three-dimensional survivals of the American Industrial Revolution. The visitor enters the exhibit through a recreation of the 1851 London Crystal Palace, where American technology first gained world recognition. Passing through the Crystal Palace, the visitor is confronted with a montage of pictures of industry: the men and women and factories and machines behind the American success at the Crystal Palace. The next sections provide background on America before the Industrial Revolution, concentrating on America's "wooden age" and its artisans. Into that scene was brought technology from abroad. Americans adapted this foreign machinery to fit American needs and changed the country to better make use of the new machinery. Beyond this section on "Transfer of Technology" lies the largest section of the show, entitled "Mechanization." Here, about a dozen examples of important new machines, new forms of industrial organization, and other influences on the American Industrial Revolution are shown. The show concludes with sections on proposed utopian alternatives to industrialization, a look at America in 1860, and an epilogue that draws comparisons between the first Industrial Revolution and what some have called the second Industrial Revolution of today.

Telling the story of the Industrial Revolution in American is only one of the goals of the exhibit. Another is to reveal something of the nature of technology and the relationship between mechanization and industrialization. "Engines of Change" will serve as an introduction to the exhibits about the history of technology at the museum, and so it is appropriate that a visitor could apply what he or she had learned about technology to other exhibits.

For this exhibit, the museum is borrowing very little, drawing on its own unsurpassed collection of artifacts of early American industry.

Among the objects that will be shown in the exhibit are the oldest operable locomotive in the world, the "John Bull"; the only surviving piece of the first steam engine in the New World; machinery built by Samuel Slater and used in the first successful textile factory in America; and the earliest surviving marine steam engine, invented by John Stevens for the steamboat *Little Juliana*. Not every object in the exhibit is the first, the oldest, or the most important. Each, though, has this in common: it reveals in its three-dimensional reality something of the ineffable truth of the historic moments of which it was part. Every historical object contains within it the history of the times in which it was made and used, and through which it has survived.

The job of the exhibit historian is twofold, historical and museological. The historical task is first: to undertake the research necessary to draw out the historical truth of the object that is, to discover the ways in which history is reflected in it. The museological task follows closely: to discover ways of exhibiting that history to the museum visitor. This work is a search after historical facts and objects with which to document those facts. The exhibit historian shares with the academic historian the job of determing the contexts of an object, and choosing which contexts are important, that is, which reflect the currents of history that the historian believes significant. He or she goes beyond the academic historian in finding the objects and evidence to recreate those contexts.

The central task of preparing a history exhibit is a historical one. First, objects must be selected to speak to the historical points we want to make. Appropriate contexts for each object must be determined and then researched. The historian must discover how each object fits into the history presented. The sources and the techniques of historical research needed for this type of museum exhibit are identical to those employed in academic history. All the tools and tricks of the historians' trade must be employed to draw out from a mute object the history of which it was a part.

Objects of great significance often have been researched extensively; for these, much of the historical information needed can be found in secondary works—carefully checked in primary sources, of course. Research for objects of lesser significance requires many of the techniques of the "new social history," such as the detailed examination of credit registers and manuscript census listings. The techniques for discovering the life histories of machines are not that different from those used for finding the life histories of "anonymous" individuals, though with the added evidence of the artifact itself. Revealing the true story of any object is historical detective work; it requires not only the search for facts but also the compounding of hypotheses. The end result of the research could as well be an article as a set of exhibit labels, and indeed, several of the objects researched for this exhibit will be the focus of articles or parts of books.

Finding the history in the object is only the first step. Next the historian must find the documents, both two- and three-dimensional, that prove, illustrate, and exemplify that history. The museum exhibit is much more than a book, in that the historical points must be made not only in words but in artifacts as well. The way in which the historical truth of objects is conveyed to visitors to "Engines of Change" is simple: we attempt to surround each object with as much of its original context as we are able.

Some objects are surrounded with context in the form of period rooms: a loom is put into a weaving room, a lathe into a period machine shop. Other objects are provided with a "paper context," the documents which governed their creation or use surrounding them: the patent application for an 1842 pin machine and the incorporation papers of the company that used it to make a point in history. Still other objects are given an artifactual context: an early rifle is shown with the Blanchard lathe used to produce its stock and the kit of gauges used by the inspector who approved it. These types of context, of course, are not mutually exclusive. In front of the textile mill room is a petition from the mill girls demanding a shortened workday as well as some of the handtools they used to tend the loom. Shown alongside the "John Bull" is a watch used by the conductor on the line, the wooden drive wheel that was early replaced with a metal one, a book of rules for employees, timetables, and a copy of the agreement between the manufacturer and the railroad that purchased it, as well as a video of the locomotive in operation.

This contextual style of presentation accomplishes several purposes. It makes each artifact in the exhibit part of some historic moment or movement. It brings each artifact to life; historical context is by its nature human context, and most visitors to the museum are more interested in people than in machines. Most important, it makes the exhibit fundamentally historical. The artifacts are not presented as objects of primarily aesthestic value or technological knowledge, although both of these are secondary messages, but as objects of history.

AN EXAMPLE: JOHN HOWE'S 1842 PIN MACHINE

The process of finding and recreating appropriate contexts for each of the artifacts in the show is the central work of the historian. An example shows the users and techniques of history in this sort of museum exhibit. One artifact that will be in "Engines of Change" is a pin-making machine invented by John Howe in 1842 and used at the Howe Manufacturing Company in Derby, Connecticut. The pin machine, which has been at the museum for many years, is one of the oldest pieces of automated industrial machinery extant. It will appear in the exhibit in the "Mechanization" section. A number of points are made in this section. The presence of the Howe pin machine should speak to:

1. the technological ingenuity that was applied to factory production
2. the skills needed to produce complex machinery
3. the skills needed to run the machine; more generally, the nature of work at the pin factory

4. the economic and business resources that went into setting up the
   pin factory
5. the relationship of the pin industry to other industries and to larger
   economic and political movements, e.g., urbanization and government regulation

Each of these aspects of the industrial revolution affected Howe, the
Howe Manufacturing Company, and the Howe pin machine. The
exhibit historian's job is to discover those effects and to present them for
the public.

The machine's invention was the first object of research. The museum
had in its collections the patent model for the machine—a model which,
in its differences from the machine, was revealing of the changes
between idea and implementation. The original patent application, as
well as an earlier patent for another pin machine Howe invented, was
found at the National Archives. Readings in mechanics' magazines and
the *Reports* of the Commissioner of the Patent Office revealed something
more about the machine's invention and early use. Research at a local
historical society turned up the diary John Howe kept on his trip to
Europe to examine other pin-making machines. Fortuitous reading,
unrelated to the original question, and the keen eye of associates at the
museum, revealed that Howe had gone to the Whitworth machine shop
in London and the R. Hoe and Company machine shop in New York for
help in constructing the machine.

The social setting of the machine was the next context for investigation. No company papers could be discovered. I wanted to know who
ran the machine and what their day was like. To present the machine
without mentioning the men or women who spent long days tending it
would be to neglect an important part of its history. Close examination
of the manuscript census of population of Derby, Connecticut, allowed
me to get at the workers in the pin factory. A statistical summary as well
as some reset listings from the census will allow us to present this
information to the visitors. What was it like to work there? Again, there
are no direct sources. A visit to the site of the factory, now demolished,
gave a feel for the setting; a visit to a modern day pin factory gives some
feeling for the work; insurance maps showed the interior geography of
the factory. The patents awarded to men who worked at the plant—
especially the requests for patent extensions, which include narratives of
the circumstance of invention—revealed some of the technological,
economic, and organizational forces at work in the factory.

This part of the investigation profited from the evidence of the
artifact itself. Because it was impossible to have the machine shown in
operation in the exhibit, it was decided to produce a videotape of the
machine in operation. To do this, we first had to put the machine in
working order—no small job. Months of work by the museum's Division
of Conservation allowed a degree of operation sufficient to edit into a
videotape, and also a glimpse into the work of the operative who tended
the machine 140 years ago. We discovered that a single mechanical
mishap would result in an unending supply of misshapen pins and, thus,

we learned something about the constant alertness the operative must have had. Evidence from running the machine showed some of its faults and helped to explain the course of invention in the pin industry.

Who invested in the pin factory? The business context is one to which this exhibit pays some attention, for corporations and unincorporated partnerships were essential to the machinery of the Industrial Revolution in America. A letter to the New York State Archives led to the discovery of the certificate of incorporation of the Howe Manufacturing Company. Not only might this be used for display, but it also provided the names of the men who put up the money needed to build the machines and the factory, hire employees, and buy materials. The Dun and Company registers at Baker Library, Harvard Graduate School of Business Administration, revealed the capital and profitability of the company. Histories of the pin industry and the autobiographical notes compiled by John Howe told something of the day-to-day problems of running the company. Letters from the directors of the firm to their local congressmen revealed their dislike of the tariff on the imported brass wire the company used.

The final object was the product: pins. Though the exhibit concentrates on the technological side of the Industrial Revolution, not the consumer aspect, we show products here and there to make the industrial more familiar. By chance, the museum had in its collection a set of pins produced by the Howe Manufacturing Company, as well as some advertising. By good chance, the advertising played up the "Made in America" aspect of the pins, reinforcing the point about the importance of the tariff.

The end result of this research is a small piece of the exhibit. Centrally located in it is the pin machine, hooked up to a power transmission belt so that it might occasionally be run. A general label briefly explains its history and importance. Surrounding it are five labels, each with a number of objects:

Labels	*Objects*
"Who invented this machine?	patent model
	patent drawing
	portrait of John Howe
"Who used this machine?"	reset 1860 Derby census
"Who owned the company?"	Howe Mfg. Co. letterhead
	Howe Mfg. Co. advertisement
"Government and the pin industry"	tariff petition
	letter to congressman
"How the machine works"	video of machine in operation
	package of pins

Each of these labels and its associated artifacts explains some important aspect of the American Industrial Revolution.

This summary of the contexts of one artifact in the show, and the historical and museological work necessary to discover and present them, might be retold dozens of times. Every major artifact in the show has its own story, or rather its own set of stories. The central job of the historian in this kind of exhibit is to find these stories and good ways, verbal and artifactual, to present them to the visitors to the exhibit.

MUSEUM HISTORY, ACADEMIC HISTORY, AND PUBLIC HISTORY

The history done for this kind of Smithsonian exhibit does not differ all that much from history done for scholarly purposes. The same criteria could be used to judge the two sorts of history: thorough, creative use of sources; attention to the broader questions of history; careful use of evidence and imaginative creation of hypotheses; and original and interesting presentation. Much of the work done for the exhibit is also useful in writing the book that will be published to accompany the exhibit.

It is in the work that takes place on either side of the research that the public history of the museum differs from the scholarly history of the academy. Negotiation and compromise accompany the initial formulation of the problem in the joint effort of the museum historian much more than in the individual effort of the university professor. After the research comes more team effort, this time with designers, curators, fund raisers, public relations people, exhibit builders, audio-visual specialists, special events coordinators, and on and on. One need only glance at the occupations outlined in the museum's telephone directory to see the complexity of the work of putting together an exhibit. If, one hundred years from now, I were doing an exhibit on putting on an exhibit at the National Museum of American History in the 1980s, I would use this as one of my artifacts.

An example shows some of the aspects of the teamwork that goes into the final product. Accompanying every major exhibit at NMAH are a variety of programs, produced by the museum's Department of Public Programs. Some take place within the museum: docents give tours or offer educational programs; a series of lectures or movies is scheduled; musical events are arranged. Others take place outside the museum: slide shows are packaged for historical societies and libraries; teachers' guides to material are written for classroom use; special events are organized.

The most important public program is, of course, the exhibit itself. The Department of Public Programs also takes responsibility for exhibit evaluation, collecting public response that might be helpful in building future exhibits. Sometimes exhibit evaluation goes on while the exhibit is in process, small parts of the exhibit being tested to check public response to themes and presentation.

The show's curator and historian work with the Department of Public Programs in planning events and undertaking evaluation, just as they work with all of the other groups involved in putting on the exhibit.

They must balance the time devoted to these affairs with the time necessary for research, writing, artifact selection and acquisition, management, and budgeting. The amount of time spent away from historical work is enough, sometimes, to make one wish for the privacy of the ivy tower, where one's work is one's own, where considerations of public appeal are much less strong, where there is only one's own conscience and the community of scholars to please. But, as any academic historian will admit, that vision of the ivy tower is a fantasy vision. Though from afar the towers of academe appear a wonderland of scholarship, in academia as well as in the museum there are distractions from the scholarly work of the historian. The distractions are different, but they are no less real, no less time-consuming.

But those distractions, in both academic and public history, are only that—distractions. There is another, much more important, fantasy vision that the public historian and the academic historian share. That fantasy—and I am convinced that it is more than that, that it is a reality— is that the work of the professional historian does make a difference. To understand history is to take the first step toward understanding civilization, culture, and humanity. And to teach it, whether in the classroom or in the museum, is to give that understanding to others. What better payoff could there be for the occasional distractions of working as a historian?

To work in the National Museum of American History is to have the chance to teach the American people about history. The history we make available to our visitors is real history—history in all of its complexity, with its positives and negatives, its ups and downs. Historians at the Smithsonian, and indeed at any museum, have a chance to tell the most important audience of all something about the forces that shaped their past and continue to shape their life. That understanding is liberating and empowering, for it is knowledge that allows people to understand their society and themselves. The chance that some of the museum's visitors, after passing through "Engines of Change," might better appreciate America's history, the workings of industrial and technological change, and the impact of that history on their own lives—that makes it all worthwhile.

The opinions expressed in this paper are those of the author, and do not necessarily reflect those of the National Museum of American History, the Smithsonian Institution, or the other individuals associated with the "Engines of Change" exhibit.

John W. Durel is assistant director for research and curatorial services at Strawbery Banke and holds a Ph.D. in American History from the University of New Hampshire. He has held the posts of assistant director for education and research and director of education at Strawbery Banke. Dr. Durel has published in Nineteenth Century *and* Historical New Hampshire.

THE PAST: A THING TO STUDY, A PLACE TO GO

John W. Durel

Eleven miles from the University of New Hampshire there is an outdoor museum called Strawbery Banke. The museum, which is in an old waterfront neighborhood in the port city of Portsmouth, had originated in the 1950s as an alternative to an urban renewal project. A group of preservationists had saved about thirty buildings from demolition, acquired a few others, and opened the area as a historic site. By the early 1970s the public could visit over a dozen of the buildings, not all restored, and see furnishings, exhibits, and craft demonstrations.

In 1973 I entered graduate school at the university and lived a few blocks from the museum. The place intrigued me. The kind of history I saw there was certainly very different from the history I encountered at the university. It was an antiquarian approach, lacking the intellectual rigor of the academy. Yet it had value. History in the classroom seemed remote and lifeless. At a place like Strawbery Banke the past had an immediate sensory appeal. One could see old buildings and furnishings, and with imagination experience the past.

This contrast between history in the academy and history in the museum has existed for over a century. In the late nineteenth century academic history became a professional study in its own right, and not merely an adjunct to literature. Inspired by developments in the natural and social sciences, historians like Henry Adams and Frederick Jackson Turner began to look to various scientific methods and models for ways to investigate the past.[1] For them, and for the profession that followed in their wake, the past was primarily something to be studied.

But for most Americans the value of the past lay not so much in the lessons that it might teach as in the way it made one feel. This notion was rooted in nineteenth-century Romanticism, which emphasized the emotional appeal of the remote and the heroic.[2] This led Europeans to visit ancient shrines, the ruins of castles and cathedrals. Americans, without a long history of their own, turned at first to Europe. But by the middle of the century they began to create their own historic shrines, beginning with George Washington's Revolutionary War headquarters in Newburgh, New York, and then with his plantation home in Virginia.[3]

The idea that the past was a place to go gained considerable momentum toward the end of the nineteenth century and into the twentieth. At the same time that the historical profession was taking shape in the academy, numerous local historical organizations and museums appeared. Americans became interested in ancient landmarks: the site of an early Indian raid, the location of a town's first house, or a place where George Washington slept. As an example, Portsmouth, which had been a thriving seaport in the eighteenth century and nothing special in the nineteenth, became a "historic" attraction for summer visitors, complete with a guidebook to local landmarks, as early as 1876.

By the 1920s this approach to history found dramatic expression in the creation of Colonial Williamsburg, one of America's first outdoor museums. There were earlier outdoor museums, most notably the world's first, Skansen in Stockholm, Sweden.[4] In Williamsburg the idea originated with William Goodwin, rector of Bruton Parish Church which had been built in 1715, heavily altered in 1839, and restored by Goodwin in 1903.

Before the American Revolution Williamsburg had been an important political and social center, the capital of the province of Virginia. In 1780 the government moved to Richmond, and Williamsburg became just one among many tidewater towns. In time many colonial buildings disappeared; both the Governor's Palace and the capitol were destroyed by fire. But others survived, in part due to the absence of prosperity. By the early twentieth century Williamsburg was an American version of an ancient ruin, or as an early Colonial Williamsburg guidebook later called it, a "pleasingly decayed colonial city."[5]

It was not the decay that prompted Goodwin to come up with a scheme to restore the entire colonial city. Rather it was the threat of modernization. During World War I the town served as a supply base for nearby ammunition manufacturing plants and during this moment of prosperity

> . . . "The Duke of Gloucester Street became a teeming highway of concrete; great posts to carry wires and cables were raised on every hand; the empty spaces in Williamsburg, which were the sites of forgotten buildings and gardens, began slowly to be filled with shops, and stores, and with stations for gasoline." . . . Williamsburg was becoming a "highway town."[6]

Goodwin planned to save Williamsburg from this modern fate and restore it to its former dignity. In 1926 he was able to gain the interest and financial support of John D. Rockefeller, Jr. Over the next decade they purchased almost the entire area that had formed the colonial town, tore down or removed nearly 500 post-colonial structures, restored 67 surviving colonial buildings, and built nearly 100 replicas on extant colonial foundations. They then furnished the houses, recreated gardens, hired guides, and opened the town to the public. Their hope was to "revive and retain something of the strength and beauty of

Figure 1. U.S. Army tank on Main Street (now Duke of Gloucester Street) in Williamsburg, Virginia. World War I brought prosperity to the sleepy southern town, prompting the Rev. W. A. R. Goodwin to launch a plan to restore the place to its colonial appearance. *Photograph from a private collection.*

another age, something of the spirit of the men who lived in it and made it great."[7]

Another major American outdoor museum came into existence in the 1920s and 1930s. For some time Henry Ford had been collecting things: watches and clocks that he liked to repair; objects associated with Thomas Edison, his life-long hero; and things he remembered from his childhood, like copies of McGuffy's *Eclectic Readers.* By the mid-1920s this activity had grown into a desire "to have something of everything" with the intention of creating a museum to "reproduce the life of the country in its every age."[8] The result was the Edison Institute, made up of an outdoor museum called Greenfield Village and a large indoor museum now called the Henry Ford Museum.

Unlike Colonial Williamsburg, Greenfield Village was not intended to represent a specific place in the past. Ford's architect based early plans on typical New England villages, with public buildings situated around a common green. But Ford made many changes as the project developed. The village green remained a prominent feature, but equally important was the restoration within the village of Edison's entire Menlo Park, New Jersey, "invention factory." In the end the form and content of Greenfield Village were the result of numerous decisions made by Ford.

For Ford the village was not an end in itself but rather a means to attain a greater goal, a reordered society of the future. As Steven K. Hamp has noted, "As [Ford] grew older, his focus progressively shifted from problems of a mechanical engineer to those of a social engineer."[9] He originally planned for 300 people to live and work in the village; and he established a school system which at its peak enrolled students from kindergarten through post–high school technical levels. Greenfield Village was to be a learning laboratory, where students attended a one-room school house and visited the shops of Edison, the Wright brothers, and other model leaders of technology. This dream died with Ford, and in later years Greenfield Village came to be seen as a fanciful version of the past created by a wealthy antiquarian.

In the decades following the openings of Colonial Williamsburg and Greenfield Village numerous similar projects appeared. The pattern had been established: a person or group of people interested in preserving old buildings and artifacts, and often the way of life that such things represented, created a setting in which to display the things. Usually they had some educational purpose in mind, whether it was simply the notion that a visit to such a place was by its nature beneficial, or a more sophisticated idea about learning practical skills and values through the study and use of artifacts. The projects varied greatly in size, subject, and format. Some, like Iowa Living History Farms, focused on individual farmsteads. Others, like Old Sturbridge Village in Massachusetts, portrayed a whole community. Many were simply eclectic collections of buildings, arranged according to whim rather than research. With few exceptions, they depicted rural, or at least preindustrial life. Most, like Greenfield Village, involved the movement of structures from their original sites to the museum, although a few followed the Williamsburg model of restoration *in situ* and possibly the replication of missing buildings.[10]

Emerging from these places was a form of presentation that Jay Anderson has called an "American way of history."[11] The founders of similar institutions in Europe generally were content only to display the buildings and artifacts, but in America there was great interest in the recreation of the activities that once took place in the historical environments. Beginning with Colonial Williamsburg's use of costumed guides in the 1930s, American outdoor museums have sought to present what has come to be called "living history."

Until the latter half of the 1960s these outdoor museums generally preserved and presented the past in terms irrelevant to academic historians. Then came the "new social history," a surge of interest on the part of historians in the daily lives of ordinary people. Inspired by the work of French social historians, young American scholars began to examine early American families, communities, and life experiences. For the first time a sizeable group of historians in the academy was addressing topics that had long been in the sphere of the outdoor museum.

A few of these scholars, sensing that there was more value in teaching history in the "real world" than in an "ivory tower," went to work in outdoor museums. They found in these recreated settings the physical context in which families and communities once existed, and saw an opportunity to explore past life in all its aspects.[12] Other historians, while not actually going to work in the museums, tentatively began to use artifacts and the restored environments as evidence. John Demos, for example, made use of the recreated historical setting at Plimouth Plantation in Massachusetts in writing *A Little Commonwealth,* a book that became immensely popular in college classrooms in the 1970s.[13]

The few historians who entered the museum field in the late 1960s were followed by many more in the next decade, as opportunities for employment in the academy diminished. Most did not find jobs strictly as historians, for few museums could afford to hire people just to do research and teach. Instead they filled positions as educators, interpreters, curators, and administrators. But their presence has made a difference in the way history is done at outdoor museums.

One change has been a shift in emphasis away from the elite and the unusual toward the common and the ordinary. Most museums had a tendency to present the story of someone of note, either on the local or national level. There was also a predilection for displaying things that were valued for their age, their quality, or their association with a notable. Ordinary people and common artifacts were part of the setting, but only as a backdrop to the main story. This has begun to change as museums and their audiences have become interested in the new social history. Even Colonial Williamsburg has redirected its interpretation away from the story of the "great patriots" to the process by which eighteenth-century Virginians, black and white, rich and poor, male and female, became Americans.[14]

There has also been some movement away from certain romantic or comforting views of the past. Colonial Williamsburg is noted still for its freshly painted houses and clean streets, but Plimouth Plantation has recreated a setting complete with dirt and weeds. Instead of simply honoring the Pilgrim Fathers, the museum portrays the lives of real people undergoing the hardships and pleasures of life in an early settlement. To be sure, Myles Standish and William Bradford are there; but they are there as their contemporaries saw them, and not as later generations came to see them.

The program at Plimouth Plantation represents in the extreme the most significant development of the 1970s. There is now greater emphasis on getting it right, on recreating the historical setting as accurately as possible, and on presenting the past on its own terms. Few museums have gone as far as Plimouth, where the desire to recreate has led to the wholesale adoption of a first-person mode of presentation, in which staff members play the roles of historical characters, speaking in period dialect. Visitors encounter seventeenth-century English settlers going about their daily and seasonal tasks, much as an anthropologist might observe villagers on a remote Pacific island. More often museums have adopted the first-person mode as a discreet component of a more conventional presentation. At Colonial Williamsburg, for example, one occasionally encounters on the streets an actor portraying a merchant, a servant, or a slave.

Even in cases where museums have not ventured into this form of presentation, there are few that have not revamped an interpretation program or refurnished a house in recent years. The desire to recreate the past accurately has led museums to critique and to disassemble earlier antiquarian versions. These museums have also spent considerable energy and money disguising water fountains, restrooms, electrical outlets, and other twentieth-century fixtures necessary to the operation of a museum.

Such steps can help a museum-goer imagine life in the past. However, although these historical environments appear to be real, in the words of Darwin Kelsey of Old Sturbridge Village, they are "only accounts of the past and not the past itself. . . . They are subjective, as any 'model' produced in the arts, humanities, or sciences."[15] The best are based on sound and extensive scholarship, but all are ultimately someone's version of the past.

The accurate recreation of a past environment was the dominant thrust at outdoor museums during the 1970s. This was a problem for Strawbery Banke. Founded in the late 1950s, Strawbery Banke took Colonial Williamsburg as its first model. The link with Williamsburg was more than figurative, for the new museum hired the Boston architectural firm of Perry, Shaw, Hepburn, and Dean, whose senior partner, William G. Perry, had been the architect for Williamsburg. In the early plans for Strawbery Banke and even today in certain buildings and in certain landscape features, one can glimpse elements of Colonial Williamsburg.

But Strawbery Banke did not become a recreated colonial town. The cost of preserving over thirty buildings, most of which still stood on their original foundations, and the absense of a wealthy sponsor, militated against any dramatic recreation of the past. Instead, Strawbery Banke became primarily a historic preservation project, taking on one building at a time as funds permitted.

In 1964 the site opened to the public as a museum, with two houses restored and furnished, and with crafts demonstrations in several unrestored buildings. In another decade there were two more furnished houses, a "country store," a blacksmith shop that had been moved in from a farm in another part of the state, and displays of old tools, old photographs, spinning wheels, and architectural fragments from notable houses that had been demolished. These disparate features existed amidst many buildings yet to be restored. The museum gained a reputation as a place incomplete. A frequent comment of visitors was that the place would be first-rate when it was finished, like Colonial Williamsburg or Old Sturbridge Village. This placed Strawbery Banke in a defensive posture, leading the institution to apologize for its programs.

Old Sturbridge Village was an important model for Strawbery Banke in the 1970s. The village was a recreation of a typical New England rural community from the early nineteenth century, with emphasis on early crafts and household activities. Another model was Mystic Seaport in Connecticut, which interpreted a nineteenth-century maritime community. At various times Strawbery Banke entertained and partially implemented such things as fireplace cooking demonstrations, a restored wharf, a landscape plan to show the site as it appeared in 1830, and a crafts program that included only trades practiced in Portsmouth prior to 1850.

In looking to other museums Strawbery Banke failed to establish a clear identity of its own. This was further complicated by the fact that the accurate recreation of a historic environment, even if it had been financially feasible, was at odds with other aims. For example, when architectural historians discovered that Sherburne House, which at first glance appeared to date from the Georgian period, was actually pre-Georgian, they chose to restore the building to its earliest appearance. Thus, Sherburne House, looking the way it did about 1705, stands in its original location between two houses that were not built for another ninety years. Other houses were restored to various dates—1780, 1796, 1810, 1830—with significant architectural features usually dictating the choices. Another group of houses was not restored at all, but simply adapted for modern use, retaining twentieth-century features. Obviously these decisions precluded the selection of a single period for the site as a whole.

Indeed, the confusion over dates existed for individual houses. One, for example, named for its owner in 1850, had been restored to its appearance in 1750, and was surrounded by a landscape that showed features from 1830. The public, and even the institution itself, had trouble making sense of this.

I joined the Strawbery Banke staff in the late 1970s, at which time the institution was beginning to recognize and come to grips with its dilemma. Several of the staff had academic history training, so it seemed natural to conceive of the past as primarily something to be investigated. Realizing that such investigations often involved tracing a particular theme or topic over time, we decided to investigate and interpret a particular place—the waterfront neighborhood of which the museum was a part—over time. With this new approach the museum could stop apologizing for its inconsistencies. Even the marketing department liked it. Soon Strawbery Banke was inviting the public to take an afternoon and spend three centuries in history.

Strawbery Banke was not alone in wanting to interpret change. Iowa Living History Farms was doing so already with the presentation of farmsteads dating to different periods. Old Sturbridge Village entertained ideas of creating a nineteenth-century industrial village to contrast with its farming community. Colonial Williamsburg saw Carter's Grove, an eighteenth-century plantation where archeologists had discovered the remains of a seventeenth-century settlement, as an opportunity to trace the development of one site over several centuries. At Greenfield Village, director Harold Skramstad asserted that his institu-

Figure 2. Strawbery Banke interprets the development of a single site over several centuries. These three houses are all in their original locations. Sherburne House, in the center, appears as it did in the early eighteenth century; Lowd House to the left appears as it did in the early nineteenth century; and Drisco House, built in the 1790s, retains its twentieth century appearance. *Photograph courtesy of Strawbery Banke.*

tion's proper subject was "the history of change in American life brought about by the Industrial Revolution." "We are," he said, "we have to be, the great American museum of change."[16]

At Strawbery Banke the interpretation of the site over time made it acceptable to have elements of the museum dating to different periods, but the fact that we had such elements did not mean that we were interpreting the development of the site. The disparate elements needed something to tie them together as parts of a whole.

That required research. Most of what was known about the site was limited to the architecture of the buildings that had survived. Little was known about what was missing—vanished buildings, outbuildings, past landscape features—and almost as little was known about the people who once had lived there. Since the mid-1970s we have undertaken several archeological excavations and numerous documentary history projects, which in aggregate have yielded a better, although still incomplete, understanding of the site's development.

In the process of doing this research we discovered something equally as important to the museum as had been the decision to interpret

Figure 3. In the Sherburne House exhibit at Strawbery Banke visitors are able to view architectural evidence in order to understand how architectural historians go about piecing together the history of a building. *Photograph courtesy of Strawbery Banke.*

change. People enjoy participating in research. The archeology digs in the 1970s were conducted by professionals and students, but in 1981 we opened a dig to the public and attracted over 120 volunteers, ranging in age from sixteen to sixty. At about the same time we found that many people were eager to learn the techniques of researching the history of a house, a family, or a landscape. The important thing was that they wanted to participate in the process of investigation, and not be merely the recipients of the results.

In one of our most popular new exhibits we have combined documents, tools, and architectural features to present the evidence of changes in house construction techniques and architectural styles at the end of the eighteenth century. Significantly, Winn House, which contains the exhibit, was built in 1796 and is the primary artifact in the exhibit. Architectural features, ordinarily hidden from view, are visible. Visitors encounter not so much a thesis as a display of evidence and are encouraged to make comparisons, look for connections, and take part in the interpretation.

This approach is fundamentally different from that found at

Figure 4. In the Winn House exhibit at Strawbery Banke the house itself is the primary artifact on display. Here a cutaway of the plastered walls and ceiling exposes the house's frame. *Photograph courtesy of Strawbery Banke.*

Plimouth Plantation. There, artifacts are props, the place is a stage, and people learn by encountering performers in a carefully recreated environment. At Winn House the artifacts are evidence, the place is a laboratory, and people learn by observing, comparing, and manipulating the evidence.

The full potential of this approach has yet to be realized at Strawbery Banke. The architecture, landscape, archeological artifacts, and social history provide a rich field in which people can be active participants in the study of the past. Yet much of the current presentation is unchanged from what it was a decade ago, only in part due to the expense involved in changing established programs and exhibits. There is still sentiment within the museum for taking the more traditional living history approach, which tends to be less scholarly oriented (at least on the surface) and less demanding on visitors. At this point it is uncertain as to whether the museum-as-laboratory approach will grow or simply become another feature in a varied presentation.

Academic historians are using outdoor museums more and more as field sites for the study of particular topics such as architecture. Increasingly they see the study of material culture as a legitimate way to investigate the past. As a prime example, for many years Thomas Schlereth of the University of Notre Dame has treated Greenfield Village as a "laboratory" (his term) in which his students study a number of topics, including the museum itself as a cultural artifact.[17] The experience at Strawbery Banke raises the possibility of extending this approach beyond the organized class to the public at large.

Developing Strawbery Banke or any other outdoor museum as a learning laboratory asserts that the past, for the general public, is as much something to be studied as it is a place to go. In a way this approach is a return to Henry Ford's explicitly educational approach, although the goals and methods differ. The museum-as-laboratory combines the intellectual activity of the classroom with the sensory appeal of the historical environment. It recognizes that learning and enjoyment go hand in hand and that people want both.

The learning laboratory concept can do for history what science museums do for science: allow people to observe and manipulate evidence in order to explore certain phenomena. Just as people enjoy learning how things work in the natural world, so too do they take pleasure in discovering relationships among the things, the people, and the ideas that make up the past.

The views expressed in this essay are those of the author and not necessarily the official views of Strawbery Banke, Inc.

NOTES

1. Harvey Wish, *The American Historian* (New York: Oxford University Press, 1960), 158–208.
2. Anthony Brandt, "A Short Natural History of Nostalgia," *The Atlantic Monthly*, December 1978, 58–63.
3. Edward P. Alexander, *Museums in Motion* (Nashville: American Association for State and Local History, 1979), 88–89.
4. An excellent account of the early development of outdoor museums appears

in Jay Anderson, *Time Machines: The World of Living History* (Nashville: American Association for State and Local History, 1984), 17–33.

5. [R. Goodwin], *A Brief and True Report for the Traveller Concerning Williamsburg in Virginia* (Richmond: Colonial Williamsburg, Inc., 1936), 130. This book, written in eighteenth-century style, is itself a good example of the impulse to recreate the past.

6. Ibid., 126, 130.

7. Ibid., 149.

8. Geoffrey C. Upward, *A Home for Our Heritage* (Dearborn, Mich.: The Henry Ford Museum Press, 1979), 3.

9. Steven K. Hamp, "Subject Over Object: Interpreting the Museum as Artifact," *Museum News* 63 (December 1984): 35.

10. Mitchell R. Alegre, *A Guide to Museum Villages* (New York: Drake Publishers, 1978) lists 102 outdoor museums across America. This is a minimum number, since several are not included.

11. Anderson, *Time Machines,* 25–33.

12. Cary Carson, "Living Museums of Everyman's History," *Harvard Magazine* (Summer 1981): 22–24, describes the entry of academically trained historians into the outdoor museum field.

13. John Demos, *A Little Commonwealth: Family Life in Plymouth Colony* (London: Oxford University Press, 1970).

14. Carson, "Living Museums," 31–33.

15. Darwin Kelsey, "Harvests of History," *Historic Preservation* 28 (March 1976): 22, quoted in Anderson, *Time Machines,* 43.

16. Charles Phillips, "Greenfield's Changing Past," *History News* 37 (November 1982): 12.

17. Thomas J. Schlereth, *Artifacts and the American Past* (Nashville: American Association for State and Local History, 1980), 123.

Douglas C. Dolan is executive director of the Bucks County Historical Society, Doylestown, Pennsylvania. The society owns and/or operates the Mercer Museum, Fonthill Museum, and the Spruance Library. Prior to his appointment in Bucks County, Dolan was the executive director of the Historical Society of York County [Pennsylvania] and, before that, Bicentennial coordinator at the University of Delaware.

Dolan is a member of the Board of Governors of the Mid-Atlantic Association of Museums, a regional branch of the American Association of Museums; a member of the Board of Directors of the Pennsylvania Federation of Historical Societies; and a member of the Bucks County Museums Council.

He is a graduate of the University of Delaware with a master's degree in American History and a certificate in Museum Studies. He is also a graduate of the Williamsburg Seminar in Historical Administration and the Museum Management Institute at the University of California at Berkeley. Dolan is active in numerous professional organizations and has served as a consultant to many small museums and historical organizations.

THE HISTORIAN IN THE LOCAL HISTORICAL MUSEUM

Douglas C. Dolan

The historian employed in a local historical museum may function as a director, curator, librarian, archivist, educator, or all of the above. Local historical museums range in size from one-person operations to large operations where duties and responsibilities are clearly delineated. By far, the small historical museum is the norm across the country. A recent survey conducted by the American Association for State and Local History noted that 62 percent of the historical institutions in America had operating budgets of $50,000 or less.[1] However, local historical museums, regardless of size, share the common bond of making history real and meaningful to a diverse audience. Within the local historical museum, practicing public historians will find themselves actively engaged in historical resources management for a variety of "publics."

Traditionally, historians have gravitated to local historical museums and historical agencies as places of employment that utilized their skills as researchers and historians. From the outset, though, historians have had to develop new skills to augment their academic training and enable them to communicate a sense of the past to their audiences. These audiences may range from children to senior citizens, and they may come in contact with the museum either individually or as part of an organized activity. Each audience brings along its own set of perceptions of history and time. The challenge for historians is to discover the key that will enable them to make the transition between history as an abstraction to history as a meaningful experience for each audience group.

By its very nature, the local historical museum is concerned with the history of ordinary people, events, and happenings within a definable geographic boundary. Its focus is on a study of grassroots history. It is a history of families and communities told through the photographs, documents, artifacts, and memorabilia of a region. In an age of computers and space shuttles, the local historical museum functions as the collector and preserver of a region's history and serves as a storehouse of its collective memory. Equally important, it becomes the medium through which the past becomes alive. The historian working in the local historical museum as director/curator must be the catalyst to inspire and stimulate people to comprehend the past and its impact on the present and the future.

The challenge confronting the historian in the local history museum is to develop the means to reach these diverse audiences. Through exhibits, workshops, lectures, and school programs, the local historical museum provides avenues to explore the past. Schoolchildren can be challenged to make the transition from today to yesterday through discovery programs that encourage identifying similarities between household objects of the past and items that they are familiar with from around their homes. Exhibits of maps and photographs can document the evolution of communities or serve as focal points for seminars and workshops that draw senior citizens into discussions about their past experiences. The local historical museum is on the front lines of the grassroots history movement. It is the institution most concerned with what has been termed "nearby history."

David E. Kyvig and Myron A. Marty stated in their publication *Nearby History: Exploring the Past Around You* that "the territory of nearby history is, obviously, both a training ground and a principal workplace for public historians. In exploring the past of subjects close at hand, a person learns to identify, collect, organize, and exhibit historical materials, to analyze complex factors, to examine the relationship of the inner concentric circles of nearby situation to the outer circles of national and international development. . . ."[2] "Nearby history" involves interpreting history not as an abstraction but rather through tangible artifacts and documents. Within the local historical museum, the historian focuses not on the effects of great historical movements on a national scale but rather on their impact on the local community. In doing so, the historian is presented with the unique opportunity to study and interpret complex historical developments in terms of the daily lives of ordinary people. Within this context, the historian will function both as manager and researcher. As manager, he/she will be involved in organizing and caring for historical materials. As researcher, he/she will actively utilize historical materials to convey an understanding of history and historical trends.

Functioning as a manager, the historian working within the local historical museum actively collects, catalogs, and maintains a wide range of historical artifacts. The historian may have the title of director or curator, historian, or librarian. Indeed, in the small local historical museum, these positions may be blended together or even vested in one individual. However, the professional staff member within a local historical museum will have the chief responsibility to guide the growth and development of the collections and plan and implement interpretive programming. In carrying out these responsibilities, the professional staff members must combine the knowledge and sensitivity of a historian with the organizational and planning skills of a manager. Within the established guidelines and purposes of the museum, staff members seek out new acquisitions that will enhance the collections while educating individuals, business persons, community leaders, and others to the importance of preserving the tangible records and artifacts of the past.

Because the local historical museum functions as a repository of historical artifacts and memorabilia, the historian must manage the collections in a manner consonant with professional standards. This will ensure that collections are maintained adequately and are accessible to researchers and museum personnel. Objects that are accepted into the collection need to be assigned a discrete number which is recorded in accession records. Information about an object's composition, place of origin, date, use, provenance, and relationship to the museum, and so forth, must also be recorded. In some cases, objects will require extensive historical research as part of the cataloging process. In other cases, the associational relationship may be more important than the object itself. Records on object condition, location, and donor are all part of an integrated record system that allows the historian to utilize objects in the study of history. Over the years, museums have developed various systems to record the essential documentation of objects. The historian interested in guidance in this area would do well to consult the publications of the American Association of Museums or the American Association for State and Local History.

The local historical museum should be devoted to telling the entire story of the history of its region. One dilemma that confronts the director/curator stems from the establishment of arbitrary cutoff dates dealing with the artifacts and records of the more recent past. Too often in the local historical museum, history is perceived as ending with the Civil War, or, perhaps, with the close of the nineteenth century. The result is that a coherent policy for collecting readily available examples of recent history is lacking. Not only does this practice leave an important gap in a museum's collections, but also it does a grave disservice to future historians. Surely, 100 years from now, the miniskirt and denim jacket will be as important cultural artifacts as an eighteenth-century brocade coat or hoop skirt. Since museums are timeless, collecting policies should recognize the continuum of local history in a region.

With a focus oriented toward local history, it is only natural that an individual working as a director/curator of a local historical museum will on many occasions come into contact with professionals throughout the community in matters dealing with local history. Of course, the museum professional often will be dealing with teachers of history and social studies on the local elementary, secondary, and college levels in the development of educational and historical research projects. In some cases, it will be easy to develop projects out of the needs and interests of both parties. At other times, however, the museum professional will be challenged to find ways to utilize historical artifacts to complement classroom teaching. Cooperative projects between schools and the museum that allow students to work with primary historical materials and artifacts as the basis for research projects can provide a tangible link between broad historical concepts and the realities of the past. For example, students, working with museum staff, can be utilized to survey historical inventories and vendue lists to develop a composite representative list of household furnishings in a particular region during a specific time period. The museum, through its historical collections, provides the evidence for students to better comprehend the historical theories taught in the classroom. It can turn the two-dimensional pages of a historical textbook into a three-dimensional experience.

In addition to teachers and students, the director/curator of the local historical museum will have dealings with professional researchers working on historical projects. Often these projects will extend far beyond the scope of the local historical museum and its collections, but they provide important opportunities for a better understanding of the effects of large-scale historical trends in the local historical museum. Indeed the professional researcher will often find that within the local historical museum's collections are the artifacts and documents that provide the best illustrations in human terms of the realities of the great historical movements on the local scene. Neither the professional researcher nor the academic historian should overlook the treasures housed within the local historical museum.

It should be noted that the bond of understanding between the public historian and the academic historian is weak at times. Traditionally, the academics have perceived "public historians" as less than scholarly in their pursuits. In some respects, this criticism has been justified as museum curators and exhibit designers have tried to take historical concepts and themes and neatly package them in concise museum exhibits and interpretive publications. A problem that museums must confront is the real tendency of oversimplification and strict periodization. Noted historian Thomas J. Schlereth states, "Rigid periodization in museums and textbooks provokes historical truncation in the mind of the visitor or the reader. . . . The use of the decade or the century . . . as the only parcels of human history has induced us to divide the American past into artificial vacuous categories of period settings, period displays, period rooms, period houses and period environments."[3]

The advent of "public history" and its acceptance by academics as a legitimate pursuit for the history scholar provide an important opportunity to explore ways to incorporate current historical thinking into the development of exhibits, programs, and publications of local historical museum interpretation. In fulfilling their function as researchers, historians in the local historical museum are confronted with the very difficult problem of blending subtle, complex historical trends into the museum's educational programs in a manner that encourages participants to think about the larger issues. In doing so, the historians need to familiarize themselves with the current level of interpretive thinking by academic historians and to incorporate those historical theories into the museum's interpretive efforts. The historians involved in the local historical museum should avail themselves of the same primary historical resources and proven research methodologies as their academic counterparts. On the other hand, academic historians need to respect the important role that tangible objects can play in focusing an individual's or group's attention on historical trends and their meaning.

Academic historians and teachers are by no means the only professionals that one deals with in the position of director/curator of the local historical museum. The museum's professional staff often find themselves called upon as the history experts for comment on projects ranging from building restorations to the development of community identity and image for marketing efforts. Urban planners, architects, economic development specialists, tourism promoters, and even politicians recognize local history as an economic asset. One needs only to look at the tremendous impact of the Bicentennial upon communities, big and small, all across this nation to see graphic proof of this fact. Unfortunately, recognizing the economic advantage of history and being able to use history in a sensitive, accurate manner do not always occur at the same time. Nonhistory professionals and politicians may sympathize with the historical aspects of any issue but should not be expected to be the chief advocates of these aspects. This is a role that the local historical museum can fulfill.

The history professional from the local historical museum is a valuable partner to any professional team addressing issues that impact on the community. In small communities, where limited resources preclude the hiring of a history specialist directly, the local historical museum professional can provide valuable insights into the cultural and social forces that are at the heart of the historical background of any issue. In cases dealing with the recycling and restoration of old buildings, many times the staff of the local historical museum may be called upon to provide input on historical questions. Even the development of tourism brochures promoting the local region might necessitate the involvement of the local historical museum in defining the area's historical image that is to be projected. Many a local tourism agency has had to be educated to understand that their "colonial" image does not describe the historical realities of the town or region that may, in fact, be a post–Civil War Victorian town. The local historical museum staff can and should be involved in dispelling historical myths and providing accurate historical information.

The local historical museum staff performs an important function for community leaders and activists. Staff members can work with interested parties in understanding historical trends and their relationship to current and future events. Further, they can help bring the history of the community into the decision-making process of planners and political bodies. Thus, history can be at the very foundation of understanding the impact of larger events upon the community or region. Historical consideration can affect economic issues on the local level. In fact, the local historical museum may be called upon to provide the stamp of approval—the mark of historical authenticity—to nonmuseum projects and ideas. When called upon in these situations, the museum staff members will find themselves dealing with individuals whose concept of history may be a mix of myth and reality that will require the skills of a historian and a diplomat to unwind.

A student who is interested in working in a historical museum would do well to read G. Ellis Burcaw's *Introduction to Museum Work* (Nashville: American Association for State and Local History, 1975) and Edward P. Alexander's *Museums in Motion: An Introduction to the History and Functions of Museums* (Nashville: American Association for State and Local History, 1979). Both publications provide valuable insights into museums and the museum profession. Together, they give not only a historical perspective but also an understanding of the complex issues involved in the daily operation of a museum, large or small.

One simple way that a student can explore the museum profession and, at the same time, gain some valuable experience, is by becoming a volunteer at a local historical museum. Volunteers are the foundation of the small historical museum. A recent survey by the American Association for State and Local History noted that almost 40 percent of America's historical organizations have no paid staff whatsoever and another 11 percent have only one paid employee.[4] Obviously, the work being done by these organizations is largely dependent upon volunteers. The museum field is one profession in which volunteer experience can count equally as well as a paid position in terms of acceptable work experience. Students should identify the volunteer opportunities available in their own local historical museums and take advantage of them. This step not only provides valuable hands-on experience but also, perhaps, a foot in the door for future employment.

Another technique that will help students learn about career opportunities in museum work is to conduct a series of informational interviews with persons already employed in the museum field. By this method, students can get first-hand information on the nature of professional duties and responsibilities along with some personal insights into the museum field. Museum professionals are like anyone else and will be flattered that someone is interested enough to seek their opinion. A good interviewer may be able to draw out some very candid observations and comments on museum work. This information could prove very helpful in defining career goals.

One important consideration for anyone thinking about a museum career is that compensation levels are low. In the small historical museum, director and curator salaries are often at or below the level of a college instructor or assistant professor, with entry-level professional salaries often below the level of beginning school teachers. Combined with benefit packages that are virtually "no-frills," the museum profession is not a fast track to riches. In fairness, it should be noted that salaries are rising, albeit slowly, but it is an underpaid profession.

The other important trend a student should be aware of is the rising educational level of professionals in the field. For many years, historical museums were the bastion of the interested layman and amateur historian. Not so today. Even in the small historical museum, an undergraduate degree is virtually essential, and more and more beginning professionals are coming to the field with master's or doctoral degrees in history or a related academic specialty. Students should realize that the job market in the museum profession is very competitive. It would be in their best interest to pursue graduate work in their chosen academic field. Indeed, many employers will look for a candidate with a master's degree, and a doctorate is highly recommended for a curator position. There is always a large pool of candidates for any opening in the museum profession. Students who can arm themselves with a graduate degree and some practical experience, either through volunteer work or an internship, will be better prepared to compete successfully for that all-important first job.

In addition to a sound background in history, the individual seeking a career in the historical museum field should have other personal and technical skills. An individual should be a skillful manager with good organizational skills. Whether managing the collections, education projects, volunteers, or the entire museum, familiarity and knowledge of management theory and techniques will serve the historian well. The characteristics of management situations within a not-for-profit environment are unique and affect all facets of operations. Classroom exposure to the fundamentals of management theory would provide a solid foundation.

Another equally essential asset for any individual contemplating a career in the historical museum field is to develop the skills necessary for working with people. Interpersonal relationships are at the heart of any endeavor within this field. By its nature, the museum profession is very labor intensive. One needs to have an ability to work with people of diverse ages, backgrounds, and interests. From trustees to volunteers to schoolchildren and the general public, one deals with a variety of people on a daily basis. Whether through written or spoken means, an individual must develop the skills to communicate ideas and concepts clearly. Further, the communication process also requires an individual to listen attentively. Feedback from various audiences, whether visitors to an exhibit or children in a school program, is an important part of the evaluation process within the museum field. Because a historian will deal with groups with different conceptions of history and time, the ability to listen will enable a historian to bridge these conceptual gaps and develop more meaningful historical experiences.

Anyone who contemplates work in a local historical museum needs a working knowledge of the fundamentals of museum operations and philosophy. Museum ethics and standards have been established and endorsed by the profession as a whole. Numerous publications have been written on specific issues ranging from collections care and record keeping to the history and philosophy of museums, and a working familiarity with this body of knowledge is essential. Museums are complex educational organizations that require an understanding of their basic nature. Fortunately, there are many fine graduate-level museum studies training programs associated with universities and colleges across the country. In many cases, students can avail themselves of this specialized training while pursuing a graduate degree in their chosen academic field of study. This will provide a student with a balanced knowledge of museum practices and advanced historical studies.

One important aspect of any museum studies training program is the provision for internships. This provides students with hands-on experience within a museum setting and allows them to apply skills learned within the classroom to real problems. Internships come in many forms, from one week to a full year, paid and unpaid. Students evaluating various museum studies programs would do well to examine closely their internship policies and placement procedures. Successful internships should provide a meaningful experience for both the student and the host institution. An internship should allow a student to experience the day-to-day activities within a museum as a member of the regular staff.

A professional employee of a small local historical museum will at times feel like a jack-of-all-trades. Researching and designing exhibits, developing slide lectures, and organizing workshops will call into play a host of technical skills. Knowledge of audiovisual equipment and photography would be helpful. An understanding of the printing industry and how to work with printers will smooth the development of brochures and publications resulting from historical projects. Fabricating small exhibits and displays requires manual dexterity and some ability to use hand tools. Of course, the rapid evolution of the personal computer has brought this tool within the realm of the small museum as an aid in collections management and word processing.

Working in a local historical museum is both challenging and rewarding. It is an environment that requires a self-starter who can establish goals and strategies to attain them. It is also a field that rewards patience and perseverance. Because resources are always limited, one must also have a high tolerance for frustration. In some cases, frustration comes from the inherent conservatism of boards of directors and volunteer groups as new ideas and projects are put forward. However, the frustrations are easily forgotten in the joys of successful projects that make history a personal and real experience. And, of course, the best antidote for frustration that anyone can have is to maintain a good sense of humor! This asset may be the most beneficial one for any individual who works in a nonprofit organization.

The historian employed as director/curator in the local historical museum will wear many hats. Functioning as manager and researcher, historians will have the opportunity to guide the growth and development of a nonprofit organization dedicated to preserving the heritage of a local area while at the same time utilizing their knowledge of history and research techniques in the design and implementation of educational programs. Although resources are traditionally limited, the local historical museum provides the perfect environment for the creative, imaginative historian who wants a "hands-on" approach to making history come alive. In the local historical museum, history is not an abstraction. It is very real and always "nearby."

NOTES

1. Philips, Charles, and Patricia Hogan, "Who Cares for America's Heritage?" *History News* 39 (September 1984): 8.
2. Kyvig, David E., and Myron A. Marty, *Nearby History: Exploring the Past Around You* (Nashville: American Association for State and Local History, 1982), 12.
3. Schlereth, Thomas J., "It Wasn't That Simple," *Museum News* 56 (January–February 1978): 38.
4. Phillips, Charles, and Patricia Hogan, "The Wages of History," *History News* 39 (August 1984): 7.

SUGGESTED READING

For anyone seeking to learn more about museums and the museums profession, the following publications may prove helpful: Edward P. Alexander, *Museums in Motion: An Introduction to the History and Functions of Museums* (Nashville: American Association for State and Local History, 1979); G. Ellis Burcaw, *Introduction to Museum Work* (Nashville: American Association for State and Local History, 1975); American Association for State and Local History, "So You've Chosen to be a History Professional . . . " (Nashville: American Association for State and Local History, 1978); American Association of Museums, *Museums for a New Century* (Washington, D.C.: American Association of Museums, 1984); Dorothy Weyer Creigh, *A Primer for Local Historical Societies* (Nashville: American Association for State and Local History, 1976); Ronald L. Miller, *Personnel Policies for Museums: A Handbook for Management* (Washington, D.C.: American Association of Museums, 1980); Ralph H. Lewis, *Manual for Museums* (Washington, D.C.: Government Printing Office, 1976); and American Association of Museums, *Museum Ethics* (Washington, D.C.: American Association of Museums, 1978). See also the related essays in this book by Gerald George entitled "The Perils of 'Public' History: An Imaginary Excursion into the Real World" and by Steven Lubar entitled "Public History in a Federal Museum: The Smithsonian's National Museum of American History."

For a biographical sketch of Gerald W. George, see his essay, "The Perils of 'Public' History," elsewhere in this book.

THE AMERICAN ASSOCIATION FOR STATE AND LOCAL HISTORY: THE PUBLIC HISTORIAN'S HOME?

Gerald George

If you are contemplating a career in public history, you will, sooner or later, run onto—or up against—the American Association for State and Local History (AASLH).

The first encounter may come on your very first day in class, if you happen to be handed an assigned reading list that includes G. Ellis Burcaw's *Introduction to Museum Work*, or Kenneth W. Duckett's *Modern Manuscripts: A Practical Manual for Their Management, Care, and Use*, or *Ordinary People and Everyday Life: Perspectives on the New Social History*, edited by James B. Gardner and George Rollie Adams—all among the standard texts published by the AASLH Press. But the diversity of that booklist itself, and its apparent lack of relation to state and local history *per se*, may well make you wonder just what, exactly, AASLH is.

Your bewilderment likely will grow as the semester or quarter progresses. On a day when you discover that the slide-tape program shown by the professor in class is one of a series available from AASLH on historic house conservation, you may conclude that the association serves primarily historic houses. But the next week your professor may show an AASLH videotape on something such as "Interpreting History Through Pictorial Documents." And the following week there may be a class exercise using material in an AASLH independent study kit on, say, "School Programs and the Museum." At that point you may well start to wonder—does AASLH itself know what it is?

On and off through your university program, you probably also will encounter scores of AASLH technical leaflets, which offer advice on everything from accounting practices for historical societies to methods for detecting and preventing wood deterioration. Included is a leaflet that you as a public history student may especially want to read, on "Using Consultants Effectively," because you are likely to be debating whether to seek a history job in a public institution or to set up as a consulting historian on your own. However, many of the leaflets will seem so restricted to beginner-level fundamentals—"Methods of Research for the Amateur Historian," for example—that you may begin to think of AASLH as chiefly for amateurs; after all, much local history and historical society work has been the province of history buffs.

Figure 1. The AASLH Press is one of the leading publishers of books for the museum and historical society professional, and a valuable source of publications for history students, teachers, and amateur historians. *Chris Fenoglio, photographer.*

But then, in some advanced class, you will try to grasp the principles of a computer printout volume entitled *Nomenclature for Museum Cataloging*, by Robert G. Chenhall, which AASLH published to help sophisticated museums standardize their collections terminology. And in anticipation of becoming a professional historian off-campus, in either a firm or an institution, you will consider whether you can afford the

Figure 2. AASLH's independent study programs provide comprehensive instruction in vital areas of museum and historical agency work. Developed for
personal study at home or at work, each kit contains a study guide, supplemental
reading materials, tools, supplies, and lesson assignments. Written by experts,
packaged for convenience, AASLH independent study programs provide an
excellent way for historical agency and museum workers to develop specialized
skills.

AASLH six-volume *Bibliography on Historical Organization Practices,* which
the editors, Frederick L. Rath, Jr. and Merrilyn Rogers O'Connell,
clearly prepared as a career tool for professionals. And then may come
your first trip to an AASLH annual meeting, after you discover the
student discount on registration fees. There you will rub shoulders with
pros from Colonial Williamsburg, the National Park Service, and the
major state historical societies, as well as with staff of smaller places—and
with relatively few amateurs. And you may wonder about AASLH all
over again.

Well, as graduation approaches, you may turn with increasing regu-
larity to the AASLH bi-monthly magazine, *History News,* where job
opportunity advertisements are regularly found. That may even lead
you to peruse articles in the magazine, such as "Public History's First
Ph.D. Puts Her Skills to Work Outside the Academy," among other
public history pieces. And then, at last, it may fully dawn on you—yes, of
course, that's it—*that* is why AASLH produces such a bewildering variety
of stuff! It is because of the variety of things people need to know,
amateurs or professionals, if they practice history for the public off-
campus, rather than teaching and doing academic research. AASLH is

Figure 3. *History News,* the bi-monthly magazine published by AASLH, covers the news and issues affecting today's historical agency and museum workers. The magazine includes a mix of exciting in-depth feature articles and regular columns that carry professional and practical information.

about history in all its public aspects. Yes, the American Association for State and Local History is really, never mind the name, the American Association for Public History.

ORIGINS OF THE DEBATE ON PUBLIC HISTORY

Alas, you may have just made your first major professional mistake. For in the glow of the revelation just reached, as described above, you might write to one of the employers who has advertised a job in *History News* and say: "I am now a trained public historian, ready to pursue my career in a public history institution such as yours."

There is a chance that rejection could come from that alone. For if you had read further in *History News,* you would have discovered a further division or confusion within the American Association for State and Local History. Some of the leading, veteran members of AASLH have opposed and even felt insulted by the term "public historian" and the entire concept of "public history." Such opposition has come not just from intellectual conservatives or professional curmudgeons; indeed, one of the personally most tolerant and professionally most revered of former state history directors summed it up in a letter to me as follows:

> As an old-time historian who busied himself for decades with meeting the public and trying to serve them, writing, helping to establish policies for the people and their legislators, giving out historical information and advice as called upon, keeping doors open, picking up unwanted trash from the grounds, calming personalities, and stuffing envelopes, what could be more "Public Historian" than this kind? So, I'm still puzzled by the appearance of the special *Public Historian* of the 1980s.

Within AASLH, the controversy first surfaced openly in the May 1979 issue of *History News,* which we devoted almost entirely to articles about "the phenomenal growth of the public history concept" and "the important implications it holds for the work of state and local history." Included was a staff-written article about the "public history movement" and its advocates overall, plus "A Case for Public Historians," by Larry Tise, himself a state history agency director and subsequently elected to a seat on the AASLH governing council, plus an editorial by me, rather provocatively entitled, "Take a 'Public Historian' to Lunch."

The general article described, among other things, the rise of "public history" graduate programs in the 1970s at institutions such as the University of California at Santa Barbara, where Professor Robert Kelley and colleagues hoped to prepare history graduates for professional involvement in social decision making, "bringing the historical consciousness into a working role in the daily conduct of affairs," a "purpose honorable in character and elegant in its dimensions." In an equally visionary spirit, Dr. Tise wrote in *History News:*

> . . . Mark the year 1978 as the year in which a phenomenon known as "public history" burst forth generally and publicly in the United States as a new reality in the field of history. Rarely in the course of the development of any discipline or of any profession has such an occurrence been more badly needed or more timely. But whether it will succeed in bringing new life to the sagging fortunes of the history profession or meet the challenges of a viable public history for the American nation . . . ay, there's the rub. . . .

My editorial more mincingly observed that, if nothing else, the "phenomenon" offered "a new opportunity" for "rebuilding the bridges between those who work with history outside the schools and those who work in academic research and teaching. . . ." And I asked AASLH members to respond sympathetically.

Unfortunately, *History News* was too small at that time to have a letter-to-the-editor column, which we could have filled with "public history" arguments from a variety of viewpoints. Some historical agency veterans resented not only the implication that "public history" was something new, but also the seeming assumption by historians in academe that they had discovered or invented it. Moreover, some young historians working off-campus resented being called "public historians," which sounded like less than the real thing.

History News continued to encourage AASLH members to confront the issues involved. In June 1980, for example, the magazine ran a report by Alan M. Schroder, who had unearthed a six-volume series of monographs that the State Historical Society of Iowa had published between 1912 and 1930 as an "Applied History Series." The older "applied history" seemed remarkably similar to the "new" public history. The controversy continued also to provide subject matter for sometimes heated sessions at annual meetings of AASLH. And in October 1982, *History News* provoked a fresh outburst with an article on the first person to earn a doctorate from the Santa Barbara program: "Gayle Clark Olson, History Entrepreneur." It was a candid report about problems as well as opportunities that students were encountering in such programs and in marketing their skills after graduation. In response, Professor Kelley, himself formerly a historian in the Air Force, who had coined the term "public history" in 1975, while "thinking about the new directions the profession should be heading," wrote a long letter to the editor about the "wearing experience" of creating a new program "designed to give our students a 'generalist' understanding of the many things public historians do." He asserted that "no one had ever done before what we were trying to do," that "we had to learn everything, from the first step," and that his program was "brand-new, with absolutely no precedents to go on, no useful parallels anywhere else. . . ." Which in turn provoked a rebuke from William T. Alderson in a letter to the editor that concluded:

> If, on the other hand, Kelley is using the everchanging and constantly broadening definition of public history that refers to almost everything the historian does outside of a classroom, he is ignoring the truly pioneering programs developed by the late Ernst Posner in archival training, the late Charles Montgomery who began the Winterthur program in Early American Culture, Earle W. Newton who ran a program in Historical Administration at Radcliffe College in the 1950s, Louis C. Jones who established the Cooperstown Graduate Program, Edward P. Alexander who was the prime mover in establishing the Williamsburg Seminar for Historical Administration in 1957 and a host of others—including the American Association for State and Local History—all of which provide precedents and parallels and several of them a quarter of a century of experience upon which to draw. . . .

The short quotations above don't do justice to the positions taken by either Dr. Kelley or Dr. Alderson. But they make this point: Dr. Alderson, before heading the museum studies program at the University of Delaware and then the Strong Museum, had spent fourteen years as director of AASLH itself. Obviously during that time AASLH had not conceived itself as an American Association for Public History. Nor, apparently, had Professor Kelley and his colleagues thought of it as such.

DIFFERENT PERSPECTIVES ON PUBLIC HISTORY

Oh well, you may at this point argue, the differences after all seem merely semantic and the argument only territorial. Whatever AASLH called itself, and however much antipathy some of its leaders may have had toward the term "public history," the association has in fact provided technical literature, educational seminars, and other services for people practicing history in some public rather than academic forum—a museum, archives, library, historical site, preservation group, historical society, or independent research activity. The new university programs simply moved formally into AASLH's field and gave it a new name.

The only real differences, you could argue further, were in emphasis. Professor Kelley's program at Santa Barbara had emphasized the concept that historians could be trained to provide a kind of perspective and analytical skill needed by government agencies and private businesses. Public historians could contribute to policy decisions by contracting for environmental impact studies, by producing research on the historical background of social problems, and by organizing archival materials and writing histories for businesses and other private or public institutions. AASLH, on the other hand, had usually focused its publications and programs on the historian at work in a historical society, museum, or other institution whose primary business was history. And unlike the universities, which hoped to expand professional opportunities for trained historians, AASLH was just as interested in helping the amateurs and volunteers on whom hundreds of local historical societies and museums depended.

Differences in emphasis could be seen again when AASLH, alarmed at what seemed a sudden proliferation of ill-conceived "public history" training programs in universities in the early 1980s, published standards identifying the content such programs would realistically need to prepare students adequately and responsibly. Included was insistence on substantial internships in historical agencies for students, which university program heads sometimes felt unwilling or unable to provide. The AASLH emphasis on extensive hands-on experience often seemed unreasonable if not irrelevant in academe.

Moreover, those already in the field who called themselves public historians often felt in the minority among historical agency and museum people, and uncomfortable with or ambivalent about AASLH, which did not particularly try to accommodate their special interests. Few if any hesitated to find out about and make use of AASLH resources, particularly technical publications from the AASLH Press. But, only a small percentage actually joined the association, and fewer still came to its annual meetings or otherwise participated in its affairs. Instead, they formed organizations of their own, such as the National Council on Public History, and fought within the academic associations, most notably the Organization of American Historians (OAH), for the professional recognition and influence they felt they should have. It quickly became clear that, however far the work of such "public historians" might take them from the campus, their standards for professional achievement and self-esteem remained within it. "Real" historians are recognized by their intellectual products, chiefly in writing, right? But AASLH offered no scholarly journal and few annual meeting sessions at which formal papers could be read or subjects other than administrative, curatorial, or institutional matters discussed. Better to publish articles in the new *Public Historian,* which had the format of a scholarly journal, or seek space on the OAH annual meeting program side by side with university scholars, than try either to transform AASLH or accept such routes as it offered to recognition for historians and others indifferent to the preferences of professors.

Thus, in retrospect, the essential positions represented by Professor Kelley and Dr. Alderson both seem more or less right: historical organizations were indeed full of trained (as well as untrained) historians engaged in a whole range of "public history" activities long before that term was coined or university programs using it were begun. But previously the historian who went into off-campus historical activities often became also an archivist, a curator, a librarian, an interpreter, a preservationist, a museum educator, a site superintendent, or an agency administrator. And some such specialties had their own professional organizations, training programs, and ladders to status. What the public history movement emphasized at the outset was the employment outside academe of historians whose primary activity remained research, professionally linked with those who stayed in the classrooms and libraries of the university. Only later did the term tend to get expanded to cover any history-related activity not centered on formal education. And the more amorphous the term became, the more it was resented by some historians off campus who felt academics were co-opting them in the spirit with which Columbus "discovered" "Indians."

AASLH DEFINES ITSELF

If AASLH was not and is not, after all, the American Association for Public History in the narrow sense, what, then, is it? Those questions are not easy to answer either, because in the 1980s AASLH seemed to be having its own "identity crisis." In fact, that was partly because the public history movement, however defined, was having considerable effect on AASLH.

That is, a number of new movements in the 1970s and early 1980s did. For the public historians were not the only new group to emerge around the edges of what AASLH had more or less assumed to be its tent. The National Trust for Historic Preservation, which itself was founded after

AASLH, spawned a new Historic House Association. Other new groups sprang up under the aegis of the American Association of Museums, some of whose leaders tended erroneously to regard AASLH as the history museum group within its own voluminous tent. State and regional museum associations grew and increased in number. Also such separate groups as the Museum Stores Association, the National Council for Preservation Education, and the Association for Living Historical Farms and Agricultural Museums came into being. In the records field, the Society of American Archivists, which predated AASLH and had some membership overlap with it, had become flanked by such groups as the Association of Records Managers and Administrators and the National Association of State Archives and Records Administrators. All of this professional ferment, this assertion of professional specialty identification, of which the public history movement was a part, put pressure on AASLH to consider who, if anyone, it really did represent.

The question was compounded rather than answered by the clear evidence that AASLH certainly was representing somebody, because its membership kept rising through the 1970s and into the 1980s, peaking at around 8,000 individuals and institutions in 1983. We knew also that the historical organization field itself had been growing: The AASLH *Directory of Historical Societies and Agencies in the United States and Canada* identified 3,300 such organizations in 1970, more than 4,000 by 1978, nearly 6,000 in 1982, and 13,000 in 1986.

In 1981, the Executive Committee and I "retreated" for a few days to a remote and hospitable historic site in Maryland to think about it. And there, as the first step in preparation for a new three-year plan that eventually engaged all AASLH committees and the council as a whole, we decided that we didn't want to focus on anybody in particular. We wanted to carry on the mission to promote grassroots historical activity that had been at the heart of AASLH from its start. The lengthy "purpose" clause of the AASLH Constitution had long called for encouraging the preservation and use of local history broadly. The founders in 1940 had stressed the need to "promote a broad program of historical work for the American and Canadian people. . . ." And we gave ourselves again, at least tentatively, a similar mission statement:

> The purpose of AASLH is to help individuals and communities, especially through their historical organizations, identify, save, and use their significant historic resources.

That was a banner (or more accurately, perhaps, a quilt) under which the history-minded of many stripes could enlist, including public historians of the new kind. The statement was written, obviously, in a socially crusading rather than a profession-promoting spirit. Our eyes were on the end desired—the use by communities, for research, education, and enjoyment, of all kinds of historic resources: documents and manuscripts, museum artifacts, historic sites, and structures. If one recognized that all those things were part of the historical record, then archivists *and* museologists *and* preservationists *and* historians, both professional and amateur, public and scholastic, could see their work as all part of a common cause.

But secondly, at least, the consensus statement did take cognizance of historical *organizations* as the chief vehicles to produce the desired end. And in fact, when we got down to setting specific objectives for AASLH in the three-year plan, we focused not on individuals or communities but on the kinds of help historical organizations themselves would need as they served their constituents with history. In that sense we became conceptually the American Association for Historical Organizations. Which, as staff director, I, in a misguided moment, actually, publicly proposed.

WHAT IS IN A NAME?

In a special editorial in *History News,* I put the question to the membership: "Is the 'American Association for State and Local History' a proper, useful, accurate, still-serviceable name?"

On the negative side there were practical problems with it, I reminded the membership:

> You all know the usual objections: It hardly rolls trippingly off the tongue. It admits of no easy acronymic shorthand, though some of you have tried by calling us "ashlash" or "assla" or worse. And by the time you say the whole thing, the person who inquired about it often is asleep or has moved on to some other corner of the cocktail party. Our name is not an *easy* form of identification.

Next, I detailed public relations problems caused for us by a name that sometimes conveyed only notions of parochial narrowness to busy officers of grant-making institutions, when they could grasp what we were about at all. Indeed, I argued, the name misrepresents us by emphasizing a certain field of study rather than certain kinds of institutions—historical organizations generally. Is Andrew Jackson's Hermitage in Nashville a state or local historic site? the Smithsonian Institution? the Winterthur Museum? In those institutions we have many good members, I argued, but all are national as well as state or local in scope. Referring to leaders of AASLH at the time, I wrote:

> AASLH proudly represents the State Historical Society of Wisconsin, whose director is our current president; the Historic Pensacola Preservation Board, whose historical preservationist is our current treasurer; the Littleton, Colorado, Museum, whose director chairs our education committee; and the Harris County, Texas, Heritage Society, which has a trustee on our Council. But also on our Council are representatives of the National Archives, Colonial Williamsburg, and the University of Notre Dame. Many of our members are in the National Park Service, the National Museums of Canada, or ethnic and racial historical groups rather than local organizations. Looking at either our membership rolls or our *directory,* there seems no end to the kinds of historians or groups that we serve. Why not say so by changing our name?

Interestingly enough, more or less the same argument had taken place when AASLH had split off from the American Historical Association (AHA) in 1940. As early as 1904, historical society directors, most of them heading state agencies, had formed a Conference of State and Local Historical Societies, which met annually within the AHA until its leaders felt they needed an organization of their own. A special committee on plans for independence proposed such names as the "Association of American Historical Societies," to reflect the kind of membership that the new organization would in fact have. But "state and local history" prevailed in the name at the behest of state agency directors who themselves were trying to encourage grassroots historical activity in their own states and wanted an association to stand *for* that, not simply to represent those who were doing it. The new organization, they felt, should popularize history, bring together "people of all classifications who are interested in local and regional American history," give the layperson the benefit of guidance from trained historians, encourage lay historians to do local history work that professionals need to draw upon, and enlist the interest of the public at large. Not many years after AASLH began, it had founded *American Heritage*, presenting history to a broad "popular" audience, and maintained a relationship with the magazine until 1984.

Nonetheless, since the founding of AASLH the promotional job had been wildly successful. Where there had been but a few hundred historical organizations at the time helping communities preserve and appreciate their histories, now there were thousands, dealing with ethnic, racial, and special-interest communities as well as those that are geographically defined. AASLH had to concentrate its resources on helping *them* do the public relations and citizen involvement jobs, I suggested. "Shouldn't our name reflect this change?"

Nothing doing.

A few members wrote back in agreement that "the present name of the organization does not adequately describe either its scope or function," and suggested such names as "Historical Organizations of America," the "Association for Material and Cultural History," the "Association for American History," or the "North American Historical Alliance." But a thirty-year member from a historical society in Massachusetts shot back: "I wish to register my vote that the name of the Association remain unchanged. . . . Organizations such as the National Archives know when they join that AASLH represents the grassroots outfits that serve local communities as no others can or will." And a younger, academically trained museum director in Pennsylvania wrote:

> . . . If all the recent surveys and information that we have received from AASLH are correct, the overwhelming majority of historical organizations in this country still have budgets less than $100,000, still employ one or fewer people, and still focus on or appeal to a restricted, specialized subject or audience. Whether or not the staffs of those organizations are becoming more "professional," whatever that may mean, the Association is still largely

serving organizations and individuals involved in state and local history. The only people to whom a name change could appeal are the academics, who frankly neglected local history to the point of scorn until the market-place forced them to look beyond academe for employment. Why should we now want to do something more than state or local history . . . to change our name to become, in someone else's eyes, something other than what we are?

That refrain echoed repeatedly as more letters to the editor on the controversy came in. Even some that did not necessarily oppose chang-ing the name insisted that "state and local history" remain one way or another in it. And I finally concluded, along with many others, that the American Association for State and Local History is called that because, in fact, and in the hearts of its supporters, *that is what it is.*

In our time it happens that most work in state and local history tends to be done off-campus, in historical societies, sites, museums, and public agencies other than universities. AASLH can serve and has served many kinds of organizations and many kinds of historians and historical work, not excluding that of the classroom. But the study of state and local history is what AASLH legitimates. Historians of tangible things, those who work to develop the historical sensibilities of citizens about the places in which they live—they most of all see in AASLH the one organization that fundamentally is, in every sense of the phrase, *for them.*

I hope by now that it is clearer what AASLH offers to you. Whatever kind of historian you are planning to be, AASLH offers both a warning and a welcome.

The warning is not to think too narrowly about what you are going to do "out there." An immense range of opportunity is available for useful history work in the world. Hundreds of trained historians have found satisfactory careers in quite different kinds of history activities, or in moving professionally among them. Titles as well as activities may change in the moves that a historian can make. AASLH probably will continue to seem most relevant to the historian who works in an organization that focuses on a state or locality. But AASLH will try to remain of use one way or another to a broad range of history workers. And all, including you, are welcome to join in the debates that doubtless will continue in AASLH about its mission and its constituency. For associations, too, it should now be obvious, both influence and are influenced by the changing currents of human pressure that we call history.

> *Mr. George's views in this article are per-*
> *sonal, rather than those of the American*
> *Association for State and Local History.*

SUGGESTED READING

For an overview of the history and development of AASLH, the best published accounts are two articles. One is by former AASLH Director

William T. Alderson, Jr., "The American Association for State and Local History," *Western Historical Quarterly* 1 (April 1970): 175–82; the other is by George Rollie Adams, former AASLH Assistant Director for Planning and Development, "Planning for the Future, AASLH Takes a Look at its Past," *History News* 37 (September 1982): 12–18. Another useful though prejudiced account is by Walter Muir Whitehill in the chapter entitled "The Organization Men," in his book, *Independent Historical Societies: An Enquiry Into Their Research and Publication Functions and Their Financial Future* (Boston: The Boston Athenaeum, 1962), 499–520.

For the debate within AASLH over "public history," the student will find articles, editorials, and letters to the editor in *History News* 34 (May 1979): 120–26, 146–47; 35 (June 1980): 13–14; 35 (March 1980): 4; 35 (August 1980): 6; 36 (November 1981): 22; 37 (October 1982): 28–31; 38 (January 1982): 6; 38 (February 1983): 6–7; 38 (March 1983): 5; 38 (April 1983): 6; and 38 (June 1983): 6.

For the debate over the name of AASLH, the student will find statements by the author in an article, "What's in a Name?" *History News* 39 (January 1984): 34, and in editorials in *History News* 39 (April 1984): 5; and 39 (August 1984): 4. Responding letters to the editor appear in *History News* 39 (March 1984): 5; 39 (April 1984): 5–9; 39 (May 1984): 4–5; 39 (June 1984): 5; and 39 (July 1984): 5–7.

The AASLH "Standards for Historical Agency Training Programs" was published in pamphlet form and also as an insert in *History News* 36 (July 1981). It and other AASLH books and leaflets mentioned in this article are available from the AASLH Press, 172 Second Avenue, North, Suite 102, Nashville, Tennessee 37201.

IN PUBLIC PROJECTS

Cynthia J. Little currently is the director of education at the Historical Society of Pennsylvania where she has responsibility for designing, planning, and implementing the society's programs for school age groups and adults. Previously she was executive director of the Philadelphia Area Cultural Consortium, a not-for-profit agency specializing in adult public programming exploring the history of Philadelphia. Through the consortium she has served as executive producer of a one-hour historical dramatic film on the life of Lucretia Mott. In the early 1970s she co-founded the first women's history tour company—Feminist Tours—specializing in walking tours emphasizing women's history in Philadelphia.

Little holds a Ph.D. in History from Temple University and an M.A. in Latin American Studies from the University of London. She did her undergraduate work in history at The George Washington University. She received a Fulbright scholarship in 1974 to spend a year in Argentina doing dissertation research. She also received a Social Science Research Council grant to participate in a summer institute in Mexico, examining feminine perspectives on Latin America. In 1979 she was asked to participate in the Sarah Lawrence summer seminar on women's history for leaders of the national women's movement.

CELEBRATING 300 YEARS IN A CITY OF NEIGHBORHOODS: PHILADELPHIA MOVING PAST

Cynthia Jeffress Little

During 1982 Philadelphia marked the 300th birthday of its founding by William Penn with a year-long celebration encompassing everything from historical poster contests in the schools to a visit by the tall ships. This city-wide extravaganza offered everyone an opportunity to participate in some type of history-related program or event. For public historians the tercentenary presented numerous opportunities as well as challenges. This essay will describe and assess the planning and implementation phases of the city's major community history project, "Philadelphia Moving Past" (hereinafter PMP), a traveling history event. This exceptionally popular project, which appealed to people across all lines of class, education, and age, is an excellent case study on public history in the context of a major civic celebration.

THE PLANNING PROCESS

Responsibility for the overall planning and coordination of the tercentenary rested with the Century IV Celebration Committee, an

appointed body representing the citizens of Philadelphia. Its membership included leaders of twenty community groups and institutions,
fourteen public officials, and six mayoral appointees. The Century IV
staff carried out the committee's policies by drawing upon the city's
extensive resources in the areas of management, equipment, and
promotion. In late 1980, Century IV officials asked the Philadelphia
Area Cultural Consortium and the Center for Philadelphia Studies at
the University of Pennsylvania to join with them in designing a city-wide
community history project. The cultural consortium brought to this
project four years of public programming encompassing tours, lecture
series, workshops, performances, and exhibits focusing on Philadelphia's history since 1800. The Center for Philadelphia Studies
through its Philadelphia Social History Project had spent a decade in a
collaborative research effort exploring the history of industrialization
and urbanization. Much of the data resulting from this project was easily
adaptable for a "hands on" public history project. A Chairman's Grant
from the National Endowment for the Humanities for $17,500 and a
$12,000 cash award from Century IV allowed the planning process to
begin.

The core planning committee consisted of veterans of numerous
public history projects; thus, the need for early and careful planning was
recognized at the outset. The committee consisted of Michael Frisch
(SUNY Buffalo), Henry Williams (Center for Philadelphia Studies),
Nancy Moses (Century IV), John Alviti (Atwater-Kent Museum), and
this author representing the cultural consortium. Four of the members
had advanced training in history at the Ph.D. level and one had
completed a degree in museum studies. This funding enabled the
committee to hold weekly meetings over a six-month period, to consult
with designers and scholars, to visit other community history projects,
and to meet with representatives of neighborhood organizations.

Throughout the planning process the core committee struggled with
how to respond to three often conflicting perspectives. Designers and
public relations people emphasized their desire for an entertaining and
visually appealing creation. Meetings with neighborhood groups underscored concern that the project enhance their already planned events
such as block parties and library anniversary celebrations. Moreover,
they stressed the importance of activities which focused on the history of
their particular area. Sessions with scholars always highlighted their
interest in promoting further understanding of the city's present and
future prospects through a serious engagement with the past. The
committee's challenge at this juncture was to develop a project that to
some degree satisfied each of these constituencies.

The proposal the committee submitted initially to the National Endowment for the Humanities and later to other potential funders had
three major components—a historymobile, urban issues tours, and an
urban public history institute. Although each element could stand on its
own, all were grounded in a single set of concepts and drew on similar
scholarship and documentation. Each component addressed the needs

the various constituencies had expressed during the planning process. All aspects of the project reflected a sustained and high level of community involvement.

The historymobile was envisioned as a traveling history event with exhibits and programs for presentation throughout the city. A refitted bus was to serve as the base of operations, holding modular exhibits, interactive workshops, a presentation stage and other elements capable of being set up at any site or event. Three general theme exhibits, each composed of two or three kiosks, would introduce visitors to: "The Bigger Picture"; "What Is a Neighborhood?"; and "Daily Life in Perspective." A fourth theme of "Past and Present" was to be woven through all the exhibit copy. A workshop area would offer the public an opportunity to use primary source materials such as the Philadelphia 1880 census, the 1895 ward atlas, and nineteenth-century business directories. Structured group activities relating to this documentation were to include constructing a map of six neighborhoods using the data base of the Philadelphia Social History Project. As participants filled in the information, a highly visible, graphic profile of that neighborhood one hundred years ago would emerge. Supporting this activity would be brief neighborhood history booklets for the six target areas.

Using the public's own experiences to engage them with the past shaped the "Neighborhood Origins and Destination" installation. This was to be a giant billboard-sized map of Philadelphia to which visitors would affix color-coded tape indicating the location of their present neighborhood, where they grew up, and where their families originally lived. This map would graphically illustrate the individual's relationship to the city as a whole. On-site interpreters would help visitors to understand the generational, cultural, social, and economic circumstances which propel people to move to a particular neighborhood at a given time. The "People Wall" and the "Neighborhood Family Album" were intended to build on individual and neighborhood reminiscences rather than on concepts such as urban mobility. The "People Wall" was to be a traveling community self-portrait focusing on people of the neighborhood, daily life, family, and work in 1982. As the montage grew, viewers throughout the city could have an opportunity to share in the diversity of people, places, and experiences. Using the same kinds of documentation except with a historical focus, the "Neighborhood Family Album" was to be an exhibit-in-process. Staff at an on-site accession booth would interview potential donors of artifacts and documents, identifying and describing them for files of what might be donated. Such interviews also would attempt to cull out good prospects for oral history interviews. Not only would this format create a base for future history projects, but it also would provide another structured opportunity for staff to engage the public in discussions about the past.

Complementing and serving as a bridge to the historymobile would be the urban issue tours. Past efforts on the part of the cultural consortium had demonstrated the effectiveness and popularity of this format for presenting the city's history. Whereas the earlier cultural consortium tours had focused on specific neighborhoods or classical historical themes, the tours planned for this project would trace the roots of contemporary problems. This approach offered opportunities for comparison and contrast both along geographical and historical dimensions. Over the course of the project, the organizers hoped to offer four core tours given on a regular basis and a series of longer and more complex tours offered on a one-time basis. Core tour themes would include "Fate of the Industrial City," "Abandonment and Reconstruction," "Centre-Square, Heart of Downtown," and "Ethnic Succession Along South Street." The special tours might have included such topics as "Green Space in the City," "Transformation of the Economy," and "Future of the Waterfront." Guides for these and other similar tours would have been drawn from the local pool of academic humanists with expertise in Philadelphia history and experience in public programming. Publicity for the tours would go through standard channels as well as through the historymobile and the city's special Century IV promotional campaign. Planners anticipated that revenues from the urban issue tours would cover some of the expenses associated with offering these events. Audiences for these tours would have been drawn from a wide general public including both residents and tourists.

The final component of the project, the three-week Institute in Urban Public History for teachers and neighborhood history buffs, had two objectives. In the short run, the institute would offer valuable training to participants. These people would be relied upon to assist in preparations for the historymobile's fall visit to their respective neighborhoods. In the long run, training received at the institute would ensure a core of two or three skilled humanists-in-residence with knowledge and city-wide institutional contacts to tap for future public history and research projects.

Curriculum for the institute would parallel the themes developed in the historymobile exhibits and research data as well as in the urban issue tours. Morning sessions would focus on historical theory and substance related to the week's theme. Institute staff and visiting scholars would make presentations elaborating each theme. Afternoons would include field trips to local archives and museums as well as discussion sessions emphasizing the application of the participants' knowledge to public settings such as block parties and school assembly programs. To encourage participation in the institute, the core committee hoped to offer small stipends and additional sums to sponsoring neighborhood organizations and schools to help cover the cost of materials and other expenses necessary to mount their fall history celebrations, the culminating project for each institute participant.[1]

The total budget for the project, including $112,018 in cost-sharing, was $336,893 of which the committee requested $120,000 from the National Endowment for the Humanities. The rejection letter from the endowment noted that reviewers and panelists had sharply divided on this proposal, with some finding it too popular and theatrical while others found it not popular enough. Clearly, no one found it just right. This negative decision came as a decided blow to the committee members, but it did not kill the project. Soon a new fundraising strategy emerged and within a short period of time monies had been secured from the Sun Company for the historymobile and from the Pennsylvania Humanities Council for the institute and scholars to accompany the historymobile.

ORGANIZING PHILADELPHIA MOVING PAST

Reduced support for the overall project forced the committee to make painful cuts such as eliminating the urban issue tours, shortening the institute to two weeks, and doing away with the fall history festivals in the institute's participants' neighborhoods. With the historymobile, the exhibit kiosks were retained along with the presentation stage and parts of the research area. Components requiring high fabrication and labor costs, such as the "People Wall" and the "Neighborhood Family Album," were removed. Staff for the historymobile was reduced to three people responsible for everything from working out arrangements with sponsoring organizations to setting up and disassembling the exhibit kiosks. Planners had hoped that a core of regular volunteers would supplement paid staff; this proved to be wishful thinking as volunteers did not find the physically demanding work and often long hours in the hot sun appealing. Problems aside, the historymobile—Philadelphia Moving Past—went on the road in June 1982, bringing its popular program to forty-seven neighborhood events over a five-month period.

Using the cultural consortium and Century IV networks of community contacts along with standard public relations strategies, the process of soliciting applicants for PMP visits began. Initially staff had to be quite persuasive to convince neighborhood groups to schedule PMP at their block parties, but after a few successful events more groups wanted the historymobile than there was time available. Organizers worked to balance visits to include large festivals, block parties, and school and library celebrations. Geographic, ethnic, and socio-economic considerations also entered into decisions on the final roster. Prior to every PMP visit, one organizer had lengthy conversations with neighborhood contacts and sometimes made site visits. Preparation for a PMP visit also included finalizing arrangements with performers, recruiting a historian, looking for volunteer help, and familiarizing the three staff members with the history of the area to be visited.

The days PMP made appearances were busy ones from arrival until departure. Setting up the exhibit portion entailed unloading and assembling seven to nine collapsible steel-framed kiosks measuring $10\frac{1}{2}'$ by 96″ square. The silk-screened nylon skins covering the steel frames contained the visuals and exhibit copy. A staff member perched in the top of the kiosks attached the skins to the frames with velcro strips. Twelve-foot wide bright blue canopies held in place by four steel poles topped the kiosks on windless days. To steady the kiosks, trash cans filled with water sat on platforms inside each frame. One or two kiosks had tape decks suspended inside the frames playing a medly of upbeat contemporary Philadelphia theme music. As the designer, Jim Hamilton, promised, the kiosks worked well everywhere—in parks, on streets, in parking lots, and in shopping malls and libraries. The larger-than-life quality of the kiosks meant that their presence always drew a crowd because they visually announced that something special was about to happen.

For the three full-time PMP team members, Pam Kosty, Janusz Mrozak, and this author, the assignment proved to be one of continual challenge. For Mrozak, an urban planning student at the University of Pennsylvania, this summer job entailed learning to drive a city bus in places meant only for small cars. Kosty, the outreach coordinator for the cultural consortium with a B.A. in American Studies from Oberlin College, and this author discovered the joy and pain of pumping iron as muscles became more defined with each PMP event. Tapping water hydrants, directing traffic, and repairing tape decks became second nature for the PMP team members. Breaking set during sudden rain and wind storms offered the team opportunities to demonstrate speed and dexterity. The true meaning of patience and perseverance became clear on days when the line of people waiting to discover who lived in their house in 1880 remained thirty deep after six hours with temperatures in the 90s. Friends became those who brought food and drink on busy days, braved the history booth for fifteen minutes, and showed up in time to help break the set and load up the bus. From start to finish, PMP tested this group's physical constitution, flexibility, and sense of humor.

Before the city bus lost its brakes on a hill in mid-summer and PMP reduced its load to fit into a van, the crew set up a presentation stage which used the bus as a backdrop. Whether on a stage or on the pavement, the PMP shows went forward. Sponsoring neighborhood organizations discussed with the PMP planners the type of performances and other activities they wanted for their visit. The availability of money to hire performers varied throughout the summer, meaning that some events had more elaborate shows than others. PMP offered a puppet show, a musical skit on black history, a mime, and various musicians as possible choices. History-related games such as Phila Bingo and the team game Phila History race offered audiences opportunities to test their knowledge about the city's history while competing for prizes, usually history books donated by local museums. Some groups used this structured time during an event to recognize the street's oldest residents, to salute a local politician, or to solicit support for projects such as Town Watch and Clean-Up Days. A master of ceremonies, sometimes a hired extra, but most commonly one of the three regular staff members, whipped up enthusiasm and an audience for the performances and ceremonies as well as directed people to the history booth.

The star attraction of PMP was the research area commonly known as the history booth. This aspect of the PMP program offered the public an opportunity to discover who lived in their house in 1880. Copies of the enumeration booklets from the 1880 Philadelphia census accompanied

Figure 1. Learning Philadelphia history through Philadelphia Moving Past. *Photograph courtesy of the Historical Society of Pennsylvania, Lou Meehan, photographer.*

by computer printouts for most residences directed the researcher to the correct booklet and page number. The rapidity with which staff could locate information gave this exercise an almost magical quality. The personal nature of this information which included name, age, race, sex, and occupation as well as the country of origin for the individual and his/her parents captivated the public. Official PMP "Historic Property Certificates" detailing information about the former residents of a house became much sought after souvenirs in all neighborhoods. Many visitors asked for extras in order to have them done in calligraphy and framed for display in their own home or to give as gifts. Real estate agents and others not convinced these certificates were just souvenirs, and thus would not offer the bearer a tax credit, often became verbally aggressive when staff could not locate the desired property.

Because Philadelphia is an old city with numerous stable, close-knit neighborhoods pre-dating 1880, many visitors found the residents of their current home or the one in which they or their parents had grown up. In neighborhoods such as Fishtown, Fairmount, and Manayunk, several people always found relatives or close family friends in the 1880 census. For some the emotional nature of this encounter with the past moved them to tears. Others became so excited that they began to beckon all within shouting distance to come and see their "historic" family. Many wanted to know how they could learn more about their family history. Others engaged the staff in lengthy conversations about various aunts, cousins, and in-laws. Because the majority of those discovering relatives in the census were senior citizens, they welcomed the opportunity to share not only their family's story, but also offered interesting insights and information about changes in the area during their lifetime. These rather special finds of friends and relatives in the 1880 census were the exception, but the excitement they sparked kept the history booth going at full pace until sunset or the staff collapsed from exhaustion.

Even though the PMP visits to neighborhoods with primarily post-1880 housing did not generate the same level of excitement as the older areas, the history booth staff never lacked for a steady stream of interested customers. In these newer areas staff depended on enlarged 1895 Philadelphia ward atlas maps to capture the public's imagination about the past. These detailed maps, laminated and mounted on foam board, continually fascinated visitors of all ages, ethnic backgrounds, and educational levels. Since a large number of the city's homes were built between 1880 and 1895, many people found their house on one of the fifty-two maps in this series or at least saw that their street was in line for development. The profile of residential sections as well as businesses and industrial areas which the maps offered provoked many discussions. Although the maps often kindled conversations of a purely nostalgic nature, some visitors were interested in more thought-providing exchanges. The graphic evidence of Philadelphia's once prosperous manufacturing sector prompted speculations as to why that part of the economy had declined and what was the future for jobs in this region. The identification of neighborhoods with specific ethnic groups through churches and synagogues stimulated discussions about which groups lived where and why, as well as the factors which pushed one group out and brought another into a given area. These exchanges added a level of serious consideration about the meaning of the city's past for the present often not obvious in many tercentenary projects which had a purely celebratory nature.

The history booth had a variety of other research materials for the public to examine. Copies of the 1880 and 1890 Philadelphia city directories gave visitors an opportunity to find relatives in print as well as the chance to experience using a basic historical research tool. Just as the census information and the ward atlas maps had sparked lively discussions, the city directories drew people into wondering why more women did not appear in the pages and to ponder the nature of the many unfamiliar occupations. The business and manufacturing census printouts at the history booth generally were overlooked except by a small number of visitors who appeared to have specialized interests and some training in history. The lack of personal appeal inherent in this type of information kept it from being in great demand. A computer printout grid dictionary with data such as total population figures for an approximately five-block square in 1880 Philadelphia attracted some attention. Because of the amount of staff time required to explain the grid dictionary's mysteries, its use was restricted to events with smaller crowds and essentially nonresidential areas in 1880.

Complementing the research materials was a wide assortment of free handouts such as self-guided historical walking tours and pamphlets from a series of neighborhood history exhibits, all products of earlier cultural consortium projects funded by the National Endowment for the Humanities. Other local organizations, museums, and historical societies provided free books and pamphlets with a historical focus; most did not have a neighborhood history focus. The free handouts proved to be not only a drawing card for the history booth, but a way to keep visitors occupied and reasonably patient while waiting their turn to look at the research materials.

Midway through the project two consecutive grants from the Pennsylvania Humanities Council enabled PMP occasionally to hire local academics with expertise about the city's history to spend time at the history booth. Visitors clearly enjoyed meeting academics and having an opportunity to engage them in debates in informal and familiar settings. These question-and-answer sessions using PMP research materials as departure points for discussion often educated the "van historians" as much as the public. Even though PMP recruited academics experienced in working with the general public, some fared better than others in this unusual setting. A few took to working the history booth with gusto and immediately struck up exchanges with visitors and encouraged those who seemed hesitant to come over to see what was offered. Others were passive and expected the regular PMP staff to facilitate their interactions with the public. On the whole, the staff welcomed having an additional informed person to work the history booth, especially on busy days. Integrating academics into this setting clearly augmented PMP's ability to offer the public an informative and thought-provoking experience.

The colorful exhibit kiosks provided not only a visual backdrop, but also the story line which complemented the materials at the history booth. The planning phase for this part of PMP was so fraught with dissension that arguments centering on the amount and content of the story line delayed the overall project several weeks. The designer, Jim Hamilton, who came to PMP with years of experience doing theatrical sets and industrial exhibits, wanted minimal copy and all ideas to be presented in a direct and simple manner. Academics, on the other side, insisted that more of the city's history be told and that the process of change over time be emphasized. The former contingent accused the latter of wanting to "to put a book on the wall" which no one would read, much less understand. The academics viewed the designer and public relations representative's idea as superficial and worthless for conveying any real sense of history. The other part of the conflict centered on selecting the visuals for silk screening and photographic collages. Several painful sessions reviewing slides selected by an academically oriented researcher with little visual sense emphasized the distance between the two sides. Ultimately the planning team reached workable compromises, but only after several people considered withdrawing from the project.

As is the nature of compromise no one was completely satisfied, yet almost everyone was able to live with the result.

Each of the nine exhibit kiosks highlighted a specific theme or offered facts related to the city's past, present status, or prospects for the future. The lead kiosk, headlined "We the Neighborhoods," had a large city map designating all 105 Philadelphia neighborhoods by number; the adjacent panel had the key with the corresponding names. Because neighborhood boundaries reflect social and political biases, agreement as to the location and even the names of neighborhoods was a source of much lively debate. For Philadelphians who have difficulty imagining their neighborhood as part of a larger whole, the map panel offered a graphic reminder of the relationship of the parts to the whole. Because 1982 was a year of celebration, one kiosk, titled "Philadelphia Fabulous City of Firsts," included a national and international historical time line and a list of usual and unusual Philadelphia firsts. Kiosks focusing on historical themes had headlines such as "The Neighborhood Was Community" and "The Neighborhood Was Industrial." These kiosks told the story of the city's industrial/manufacturing past, the relationship of work to home, the formation of identifiable ethnic communities, and the components of the household economy. As with all the kiosk panels the story line was kept simple and had a lyrical quality to it for easy reading. The final three kiosks exploring the contemporary situation were headlined "What's Our Future?", "Neighborhoods Now–Jobs," and "City Services." These panels presented facts such as that Philadelphia had 2,200 miles of streets and 26,783 fire hydrants. The importance of maintaining the city's services and infrastructure in good condition as a way to enable Philadelphia to maintain a competitive edge over other cities was emphasized. The job-related panels posed questions such as where will Philadelphians find work in the coming years now that its traditional industrial sector has declined. Together and individually the exhibit kiosks offered information or posed questions of interest to a wide variety of visitors.

Philadelphia Moving Past did its final event for Century IV in late October 1982. At this point the project had become so popular and well known throughout the city that groups continually tried to book it for the coming year. Century IV donated the history booth materials to the Historical Society of Pennsylvania and the kiosks to the Port of History Museum of the City of Philadelphia. Since 1982 the Historical Society of Pennsylvania has scheduled regular times for opening the history booth to the public. It also has brought the kiosks and the history booth back together for special events such as the ten-day gala marking the opening of Gallery II, a downtown urban shopping mall. In the summer of 1984 PMP lived at another shopping mall where the history booth was opened on weekends. The Education Department at the Historical Society of Pennsylvania continually uses the history booth materials in many of its lessons for school and college groups as well as teacher workshops. Researchers, both historians and genealogists, periodically check this data source. For the historical society, having stewardship over the

Figure 2. Locating your neighborhood through Philadelphia Moving Past exhibits. *Photograph courtesy of the Historical Society of Pennsylvania, Lou Meehan, photographer.*

history booth materials has made the institution much more appealing and visible in the larger non-scholarly community. The legacy of PMP over a two-year period indicates that this project's life will extend well into the future.

CONCLUSIONS

Most communities could mount a PMP-like history program for a civic celebration or educational outreach series. Obviously, older communities with a wealth of processed historical data have clear advantages over newer, less researched areas. A diversified and creative planning team will be able to find ways to work with existing resources in innovative ways. Experience with PMP suggested that the following guidelines must be adhered to for this type of project to be successful. The planning process must seriously engage from the outset input from designers, community representatives, project personnel, academics, and public relations specialists. The project has the greatest chance of succeeding when it enhances another event or larger celebration with a preexisting audience. Historical materials selected for presentation must engage the audience in a personal way by offering specific information the public can relate to their family, home, work, ethnic group, or immediate neighborhood. Historical information which deals with larger issues in an abstract manner can be presented, but must demonstrate the connection to the individual experience for maximum impact. The personal ingredient is essential with a broad general public. Offering visitors some kind of tangible souvenir, such as the historic property certificate, increases the project's legitimacy and importance as well as functioning as a form of advertising. The exhibit component of any out-of-doors, traveling exhibit must visually announce the event and draw crowds to it as well as offer visual and printed information elaborating the historical message. The exhibit and other components of the show must be relatively easy to assemble, use, break down, and repair if the apparatus is going to last throughout the duration of the project and beyond. Because this kind of civic celebration project is not "school," the public must first perceive it as entertainment. Thus, having performers as part of the day's agenda helps draw and keep audiences. Finally, no PMP-like project will succeed without the support of hardworking, well-informed, humorous staff members who can imbue the experience with their collective elan even when the exhibit kiosks are taking off like rockets during a windstorm.

Large-scale historical programming for civic celebrations must balance the requirements of three major constituencies—funders, politicians, and voters. Those who ignore this reality have their heads in the sand or live in ivory towers. Their approach may be very pure and traditionally academic, but it will not bring a project money and audiences. The public historian who takes this advice to heart must then accept the challenge of developing programs which impart a sound sense of history in an engaging way. PMP successfully combined the needs of the three main constituencies and also satisfied the scholars' desire to offer an intellectual experience. Visitors had a rare opportunity to work with primary source materials about their neighborhoods and discuss local history with experts in a familiar setting. Not everyone got more than an emotional, nostalgic experience from PMP, but many did. All participants came away from this history event aware that history touched their lives and those of their families, neighbors, and the city in fundamental ways.[2]

> *The views expressed in this article are those of the author and are not necessarily those of the Philadelphia Area Cultural Consortium or the Historical Society of Pennsylvania.*

NOTES

1. Century IV Celebration, City of Philadelphia, Center for Philadelphia Studies, and Philadelphia Area Cultural Consortium, *A Proposal for A Tercentenary Community History Project* (Philadelphia: n.p., 1981), 3–25 passim.
2. For an additional approach to public celebrations, see George McDaniel's essay entitled "Folklife Festivals: History as Entertainment and Education" elsewhere in this book.

George W. McDaniel serves as director of education, interpreta-tion, and public programs at the Atlanta Historical Society. He has a B.A. (History) from the University of the South, an M.A.T. (History) from Brown University, and a Ph.D. (History) from Duke University.

He is a Vietnam veteran and a former Peace Corps Volunteer in Togo, West Africa. He has worked with the Festival of American Folklife and directed numerous festivals, including the Mid-South Folklife Festival. His recent book Hearth and Home: Preserv-ing a People's Culture, *the product of his work in public history, won an Honor Award from the National Trust for Historic Preservation.*

FOLKLIFE FESTIVALS: HISTORY AS ENTERTAINMENT AND EDUCATION

George McDaniel

"Cotton farm life was hard. You had to work long hours, but it provided a living. I worked just as hard as any of my hands. I got up at dawn and worked 'til dark. I believe that if you work hard, you get what you earn. Hands on my place could garden, raise hogs and chickens, and could do pretty well if they had the initiative. At settling up time, they'd even have money to put away, but most of them spent it just as fast as they got it. That wasn't my fault. I treated them fairly."[1] This description from a cotton planter's point of view is but one of a series of pictures of traditional cotton farm life presented to an audience of several hundred at the Mid-South Folklife Festival which took place in Memphis, Ten-nessee, in the summer of 1982.

A black tenant farmer who grew up on a cotton farm nearby replied, "Well, I'm sure it wasn't like this on your place, Mr. Johnson, but on our place we hardly had a chance at all. We planted the cotton and the man kept the books. Planted cotton all the way up to our back doorstep, worked from can to can't, but we hardly got a thing. We had initiative, that wasn't the problem. Things were just set up so that us tenant farmers couldn't get ahead. So we took the initiative and left. That's why I'm not farming today."[2]

As a result of these different pictures that were presented, the audience at the Mid-South Folklife Festival was not offered a simplified portrait of the past, but learned about the issues historians grapple with in trying to decipher America's history. Participants in the same event bring to bear different perspectives upon that event, and it is the

Figure 1. Les Scott introduces students to traditional music at the Atlanta Historical Society's Folklife Festival. *Photograph by William F. Hull. Courtesy of Atlanta Historical Society.*

historian's job to weigh these perspectives carefully and interpret them. The workshop on cotton farm life did not just happen. It was the result of careful planning by professional historians who used their training in southern history to select the major themes of the festival, choose the participants whose backgrounds represented different perspectives on those themes, and moderate the workshop to facilitate the exchange of contrasting recollections. The presence of historians was vital in order to ensure that the discussions did not lapse into nostalgia. As a result of this forty-five minute exchange from which I have quoted from only two of the participants, a young man commented, "This is fascinating. I came to the festival to be entertained, and now I've also been educated."

It is this combination of education and entertainment that makes festivals a unique "classroom" for the teaching of history to the general public (Figure 1). By working with festival producers, many of whom are professional folklorists, historians can help ensure that festivals are more than nostalgic crafts demonstrations or old-time music concerts and that interpretations of historical issues which shaped the culture are inter-woven throughout the event. These issues, such as race, class, gender, politics, and economics, manifest themselves in the work and life of everyday people. By presenting folklife within the context of these issues, the historian can inspire thoughtful consideration by the public of

Figure 2. William Diggs entertains and educates at the Festival of American Folklife at the Smithsonian Institution. *Photograph by George W. McDaniel. Courtesy of George W. McDaniel.*

issues often taught in textbooks as apart from personal or community life.

Since a folklife festival is inherently grassroots in character, it provides a perfect opportunity to teach the public of the rich mosaic of America's indigenous and ethnic cultures (Figure 2). Each has contributed its own distinctive traditions to the nation's fabric and can be illustrated through music, crafts, oral histories, and foodways. Further, the heritage of new immigrants can be showcased to underscore the fact that America was, and still is, a nation of immigrants. As a result, the local citizenry, whether students, teachers, or lay persons, can see the larger picture of their culture, and out-of-town visitors can learn of a more authentic identity than that offered by most tourist attractions.

PRODUCING A FOLKLIFE FESTIVAL

Festivals vary in size and format, but a successfully produced festival is more or less the result of the judicious combination of the same ingredients. To facilitate the aspiring public historian's efforts to work with festivals, a checklist of key points is offered. The Mid-South Folklife Festival will serve as the specific model, since it was derived from the successful production of previous festivals, including three local festivals sponsored by the Center for Southern Folklore, the North Carolina

Folklife Festival, and the Festival of American Folklife produced by the Smithsonian Institution. This checklist is by no means exhaustive. Rather, it is intended to introduce the historian to the components of festival production, ranging from funding to programming, to make the aspiring public historian sensitive to the different types of skills necessary to an educational and entertaining festival.

PURPOSE

The first consideration in planning any festival should be careful analysis of its purpose. A folklife festival can serve as a way to teach the community about itself—the similarity and diversity of its people—by presenting their music, crafts, foodways, occupational lore, and ways of life (Figure 3). By doing so, a festival can strengthen the sense of identity of individuals and of the community as a whole. In order to make citizens from all walks of life feel a part of the festival, it should be planned so that a variety of cultural resources are featured. Music, crafts, and ways of life representative of the majority culture serve as main popular attractions and as opportunities to teach the public of the principal historical issues and cultural traditions that have shaped the region. A common shortcoming of conventional festivals is that only rural, "old-timey" music or ways of life are presented, reinforcing the misconception that traditions shape the life of only a select few, instead of all. Inclusion of the majority culture permits most citizens to come and see something of their own heritage reflected.

In addition, less popular or neglected resources should be brought to light to make visitors aware of how much more needs to be learned about their community. For example, at the Mid-South Folklife Festival, historians and folklorists on the staff discovered persons who had actually lived on Mud Island, the festival site in the Mississippi River a short distance from the Memphis shoreline. In oral history workshops these river families described the river, its islands, and shoreline as a home and a workplace, using family photographs, artifacts, and their own paintings produced from memory to illustrate the historical landscape and ways of life (Figure 4). Their descriptions evoked a community of hundreds of families who lived up and down the river in tents and houseboats, and they taught the public of a chapter in the history of the Mississippi and of the region not available in museums or books. All regions possess similar neglected but vital resources, and festivals offer the chance to give them the public attention their history deserves.

Festivals can also help build bridges among the different social groups of a community, which have often been isolated and divided from one another. Ways of life of different ethnic groups can be presented. At the Mid-South Folklife Festival, Euro-Americans and Afro-Americans demonstrated their crafts alongside one another, thereby conveying the similarity and diversity in southern culture. They were joined by recent immigrant craftspersons, such as the H'Mongs from Cambodia; this

Figure 3. Marie Rogers demonstrates traditional methods of making pottery, a vital craft in preindustrial America. *Photograph by William F. Hull. Courtesy of Atlanta Historical Society.*

juxtaposition enabled the newcomers to learn of the traditional culture in the region and introduced their culture to the indigenous population.

A festival also serves economic purposes, and organizers should be quite clear about these if they expect to produce a festival again. In Memphis the Mid-South Folklife Festival was a highlight of the recent revitalization of the city, introducing many suburbanites to the historical character of the city's downtown district, and spurred the development of tourism, a burgeoning contribution to the Memphis economy. Downtown merchants, many of them small shopkeepers, profited from the positive publicity and from the numbers of people who attended. Musicians, craftspersons, and artists benefited not only from the pay, but from the public exposure, sales of crafts and recordings, and further job offerings. The Center for Southern Folklore, sponsor of the festival, was provided with a major opportunity to present its work to the public and thereby to strengthen its local identity. Moreover, it generated income from admissions, crafts sales, and concessions and reinforced its credentials for funding requests from public and private sources. Further, the City of Memphis, which operates Mud Island as a park, and which served as a co-sponsor, profited from record sales of admissions and merchandise.

Figure 4. Oral histories, family photographs, and paintings by participants portray traditional ways of life on the Mississippi River at the Mid-South Folklife Festival. *Copy photograph by George W. McDaniel. Courtesy of Anne McDaniel and Center for Southern Folklore Archives.*

STAFF

Behind every good festival lies a creative, thoughtful, and skilled staff. A festival is never a one-person operation. In the planning stages, a multifaceted, cohesive staff must be designed, and the following questions addressed: How is the staff to be structured, and who will design the festival? What personnel are needed for research, programming, design and construction, publicity, fiscal management, sales, sound, lighting, security? Experience counts, and if the personnel on hand are unfamiliar with these assignments, consultations with persons with first-hand experience as well as readings are essential. In addition to staff, in what areas are volunteers needed, how many are required, and how will they be recruited, organized, and rewarded? Are there existing organizations with which alliances could be formed and which could provide personnel or services? For example, at the Mid-South Folklife Festival, Boy Scout troops volunteered to assist with setup and cleanup, while the city park, Mud Island, contributed personnel and logistical services for sanitation, electricity, lighting, staging, security, and admissions in return for a portion of admissions and crafts and merchandise sales.

FUNDING

No festival can succeed without sound funding, and a historian considering work with a festival needs to be creative and thoroughly knowledgeable about funding sources. Conventional sources include the federal government, such as the National Endowment for the Arts or the National Endowment for the Humanities, the state government such as the state's arts and humanities council, and national and regional foundations. The historian should be aware that arts councils are more likely to fund artistic performances, while humanities councils are more likely to support interpretive programs and exhibits. Corporations and labor unions, seeking to demonstrate their positive community contributions, are also excellent funding sources. And their contributions may not always be in the form of a check, but rather through in-kind contributions such as free publicity, materials, or services. For example, at the Mid-South Folklife Festival, the Coca-Cola Bottling Co. of Memphis contributed a major grant, but also gave one thousand posters as well as banners and backdrops for all the stages. The Memphis Hardwood Lumber Association contributed lumber for all stage construction as well as exhibits and demonstrations of traditional occupational lore of the lumber industry.

In order to maximize the use of limited funds, it is often more advantageous to join existing community celebrations rather than create new festivals. Most communities already have such events in place, attracting hundreds or thousands year after year. The historian should evaluate these events creatively and pragmatically, considering ways in which the community's heritage could be presented more authentically. In 1981, for example, the Center for Southern Folklore co-sponsored such an event, the Sorghum Days Folk Festival, which had been organized by Anderson Farms for many years as a strictly commercial crafts festival in DeSoto County in rural northern Mississippi. Drawing from its research of folk art, music, and crafts in the area, the center featured local traditional musicians and craftspersons who had been neglected in favor of commercial craftspersons from outside the community who could pay the entrance fees. These indigenous quilters, basketmakers, woodcarvers, and chairmakers, to name a few, demonstrated their traditional crafts and sold their wares, while blues, gospel, and traditional string band musicians showcased their talent. Oral history workshops, focusing on traditional ways of life, brought together white and black craftspersons on an equal basis for the first time in the county and presented the differences and similarities in their heritage. Thus, with a minimum of funds, staff, and publicity, the Center for Southern Folklore was able to present a community's heritage to hundreds of residents and out-of-town visitors simply by enriching an established popular event.

RESEARCH

Research is a vital preliminary step in the production of any successful festival. Before major funding can be acquired, there must be a clear

Figure 5. Dr. David Evans moderates a workshop on traditional music with artists, left to right, Hammie Nixon, Othar Turner, and Lonnie Glosson. *Photograph by Pete Ceren. Courtesy of Center for Southern Folklore Archives.*

concept of the heritage to be interpreted, and the resources with which to do so. In fact, it is this overall historical context that is missing from many festivals with the result that visitors see a crafts demonstration here or listen to delightful music there, but do not learn how these traditions reflect the culture as a whole or what major social, economic, or political issues shaped the culture.

It is the historian's task to research the history of the area, locate the persons who exemplify these themes, and develop creative programs that weave the themes together into an interpretive tapestry. At the Mid-South Folklife Festival, blues musicians, for instance, not only entertained audiences with their music but in oral history workshops moderated by professional historians, they discussed life in the rural South during the era of segregation and how these conditions influenced their music and career (Figure 5).

PUBLICITY AND MARKETING

With the research under way, staff in place, and funding at hand, the festival begins to become a reality. But in order for the work to have been worthwhile, there has to be an audience. In the eyes of many, the festival's success will be judged by the size of the crowd. While not specifically trained in advertising or marketing, the historian is not without allies. Newspaper, radio, and television are often anxious to help promote community events, and creative research inevitably produces feature stories of significant interest. Further, the historian has been trained to interpret the significance of events or persons, and this is an excellent background for writing news releases that capture the attention of editors.

The historian should be aware, however, that publicity is a distinct skill and should consult with professionals. Depending upon financial circumstances, publicity professionals may be contracted as consultants to develop a plan that would be implemented by the staff, or they may be hired full time to supervise the publicity campaign throughout. At the Mid-South Folklife Festival researchers located scores of musicians, craftspersons, and storytellers and wrote publicity descriptions of each, identifying their craft, life history, and significance for the publicity director on staff. One particularly effective example was a traditional Mississippi River commercial fisherman, Ernest Willis, whose handmade boat lay abandoned in the banks of the river near his house. When researchers excavated the boat and trailered it to the festival site, the public relations director arranged for a television crew to film the excavation and to interview Willis, a character of local renown. As a result, people throughout the region learned of a fascinating character to be featured at the festival and the local populace learned that one of their own was to be featured. And Willis, basking in the fame of being on television, became one of the principal promoters, as he told everyone who just might have missed him on television about the festival.

PROGRAMMING

Programming is the historian's interpretive statement. It is here that the historian must evaluate the research and select the subject areas, participants, exhibits, and performing arts that portray the region's heritage. The historian should bear in mind that in programming as in writing it is better to produce a small thing well than something large sloppily. Not everything can be presented, and a festival, like an essay, needs editing. Furthermore, a festival should have a carefully orchestrated movement, beginning with attractive programs that hook the audience and continuing with ones that engage a variety of interests and build to a grand finale.

To produce successful programs, the historian should also appreciate the capabilities of the participants and the interests the audience brings to the festival, including not only the unique aspects of a community but the commonplace as well, so that all people feel a part of the event.

At the Mid-South Folklife Festival analysis of research resulted in the selection of three themes as illustrative of the development of the region—cotton, the timber industry, and the Mississippi River. Crafts, occupational lore, and ways of life related to these were portrayed in three heritage pavilions—the site of exhibits, demonstrations, and oral

Figure 6. Mississippi Delta blues artists James "Son" Thomas (center) and Sam Chatmon (right) lead festival visitors in a jam session in the "Backstage" area of the Mid-South Folklife Festival. *Photograph by Pete Ceren. Courtesy of Center for Southern Folklore Archives.*

history workshops. In the cotton pavilion, for instance, the story of cotton was told from field to fabric as interpreted by participants who ranged from cotton farmers, sharecroppers, and representatives of the Southern Tenant Farmers Union, to cotton ginners and traders and to quilters, embroiderers, and other craftspersons who worked with cotton. The music of the South, celebrated around the world, was featured on one large stage, two smaller ones, and in one dance pavilion with flooring. A "Backstage" was designed, where the performers, according to a prearranged schedule, were to jam with festival-goers, who in the publicity were encouraged to bring musical instruments and thereby personally participate in the living traditions of the region (Figure 6).

Since foodways are vital statements of cultural identity, concessions were set up representing the range of southern cuisine from barbecue and fried catfish and hush puppies to ethnic specialties from the Italian, Jewish, and Chinese communities in the region. This variety of foodways reinforced the point made in the music concerts and heritage pavilions that southern culture is not monolithic, but rather a tapestry of subcultures, and visitors were able to learn this personally as they sampled the foods. In addition, visitors learned of the historical context of foodways in oral history workshops (Figure 7). For example, Herbert Harding, the concessionaire of catfish, explained his current occupation as the result of his growing up in the Mississippi Delta, where his parents held fish

Figure 7. John Grisanti leads a cooking demonstration of traditional Italian cuisine at the Mid-South Folklife Festival. Note use of mirror above table for viewing by audience. *Photograph by Pete Ceren. Courtesy of Center for Southern Folklore Archives.*

fries on Saturday nights, cooking in washpots in the yard with itinerant blues musicians providing the music for the folks who danced on the swept yard. Such events supplemented his parents' meager income as sharecroppers, he pointed out, provided a living for musicians, and served as a meeting, courting, and entertaining place for the community. At his own restaurant in Memphis, he explained, he has continued this tradition, holding fish fries in the parking lot on Saturday nights with local bands providing dance music. Descriptions such as this were then linked by the moderator to others to reinforce the point that strategies of making do were integral to rural southern culture and to show that contemporary urban life in the South was a creative blend of rural and urban traditions.

Contracts are vital to successful programming because the establishment of agreements in writing diminishes the likelihood of misunderstandings. Despite the best of intentions, oral agreements are fallible and can lead to serious, unwarranted disagreements which can wreak financial and emotional havoc with participants or producers. To prevent this, one should explain in simple terms the following points in a contract and review it with a lawyer: the place, time, and dates of participation; types of performances to be provided (music concert, crafts demonstration, oral history workshop, etc.); fees to be paid as well as terms regarding travel, room, and board; insurance and responsibilities for possible injury or property loss; rights to photographs, video-tapes, films, and recordings; cancellation policies; and sales of crafts and recordings at the festival. The contract should be accompanied by a courteous, explanatory letter, and upon acceptance, followed by a hospitality packet including, for example, participant identification badges, a map, and instructions explaining all aspects of festival participation.

An integral feature of programming is publication of a festival catalogue. Depending upon financial circumstances, this may be an inexpensive handout with only a brief interpretive statement, schedule, and list of artists. Or, it may be a more polished publication with a variety of illustrations, selections from oral histories, and essays by scholars interpreting the principal cultural themes of the festival. It is vital that all participating artists and contributors be credited since the festival is very much the product of their support. Advance consultation with local teachers and inclusion of study questions and bibliographies can make the festival program an important resource for continued use by schools.

PRODUCTION

Up to this point the historian has been the expert in planning the festival, but when it comes to construction, sound, lighting, electricity, and other aspects of production, the historians should turn to technical professionals. It is important to consult with technicians who have substantial experience in producing festivals and are well acquainted with the variety of problems that inevitably arise. The following questions provide a sample checklist and are not in order of priority since many are interrelated.

1. What is the layout of the festival? How will the flow of traffic be directed? Where should interpretive workshops, exhibits, crafts demonstrations, concessions, and concert stages be located so they do not interfere with one another in terms of aesthetic appearance, sound, and crowd control? What opportunities or problems does the natural landscape present?
2. How will the stages, crafts demonstrations, concessions, and workshops be designed so they are both functional and attractive in appearance?
3. What are the sound, lighting, and electrical requirements for each area?
4. How are the exhibits of photographs and artifacts to be designed and produced? How will they be used after the festival?
5. How will the needs for transportation and communication for staff and participants be met?
6. What provisions have been made for parking for festival-goers, staff, and participants?
7. What types of signs will be used to identify areas of the festival?
8. Have the regulations of the health, police, and fire departments, and the needs for public sanitation been met?

9. Have provisions been made for proper security?
10. What provisions have been made for hospitality—that is, the room, board, transportation, and tokens of appreciation for artists and volunteers?
11. How is the festival equipped to meet the needs of the elderly or handicapped?
12. What provisions have been made for the unexpected, such as accidents, rain, extreme heat, or other changes in the weather?

The rule of thumb in producing a festival is to place oneself in the diverse roles of festival-goers, participants, and staff and to anticipate the interests and needs of each.

DOCUMENTATION

The festival is the fruit of the historian's research and analysis. Often festivals are only seen in terms of the present day, yet the resources at the festival can yield long-term benefits if properly documented. Participants present traditional crafts, stories, and music, much of which cannot be replicated by younger practitioners. Further, the exchange of ideas and recollections in interpretive workshops is lost unless recorded at the time, making documentation vital for future scholarly use. In addition, documentation can be used to demonstrate the quality of the festival to financial contributors and assist in securing continued funding. In documenting a festival, the historian should consider all the effective means available today, such as audio-tape, photography, and videotape. All documentation should be properly identified, accessioned, and archived. A common mistake is to neglect sufficient funds and personnel for this purpose.

EVALUATION

Evaluation should be incorporated into the initial planning so that results of the festival can be accurately measured against its purposes. The advice of a marketing professional is helpful in producing an evaluation plan that would yield reliable results. Broadly speaking, evaluation criteria should include but not be limited to the following topics: What was the attendance? Was the intended audience reached? What sample of the population was present? Did the audience enjoy and participate in the crafts or cooking demonstrations, oral history workshops, and concerts? Which were the most popular or effective? Which needed to be modified or omitted? How was the festival reviewed by professional historians, folklorists, or other scholars as well as by print and television media? How did festival participants, volunteers, and staff appraise the festival? How did the festival contribute to the financial stability of the sponsoring organization? Are the staff and financial contributors willing to support a festival again?

As with teaching, successful festivals are the result of constant work, evaluation, and creative revision. And they reward with intense satisfaction. When a historian creates an occasion in which thousands come together to participate in their heritage, it is a grand moment. But there are smaller moments as well—when an elderly lady taken for granted in her local community receives the recognition her craft deserves; when persons who worked the land for years stand a bit taller and prouder as they relate their trials and tribulations and "how we made it through"; when blacks and whites, so long divided by race, see afresh the shared elements of their heritage, of their human condition.

In 1978 I interviewed a 100-year-old man about southern history. He lived only 200 yards behind a school, yet not once had a teacher or student approached him. He was taken for granted. Later, when I returned, he had passed on. There is no retrieval of the history those students lost. Two years later, I visited an elderly quilter living by herself with a collection of family-made quilts and photographs dating back for more than 130 years. I featured her collections and her work in local festivals, the Mid-South Folklife Festival, and the Folklife Festival at the World's Fair in Knoxville. As a result of this recognition, she is no longer taken for granted, and the story of her family, told through her quilts and photographs, is being written into the county history. So the real success of a festival is not only measured by the numbers in attendance or by the volume of applause, but by the extent to which the community learns about and teaches its history.

NOTES

1. A. K. McCalla, panel discussion at the Mid-South Folklife Festival, Mud Island, Memphis, Tennessee, 14 August 1982.
2. George Staub, panel discussion at the Mid-South Folklife Festival, Mud Island, Memphis, Tennessee, 14 August 1982.

SUGGESTED RESOURCES

The literature on the subject of folklife festivals is meager. The only complete guide to festival production, and an excellent one, is Joseph T. Wilson and Lee Udall, *Folk Festivals: A Handbook for Organization and Management*, (Knoxville: University of Tennessee Press, 1982). The *Journal of American Folklore* features periodic analyses of the theory and production of festivals as well as reviews of specific endeavors. Catalogues from major festivals such as the Festival of American Folklife produced by the Smithsonian Institution or the Border Folk Festival produced by the Chemizal National Memorial in El Paso, Texas, shed light on programming and interpretation.

The best source of assistance is public folklife organizations whose experienced staff can offer invaluable guidance. Many states have state-employed folklorists, often associated with the state arts councils, whose job is to document and interpret folklife in the state and educate the public about its folk heritage. National organizations are also excellent sources, among them being the Folk Arts Program of the National Endowment for the Arts, the American Folklife Center at the Library of Congress, the Office of Folklife Programs at the Smithsonian Institution, and the National Council for the Traditional Arts in Washington, D.C.

IN GOVERNMENT AND
PUBLIC WORKS

A Ph.D. graduate of Duke University, Martin Reuss is the senior civil works historian for the U.S. Army Corps of Engineers. He specializes in the history of inland navigation, flood control, and hydraulic engineering. He has served as the principal editor for two series published by the Corps of Engineers, one dealing with environmental history and the other covering the development of navigation in U.S. ports and rivers. Dr. Reuss has published articles in various historical journals and is the author of Shaping Environmental Awareness: The United States Army Corps of Engineers Environmental Advisory Board, 1970–1980.

PUBLIC HISTORY IN THE FEDERAL GOVERNMENT

Martin Reuss

"The function of news," wrote Walter Lippman, "is to signalize an event; the function of truth is to bring to light the hidden facts, to set them into relation with each other, and make a picture of reality on which men can act."[1]

Historians in the federal government have special reason to heed Lippman, for their primary audience consists of senior executives who use history to develop a better informed and more responsible public policy. No historian, least of all a federal historian surrounded by a massive amount of documents, can be sanguine about always serving truth well. But serve they do. Federal historians need to know the truth, the "hidden facts" to explain what really happened in the Tet Offensive and why; all the documents must be examined to reach judicious conclusions on the near tragedy at Three Mile Island; records must be studied to gain insights into what was done rightly or wrongly in disposing of hazardous waste material. Federal historians are called upon to examine all these subjects and more; the same analytical and research skills they apply to contemporary issues are used in writing more traditional histories. Flexibility is the key. An agency historian might study the immediate background of some current policy debate while concurrently doing research for a book on early nineteenth-century agency history. At its best, the position of federal historian offers the opportunity to do significant research while contributing to an informed and balanced policy. Of course, there are frustrations: archival documents that are classified for no apparently good reason; policy makers who do not care at all about history or who wish to use historians as public affairs officials; and, conversely, the need to postpone a project in order to respond quickly to executives demanding certain analyses or information. Genuine satisfaction can be gained, however, when senior executives seek historical guidance and actively support historical programs.

THE DEVELOPMENT OF FEDERAL HISTORICAL OFFICES

Although "public history" is a relatively recent term, there has been historical work in the federal government since at least 1863, when Maj. Gen. Henry W. Halleck, commander of the Union Army, initiated a project to collect and publish Civil War military records. This program was later broadened to include all the important records of both the Union and Confederate armies. It was reorganized under Capt. Robert N. Scott, who became head of "The Publications Office, War Records" in 1877. Scott separated the proposed volumes into four series: operations, prisoners of war, miscellaneous Union records, and miscellaneous Confederate records. The volumes, totaling 128, of which 111 dealt with operations, were published between 1881 and 1901. Entitled *The War of the Rebellion: A Compilation of the Official Records of the Union and Confederate Armies*, the project was the first genuine historical effort sponsored by the federal government.[2]

The Navy was not far behind the Army in its efforts to record the past. After the Civil War, Prof. James Russell Soley, director of the Navy Department Library, systematically began to collect and preserve naval records pertaining to that war. In 1884, Congress recognized Soley's effort by appropriating $2,640 to hire one clerk and two copyists. At the same time, library and records functions were consolidated in a new Office of Library and Naval War Records. Ten years later Congress appropriated $15,000 for printing expenses, and the first volume of the *Official Records of the Union and Confederate Navies in the War of the Rebellion* appeared. Volume 31, the last in the series, was published in 1927.[3]

While the Army deserves credit for creating the first project specifically intended for historical purposes, other federal agencies established programs that utilized historical skills but were not intended primarily to serve historians. For instance, the skills of a historical documentary editor were needed to edit treaties and laws for the Department of State. This function began under Secretary of State Thomas Jefferson's leadership in the late eighteenth century. The first volume in the official series *Foreign Relations of the United States* was published in 1861.[4] Another example is the creation of the Office of Farm Management in 1905 in the Department of Agriculture. Utilizing a "historical-geographical" approach, the office studied both existing and past farm conditions. Its purpose was to utilize this knowledge to develop more efficient systems of farm management.[5] This may be the first example of "applied history" in the federal government.

World War I stimulated interest in historical work within the federal government. In 1917, the Secretary of Agriculture directed the Office of

Farm Management to ascertain the war's impact on the world's supply of wheat. That effort, which evidently sought to identify historical trends, helped lead to the creation in 1919 of an agricultural history and geography group within the Office of Farm Management. This group studied "the trend of agricultural development, shifts of agricultural production, relation of foreign conditions to American agriculture, supervision of the Atlas [of American Agriculture] and land utilization."[6] In 1921, Secretary of Agriculture Henry C. Wallace merged the Office of Farm Management with the Bureau of Markets and Crop Estimates. The following year the newly formed bureau was named the Bureau of Agricultural Economics. One of the offices within the bureau was the Division of Statistical and Historical Research. Headed by O. C. Stine, the division took its historical responsibilities seriously. Already in 1919, Stine had actively promoted the establishment of an Agricultural History Society. In 1927, the society began publishing *Agricultural History*, the only American journal dedicated to that particular field. Stine hired Everett E. Edwards as editor. Wayne Rasmussen succeeded Edwards in 1952. By that time the bureau had two other historians in addition to Rasmussen.[7]

Not surprisingly, the Army's historical efforts substantially increased during World War I. Maj. Gen. Tasker H. Bliss, Army Chief of Staff, urged the establishment of a historical office in Washington, D.C., in a memorandum to Newton D. Baker, the Secretary of War, on January 2, 1918. Bliss thought the office should employ both civilian and military historians. The history "would record the things that were well done, for future imitation [and] it would record the errors as shown by experience, for future avoidance."[8] Baker approved Bliss's recommendation. Consequently, on March 5, 1918, the Army created a central historical office under the direction of Lt. Col. Charles W. Weeks. Established to write the history of the Army's involvement in the "Great War," the office has been in continuous existence since 1918, although it has undergone various reorganizations, name changes, and new mission assignments. Today it is known as the United States Army Center of Military History.[9]

Also during World War I, Secretary of the Navy Josephus Daniels ordered the formation of a historical section in the London headquarters of U.S. Naval Forces in Europe. The section collected reports, diaries, and other materials of potential historical significance. Meanwhile, in Washington, D.C., the Navy created another historical section, with interest in only World War I records and completely separate from the Office of Naval Records and Library (the title since 1915). The records of the London section were transferred to the Washington, D.C., historical office after the war. In 1921, Capt. Dudley Knox became head of both the Office of Naval Records and Library and the Historical Section, although the two offices were located in different buildings in Washington.[10] He became the "driving force" of the Navy's historical program for the next quarter of a century.[11] In 1927, the Historical Section was absorbed into the Office of Naval Records and Library.

Three years later, the Secretary of the Navy assigned Knox the additional duty of curator for the Navy Department.[12]

With the active support of President Franklin D. Roosevelt, a former Assistant Secretary of the Navy, Knox initiated a publications program dealing with the Navy's early history. Between 1935 and 1938, a seven-volume series appeared entitled *Naval Documents Related to the Quasi-War Between the United States and France: Naval Operations from February 1797 to December 1801*. Between 1939 and 1944, six volumes were published of *Naval Documents Related to the United States Wars With the Barbary Powers: Naval Operations Including Diplomatic Background from 1785 through 1807*. World War II forced the indefinite postponement of similar projects dealing with the Revolutionary War, the War of 1812, and the Mexican War.[13]

The Historical Adviser's office at the Department of State was not created until 1929, and only after professional historical societies had lobbied the department to develop a more ambitious historical program. Again, this pressure was partly a response to the demand for the publication of diplomatic records pertaining to World War I. The Historical Adviser expanded the *Foreign Relations* series and initially focused on the publication of the records of the 1919 Paris Peace Conference. After World War II, the renamed Division of Historical Policy Research embarked on an even more ambitious program. In 1946 the division employed some sixty people who were primarily responsible for preparing a variety of publications including *Foreign Relations, Statutes at Large, Treaties and Other International Acts, Register of the Department of State, Territorial Papers*, and the Department of State *Bulletin*.[14]

Wars have served historians well, and this is probably particularly true of federal historians. Just as World War I had generated concern for accurate historical records, World War II increased the bureaucracy's historical sensitivity. On March 4, 1942, President Franklin D. Roosevelt endorsed a plan for federal agencies to write "accurate and objective" accounts of their wartime experiences.[15] Many agencies took the directive seriously. As a result, today there exists in the National Archives myriad historical accounts of agency World War II activities. Some eventually found their way into print.[16] Many were not written by professional historians. In a few cases, however, Roosevelt's charge resulted in both more and better historians being employed by the federal government.

During World War II, the Department of Army Historical Branch was primarily involved with publishing short studies of various combat operations. Nine three-man teams were sent overseas to collect information for these studies. Meanwhile, some work was done with the Navy on joint Army-Navy operations, although the branch opposed an overall popular history of combined military operations. It thought each service should prepare its own popular history. On November 9, 1945, Secretary of War Robert P. Patterson directed the Army Chief of Staff to transfer the Historical Branch to a new Special Staff Agency within the Pentagon. A general officer was assigned to head it. A little over three months later, the Secretary of War approved a plan that had undergone numerous changes since it had first been proposed in 1943. That proposal was to publish an official "Army in World War II" series that would run to about 120 volumes. The responsibility for carrying out this proposal was given to the new Special Staff Agency. In 1950 the Historical Branch was renamed the Office of the Chief of Military History. While engaged in numerous special studies for the Department of Army, the office's chief activity in the two decades following World War II was the completion of the World War II volumes.[17]

Captain Knox of the Navy did not attempt simply to collect a massive amount of material pertaining to World War II, but to organize it according to established archival principles. During the war, he staffed his war record archives with academicians, who came to him as Naval Reserve officers. Knox's far-sighted organizational efforts enabled Rear Adm. Samuel Eliot Morison to complete his fifteen-volume *History of United States Naval Operations in World War II* fifteen years after the war's conclusion, an outstanding accomplishment. In 1944, Secretary of the Navy James Forrestal established an Office of Naval History "to coordinate the preparation of all histories and narratives of the current wartime activities in the naval establishment in order to assure adequate coverage to serve present and future needs and effectively to eliminate nonessential and overlapping effort."[18]

One can identify several major reasons for the development of historical offices during the last forty years. First, concern with a proper record of the government's wartime activities continued. One manifestation of this was the continued funding of publications dealing with World Wars I and II. Another indication was the strong directive President Harry S. Truman issued on January 29, 1951, mandating that federal agencies record their experiences during the Korean conflict.[19] Second, agencies created historical offices to assist in the celebration of agency anniversaries. This was true of both the Atomic Energy Commission (AEC) and the Department of Labor. In 1957, AEC Commissioner Lewis Strauss decided that an agency history should be written to celebrate the commission's tenth anniversary. Richard Hewlett, who was already employed in the Division of Finance in the agency, became Strauss's choice to write the history. What Hewlett began has expanded into a sizeable operation. Under the AEC's successor organizations, the Energy Research and Development Agency and, finally, the Department of Energy, the Historian's Office has provided a number of historical services including the establishment of an agency archives and the creation of an oral history program.[20] The Department of Labor established a Historian's Office as a permanent office in 1962, a year before the department's fiftieth anniversary, in order to prepare material for the commemoration. The office has been a part of the department's organization ever since. It prepares numerous studies of interest to the department, maintains an oral history program, reviews public affairs programs relating to history, and ensures that the agency keeps an ongoing history of its significant activities.[21]

The Smithsonian Institution had an altogether different reason for increasing its interest in history. Although it had long been involved in research that bordered history, only after World War II did its staff include professional historians, primarily in the area of the history of science and technology. These historians helped in the remolding and expansion of the old United States National Museum. The National Museum's successors today include the National Museum of American History and the Air and Space Museum, both of which employ professional historians. Additionally, the Smithsonian has employed a number of art historians to help organize and exhibit its priceless art collections.[22] Committed to fundamental research, nearly all of the Smithsonian's historians have made important contributions to the literature of their particular field while engaged in the preservation and exhibition responsibilities of the institution.

Still another reason for the increased agency involvement in historical matters was to use history to fight proposed organizational or policy changes. An example is the increased interest the Marine Corps showed in its historical program during the unification battle preceding the passage of the National Security Act of 1947. Afraid that the service might be subordinated to another branch of the armed forces, Marine Corps officials strengthened the historical office in order to produce a series of monographs dealing with the role of the Marines in the Pacific during World War II.[23]

The manner in which a historical office is established is more than a simple curiosity. It tells us much about what value senior bureaucrats place on history. Many historical offices were created to ensure that a particular—almost invariably, successful—story was told, whether it be of a wartime victory or an agency anniversary. The fact that these offices have survived and been assigned other duties suggests that the bureaucracy is learning the value of an accurate and reliable written record.

Unfortunately, the factors that gave rise to a new historical office have occasionally inhibited innovation. Historians in an office created to celebrate an anniversary, for instance, may feel that their charge does not extend to the development of background reports on current issues. Another agency's historians, preoccupied with recording the epic battles of World War II, might believe it beyond their purview to address the problems of a peacetime army. In short, agency historical offices can be captured by their own history. Sticking closely to their original charter, the official historians fail to educate their superiors about other benefits that a historical perspective confers. They do not look for ways of selling their craft and forget that, as new issues emerge and new organizations appear, historians must continue to educate each bureaucratic generation.

THE CONTROVERSY OVER OFFICIAL HISTORY

With the growth of federal historical programs during World War II, many historians, particularly from the academic community, began to raise concerns about "official history." There is some irony in this since academic historians and historical societies had been among the most outspoken advocates of government-sponsored history when federal historical programs were first being established.

The controversy first received widespread attention toward the end of World War II. Because federal agencies were directed to document and analyze their wartime activities, "official history" came to mean principally an account of contemporary events in which the writer, an agency employee, partly participated or at least observed. The question of objectivity was then aimed at two different issues. First, could an agency historian be impartial? Second, could contemporary history be sufficiently analytical? It is a controversy that time has not diminished.

In a 1945 publication of the Social Science Research Council, the eminent University of Chicago historian Louis Gottschalk, later president of the American Historical Association, listed three objections to histories of the "recent past."[24] First, the best sources—the 'most intimate and confidential ones'—are seldom available. Second, impartiality is difficult to obtain. Third, true perspective on what is important can be developed only in the long run.[25] Gottschalk admitted that some contemporary (public?) historians such as Thucydides, Suetonius, Voltaire, Napier, and others may have made significant contributions, but he closed his discussion by expressing special concern about official histories. "As a general rule," he maintained, "*official histories* must be treated with caution." He went on to say:

> Not only are they liable to reveal the weaknesses inherent in investigations of subjects of current interest; they are also often likely to be largely secondary in nature, since they are based upon information only partly obtained by the author at first hand, if indeed they are not wholly dependent upon the analysis of others' testimony. Whenever they are in fact primary, they suffer from the shortcomings characteristic of memoirs, especially from the tendencies to suppress embarrassing, incriminating and confidential information, and to present apologia.[26]

Because many historians have accepted, in one form or another, Gottschalk's indictment of official history, it is worthwhile to respond to his criticism.

The question of the availability of reliable data is easy to answer. While there have been occasions when important material has been accidentally or purposely destroyed, in general federal historians do not suffer from a lack of data but from just the reverse. There is an overwhelming amount of archival material available, and much concerns the "recent past." The number of documents in the permanent possession of the National Archives has increased more than tenfold since 1938. The most recently retired documents are generally stored in Federal Records Centers, where they remain agency property until the National Archives accessions them or they are destroyed. Besides having access to the National Archives and the Federal Records Centers, federal historians can often examine agency files that contain data going back several

years. Access to so-called private files of agency executives—often
containing official correspondence—is another matter and urgently
requires legislative clarification. Constraints on access usually are confined only to highly sensitive material that involve current policy
problems, legal concerns, or questions of national security, although
recent presidential directives allow using the classification stamp more
promiscuously. Given the time and the means, there is no reason why
federal historians cannot exploit a wealth of archival material to develop
a well-balanced picture of agency activities. When time, budgetary, or
other considerations necessarily constrain the scope of the research, the
history must be limited accordingly.

The question of perspective and balance is more difficult. Some argue
that constant contact with some of the "actors" in a contemporary,
official history could prejudice a historian's view. Just the opposite might
be true. Interviews with principal participants reveal insights and
information that often cannot be garnered from the written record. In
this regard, Gottschalk might well have been instructed by Alexis de
Tocqueville, who wrote of writers of contemporary history:

> But what these writers know better than does posterity are the movements
> of opinion, the popular tendencies of their times, the vibrations of which
> they can still sense in their minds and hearts. The true traits of the principal
> persons and of their relationships, of the movements of the masses are
> often better described by witnesses than recorded by posterity. These are
> the necessary details. Those close to them are better placed to trace the
> general history, the general causes, the large movements of events, the
> spiritual currents which men who are further removed may no longer find,
> since these things cannot be perceived from the memoirs.[27]

In short, properly used, interviews will lead to better, more balanced
history.

A more important stricture holds that agency historians do not have
the freedom to criticize their employer. There are cases when pressures
have been put on agency historians. Nevertheless, such incidents appear
uncommon and probably occur no more frequently than in academia.
One way of helping to offset pressures, real or otherwise, is to educate
officials about the writing and research standards that all professional
historians share: balanced and fair interpretation of all available evidence, honest and forthright conclusions, clear writing, accurate quotations, and proper citations.[28]

At the same time, it must be understood that the imperatives of time
and money occasionally limit research and writing in the government.
Not every history can be on the grand scale if it is to serve policy makers
in a timely fashion. This is particularly true of background studies to
contemporary issues. A policy maker desiring such a report wants it
when the issue is under advisement, not two years later. What separates
academic from public history is not the standards or even the training.
It is the audience and the short deadlines. Government historians must
respond in a timely manner, and they must make their histories

understandable and useful to the people who employ them. Ideally, these histories will be both helpful to the bureaucrat and acceptable to fellow historians—but the ideal will not always happen.

The argument over the merits of contemporary—and especially official—history will undoubtedly continue. Federal historians will remain engaged in the debate since it directly bears on the degree to which professional historians outside of the government accept their work. However, as a matter of practical significance, the discussion is moot. One of the chief justifications for having federal historians at all is to write down the history of the "recent past." What is important is that such history is done professionally and that it serves the needs of the agency.

USING FEDERAL HISTORY TO UNDERSTAND THE PRESENT

Is it enough to document and analyze the past, or is it appropriate to generalize in order to provide guidance for the future? Implicitly or explicitly almost every federal historian is asked this question, especially when writing reports on current issues. The problem is complex because many policy makers believe that the main value of history is to prevent future mistakes; historians are not fulfilling their responsibility if they use their knowledge only to enlighten and not to *instruct*. These managers want historians to do one or more of the following: 1) develop generalizations of universal validity; 2) argue by analogy and focus on situations in the past that may shed some light on the present or future; and 3) identify historical trends that may affect the agency.

To some extent, all three of these approaches, particularly the first one, are unsettling. Many historians do not believe that they should be the ones to draw lessons from history; that is better left to statesmen and politicians. The historian's duty, runs the argument, is solely to reconstruct the past as accurately and comprehensively as possible, and the attempt to compare epochs or events inevitably leads to as many erroneous conclusions as useful insights. This is a forceful argument, but too conservative to serve the needs of many historians in the federal government. If federal historians cannot persuade their superiors that knowledge of history is critical to understanding current questions, they have failed their most important function.

The issue of developing "universal" generalizations is as much a subject for analytical philosophy as historiography. While historians generalize all the time when describing the past, they are more circumspect in generalizing about the future. They believe that such generalizations exceed the authority of the profession. For example, without fear of scandalizing his colleagues, a historian may assert that military alliances in the past generally lasted only as long as the common fear of the opponent exceeded mutual suspicion within the alliance. If the same historian were to suggest that this tendency seems universal, applicable to the future as well as the past, he would undoubtedly find himself quarreling with his more cautious colleagues. Yet, these kinds of generalizations, given with adequate caution about the unique and unusual, can offer helpful insights to senior officials.

The use of analogy to interpret the past has long been a historical device. Indeed, the search for analogies motivates much historical research, leading inevitably into comparative histories on everything from revolutions to family planning. When one looks for analogies to describe the present, however, the danger is that, instead of using the past to focus on current issues, the biases of the contemporary world (and of one's historical training) will define the choice of analogies. It is not easy to use historical analogies in a way that is intellectually satisfying; or, conversely, the way is too simple if one is unaware of the occasionally abstruse, "hidden" differences separating one event from another. When asked to do so, the public historian must use analogy, but carefully and sparingly. The person requesting the study must be made aware of differences as well as similarities.

Perhaps the most valuable information historians can give policy makers is the identification of historical trends. Some historians are not comfortable with the idea of working with trends. To do so de-emphasizes the importance of the individual and exaggerates the influence of the environment. One looks for the common and pays scant attention to the unique. Unfortunately, all this is foreign to the training of many professional historians. Yet, new questions seem to stretch the applicability of earlier heuristic principles. An age of popular culture, mass movements, and unparalleled threats to mankind requires new ways to understand itself. Political scientists, sociologists, lawyers, "investigative journalists," and, occasionally, criminals have sought to interpret modern life for us. It is important that historians not leave the field to others. Rather they need to employ their traditional training, and the insights borrowed from other disciplines, in an effort to understand the complexities of modern life. The public historian must use his skills to help the policy maker plan for the future. This does not mean the historian needs to become a soothsayer, but he should possess good analytical ability. Like all competent historians, he must separate the significant from the superficial and identify the major forces and events that have shaped a given historical period and place.

THE HISTORICAL OFFICE IN THE FEDERAL GOVERNMENT

Today, federal historians (GS-170 occupational series) are distributed throughout the government. Most are employed in historical offices. Others work in offices that utilize their historical abilities for policy analysis or other kinds of staff work. About half are located in agency headquarters in the Washington, D.C., area. There are about 25 in the Department of State, 10 in the Department of Agriculture, 50 in the U.S. Army Center of Military History, 9 in the Marine Corps Historical Center, 17 in the Naval Historical Center, 20 in the Office of Air Force

History, and 30 in the Department of the Interior, including the Bureau of Indian Affairs, the National Park Service, and the Historic American Buildings Survey and Historic American Engineering Record Division. Other federal entities employing historians include the Department of Labor, National Aeronautics and Space Administration, Nuclear Regulatory Commission, Central Intelligence Agency, Federal Emergency Management Agency, U.S. Arms Control and Disarmament Agency, Government Printing Office, Bureau of the Census, Social Security Administration, Department of Energy, Library of Congress, Smithsonian Institution, National Historical Publications and Records Commission, Federal Bureau of Investigation, Office for the Bicentennial of the United States House of Representatives, and the United States Senate Historical Office.[29]

The majority of historical offices are not located in Washington, D.C., however, but are spread throughout the country. Quite a number are located in subordinate agencies. By far the largest number of such offices are within the Department of Defense. The Army has 78 historians in 43 field offices in the United States, Europe, and the Far East. The Air Force employs nearly 200 historians at bases throughout the world. Outside of the Department of Defense, the largest number of "field historians" are within the Department of the Interior. Nearly 100 historians serve the National Park Service in areas outside of Washington, D.C.[30]

It is clear from what has already been noted that federal historians are involved in a great many activities. Generally, the larger the historical office, the more defined are the duties of individual employees. Many offices employ nonhistorians. In a 1981 survey, the Society for History in the Federal Government sought to identify the various occupational groups in federal history offices and projects. Data was obtained from 125 offices, including a large number from the National Archives and Records Service (NARS). The two largest professional classifications were historian (GS-170) and archivist (GS-1420), with 36 and 39 percent, respectively, of the total number of employees reported.[31] These figures are skewed, however, because, of the 359 archivists reported, over 300 worked for NARS. The other major occupations found in the 125 offices (and the number of offices in which they were found) were librarian (12), archives technician (26), museum curator (17), museum specialist (13), military officer or enlisted person (9), anthropologist (1), editor (3), park manager/ranger (1), technical information specialist (2), technical writer/editor (1), and writer/editor (2).[32]

The number of occupations suggests the wide variety of responsibilities federal historical offices may have, but it does not accurately reflect the number of professionally trained historians in the government. There are those historians employed as policy analysts or writers; and, even within historical offices, a significant number of professionally trained historians occupy positions as archivists, editors, museum specialists, and cultural interpretation experts. The number of GS-170 historians found in the 125 offices was broken down as follows:[33]

Distribution of Historical Offices And Projects by Numbers
of Historians (GS-170) in Each Office

No. of Historians	No. of Offices	Percentage of all Offices
0	26	21
1	39	31
2–4	46	37
5–8	6	5
9–30	6	5
Over 30	2	1
Totals	125	100

The historians were employed in 99 of the 125 offices. An analysis of
their GS grades revealed the following range:[34]

GS Grade	Number of Historians
5	1
7	16
9	30
11	69
12	112
13	56
14	35
15	24
Senior Executive Service	10

One reason why GS-170 historians were not found in more historical
offices is that a few offices administer activities that the Office of
Personnel Management does not characterize as historical, i.e., in the
GS-170 series. These include certain kinds of historic preservation,
federal museum, and cultural interpretation work, activities discussed
elsewhere in this book. It need be noted here only that federal historians
are involved in these enterprises. The Center of Military History, for
instance, administers one of the largest federal museum systems—
sixty-seven army museums spread around the world. Indeed, this
number is exceeded only by the National Park Service, which has over
200 reception centers around the country.[35] These centers often incorporate small museums in order to explain the significance and development of their respective park sites. Historians involved in museum,
preservation, or cultural interpretation work often require knowledge of
archeology, architecture, and federal and state laws dealing with the
recovery of cultural resources.

A number of professional historians work as documentary editors. At the Smithsonian Institution a staff is editing and publishing the papers of Joseph Henry, the first Secretary of the Smithsonian. Historians working on the United States Supreme Court Documentary History Project are selectively editing and publishing papers dealing with the first ten years of the court's history.[36] Documentary editing requires patience, attention to detail, and, of course, excellent writing skills. Those who have the aptitude can find a substantial reward in illuminating people and institutions through the collection and publication of carefully edited records.

A suggestive, but hardly all-inclusive, list of the various functions of historical offices follows:

1. Write and publish agency history.
2. Respond to inquiries from the agency, the public, Congress, and other government offices.
3. Conduct an oral history program.
4. Write studies and reports.
5. Support public affairs activities.
6. Administer a contract history program.
7. Administer a museum or a museum system.
8. Edit documents.
9. Develop and implement cultural interpretation (mainly in the National Park Service).
10. Be involved in cultural resources management, including writing environmental impact statements, surveying historic buildings, and historic preservation activities.
11. Preserve and inventory historical materials, possibly including audio-visual sources.

An additional responsibility for some headquarters historical offices is the supervision of the historical program of subordinate offices. This usually means developing a policy statement for an agency-wide historical program, ensuring adherence to the policy, and reviewing histories done at lower levels. For instance, the United States Army Corps of Engineers requires that each regional office and laboratory prepare a history. Altogether, this entails the preparation of more than fifty such histories, most done on contract, generally by academicians. Some are done by historians who may be employed temporarily or permanently by these subordinate offices. Each time a history is prepared, it is sent to the main historical office in the Office of the Chief of Engineers at Fort Belvoir, Virginia. There the drafts are carefully read and either disapproved or approved for publication. The final printed product is generally published by the Government Printing Office, although entirely funded by the Corps of Engineers. Updates are required every five years.

The Center of Military History supervises a different kind of program. It requires each Army historical office to submit an annual historical review. These documents are printed by offset at the various installations supporting historical offices. Copies are distributed to other historical offices, the Army Library, the Command and General Staff College, Army War College, and other appropriate institutions and agencies.

For historical offices to fulfill all their various assignments is a formidable task. Even a well-staffed historical office may find it difficult to perform six or seven functions concurrently. All federal historians must carefully decide their priorities and convince their supervisors that the priorities deserve support, even if certain other tasks must remain undone or delayed. This does not mean that historians should always begrudge new tasks—an inquiry from the agency head, for instance, ought not remain unanswered—but in those cases they must explain to their supervisors how the new assignment will postpone completion of others.

Much of what happens in a federal historical office is what Richard Hewlett calls the "essential tension," borrowing a line from Thomas Kuhn.[37] Federal historians face the essential tension of reconciling historical writing with historical services. Historians like to write history; and the bigger the project, the more attractive it is. In the federal government, institutional history has long held sway. Today, more federal historical offices are turning to shorter histories that more closely bear on current policy issues. No matter which kind of history he is writing, the historian can be frustrated by demands endemic to his office: a private citizen writes in for some piece of arcane information; some congressman wants to know why the agency was not more responsive *twenty years ago*; or a senior official desires a short background paper on a current crisis. Requests such as these necessarily take the historian away from his project. Even though the resulting research may be interesting and worthwhile, the historian is frustrated and must readjust schedules and momentarily change priorities. Historians unwilling or unable to be this flexible should not apply.

BECOMING A FEDERAL HISTORIAN

Before seeking a position as a federal historian, one should be aware of what a successful career will require. As indicated above, flexibility is very important, as is the ability to research and write well and quickly—the days of the federal historian babying one book for twenty years are passing. Most upper-level positions require a doctorate degree, and the majority of historians employed at the GS-11 level or above have a substantial amount of graduate school education.

The first thing that one has to do to become a federal historian is to fill out a Standard Form (SF 171), "Personal Qualifications Statement." It is available at any local branch of the Office of Personnel Management or at agency personnel offices. It is important to fill out these forms carefully and completely. Modesty is no virtue in this case. Activities that may seem peripheral or insignificant should be included. There is no telling what may attract a future employer.

A SF 171 form will require the applicant to list those places where he or she would like to work. If at all possible, the selection should not be limited to one's own immediate area or to Washington, D.C. It is difficult—though not impossible—to find immediate employment in Washington. Usually, it is better to obtain experience and seniority elsewhere and then, if one desires, to transfer to Washington. Historical offices are scattered throughout the country. Many are located on Department of Defense installations. The chances of finding employment are improved if one is willing to settle for a less attractive geographical location.

Those interested in employment with the federal government should find out all they can about various historical offices. Many offices are listed in the *Directory of Federal Historical Programs and Activities* jointly published by the Society for History in the Federal Government, the American Historical Association, and the National Coordinating Committee for the Promotion of History. This guide is invaluable. It briefly describes the work of each office, gives telephone numbers and addresses, and lists the personnel. A copy may be obtained by writing to the Society for History in the Federal Government, Box 14139, Benjamin Franklin Station, Washington, D.C. 20044. Job-seekers should not hesitate to contact offices about possible positions and to send a completed SF 171 with the cover letter. They should try to get on mailing lists for job openings. These lists are prepared by agency personnel offices. Also, they must be on the lookout for announcements in the professional journals and newsletters.

A good way of gaining experience in federal history without becoming a government employee is to work as a contract historian for an agency historical office. Besides learning how to do research in federal records, one can gain useful knowledge about the way an agency operates, how it is organized, and what "language" (acronyms, "initialisms," etc.) it uses. Moreover, the contractor's work may be published by the Government Printing Office or even occasionally by a commercial or academic press, depending on various arrangements and regulations. Also, experience as a contractor will undoubtedly benefit an applicant for a permanent position in a historical office. Many offices will advertise forthcoming contracts in the *AHA Perspectives* or in other professional publications. By law, most contracts are advertised in *Commerce Business Daily*, a publication of the Department of Commerce in which government contracts of all types are listed. University libraries and even history departments should seriously consider subscribing to this newspaper. It is the only way of ensuring awareness of currently available contract work.

Being a government historian can be an enormously satisfying experience. The government historian is usually the first to tell the nation about an agency's past performance. The historian is the first to work with agency archival records, and whatever is revealed depends on the historian's objectivity and thoroughness. Moreover, the opportunity to develop analyses and background papers that may influence important policy decisions is a challenging responsibility unlike anything most academic historians will ever do. But the federal historian's most important task is to ensure that government officials retain a historical awareness—a sense of place and proportion that will lead to wise and informed decisions. In the daily routine of the bureaucracy, it is easy to forget about these special responsibilities. This does not lessen the challenge. Popular government depends on the free exchange of information. Government historians can help ensure that the process works.

The views expressed in this essay are those of the author and do not reflect those of the U.S. Army Corps of Engineers, the Department of the Army, or the Department of Defense.

NOTES

1. Cited in Joan Hoff Wilson, "Historians, Archivists, Journapolitics, and the Writing of Contemporary History" (An expanded version of a paper delivered at the Ninety-fifth Annual Meeting of the American Historical Association, Washington, D.C., 28 December 1980).
2. Stetson Conn, *Historical Work in the United States Army, 1862–1945* (Washington, D.C.: Government Printing Office, 1980), 1–5.
3. William James Morgan and Joye L. Leonhart, *A History of the Dudley Knox Center for Naval History*, with an Introduction by Rear Adm. J. D. H. Kane, Jr., USN (ret.) (Washington, D.C.: Government Printing Office, 1981), 3–4.
4. *The Federalist* (Newsletter of the Society for History in the Federal Government) 3 (September 1982): 1.
5. Ralph Thomas Fulton, "A Short History of the Agricultural History Group, National Economic Analysis Division, Economic Research Service, of the United States Department of Agriculture" (Unpublished report, April 1975), 5. The term "historical-geographical" was used in Henry C. Taylor and Anne Dewees Taylor, *The Story of Agricultural Economics in the United States, 1840–1932*, (Ames, Iowa: Iowa State College Press, 1952), 316, as cited in Fulton, "A Short History of the Agricultural History Group," 5. I am grateful to Mr. Fulton for allowing me use of his unpublished manuscript.
6. U.S. Department of Agriculture, "Handbook of the Division of Statistical and Historical Research," 1941, 2. Unpublished article in the Agricultural History Group files, as cited in Fulton, "Agricultural History Group," 9.
7. Fulton, "Agricultural History Group," 9–14, 16; *The Federalist* 3 (June 1982): 1, 6.
8. Cited in Conn, *Historical Work in the United States Army*, 15.
9. Ibid., 16–18.
10. Morgan and Leonhart, *Dudley Knox Center*, 5–6.
11. Ibid., 6.
12. Ibid.
13. Ibid., 6–7.
14. *The Federalist* 3 (September 1982): 1.
15. Cited in Conn, *Historical Work in the United States Army*, 79.
16. For a very informative examination of one agency's experience in writing its wartime history, see John J. Rumbarger, "The War Production Board and

Historical Research: Some Observations on Writing Public History," *The Public Historian* 6 (Spring 1984): 5–19.

17. Conn, *Historical Work in the United States Army*, 91–94, 113–20, 158.
18. Cited in Morgan and Leonhart, *Dudley Knox Center*, 8.
19. Conn, *Historical Work in the United States Army*, 185.
20. *The Federalist* 1 (Fall 1980): 1–2.
21. Judson McLaury, Department of Labor Historian's Office, telephone conversation with author, 11 September 1984.
22. Nathan Reingold, Joseph Henry Papers, Smithsonian Institution, telephone conversation with author, 10 September 1984.
23. Jack Shulimson, Marine Corps Historical Center, telephone conversation with author, 13 September 1984.
24. Louis Gottschalk, "The Historian and the Historical Document," in Louis Gottschalk, Clyde Kluckhohn, and Robert Angell, *The Use of Personal Documents in History, Anthropology, and Sociology*, Bulletin 53 of the Social Science Research Council, 1945, 3–75.
25. Ibid., 21.
26. Ibid., 22.
27. Cited in John Lukacs, *Historical Consciousness or the Remembered Past* (New York: Harper & Row, 1968), 96–97.
28. These standards are a paraphrase of those given in "Principles and Standards for Federal Historical Programs," a statement that the Executive Council of the Society for History in the Federal Government formally adopted on behalf of the society in December 1984.
29. This is an incomplete list. For more details, see the *Directory of Federal Historical Programs and Agencies* (Washington, D.C.: Society for History in the Federal Government, American Historical Association, and National Coordinating Committee for the Promotion of History, 1981). Too late for use in preparing this essay, an updated version of the directory was published in September 1984.
30. Edwin Bearss, National Park Service, telephone conversation with author, 17 September 1984; Brooks Kleber, U.S. Army Center of Military History, telephone conversation with author, 30 September 1984; and Grant Hales, Office of Air Force History, telephone conversation with author, 9 October 1984.
31. *Directory of Federal Historical Programs and Activities*, 60.
32. Ibid., 61. These figures are derived from a table titled "Grade Distribution of Persons in Professional Classifications in Federal Historical Offices and Projects."
33. Ibid., 63.
34. Ibid.; figures derived from table on p. 61.
35. Michael Vice, U.S. Army Center of Military History, telephone conversation with author, 30 September 1984.
36. Larry Paszek and Jack Neufeld, "Interview with Maeva Marcus, Supreme Court," *The Federalist* 5 (March 1984): 1, 7.
37. *The Federalist* 1 (Fall (1980): 1–2, 7–8.

Thomas P. Ofcansky is currently serving as African Affairs specialist with the Center for Aerospace Doctrine, Research and Education at Maxwell Air Force Base. Previously, he was a historian with the Air Force Communications Command, Scott Air Force Base, Illinois. He has held similar positions with the Military Airlift Command, Dover Air Force Base, Delaware, and the Tactical Air Command, Langley Air Force Base, Virginia. Apart from his interest in the Air Force History Program's development, Dr. Ofcansky has published numerous articles about Air Force history and military affairs in eastern and southern Africa.

His papers about East Africa's colonial history have appeared in numerous journals and magazines, including Africana Journal, History in Africa, *and* Journal of Forest History. *West Virginia University Press will publish his forthcoming book about the history of game preservation in East Africa. Dr. Ofcansky holds a Ph.D. in African History from West Virginia University.*

THE HISTORY OF THE UNITED STATES AIR FORCE HISTORY PROGRAM

Thomas P. Ofcansky

The United States Air Force has the most extensive applied history program in the world, with full-time professional historians and civilian and military personnel serving at installations in the United States, Europe, Asia, and Australia. The program's origins can be traced back to the closing days of the First World War. In February 1918, the War Department established the Historical Branch of the General Staff to write a history about America's participation in the war. Shortly thereafter, Gen. John J. ("Black Jack") Pershing, Commander-in-Chief of the American Expeditionary Force, created a historical unit in his headquarters. Various U.S. Army elements, including the Services of Supply, Air Service, American Expeditionary Force, subsequently adopted historical reporting procedures that enabled air unit historians in England, France, and Italy to write and submit monthly histories.[1]

The information in these histories, along with orders, bulletins, memoranda, statistical data, official statements by field commanders, and other related documents, formed the basis of the "Final Report of the Chief of Air Service, American Expeditionary Force." At approximately the same time, the author of that study, Col. Edgar S. Gorrell, Assistant Chief of Staff, Air Service, American Expeditionary Force, started work on a multivolume "History of the Air Service." Unfortunately, he never finished it because of funding cutbacks. Consisting of 280 volumes of narrative and documents, the collection, now on deposit in the National Archives, came to be known as "Gorrell's History." It remains one of the richest documentary sources on World War I aviation. The historical significance of "Gorrell's History" prompted the Office of Air Force History, presently located at Bolling Air Force Base, District of Columbia, to publish selections from this history in a four-volume series entitled *The U.S. Air Service in World War I.*[2]

1918–1941

During the inter-war period, Army historical activities operated under the direction of the Army War College's Historical Section. Regulations required all Army units, including aviation, to submit periodic historical reports. Despite the fact that interest in general aviation history, lineage, honors, and battle participation grew significantly after World War I, Army records lacked adequate documentation about aviation squadrons and group activities. Consequently, there have been few official publications about this important era. With the 1983 appearance of Col. John F. Shiner's *Foulois and the U.S. Army Air Corps, 1931–1935*, however, the Office of Air Force History started to bridge this gap. In the near future, the Office of Air Force History will publish Maurer Maurer's *Aviation in the U.S. Army, 1919–1939.*[3]

1942–1949

Because of the loss of so many World War I records and the need to document the country's military activities, the United States government was greatly interested in maintaining a record of military activities during the Second World War. On March 4, 1942, President Franklin D. Roosevelt wrote to Harold D. Smith, Director of the Bureau of the Budget, ordering each war agency to prepare "an accurate and objective account" of its wartime experiences. Subsequently, Gen. Henry H. ("Hap") Arnold, Commanding General of the Army Air Forces, issued a statement supporting Roosevelt's action:

> As you know, history is often a step-child, relegated to some distant date in the future and consigned to the treatment of professors and researchists who necessarily deal with the subject in academic fashion. We don't want that to happen this time; we want the public now and after the war to understand what airpower really is; we want credit to go where credit is due. We have assembled a group of competent historians who are already hard at work with the objective of compiling a definitive history of every unit and every phase of our activity from the beginning to the end of the war.[4]

To accomplish this goal, the Army Air Forces organized a Historical Division under Air Intelligence and assigned it the task of preparing a comprehensive history. In September 1942, Col. Clanton W. Williams reported for duty to the Historical Division on leave from the University of Alabama. Eventually, he became the Army Air Forces Historian, which was comparable to an academic dean, and started building a staff of professionally trained civilian and military historians for service in the continental United States and overseas.[5]

To assure a proper and usable selection of documents, Colonel Williams placed historians in key command posts, the most important of which was the Army Air Forces Headquarters. In addition, he assigned qualified historical personnel to the headquarters staff of each numbered air force and command. These historians collected documents that otherwise would have been lost, compiled histories, and wrote numerous monographs during and after the war. These materials not only served as guides for ongoing and future operations but also preserved the Air Force's corporate memory.[6]

Another methodology designed to enhance the quality of historical reporting concerned procedures, adopted on August 1, 1943, for the collection of all significant information affecting the organizations, plans, and operations of the Army Air Forces. Under these guidelines, each historian prepared a brief, daily narrative summary of the preceding day's events. To make the work more relevant to future Air Force needs, the regulation directed historians to incorporate accounts of official discussions, communications, and conferences relating to a unit's activities as well as interpretations, evaluations, critical analyses, and personal views of key personnel. Finally, historians attached to the daily summaries historically significant studies, reports, and documents.[7]

During the war's later stages, a special civilian advisory committee, which consisted of Professors Richard A. Newhall of Williams College (chairman), Joseph R. Strayer of Princeton University, and John A. Krout of Columbia University, approved a project known as "The Seven Volume History." The committee maintained that this history should be written in a scholarly fashion for those readers who had a serious interest in the study of the air war. Rather than giving the herculean task of preparing this history to one historian, the three academicians recommended a cooperative effort. To oversee this mammoth undertaking, the advisory committee selected two editors who not only had served with the Historical Division during the war but also had retained strong ties with the academic community: Wesley Frank Craven of Princeton University and New York University and James Lea Cate from the University of Chicago.[8]

In December 1945, Lt. Gen. Ira C. Eaker, Deputy Commander, Army Air Forces, and Chief of the Air Staff, authorized the editors to open negotiations with the University of Chicago, which eventually agreed to sponsor and publish the history, provided there was no "suppression or distortion of significant facts." The volumes, written by a staff of thirty-four historians, appeared sporadically throughout the 1948–58 period under the series title of *The Army Air Forces in World War II*. Largely because this history was out of print and represented the only comprehensive account of the use of American land-based air power during the Second World War, the Office of Air Force History reprinted the seven volumes in 1983.[9]

The wartime history program ended in September 1946. From the millions of documents prepared and collected by all echelons of the Army Air Forces, the Historical Division assembled a sizeable reference collection of the most useful documents. Moreover, its personnel wrote numerous histories and monographs about the units, commands, and numbered air forces that had participated in the war. By mid–1948, the Historical Division, now committed to using this raw data to write more scholarly histories, had been renamed the Air Historical Group and had become a permanent part of the United States Air Force.[10]

In September 1949, the Air Historical Group moved from Washington, D.C., to the Air University at Maxwell Air Force Base, Alabama, to be in the same locale as the Air Force archives and was reorganized as the United States Air Force Historical Division. To facilitate its operations and to provide Air Force Headquarters with a historical office, the United States Air Force Historical Division Liaison Office commenced operations in Washington, D.C., on September 12, 1949. For approximately the next twenty years, the history program's organizational structure remained unchanged.[11]

1949–1969

During these two decades, an increasing number of government officials and senior military officers recognized the value of the history program's contribution to the Air Force. In January 1951, for example, President Harry S. Truman, in the midst of the Korean War, reaffirmed President Roosevelt's 1942 directive to maintain an active military history program and directed that military historians should have "full access to source materials." On June 24, 1959, Gen. Thomas D. White, Air Force Chief of Staff, acknowledged the necessity of ensuring that pertinent events were well recorded for "the citizenry and commanders of tomorrow." He also pointed out that:

> for utility value today, for our research purposes in the near future, and for posterity's study in more distant times, the history of the Air Force is vitally important. The [histories] will always remain in fixed relation to the efficiency of contemporary record-keeping. Every aspect, fact, and thought behind our current decisions and our position on national defense organization, weapons system development, and other controversial matters must be completely and accurately recorded now, while our files and faculties are full and functioning.[12]

Approximately six years later, on March 8, 1965, Gen. William H. Blanchard, Air Force Vice Chief of Staff, reiterated the service's commitment to history. In a memorandum to various commanders, he noted that the histories and specialized research services provided by the Historical Division were "among our most valuable management tools." Additionally, General Blanchard indicated that accurate and properly written histories were instrumental throughout the Air Force "in preventing the repetition of mistakes and the continuation of inefficient or uneconomical practices, as a basis for proper mission review and assessment, and as a major support to sound planning, programming, and decision-making."[13]

The 1946–69 era also witnessed the beginning of a book publishing program. In addition to the Craven and Cate series, one of the more important books to appear was Frank Futrell's *The United States Air Force in Korea, 1950–1953*. In this seminal study, the author, who had served as historical officer of the Army Air Forces Tactical Center, Orlando, Florida, and assistant historical officer of Headquarters, Far East Air Force in the Philippines, presented a valuable narrative of Air Force activities and an interpretive analysis of the operations. Moreover, Futrell discussed the war's impact on Air Force doctrine, procedures, and organization. Even today, the book, a revised version of which was published by the Office of Air Force History in 1983, is recognized by many historians as a model for official operational military histories.[14]

Another prominent book written in that period was *A History of the United States Air Force, 1907–1957*, edited by Alfred Goldberg of the Historical Division Liaison Office. It was written to commemorate the fiftieth anniversary of military aviation in the United States and the tenth anniversary of the United States Air Force. The book covered everything from the use of balloons in the late 1700s to the advent of jet aircraft as well as the use of American airpower in three wars, including the men, their missions, and the tools with which they fought. To prepare this history, Goldberg assembled an eight-man staff from the Historical Division's offices in Washington, D.C., and Maxwell Air Force Base.[15]

Another of the history program's major contributions in the 1949–69 period was the hundreds of classified and unclassified monographs, chronologies, and special studies written by scores of field and headquarters historians. Taken as a whole, these works, which ranged in length from a few dozen pages to several hundred, delved into nearly every possible aspect of Air Force history. Apart from dealing with lesser known episodes of World War I and II, several of them addressed highly complex, technical matters. For example, historians who worked for Air Force Systems Command, which was responsible for air research and development, wrote about topics as esoteric as *The BOMARC Nose Room Test Facility* and as important as the *Growth and Development of the Atlantic Missile Range, July 1950–June 1960*. Additionally, historians assigned to the United States Air Force Historical Division Liaison Office wrote many "blue cover" monographs that chronicled the history of Air Force policies and programs and emphasized the work done at the air staff level.[16]

To furnish timely, analytical studies of Air Force operations in Southeast Asia in 1962, the Air Staff established the Contemporary Historical Examination of Current Operations, known as CHECO. Under this program, historical teams deployed to combat zones to interview participants and gather documents. The material in turn provided an unprecedented insight into the Vietnam War and enabled historians and interested military personnel to write scores of Project CHECO Southeast Asia reports and monographs. In addition, the Office of Air Force History used information gathered by the CHECO teams to start preparing a series of books dealing with the air war in Southeast Asia. Eventually, because of CHECO's superior performance in Vietnam, the Office of Air Force History stationed additional teams in Europe, the Pacific, and at the United States Air Force Historical Research Center.[17]

1969–1976

In January 1969, acting on the recommendation of a special advisory committee, Gen. John P. McConnell, Air Force Chief of Staff, ordered the reorganization and the expansion of the Air Force history program. He believed this was necessary to provide "an accurate and detailed accounting to the American people of Air Force activities, particularly its role in Southeast Asia." On 15 January 1969, General McConnell recalled Maj. Gen. Richard A. Grussendorf to active duty, assigned him as Chief of the Office of Air Force History, and directed him to establish a long-term program that emphasized publication of scholarly historical books, monographs, and special studies. General McConnell also maintained that, to support the revised program, it was imperative to stress the writing of supporting monographs and topical studies, especially within the major commands.[18]

In terms of organizational structure, General McConnell declared that, instead of reporting to the Office of Information, all command history offices (e.g., Strategic Air Command, Air Force Systems Command, and Air Training Command) would be responsible to the newly created Office of Air Force History, which furnished central policy and guidance. The United States Air Force Historical Division at Maxwell Air Force Base, redesignated in 1972 as the Albert F. Simpson Historical Research Center and now known simply as the United States Air Force Historical Research Center, remained an element of the Air University, with operational control provided by the Office of Air Force History, until it became a direct reporting unit in 1979.[19]

The final issue General McConnell addressed concerned wing histories, especially from those units that participated in or directly supported American operations in Southeast Asia. The most important change was to emphasize quality coverage of such items as significant daily events, operational techniques, and tactics to furnish an information base for "meaningful and interesting" Air Force histories. He therefore charged all appropriate wing commanders with responsibility for assigning competent personnel at the command or operational level and for reviewing the history's accuracy and completeness. In some cases, General McConnell pointed out, a full-time historian(s) may be required to accomplish this task. Therefore, in view of the program's expanding requirements, he ordered a thorough review of personnel requirements and authorizations.[20]

During the 1969–76 period, the book publishing program became more systematic. First to appear was Maurer Maurer's *Combat Squadrons of the Air Force, World War II*, which listed 1,226 combat squadrons active between December 7, 1941 and September 2, 1945. In addition to containing official lineage statements, this book included information about assignments, stations, aircraft and missiles assigned, operations, service streamers, campaign participation, decorations, and emblems. In 1971, the Office of Air Force history published Carl Berger and Mary Ann Cresswell, *United States Air Force History: An Annotated Bibliography*, which was a selected sampling of literature covering military aviation from the Wright brothers' delivery of the Army's first aircraft to the Vietnam War and the United States Air Force's missile program. *The Army Air Forces in World War II—Combat Chronology*, by Kit C. Carter and Robert Mueller, was patterned after an earlier Army publication and was written as a companion volume to *The Army Air Forces in World War II*; it chronicled significant operational events from December 7, 1941 to September 15, 1945. Bernard C. Nalty's *Air Power and the Fight for Khe Sanh*, which was the first published historical monograph about the United States Air Force's role in Southeast Asia, analyzed air operations, airlift, unified control of air power, and uses of electronic sensors. Another 1973 study was a useful reference work by Lawrence J. Paszek, entitled *United States Air Force History: A Guide to Documentary Sources*, which surveyed public and private depositories containing Air Force-related materials. The remaining book was a collection of first-hand accounts by fighter crews who flew combat missions over North Vietnam, entitled *Aces and Aerial Victories—The United States Air Force in Southeast Asia, 1965–1973*, edited by James N. Eastman, Jr., Walter Hanak, and Lawrence J. Paszek.[21]

1976–1981

In September 1976, the Air Staff recalled to active duty Maj. Gen. John W. Huston, a reservist who had served for twenty years on the United States Naval Academy faculty, the last five as chairman of the history department, to serve as Chief of Air Force History. During his tenure, which lasted until 1981, the Air Force History Program grew significantly in terms of expanding the book publishing program, keeping histories relevant to user needs, and providing varied services to the Air Force. According to a statement General Huston gave to *Airman* magazine shortly after returning to active duty:

> We're not writing and collecting histories just to build an empire. If our histories are not serving the Air Staff, if they're not showing a unit commander how not to reinvent the wheel, then we're not doing our job. History is an important management tool. Some of our most beneficial histories are not necessarily about what we have accomplished, but about what we have failed to accomplish and why.[22]

Within five years, the history program had published seven major studies, one of which was previously discussed: the four-volume *The U.S. Air Service in World War I*. Alan M. Osur's *Blacks in the Army Air Forces During World War II* and Alan L. Gropman's *The Air Force Integrates, 1945–1964* examined the black experience in the Air Force. *The United States Air Force in Southeast Asia, 1961–1973—An Illustrated Account*, edited by Carl Berger, described most major aspects of air operations in Southeast Asia as well as discussing the deeds of individual United States Air Force Medal of Honor winners. Roger P. Fox's *Air Base Defense in The Republic of Vietnam* was a more detailed book exploring United States Air Force efforts to defend ten key bases in South Vietnam. The Office of Air Force History also released two reference works entitled *An Aerospace Bibliography* compiled by Samuel Duncan Miller and Marcelle S. Knaack's *Encyclopedia of U.S. Air Force Aircraft and Missile Systems; Volume I, Post-World War II Fighters*. Historians assigned to the Office of Air Force History also started work on numerous other books dealing with the Vietnam War and other Air Force history topics.[23]

One example of keeping histories relevant to user needs concerned the temporary relocation of personnel from one air base to another in the United Kingdom while civil engineers resurfaced runways. The historian studied the move's impact on the unit mission, dependent schooling, bus transportation, mess and support service, as well as a variety of other areas. He then wrote a sixty-page monograph explaining the problems associated with moves of this type. The Office of Air Force History made his findings available to other commanders facing similar situations so they could learn from someone else's experiences.[24]

At the unit level, where this particular history was written, historians are enlisted personnel, usually ranging in rank from airman to senior master sergeant. Even before 1976, training normally consisted of completing a college-level historical methodology course at Maxwell AFB, Alabama, which focused on document evaluation and interviewing techniques. Enlisted historians usually are assigned to wing units as members of the commander's staff. After proper coordination, histories are forwarded through the chain of command to the appropriate numbered air force, major command, United States Air Force Historical Research Center, and then to the Office of Air Force History. Histories also are placed on deposit with the National Archives for future researchers.[25]

The kinds of services the history program provided to the Air Force also expanded during the 1976–81 period, especially as far as the field program was concerned. One of the most important activities field historians performed was writing articles for base newspapers or Air Force publications, such as the *Air University Review*. Others organized lectures or special study groups for military and civilian personnel to examine the growth and development of Air Force history. Many field historians represented the Air Force in the academic community by attending conferences, by advising unemployed historians of the job prospects in the Air Force History Program, and by contributing articles to local publications. In general terms, historians became more active in disseminating information to all ranks of Air Force personnel; indeed, field offices together answered, and continue to answer, thousands of information requests each year in addition to writing quarterly or annual histories.[26]

During 1976–81, the Air Force History Program also made a concerted effort to expand the personal papers collections of Air Force officers, enlisted personnel, and civilians. To that end, General Huston wrote to more than 135 retired general officers seeking their donations. One of the more notable acquisitions was the diary and personal letters that Lt. Gen. George E. Stratemeyer wrote while he was Commanding General of the India-Burma sector and Air Advisor to the Commanding General, China-Burma-India theater during World War II. General Huston also secured the private papers of General of the Air Force Henry H. ("Hap") Arnold, who was perhaps most responsible for building the modern Air Force. Additionally, the Office of Air Force History managed to obtain several other valuable documentary collections, such as the minutes of the first Air Staff meeting held in 1949, after the Soviet Union exploded the atomic bomb. Moreover, the Air Force History Program worked to enlarge the oral history program, persuading many retired senior leaders to record their thoughts and reminiscences on tape. As a result, by 1978, the oral history collection totaled more than 1,200 interviews with former chiefs of staff, secretaries of the Air Force, and past commanders of major commands.[27]

1981 TO PRESENT

In August 1981, Dr. Richard H. Kohn, a civilian historian who had taught at the City College of New York, Rutgers University, and the Army War College, took over as Chief of Air Force History. Since then, the history program has substantially expanded the range of services it provides to the Air Force. Book publishing output has grown considerably, with approximately ten to twelve original and reprint titles appearing annually. To ensure scholarship and accuracy in all official publications, the Office of Air Force History Publications Committee was established to administer rigorous review procedures. Accordingly, the committee, composed largely of senior Air Force historians, approves field monograph proposals and all books to be published by the Office of Air Force History. After a particular study is approved, the Publications Committee chairman subsequently convenes seminars to review the final draft of a monograph; or in the case of books, to review individual chapters, and ultimately the final manuscript. The committee also oversees the Office of Air Force History's Long Range Publication Plan, which is updated every few years.[28]

Since 1981, the Air Force History Program has significantly improved its professional reputation not only in the Air Force and the federal government, but also in the civilian academic community. Thanks to aggressive recruiting campaigns at professional meetings such as the

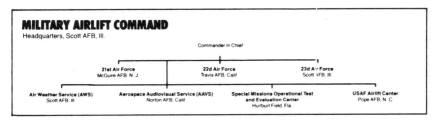

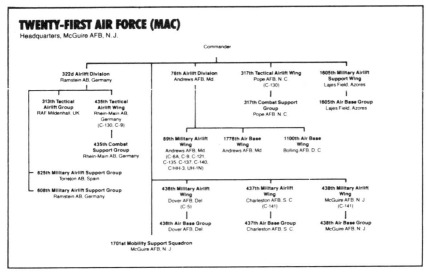

Figure 1. Air Force organizational system. *Air Force Magazine* 67 (May 1984): 107.

annual American Historical Association convention, the history program attracted increasing numbers of professionally trained historians. To speed the selection process for all permanent historian positions, the Office of Air Force History created the Historian Civilian Career Program in 1984 to serve as a central clearing house for matching Air Force historians with vacancies throughout the United States and overseas. Moreover, at the 1984 Worldwide Air Force Historians Conference, held at the Air Force Academy in Colorado Springs, Dr. Kohn launched the first comprehensive review of the entire history program, to enhance its utility to the Air Force.[29]

The Air Force History Program also has continued to diversify the kinds of services it provides the Air Force. One of the most important activities in this area concerns Project Warrior, which Air Force Chief of Staff, Gen. Lew Allen, Jr., started in 1982 to emphasize leadership over management, and the Air Force's fighting heritage. The project's goals are to ensure that personnel are aware of the Air Force's wartime roles and missions and understand the theory and practice of war, with special emphasis on air power contributions. Since Project Warrior's inception, an increasing number of historians has supported these objectives by publishing appropriate articles and pamphlets and engaging in numerous history-related activities such as organizing or conducting voluntary study groups about airpower and aviation history. Many historians also serve as Project Warrior points of contact at their base or installation. For its part, the Office of Air Force History started publishing a continuing series of historical studies in support of Project Warrior, one of the most recent being a reprint of the 1946 study, *Condensed Analysis of the Ninth Air Force in the European Theater of Operations.* Lastly, as the Office of Air Force History's contribution to a Project Warrior lecture series, Dr. Kohn instituted a general officers' study group which meets on a monthly basis at the Pentagon.[30]

Additionally, the Office of Air Force History improved the program's relationship with the Air Force Historical Foundation, a nonprofit independent organization "dedicated to the preservation, perpetuation, and publication of the history and traditions of American aviation, with emphasis on the U. S. Air Force." Apart from asking all historians to support the foundation's annual membership drive, the Office of Air Force History encouraged them to consider, "as a matter of professional activity," contributing an article or book review to its quarterly journal, the *Aerospace Historian.* Dr. Kohn believed this would help increase the Air Force's historical mindedness and the general reading public's knowledge about airpower. To increase visibility within the military, the Office of Air Force History agreed to submit a series of historical articles on a regular basis to *Airman* magazine, one of the Air Force's most popular periodicals.[31]

The four divisions of the United States Air Force Historical Research Center, whose archival collection presently consists of more than 45 million pages of material pertaining to Air Force history, also grew during the post-1981 period. As part of an ongoing project, the Reference Division succeeded in declassifying more than 85 percent of the center's pre-1955 holdings and microfilming almost all of its archives. The Oral History Division expanded the end-of-tour report program and added numerous valuable items to the personal papers and oral history collections. Offices and organizations throughout the Air Force have relied more and more on the Reference Division, which, among other things, prepares lineage and honors of Air Force units, determines aerial victory credits, and writes books and papers on a wide variety of topics. In 1983, the Technical Services Division announced that the Inferential Retrieval Index System had become operational. Current plans call for the center's archival collection to become accessible in 1986 through remote terminals throughout the Air Force.[32]

Thus, it is evident, at least for the foreseeable future, that the Air Force History Program will continue to look for new ways to disseminate historical information to the Air Force. This is not to suggest, however, that its basic mission will change; on the contrary, field historians still will be expected to collect historically significant documents and to write quarterly or annual histories, monographs, and special studies. The Office of Air Force History will continue to emphasize book publishing and Air Staff support while the United States Air Force Historical Research Center will devote much of its time to collection and automation. What is certain to change is that the Air Force History Program will become more dynamic and user oriented so as to better support the Air Force and inform the public.

> Public History: An Introduction, *published by Krieger Publishing Co., Inc., a private firm, is in no way connected with the Department of the Air Force. Opinions expressed by the publisher and writers herein are their own and are not to be considered an official expression by the Department of the Air Force.*

NOTES

1. This article would not have been possible without the advice, support, and guidance of numerous Air Force and Army historians, including Dr. Richard H. Kohn, Grant M. Hales, Col. John F. Shiner, Dr. Joseph P. Harahan, Herman S. Wolk, Jacob Neufeld, Robert W. Rush, John T. Bohn, Dr. Thomas S. Snyder, and H. O. Malone.
2. Maurer Maurer, ed., *The U.S. Air Service in World War I*, 4 vols. (Washington, D.C.: Government Printing Office, 1978–79).
3. John F. Shiner, *Foulois and the U.S. Army Air Corps, 1931–1935* (Washington, D.C.: Government Printing Office, 1983).
4. Letter, Roosevelt to Smith, 4 March 1942, in author's collection; Arnold quoted in memorandum, "Attachment to Suggestion ASD 73–71," n.d., in author's collection.
5. Wesley Frank Craven and James Lea Cate, eds., *The Army Air Forces in World War II: Plans and Early Operations January 1939 to August 1942* (Washington, D.C.: Government Printing Office, 1983), ix.
6. Ibid., ix.
7. Ibid., xii–xiii.
8. Ibid., xiii.
9. A total of thirty-four civilian and military historians contributed to this project. They included James Lea Cate, University of Chicago; Wesley Frank Craven, Princeton University and New York University; E. Kathleen Williams, University of Chicago; Richard L. Watson, Duke University; William A. Goss, City College of San Francisco and College of San Mateo; John D. Carter, West Virginia University and Headquarters, United States Air Force; Kramer J. Rohfleisch, San Diego State College; Herbert Weaver, Georgia Teachers College and Vanderbilt University; Arthur B. Ferguson, Duke University; Alfred Goldberg, Air Historical Group; Thomas J. Maylock, Air Intelligence Division; Albert F. Simpson, Air Historical Group; John E. Fagg, New York University; Joseph W. Angell, Pomona College; Robert H. George, Brown University; Robert T. Finney, United States Air Force Historical Division; Harris Warren, University of Mississippi; David G. Rempel, San Mateo Junior College; Martin R. R. Goldman, United States

Air Force Historical Division; James C. Olson, Nebraska State Historical Society; Major Bernhardt L. Mortensen, Air Force Historical Division; Harry L. Coles, Ohio State University; Lee Bowen, United States Air Force Historical Division; Frank Futrell, United States Air Force Historical Division; Woodford A. Heflin, Air University; James Taylor, Southwest Texas State Teachers College; Chauncy E. Sanders, United States Air Force Historical Division; P. Alan Bliss, Directorate of Intelligence, Headquarters, United States Air Force; Arthur R. Kooker, University of Southern California; Thomas H. Greer, Michigan State College; Frank H. Heck, Centre College of Kentucky; Jonas A. Jonasson, Linfield College; George V. Leroy, University of Chicago; and Kathleen Williams Boom, University of Tennessee Extension Division, Memphis Center.

10. Air Force Regulation 210–1, "USAF History Program Policy and Requirements," 26 August 1984, 1–2.

11. Ibid.

12. Quoted in memorandum, "Attachment to Suggestion ASD 73–71," n.d.

13. Letter, Blanchard to Strategic Air Command et al., 8 March 1965, in author's collection.

14. Frank Futrell, *The United States Air Force in Korea, 1950–1953* (Washington, D.C.: Government Printing Office, 1983).

15. Arthur Goldberg, ed., *A History of the United States Air Force, 1907–1957* (New York: Arno Press, 1972).

16. For additional monograph titles, see Jacob Neufeld, *The United States Air Force History: A Guide to Monographic Literature, 1943–1974* (Washington, D.C.: Office of Air Force History, 1977).

17. Harold Newcomb, "A Memory in Words," *Airman*, June 1978, 6–7.

18. Letter, McConnell to Coira, 15 March 1969, in author's collection.

19. Ibid.; and "Look It Up," *Air Force Times*, 20 February 1984, 43.

20. McConnell to Coira, 15 March 1969; and "Look It Up," 43.

21. Maurer Maurer, ed., *Air Force Combat Units of World War II* (Washington, D.C.: Government Printing Office, 1983); Carl Berger and Mary Ann Cresswell, *United States Air Force History: An Annotated Bibliography* (Washington, D.C.: Government Printing Office, 1973); Kit C. Carter and Robert Mueller, *The Army Air Forces in World War II—Combat Chronology* (Washington, D.C.: Government Printing Office, 1973); Bernard C. Nalty, *Air Power and the Fight for Khe Sanh* (Washington, D.C.: Government Printing Office, 1973); Lawrence J. Paszek, *United States Air Force History: A Guide to Documentary Sources* (Washington, D.C.: Government Printing Office, 1973); and James N. Eastman, Jr., Walter Hanak, and Lawrence J. Paszek, eds., *Aces and Aerial Victories—The United States Air Force in Southeast Asia, 1965–1973* (Washington, D.C.: Government Printing Office, 1973).

22. Quoted in Harold Newcomb, "A Memory in Words," *Airman*, June 1978, 1–2.

23. Alan M. Osur, *Blacks in the Army Air Force During World War II: The Problem of Race Relations* (Washington, D.C.: Government Printing Office, 1977); Alan L. Gropman, *The Air Force Integrates, 1945–1964* (Washington, D.C.: Government Printing Office, 1978); Carl Berger, ed., *The United States Air Force in Southeast Asia, 1961–1973—An Illustrated Account* (Washington, D.C.: Government Printing Office, 1977; revised edition, 1984); Roger P. Fox, *Air Base Defense in The Republic of Vietnam* (Washington, D.C.: Government Printing Office, 1979); Samuel Duncan Miller, *An Aerospace Bibliography* (Washington, D.C.: Government Printing Office, 1979); and Marcelle S.

Knaack, *Encyclopedia of United States Air Force Aircraft and Missile Systems: Volume I, Post–World War II Fighters, 1945–1973* (Washington, D.C.: Government Printing Office, 1978).

24. Newcomb, "A Memory in Words," 3.
25. Air Force Regulation 210–1, *Historical Data and Properties: USAF History Program Policy and Requirements* (Washington, D.C.: Department of the Air Force, 1984), 5.
26. Grant M. Hales, Senior Historian for Field History Program, interview with author, 2 February 1985.
27. Ibid.; and Newcomb, "A Memory in Words," 5.
28. Richard H. Kohn, AF/CHO Publications Committee: Responsibilities and Procedures, 5 June 1984, in author's collection; and Herman S. Wolk, Chief, General Histories Branch, interview with author, 20 March 1985.
29. Grant M. Hales interview; and Letter, Kohn to Alaskan Air Command et al., 6 April 1984, in author's collection.
30. Valerie Elbow, "The Warrior Spirit," *Air Force Magazine* 66 (October 1983): 54; and *Condensed Analysis of the Ninth Air Force in the European Theatre of Operations* (Washington, D.C.: Government Printing Office, 1984).
31. Newcomb, "A Memory in Words," 8; and Grant M. Hales interview.
32. "USAF Historical Research Center," *Air Force Magazine* 67 (May 1984): 152, 155.

Larry E. Tise, executive director of the Pennsylvania Historical and Museum Commission, is a native of Winston-Salem, North Carolina. He received the A.M. and Master of Divinity degrees from Duke University and his Ph.D. in American History from the University of North Carolina at Chapel Hill in 1974. From 1975 until 1981 he served as director of the North Carolina Division of Archives and History at which time he moved to his current position. In addition to books and articles on the American Revolution, North Carolina history, and church history, he has written extensively on the nature of public history, particularly on the state level. His articles have appeared in History News, The Public Historian, *and elsewhere. He has also served as president of the National Conference of State Historic Preservation Officers, the National Association of State Archives and Records Administrators, and as chair of the National Council on Public History.*

THE PRACTICE OF PUBLIC HISTORY IN STATE GOVERNMENT

Larry E. Tise

There are more similarities than dissimilarities in the practice of history at all levels of government whether one speaks of federal, state, or local government in the United States. The practice of history at the federal level or within the confines of a tiny borough in the backwaters of Pennsylvania or Kentucky involves the same principles, the same challenges, and the same difficulties. Wherever one practices history in government, it is essential that the historian be mindful of the canons of historical scholarship; the political process in all of its curious manifestations swirls constantly overhead; the limited financial resources are never sufficient to provide adequately for cultural programs; and Ezekiel-like wheels of bureaucracy grind discouragingly.

There is nevertheless a uniqueness to the manner in which the practice of history has developed within governments. There are a host of opportunities to affect the study, practice, and interpretation of history on the state level not feasible for the individual historian or the historical agency on other levels. It is instructive and useful for any historian contemplating history work within government to appreciate and understand both the essence of the practice of history at all levels of government and the special opportunities within the context of state government.

Within state governments in the United States most history work is pursued within the confines of a variety of agencies or subagencies which are responsible for one aspect of history or another. Very few state agencies have the luxuries often found in many federal government agencies, such as their own history office, historic preservation officer, or cultural resources management office. And unlike local governments which by and large have not developed historical agencies (except in the case of the larger cities), state governments have generally acknowledged that they have some responsibility in the area of historical programming or management that includes at least archives and records management, historical publications, the creation and management of historical monuments and markers, the restoration and interpretation of historic sites or historical parks, the fostering of historical museums, and the administration of a state-based historic preservation and archeological management program.

While the size of such programs may vary radically from state to state depending upon a number of historical or social and economic characteristics, one can expect to find somewhere in state government an agency or series of agencies fostering within the state each of these now traditional forms of public history. In some states—Pennsylvania, Ohio, North Carolina, and Minnesota—all of these historical functions are combined in one large historical agency. In New York, Massachusetts, Tennessee, and California these various historical functions are spread across nearly as many different agencies and offices, although each in its own respect may be as strong and productive as the similar functions in those states where all historical functions are combined in one agency. Regrettably, however, in most states historical functions are located in a few relatively small and frequently poorly endowed offices.

While there are radical differences in the size and capabilities of historical programs among and within the states, there are some similarities among clusters of states in the type of historical institutions serving their citizens. The oldest type of state historical institution, and until the twentieth century the most common, was the privately funded and controlled but publicly minded state historical society. Most of the states in New England and the Northeast and many in the Midwest developed state-wide individual membership historical societies frequently shortly after they became states. Among the New England states, historical societies began to emerge during the last years of the eighteenth century and the opening decades of the nineteenth. In the Midwest, historical societies were formed almost as part and parcel of the achievement of statehood.

Although most of these publicly minded historical societies remained under private control until the twentieth century, they early became the beneficiaries of partial public funding in return for preserving the historical records of the state or commonwealth and other special services. With the rapid growth of government at all levels during the twentieth century, these quasi-public history institutions increasingly came under the control and eventually became virtual creatures of state government. By the early 1980s those that provided public history services for the states—while they might have preserved their independent charter and private board of directors—had become so dependent upon state governments for financial support that they fell subject to the same budgetary, personnel, and legislative control as state historical agencies which were considered full-fledged parts of state government. Such has been the case particularly in the Midwest states of Ohio, Wisconsin, and Minnesota where large privately chartered state historical societies provide nearly all historical programs within each state. In other states where the state society chose not to provide a full range of historical services to the peoples of the state, the society has been overwhelmed and obscured by the growth of publicly funded historical agencies. Such would be true of the Historical Society of Pennsylvania, the Massachusetts Historical Society, and the Maryland Historical Society.

During the early years of the twentieth century when state governments began to grow in size and complexity and when the historical profession began a concerted push to develop state history programs in the areas of archives and historical publications, many of the former private state historical societies began the long slow conversion to become public history institutions. At the same time in those states where such societies did not exist or where the existing state societies did not wish to take on essentially public responsibilities several other forms of state history institutions began to emerge. In some states, North Carolina (1903) and Pennsylvania (1913), publicly appointed commissions were established to oversee the development of state history programs. Such commissions were a cross between the privately chartered historical society and fully publicly controlled state agency. With citizen members usually appointed by governors and in some cases representing in ex-officio capacities existing historical societies and various colleges and universities, the early commissions began the process of building the first full-fledged state historical programs in the nation utilizing a small mix of private sector input with a majority of funds provided by state treasuries.

In other states, particularly in the area of the old southern Confederacy, a slightly different form of state historical program began to emerge. Departments of archives and history were created by state law in Alabama, Mississippi, and Georgia among other states. Although some of the departments had executive boards along the lines of the other state historical commissions, most were developed as full-fledged departments of state government usually under the auspices of the governor's jurisdiction. This form of governance for state history programs became sufficiently attractive that it remains the virtual pattern for the administration of state history through the states of the Old South. North Carolina's Historical Commission became such a department in 1945. South Carolina and Florida followed the same pattern when they created consolidated state history agencies years later. Under this form of governance such departments became among the strongest state history programs in the nation even though they frequently lacked the private sector, citizen involvement of the publicly funded state historical societies or the citizen controlled state historical commissions.

More than half of the states have what might be considered single state historical agencies either in the form of a state historical society, a historical commission, or a department of archives and history. The remaining states have history programs dispersed among a number of agencies depending upon their historical traditions, geographic location, and constitutional nature. Some states that once had consolidated programs have seen elements of the state's history program shifted to other departments where they could be more easily managed, controlled, or developed. States with historically dispersed programs include Massachusetts, New York, Virginia, Indiana, Illinois, Louisiana, Texas, and California. States in the Far West generally have dispersed programs. States with elected cabinet officers, particularly a secretary of state, tend to have archival and historical programs under the aegis of that office. States that have undergone severe development pressures over the last quarter century or which have strong traditions of conservation and recreation have tended to locate historic preservation programs in departments dealing with environmental resources or transportation.

Historical program functions in those states that do not have consolidated historical programs are likely to be found in some of the following offices or agencies. Archival programs are frequently associated with secretaries of state, state libraries, or possibly with state general service agencies. Records management programs are frequently connected with general service or state administration agencies. Historical publications may be issued by the secretary of state or the state library. Monuments and historical markers may be the responsibility of state parks or transportation agencies. Historic sites, if not under the state historical society, may be included in the state park system, or may be held by a state historical trust such as the Maryland Historical Trust or the Virginia Landmarks Commission. Historical museums may be operated by the state park system, may be associated with a strong state museum, or may be connected with the state education department. Historic preservation and archeological resources management are perhaps the most widely dispersed forms of state history programming. If not in the state historical agency, they may be under the secretary of state, an independent commission, the state historical trust, the environmental resources agency, state parks, transportation, education, and perhaps other locations.

Wherever state historical programs may be located within state governments, the work of the individual programs from state to state varies very little. While the conditions under which they are forced to operate may be radically different, the essence of their work remains relatively constant wherever one might go. An introduction to a particular historical program in one state will normally reveal the aspirations if not the actual work responsibilities of the program in nearly every other state.

State archives are generally institutions that receive, arrange and describe, preserve, and make available for public use historical records of the state government. Some state archives also serve the same function for all of the subdivisions of state government including county and municipal governments. Some, in addition to serving as the repository for governmental records, actively seek out and collect large bodies of private manuscript material. Nearly all state archives operate some form of micrographics service transferring paper records into some microform for more compact storage or easier reference. Nearly all have some form of conservation program preserving those records which have deteriorated. Nearly all handle a variety of forms of records from paper to microform, from photographic negatives to prints and posters, and from film to video and computer tape. Nearly all prepare finding aids for researchers and maintain reference or reading rooms where historical records may be consulted under secure circumstances. Nearly all seek to maintain storage facilities that are secure against theft, atmospheric conditions, and fire.

More than half of the state historical or archival programs in the nation are involved in records management programs. In the area of records management the historical program seeks to get other agencies of government to maintain a constant inventory and filing system for current, noncurrent, and historical records. With records under proper management control it is possible to prepare records retention and disposition schedules for all records series. Certain records have only temporary use and may be disposed of within a year of their creation. Others have temporary administrative value and need only be retained so long as there is an administrative need for them. Still others may be deemed by the archivist or historian as of permanent historical or archival value and be scheduled almost from the instant of creation for eventual transfer to the state archives. Whatever the form of records, it is the responsibility of the state history program to manage the records of the state from creation to final disposition.

Historical publications programs vary considerably in the type of product produced, but relatively little in the historical methods to be applied. Some state historical agencies merely produce brochures, pamphlets, and leaflets on various aspects of the state's history or on the various historic sites and museums of the state. Others seek to publish popular historical magazines in full color. Still others publish the state's scholarly historical journal. In terms of books, some publish only historical monographs either carefully documented or for popular consumption. Others publish only edited historical records of great historical figures within the state or events important in the state's history. Some produce massive documentary publications such as the North Carolina and the South Carolina Colonial Records projects. Others produce biographical directories of general assemblies and state leaders and official state manuals. Only a few of the major state history programs seek to produce all of the foregoing types of publications.

Nearly all states have some form of state monument or historical marker program. From the conclusion of the Civil War until the development of a national highway network, states regularly created monuments of various sizes and shapes to commemorate early leaders, military heroes, and famous events. They were placed in cities, towns, at important intersections, on battlefields, and sometimes at nearly hidden and remote locations where historical events occurred. During the 1930s while automobiles still traveled at relatively low speed, many states began creating vast programs to fabricate historical markers that could be read as automobiles passed by. Some states have vast marker programs today with their familiar shapes and now inscrutable legends scattered along all of the principal roads and highways of the state. Each monument or marker had to be researched and approved by the state history program. And once erected or placed it had to be maintained, cleaned, and frequently repainted. Historical programs, therefore, not only research the claims of historical significance and precedence, but also must maintain the monument or marker that resulted from local interest and eager research.

All states have historic sites owned and operated by state government. Whether they fall under the auspices of the consolidated state historical agency or under some other agency, all must be researched both in documentary records and in terms of the material remains at the site above and below ground. They may include battlegrounds, birthplaces of the great and famous or infamous, typical homesteads of early settlers or frontiersmen, elegant homes of the creative or rich, industrial and technological sites, archeological sites, burial grounds, and even engineering landmarks such as covered or stone arch bridges. Once they come into public ownership they must usually be restored based on careful research and planning, furnished and interpreted to the visiting public, and maintained both against the ravages of weather and of the visitors for whom they have been preserved. As in the case of the private home or commercial structure, grass must be mowed, hinges oiled, bathrooms cleaned, and furniture polished. State historical programs must have the capability of performing all of these responsibilities whether they be deemed purely historical in nature or not.

Nearly all states have historical museums, even if only the solitary state museum. Some have vast state-owned museum systems such as in Pennsylvania where the Historical and Museum Commission operates not only the State Museum of Pennsylvania but also large thematic museums devoted to military, agricultural, mining, lumbering, railroading, and petroleum history. Other states may have one or two specialized museums dealing with particular facets of the state's past such as the Circus World Museum operated by the State Historical Society of Wisconsin. But whatever the size and shape of the museum system, certain historical functions are common to all of them. All collect objects and artifacts of historical or artistic significance and materials representing lifestyles in various eras and occupations. They must properly accession, document, store, and preserve those objects either for future purposes of study or exhibition. They must develop exhibits making use of historical research and items from the collection. All must prepare interpretive and educational programs for the visiting public. Depending upon the scope and purposes of the museum's program the historical agency may also operate storage facilities, conservation centers, sales facilities, exhibit shops, and custodial and security forces beyond the mere curatorial function of the historical museum.

Every state has a historic preservation program and an archeological resources management program. This is because the federal government through the National Historic Preservation Act of 1966 and its various amendments has opted to operate the national historic preservation program in partnership with state and territorial governments. Either within the state historical agency or somewhere else, the State Historic Preservation Officer is responsible for carrying out the mandates of both federal and state historic preservation laws within the state. Although some states had developed historic preservation offices prior to 1966 usually in association with their historic sites programs, as a result of the national act and the way in which it has been administered one will find greater uniformity in size, workload, methods, and objectives among State Historic Preservation Offices than any of the other facets of public history on the state level.

Every historic preservation office must administer a program of federal grants within the state, identify historic properties and archeological sites, actively nominate those deemed significant to the National Register of Historic Places, maintain an environmental review program to determine the effect of state and federally funded projects on historic properties, and stage educational programs to promote the causes and methodologies of historic preservation. Most states also participate in the review of certified rehabilitation projects making use of federal and sometimes state tax incentives. Some states carry on active historic property inventory programs. Some mount archeological reconnaissance surveys. Some investigate particular historic properties or archeological sites. A few states maintain underwater archeology programs. Others maintain active restoration consulting operations. At least one conducts an active preservation training center such as the Stagville Center of the North Carolina Division of Archives and History. Most either cooperate with or administer a state preservation society. A few operate revolving funds or revolving fund corporations to purchase and resell endangered historic properties.

Because of historical precedents the relationship of state historical programs to archeology may sometimes be confused. States that had strong archeology study centers at state universities or major museums prior to 1966 may have divided authorities in the realm of both prehistoric and historic archeology. In such states as South Carolina, Arkansas, Illinois, and most of those in the Far West, major archeological research proceeds from universities whereas in many eastern states the state archeological center is likely within the state historical agency. In all states, however, the state historic preservation office finds that it must deal with growing numbers of contract or consulting archeologists and increasingly in other disciplines as well where professionals are developing livelihoods in conducting surveys and mitigation studies in the path of federally assisted development projects such as highway and dam construction.

Whatever the shape of the state historical agency, wherever it may be located in state governments, and however large its scope or mission, there are certain unalterable facts about the life and working conditions of the organization and the people who work within it. All of them are greatly influenced and their heads perhaps hired and fired by state governors. Even in those states where public history is conducted by a privately chartered historical society, changes in administrations can have dramatic effects on the direction and operations of the state program. By the same token all state history programs live in one measure or another on the goodwill and support of the state's general assembly. By controlling the purse strings of the public treasury and by constantly responding to various national and local currents to restrict taxes, control spending, eliminate waste, or expand services, the actions of the state assembly can and do shape the type of service the historical agency can render. Moreover, between the state historical program and the governor and general assembly there is always some entity usually known as the Department or Office of Administration or Budget that further exacts control and can modify the abilities and behavior of a state history program.

All of these are but concrete expressions of the much larger political environment in which a state historical agency must operate. Although it generally is a relatively small budget agency in the total context of state government, it is subject to the same fickle whims of the political process and contemporary currents within the state. Occasionally some of its interests or pursuits can become causes célèbres that can bring down the entire political system upon the agency and its head. Such a case might result from the efforts of the historic preservation program to protect a historic building or an archeological site in the pathway of a major highway corridor being demanded by the citizenry of the state. The same can result from the refusal of the historical agency to accept or endorse a historical project that has popular support and according to folklore is associated with someone famous, like Daniel Boone, for example, but is without verifiable historical evidence.

But the political process in which state history work is done can offer up rewards as well as pose obstacles. The same system that can cause a highway project to humble the historic preservation program can be used to promote the causes of history. The same system that is used to restrict funds for unpopular programs can be used to promote allocation of funds to historical endeavors that have been sold to the public or have been proved beneficial to some segment of the society or economy. The same system that can prevent controversial causes from being converted into law can be used to thwart the efforts of politicians who have single-minded projects and proposals that can be destructive to history. Effective state historical program administrators must learn early on that the political environment in which they work is the norm wherever one works in the governmental sector. One must learn to take advantage of the benefits of the system as well as be aware of its blunt potential destructiveness.

Whereas it was perhaps once possible for state historical agencies to operate as nonbureaucratic institutions in a bureaucratic sea, such is no longer feasible or advisable. With the growth of government following the Second World War and with the reaction against big government that followed in the 1970s, it has become essential for historical agencies to become the best possible practitioners of bureaucratic systems. At nearly all levels of the history program it is necessary for administrators and professionals to understand budget and spending regulations, personnel rules and practices, contracting procedures, and all the rest that goes along with a highly sophisticated and productive bureaucratic system. Instead of abhorring bureaucracy it is incumbent upon historians and history administrators to understand that carefully ordered administrative systems are necessary by-products of the legal framework in which government is required to operate. That it is more complicated to accomplish tasks in government and that the cost of doing things is more expensive in government than in the private sector are givens that must be understood and conquered instead of causes for resignation and defeat.

Among the opportunities that inure to state historical programs and are not present in other types of governmental institutions are the opportunity—and the challenge—of developing private sector support. It would be folly for a government welfare agency to seek contributions from corporations and individuals to enhance the level of funds given to welfare recipients, for a transportation agency to seek volunteers to help repave roads, or for a defense agency to seek corporations who would donate design services for a new weapon system. However, it is possible for the state history agency to seek and obtain corporate and individual donations to assist with many projects and programs. The acquisition of objects and artifacts, the funding of conservation activities, the arrangement of records, the publication of books, the sponsorship of educational programs, and payment for the research and preparation of an exhibit are just a few activities commonly funded through private contributions in state history programs.

The same is true with volunteerism. While the eighteenth-century pattern of donating so many days a year to the improvement of the public roads is a practice long forgotten, volunteers abound in considerable numbers in and around state history agencies. In 1984 the Pennsylvania Historical and Museum Commission had more than 9,000 volunteers who donated more than 99,000 hours of service in conducting museum tours, assisting with curatorial activities, operating sales facilities, preparing bulk mailings, and holding special events from fairs to picnics to exhibit openings. Most come to the program through nonprofit associate groups formed just for the purpose of recruiting intelligent and capable people to carry on activities frequently on a paying basis to supplement and enhance the state-funded core history program.

While defense contractors would laugh at the notion of donating design services to government, architectural and engineering firms are frequently happy to donate their special talents in the cause of history to state history programs. When special talents are needed in any realm of his work, it is not always necessary for the history administrator to turn to the general assembly for more funds. For almost every need of the history program there is a potential donor for the service, the material, the item required—almost none of which could be secured in the same quality through government-regulated purchasing and contracting procedures.

One of the great challenges and opportunities available to the historian or other professional working in the context of a state history program is that of working both in the public and private sector, of working with contractors and with charitable institutions, of meeting head to head with the chiefs of corporations and foundations and tapping the American tradition of philanthropy for the sake of history. Whereas it was once possible for the historian to bury himself or herself in the technical minutiae of dealing solely with historical objects, records, or properties, it is presently necessary for every professional working in history on the state government level to double as administrator and promoter as well. It is essential for every researcher and every archivist and every curator to develop his or her area of special knowledge and expertise with a mind toward its marketing and sales potential.

Unfortunately very few professional training programs in the realms of history or even public and applied history, in the realms of archives and museology, or in the realms of architectural history and archeology properly fit the aspiring professional for the work that lies ahead in the state history program. Indeed, the paucity of usable training in these programs and the feebleness of the mindset that many history and history-related students acquire in their professional training programs have frequently served as detriments to their promotion and advancement in state history programs. To deal with the realities of operating contemporary governmental history programs, many with professional training in history are passed over for more suitable individuals steeped in economics, business, management, and administration. Until historians are better equipped in both outlook and varied areas of technical competence, the pattern of declining numbers of history-trained individuals in state history programs is likely to continue.

It should be emphasized, however, that the historian working in state government is in a special, enviable position. From the seat of the state history program it is possible, even mandatory, for history administrators to work with colleges and universities to upgrade and refocus history undergraduate and graduate curricula. In Pennsylvania, North Carolina, and South Carolina the state history programs work with all colleges and universities in the state to administer cooperative programs in applied history, bringing together academicians and public historians and providing substantial internship possibilities for aspiring students. The rising tide of communication between state government historians and academic historians must continue.

State government historians also have the opportunity of working with the professional and quasi-professional history associations in their states. By assisting such organizations in their membership, publishing, and conference activities, it is possible for the state government historian to influence the future shape of the history craft and to raise the awareness and understanding of historians working in academic settings. Moreover, in greater numbers state historians are making their presence known in the national professional associations, explaining the nature of public history as it is practiced in state government. To the extent that the channels of communication are further opened, professional historians will be able to reinfiltrate and guide the destinies of state history programs.

The practice of public history in state government is not unlike the pursuit of history in any level of government. Agendas are determined in the fine interplay between political and professional concerns. Timetables for the completion of history projects are prescribed by the availability of resources and the needs of the agency. Historians are stretched far beyond the bounds of anything they were prepared to do when they made the choice of becoming professional historians. Professionalism itself is challenged by the demands of making deadlines and forcing the products of research and interpretation to fit into small spaces and alien formats. By the same token history professionalism can reach its highest degree of achievement and service as professional historians make use of their knowledge of history, their commitment that history shall be presented accurately and faithfully—at the same time fully aware that their audience will take greater notice of the squeaking hinge and the unmowed grass than of the products of their most creative insights into the past.

SUGGESTED READING

There are few sources related to this topic. For information on state archives, see Ernst Posner, *American State Archives* (Chicago: University of Chicago Press, 1964). Larry Tise has also written several articles related to this topic. See, for example, his "The Philosophy and Practice of Public Historical Administration," in *Carolina Comments* (January 1978); "State and Local History: A Future from the Past," *The Public Historian* 1 (Summer 1979): 14–22; "The Future of Public History," *The Public Historian* 2 (Fall 1979): 58–64; and "Jacques Cousteau, the USS *Monitor*, and the Philosophy and Practice of Public History," *The Public Historian* 5 (Winter 1983): 31–45. A condensed version of this essay appeared in *History News* 40 (September 1985): 16–21 in "The Politics of State History" by Charles Phillips.

Roy H. Lopata received a Ph.D. from the University of Delaware in 1975. Prior to his appointment as planning director for the City of Newark, Delaware, in 1977, he served as administrative assistant to Newark's city manager. The Newark Planning Department is responsible for zoning and land use regulation, economic and community development, historic preservation, transportation planning and public transit operations, environmental protection, planning for capital expenditures, and demographic data gathering and analysis. In addition, the Planning Department assists the city manager's office with public and press relations, labor and personnel relations, records management, and financial planning. Mr. Lopata has published in The Public Historian, Public Works, The International Transportation Engineers Journal, The Dictionary of American Biography, The Journal of the American Planning Association, Small Town, *and was a contributor to the annotated public history bibliography,* The Craft of Public History.

RED TAPE TIPS:
THE HISTORIAN IN CITY HALL

Roy H. Lopata

Of the approximately 110 million Americans in the civilian labor force, almost 16 million work for governments. In other words, about one out of every seven employees in the United States is a public servant of one kind or another. These 16 million are employed by 82,688 units of government, including 31,041 counties, 19,083 municipalities, 16,748 towns and villages, 15,032 school districts, 28,733 special service districts and agencies, 50 states, and, of course, 1 federal government. Over nine million governmental workers serve local governmental agencies—that is, they work for one of the various kinds of governmental units but not the fifty states or the United States. Interestingly, in 1980, American colleges and universities granted 2,367 master of arts degrees and 712 doctor of philosophy degrees in history, and only a small few of these historians found employment as one of the 16 million in government.[1] And of those who held federal, state, or municipal positions, most worked at tasks specifically designated for those with historical training as "historians" or "preservationists." Hardly any of these historians served as administrators, managers, staff assistants, or in similar positions, performing tasks not directly linked to the study of the past. Perhaps that is as it should be. . . .

In the first issue of *The Public Historian*, Editor G. Wesley Johnson, Jr., called government, "The most essential sector for the Public Historian."[2] And in the same issue Robert Kelley argued that:

> Because the historical mode of thinking has been professionally located almost solely within the academic community, where it has been put to use on matters far distant in time, history has been thought to be like the arts and the humanities. That is, it is thought to produce things which are interesting, which are essential to the human spirit, but which are not immediately useful. The cultivated mind should have knowledge of history, that is an accepted truism. History's connection with the real world, however, has been thought to be limited to such sophisticated fields as foreign policy or the conduct of government within the White House.
>
> This is the fundamental misconception which must be swept away. The historical method of analysis is not simply relevant to the fate of nations, or to issues of peace and war. It is essential in every kind of immediate, practical situation.[3]

Kelley goes on to describe various hypothetical situations where historical perspective or the historian's tools would be helpful in day-to-day governmental problem solving. He concludes by noting that public history will reach fruition when historians by the thousands serve throughout our society and when "their potentiality is widely recognized and they are permanently employed as practicing public historians and not simply as academic historians carrying out an occasional task of public service."[4] In other words, while historians in governmental service have been primarily consigned to archival management, historic preservation, and neighborhood conservation—that is, examining, recording, and preserving the relics of our civic past—historians could, so Johnson and Kelley maintained, utilize their skills in areas of public service problem solving without obvious and direct historical components.

Thus, Johnson, Kelley, and other public history pioneers seemed to sense, almost intuitively, that those who write the story of human affairs could contribute, in some ways, to making the story themselves. Perhaps, then, historians could fend for their share of the 16 million available governmental positions. Surely, of course, they could not compete for technical or specialist positions—botany, geology, or veterinary medicine, for instance, would have to be left to others—but certainly there appeared to be no good reason for historians to shun jobs held by geographers, political scientists, planners, sociologists, economists, or public administrators.

And, not so surprisingly, the pages of the issues that followed the first issue of *The Public Historian* fulfilled the editor's prophecy. Articles appeared describing the day-to-day contributions of historians in growth management, cost benefit analysis, city planning, public works, environmentalism, records management, transportation planning, municipal finance, policy analysis, and so on.[5] Yet, until one actually experiences it, the notion that historians can successfully handle the routine and more complex aspects of municipal management administration, as well as the tasks traditionally assigned to historians, remains difficult to understand or accept. Certainly, *The Public Historian* has effectively outlined the talents historians possess which are applicable to careers in government. And moreover, since the experiences of historians in local public administration have begun to coincide with those of other public officials, public history students can expect that generalizations about public administration and management will apply to their future careers as well as to those of students trained in the more traditional routes to government service.

What, then, are the components of public administration? What does managing, supervising, directing, or administrating in a local governmental setting mean? What are the various roles municipal bureaucrats must learn to play? What skills need to be mastered for service in local public administration? And finally, how does the historian manage to manage in a municipal or local government?

Local public administration positions normally are said to include city managers, department heads, planners, senior staff of regional councils, directors or staff members of research or service organizations, community or neighborhood action agencies, service agencies, and officials in state and federal programs concerned with urban problem solving. These public administrators indicate that they spend most of their time coordinating the work of experts or specialists. That is, the local governmental administrator summarizes and implements primarily on the basis of technical expertise supplied by others. The administrator must serve as a consensus builder, salesperson, and manager of conflict. This is so because, unfortunately, neither the experts one relies upon nor the public one serves always agree. In fact, one can count on the opposite. Thus, those in policy-making or directive positions in government or in institutions related to governmental activities spend most of their time attempting to guide their organizations in the face of continually changing circumstances, while ensuring that the organization's various facets function together smoothly.

Beyond that, the demands on the administrator's time, energy, and emotions arising from the multidimensional aspect of local governmental service, require the ability to analyze data, sift through conflicting advice and opinion, and handle people. In the meantime the local public administrator must live and work in a media fishbowl. Public administration is, after all, the people's business. This means, of course, that the budding public historian-administrator must be ready to forsake quiet hours in the archives, the luxury of writing limited only by the canons of scholarship, and academia's intellectual ferment. Yet, despite the pressures of an often irate citizenry, inquiries from confused reporters, and the constraints of real deadlines, local public administrators have the opportunity to make a difference, to see the fruits of their labor. Most importantly within this context, public historian administrators have the opportunity to utilize their historically based understanding of human nature, and of the values that motivate individuals, their knowledge of the roots of urban problems, and their sense of the various, and often competing, social, economic, and political policies that form the basis of urban programs and policies.[6]

In general, then, the administrator or staff member in local public administration must develop a capability to visualize beyond the present circumstances, problems, and controversies, and to focus on the larger institutional strategies in order to reach goals normally articulated by the public's representatives—elected officials. Yet, implementation of grand strategies coincides with managing the more mundane public service routine. The personality of the successful administrator, therefore, requires flexibility, as well as the combination of the pragmatic with the philosophical. In other words, good public administration at the local level remains an art rather than a science.[7]

Historically, the difficult task of teaching the art of public affairs has been assigned to university and college schools of government, political science, urban affairs, business, and law. Today, these programs usually include course work in identification and definition of urban problems, analysis of problems and alternative solutions, choosing most feasible programs, translation of decisions into action, and assessment and evaluation. In addition, public administration students examine the values and ethics of public decisions and actions and learn the process of government and policy analysis techniques. They also study technology and society; organizational theory and development; community relations; statistics, personnel and management systems; and finally, public administration theory.[8] Often this course material is presented in seminar format, with case studies of specific urban problems and policies forming the basis for discussion, analysis, and further research.

Because such educational programs normally do not, and probably cannot, provide training in specific and more technical disciplines, historically educated public administrators will find that the abilities and skills developed during their graduate school experience are not dissimilar from those of their colleagues. This is not to imply that historians necessarily will be better prepared for governmental service, but only that the education historians receive will not be a handicap. Of course, historians who broaden their education with course work and/or reading in public affairs or public administration subject areas will feel more immediately comfortable in the public service environment. And conversely, public administration students will understand urban problems and urban decision making from a wider perspective with some training in history.

No matter how intensive the preparation, however, graduates soon discover that service in local government remains best understood through experience. In this context noted planner Frederick Bair's description of day-to-day governmental service is particularly relevant:

Each citizen may know of one of two or half of dozen things which he thinks . . . public officials should do something about immediately. Taken all together these problems become a fearsome thing. . . . Low flying airplanes, barking dogs, beautification, sewage treatment plants, hospitals, highways, parking, traffic, street lighting (both too much and too little), overflowing

septic tanks, zoning, parks, playgrounds and recreational programs, business (more or less), foilage diseases, budgets, fire protection, mosquitoes,
billboards, noise, garbage and trash disposal, schools, swimming pools,
police protection, community centers, welfare, day nurseries, bond issues,
holes in the pavement, standing water, legal problems, fallen trees, fund
drives, dust, smoke, industrial promotion, public finance, tourist promotion, accident prevention programs, livestock at-large, building permits,
speeding, loitering, too much control on me and too little control on other
people, threats to constitutional liberties, high assessments on me and low
assessments on the neighbors, job requests, low water pressure, fish in the
sink, subdivision regulation—you haven't lived life to the full until you have
been a public official.[9]

Fortunately, in order to understand the bewildering array of tasks
confronting the local public administrator, the essential elements of
municipal management can be grouped together in general skill or task
categories. On the other hand, categorization, by definition, tends to
obscure the chaotic, disorganized, and contradictory aspects of life at city
hall ably captured by Bair.

Despite this caveat, an examination of municipal management's components remains crucial for historians contemplating careers in local
governments. To begin, one of the most critical, and at times vexing,
aspects of local government administration (and business for that
matter) is personnel management. Because personal services normally
consume over half the operating budgets of cities and city-related
institutions and organizations, the effective management of people
remains the key to providing local services at reasonable costs. Moreover, because personnel administration covers all aspects of government's human resources, all managers—chief administrators, assistants,
department heads, foremen, and so on—must devote a considerable
portion of their time to people-oriented tasks.

Personnel administration, although varying to some extent from city
to city, normally covers a wide spectrum of tasks and duties. These
include job applicant recruitment; employee selection through interviews and testing; appointment; performance evaluation, motivation,
and discipline; position classification and pay administration—that is,
ensuring that pay is adequate to recruit quality employees but not
beyond the local market or the ability to pay; labor relations, primarily
involving collective bargaining, grievance procedures, mediation and
arbitration, and related legal issues; and finally, employee development,
including on- and off-site training programs, and continuing education.
Obviously, this is only a cursory review of the personnel aspect of local
government. But above all, handling employee relations requires the
ability to work with people and to understand that because no two
employees are alike, every situation and personality will vary. Personnel
management then best exemplifies the nontechnical aspect of governmental service; that is, experience rather than education is crucial for
success in employee management and supervision.[10]

Because cities strive to provide the best possible service at the lowest possible cost, financial administration is the fulcrum upon which munic-ipal government rests. The taxpayer revolts of the 1970s, cutbacks in federal assistance, and the ever-increasing demands for municipal service, have made managing local revenues increasingly difficult and complex. Public historians contemplating urban oriented careers ought to consider some training in statistics, accounting, fiscal analysis, or related fields.

Municipal financial management primarily involves developing both operating budget documents—the "annual budget" and the "capital budget" (consisting traditionally of capital improvements required for a five- or six-year period). This budgetary process involves a series of decisions focusing on the organization's goals; the level of services desired; evaluation of facilities and need for repairs, improvements, and expansion; revenue availability including the potential for new revenue sources; and budgetary data and related information gathering. Because of the constraints of balanced budget requirements and limited reve-nues, and the inherent difficulties in starting anew for each budget cycle, most governments rely on last year's budget as a base from which to work. Dissatisfaction with this form of incremental budgeting, however, has led to a series of management innovations which purport to improve governmental budgetary effectiveness. These new systems usually sug-gest starting from scratch each year and examining all the components of municipal departments and programs. Whether known as "Zero-Based Budgeting" or PPBS (Planning-Programming-Budgeting Sys-tem), or "Strategic Planning," these reforms have not, as yet, produced the revolutionary consequences expected by their proponents, but they do help formulate a somewhat broader context for budgetary planning and decision making.

Financial administration also requires budgetary implementation, meaning primarily the monitoring of expenditures to ensure that they follow the requirements of the adopted budget. This is accomplished through central purchasing and procurement departments, or closely controlled departmental purchasing; quality control; revenue resource analysis, through up-to-date property assessments; cash flow manage-ment, regulating the flow of cash in and out to ensure that cash requirements remain relatively fixed; utilities revenue projections; and the ongoing evaluation of programs to ensure that funds are being spent as proposed. Although many of the budgeting tools are taught in public affairs and graduate programs, as in the case of personnel administra-tion, effective financial management requires time and experience on the job.[11]

Planning and development have become increasingly important task areas for municipal managers and staff. Planning of one form or another is handled by mayors' offices and assistants, city managers, planning directors and their departments, financial officers, budget directors, and public works and utilities departments. In general, planning for municipalities or organizations refers to deciding in advance "what the organization will do in the future, who will do it, and how it will be accomplished."[12] In addition, planning also refers to municipal planning departments' traditional role of regulating growth and development through comprehensive planning, zoning, and subdivision regulations.

From the administrative or organizational standpoint, planning begins with the commitment to plan—which is hard to avoid since it normally involves nothing more than deciding to initiate a new program or continue an old one. Once the commitment is made, the local public administrator evaluates the organization's future and that of the community, within the context of community-wide goals or values. This evaluation—which is sometimes quite explicit through formal study or more simply a conclusion that, for example, the streets should be cleaner—is followed by a determination of objectives and priorities. The setting of specific objectives and priorities evolves into plans for action, and, finally, implementation of new, improved, or continuing programs to meet the previously determined policies and goals. Satisfactorily accomplishing this planning process for the more than routine projects typically involves the gathering of data about the locality involved, some form of forecasting community needs assessment, and the evaluation of the availability of resources in the form of infrastructure, manpower, and revenues.

As noted earlier, the land use regulatory aspect of municipal management, usually conducted by city planning departments, is primarily based upon comprehensive plans, zoning codes, and subdivision regulations. In theory, comprehensive plans attempt to provide optimum long range proposals for the use of real estate within the community. Often, however, the plans become splotches of color on wall maps that are ignored or are soon out of date. Most planning departments today, while paying lip service to zoning "in accordance with the comprehensive plan," accomplish the original intent of the process by the more informal, but sometimes more effective integration of transportation, capital budgeting, housing, and related planning into rezoning decisions and subdivision approvals. In any case, zoning ordinances, whether based on comprehensive plans or not, separate municipalities into districts where various classes of uses are permitted—residential, commercial, and industrial—and provide the "area" regulations for the use categories—that is, minimum distances between buildings, setbacks, side and rear yards, required parking spaces, and so on. Subdivision regulations establish the requirements for the division of large vacant parcels into lots for development and, in addition, provide the construction standards for streets, curbs, sidewalks, water and sewer lines, and related "public improvements."[13]

Although planners traditionally spend considerable time on comprehensive planning, zoning, building design, and the subdivision process, the deterioration of many of our urban centers, especially in the Northeast and Midwest, has resulted in a reorientation toward the maintenance of facilities and urban renewal. Thus, planners in cities like Boston, Cleveland, or Milwaukee would supervise urban redevelopment, or community development and housing programs, in response to the local housing stock's deterioration or the flight of business and industry to the Southwest and overseas. Interestingly, however, even younger cities like Denver and Phoenix have been forced to turn some of their attention away from growth to redevelopment and to the reconstruction of streets, sidewalks, water and sewer pipes, roads, public transit systems, and so on. On the national level, the projected gap between anticipated revenues for these basic infrastructure needs approaches $450 billion through the year 2000. Thus, as our cities mature, planners have been forced to deal with problems caused by population decline, increasing ethnic diversity, shrinking tax revenues, endemic poverty, racism and discrimination, reduced industrial employment opportunities, aging housing stock, and deteriorating service delivery systems.[14] Obviously, while planning for the metropolis has changed, the scope of the task ahead for planners and city administrators remains formidable.

As a result of the shift in focus from growth management to redevelopment, a sub-discipline of planning, economic development, has emerged. That is, the previous emphasis on controlling business and land development has been, to a large extent, replaced by a new effort to forge private sector–public sector links. Federal funding, in particular the use of Urban Development Action Grants (so called "UDAGS"), has served as a catalyst for the rebuilding of central business districts and the revitalization of industrial zones. As a result, planners now must have some knowledge and understanding of various economic development and fiscal management concepts. These include: leveraging—using public funds to induce private spending; program packaging—ensuring that all necessary paperwork, agreements, zoning approvals, public and private loans, and so on are pulled together to initiate projects; targeting—ascertaining whether economic development assistance, in whatever form, fits the community and the location chosen; landbanking—providing or holding parcels of land for developmental purposes, often with the provision of utilities; cost benefit or risk benefit analysis—the weighing, for example, of the cost to provide services or public financing against the revenues, jobs, etc., to be derived from projects; environmental quality—ensuring, insofar as possible, that redevelopment does not negatively impact air, water, or community resources; and economic base analysis—evaluating local and regional economies.[15]

This brief survey of some of the local public administrator's tasks just begins to touch upon the nature of contemporary municipal management. Historians in city government may also find that they will need to become familiar with the public and press relations, intergovernmental programs and policies, health and human services management and planning, parkland and recreation program management, fire protection, public transit and transportation planning, citizens' participation, and municipal law and related legal issues.

Historic preservation, community and local history, records and cultural resources management—these remain the primary tasks for the few serving in local government with historical training. Fortunately, because cities and interested citizens have become increasingly concerned with preserving our urban heritage, historians have been able to move to the forefront of the historic preservation and neighborhood conservation movements. Thus, in one sense, public historians in local government have simply changed the locale of their work from the university to city hall; that is, the public history idea has fostered and encouraged employment of historians in government to research and write internal institutional histories, to collect and preserve materials, or to write the histories of the communities that these local governments serve. But this aspect of public history, although obviously important in terms of historians' career aspirations, and the furtherance of historical knowledge, has not been stressed here. Rather, the broader implication of the emergence of public history, the notion that historians can serve in public arena positions of varying responsibility without obvious and direct historiographical components, has been this essay's central theme.

Experience and the available literature indicate that government service at the administrative level requires generalists. In fact, the problem of overspecialization in governmental service training has plagued public administration for years. For example, in 1913, Brooks Adams maintained that administration cannot be adequately handled by specialists because, "of the intellectual isolation incident to specialization." And he commented further that, "generalization is not only the faculty upon which social stability rests, but is, possibly the highest faculty of the human mind."[16] More recently, Frederick C. Mosher concluded that: ' . . . as there is deepening of specialization in government and in education, there is a geometrically increasing growth in the need for people capable of visualizing longer and broader goals, of identifying the interconnections of different specialized activities, and of coordinating and integrating specialized activities towards those goals."[17]

Repeatedly, educators in government and political science have been told that they should "place least importance on knowledge relating to technological innovation, engineering principles, the special services rendered by government, and the principles of governmental planning."[18] The sentiment is nearly universal—the governmental manager need not be a specialist; in fact, he or she will do better as a generalist, examining the broader picture from the widest perspective with the fewest possible preconceived notions. Generalists are presumably more adaptable and, thereby, better prepared for the future. Conversely, in the words of physicist Leo Szilard, "if you are an expert, you believe that you are in possession of the truth, and since you know so much, you are unwilling to make allowances for unforeseen developments."[19]

Thus, the public history idea—the notion that nonspecialists with historical training can effectively serve in policy oriented positions— corresponds quite well with the image public administrators have of themselves and of the kind of training that best prepares them for government. In the meantime, as public history has evolved, the crude

notion of applying history's truisms directly to policies and programs has
been refined to reflect the understanding that historians, rather than
bringing useful analogies to bear on the present, instead provide the
intellectual awareness of the continuity inherent in civic matters. Events,
problems, or opportunities do not spring up whole out of nowhere.
Things connect through time, sometimes haphazardly, but linked nevertheless. In this regard, Otis Graham comments that:

> If we (historians) develop skill at anything, it is the ability to discern which
> parts of the received heritage of any contemporary moment retain or even
> gain in force and momentum, and which tend toward debility. Every
> moment, and of course the future, is composed of strands from the past,
> but these are never of equal vitality. Reasoning by simple analogy confers
> on every part of the inherited past—all institutions, practices, ideas,
> organizations, memories—the same force and effect they possessed when
> last they meshed. . . . Historians . . . know that time enervates and initiates
> as it moves, that it undermines many a fighting faith before that is fully
> known, and launches new forces of unsuspecting power. The trick . . . is to
> know when the hand of heritage is heavy or light, and where. This assists us
> in accounting for uneven rates of change, perceiving when situations are
> open for movement and innovation, or jelled and stalemated against
> change.[20]

In other words, the historian, or governmental official with historical
sensibility, ought to be better prepared to experiment, to compromise,
and to cope with the untidiness, confusion, and loose ends of political
life.

And, parenthetically, because of the chaotic and unpredictable nature
of governmental service, planning and management staffs tend to be
made up of individuals educated in a wide variety of disciplines. The
American Planning Association, for example, notes that,

> . . . the staff engaged in program planning tends to be virtually indistin-
> guishable and interchangable. Newcomers to the operation are frequently
> perplexed by their inability to identify the specific professional background
> of staff people. They all seem to be bright, articulate, on top of current
> problems, well-versed in the current managerial argot. As is often the case,
> what they were or where they trained is less important than what they can
> do.[21]

Ironically, although the generalist training of public administrators is
understood and appreciated within government, many historians, especially in academia, reject public history insofar as the term applies to the
usefulness of the historical approach for legitimizing careers outside the
classroom.[22] Unfortunately, historians often forget that self-imposed
limitations on their vocational aspirations will surely become barriers
impossible to surmount. Certainly, the "lessons of history," in the broad
rather than specific sense, are not taught for their own sake. They are,
one trusts, supposed to tell us how civilizations, nations, or communities
lived and, within the parameters outlined through historical scholarship,
will live. While historians in public service, like their counterparts

trained in law, political science, or urban affairs, must rely on engineers and other specialists for technical and scientific advice, paraprofessionals and secretaries for office management and information distribution, and foremen and work crews for refuse collection or street paving, they also must depend on their own abilities and knowledge for managing programs, developing and evaluating policies, and planning for the future. And, thus, is it not wise for historians to fall back upon what they know when seeking guidance in public affairs? In other words, to rephrase Satchel Paige, "Look back, you might be going in circles."

NOTES

1. U.S. Department of Commerce, Bureau of the Census, *Statistical Abstract of the United States, 1982–83* (Washington, D.C.: Government Printing Office, 1982), 167, 294, 303, 378. Calculating the exact number of governmental employees with historical training of one kind or another is a difficult, if not impossible, task; suffice it to say that there are enough of them to establish the fact that more historians could succeed in public administration.
2. G. Wesley Johnson, Jr., "Editor's Preface," *The Public Historian* 1 (Fall 1978): 6.
3. Robert Kelley, "Public History: Its Origins, Nature, and Prospects," *The Public Historian* 1 (Fall 1978): 17.
4. Ibid., 17–19.
5. See Arthur M. Johnson, "Transitions to Public History: The Example of the Maine Balanced Growth Project," *The Public Historian* 1 (Winter 1979): 41–49; Stephen D. Mikesell, "Historical Analysis and Benefit-Cost Accounting: Planning for the New Melones Dam," *The Public Historian* 1 (Winter 1979): 50–65; Roy H. Lopata, "Historians in City Planning: A Personal View," *The Public Historian* 1 (Summer 1979): 40–44; Richard J. Cox, "Reappraisal of Municipal Records in the United States," *The Public Historian* 3 (Winter 1981): 49–63; Mark S. Foster, "The Automobile in the Urban Environment: Planning for an Energy-Short Future," *The Public Historian* 3 (Fall 1981): 23–31; Roy H. Lopata, "Small Cities Planning from a Historic Perspective: A Case Study of the Municipal Response to Tax-Exempt Landholdings," *The Public Historian* 4 (Winter 1982): 53–64; and Peter N. Stearns, "History and Policy Analysis: Toward Maturity," *The Public Historian* 4 (Summer 1982): 5–29.
6. Robert R. Cantine, "How Practicing Urban Administrators View Themselves: An Analysis of the Workshop Deliberations" in *Education for Urban Administration*, ed. Frederic N. Cleveland (Philadelphia: The American Academy of Political and Social Science, 1973), 5, 10, 11; Graham W. Watt, Robert R. Cantine, and John W. Parker, "Roles of the Urban Administrator in the 1970s and the Knowledges and Skills Required to Perform These Roles," in *Education for Urban Administration*, 67, 75; and Thomas J. Davy, "Education of Public Administrators: Considerations in Planning and Organizing Graduate Degree Programs," *Public Management*, February 1971, 5.
7. *Public Management*, April 1983, 9.
8. Thomas J. Davy, "The University and Pre-Entry Professional Education for Urban Administrators: What Should We Teach? How Should We Teach," in *Education for Urban Administration*, 197–99; and Division of Urban Affairs and Department of Political Science, *A Program Design for a Master's Degree in Public Administration* (Newark, Del.: University of Delaware, 1975), 38–39.

9. Frederick H. Bair, Jr., *Bair Facts* (Trenton, N.J.: Chandler-Davis Publishing, 1960), 4.

10. W. Donald Heisel, "Personnel Administration," in *Managing the Modern City*, ed. James M. Banovetz (Washington, D.C.: International City Management Association, 1971), 318–46; Cantine, "Practicing Urban Administrators," 13; and James E. Jernberg, "Financial Administration," in *Managing the Modern City*, 347–76.

11. John K. Parker, "Administrative Planning," in *Managing the Modern City*, 238.

12. Ibid., 238–54.

13. William Lamont, Jr., "Subdivision Regulation and Land Conversion," in *The Practice of Local Government Planning*, ed. David S. Arnold (Washington, D.C.: International City Management Association, 1979), 389–415; Richard F. Babcock, "Zoning," in *The Practice of Local Government Planning*, 416–43; and Clifford L. Weaver and Richard F. Babcock, *City Zoning: The Once and Future Frontier* (Chicago: American Planning Association, 1979), 260–69. See also F. Stuart Chapin, Jr., *Urban Land Use Planning* (Urbana: University of Illinois Press, 1965); and Mel Scott, *American City Planning* (Berkeley: University of California Press, 1971).

14. Chester C. McGuire, "Maintenance and Renewal of Central Cities," in *The Practice of Local Government Planning*, 467–98; see also U.S. Congress, Joint Congressional Economic Committee, *Hard Choices: A Report on the Increasing Gap Between America's Infrastructure Needs and Our Ability to Pay for Them* (Washington, D.C.: Government Printing Office, 1984).

15. Stephen B. Friedman, "Economic Development: The Planning Response," in *The Practice of Local Government Planning*, 588–99.

16. Brooks Adams, *The Theory of Social Revolution* (New York: Macmillan, 1913), 207–08.

17. Frederick C. Mosher, "End Product Objectives of Pre-Entry Professional Education for Urban Administrators and Their Implications for Curriculum Focus," in *Education for Urban Administrators*, 151–52.

18. Watt, Cantine, and Parker, "Roles of the Urban Administrator," 75–76.

19. Quoted in Gregg Herkew, *The Winning Weapon: The Atomic Bomb in the Cold War, 1945–1950* (New York: Alfred A. Knopf, 1980), 339.

20. Otis L. Graham, Jr., "The Uses and Misuses of History: Roles in Policymaking," *The Public Historian* 5 (Spring 1983): 11.

21. Melvin R. Levin, "Bumpy Roads Ahead," *Planning*, July 1979, 30.

22. One of the best (or worst, depending on your point of view) of the genre appeared (remarkably) in *The Public Historian*: Terence O'Donnell, "Pitfalls Along the Path of Public History," *The Public Historian* 4 (Winter 1982): 65–72.

Howard Rosen is executive secretary of the Public Works Histor-
ical Society, which is headquartered in Chicago, Illinois. Rosen has
his Ph.D. from the University of Chicago, where he specialized in
European military and technological history. He has had a
longstanding interest in historical and contemporary technology
and society issues. He is co-author of Engineering and Social
Responsibility: A Select Annotated Bibliography *(1980)*
and numerous articles and papers on topics in the history of
engineering and public works.

Before joining the staff of the Public Works Historical Society,
Rosen taught the history of western civilization at Stanford
University and was a member of the Program in Values, Tech-
nology, and Society. At the Illinois Institute of Technology, he
taught courses on the history of technology and engineering,
engineering ethics, and industrial culture. He was elected secretary/
treasurer of the Liberal Studies Division of the American Society
for Engineering Education.

In his current capacity, Rosen edits a quarterly newsletter and a
monthly biographical article, "People in Public Works," for the
American Public Works Association Reporter. *He has conducted*
and edited oral histories and the public works issue of Cobblestone *magazine for children. In addition, he has organized and*
participated in many public programs. He is currently preparing
to teach a graduate course on public works administration and is
working with the Canadian Public Works Association to develop a
History of Public Works in Canada. *Rosen is a member of the*
Board of Directors of the National Council on Public History.

PUBLIC HISTORY AND PUBLIC WORKS

Howard Rosen

The field of public works comprises the design, construction, and maintenance of structures and facilities which government at all levels provides so that services essential to the functioning of organized society are available. Public works professionals blend engineering skills with the techniques of public administration. Successful practitioners have technical competence in a number of areas, combined with the ability to manage effectively in a public and often political environment. Most of the 23,000 members of the American Public Works Association are civil engineers who entered public service and acquired their nontechnical skills while on the job. Few have degrees in public works administration. Those responsible for the management of socially significant and capital intensive operations have rarely received much public attention. They have certainly not been given the historical recognition they deserve.

Public works professionals can benefit greatly from the contributions of history. Through the preservation and analysis of documents and the preparation of selected case studies, historians provide them with the lessons of examined experience. Public works historians help to ensure that advances in the field will be cumulative: that the lessons of experience will be learned, not lost. But this is not to say that public works history serves the profession only by focusing on the positive successes. For practicing professionals to have a better understanding of the ways in which processes and practices actually evolve over time, it is essential that they be presented within historical context, including the inevitable problems and failures that trial and error approaches produce as well. Such case studies, utilizing historical methods, can become an effective part of the continuing professional education of people in public works.

As in the case of other types of public history, simply doing historical research and writing is not adequate. To be effective, the information has to be prepared and presented in a manner that makes it readily usable. Applied history, as a form of public history, is as different in form and content from "pure" academic history as engineering differs from science. There is much overlap in both instances, and while the fields are not separate, they remain distinct. In neither case is the simple "application" of the "pure" sufficient. For public works historians, the challenge is to be able to design their specific historical efforts so that they will be suitable to the needs, perspectives, and mentality of public works engineers/administrators.

Public works historians offer practitioners a range of information not available to them otherwise. While functioning in different ways, working in various capacities and types of organizations, the public works historian generally can preserve institutional memory and contribute to the profession's continuity and to an appreciation of its heritage. As public works facilities and structures function in a community over long periods of time (often an entire generation or more), it is essential for those who are responsible for planning them to have an understanding of historical context. In the engineering-based field of public works, the historian helps to examine the long-term interaction between technology and society. The examination of these historical interactions allows practitioners to anticipate trends and plan more effectively. By giving them a greater understanding of the broad social, political, and economic context in which they must operate, it also enables them to better communicate with the public in general.

Public works historians address public works professionals, the general public, or the community of historians. The determination of which audience should be addressed and how best to do it is largely the function of the historian's own affiliation. Public works historians are employed by public works agencies, by museums, state and local historical societies, or they work on public works projects as independent contractors or while maintaining a university affiliation. Those historians who work as full-time employees of a public works department or agency are usually charged with responsibility for projects directly related to the particular needs of the professionals within the organization. As in the case of the historical program of the U.S. Army Corps of Engineers, the USDA Forest Service, and various state departments of transportation, public works historians are employed to provide an in-house capability for document preservation, project histories, and staff oral histories. To a certain extent, they also prepare exhibits, audio-visual programs, and other publications intended for an external audience. Historians employed by public works agencies can also be expected to provide background documentation relating to a proposed project, legislative hearings, or public policy issues in which the agency is involved. As full-time employees such public works historians are at times called upon to contribute materials which will be of direct, practical benefit to the organization. In such cases, when the audience is internal, the language and form of historical presentation may differ substantially from what is commonly expected by the historical community. In these instances, the measure of effectiveness, however, should be evaluated by the ability of the historical document to do its intended job. While these public works historians are no less objective, analytical, or critical in the exercise of their historical judgment, and while they are as proficient in their knowledge and application of historical methods, it should be recognized that as employees they are not always completely independent in the choice of projects in which they are expected to work, nor can they operate exclusively on the basis of peer review. Public works historians who value the ability to be integrated fully into an ongoing organization to bring historical perspective into the decision-making process accept the need to occasionally work on assignments that demonstrate the practical benefits that history can provide.

Historians who develop exhibits, programs, or publications on public works for state and local historical societies or museums have the opportunity to take something which is otherwise a part of common everyday experience and make it special. Having a focus on a community's water supply, wastewater treatment, streets, bridges, solid waste collection and disposal practices, utilities, public buildings, and parks helps the public understand historical evolution. It also provides them with insights and historical perspectives on issues of direct and immediate importance to the community. Choices relating to the future of the infrastructure can be better informed as a result.

THE PUBLIC WORKS HISTORICAL SOCIETY

The Public Works Historical Society serves as the umbrella organization for all public works historians. It is composed of a unique blend of practicing public works engineers/administrators with professional historians. Since its founding in 1975, it has itself published many key works in the field and encouraged the production of numerous others.

Figure 1. Pittsburgh horsecars crossing the Sixth Street Bridge (built by John A. Roebling) in the 1870s. *Photograph courtesy of Carnegie Library of Pittsburgh, Pittsburgh Photographic Library.*

The History of Public Works in the United States, 1776–1976 is the standard text for the entire field. The bibliography, *Public Works History in the United States: A Guide to the Literature,* is the most important research tool now available. The respected series, *Essays in Public Works History,* represents important case studies on water resources, transportation, solid waste, municipal engineering, parks, and planning. Many of the essays have been used in courses in urban history and public administration. The society continues to publish a series of oral histories with major figures in public works history. In addition to publishing a quarterly newsletter and a monthly biographical article, "People in Public Works," for the *APWA Reporter,* the society regularly sponsors programs and presentations at professional meetings and works with museums, libraries, and state and local historical societies to enable them to include public works themes and materials in their own programs. In 1986, the society will inaugurate the Abel Wolman Award to be presented annually to the best book in public works history.

The origin of the Public Works Historical Society, which now numbers over 1,300 members, is to be found in the Bicentennial project initiated by the American Public Works Association. In 1975 APWA resolved to publish a history of public works "so that future generations may benefit from a comprehensive review of public works in perspective." When Michael Robinson, Suellen Hoy, and Ellis Armstrong began to work on

Figure 2. Former U.S. Senator Jennings Randolph receives a copy of "An Interview with Jennings Randolph," a publication of the Public Works Historical Society, from John Greenwood, Chief Historian, U.S. Army Corps of Engineers. Randolph was a key supporter of public works legislation, including the Federal Aid to Airports Act (1946), the Accelerated Public Works Act (1962), and the Solid Waste Disposal Act (1965).

the Bicentennial history, many important areas in public works were seriously deficient in historical literature.

> There has since been a proliferation of case studies of major public works projects and systems, analyses of the policy and legislative context of infrastructure evolution, and efforts to group the influence of public-funded technologies on human habitats and economies. Furthermore, the Society has had an inestimable influence in bringing public history 'out of the closet' and making non-academic careers a legitimate and respected part of the history profession.[1]

As a result of the continuing efforts of dedicated professionals and historians, public works is now established as a legitimate field for historical scholarship.

Today, the activities of the society are shaped by a set of specific goals and objectives which were adopted by the Board of Trustees in 1984. Historians who contribute to attaining any of these goals would be regarded as major contributors to the field of public works history. The goals are as follows:

1. Foster increased understanding and appreciation of public works history.

2. Work closely with APWA and its various entities to provide public works professionals with the benefits of historical perspectives.
3. Encourage the preservation of historically significant public works structures and records.
4. Introduce public works history into the activities and programs of selected public agencies, schools, libraries, and museums.
5. Establish continuing liaison with historical and public works related organizations.
6. Promote public works history through appropriately designed courses in public works administration, engineering, and history.
7. Promote relevant historical information to enhance the quality of decisions regarding public works programs.

Each of these goals involves different activities and audiences. Achieving them effectively requires different skills as well. Public works historians can thus contribute in numerous ways to the effort to enhance the field.

As these goals suggest, communicating with public works engineers/administrators constitutes a major effort of the society. This is a challenge for historians and is one which can be approached in three different ways:

1. By traditional historical studies on public works topics that are thoroughly researched, documented, and footnoted. Such scholarly studies can be provided by university-based historians or by public historians under contract.
2. By focused case studies intended to provide historical information of a utilitarian kind.
3. By historical programs, projects, and publications designed to enhance the historical sensitivity of practitioners.

The first approach is easier for professional historians to produce but more difficult for public works practitioners to appreciate. Yet, without a body of scholarship on which to draw, the approaches and goals of the society would be difficult to implement. By succeeding in the effort to encourage scholarly research on public works topics, it becomes possible to include public works-related issues in courses in history and related disciplines. The recognition of the interdisciplinary character of public works and the significance of the field to many other academic and contemporary concerns will prove to be a long-term benefit to the profession. Getting large numbers of practitioners, however, to themselves be motivated to read and appreciate such works is a difficult matter. Convincing them simply to support such efforts has been one of the goals of the society, as has convincing traditional historians to focus their research on public works topics.

The second approach represents the attempt to tailor history to the specific needs of practitioners. In order to accomplish this, it is important to design the studies in advance so that the results can be presented most effectively. This may require close prior communication with the practitioner community so that their particular needs, rather than gaps in the historical literature, serve as the focus. The Public Works Historical Society, by bringing together historians and practitioners, offers the opportunity for both to better understand each other. By understanding clearly the needs of decision makers and administrators (those responsible for management, operations, and maintenance, as well as policy), historians can provide them with valuable materials intended to be of direct practical benefit.

The third approach is that which provides the link between this technical profession and the general public. Since the historical dimensions of public works are not very well understood, this approach can stimulate other forms of historical research. It is also the approach which serves to educate the public regarding public works. Every community has its own important public works history to tell. The better the story is told, the greater the general understanding of the nature and character of public works, their evolution over time, and the issues which surround them in the future. Simply telling the story of how a city works, in terms of its water supply, wastewater and sewerage, solid waste collection and disposal, transportation system, public buildings and grounds, etc., is one of the most important and can be one of the most compelling of stories. Museum exhibits in North Carolina and Baltimore, Maryland, have done this particularly well, having a major impact on teachers, students, and their parents. The public works issue of *Cobblestone* magazine (August 1983) was directly intended to educate the younger audience. History in these instances tends to be introductory, with an emphasis on visual elements. Narratives of this sort tend to be somewhat antiquarian. But telling a story in this way can help in the process of building up a larger body of historical literature. The objective, in this instance, is to produce histories which go beyond the practical. As Raymond Merritt noted,

> history provided people with much more than just another tool to implement their planning, promotion and productivity. History could also provide a new substance, a new meaning, a clear understanding that could not be measured by a 'cost-benefit' ratio:. . . . The Public Works Historical Society. . . . has become an opportunity for such people in public works, as well as those outside the profession, to explore the meaning of living a creative life in a technological society.[2]

THE AMERICAN PUBLIC WORKS ASSOCIATION AND PUBLIC WORKS HISTORY

Public works historians thus have many different ways and purposes in preparing their work to reach public works practitioners, the general public, or other historians. Within the context of ongoing programs and activities of the Public Works Historical Society, there is the opportunity to adopt any or all of these approaches. Possibly the greatest opportunity is provided by the affiliation of the society with the American Public Works Association. Under the leadership of many of its most prominent members, such as Ed Cleary, Myron Calkins, Ellis Armstrong, Eugene

Peltier, Herbert A. Goetsch, and Dr. Abel Wolman, and its executive director since 1958, Robert D. Bugher, this organization has been in the forefront of the effort to encourage the integration of historical perspectives into the conduct of their professional activities.

APWA is composed of sixty-two local chapters throughout the United States and Canada. Most have designated chapter historians to work with the society, and many have undertaken projects relating to the history of public works in their communities. Each year the association presents a Heritage Award to that chapter which has undertaken the best historical program during the previous year. This prestigious award, which carries with it a stipend of $1,000, is presented annually at the International Public Works Congress and Equipment Show. The society plans to present an annual award to the best publication in public works history. APWA is also composed of seven Institutes for Professional Development, representing the key functional areas within public works: administrative management, municipal engineering, equipment services, solid wastes, transportation, water resources, and buildings and grounds. The society has initiated historical projects with several of the institutes and is currently planning to publish an annual collection of articles on specific topics within these functional areas. Working with the geographical and functional elements of APWA gives public works historians access to people and documents which otherwise might not be accessible.

CONCLUSION

The historian's training is an invaluable asset in working well with public works professionals. They have already demonstrated their talents as employees of APWA.

> During the past decade, APWA has employed some eight historians either in full-time or part-time positions. . . . historians have worked in all APWA fields: research, publications, membership, chapter affairs, institutes, education, and management. They have been valuable employees who have demonstrated the versatile skills and capacity for work essential for success in any professional association.[3]

The historian's ability to conceptualize, write, edit, conduct research, and communicate will be a firm foundation for anyone interested in entering the field of public works.

Beyond the general skills of the historian and the specific knowledge of the field of public works, the potential historian of public works should attempt to acquire an understanding of the physical and organizational dimensions of public works activities. What is it that public works professionals do, how do they do it, and why? Some hands-on experience with city crews patching potholes in the summer, clearing snow in the winter, hauling and disposing of household wastes, seeing a water treatment plant or pumping station in operation, understanding what's underground in a modern city, knowing where water comes from and where it goes—all these and a myriad of other essential public works functions should be understood in three-dimensional, human terms by the historian. Armed with such knowledge, the public works historian can well serve the various publics to be addressed.

Since public works involves government sponsored and supported projects, they inevitably contain a political dimension. The ethical issues which the public works historian tends to confront are not fundamentally different from those which any professional working in a political context also confronts.[4] Organizations generally do not wish to support the publication of documents that make them look bad. In an era of regulation and litigation and charged debates over water rights, land use, environmental quality, and toxic wastes, those with responsibilities in these areas are understandably sensitive to criticism. Yet the importance of the public works infrastructure to the economic and social fabric calls for objective, thorough documentation to provide decision makers with adequate information.

Long neglected, the future of public works history now looks promising. Reviews of publications in the field in major historical journals have focused greater attention in this area. Public works has been a topic of panels on the programs of national meetings of major historical societies. Government agencies and foundations have recently supported historical research on public works. There should be more opportunities for trained public works historians in museums, state and local historical societies, government agencies, and professional associations. In addition, "the currently publicized infrastructure 'crisis' provides us with a unique opportunity to draw upon the lessons of the past, and using the capabilities of the Public Works Historical Society, to provide policy makers with relevant historical public works information which lead to more effective decisions and thus enhance the public service."[5] With opportunities like these, public works constitutes a significant field for public historians.

NOTES

1. Michael C. Robinson, *PWHS Newsletter* 35 (Spring 1985): 14.
2. Raymond H. Merritt, "Reflections," *PWHS Newsletter* 35 (Spring 1985): 2.
3. Robert D. Bugher, "Historians in Professional Associations," *The Public Historian* 5 (Summer 1983): 81.
4. See *Values and the Public Works Professional. A Workshop Preceding the 1978 International Public Works Congress and Equipment Show of the American Public Works Association* (Chicago: American Public Works Association, 1980).
5. Herbert A. Goetsch, "Reflections," *PWHS Newsletter* 35 (Spring 1985): 15.

SUGGESTED READING

The Public Works Historical Society has published a series of *Essays in Public Works History*; individual titles include Roger Daniels's "The Relevancy of Public Works History: The 1930s—A Case Study"; James O'Connell's "Chicago's Quest for Pure Water"; Edward C. Carter II's,

"Benjamin Henry Latrobe and Public Works: Professionalism, Private Interest, and Public Policy in the Age of Jefferson"; Able Wolman's "George Warren Fuller: A Reminiscence"; Martin V. Melosi's "Pragmatic Environmentalist: Sanitary Engineer George E. Waring, Jr."; Larry D. Lankton's "The 'Practicable' Engineer: John B. Jervis and the Old Croton Aqueduct"; Joel A. Tarr's "Transportation Innovation and Changing Spatial Patterns in Pittsburgh, 1850–1934"; David L. Nass's "Public Policy and Public Works: Niagara Falls Redevelopment as a Case Study"; Todd A. Shallat's "Fresno's Water Rivalry: Competition for a Scarce Resource, 1887–1970"; Marilyn Weigold's "Pioneering in Parks and Parkways: Westchester County, New York, 1895–1945"; Louis P. Cain's "The Search for an Optimum Sanitation Jurisdiction: The Metropolitan Sanitary District of Greater Chicago, a Case Study"; Jeffrey K. Stine's "Nelson P. Lewis and the City Efficient: The Municipal Engineer in City Planning During the Progressive Era"; Carol Hoffecker's "Water and Sewage Works in Wilmington, Delaware, 1810–1910"; and Eugene P. Moehring's "Public Works and Urban History: Recent Trends and New Directions."

The society has recently published "Infrastructure & Urban Growth in the Nineteenth Century," which contains studies by Ann Durkin Keating ("From City to Metropolis: Infrastructure & Residential Growth in Urban Chicago"), Eugene P. Moehring ("Space, Economic Growth & The Public Works Revolution in New York"), and Joel A. Tarr ("Building the Urban Infrastructure in the Nineteenth Century: An Introduction").

In addition to the two major surveys mentioned in the essay, *The History of Public Works in the United States, 1776–1976* and *Public Works History in the United States: A Guide to the Literature*, the Public Works Historical Society has published interviews with Jean Vincenz, Samuel A. Greeley, Samuel S. Baxter, Edward J. Cleary, William D. Hurst, and Jennings Randolph.

Information about all Public Works Historical Society publications is available from the society at 1313 E. Sixtieth St., Chicago, Illinois 60637. The society also sponsors a Public Works Historical Society Bookclub, offering discounts on relevant books published by universities, commercial presses, and private foundations that cover topics of interest to those studying the history of public works.

IN THE
NATIONAL PARK SERVICE

Heather Huyck received her B.A. degree in American History from Carleton College and her M.A. in Cultural Anthropology and Ph.D. in American History from the University of Minnesota. She first worked for the National Park Service as a seasonal employee in 1971, following years of traveling through the parks with her journalist mother. She has worked in several parks, in the Division of Interpretation and Visitor Services as an interpretive specialist for cultural resources in the Washington, D.C., office of the National Park Service and is currently chief of the Division of Resources Management, National Capital Parks-Central in Washington, D.C. Dr. Huyck has been active in the Organization of American Historians and the Society for History in the Federal Government and has published or presented papers in the areas of women's history, oral history, and the National Park Service.

Dwight T. Pitcaithley is the regional historian for the National Park Service in Boston, Massachusetts. A native of New Mexico, he received his Ph.D. from Texas Tech University in 1976. Following three years as a historian in the Southwest Regional Office in Santa Fe, New Mexico, Dr. Pitcaithley accepted his present position where he is involved in the planning, management, research, and interpretive aspects of historic preservation in the Northeast.

NATIONAL PARK SERVICE: HISTORIANS IN INTERPRETATION, MANAGEMENT, AND CULTURAL RESOURCES MANAGEMENT

Heather Huyck and Dwight Pitcaithley

Quite recently a historic preservationist questioned why the National Park Service (NPS) had jurisdiction over so much history, saying vehemently, "But they're about *parks*, not history." His concept of parks included Yellowstone and Yosemite, but ignored the Chesapeake and Ohio Canal, Tuskegee Institute, and Castillo de San Marcos. Actually, the National Park Service has administered historic sites since the 1930s—only fifteen years after its creation. Since then, cultural areas in the NPS, archeological as well as historic, have increased to 60 percent of the total sites, with 100 million visitors in 1983—a lot of history. In addition, the external programs the NPS administers include the National Register of Historic Places, the National Historic Landmarks

Program, Technical Preservation Services, and tax act certification—more history. Even parks best known for their natural resources—Yosemite, Yellowstone, and Shenandoah—contain significant cultural resources.

Central to the NPS approach is the 1916 Organic Act, which established the National Park Service to conserve the natural and cultural resources within its national parks, monuments, and reservations "unimpaired for the enjoyment of future generations"—neatly summarizing the dilemma of current use and future preservation, as well as legislating conservation as the core of the National Park Service.

When the NPS was created, it assumed responsibility for thirty-seven diverse areas with only three—El Morro, Tumacacori, and Sitka national monuments—established for their historical significance. Today the system comprises roughly 330 different areas; more than half commemorate historical events, personalities, and ideas. Valley Forge, Scotts Bluff, and William Howard Taft's home only begin to illustrate the diverse kinds of historic sites under National Park Service management. The evolution the service has undergone in the nearly seventy intervening years has created numerous opportunities for historians with undergraduate as well as graduate degrees. Although there are about 130 service employees officially called "historians," the total number of interpreters, managers, and various specialists who manage, preserve, and interpret historic places is many times that number.[1]

Horace M. Albright, the first assistant director of the NPS and director between 1929 and 1933, deserves credit for expanding the NPS into the area of historic site management and establishing the need for historians with their unique skills and perspectives. His personal interest in history and professional desire to place the fledgling service on a firm footing in the eastern part of the country thrust the agency into the field of historic preservation. The establishment of the George Washington Birthplace National Monument and Colonial National Monument (presently Colonial National Historical Park containing Jamestown Island, Yorktown Battlefield, and a twenty-three-mile parkway connecting them) set the stage for the service's first historians—two at Colonial and one in Washington, D.C. Albright selected Verne E. Chatelain, chairman of the history and social sciences department at Nebraska State Teachers College in Peru, to head the nascent historical program. Although the new historian reported to the assistant director in charge of research and education, the rapid increase of historic sites under NPS jurisdiction soon forced Chatelain to deal with a wide range of issues related to historic site development and administration.[2] As the principal historian in the service, Chatelain oversaw all aspects of the historical program, from reviewing the suitability of sites for inclusion in the National Park System, to establishing a research program for the newly established sites, to monitoring and supervising all facets of the development of historic sites.

In less than a year Chatelain hired thirty-five historians to provide the historian's perspective not only to park service historic preservation projects, but also to the dozens of Civilian Conservation Corps restoration and reconstruction projects under National Park Service control at state historic sites. In 1935, the value of the various skills offered by historians and their worth to the growing system was recognized by the establishment of the Branch of Historic Sites and Buildings as a separate entity within the Washington, D.C., office.[3] From this modest beginning the role of historians in the NPS has grown to a point where they can be found at all levels of the organization performing a variety of duties.

The NPS today is a strikingly diverse land-managing agency. Spreading from Guam to Alaska to the Virgin Islands it encompasses sites from all periods of the nation's history and prehistory. The efficient management of these diverse and often complex parks requires the service to employ people from many different occupations. National Park Service "vacancy announcements" regularly advertise for park rangers, architects, contract specialists, tree workers, curators, and superintendents, as well as wastewater treatment specialists and realty clerks. Park rangers have a surprising assortment of duties and routinely are expected to exercise many skills.

Where does the public historian fit in all this? Like many federal bureaus, the National Park Service is organized by regions. Its 337 different areas are managed by superintendents or site supervisors who answer to ten regional directors who, in turn, report to the director in Washington. At each level—park, regions, Washington, D.C.—historians work to ensure the accurate preservation and interpretation of roughly 10,000 structures and ten million artifacts.

Interpreters—who interact with the public through their walks, talks, and programs—serve as the front line in sharing the country's heritage with the public. Researchers provide information about the resources and clarify their significance. Because the NPS deals with *tangible* aspects of our past—landscapes, structures, artifacts, and sites— research is oriented to specific sites and features. The gallows and courtroom at Fort Smith make frontier justice vivid; the animal trophies, oriental carpets, and early telephone at Sagamore Hill make Theodore Roosevelt more real. Resource managers work to maintain park resources as "unimpaired" as possible. Concerned with historic preservation and its associated principles and skills, resource managers also cope with subjects generally foreign to historians such as pest control and climate control. These become an immediate concern if termites are threatening a historic structure, or excessive humidity is damaging a collection's artifacts. Suddenly, issues of security, fire control, and inventory become germane, even essential, to the perpetuation of irreplaceable resources. Park managers bring together this conglomeration and add various other concerns as well. Historians also serve as managers in central offices administering a variety of historic preservation programs.

INTERPRETATION

Interpreters serve as the public face of the National Park Service, as they provide the walks, talks, and tours that the public has come to expect at parks. Interpretation, a term often used within the NPS and as frequently confused outside it, refers to the various methods employed to convey the history and significance of park resources to the public. As such, interpretation includes everything from the personal services of house tours, living history demonstrations, and campfire programs, to nonpersonal services—films, park newspapers, visitor center exhibits, park brochures, and handbooks. All of these help visitors understand park resources and their historical significance. Because major historical events have so often occurred in locations which appear ordinary to the uninformed, interpretation serves the major purpose of making the pastoral village again belch with the iron furnace's soot and smoke, or the dogwood-studded woods noisy with battle, or the quiet elegant parlor ring with spirited discussion. Such explanations also enlist visitor assistance in protecting the resource. Because the public learns so much of its history here, interpretation must be of the highest quality, well-grounded in scholarship, and professionally communicated.

Interpreters bear the brunt of the public's delight, peculiarities, and ire, often learning new aspects of their sites on an intense daily basis. As in classroom teaching, the requirements of communication result in a clarified understanding for the communicator. Unlike classroom teaching, the audience's diversity forces interpreters to be flexible in their approaches. The diversity of visitors cannot be overstated.

The traditional interpretive tour led by a park guide or ranger is the most common form of park interpretation. Programs, whether for school groups, senior citizens, or at campfire, interpret a wide range of the nation's history. Special events, such as the annual fiesta at Tumacacori or commemorations of centennials, bicentennials, or even quincentennials, match historical interpretation with public enthusiasm. Living history with interpreters dressed in period costumes uses the past's approximation to evoke the present's understanding. Demonstrations include ironworking, farming, black powder shoot-ups, and period cooking. Theatrical techniques are regularly used in several parks. At the Nelson House in Colonial National Historical Park, actors interpret the story of the Yorktown surrender in the sparsely furnished house. All of these approaches, as well as the simple-but-powerful presence of uniformed rangers, provide ways to convey history and impart the unique importance of the resources.

Interpretation has many other faces as well. Best known are the visitor centers which dot the country providing exhibits, introductory movies, books, and brochures on their parks. Visitor centers put sites in their larger historical contexts. Exhibited artifacts, ranging from George Washington's tent to a mountaineer's loom, from letters to totem poles to Civil War minie balls, give visitors an opportunity to understand past

Figure 1. National Park Service historian uses illuminated map to explain Battle of Fredericksburg to visitors. *Photograph courtesy of National Park Service.*

people and events. Visitor centers' bookstores—which sell some $8 million worth annually—help visitors gain more indepth knowledge of the nation's history. Sites lacking visitor centers, like the Alaska coastal packet *Balclutha* or the Washington Monument, substitute signs and interpreters. While visitor centers house many kinds of interpretive media, wayside exhibits, historic trails, and tour roads necessarily leave buildings behind. Visitors can choose the form, intensity, and subject matter of interpretation they prefer. Such choices make for receptive audiences and force good interpretation. This diversity of approaches matches the audiences it serves.

The National Park Service has constructed many of its own exhibits, designing them in Harpers Ferry, West Virginia. That center also combines historical information about a site's importance, its tangible remains, and ways to visit them through its publication of interpretive handbooks and monographs. In addition, the center produces posters, park brochures, and films. A recent film on Antietam focused not on the battle itself but on Lincoln's visit there a few days later and his issuance of the preliminary Emancipation Proclamation. These products, all involving history and historians, contribute to the National Park Service's professional reputation.

WASHINGTON PROGRAM MANAGEMENT

Today the Office of the Chief Historian provides general policy direction on historical matters throughout the system, reviews history

Figure 2. Historian with young visitors at Fredericksburg Battlefield Visitor Center. *Photograph courtesy of National Park Service.*

reports and interpretive media to ensure that they are accurate and meet the canons of historical scholarship, researches the history of the National Park Service, and administers the research arm of the National Historic Landmarks Program. A product of the 1935 Historic Sites Act, the National Historic Landmarks Program surveys historic and archeological sites, buildings, and objects for the purpose of "determining which possess exceptional value as commemorating or illustrating the history of the United States." The historians who manage the landmarks program conduct theme studies that group historic resources within historic themes and recommend to the National Park System Advisory Board those sites and structure that best exemplify particular themes, such as "Man in Space" and "War in the Pacific."

REGIONAL PROGRAM MANAGEMENT

Each of the ten regions of the NPS employs a regional historian who, with a regional archeologist, curator, and historical architect, oversees cultural resources management concerns. The regional historian participates on planning teams for the development of individual sites, assists park superintendents in identifying research needs, monitors historic building inventory and research projects, and reviews the final product to ensure historical accuracy and relevance to the specific park. Responsibility for legislative compliance with various laws and executive orders pertaining to cultural resources management—particularly the National Historic Preservation Act of 1966—often falls to the regional historian who consequently maintains a close working relationship with relevant State Historic Preservation Officers and the President's Advisory Council on Historic Preservation. The National Historic Preservation Act of 1966 mandated the appointment of a State Historic Preservation Officer in each state to oversee the state's historic preservation program. The act also created the Advisory Council on Historic Preservation that advises the president and Congress on matters relating to historic preservation, encourages public interest and participation in preservation activities, and works with federal agencies in the execution of their preservation responsibilities. The regional historian also works with each region's division of interpretation, reviewing drafts of interpretive brochures, wayside interpretive exhibits, park interpretive handbooks, and museum displays for accuracy and balance.

Parks are planned and run using a multiplicity of documents. Developing those plans is one of the most critical aspects of the regional historian's job. Through the planning process, the tone for a historic site's future is established. General management plans, development concept plans, and interpretive prospectuses are three of the basic plans that provide direction to park managers in the administration of their parks.

Many issues face the park service as it tries to reconcile existing historic fabric with past events. Often, the physical evidence of history has been altered over time. Chapels become opera houses, then car dealerships, now laundromats; fields and orchards surrounding elegant Victorian homes now buzz with freeways. History's tangible and intellectual aspects must be balanced by park service historians. The past's physical remnants—the cultural resources of landscapes, structures, and artifacts—seldom coincide with their interpretive capacities, the history those resources represent whatever their present condition or form.

From the cultural resources management perspective, one of the thorniest planning issues is the restoration dilemma. Should a structure or a site be restored to a particular period in the past? Even in the most straightforward of situations, there is an urge to remove architectural elements that clash with the twentieth century perception of the visual past and to put back certain architectural elements that once were part of the building but were later removed or changed. The significance of the site; the ability of the visitor to understand the historical associations of the site in its present condition; and the extent of architectural, archeological, and historical evidence on the evolution of the site or structure must all be considered.

The designation of a "historic period" for the site marks the first step. Each property has its own unique history when it attained significance because of its association with a person or an event. In some instances, this is one brief moment in time. Examples include Ford's Theater in Washington, D.C., the site of the Lincoln assassination; the 1869 meeting of the Union Pacific and the Central Pacific railroads at Promontory Point, Utah; and the Wilmer McLean House at Appomattox Court House, Virginia. But for most sites, the period of historical significance stretches for years and, sometimes, centuries. The importance of the Adams house in Quincy, Massachusetts, is its ownership by four generations of the family. Hubbell Trading Post in Ganado, Arizona, owned and operated by the same family from 1878 until its 1967 acquisition by the National Park Service, typifies Navajo Reservation trading posts. The Kinderhook, New York, home of Martin Van Buren has been restored to its appearance in 1862, the year of Van Buren's death, because changes made to the property by subsequent owners of the site were not of sufficient historical or architectural importance to warrant preserving.

Ellis Island—now undergoing restoration and development—served as an immigration, detention, and deportation center from 1900 until 1954. Its use as an immigration center peaked in 1907 and declined dramatically after the Quota Act of 1921 and the Immigration Act of 1924. National Park Service historians and planners must confront the question "Should the island be restored to 1907 to depict the major period of immigration, or should it be restored to 1954, with all of the changes its use as a detention and deportation facility necessitated, or perhaps even to its original configuration in 1900?" How to interpret the 1892–1897 immigration facility destroyed by fire adds yet another dimension to the planning equation. Interpretive needs and management considerations—safety, visitor circulation routes, office and exhibit space, resource preservation and protection—all affect the final decision.

PARK MANAGEMENT

Resources and visitors do not magically exist or coexist. Their needs are often immediate, persistent, difficult, and contradictory. Political pressures are often relentless. Funding is seldom sufficient and the state of knowledge changes constantly. Older cultural resources management methods often seem questionable and sometimes even irresponsible. Management has the challenge of balancing all these forces and guiding the park's direction. Park managers prepare budget requests, cope with budget allotments, allocate and direct personnel, set priorities—all the things managers do anywhere. Management pulls together the various park functions from maintenance to public relations. If it seems further removed from the visitors and resources, it is. But its long-term effect on both is profound.

Historians who prefer to remain in research and interpretive positions risk having those without historical backgrounds determine policy for them. While academic historians increasingly accept resources management, research, and interpretation as legitimate functions of public historians, historians in management are still not always acknowledged as "real" historians. The attitude that managers, by being involved in so many fields and being so administratively oriented, should hand in their degrees, denies the key impact such managers have on our nation's historical resources.

Historians in National Park Service management positions bring their training and professional perspective to issues as well as to the specific tasks they do. Such tasks may not always be "history" directly, although they do support the preservation of historical resources. Narrow definitions of history do not suffice here; a recognition of the approach that historical training inculcates must be recognized.

Running a park entails a diverse set of skills. Parks include everything from archeological ruins to golf courses, from forts to airstrips. The range of issues superintendents must consider in running their parks resembles those of managing a small, if rather unusual, city—construction, public health, wildlife management, law enforcement, employees' quarters, concessioners who provide lodging, food, and other services for the public, as well as interpretation and resource management. Parks are complex entities full of resources which legally must be maintained in perpetuity for visitors who are by definition transient.

Historians bring a different attitude to management, one that looks back to the past for its techniques—especially appropriate when dealing with historic resources, with their earlier construction methods and materials—and forward, documenting present actions for future generations to learn how problems were, or were not, solved. Manager-historians seek, by training and instinct, the largest, broadest sets of data to solve a problem and use their training to analyze them.

Consider needed repairs to a park's seawall—hardly a topic ever considered in history graduate programs. While the engineers will jump in a boat and survey the seawall physically before recommending costly drill samples and test pits, the historians will ask "When was it constructed? How was it constructed?" and promptly head for the written record to match current problems with past construction. Obviously both approaches are necessary and complementary. Too often organizations have relied on older employees' memories instead of the written record. In so doing, they rely on individuals rather than the institution's collective memory and deny themselves access to the broad corporate record. Historians have the opportunity and the responsibility to convince management that decisions based on the recorded past can be both cost effective and more efficient. They also need to educate management to save today's records for future use.

Except for donations, money comes to the National Park Service from congressional appropriations through the Department of the Interior. Getting money for specific parks and their projects entails a long process of "selling" needs and matching various funding sources with specific projects. These funding sources have assorted rules for their use. Lump sum construction, repair-rehabilitation, cultural resource preservation programs, cyclic maintenance may all sound irrevelant to protecting the nation's heritage, but they are not. Managers must balance the competing needs of the resources and determine priorities. How they perceive the past's remnants—as requiring additional and burdensome work or as important resources to be protected and saved—and how they allocate always insufficient funds in the preservation and interpretation of the past greatly affects the public's understanding and perception of the past.

Management includes working with external groups—professionals, local citizens, contractors, cooperating associations, and concessioners. The park service's "public" ranges from curious park visitors, Civil War buffs, reenactment groups, and first amendment demonstrators to those individuals who, convinced of constant government mismanagement, appoint themselves as watchdogs. Additional "publics" include young children doing school reports ("Please send me all you have on. . . . "), dedicated volunteers, and highly organized interest groups who send their congressional representatives constant streams of recommendations on how the NPS should be run. Citizen groups become especially important when park managers anticipate changes such as the establishment of new areas or necessary but controversial actions. These individuals and organizations can serve as defenders of parks, as monitors, volunteers, and fund raisers. Parks cannot, and should not, be run without their participation.

Good management requires balancing citizen preferences, resources, and policy. Unfortunately, academic historians traditionally have not played an active role. Professional historical organizations have a vested interest in the service's interpretation of the past and can play an important role in emphasizing their particular concerns. Such groups can influence park management by using their expertise, providing other sources of assistance (as potential research contractors), and by simply being interested and asking questions. Research contractors extend the skills and personnel available within the NPS by performing services and providing materials uneconomical or unavailable from within the NPS.[4]

CULTURAL RESOURCES MANAGEMENT

Park resources are marvelously complicated in their diversity and needs. They include nearly every conceivable environmental extreme from Scotty's Castle in Death Valley to the Archbishop's House in Sitka, Alaska, to El Morro in Old San Juan, Puerto Rico. The Vanderbilt Mansion's elegance, Fort Sumter's walls, Eleanor Roosevelt's swimming pool, and Andersonville Prison all pose different preservation problems. Historic artifacts range from the personal effects of the great-and-famous to the humblest kitchen objects to the strange and unusual—champagne from the Gold Rush-era, sunken ships, historic putting greens, and potsherds.

The National Park Service's sites include both natural wonders and cultural landscapes, structures, and artifacts. The artifacts alone number some ten million; the structures range from forts and mansions to clipper ships, log cabins, the Washington Monument, canals and factories, churches, barns, bearproof pig pens, and dog houses. Such diversity demands flexibility from its custodians. While the basic principles of historic preservation and its legal mandates apply equally to this diversity, the technical problems vary greatly. NPS employees must be able to switch their efforts among these resources, a task which entails analysis of the problem, determination of where to obtain expert assistance both inside and outside the service, and matching people, funds, and needs. Resource management needs are both subtle and persistent; the slow deterioration of adobe, marble, a coastal shoreline, or a nineteenth-century quilt is quite different from the immediate and unforeseeable storm damage to a historic building or volcanic ash to museum collections.

Always the temptation to repair such damage or deterioration using modern techniques remains—being faster, less expensive, and certainly less difficult. Yet hasty repairs are often anathema to good cultural resources management: structures often contain valuable information about past building techniques and processes and the people associated with them. At Lowell National Historical Park the nineteenth-century canal system offers information about successful alternative energy forms; at Grant-Kohrs Ranch the Chinese cook's notes on the kitchen wall tell of his life and times—data as interesting as rare. In her home, Clara Barton substituted stretched muslin walls for the usual lathe-and-plaster ones—vivid evidence of her personality that provided the National Park Service an opportunity to discover the secrets of muslin hanging.

Resources management utilizes technology ranging from the most elaborate—remote sensing, X-ray diffraction, and the chemist's cornocopia—to photography and oral history, as well as quite simple day-to-day monitoring techniques.

Traditional graduate training in history has concentrated on the intellectual evidence of the past, with quantitative methods and oral history added more recently. But the analyses of material culture, archeological, and architectural evidence remain key sources of historical data little integrated into college curriculums. Yet these subjects, along with anthropology, form the basis of cultural resources management in the National Park Service and sharpen the historical perspec-

Figure 3. National Park Service interpreter at Spruce Tree House, Mesa Verde. *Photograph courtesy of National Park Service.*

tive. While no one can master all of these sources, all need to be recognized for their potential contribution.

RESEARCH

The National Park Service conducts historical research at various levels for many purposes. Although research historians are scattered in parks throughout the system, since the mid-1960s most research has been carried on at the regional level, in Washington, D.C., or at the Denver Service Center. (The role of research at the Denver Service Center is discussed in Ronald W. Johnson's essay, "History in the National Park Service: The Denver Service Center as a Case Study," elsewhere in this book).

National Park Service research seeks to support three functions: planning, resources management, and interpretation. The Denver Service Center conducts most of the research for planning; park and regional offices perform most for resources management and interpretation. Cultural resources inventories listing the historical and archeological resources of a park, and broad historical overviews (Historic

Resource Studies) that place those resources in their proper historical context are two of the most basic planning tools. (A recently prepared historic resource study for Ellis Island ran to 1,354 pages and three volumes). Using this research, planners and park and regional managers can make knowledgeable decisions about the interpretation, preservation, restoration, rehabilitation, and even the demolition of structures and land forms. Historic structure reports prepared for buildings used as historic house museums detail their structural history, describe their existing condition, and make recommendations for their preservation or restoration. Sometimes these studies significantly revise popular perceptions of the past. A 1984 study of a house in Seneca Falls, New York, believed to be the one-time home of Amelia Bloomer and congressionally authorized in 1980 to become part of Women's Rights National Historical Park, failed to uncover any documentary evidence to support the belief that Bloomer ever occupied the building.

Structures used primarily for interpretive purposes often have a historic furnishing report prepared for them which documents the furnishings used in them during a specific period or periods. If, as at Frederick Douglass' home, the furnishings remain in place, the report serves primarily to aid the building's interpretation. If the furnishings are dispersed or no longer extant, the Historic Furnishing Report serves as the basis for deciding whether to refurnish the building. The report guides the purchasing and arranging of the required objects within the structure if refurnishing is determined necessary for the proper interpretation of the site. The National Park Service maintains more than 200 furnished structures. They vary from the officers' quarters at the reconstructed Fort Clatsop (the winter base of Lewis and Clark), to Abraham Lincoln's home in Springfield, Illinois; from Carl Sandburg's home in Flat Rock, North Carolina, to the Mormon fort at Pipe Spring National Monument near Moccasin, Arizona.

Historic grounds reports also assist in the management and interpretation of historic sites by documenting an existing landscape or describing a historic one. Requiring both traditional research skills and an ability to interpret documents and photographs for horticultural information, the grounds report—particularly when used to describe an earlier period—can raise as many questions as it answers. A 1970 Master Plan for Martin Van Buren National Historic Site recommended that the grounds surrounding the main house be restored to the same period as the house, 1862, but the historic grounds report prepared by a team of historians and archeologists from Brown University found the documentary and archeological evidence inadequate to permit even a reasonably accurate restoration of the grounds.

Following other federal agencies, the National Park Service has recently reinstituted a historical program designed to research its own history. Administrative histories now being prepared throughout the service describe how the National Park Service functioned during particular eras or analyze the management of particular parks. These studies—analogous to corporate histories—enable managers to understand more completely the evolution of their site and the justification behind certain decisions and projects. A bureau historian in Washington, D.C., coordinates the administrative history program, suggests thesis- or dissertation-length topics to interested graduate students, and assists researchers in search of NPS records.

While all research undertaken in the service is designed to improve the management of the service's cultural resources, facilitate the planning process, or enable interpreters to present resources to the public with authority and accuracy, occasionally the results are so unexpected that they force a major revision in a park's development. A dramatic example of the effect research can have upon park service sites occurred in 1983 at the site of the War of 1812's Battle of New Orleans. Now part of Jean Lafitte National Historical Park and Preserve, the original battle site had been transferred in 1933 to the National Park Service from the War Department. Since then tradition held that approximately 860 feet of the American line of defense, which ran perpendicular to the Mississippi River, had been lost to river erosion and levee construction. A proposal to construct a visitor facility on the site prompted the required archeological examination of the site and the subsequent discovery of substantial structural foundations. Because historic maps did not depict any major structure in the test area, the project archeologist, aided by the bureau historian and a research historian from the Denver Service Center, reassessed the current interpretation of the maps, reread past research conducted at the site, consulted nineteenth-century accounts of visits to the site, and concluded that the battlefield's features had been misinterpreted for fifty years. Their re-examination revealed that only 247 (not 860) feet of the American line had been "lost."

Every year, the National Park Service commits thousands of dollars for scholarly research on its structures, archeological sites, artifact collections, and landscapes. A computer-maintained cultural resources management bibliography in the Washington, D.C., office currently lists more than 6,800 historical, archeological, architectural, and curatorial research reports prepared by or for the NPS since the early decades of the twentieth century.[5] Collectively these studies document the service's management of its historic resources and provide park managers and planners with data they can use to make informed decisions for the present and future management of these resources.

SUMMARY

Public historians thus function in the National Park Service in several (often overlapping) roles—as interpreters, researchers, resources managers, and program managers. Because of the specific resources being managed by the National Park Service, the NPS employee must be cognizant of and sensitive to the particular, but also comfortable with the general. In bemused tones, employees frequently say, "Join the NPS— you never know what you will do or learn next."

Historians working for the service may or may not work in the company of other historians. Specialists in biology, parks and recreation, archeology, architecture, planning, maintenance, and landscape architecture work cooperatively with historians to manage cultural resources. The historian on a planning team or at a historic site often must speak for the discipline—making the case for history. As interpreters, resources managers, and superintendents, historians deal with a variety of people with diverse professional (and non-professional) backgrounds— a definite challenge to anyone used to the relative homogeneity of academia.

Salary grades in the NPS tend to be lower than in other federal agencies. Salaries fare better, however, in comparison to academia. And anyone really absorbed in history, if they have the courage to risk sounding antiquarian, will admit the special satisfaction of having direct access to historic artifacts and structures. Sometimes, as in coping with 3 a.m. intrusion alarms or during the 1983 fire at Hyde Park, New York, when curators and rangers risked frostbite to carry historic furnishings from FDR's home into the snow, access can be painfully direct. Indeed, a public history career in the National Park Service enables one to view the profession of history in a different light, to work with resources and other specialists seldom encountered by traditional historians, and to develop skills that complement and enhance those basic to the craft of history. The historians responsible for fulfilling the National Park Service's mandate as legislated in 1916 are acutely aware of the irreplaceable nature of history's physical legacy. The preservation and interpretation of these resources require all the discipline and inventiveness the professional can muster, for these parks teach millions of visitors America's history.[6]

The views presented in this article are those of the authors and are not necessarily those of the National Park Service or the U.S. Department of the Interior.

NOTES

1. There are no statistics available for determining precisely the number of National Park Service employees with backgrounds in history. Many park interpreters in historic parks do have degrees in history; and many do not. Site managers are usually selected for their managerial abilities rather than specific historical knowledge. Most interpreters and site managers are listed in personnel records as being "Park Rangers" regardless of academic speciality.

2. In 1933, Franklin D. Roosevelt signed an executive order that transferred to the National Park Service from other federal agencies a dozen natural and some fifty historical areas. This deluge of new sites included battlefields at Gettysburg, Vicksburg, and Antietam; Fort McHenry; Appomattox Court House; and the Statue of Liberty.

3. For a complete treatment of the National Park Service during the 1930s, see

Harlan D. Unrau and G. Frank Willis, *Administrative History: Expansion of the National Park Service in the 1930s* (Denver: National Park Service, 1983).

4. Most National Park Service research is done within the service by NPS historians, but academic, public, or free-lance "contract" historians are used regularly. Opportunities for contract research for the NPS are regularly listed in *Commerce Business Daily* and local newspapers.
5. The official repository for these reports is the Department of the Interior's Natural Resources Library, Interior Building, 18th & 19th Streets at Virginia Avenue, N.W., Washington, D.C. Libraries containing cultural resources management research reports are also maintained in each of the ten regional offices, and in the 335 individual parks.
6. For related essays in this book, see Ronald W. Johnson, "History in the National Park Service: The Denver Service Center as a Case Study;" Lige Benton Miller, Jr., "History on the Drawing Board: The Historian as Developer of Interpretive Media;" Beth Grosvenor, "Federal Programs in Historic Preservation;" Janet G. Brashler, "Managing the Past in a Natural Resources Management Agency;" Barbara J. Howe, "The Historian in Historic Preservation: An Introduction," and Barbara J. Howe, "Historic Preservation: An Interdisciplinary Field."

SUGGESTED READING

Most research on the National Park Service has focused on the parks themselves and not on the service's administration of them. The recently revived administrative history program is making progress in that direction but much remains to be done. The number of published works dealing with the internal operations of the NPS are few, and those that discuss the role historians play are even more rare. Foremost in the second category is Charles B. Hosmer, Jr.,'s *Preservation Comes of Age: From Williamsburg to the National Trust, 1926–1949* (Charlottesville: University Press of Virginia for the National Trust for Historic Preservation, 1981). This two-volume study details the first twenty years of the service's administration of historic sites. The only study that treats the National Park Service as part of the federal bureaucracy is Ronald A. Foresta's *America's National Parks and Their Keepers* (Washington, D.C.: Resources for the Future, 1984). Foresta takes a critical look at the service's recent past that forces a reassessment of the popular perception of the NPS as the passive and benign keeper of monumental landscapes and treasured historic sites. A chapter titled "History Policy" explains the role of history and historians within the service.

The administrative history by Unrau and Willis cited above is the best detailed study of the agency during the 1930s. Former Chief Historian Ronald F. Lee's *The Origin and Evolution of the National Military Park Idea* (Washington, D.C.: National Park Service, 1973) is a good source for the commemoration of battlefields within the NPS, while Horace M. Albright's *Origins of National Park Service Administration of Historic Sites* (Philadelphia: Eastern National Parks and Monuments Association, 1971) provides an autobiographical account of Albright's success in moving the NPS in the direction of historic site management. Agency Historian Barry Mackintosh's *The Historic Sites Survey and the National*

Historic Landmarks Program: A History (Washington, D.C.: National Park Service, 1985) is an excellent account of these two park service programs.

The paucity of research on the historic branch of the National Park Service indicates the extent to which the subject has been overlooked as a field of academic inquiry. Although corporate histories are becoming increasingly popular among historians, there remains some hesitancy to approach the NPS using similar methods. Many topics have never been addressed or have been only cursorily explored. The role of history and historians at the park, region, and Washington, D.C., levels offers numerous research possibilities.

Ronald W. Johnson received the Ph.D. degree from the University of Missouri in 1973. He is employed at the National Park Service's Denver Service Center, where he serves as chief, General Planning Section, Central Team. Professional interests include research, cultural resources management, and planning. He has published articles in the North Dakota Quarterly, Maine Life, Midwest Quarterly, Inland Seas, *the* Red River Historical Review, *the* George Wright Forum, *and* The Public Historian. *He has read papers at meetings of the Organization of American Historians, Western History Association, Society for Historical Archeology, the National Council on Public History, and the 1982 Conference of the Council of Educators in Landscape Architecture.*

HISTORY IN THE NATIONAL PARK SERVICE: THE DENVER SERVICE CENTER AS A CASE STUDY

Ronald W. Johnson

Research history has been an important aspect of the National Park Service mission since 1931 when the agency employed its first professional historian. As Charles B. Hosmer, Jr., records in *Preservation Comes of Age*, federal-level history programs reached new importance in the New Deal years. Motivated by increased funding, innovative legislation, and supportive management, park service historians of that era left an intellectual legacy that their professional descendants strive to uphold in the mid-1980s. The purpose of this essay is to describe and analyze the current state of the agency's history program at two major offices located in Denver, Colorado, and Harpers Ferry, West Virginia. The history program helps provide a sound foundation for park planning, construction, and interpretive work. This is not to suggest that the two offices are responsible for the entire history program—important related work occurs in regional offices, in some parks, and at the Washington, D. C., headquarters, but the largest group of research historians is concentrated at Denver.

OVERVIEW

The National Park Service was established by congressional act on August 25, 1916, to manage and maintain natural and cultural areas included within the National Park System. The agency's Organic Act stated that it would be federal policy "to conserve the scenery and the natural and historic objects . . . to provide for the enjoyment of the same in such manner and by such means as will leave them unimpaired for the enjoyment of future generations." As of early 1986, the system was comprised of 337 national parks, monuments, memorials, parkways, seashores, historic sites, battlefields, lakeshores, and recreation areas, staffed by some 11,000 career and several thousand seasonal employees. These parks attracted approximately 263 million visitors in 1985.

The National Park Service is organized on a decentralized basis, with a Washington headquarters, ten regional offices, two service centers, several satellite offices, and the 337 parks (see Figure 1 for the agency's regional organizational framework). Park superintendents report to regional directors who in turn report to the director. The two service centers are supervised by managers, who report to the Associate Director for Planning and Development at the Washington office (see Figure 2 for the Washington, D.C., office organization).

THE DENVER SERVICE CENTER MISSION

In late autumn 1971 the Denver Service Center (DSC) was established during an executive department campaign to remove portions of the federal bureaucracy from Washington in order to regionalize and decentralize operations. Presently the office employs over 500 permanent, full-time personnel responsible for planning, design, and construction projects for the entire National Park Service.

The DSC has evolved as a public sector consulting firm analogous to a "think tank" operation. Prior to the creation of the Denver office, two design and construction units had been located in Washington, D.C., and San Francisco. Today the DSC extends professional services to all park managers through its annual planning, design, cultural resources preservation, and construction program. It also provides the basic concepts, documentation, and technical expertise to give National Park Service managers the necessary data to implement proposals that will result in new or improved operations and visitor use.

In support of this comprehensive mission, there are a number of specialists with advanced training in research, interpretation, and writing of history. Within the agency, historians serve as researchers, cultural resources managers, cultural resources specialists, and park interpreters.[1] Specifically at the DSC historians provide a sound foundation for the numerous multi- and interdisciplinary studies and plans that emanate annually from this office.

ORGANIZATION

The DSC is divided into three large units or teams with approximately one hundred employees each that serve three or four regions and their parks.[2] A team is comprised of three branches—planning, design, and

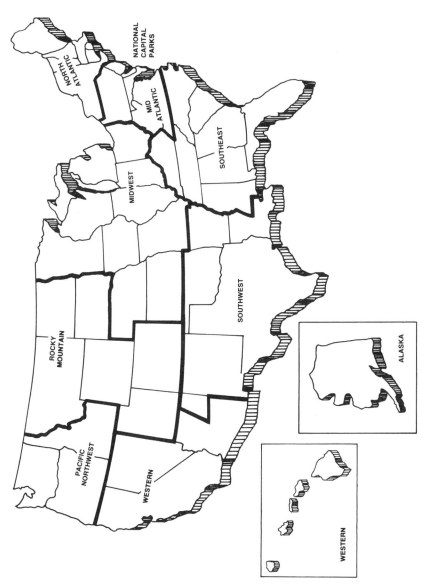

Figure 1. National Park System Regions. *Courtesy of the National Park Service.*

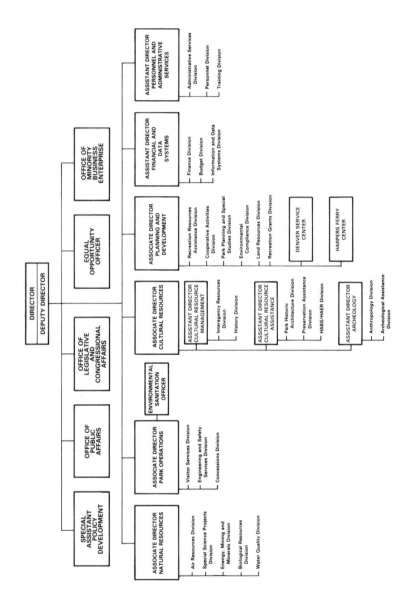

Figure 2. National Park Service organizational chart. *Courtesy of the National Park Service.*

construction. (see Figure 3 for the October 1, 1985 DSC organizational chart). The research historians have been integrated into the various planning branches, and each planning branch has three or four historians. Currently there are a dozen historians at the DSC. This constitutes the largest aggregation of research historians employed by the National Park Service.

Striving to improve effectiveness and efficiency as well as addressing external pressures exerted by the former Civil Service Administration and the present Office of Personnel Management, the DSC has been reorganized several times during its thirteen-year history. The bi-regional team configuration appeared in July 1975, but an autonomous historic preservation division existed until March 1978. After this unit had been abolished, its historians, architects, and archeologists were assigned to the then five major teams as members of a Branch of Cultural Resources. In the early 1980s three teams (Western, Southeast/Southwest, and Mid-West/Rocky Mountain) merged cultural resources with the planning or design branches—the historians and archeologists being assigned to the former, the historical architects to the latter.

Although some found their new organizational "homes" discomforting, the lasting impact forcibly drew historians into a wider context of assignments and into contact with other professionals. Research historians essentially became cultural resources specialists whether or not they accepted or internalized that fact. Another fundamental change for some historians was that their assignments and annual performance evaluations were no longer given by a fellow cultural resources professional but by a planning or design supervisor. As members of planning branches, the research historians have gained new experience preparing and managing projects hitherto considered the province of other professionals.

Thus, by early 1985 only the Northeast Team, which served the North Atlantic, Mid-Atlantic, and National Capital regions, maintained a discrete cultural resources branch. Since the DCS is an organic creature, change can occur rapidly. For example, in 1984 DSC management established a separate Branch of Cultural Resources with a supervisory archeologist responsible for the assigned anthropologist, archeologist, and historian. While the new branch had an elaborate role and function statement, the new group had minimal impact on the core teams' cultural resources activities. Instead of being project-related, this contingent's mission was programmatic in nature, involved with outreach programs.

Then in October 1985 management reorganized the Denver Service Center once again. The four teams were reduced to three, and separate branches of cultural resources were abolished. The historians were assigned to planning units, while the historical architects went to design branches. Cultural resources supervisors received new assignments as well.

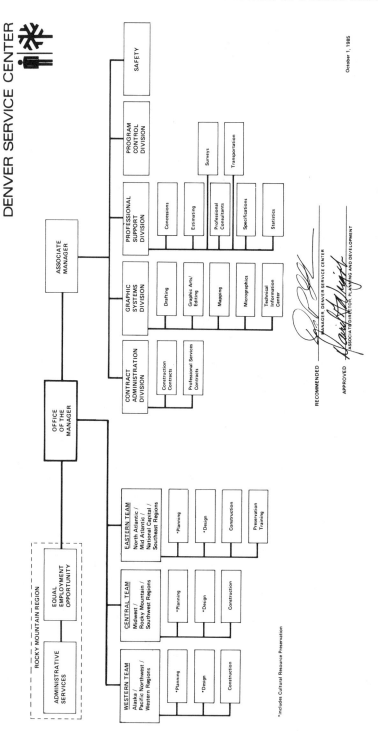

Figure 3. Denver Service Center organizational chart. *Courtesy of the National Park Service.*

MISSION

The principal reason that so many research historians are concentrated at the DSC is because by organizational definition they actively support the annual National Park Service construction program which can total $50 to $100 million. Funding to operate the office fluctuated between $36 million in 1978 to $26 million in 1982 up to $36 million in 1984 and is derived from Congressional appropriations for planning, design, and construction activities. While most units in the National Park Service are base-funded, which means that a set amount is allocated annually to operate these offices, 98 percent of the DSC's funds come directly or indirectly from specific project accounts established to accomplish agency priorities.[3]

How the research historians contribute to this work will provide the body of the essay. The historians, many of whom hold doctorates, generally are full-performance professionals at the GS-12 or GS-13 grade. Due in large part to a stable annual construction program, no research historians were hired between 1978 and 1984 following a large buildup in the mid-1970s for the Bicentennial of the American Revolution commemoration. In 1984 two doctoral-level professionals were recruited to augment a declining cadre. Interestingly, both had prior National Park Service field experience which has obviated the necessity for intensive on-the-job training.

The Denver historians work for a mission-oriented agency—not directly for the general public—although much of their output ultimately is seen by the public sector or by academia. Because historians must complete projects on a timely basis, they cannot linger over minute details or excessively hone their output. These public historians provide competent technical reports to be used by the agency's managers who, for the most part, are not historians. The historians also have ample opportunities to inform others about the importance, relevance, and applicability of their craft, and, thus, a great deal of informal teaching occurs at the Denver office. Professionals hired by the National Park Service who expect to lead a quiet and monastic life are quickly disabused of that notion as these historians participate in a wide range of activities.

The historians' work is predicated upon a comprehensive set of legislation, internal policies, regulations, and guidelines. These include the 1916 Organic Act, the 1935 Historic Sites Act, the 1966 National Historic Preservation Act as Amended, the 1971 Executive Order 11593, "Protection and Enhancement of the Cultural Environment," the revised Advisory Council on Historic Preservation *Regulations* (36 CFR Part 800), the National Park Service *Management Policies* and the *Cultural Resource Management Guideline* (NPS-28).[4] For this essay, it is not incumbent to describe or analyze these laws and policies in detail but to point out that the agency's mission is to identify, survey, evaluate, describe, and make recommendations to management concerning cultural resources. Thus, the National Park Service historians must be aware of and familiar with this sizeable list to make effective and efficient use of time and scarce funding resources.

PRIMARY PRODUCTS

Although DSC historians have become involved in a diverse range of projects, historic resource studies and historic structure reports provide the bulk of the assignments. The historic resource study is an overall treatment of a park or specific development zone within that park. The study contains a thorough history beginning with the park's regional context, its setting, applicable major cultural themes, a historical base map illustrating relevant time periods or principal events, appropriate graphics, bibliography, recommendations for future research preparation, and submission of forms documenting National Register of Historic Places eligible properties.[5] The total cost can range from less than $20,000 to $100,000 or more. For instance, the historic resource study for the recently established James A. Garfield National Historic Site in Mentor, Ohio, cost approximately $40,000 with the work having been done in about ten months, not counting review time and printing (see Figure 4). A similar project for the Ellis Island unit of the Statue of Liberty National Monument totaled more than $100,000. It was completed in eighteen months and resulted in a massive three-volume document. Funding for such work generally is derived from cultural resources preservation monies prioritized and disbursed by the Washington office or in some instances reallocated from annual park operating funds. Each year the DSC historians, often working with historical architects and archeologists on an interdisciplinary basis, produce a number of resource studies. Each project varies in length, complexity, and time of completion.

Data from these assignments are useful in a variety of ways. For example, the planners find the historic resource study an essential tool in preparing a general management plan (master plan) for a park such as Garfield. Each park is required by internal policy to prepare an approved general management plan to guide operations, development, and visitor services for at least a ten-year span. The planners extract pertinent data from the resource study to provide a historical context for their work as well as referencing all significant cultural resources such as buildings, fortifications, and roads which may have been identified, described, and evaluated by the historian.[6] The historic resource study also provides basic data for a park's interpretive program—for instance, the small folder given to incoming park visitors may have been derived from material excerpted from a history report. Park management will find this document handy in making decisions as to which historical period a park should focus on in its development, operational, and interpretive phases. Hence these studies have practical application and are not prepared to keep people busy and to collect dust.

Once this overall park history has been completed, data are then

Figure 4. Lawnfield. James A. Garfield National Historic Site, Mentor, Ohio. *William Howell, photographer. Photograph courtesy of William Howell.*

collected and used to preserve or restore particular structures in a park. This document is called the historic structure report. Such an undertaking is currently under way at the Garfield site. In this instance the historian will examine documentary data that could shed light on the origins, development, and evolution of an individual structure or an assemblage of buildings. Regarding the Garfield park, the historic resource study previously mentioned described the origins and development of the property that became the politician's farm in the late 1870s, his ownership, and what occurred at the site following the assassination in 1881. Concerning the historic structure report, the completed document will describe and analyze the structural evolution of the main house known as "Lawnfield" and several outbuildings.

As with the historic resource study, the historian will work as a member of an interdisciplinary team—architects and an archeologist contribute basic data for the final product. The historian will provide relevant documentary information in a timely manner to other team members so that the final document can be utilized for eventual preservation activities at "Lawnfield." Preservation work could include maintenance, stabilization, restoration of the main house and its dependencies, or perhaps reconstruction of missing or badly deteriorated structural elements in any or all of the buildings. Physical maintenance and improvement packages are programmed several years in advance on the basis of a project's service-wide priority. It is the responsibility of the DSC to prepare basic data to support future management decisions

Figure 5. Frame structure at Lock 38 (12 Mile Lock). Cuyahoga National Recreation Area, near Cleveland, Ohio. *Paul Newman, photographer. Photograph courtesy of Paul Newman.*

concerning the agency's cultural resources base. As with the historic resource study, time and money expenditures vary functionally with the complexity of the project. For example, a structural evaluation of a purported locktender's house on the Ohio and Erie Canal at Cuyahoga Valley National Recreation Area was completed in less than a year at a cost of approximately $40,000 (see Figure 5), while a similar project for the Glen Echo Amusement Park in suburban Washington, D.C., will total almost $150,000 due to heavy structural and engineering costs. These documents are funded by construction monies since their timely completion affects the fulfilling of service-wide priorities. Thus, the historic resource study in general and the historic structure report specifically offer fundamental support data to the annual construction program.

These research products also may be utilized in those parks with major nonpreservation construction work such as entrance roads, parking lots, trails, contact stations, electrical services, water and sewer lines, and visitor centers. In other words, the historians' product supports the complex infrastructure one finds in virtually all National Park Service areas. To develop a modern park a host of far-ranging multidisciplinary studies, reports, plans, drawings, and specifications are completed prior to actual on-the-ground construction. Thus, research historians provide a vital link in this professional developmental chain.

SECONDARY PRODUCTS

The Denver historians often become involved in a variety of other studies. In recent years a thrust at the Washington, D.C., level has emphasized the preparation of park administrative histories. Some of these special studies have been funded by cultural resources preservation monies managed by the Chief Historian's office. Administrative histories contain all pertinent data concerning a park's origins, legislative development, purpose, and salient issues affecting a site's evolution. Park managers find these documents helpful in analyzing the roots of contemporary problems, precedents established to resolve issues, and specific administrative data pertaining to a particular area. Then too, this document provides an excellent briefing statement to incoming park managers. Administrative histories are different from the data that support preservation and interpretation efforts. Thus, in recent years the agency has devoted greater attention to its own history.

Denver historians have been in the front ranks in the preparation of administrative histories. Two professionals collaborated to complete a study of park service expansion in the 1930s, and one is busy documenting the agency's involvement in the Alaska National Interest Lands Conservation Act of 1980. Two others produced a usable history of the first national military park—Chickamauga and Chattanooga National Military Park. Another historian recently finished an administrative history for Valley Forge National Historical Park by tracing its long and rich heritage as a Revolutionary War military encampment, site of patriotic rallies and pilgrimages in the mid-nineteenth century, host to three Boy Scout jamborees in the twentieth century, a Pennsylvania state park for many years, and now a National Park Service area.

In addition to normal programmed assignments, a wide range of special studies periodically surfaces. For example, by being asked to use park generated operating funds, one DSC historian wrote a detailed history of the Liberty Bell at Independence National Historical Park in Philadelphia. Although this important symbol of America's patriotic heritage is widely known and exploited in various ways, surprisingly no serious study of the bell occurred until 1984. The superintendent of the USS *Arizona* Memorial at Pearl Harbor arranged for a Denver historian to prepare a research bibliography dealing with a black seaman who survived the December 7, 1941, attack to become a wartime hero—in this instance the historian conducted the research and interviews on his personal time to give park management a usable product quickly. Other recent special studies include an oral history of a remote fishing camp at Apostle Islands National Lakeshore near Bayfield, Wisconsin; an assessment of several extant structures at Women's Rights National Historical Park in Seneca Falls, New York; and a significance evaluation of the Elias J. Unger Farm at Johnstown Flood National Memorial in western Pennsylvania. The studies listed above represent a combination of projects to support the DSC construction program as well as special assignments for the parks' interpretive and visitor use needs.

Occasionally DSC historians work on projects funded by sister agencies. In 1982–83 several professionals attached to the Southeast Team conducted an extensive field evaluation of cultural resources along the lower Mississippi River in Louisiana for the U.S. Army Corps of Engineers. Two years later preliminary negotiations got under way between U.S. Army officials and Northeast Team personnel concerning possible future technical assistance to evaluate several hundred historic structures at Fort Leavenworth, Kansas.

There are additional projects that place the historian in a different set of circumstances. In these instances historians are assigned to assist planning teams with data and periodic consultation ranging from a hurried contact to formal research and writing efforts and ongoing involvement. For example, one historian recently gathered site-specific data for an early nineteenth-century mill at Monocacy National Battlefield near Frederick, Maryland. The planning team asked for pertinent data to assess correctly the relationship of the historic scene at the time of the battle on July 9, 1864, to contemporary visitor services proposals contained in the general management plan. The planners required specific ideas and recommendations on how to preserve and interpret structural facades, buildings, roads, and the cultural landscape. In another project a historian provided a thorough analysis regarding the significance of the Potomack Canal originally started by George Washington in the 1780s near Washington, D.C. Again the planners needed basic data to forge their concepts dealing with the development of interpretive visitor services.

In these and subsequent examples the traditional research historian acts as a cultural resources specialist responsible for the identification, evaluation, protection, preservation, interpretation, and management of the physical resource base that comprises a large percentage of the agency's holdings. Research history becomes an important aspect of this expanding field, and at the DSC several historians wear both hats with ease, while others choose a more narrow application of their talents. Cultural resources management is best treated in another essay due to its breadth and influence in the public sector in recent years as the new discipline has grown rapidly since the passage of the 1966 National Historic Preservation Act expanded federal involvement in the management of cultural resources.

Other historians have been involved in the evaluation of areas considered for possible inclusion in the National Park System. The new areas program was particularly vibrant in the late 1970s when a special unit was organized to respond to the need. At that time two doctoral-level historians went into the field with landscape architects, botanists, environmental specialists, geologists, and others to assess a candidate area's cultural, natural, and recreational resources base to determine whether a recommendation for National Park Service or other disposition should follow. Historians played key roles in such projects as the Great Basin (Nevada), Columbia River Gorge (Washington and Oregon), Illinois & Michigan Canal (Illinois), Historic Camden (South

Carolina), and the Lower Mississippi (Louisiana) studies in the late 1970s and early 1980s. With the dissolution of this unit in November 1980, the responsibility was placed with the DSC teams. Evaluation of new areas has slowed appreciably in the 1980s, but the Southeast/Southwest team has evaluated certain sites linked to the early man-in-space program and the Northeast Team has evaluated a multi-county area in west central Pennsylvania for nationally significant cultural resources.

Then too, DSC historians have been sent to existing parks to conduct site surveys, record data for the List of Classified Structures, and prepare National Register of Historic Places nominations.[7] To accomplish these varied tasks, funding requests must be programmed, assignments made, fieldwork followed by research and writing to complete a study.

On another front, several DSC historians have been involved with cultural resources compliance work. A regional director is the responsible agency official for the formal response to the 1966 National Historic Preservation Act, the Advisory Council on Historic Preservation *Regulations* "Protection of Historic and Cultural Properties" (36 CFR Part 800) and the 1981 Programmatic Memorandum of Agreement between the National Park Service, the National Conference of State Historic Preservation Officers, and the Advisory Council on Historic Preservation. Several Denver office historians, however, have worked closely and cooperatively with their regional counterparts in this important procedural area. Thus, historians have consulted with various professionals to gain a clearer picture of a particular undertaking, negotiated with the State Historic Preservation Officer's staff, and have prepared drafts of case reports ultimately sent by a region to the advisory council.

According to Section 106 of the 1966 law, each federal agency must assess the effect that an undertaking could have on a property listed on or eligible for the National Register of Historic Places.[8] Hence, the proposed construction of an entrance road, visitor center, or water line could impact or affect a known or presently unknown cultural resource. All this must be resolved prior to project implementation. A comprehensive body of agency procedures has developed in this area and once again DSC historians have participated.

The historians have produced several hundred documents in the thirteen years that the DSC has existed. The budget for history and related research generally amounts to about $1 million annually for the entire office, although that figure can shift dramatically from one year to the next, and the workload can shift from one team to another. The cost of completing projects has increased as salaries and other expenses have escalated, but it must be noted that although personnel costs account for the most significant portion of project costs, these are not the only expenses incurred. Costs mount as travel, per diem, miscellaneous research expenses, supplies, and overhead (rent, management and supervision, operating expenses, and leave) are added proportionally to each project. Review time and printing costs also increase the total. Obviously these same costs are incurred no matter what organization, office, or firm prepares a study—seeming differentials appear due to accounting variances.

ASSIGNMENTS

As mentioned previously, two or three historians are located on each team; however, because of the vagaries of the annual program a historian from one team may be assigned to a project on another. Also due to flexible funding levels and periodic personnel ceilings or hiring freezes, staffing can become a creative exercise.

In addition to intra-office project or "body swapping," the hiring of re-employed annuitants has provided a method to circumvent the personnel ceilings and freezes. This approach simply means re-employing a historian who had retired, paying the individual a negotiated salary generally lower than the person received while serving full-time. Thus, a team can retain the services of a senior historian's talents for a limited period—usually two years—for those terms the retiree considers sufficient inducement.

There are two other ways to meet the workload at the DSC if one team has a surplus of assignments but is faced with a personnel deficit. A team can negotiate with a park manager to "borrow" a qualified park historian to prepare a study of limited duration with a flexible schedule. The Northeast Team successfully employed this approach in three instances in 1984, using field historians on a temporary detail basis from the Jefferson National Expansion Memorial (Midwest Region), the Clara Barton National Historic Site (National Capital Region), and Petersburg National Battlefield (Mid-Atlantic Region) with park management approval and support.

This first approach necessitates empathetic park management willing to loan personnel during seasonal slack periods, dedicated self-starting professionals, and competent DSC coordination and supervision conducted in absentia. This process works well on small-scale projects but larger studies could slow down because of mutually incompatible schedules between a park's assignments of its staff and the DSC mission-oriented approach.

There is a second method to accomplish a substantial research history program. Formal contracts can be negotiated with an academic institution or a private firm to provide a historical study within a specified time and cost. Many supervisors recommend that contracting should be considered only as a last resort after the internal capability has been fully exploited. Due to federal guidelines, the National Park Service must advertise widely on all but the smallest pieces of historical research. Prospective bidders receive a general scope of work, then respond with specific proposals. A contractor is selected in conjunction with the supervisory historian in charge of a project and with the assistance of a DSC unit called Contract Administration. The contractor generally works independently with an approved scope of work and with technical assistance from Denver personnel but with no direct daily supervision. Obviously most contractors try to prepare a usable product but occasionally produce reports that miss the mark. Beyond the initial review draft generally submitted in a timely fashion, the preparation of the final revised document consumes much time and effort; contractual products tend to languish in this phase. An external product is only as good as the park service contract representative who set up and monitored the work from the outset and who closely reviewed its progress and, when necessary, made the difficult decision to recommend nonpayment for superficial or inadequate products.

The larger issue engendered by contract history is the potential loss of expertise when the agency chooses to farm its reponsibilities to outside interests. The park service pays handsomely to enhance the credibility and production record of professionals outside its purview, when in fact it should endeavor to sustain its own cadre of research historians—a group with varying experience levels, ages, and grades who offer high caliber replacements when senior people retire, as well as professional continuity.

HOW PROJECTS START

No matter who actually performs the work, subject matter specialists designated as section chiefs organize the project and make individual assignments. The section chief system, a grassroots management approach, is utilized throughout the DSC for various disciplines. These individuals, having been promoted from the professional ranks, manage a wide range of personnel, budgeting, and project responsibilities. Pertaining to program and budgeting, the section chief annually estimates the time and personnel costs of ongoing as well as new projects. Internally at the DSC the workload analysis system has been developed and implemented as fundamental to the office-wide commitment to project management, a means to monitor effectively the Denver office's annual program. Workload analysis consists of a sequential series of forms upon which are placed time, personnel, travel, and ancillary expense estimates for each project. These forms are reviewed by team members and then in late summer funding requests are submitted to each region for approval or refusal depending on service-wide priorities established by the director, the ten regional directors, and the DSC manager. Because of scarce resources not all project requests are necessarily funded immediately. Project estimating is a finely tuned craft employed to arrive at a usable figure for funding requests that provide future assignments.

The section chiefs also make individual assignments based on expertise, experience, and name requests from regional or park clients for certain individuals for specific projects. The section chief attempts to balance lengthier, more complicated assignments with shorter, easier ones to give each historian an equitable variety throughout the year. As a project historian initiates a new study the section chief acts in a supportive role, especially with experienced professionals, while extending timely, ongoing advice, and counsel to less-experienced staff.

Although all projects are estimated through the workload analysis exercise, a few projects require intensive preliminary analysis as to what must be done. Conceptual outlines for project work come originally from park management with assistance from the regions in establishing priorities. Occasionally section chiefs will confer with park management, other appropriate disciplinary or subject matter supervisors in architecture or archeology, and their opposite numbers from a regional office to chart a course of action. Periodically individuals from different offices will promote varying perspectives on the same project concerning what should be done, how, and when—issues that could cause later difficulties if not resolved amicably at the outset.

For example, in January 1984, the Northeast Team history, architecture, and archeology section chiefs, and their supervisor convened at Allegheny Portage National Historic Site in western Pennsylvania with park, regional, and Washington, D.C., officials to discuss a large-scale historic structure report for a dozen key structural remnants. Although earlier historical research had been accomplished, the Northeast Team history section chief briefed the group on the low probability of a historian making further significant discoveries of untapped documents, but recommended that a historian should be assigned to complement the work of the other disciplines. With this in mind the group concurred that more generous funding levels should be allocated to architecture and archeology; in this instance little had been done previously on a systematic basis. Ultimately major preservation construction activity will stabilize and restore certain culverts, bridge remains, and engine house foundations along the thirty-six-mile long incline plane railroad developed to link two portions of the Pennsylvania Canal. Stemming from this significant meeting a comprehensive task directive outlining the project was prepared in February 1984, and the work got under way later that year.

HOW THE WORK IS ACCOMPLISHED

Despite the DSC's location near the Rocky Mountains, excellent means of transportation enable its historians to travel almost anywhere in the continental United States in a half-day. More remote park service units in the Caribbean, Hawaii, Alaska, and mid-Pacific require more travel time.

Once a supervisor assigns a project such as a resource study or structure report, the historian conducts preliminary background research in the Denver area such as the perusal of team files, a visit to the office's Technical Information Center—repository of all DSC studies and documents—and a quick inspection of materials held at the Rocky Mountain Regional Library. The historian also conducts preliminary telephone contacts as well as visiting the Denver Public Library and the Norlin Library at the University of Colorado in Boulder. Once this preliminary groundwork has been completed, the historian travels to the field to inspect the resources being studied, meet with local park personnel to brief them on the project, and begin research. Following this initial trip the historian prepares a draft task directive which outlines the project, background, scope of work, and research methodology. It also highlights a budget and schedule for completion. This brief document amounts to a contract between the DSC, the region, and the park to guide the work, identify crucial milestones, and incorporate accountability into the process. All concerned parties review this document prior to approval by the regional director.

Research dictates that professionals travel to the libraries and repositories that store the raw data needed to prepare the technical studies upon which subsequent park management decisions are based. Thus, on return trips, the historian can expect to uncover relevant data in diverse places such as public libraries, city or county museums, historical societies, and in deeds, tax records, and probate records at the local courthouse. Visits may be made to appropriate college or university collections that emphasize local history, and interviews are conducted with knowledgeable informants. Additional standard visits include the state library, archives, and historical societies. For example, the holdings of the Lake County Historical Society in Mentor, Ohio, the Western Reserve Historical Society in Cleveland, the Lake County Courthouse in Painesville, and the Library of Congress provided much of the data for the Garfield historic resource study. Certain national level assignments such as military posts, fortifications, and other federal installations generally require lengthy stays at the National Archives or the Library of Congress. A recently printed 1,150-page treatment of the Charlestown Navy Yard at the Boston National Historical Park stemmed from extensive research time at the National Archives. Thus, each project requires a unique approach for its successful completion.

To accomplish the DSC mission the fundamental point is that historians must be flexible to complete their assignments in a timely and cost-effective manner. Research has included the inspection of dusty municipal records stored in the dank basement of the Calais, Maine, city hall, diplomatic requests to a person interested enough to save the extant papers of the Glen Echo Amusement Park, and oral interviews with elderly Lake Superior fishermen. The work can center on careful negotiations with local enthusiasts who may control or possess important collections of data crucial to the successful completion of a study.

The historian represents the park service in the field and must be cognizant of that fact. For instance, when working as cultural resources planners, historians often meet local authorities anxious to "sell" the virtues of a particular resource—in one instance a little known minor trail in northwestern Nevada already adequately protected and interpreted by the Bureau of Land Management. Other situations demand that historian team members defend perceived unpopular planning efforts to agitated audiences at public meetings. The historian must

Figure 6. Albert Gallatin House ("Friendship Hill"). Friendship Hill National Historic Site, New Geneva, Pennsylvania. *Scott Jacobs, photographer. Photograph courtesy of Scott Jacobs.*

develop a thick skin and objective professionalism to master tense situations.

Thus, the historians' work can include almost anything from hours of tedious desk work pouring over faded copies of *Billboard Magazine* hoping to discover data pertaining to the development of the Glen Echo Amusement Park to hiking through abandoned frontier Nevada mining camps that have lost their "boom." Fieldwork may entail long hikes, visits to remote, neglected resources, and site surveys in thick woods during inclement weather. To my knowledge historians never learned these approaches in graduate school except perhaps more recently in public history-type courses and seminars.

The most successful DSC historians have been those willing and able to try new methods to accomplish the work. Those who have not learned this fundamental truth about National Park Service research have left the agency for other employment. Every project tests the historian differently—one study may have too much data, another too little in relation to available time and funding. Agency research often amounts to the discovery of obscure sources to ferret out data about little-known aspects of the nation's past. For every study that discusses the development and evolution of a site such as the Lyndon B. Johnson ranch in the Hill Country of central Texas, several crop up that force one to deal with a little known Elias J. Unger house at the Johnstown Flood National

Memorial, the Holzworth ranch in Rocky Mountain National Park, a purported locktender's house at Cuyahoga Valley National Recreation Area, or the not well-known frontier residence of statesman Albert Gallatin in southwestern Pennsylvania (see Figure 6).

Denver office historians receive on-the-job training. Some of the most successful training is accomplished informally as questions, answers, and opinions arise on a given subject. In-house training is, as it should be, job-related and pragmatic. Formal in-house training allows historians to enroll in courses such as project management, management of park development projects, cultural resources management, and equal opportunity—all geared to enhance an employee's career goals and value to the agency.

QUALITY CONTROL SUPPORTS PRODUCTION

While timely and cost-effective history studies are crucial to the mission of the DSC, quality control assumes a significant role in this matrix. Since the merger of the major teams' cultural resources branches with planning or design in the early 1980s, the issue of effective quality assurance has been met by the appointment of subject-matter section chiefs on each team to ensure acceptable production. These chiefs have been chosen for their professional credentials and ability to supervise a research program which can reach several hundred thousand dollars annually. They are responsible for supervising three to five historians and archeologists. Thus, cultural resources personnel are supervised and evaluated by subject matter experts, a feature various office reorganizations had obviated for a time.

Once a project appears in draft the history section chief is responsible for quality assurance at the team level. This individual reads and reviews the draft document, then submits it to other team members for their comments. At this point a decision is rendered whether to submit the draft study to the park, regional, and Washington, D.C., offices for their review and approval to print. Generally most documents proceed forward without difficulty but occasionally one must be retained for extensive in-house revision before being transmitted to other offices. Most advance smoothly through the review process because the section chief has been involved with the project since initial analysis, assignment of a historian, preparation of the task directive, research, writing, and review phases.

Each historical study is subjected to close scrutiny by reviewers at the DSC and in the parks, regions, and at the Washington, D.C., level. The review period usually consumes about four to six weeks, depending on circumstances, before approval is given to proceed with printing. At each office the reviewers, including the Chief Historian, scan the draft study for strict adherence to use of accepted methodological canons as well as adherence to internal park service policy outlined in NPS-28. Generally approval to print is given, but often with minor corrections or revisions to be accomplished before the document is finalized.

As a general rule DSC history documents are not submitted to external peer review due to their specialized nature and local scope, but occasionally certain studies are sent to recognized authorities. For example the 1983 historic data section of a structure report for the nationally significant Roebling Aqueduct, a precursor to the Brooklyn Bridge, located on the Upper Delaware National Scenic and National River along the New York–Pennsylvania border, was sent to Robert Vogel, a well-known expert in engineering history at the Smithsonian. In another instance, the James A. Garfield historic resource study was transmitted to the executive director of the Lake County Historical Society for review and comment. Generally these outside reviewers are professionals who are familiar with the local structure or site being discussed.

Principally due to funding constraints, history studies are printed in limited quantities usually ranging from 55 to 100 copies. Occasionally certain studies that apply to significant nationally known sites such as Ellis Island require the printing of several hundred copies. Since the work at the Statue of Liberty and Ellis Island has been spearheaded in the private sector through national funding drives led by Chrysler Board Chairman Lee Iococca, the need to disperse complimentary copies of the historic resource study is apparent.

While some limited-run studies are actually printed at the DSC, larger documents that require perfect binding are sent to a contract printer in Salt Lake City. To prepare an approved draft for printing, the history section chief or team editorial clerk will work closely with personnel from a DSC unit called Graphics Systems. This support group makes the arrangements for editing, if necessary, final typing, and graphics layout to prepare the document for printing.

History studies are distributed in various ways throughout the country. The printed documents are sent to libraries and repositories where the research was conducted, the park service archives at Harpers Ferry, the Library of Congress, and to appropriate members of the academic community. The National Technical Information Service (NTIS) of Springfield, Virginia, is provided copies of DSC history reports. Interested parties can order copies of these reports, at cost, from NTIS.

The data contained in the history studies will have a useful life in planning, design, and construction activities. The DSC documents are also used by the Harpers Ferry Center professionals to prepare interpretive folders, and the parks will extract interpretive data from a good study. In many instances park visitors receive data in printed and other visual means and through ranger talks that more than likely have been excerpted from a DSC history report. Then too, a cooperating organization such as the Eastern National Parks and Monuments Association will allocate funds to print a revised historic resource study as a publication to be sold at a park visitor center.

Some historians, depending on their personal inclination, will rewrite (on their own time) material that appears in these documents for submission to scholarly journals and regional publications. Obviously this is an excellent vehicle for park service historians to disseminate their work to build a professional reputation. Denver historians have published articles on historic canals, industrial enterprises in Maine, military activity on the western frontier, and have made significant contributions to public history. Also, research data generated by various projects is often revised for use at annual conferences sponsored by historical organizations.

ANCILLARY ACTIVITIES

Beyond their assigned programmed responsibilities many of the DSC historians have become involved in diverse extracurricular activities. For example they teach at local colleges or universities, prepare articles or monographs, and deliver papers at conferences sponsored by such groups as the Organization of American Historians, Western History Association, and National Council on Public History. The outside professional interests vary widely, e.g., women's history, military life in the West in the 1880s, local history in Wyoming, and the expanding role of cultural resources management. These historians have published in the *Journal of Western History*, *Midwest Quarterly*, *George Wright Forum*, *The Public Historian*, and many other journals. The DSC historians, although working full time in the applied sector, have endeavored to remain true to their graduate training and their craft. Often these professionals are asked to contribute to special assignments or projects that require fundamental research and writing skills; the present essay provides an example of this commitment. Finally, DSC historians have served as consultants to other government agencies and preservation organizations to provide input to various projects, plans, and studies. For example, a DSC historian assisted a University of North Dakota archeologist in the preparation of National Register nomination forms for sites at a Bureau of Reclamation project; another individual conducted a survey on a sizeable tract of land managed by the Bureau of Land Management in southwestern Wyoming.

Historians occasionally have received administrative leave and expenses to attend annual conferences to present or critique research papers. This interchange between representatives of the public sector and academia promotes a healthy professional outlet and atmosphere for Denver historians while it demonstrates the academic skills of those employed in the applied sector. Contacts made at these meetings promote professional self-esteem and an exchange of ideas and views, and encourage future public sector contracts. Today, with abundant spending cuts in the public sector, historians generally attend conferences on their own time and with their own funds. For instance, DSC historians regularly attend the Western History Association and the National Council on Public History meetings.

THE INTERPRETIVE DESIGN CENTER (HARPERS FERRY CENTER)

Located in picturesque and historic Harpers Ferry, West Virginia, about seventy-five miles northwest of Washington, D.C., the mission of this central office staffed by approximately 140 permanent employees is vastly different from that of the DSC. This office was established to consolidate the interpretive facilities of the park service and is responsible for producing all museum exhibits, audiovisual programs, and interpretive publications used throughout the agency.

Interpretation has been considered one of the primary functions in park management. Interpretive activities are accomplished in the parks by rangers, naturalists, and historians, but with more than 263 million visitors to the system in 1985, much of the interpretive work must be done through publications, indoor and outdoor museums, slide shows, and films. Annual production at the Harpers Ferry Center is immense. For example, some 21 million park interpretive folders are the responsibility of the Division of Publications with writers, some with historians' training, using such reports as the historic resource study to provide the basic data for these documents. The Harpers Ferry Center produces about one hundred major museum and audiovisual programs each year. Also located at Harpers Ferry is a unit of the Curatorial Services Branch of the Washington Office's Preservation Assistance Division which is responsible for the care and protection of 10 million historic artifacts in its collections.

The overall mission of the Interpretive Design Center is oriented toward the material culture, that is, the physical remains of our heritage. The Harpers Ferry Center provides services to the entire park service through its library, research activities, and the acquisition of graphics and artifacts. It also provides assistance to regions and parks through planning and implementation of historic furnishings projects and consultative work as well as service to the public through the National Park Service collections and an active oral history program.

Major research goes into the production of a document entitled the historic furnishings report prepared for a diverse range of structures such as houses, public buildings, ships, shops, and churches located throughout the system.[9] As does the DSC, the Harpers Ferry Center serves a nation-wide constituency. The resultant plans provide park managers with essential data to know exactly which tools, furniture, weapons, clothing, books, and utensils to exhibit. In a recent year the unit produced plans for 148 different structures at parks such as Tuskegee Institute National Historic Site (Alabama), Hopewell Village National Historic Site (Pennsylvania), and the house where President Lincoln died in Washington, D.C. These studies are the responsibility of the Division of Historic Furnishings which also requires and preserves objects people lived and worked with to help recreate the historic scene as accurately as possible. Although the professionals who prepare these documents are not traditional research historians, they have training and experience in related fields such as art history, American studies, and the American decorative arts. They employ a very practical application of history.

Other historical-related work occurs in the Library and Archival Services unit which operates the Harpers Ferry Center library and the National Park Service archives. These facilities provide library and archival assistance to the field. The library supports ongoing information needs of the media and planning divisions. It maintains a collection of 14,000 volumes in the main repository, and staff members help parks with reference work, interlibrary loans, photocopying, library and archival consultation, and training.

Staff members, some with training in history, in the Division of Interpretive Planning, contribute to the preparation and implementation of interpretive plans for client parks. These documents provide for an overall analysis of the applicable themes that pertain to a given park, present interpretive recommendations, and offer suggestions for specific types of hardware and software to accomplish the interpretive mission.

Unlike the larger contingent at the Denver office, there are fewer professionals with historians' training on the Harpers Ferry Center staff charged with responsibilities to accomplish the center's mission. A number of professionals provide direct services to history-type projects such as an interpretive prospectus and the historic furnishings report. Projects, as with the Denver assignments, are funded individually on an annual basis; hence, like a DSC employee, Harpers Ferry personnel must be extremely cost and time conscious.

As discussed in this essay, history professionals trained in scholarly methodology not only utilize their talents to complete traditional research and writing chores, but they participate in a diverse mix of projects to support the federal government's largest preservation agency. Thus, the two large central offices described in this essay complement each other's work in fulfilling the National Park Service mission to serve as the nation's principal steward of its cultural resources heritage.[10]

Dr. Johnson has prepared this paper outside of his official responsibilities for the National Park Service. It does not necessarily represent the official view of the National Park Service or the U.S. Department of the Interior.

NOTES

1. While it is beyond the purview of this paper to offer a complete exposition of the role of cultural resources specialists at the Denver Service Center, a number of historians have gained experience in this area in the past ten years. Cultural resources specialists are trained in any one of the cultural resources fields such as archeology, architectural history, history, and historical architecture, among others. See Ronald W. Johnson, "The Historian and Cultural Resources Management," *Public Historian* 3 (Spring 1981): 43–51 for a description of this activity.

2. The three teams are: Eastern, Central, and Western. Only the Eastern

group has contingents outside of Denver, including a large wing of the team with offices at Falls Church, Virginia, near Washington, D.C., a small office in New York City, and a preservation training center at Williamsport, Maryland.

3. See the Denver Service Center, *Operations Manual Part 1 General Information* (Denver, 1984) for a detailed description of the office and its mission.

4. The purpose of this applicable guideline is to expand, clarify, and apply the principles expressed in the management policies. It has been prepared as a reference and source of direction to managers, planners, cultural resources specialists, and others involved in the preservation of cultural resources in the National Park Service.

5. Applicable major cultural themes are described and analyzed in "History and Prehistory in the National Park System and the National Historic Landmark Program," which contains appropriate historical themes which should be represented in the agency's parks. These represent various political, social, economic, military, and cultural aspects of the nation's heritage, and all park service units conform to these themes.

6. Cultural resources include sites, structures, districts, objects, and historical documents associated with or representative of peoples, cultures, and human activities, either in the present or in the past.

7. The List of Classified Structures is a compilation of all park service cultural properties worthy of preservation. It includes descriptive data and photographs, proposed resource treatment strategies, and cost estimates for that treatment as well as preliminary efforts necessary to stabilize cultural properties. As an inventory of structures classified by their state of preservation and the cost treatment necessary to maintain them, it is a tool to be used in planning, programming, and budgeting. It serves as a bargaining "chip" to justify future programming needs to Congress by placing specific expenditures for history in a larger perspective.

8. The National Register of Historic Places contains a listing of districts, buildings, sites, structures, and objects that have been professionally evaluated for their local, state, and national significance. Many of the National Park Service entries to this register were first identified in the List of Classified Structures or park planning-related survey assignments. Historians use the register as a fundamental planning tool. For initial surveys, identification, evaluation, registration, compliance, preservation, and interpretation, the register influences all cultural resources management activities.

9. The historic furnishings report researches the historic appearance of furnishings and, when appropriate and justifiable, directs the accurate refurnishing of all or part of a historic structure to reflect the period or periods of significance. The furnishings report is prepared by decorative arts specialists and curators in consultation with park and regional staff.

10. Several other essays in this book relate to issues raised here. For further information on the work of a historian at the Harpers Ferry Center, see Lige Benton Miller, Jr. "History on the Drawing Board: The Historian as Developer of Interpretive Media." Also, "National Park Service Historians in Interpretation, Management, and Cultural Resources Management," by Heather Huyck and Dwight Pitcaithley, explores other roles for historians in the National Park Service. Federal preservation programs are discussed in the essay by Beth Grosvenor, entitled "Federal Programs in Historic Preservation," while cultural resources management in general is discussed

in Janet G. Brashler's essay, "Managing the Past in a Natural Resources Management Agency." The interdisciplinary nature of historic preservation is discussed in Barbara J. Howe's essay, "Historic Preservation: An Interdisciplinary Field." Howe's "The Historian in Historic Preservation: An Introduction" discusses some of the research tools available for those doing historic structure or historic resources studies.

SUGGESTED READING

Johnson, Ronald W. "The Historian and Cultural Resources Management." *The Public Historian* 3 (Spring 1981): 43–51.

U.S. Department of the Interior. National Park Service. *Cultural Resources Management Guideline NPS-28*. Washington, D.C.: Government Printing Office, Release Number 2, October 1981.

_____. *Management Policies*. Washington, D.C.: Government Printing Office, 1978.

_____. Denver Service Center. *Operations Manual Part I General Information*, Denver: Denver Service Center, July 1984.

_____. *Statue of Liberty Ellis Island Historic Resource Study (Historical Component)*, Denver: Denver Service Center, September 1984.

IN PUBLIC POLICY

David B. Mock is a history instructor at Edison Community College in Fort Myers, Florida. Previously he was a research faculty member at the Center for Needs Assessment and Planning at Florida State University, where he was engaged in planning, policy analysis, evaluation, and applied history activities. He earned his doctorate in British history from Florida State University. He is co-author of Educating Hand and Mind: A History of Vocational Education in Florida *(1985); and has authored or co-authored half a dozen articles on educational history. He has also contributed to* Biographical Dictionary of British Radicals in the Seventeenth Century *and is currently at work on a book-length manuscript on the Elizabethan Privy Council and a* Dictionary of Obituaries of Modern British Radicals.

HISTORY IN THE PUBLIC ARENA

David B. Mock

Over the past decade historians have evinced growing interest in nonacademic vocations in which they can utilize their historical skills and training. The dismal job market for academic historians encouraged this tendency during the 1970s and, although prospects for academic employment are improving once again, interest in public and applied history remains strong. Though there are several reasons for this, perhaps the most significant is the professional challenge of applying historical knowledge to real world problems. Public historians are now not only historians, but also architects, city planners, managers, and decision makers as well. Public history programs thus have prepared students well for careers whether in museums, archives, records management, or other fields closely allied to the historical discipline. Yet these programs may have been too successful. Jobs which were relatively plentiful in these fields ten years ago are much more difficult to find today due largely to federal and state budget cuts. As positions such as archivist and curator become scarcer, historians who wish to utilize their training and preparation in history may have to pursue, what are to them, "nontraditional" career paths. A variety of careers exist in the area of public policy where it is possible for historians to find personally rewarding and intellectually challenging work. Although the number of historians in this area is relatively small, they are influencing and sometimes making policy decisions for government agencies, and are demonstrating the value of historical training and generic intellectual skills.

Of all of the areas providing employment to historians, the one which may offer the greatest growth potential is that of public policy. Over the last twenty years, government has grown significantly both in size and responsibility. A 1978 directory listed 125 federal offices that employed historians in various capacities including archivist, records manager, policy analyst, and so forth. Public agencies also are interested increasingly in research, planning, and accountability—all of which benefit from the addition of historical research and analysis.[1]

Historians interested in a career in public policy could serve in two distinct capacities. First, they could be policy makers—persons either elected or appointed to public office who are responsible for making and executing public policy decisions. Thucydides, Thomas Babington Macauley, Woodrow Wilson, and Arthur M. Schlesinger, Jr., were not only prominent historians, but were also equally prominent public officials. Though the historian policy makers, who establish organizational policies or set national goals, may be less historians than public servants, they (one hopes) call upon their historical training when making decisions. A second role historians could play is that of policy advisors. Here they are often responsible for providing staff assistance of either a technical or nontechnical nature on a particular program or policy. Typical areas of responsibility include planning, evaluation, and policy analysis. These duties could be either historical or nonhistorical in nature, and thus may demand additional training outside history. This essay will explore ways in which historians can use their historical skills and training in the area of public policy, concentrating on the nonhistorical duties historians perform for public agencies. In particular, it will discuss policy analysis, planning, and evaluation.

Most public agencies engage in a number of activities that either formally or informally include planning, development, implementation, and evaluation. Whenever a new statute becomes law, an agency becomes responsible for ensuring that the intent of the legislature is enforced. For the organization receiving this mandate, this means planning the means to introduce a new program, developing it, implementing it, and finally evaluating it. For historians interested in careers in public policy, planning, evaluation, and policy analysis offer good prospects of employment.

PLANNING

Planning serves a variety of functions. It helps managers make decisions by clarifying choices, solving current and anticipated problems, and analyzing alternative courses of action. Planning thus deals with the future by trying to determine the best, most effective way to accomplish the agency's objectives, and tries to guarantee that an organization's resources are utilized properly and efficiently. In this fashion, planning can influence the allocation of fiscal, physical, and personnel resources.[2]

Planning can be categorized into tactical and strategic planning. The former is a detailed type of planning that is concerned with an organization's basic operations, procedures, and processes over a relatively short period of time. It identifies and schedules specific actions that an organization must perform in order to achieve its goals. Tactical planning is subdivided according to the length of the planning period under consideration. Annual planning forecasts the means by which the agency will fulfill its responsibilities over a twelve-month period. It is very specific, detailed, and obviously short-ranged. Long-range planning, the second type of tactical planning, is also concerned with operational matters. Because it covers periods of three to five years, it is less detailed than an annual plan.

The second major type of planning is strategic planning. Unlike tactical planning, strategic planning is oriented toward the establishment of new policies and the verification of old ones. An important element in making realistic program projections, it is not bound by a particular length of time. Instead, those who are engaged in strategic planning activities try to identify missed opportunities or new trends in order to determine whether or not the organization should change its principal goals and objectives. An example of strategic planning in business occurred when the American Can Company's strategic plan revealed that the company should broaden its perspective by recognizing that it was not in the business of "cans," but rather of "containers." This realization inspired a significant shift in the orientation and operation of that company. Likewise, a public agency may discover that it is responsible for "transportation" and not "roads," "community development" instead of "housing."

The first step in planning is to identify the problem to be solved. It is important that planners understand the problem in detail lest they misunderstand its nature and commit resources to resolving a problem that is either minor or nonexistent. Planners define and redefine the problem in various ways to guarantee that they clearly and fully understand it and to verify that its resolution is realistic. Once they identify and clearly define the problem, they seek possible goals or objectives that will correct it. At this point, they not only try to discover alternative courses of action, but also determine possible consequences that could result if a given action were taken, anticipating possible costs and benefits. The planners at this stage frequently use models and simulations in order to determine possible consequences. Once they accomplish this, they select the best means to accomplish the organization's objectives. Although they should choose the one most effective method, in reality, they seldom do. What usually interrupts the rational choice is the emergence of conflict within the bureaucracy or between the bureaucracy and the general public. Such competition prevents the adoption of an "ideal" solution as a compromise is reached and modifications of the solution follow. After the decision makers decide on the means to achieve their objective, the plan is then put into operation. The organization commits personnel, money, and other resources in an effort to achieve the objective of the plan. Later, evaluation, the final stage of the planning process, begins. In this last stage planners determine the success of the plan and of the institution in achieving its

404 THE PRACTICE OF PUBLIC HISTORY

goals. Evaluation is an important part of the planning process and will be discussed in greater detail below.

HISTORIANS AND THE PLANNING PROCESS

Historians can play an important role in the planning process not only because of their generic intellectual skills, but also because of their particular training. The planning process requires individuals to demonstrate creative thought. Such creativity is particularly important in the identification of alternative courses of action. Planning also requires an understanding of the decision-making process and a sensitivity to underlying policy issues. Historians hopefully possess both the requisite creativity and the insight to be valuable contributors to a planning team, and they have other contributions to make as well. Whether or not they have received training in the area of planning, historians have learned to select, interpret, and synthesize data using a variety of sources. Moreover, because their background and training are vastly different from those in the social sciences, historians have a unique perspective on solving problems. Since they use various sources of information in their research, they can make inferences and reasoned decisions that others might overlook. Seymour Mandelbaum proposes that historians play an integral role in the policy development or planning process because of their ability to develop models of complex systems. Historians additionally provide a time perspective to the planning process. Through their understanding of previous developments, they can explain the context surrounding the adoption of a particular policy or the making of a particular decision. In addition, they can indicate past difficulties encountered with the implementation of a policy and perhaps anticipate when, why, and where future problems may occur. It is perhaps claiming too much to propose that historians can predict the future, or that a knowledge of history can prevent the recurrence of previous problems. Whether or not historians have, as Ernest May and David Trask believe, a "predictive ability," is also questionable. What is certain, however, is that with or without such a capability, historians' knowledge of past processes and trends and their understanding of organizational change enhance planning at all levels. Otis Graham endorses this notion, claiming that planning offers "a more promising route of infiltration" for historians than a traditional history office.[3]

EVALUATION

Evaluation is another tool the policy maker uses to make effective decisions. It is a particularly important aspect of most policy analyses and influences decisions concerning the continuation of programs, the allocation of resources, and the improvement of policies and procedures. Evaluators have gained professional prominence within the last twenty years largely as a result of the far-reaching social and educational legislation of Presidents John F. Kennedy and Lyndon B. Johnson. The extensiveness of this legislation enhanced traditionally skeptical Congressional concern that federal funds be used for the purposes it specified. This skepticism led to an increased demand that state and local governments be held accountable for results. States, following the federal lead, also expressed growing concern about the effectiveness of agencies and programs. Declining fiscal resources and an increasing interest in the purposes for which funds were expended have subsequently encouraged government agencies at all levels to fund evaluation projects in order to determine whether or not resources were being spent effectively.

Evaluations are usually conceptualized as either formative or summative. A formative evaluation is used to judge a program or policy currently in operation. It tries to improve the implementation of a program, revise an organization's structure, or resolve other problems that should be corrected before a program is completed. This type of evaluation is particularly important when you consider that some programs have a "life cycle" that lasts several years. In such situations, it is unreasonable to postpone the correction of a problem until a cycle is completed or a program concluded. The formative evaluation provides important information to the decision makers and thus permits changes to be introduced while the program is still going on. The second type of evaluation is summative evaluation, which judges a program once it is completed or is at the end of a cycle of activities. This type of evaluation is used to determine whether or not the program or policy achieved its intended purpose(s). The summative evaluation is thus frequently used to establish accountability.

Evaluations serve a variety of purposes. Their principal aim is to gather and analyze information for decision makers in order to help them determine whether to continue or to terminate a program. Through evaluations, policy makers gain an increased understanding of a program or policy without attempting to judge its worth or value. Evaluations are also used to determine the extent to which objectives are being achieved or to describe, or in some instances even assess, the worth of a program. In addition, they increase public awareness about a particular program and on occasion are used by management to exercise authority over the organization.

As public agencies undertake an evaluation for various reasons, so they conduct it in various ways. The decision-making evaluation studies a specific problem or decision, focusing on the level at which decisions are made. It then tries to identify relevant questions that should be answered. Another type of evaluation is concerned with goals and the implementation and delivery of services. This type of evaluation assumes that the goals are appropriate and determines whether a given program should be continued based upon its successful accomplishment. But some evaluators disagree. These individuals endorse "goal free" evaluations, believing that it is necessary to search for both the intended and the unintended consequences of a program's implementation. They feel that this can be accomplished only if the individual conducting the evaluation is *not* aware of the organization's goals lest such knowledge bias the findings. Evaluations are thus perceived and conducted in various ways. Despite the lack of uniformity of purpose and process, all levels of government seek judgments concerning the value of public programs and the efficiency of their operation.[4]

An evaluation is composed of three basic steps. First, evaluators outline the information to be collected. They seek knowledge of goals, strategies, methods of implementation, and the results of a program or policy. Second, they collect data using questionnaires (instruments) or oral interviews (interview schedules) that are specifically developed for their purposes. They then conduct an evaluation survey or study in order to gather the data. Third, they analyze the data, interpret it, and convert it into information useful to the organization. They then present their findings and recommendations to the decision maker.

THE HISTORIAN AND EVALUATION

Although historians may be hampered by their general lack of statistical training, they can still contribute to evaluations. In fact, they can provide a special service in both formative and summative evaluations by determining whether there were some unintended results following a policy's implementation. One of the leading educational evaluators, Robert Stake, even endorses the use of "amateurs," i.e., those whose principal training has been outside of evaluation, because such individuals can provide a different analytical perspective. Stake also encourages the establishment of evaluation teams, explaining that "being a complex task, evaluation needs to mobilize many alternative methods of inquiry from the behavioral sciences and related fields of study and utilize them according to the nature of a specific evaluation problem." The use of teams permits the pooling of varied experiences and backgrounds. Such prospects are particularly encouraging for historians who might wish to engage in evaluations. Such teamwork provides a new perspective for historians, who are more often encouraged to work independently than cooperatively. The overwhelming reliance upon quantitative data is admittedly a shock for some historians, who tend to rely more heavily upon qualitative than quantitative data. Since evaluations are more likely to affect decisions if they accept the values and perspective of the decision maker, many evaluations have significant political and economic ramifications. This, too, is a new experience.[5]

Despite these potential shortcomings, historians have much to add to an evaluation activity. They can particularly benefit an evaluation study by providing a contextual (i.e., historical) background to the subject under study. In fact, one leading evaluator, Daniel Stufflebeam, has an evaluation model which includes an evaluation component which calls for information that can best be provided by historians. He noted, for example, that existing planning models do not take into account the political, economic, and social factors that surround the adoption and implementation of a policy. Because he believed that it was necessary to understand the factors influencing the creation of policies, Stufflebeam developed a model that would supersede existing models by describing the surrounding background conditions, identifying unmet needs and unaddressed opportunities, and diagnosing reasons that prevented problems from being resolved. In order to address these matters formally, Stufflebeam included "context evaluation" as the first component in his Context-Input-Process-Product (or CIPP) evaluation model. This component provides a unique opportunity to examine the goals and objectives of programs and to uncover factors influencing the administration of programs and the allocation of resources. It also helps isolate interrelated issues that are often competing for limited resources. Thus, Stufflebeam's model serves planning and evaluation by studying objectives, by identifying unmet needs and unaddressed opportunities, and by providing a rationale for selecting organizational goals and objectives. It also strongly implies the value of history in accomplishing these objectives.[6]

POLICY ANALYSIS

Historians working in the area of public policy also engage in policy analysis. Like planning and evaluation, policy analysis helps the policy maker to evaluate alternative courses of action and reach a decision.

The first step in policy analysis is to define the problem to be addressed. This requires the adoption of a carefully conceived statement that ensures that the issue to be addressed is understood and, in fact, is the correct problem to be resolved. Because of the interrelationship of many issues and because there is frequent disagreement about the nature of the problem itself, it may be necessary to redefine the problem or to modify its scope in order to bring the issue into proper focus. Once the issue is defined, the next step is to identify alternative courses of action. Although the analysts consider already existing options, they speculate about the adoption of novel approaches as well. After identifying possible courses of action, they evaluate the potential financial, political, social, and community impacts. The analysis could result in a series of scenarios or models that indicate possible consequences (both good and bad) that could occur if a given action is taken. It will certainly result in a listing of possible courses of action. The analysts then establish criteria, helping policy makers define their preferences and rank the alternatives in order of the desirability of the anticipated results. It is generally held that policy analysts should not advocate the adoption of a policy or series of policies, because it might cause them to lose their impartiality. Once the policy alternatives are identified and the scenarios written, the policy analyst's work is done.

HISTORY-BASED POLICY ANALYSIS

There are three principal steps in a history-based policy analysis: historical background, context evaluation, and policy analysis. The first stage involves acquiring the appropriate historical background. At this point, historians use traditional research methods in order to assess documentary and oral history evidence. They examine this information, analyze it for its meanings, and synthesize it in order to develop a narrative that provides decision makers with an understanding of the various factors influencing their institution. Historians attempt to discover the who, what, when, where, and why of previous events. They highlight historical patterns and trends and examine environmental influences upon policy development and implementation. They consider what policies and procedures were introduced and then clarify the results. Historians also observe consequences that encourage the adoption or adaptation of an organization, system, or policy, and those consequences that hamper adoption or adaptation. Likewise, they look for those results that had no influence and examine the historical context in which these policies and procedures were adopted and implemented, identifying political, social, and economic influences. The product of this phase is a history that enables managers to acquire a better understanding of matters such as the evolution of their organization, the impact of policies, and the influence of political intervention. The first step of a history-based policy analysis is thus quite traditional, remaining as it does within a well-established historical research methodology.

Once the historical perspective is gained, it is necessary to move on to the second step of context evaluation. Context evaluation is a natural juncture of history and policy analysis as it consciously tries to examine the historical background for policy implications. In this stage, historians employ historical analysis to examine consciously the history produced earlier for unintended results or consequences caused by the implementation of a policy. An example of this can be seen in the history of the American West, where one *intended* result of the construction of the transcontinental railroad was the establishment of a national transportation system. One *unintended* result of this accomplishment was the disruption of the migratory paths of the buffalo and the resulting decline of the Indians. Context evaluation, by looking for unintended consequences, is understandably of great value to policy analysts as well as to policy makers who wish to understand their organization or to comprehend why a given policy failed.

But, historians in the context evaluation stage also fulfill another role. While they are looking for hidden results, they are simultaneously beginning their transformation into full-fledged policy analysts. At this time, they add the hat of the policy analyst to that of the historian and begin to reevaluate the historical narrative for possible policy implications. They should be conscious at this stage of possible connections with the adoption or evolution of policies as well as with those concerning their implementation. Questions the historian–policy analyst might ask include: What was the underlying issue being addressed? What impact, if any, did the current organization have upon the implementation of a certain policy? What difference did the government make upon a policy's development? Upon its implementation? Was funding sufficient to support the achievement of the desired objective? In short, why did the program succeed? why did it fail? Understandably, answers to these questions can have a major impact upon analyses of current policies as well as a better understanding of previous ones. Such an analysis might influence a number of issues, including organizational goals and structure, staffing, training, budgeting, planning and policy formulation, and implementation. Thus, the historical narrative produced in the first stage and the analysis in the second demonstrate that history can and should be an integral part of policy analysis.[7]

With a solid understanding of the historical background that surrounded the adoption and execution of policies, with analyses of intended and unintended results, with an understanding of the resulting policy implications, the historian at last leaves the safe confines of history and ventures into the stormy, uncharted seas of policy analysis. Policy analysis, the third stage of this history-based process, requires historians to assume a new role, shedding their former identities in order to identify possible courses of action and share them with, and sometimes defend them before, decision makers.

The decision of implementing the recommendations rests with the public officials who determine how, when, and if to act. Analysts may believe strongly in the value of their recommendations, but managers have responsibility for the success of their organizations and thus are free to accept or disregard a recommendation. There are countless reasons for decision makers to ignore the analyst's counsel. They may not believe a given course of action is economically, politically, and technologically feasible, or ethically acceptable. They may reject it because it is not in keeping with their "gut feelings." They may listen instead to the "boys in the back room" who want them to adopt another approach, or heed the advice of other analysts, or even to finance another study that will come up with a set of "right" recommendations. Of course, it is also possible that the decision makers will accept the analyst's findings and conclusions and agree to implement them unchanged. But, the fact remains that although the analysts provide their best services, the presence of politics, whether in the form of formal lobbying or back room deals, may prevent the adoption of the one best solution. Pride of ownership will certainly cause the policy analysts to care about the fate of their recommendations, as they leave the client with a list of recommendations to consider and with decisions to make.

HISTORIANS IN THE PUBLIC ARENA

Historians have been increasingly active in applying history to public policies. They have been particularly effective in areas of social and educational matters as is demonstrated by even a cursory glance through such journals as *The Public Historian* and *The Journal of Social History*. These journals have published a number of historical studies on such diverse areas as educational testing, nutrition, mental health, retirement, urban transportation, pollution control, and vocational education. While it is difficult to generalize from such diverse areas of research, it is apparently no longer unusual for policy studies to include a historical perspective. A recent book on special education, for example, included a chapter on the history of special education policies. In another instance Daniel P. Restick studied the history of educational testing and endorsed the utility of his study to educational planners. Richard Phelps examined the history of the Transient Bureau of the 1930s before suggesting the practicality of a federal policy to relocate unemployed workers to areas where jobs were plentiful.[8]

Other historians have provided histories of use to policy makers. Edward D. Berkowitz served as a historian for a project of the Office of Planning and Evaluation of the U.S. Department of Health, Education, and Welfare in the late 1970s. His research provided a historical perspective on vocational rehabilitation, workers' compensation, and disability insurance—three areas of major concern to HEW policy makers. Berkowitz reported that history had something to say to policy analysts as he made policy recommendations based on his historical narrative.[9]

Robert Stakenas and I have also made policy implications based on a historical narrative. In our case the subject was vocational education in the state of Florida. We discovered a number of relevant issues including traditional differences in determining the size and nature of the area to be served by vocational education, growing problems in coordinating the delivery of vocational programs, and increasing tensions between state legislators, local school officials, and the Division of Vocational Education. Thus, the historical perspective has been used with much interest and apparent success to understand better the evolution of public policies and programs.[10]

There has been less involvement, or at least less publication of historians' involvement, in planning and evaluation. It is difficult to determine whether this is due to a general failure of historians to engage in these activities or to the fact that planning and evaluation studies tend to produce in-house documents that, while valuable, do not lend themselves easily to publication in professional historical journals or to presentation at historical conferences. My own involvement in planning and evaluation projects has been much less historical than analytical and managerial. While I believe that a better evaluation resulted from my participation and that of another historian, it is too early to assess the value of contributions of historians to these activities.

Historians have thus been busy in the arena of public policy. While judgments about the utility of the resulting studies or the relative satisfaction of policy makers can only be made on an individual basis, there appears to be a growing interest in including a historical component to policy studies. Perhaps the two best indicators of success are the length of a relationship between historians and clients and the number of clients the historians serve. If these criteria are correct, then we have reason to be cautiously optimistic.

CONCLUSION

In recent years, historians have been aggressive in recommending the benefits of history to policy makers. Commending their discipline's contributions of providing a time perspective and institutional memory, testing analogies, and assessing trends, historians propose the direct applicability of history to public policy. Such claims may be overstated, however. Most histories are written *by* academic historians *for* academic historians and rarely focus on the specific set of circumstances and questions that concern the policy maker. As Edward Berkowitz has shown, it is not the quality of the scholarship that is at issue, but rather the scope and focus of such works. A different type of analysis is required from that found in a standard biography or institutional history. Historical analysis that enables us to understand "what really happened" is important, but such analysis is not enough to satisfy the decision maker's concerns about the possible impact of a given policy. If history is to be used to improve public policy, it must address the questions asked by policy makers and provide answers that cannot be acquired through other, nonhistorical approaches.

Although historians can contribute significantly to public policy decisions, individuals interested in pursuing careers in the area of public policy should be aware of potential difficulties. First, and perhaps most significant, engaging in evaluation, policy analyses, or planning activities may require historians to forego being historians because of a possible loss of objectivity. Long hours spent on evaluations or other activities may also consume most of the workday, pushing personal historical research into the evenings and weekends. A second problem may be that historians will have to take a stand on a public issue—not perhaps as historians, but as planners or evaluators. A third difficulty is that historians should recognize that they will have to compete for these jobs against political scientists, economists, sociologists, and other social scientists. Given the natural social science bias of many policy analysts, planners, and evaluators, initial employment may be difficult to secure. The best prospects will be with those agencies interested in including a historical component to policy studies and with those agencies that are aware that the historical context would enhance social science models and conceptual frameworks. Finally, historians might have to acquire additional methodological and analytical skills. Because many policy analysts are social scientists, humanities-oriented historians should expect to learn about and possibly adopt some of their techniques, such as conceptual frameworks, models, and flowcharts. Another necessity is to understand the intricacies of techniques such as strategic, annual, and long-range planning; needs assessment; and formative and summative evaluation. A greater professional flexibility is required, as well as the intellectual curiosity to explore different fields. Yet for historians interested in facing these challenges, public policy will offer a rewarding career.[11]

NOTES

1. Federal Government Resource Group, National Coordinating Committee for the Promotion of History, *Directory and Survey of Historical Offices and Programs in the Federal Government* (Washington, D.C.: American Historical Association, 1978).

2. E. S. Quade, *Analysis for Public Decisions* (New York: Elsevier, 1975), 1–49; Edith Stokey and Richard Zeckhauser, *A Primer for Policy Analysis* (New York: W. W. Norton and Co., 1978), 320–29; and Roger Kaufman and Bruce Stone, *Planning for Organizational Success: A Practical Guide* (New York: John Wiley and Sons, 1983), 1–17, 162–63.

3. Otis L. Graham, Jr., "The Uses and Misuses of History: Roles in Policymaking," *The Public Historian* 5 (Spring 1983): 5–19; Charles E. Lindblom and David K. Cohen, *Usable Knowledge: Social Science and Social Problem Solving* (New Haven: Yale University Press, 1979); Seymour Mandelbaum, "The Past in Service to the Future," *Journal of Social History* 11 (1977): 193–205; David F. Trask, "A Reflection on Historians and Policymakers," *The History Teacher* 9 (1978): 219–26; and Ernest R. May, *"Lessons" of the Past: The Use and Misuse of History in American Foreign Policy* (New York: Oxford University Press, 1973).

4. George F. Madus et al., eds., *Evaluation Models: Viewpoints on Educational and Human Services Evaluation* (Boston: Kluwyer-Nijoff Publishing, 1983); and Blaine R. Worthen and James R. Sanders, eds., *Educational Evaluation: Theory and Practice*, 4th ed. rev. (Belmont, Calif.: Charles A. Jones, 1973).

5. Robert E. Stake, "The Countenance of Educational Evaluation," in *Educational Evaluation*, 106–28.

6. Daniel L. Stufflebeam et al., *Educational Evaluation & Decision Making* (Bloomington, Ind.: Phi Delta Kappa, 1971), 218–20; and Lindblom and Cohen, *Usable Knowledge*, 8.

7. Several individuals suggest the value of history in policy analysis. Cf. Graham, "Uses and Misuses," 5–19; W. Andrew Achenbaum, "The Making of an Applied Historian: Stage Two," *The Public Historian* 5 (Spring 1983): 21–46; Peter N. Stearns, "History and Policy Analysis: Toward Maturity," *The Public Historian* 4 (Summer 1982): 5–29; Edward D. Berkowitz, "The Historian as Policy Analyst: The Challenge of the HEW," *The Public Historian* 1 (Spring 1979): 17–25; Robert G. Stakenas and David B. Mock, "Context Evaluation: The Use of History in Policy Analysis," *The Public Historian* 7 (Summer 1985):43–56; Mandelbaum, *"Lessons" of the Past*, 193–205; and Trask, "Reflection," 219–26.

8. Richard Phelps, "Facilitating the Interstate Migration of Unemployed Workers," *The Public Historian* 4 (Spring 1982): 57–69; Vivek Bammi, "Nutrition, the Historian, and Public Policy: A Case Study of U.S. Nutritional Policy in the Twentieth Century," *Journal of Social History* 14 (1981): 627–48; Gail Buchwalter King and Peter N. Stearns, "The Retirement Experience as a Policy Factor: An Applied History Approach," *Journal of Social History* 14 (1981): 589–625; Daniel P. Resnick, "Minimum Competency Testing Historically Considered," *Review of Research in Education* 8 (1980): 3–29; Marvin Lazerson, "The Origins of Special Education," in *Special Education Policies: Their History, Implementation and Finance*, ed. by Jay G. Chambers and William T. Hartman (Philadelphia: Temple University Press, 1983), 15–47; Joel A. Tarr, "Urban Transportation: History and Planning," *American Public Works Association Reporter* 44 (December 1977):

14–16; and Martin Rein, *Social Science and Public Policy* (New York: Penguin Press, 1976).

9. Berkowitz, "Challenge of HEW."

10. Stakenas and Mock, "Context Evaluation"; Robert G. Stakenas, David B. Mock, and Kenneth M. Eaddy, *Educating Hand and Mind: A History of Vocational Education in Florida* (Lanham, Md.: University Press of America, 1985).

11. For a different approach to history and public policy, see Edward D. Berkowitz's essay entitled "History and Public Policy" elsewhere in this book.

Edward D. Berkowitz serves as an associate professor of history and directs the Program in History and Public Policy at the George Washington University. His research centers on history and social welfare policy. He is the co-author of Creating the Welfare State *(1980). His current assignment involves writing a book on public policy toward disability for the Twentieth Century Fund.*

Before coming to George Washington University, Berkowitz was a senior staff member on the President's Commission for a National Agenda for the Eighties, a policy analyst at the Department of Health, Education, and Welfare, and the first John F. Kennedy Fellow at the University of Massachusetts.

HISTORY AND PUBLIC POLICY

Edward Berkowitz

In the simplest sense, history and public policy suggest a new career option for historians. Many people use training in history as the educational base for a career in the field of public policy. They work in federal, state, and local agencies, and also in trade associations, think tanks, and the many other institutions that contribute to the conduct of public policy. Such people find the abilities to perform research, to write coherently and quickly, and to use history as a means of identifying and classifying programs as very valuable tools in the performance of their daily activities.[1]

In a different and more subtle sense, history and public policy serve as the basis for a new type of history, one that relates the past more explicitly to the present and one that generates information for participants in the policy process. In this essay, I want to consider history and public policy in this second sense of the term.

There need be no disjunction between public history and the presumably private history that is practiced by academics. Public history, intent on seeking clients for specific products, has left intellectual commentary on the issues of the day to the academy. Instead of drawing a line between the spheres of public and private history, the historical community might find it more useful to create a common methodology for history that relates to public policy. Such a methodology might prove useful both for academics and for historians who work in the public sector.

The search for such a methodology suggests a plan of attack for this essay. The first task consists of explaining some of the weaknesses of conventional history for the conduct of public policy. The second task involves defining the need for the use of history in the conduct of public policy, and the final task concerns the formulation of some practical rules for doing history as it relates to public policy.

ACADEMIC HISTORY AND PUBLIC POLICY

Reading through the academic journals and reviewing the titles of history books, one senses the claustrophobic nature of much of American history. The literature is sometimes so narrowly focused that it might be characterized as a series of answers to questions which historians have themselves posed and in which the larger society may take little interest. Recent years have brought about calls to open up the process of historical interpretation, to reach outside of the academy for an audience and for significant questions. If historians want to render a service to the community around them, they might attempt to supply a historical perspective on contemporary questions.

Three relatively recent books give a sense of the general effort to open the process of historical interpretation. William Graebner, James Patterson, and John Garraty have written books that chronicle events over long periods of time. All of the books reach from the relatively distant past almost to the present. Each of the books recognizes the importance of change over time and the accompanying need to place events and attitudes into particular time periods, yet each also realizes the need to link descriptions of the past with perceptions of reality in the present. James Patterson, in his book on America's response to poverty, came closest to expressing this faith in its purest form. "Nothing—good times or bad, liberal or conservative administrations, demographic and social change—had a greater long-range impact on the structure of the American welfare state, than the jerry-built structure with which it began," Patterson writes.[2]

In this quotation Patterson hits upon an insight of vital importance for the conduct of history and public policy. The origins and early life of an institution go a long way toward determining its future development. Policy makers, therefore, sometimes require the services of someone who is trained to determine the origins of a particular program. Failure to engage in this exercise of meshing a program's objectives with a program's history often leads policy into impossible situations.

Examples abound of policies that have failed because programs have been asked to step outside of their histories and do things they were never designed to do. In 1967, for example, Secretary of Health, Education, and Welfare John Gardner expected a program that had a historical aversion toward welfare recipients to work with them and end the rise in welfare expenditures. Around the same time, officials in HEW hoped to use the Aid to Families of Dependent Children program as a vehicle of workfare. The officials expected a program that had been designed to keep mothers at home with their children to serve as a means of getting mothers into the labor force. Both of these efforts failed, the victims in part of failure to appreciate the lessons of history.

Such mundane concerns matter little to the academics who write public policy, since they have their own, often quite legitimate, concerns. Since academics have their fellow academicians in mind as the audience for their work, they fail to obey rules that might make their work more palatable to policy makers. In this regard, one might consider William Graebner's *A History of Retirement: The Meaning and Function of an American Institution, 1885–1978*. Graebner makes an important argument about retirement, one that is typical of much of the current writing on history and public policy. He argues that retirement, considered as an idea, serves the needs of the American economy over time.

The development of this argument merits some consideration. According to Graebner, a process of age discrimination in American industry began in 1885. Older workers lacked the capacity to keep up the pace of production during the shortened and scientifically managed working day. After 1915 feelings toward older workers became more ambivalent. If these workers were less efficient, they were also sources of stability, anchors against strikes and other forms of disruptive activity. Retirement marked a rational response to the needs of industry: it took the decision to remove superannuated workers from the hands of individual foremen and made the decision more automatic, and in the conventional wisdom of the day, also more efficient. It would, at one and the same time, ensure a younger work force and bring stability to labor relations.

Building on this foundation, the state acted to consolidate retirement as an American institution during the first three quarters of the twentieth century. The process began with the creation of a retirement law for federal workers in 1920, continued with the passage of two railroad retirement laws in the early New Deal, reached a climax with the introduction of the Social Security Act in 1935, and continued with various tax and pension laws well into the 1970s.

In the 1970s, however, influential capitalists and government leaders began to rethink the connection between retirement and efficiency. Instead of a source of cost-saving, it came to be regarded as one reason for America's inability to compete in a deteriorating international economy. As the conventional wisdom changed, a new efficiency replaced the old; new laws reversed the relationship between age discrimination and retirement.

So much about this argument is admirable. It possesses an innate elegance, and it reveals Graebner's considerable creativity and intelligence. On the other hand, policy makers who have to deal with the present system of programs experience difficulty when they try to locate their piece of the present in Graebner's vision of the past. In this regard, Graebner's analysis of the Social Security Act illustrates the more general problem. His interpretation differs from the conventional analysis. In the usual narrative, the Social Security Act of 1935 becomes a flawed, yet precedent-setting exercise in social welfare. Although the act may have contributed to a recession in 1937 and 1938, it developed into America's leading vehicle for income redistribution and, without question, into America's most important social program. Graebner, with his penchant for originality, does not see it quite that way. Instead he views social security as part of a continuing effort to solidify retirement as an American institution; it helped to remove the elderly from the labor force by providing them with a modicum of security and penalizing them for working past the age of sixty-five. Graebner notes that social security, like railroad retirement and the civil service acts before it, exemplifies a "surrogate welfare state" and not a "real welfare state," providing benefits out of general revenues.[3]

    Although creative, this piece of analysis does not help current policy makers. They are grappling with the problem of controlling the growth of entitlements. They seek ways to limit expenditures for social security. Traditional defenders of social security recognize that a battle is under way for the preservation of this program, a program that is considered too liberal. To place Graebner's analysis in the middle of the current discussion would cause the debaters to regard him as though he had walked in from the moon. The more perceptive among them would understand that Graebner had simply pushed the concerns of the 1930s forward into the present day. His history has made little attempt to explain the modern policy dilemma.

    Like many academic historians, Graebner regards social security as a metaphor. Policy makers see social security as something real, the smallest part of which now costs $18 billion. For Graebner the origins of the program in 1935 set the terms for its subsequent development. Yet the program now bears a closer resemblance to the Social Security Amendments of 1939, amendments that brought the program much closer to a real welfare state rather than a surrogate one. Preoccupied with the need to create a master interpretation, Graebner indulges in institutional history on a very selective basis. He misses the 1939 amendments. The historian who wishes to analyze public policy needs to take institutions more seriously and to realize that institutions have lives of their own. These institutional lives hold important consequences; they amount to nothing less than public policy itself.

    I do not mean to suggest that historians of public policy need to produce limited institutional accounts of programs and policies. This error is one that many historical offices in the federal government make. They regard history as a straightforward narrative of events, one that focuses on a particular battle, agency, or program. Such efforts fight battles but lose wars. They fail to reveal the richness of public policy, the complex connections that motivate change over time. To be successful, history has to analyze events rather than simply to chronicle them. At the same time, historians who wish to speak to policy makers have to direct their analysis at something the policy makers can recognize in the present. They have to accept the preoccupations of present-day policy makers as points of departure, rather than dismissing those preoccupations as unworthy of their attention.

    James Patterson's *America's Struggle Against Poverty* illustrates how helpful historians can be if they set their mind to it. I offer this book as a useful model for students of history and public policy. Most of the others that I would cite are written by other social scientists: political scientist Martha Derthick on social security and sociologist Paul Starr on medicine. Patterson's book belongs in this distinguished company because although he pays attention to intellectual history, he also devotes space to the public programs designed to alleviate poverty. He appears to recognize the truth of an important observation about contemporary public policy; policymaking and program extensions have acquired, in Martha Derthick's words, "a continuity, momentum, and political logic of their own." Furthermore, the public programs and the related components of public policy may themselves dictate the content of contemporary politics. In Theodore Lowi's words, "policy determines politics."[4]

The lesson of these insights is simple to state. Providing a historical perspective on a current issue means coming to grips with the set of public programs that affect the issue. Patterson's discussion of the negative income tax, for example, recognizes that this good idea was defeated in part by people who benefited more from the disarray of the present system than they would from a new, rationalized system. Among those people were the welfare recipients themselves. Only someone who understands the present system of overlapping programs—someone in touch with the reality of the system rather than a cursory description of the system—could make such a statement.

If this example is too complicated for someone outside of social welfare history to comprehend, consider another and more fundamental one. Patterson concludes his book with the observation that by the 1970s a wide number of welfare programs had developed "helter skelter and overlapped in ways that few people had foreseen and fewer yet could untangle."[5] One suspects that few people can untangle these programs; the task requires the craft of history, with its unique ability to add the clarifying dimension of time to discussions of public policy.

Time clarifies, but it also distorts. In this regard, John Garraty's *Unemployment in History: Economic Thought and Public Policy* comes to mind. His account has the broadest scope of the three studies. His perspective is international; his time span ranges from the beginning of civilization to the present. As an intellectual exercise, the results are intriguing; as an exercise in history and public policy, the results are not as convincing.

Garraty does make one important contribution, one that intellectual historians can often bring to discussions of contemporary issues. He understands that unemployment, like childhood or like domestic privacy or old age, is a historically determined concept. Although people have been idle, they have not always been unemployed.[6] That idea arrived in the nineteenth century. Contemporary observers, with their instant perspective and their impatience with change over time, regard unemployment or the other objects of their attention as immutable, as a permanent fixture on the agenda of public policy. They fail to see how many public policy concerns are invented. Indeed, the insight that things change over time, that nothing except the most elemental things are fixed, stands as one of the most powerful that historians can offer. The insight expands the imagination of contemporary policy makers.

Although Garraty does well with this effort to blend French-style long-range history with more pragmatic, short-termed American history, he leaves current events to economists. He writes with exceptional eloquence of Ricardo and the other classical political economists, waits for Keynes to arrive, and then closes his book with some general comments on inflation. As a result, his book contains much more information on the distant past than on the recent years.

This feature of Garraty's book underscores the difference in outlook between the policy analyst and the historian. The policy analyst has the impression that things evolve from simplicity in the past to complexity in the present. Confronted both by simplistic visions of the past and masses of data that describe the present, the policy analyst has no other choice. Historians, by way of contrast, have the opposite perspective. The materials they have mastered and whose use separates them from practitioners of other disciplines exist in greater abundance for the distant rather than the recent past. As historians approach the present, their magic wears off.

Furthermore, historians want their narratives to reach conclusions. Writers of all types do great violence to the truth in this regard as they search for a satisfying resolution to the particular search for order in which they are engaged. Only writers of fiction can end their books with no qualms. In the case of the historian, the need to tie the ends together creates a tendency to make the present appear less complex than the past. It is as if historians and policy makers view the process of change from opposite ends of a megaphone: the view of the policy maker widens from the past to the present, and the view of the historian narrows.

It is almost as if historians wish to be just as foolish as everyone else when it comes to speculations about the present. Yet, for all of the academy's efforts to distance itself from the consequences of its analysis, practitioners of public policy still express a desire for a useful past. Not only does this desire exist, its existence goes beyond the merely ceremonial to reach the contents of public policy itself.

That distinction between the ceremonial and the real bears some discussion. By ceremonial, I mean history that glorifies an aspect of the past for a political reason. No one objects to the use of history in its ceremonial sense. Examples abound. A bureau or program approaches an important anniversary and wishes to boost moral among its employees and supporters by reminding them of the bureau or program's accomplishments. As a means of political survival, it wishes to wrap itself in its past. Often the decision to indulge in this nostalgia occasions a scramble among political rivals to cast the past in acceptable terms. Often the fear that the favorable sentiment that the flag-waving exercise will create causes those who oppose the bureau or program to attempt to block the entire exercise.

One can observe this kind of thing in the fiftieth anniversary of social security. One strong program supporter has commissioned a special postage stamp to celebrate the occasion, and he encourages colleges and universities to engage in scholarly commemorations of the signing of the Social Security Act in 1935. The Reagan administration, on the other hand, dragged its feet on the matter, fearing that the program supporters will use the historical exercise as a means of beating the administration over the head.

An even more politically charged example concerns establishing a holiday in celebration of Martin Luther King, Jr. Although the eventually favorable decision hinged on political factors, much of the debate concerned the accomplishments of Dr. King. What sort of historical figure was he? The need for historical research on this question appeared obvious, although the identity of the person doing the investigation predetermined the outcome of the investigation. One's feelings about Dr. King were in the most literal sense matters of faith, and the inquiry into Dr. King's life became a matter of religion.

The fact that so much of the work that links public history and public policy falls into the realm of ceremony has occasioned the sharp gap between public and academic history. A company wants an anniversary history written or a public program wishes to commemorate its centennial. A government agency writes official commentaries on the agency's past and runs a museum on the side. No wonder that the question of ethics has come to preoccupy the public history movement; no wonder people question the validity of public history: it has come to mean history for hire. The academics object to this type of history because perfect freedom has come to define the role of the academic in America. History for hire, with actual politics taking the place of the no less political but supposedly impartial practice of peer review, violates this image of the historian.

We have already seen, however, that the academics, left to their own devices, have not produced a great deal of history that is useful. Both public historians and academics need to realize that history can do more than sentimentalize or celebrate the past. The possibility does exist of creating a past that policy makers can use. Here again examples abound.

All practitioners have a fascination with their role in history. They want to understand how their efforts relate to previous efforts, and they wish to speculate on the validity of these previous efforts as omens of their own success or failure. Used in this sense, history passes beyond the merely ceremonial. It becomes a means of analyzing current efforts and predicting the future.

This glowing rhetoric needs to be tempered by reality. The past does not lie out there like a ripe melon ready to be plucked and eaten. Instead, it comes wrapped in a cover of complexity and ambiguity, and thus historians need all of their skill if they wish to unwrap this covering. Before the historian even undertakes the exercise, he often has to put his own sense of history aside and to immerse himself in the convoluted world of public programs.

The rhetoric, although now tempered by a sense of reality, requires reduction into a coherent and concrete example. Let us consider recent developments in the vocational rehabilitation program as one example among many that could be cited. Vocational rehabilitation, it turns out, is a public program, begun in the 1920s, that offers medical care, counseling, and other services to the handicapped in an effort to make them employable. The program operates on a combination of federal and state funds. States run the program with some supervision from the federal Department of Education.

For most of the program's history, it has limited its efforts to people who stand a good chance of getting a job. Recently, however, a number of complicated factors such as the more general trend toward the deinstitutionalization of the handicapped and the emergence of the handicapped as a vocal minority have led to the creation of another program goal. Instead of employment, this new goal emphasizes independent living.

As the example proceeds, one begins to appreciate how complicated the description of public policy can become. All of the programs are surrounded by a tough skin of detail. In order to master the way in which the program operates and even to begin to understand how it has changed over time, the absorption of these details becomes necessary. This program, one might add, represents a mere speck in the bureaucratic universe, a one billion dollar bit of decimal dust in a far larger budgetary world. Each of the specks, however, has its own history, and historians have, for the most part, neglected almost all of them.

The conventional wisdom goes that we live in a conservative age in which people are beginning to rethink their commitment to the large and generous government provision of social welfare services. Much of the money that we throw at problems fails to stick. Instead it lands in what Arthur Okun called the leaky bucket of income redistribution. The conventional wisdom holds that the concept of entitlement poses a threat to the economic health of the nation by foreclosing the President's economic control over the budget and ensuring the perpetuation of a large and menacing federal debt.

When politicians grapple with matters down in the decimal dust, the conventional wisdom becomes more difficult to grasp. The connection between the specks in the bureaucratic universe and more general social trends becomes more difficult to observe. Vocational rehabilitation, contrary to our general sense of current events, has had its budget increased in recent years. The goal of independent living, an amorphous goal of the precise sort that President Richard Nixon had in mind when he complained of throwing money at problems, has been strengthened. Even more important and less intuitive is a recent decision, codified in the most recent vocational rehabilitation law, to make client assistance programs mandatory in all of the states.

With the inevitable penchant for acronyms, people speak of the CAP program. This program, mere millions in this land of billions, establishes a system of advocacy and appeal for rehabilitation clients. If a person goes to the program and becomes dissatisfied, he can take his case to the person called the advocate. Together they can petition the program to change its decision. If not pleased with the result, the person and the advocate can press their case all the way to the courts. The CAP program, then, strengthens the notion of entitlement in an age that disparages the very concept. It allows a federal program, in a sense, to sue itself at federal expense.

I mention this CAP program for two reasons. First, it shows the counterintuitive quality of history and public policy. It demonstrates that grand generalizations do not apply to all aspects of public policy. Entire lives are lived and careers are formed on the spacious grounds of the exceptions to the general rules. Second it illustrates a need for history.

When the new advocates arrive at their offices in the old vocational rehabilitation program to start the CAP programs, they will want to know about the program with which they are dealing. What better way to describe and analyze the program than through its history? The vocational rehabilitation program, after all, has developed its own traditions and priorities in the sixty-five years of its existence. If the advocates fail to understand those traditions and priorities, they will find themselves as strangers in a strange land, unable to be effective advocates for change. Their ability to advance clients' interests will be undercut. With the proper sensitivity, the program's history can also reveal the inherent conflict between a program that has stressed the independence of the counselor and a program that now needs to accept the existence of outside advocates. In the program's traditions, the counselor has the right to accept or reject an applicant for the program's services and to determine what constitutes a reasonable vocational goal. Both the rehabilitation counselor and the advocate in the CAP program consider themselves as professionals who act in the handicapped client's best interests. The potential for a clash between the two forms of professional expertise appears obvious.

An appreciation for history can help to mute the conflict and to direct it into more constructive channels. Faced with the problem of training advocates for the CAP program, a national organization has made a decision to use history as a tool of analysis. Prospective participants in the CAP program receive an analysis of the program's history. The reaction of one trainee was revealing. "I had thought," she said, "that my frustrations with the vocational rehabilitation program were personal and reflected my weaknesses. Now I see the problem in systemic terms. It's not me; it's the system."[7] History helps people to see the system. Not only do they feel better about themselves, they also operate better in the system.

NUTS AND BOLTS

Having made a general case for history and public policy as both unique and useful, I now come to my third and final task: I need to offer advice on how to do it. This last task becomes the hardest of the three. Historians, I suspect, feel uncomfortable in the role of Ann Landers.

History remains a craft to which no hard and fast rules apply. It depends upon developing a vocabulary of facts and ideas and storing them in one's memory. When called upon to undertake a specific piece of analysis, historians collect new facts, often putting them on note cards. They then match the new facts on the cards with the older facts in their memories, make some connections, and then perform the mysterious process of transforming their newly augmented store of relevant ideas into a synthetic and coherent account or narrative. This narrative, stored on paper, soon acquires a life of its own.

Doing history, like writing a novel, constitutes a highly personal exercise. In the case of academic historians, I have noticed that most appear to require privacy. They write letters in the office and history at home, much like novelists who reserve their private hours for fiction and their more public hours for essays. Historians engage in a creative act that they would find difficult to explain. Historical narratives appear to find themselves in the author's mind. In this sense, historians often describe the act of writing as an out-of-body experience, as one who says, "the words came so fast that they scared me."

The fact that good history represents a creative act undercuts discussions of methodology. A friend of mine describes a conversation in which he was asked to describe his methodology. He hesitated, contemplating visions of the Annales school and the long-range view of history. Then he discovered that his questioner had in mind something different. Did my friend use yellow pads for notes or three-by-five note cards? In a similar manner, a methodology course at a prestigious university was concerned for many years with such questions as the margins that a proper rough draft, an interesting contradiction in itself, should have.

Students should, therefore, discount all advice. The best way to do any type of history is to do it. Rules of style represent the antithesis of creativity and hence of individual style. Nonetheless, the practitioner of history and public policy might keep in mind three simple rules.

First, the present makes sense. Almost alone among policy analysts, historians see the inevitability of the present. They do not decry gaps, overlaps, and other inefficiencies in our approach to a particular problem. Historians are in the business of having the present make sense and that is a valuable corrective to a policy process that tries to capture the past and use it for its own purposes.

Second, historians understand that the present follows from the past. They can see today in relation to yesterday and can determine whether the past places a constraint upon the present. This ability gives them the power to spot what might be called the ironic anachronism such as the example cited earlier of asking the AFDC program to become a vehicle for workfare.

Third, good historians realize that the future is different than the present. Each moment is unique; it has never happened before. Because we cannot live with the resulting insecurity, we try to control the future by relating it to the past. We do this instinctively, and we project our visions of the past onto others. Ronald Reagan has a faith in America justified by his past and believes that American institutions, such as the family, will persevere; others with different backgrounds see things differently.

Because we cannot deal with the uniqueness of events, we tend to form analogies. Often these analogies do us a great disservice and limit our ability to respond to events. As Ernest May has noted in what is perhaps the single most influential book in the field of history and public policy, the events of the Korean War looked to President Truman like the events of the late 1930s leading to World War II.[8] The President reacted accordingly. The Munich analogy was powerful: force needed to be met with force.

Although historians appear comfortable with May's point about the Munich analogy, they refuse to carry the wisdom to current events. Today we are the captives of the Vietnam analogy that holds that American intervention in wars of national liberation is counterproductive and bound to fail. The prevailing wisdom, then, suffers from lags, just as our domestic policy reflects programs created a long time ago. Brezhnev dies, and we immediately compare the situation to the one that prevailed at the time that Khrushchev left power. Because the future differs from the present, historians have to learn how to control these and similar analogies.

I suspect that these rules seem disappointingly thin. Still, the diversity of public policy and the craft of history make generalizing a difficult process. It may be sufficient to say that history and public policy demand that both the past and the present be taken seriously. Despite an inattention on the part of the history profession, policy makers continue to demand a usable past for reasons other than the narrowly political and ceremonial. Although there are no hard and fast rules on doing history and public policy, it merits the attention of the public and private historical communities. The possibilities are virtually limitless, and the wider participation of historians will only improve the field's performance.[9]

NOTES

1. Edward Berkowitz, "History, Public Policy and Reality," *Journal of Social History* 18 (Fall 1984): 79–89.
2. James T. Patterson, *America's Struggle Against Poverty* (Cambridge, Mass.: Harvard University Press, 1981), 56.
3. William Graebner, *A History of Retirement: The Meaning and Function of an American Institution, 1885–1978* (New Haven: Yale University Press, 1980), 70–71.
4. Martha Derthick quoted in James T. Patterson, *Struggle*, 168; Lowi quoted in Lawrence D. Brown, *New Policies, New Politics: Government's Response to Government's Growth* (Washington, D.C.: The Brookings Institution, 1983), 1. See also Martha Derthick, *Policymakers for Social Security* (Washington, D.C.: The Brookings Institution, 1979).
5. Patterson, *America's Struggle*, 168.
6. John A. Garraty, *Unemployment in History: Economic Thought and Public Policy* (New York: Columbia University Press, 1978), 73.

7. Personal communication from Ethan Ellis, director of training for National Association of Protective and Advocacy Services, October 1984.

8. Ernest R. May, *"Lessons" of the Past: The Use and Misuse of History in American Foreign Policy* (New York: Harper & Row, 1973).

9. For an introduction to the role of the historian in public policy, see David Mock's essay, "History in the Public Arena," elsewhere in this book.

IN BUSINESS

Philip F. Mooney has managed the Archives Department of The Coca-Cola Company in Atlanta, Georgia, since 1977. Prior to joining Coca-Cola, he served as library director at The Balch Institute of Ethnic Studies in Philadelphia and as an archivist at Syracuse University.

He has been active in the Society of American Archivists and has served as an instructor in the annual Business Archives Workshop since 1979. He has published articles in the field of business archives and ethnic studies in the Drexel Library Quarterly, Proceedings of the Sewanne Economics Symposium, American Archivist, *and* Provenance.

THE PRACTICE OF HISTORY IN CORPORATE AMERICA: BUSINESS ARCHIVES IN THE UNITED STATES

Philip F. Mooney

About 2000 B.C. a guild of Assyrian merchants established a central depository for the records of their commerical activities, marking the establishment of the first business history collection. Family mercantile records, banking documents, and notarial files later became useful resources for the study of commerical development, but the more widespread acquisition of business records for scholarly use did not occur until the early twentieth century when public archival agencies throughout western Europe began to establish regional centers for the collection of business records. Not until the establishment of the Business History Society at Harvard University in 1925 and the pioneering collecting work of the Harvard Business School in the same period did American institutions begin to regard business history as a legitimate academic pursuit. The establishment of graduate business schools and the resulting demand for primary research materials ultimately led to the formation of strong business collections at major academic libraries throughout the United States.[1]

The formation and development of internal archival units within corporate organizational structures is an even more recent phenomenon. Germany's Krupp Company established the first business archives in 1905 when that firm was preparing a formal history. Almost four decades later, the initial American program began when the Firestone Tire and Rubber Company hired archivist William Overman to ensure that valuable historical records were not destroyed as part of a records management program. Still, the Firestone example did not stir many other corporations to follow their lead. By 1960 only fifty-one companies reported archives of any sort, and only a handful employed a full-time archivist.[2] In many firms librarians performed an archival function, while in others the records manager had the responsibility for determining which records to class as historical.

While archival development was slow, history was not entirely neglected in corporate America. A 1943 study conducted by the American Association of Museums identified eighty businesses that supported internal museum programs. Cost justified for their public relations value and for their utility as a visible history of patent, engineering, and trademark use, they generally developed at manufacturing firms that had prided themselves on a tradition of excellence. As with existing archival units, many of the collections were administered by retirees or "well-intentioned" librarians.[3]

Most of the museums identified in the AAM study occupied a small parcel of space in the corporate headquarters with limited public access. The skills of the historian manifested themselves only in the selection of the objects to be displayed and in the development of related publications. In many cases the museum and archival functions gradually merged, accounting to some degree for the rapid growth that has occurred over the last quarter century in business archives.

In surveys conducted by the Society of American Archivists, corporations claiming archives numbered 133 in 1969, 196 in 1975, and over 200 by 1980, ranging from the single file drawer of newspaper clippings and ephemera to well-organized historical units. The surveys did not attempt to make qualitative evaluations of the respondents. A number of popular business publications, summarizing survey data, have mistakenly interpreted these figures as signaling an emerging frontier for historians in the future.[4] In fact, while significant growth has occurred within the field, only sixty full-time archivists were identified in the same survey.[5]

The five dozen corporations supporting internal archival departments represent a cross-section of American businesses including consumer product companies like Coca-Cola, Sears, Procter and Gamble, Kraft, Weyerhaeuser, Corning, Walt Disney, and General Mills; financial institutions such as Chase Manhattan, the New York Stock Exchange, Wells Fargo, Nationwide Insurance, Bank of America and Cigna; high-tech industries like United Technologies, Control Data, Mitre, and Texas Instruments; John Deere and International Harvester representing the transportation industry; and institutions like the *Los Angeles Times*, Colonial Williamsburg, Educational Testing Service, and the J. Walter Thompson advertising agency which stand alone within their industry segments. While the diversity of this selective listing is apparent, all of these institutions are large, well-established entities which can easily support historical services as part of the corporate overhead. Smaller firms can rarely rationalize such expenditures unless they can be linked to their informational or records management functions. In such instances, the archives is usually positioned as a smaller element of a corporate library system or records program.

The rationale for the establishment of an archives can differ dramatically among corporations, but major reasons include the celebration of an anniversary or special event, the production of a corporate history, the needs of internal departments for immediate historical information, pending litigation and/or the specific directive of a chief executive officer. The programs at Wells Fargo, Chase Manhattan, and Control Data began when management recognized that an organized historical collection would make the decision-making process easier because they would have access to the records of past management practices. At American Telephone and Telegraph, the process of producing a major historical study stimulated the formation of the archives, while a Canadian anniversary celebration and the resulting search for packaging samples motivated General Mills to the same decision. At Coca-Cola, the need for documentation in a 1941 trademark case underscored the need for the formal maintenance of a historical collection. Regardless of the initial impetus, successful programs are those that have clearly positioned their long-term functions as relevant contributors to stated corporate strategies.

In some cases business leaders, hoping to preserve the record of their accomplishments, have initiated archival programs by executive fiat. With such a limited statement of purpose, those archives serve the same function as pyramids for the pharaohs. Without a life of their own or broad-based internal support, they are doomed to extinction when a new management group with a philosophy oriented toward a different goal assumes control of the firm.

Unless management clearly perceives the archives as a vital, progressive, contributory information center that renders direct support to the business, its long-term existence is unlikely. While historical consultant George David Smith has suggested that corporations are "hungry" for history and that studies of past actions are "therapeutic" for industries facing hard decisions in times of great turmoil, Deborah Gardner, archivist of the New York Stock Exchange, pinpointed the more basic concern facing practicing archivists when she observed that the corporate sector does not readily perceive itself as having a historical function.[6] To the degree that the archivist can identify the benefits of history to the parent body the more successful and secure the archival program will become.

The organizational structures most prevalent in American corporations position the archives within an administrative services group, in a public relations department, or in the office of the corporate secretary. Like other organizational units, the form and positioning of the archives strongly reflect the business function. Companies with a strong consumer products orientation often perceive the archives as a valuable public relations vehicle, while financial institutions may find that the office of the secretary may require more frequent access to historical files for the completion of important projects. Administrative placement offers even more functional flexibility ranging from strategic planning to centralized information management.

Figure 1. Archives storage area. Wells Fargo Bank Archives. *Photograph courtesy of Wells Fargo.*

All of these structures can operate equally well provided that the archivist has access to decision makers. Ideally, the archivist should have the title of department head, manage an independent budget, and report directly to a corporate officer. The archivist should be able to communicate to senior management on a regular basis and to receive feedback on programs in a timely fashion. The desired objective is to reduce the number of layers through which information must travel.

Rather than simply serving as the corporate memory, the archives must render valuable practical services to business that could not be easily secured from other sources. The functions of the office must be directed toward the achievement of goals and objectives that are positive, pro-active, and consistent with the corporate culture of the institution. To accomplish this, the archivist must truly be a practitioner of applied history, and ongoing programs must withstand the harsh empirical testing of skeptical business associates. While continuing to exercise the analytical techniques of the historian, the corporate archivist also must possess strong communications skills to properly position the department, its purpose, and activities. The tenure decision in the business world is not restricted to the individual; it is expanded to include his organization. "Produce or Perish" is substituted for the traditional "Publish or Perish."

Archives do not exist in a corporate vacuum; they demand relationships with other departments and functions. These linkages expand bases of operation, allowing the archivist to manage historical resources and to achieve results that are both understandable and measurable. Ties to areas such as marketing, advertising, public relations, human resources, training, legal, strategic planning, stockholder relations, research and development, and publications establish a strong user network for cooperative program development.

Marketing plans for the 1980s are based on programs that have succeeded in past decades. The glitter and packaging surrounding the promotion may change, but its essential shape and content hardly vary. An office that can supply detailed data on previous business achievements can help to plot new campaigns that hold the promise of similar results. Similarly, an analysis of disappointing or disastrous promotions can alert marketing strategists to the perils of poorly structured programs. Sales promotions files, packaging and advertising samples, sales aids, and financial reports help companies like General Foods, Sears, Kraft, and Ford to capitalize on successful ideas while avoiding the pitfalls that caused other campaigns to falter.

In a highly technological age, complex corporate organizations and highly mobile work forces have combined to eliminate heritage and tradition as factors in the formation of corporate policy. The effects of merger, acquisition, litigation, and records management also have contributed to corporate memory shortages. As a counterweight to these trends, the archives can provide access to the policies, standards, philosophies, and environment that influenced previous decisions and can recapture critical strategic information that helped shape the business.

Wells Fargo Bank offers a unique case study in applied history on the corporate level through its support of over a dozen members of the archival staff who routinely prepare detailed analytical reports on financial policies and procedures and publish an impressive series of monographs on regional banking history. The archives also staffs three history museums in major California banking centers as visible testaments to the impact of the corporation on the state's financial history.[7] Some archival programs, such as that at Control Data Corporation, prepare and distribute departmental histories to new employees, while Chase Manhattan Bank and Weyerhaeuser have initiated oral history programs to supplement their written records and to improve the overall quality of documentation.

The use of archival materials in employee orientation programs, training sessions, company films, and audiovisual presentations underscores the importance of heritage and tradition and helps the work force to develop an appreciation and understanding of the factors that have shaped the business. Successful business archives promote the use of departmental resources as primary training tools and vigorously publicize their availability to communications specialists. Archives such as those at General Mills, Cigna, and The Coca-Cola Company also have developed attractive and educational exhibits that provide still another opportunity to communicate the corporate success stories directly to employees, their families, business guests, and the general public. When Nabisco Brands, Inc. discovered over 1,500 original pieces of advertising art in a company warehouse, their archivist developed an exhibition of the paintings for internal showings and then proceeded to make them available in a traveling exhibit that is still in circulation.

A well-managed archival collection will provide perspective on business decisions, allowing companies to understand how they have proceeded from point A to point B. The records will outline the development and implementation of business strategies and will serve to motivate both employees and customers. Executives will make better decisions with a grasp of the institution's development, and employees will gain a better understanding of the company's policies.[8] At the Salt River Project, a public utility, a major archival focus is on issues that historically have impacted the firm's operations. Armed with detailed analytical reports, the office of strategic planning can anticipate problem areas and take corrective action to deal with them.

One of the most tangible and cost-effective justifications for a corporate archival program stems from the protection it affords in matters of litigation. The preservation of the firm's trademarks, slogans, advertising, and promotional concepts often depends on the ability of the archives to document in court a prior, exclusive, or continuous use of the marks. Since the weight of the documentary evidence provided to the court can often be the compelling factor in a judicial decision, the availability of a cohesive body of advertising and marketing documen-

Figure 2. Corporate exhibits can be useful for employee training and public relations. This is a corporate exhibit housed in the headquarters of The Coca-Cola Company in Atlanta. *Photograph courtesy of The Coca-Cola Company.*

tation has a strong positive impact on the company's legal standing. Similarly, records maintained by the company can yield valuable support data in liability, ingredients, or technical cases that require strong defense strategies. In the legal area alone, the businesses can recoup the total costs of staffing and maintaining an archives. Since the trademarks of the corporation have a value in real dollars, usually expressed as a line item in the firm's annual report, the importance of preserving documentary records forms the first line of defense in many legal proceedings.

From a public relations standpoint, the archives offers myriad opportunities to disseminate corporate messages to widely diverse audiences. The preparation of corporate histories, annual reports, magazines, and other specialized publications often demands accurate and complete historical data, coupled with well-organized visual resources. For example, Gerber, Sears, and Ford have mined archival resources to produce colorful and informative specialized publications to mark anniversary celebrations of note. Additionally, many corporate archivists use the research data they assemble in the course of handling reference requests to prepare historical features for company publications and brochures. The regular exposure achieved in these house organs serves as a continual reminder of the archival presence that can generate even more clients and support. From this same resource base, textbook, newspaper, and magazine writers, together with their colleagues from the electronic media, can develop feature articles and background features on aspects of company history and illustrate them with appropriate images. With creative collections management, companies like Corning Glass, with photographic holdings in excess of 150,000 negatives, can fashion positive public relations placements that enhance the public's understanding of the business and its operations.

Successful corporations understand their consumers and respond to their needs. Successful archival programs embrace the same philosophy in establishing their priorities and in marketing their services. Outreach programs can help to stimulate an awareness of corporate products and services in unique ways. At the New York Stock Exchange archivists have conducted lunchtime programs on the history of Wall Street, while Anheuser-Busch, International Harvester, and Walt Disney have developed timely response mechanisms for answering historical or nostalgic inquiries from consumers, and have prepared exhibitions of artifacts and historical documents that have reached consumers in a very personal and direct fashion. As an instrument for informal education, exhibits can both inform and entertain the viewer as they allow the corporation to place its marketing, advertising, and technological achievements in the public spotlight.

Procter and Gamble has gone one step further by producing a series of educational pamphlets designed to supplement social sciences curricula at the junior and senior high school levels. Through the use of photographs, advertising, letters, and documents drawn from the archival collection, these impressive publications position economic history in a very positive fashion while exposing the students to primary source material.

In a few cases, consumer product companies like Sears and Anheuser-Busch can directly influence sales and marketing programs through the development of packaged goods employing nostalgic themes. Trays, posters, glassware, and memorabilia decorated with designs drawn from archival collections remain staples of the marketing arsenal for sales promotion efforts. Trademark licensing offers still another avenue for revenue accrual, whereby a corporation in return for a royalty allows other manufacturers to use its trademarks and artwork on numerous classes of goods for retail distribution. The availability of strong reference files for licensees enhances the quality of the overall program and directly impacts on the income returned to the corporation.

While the basic tasks of the archivist to acquire, appraise, process, describe, and reference records do not differ radically from those of associates working in the nonprofit arena, the major functions of any corporate archives are inwardly directed. With few exceptions, the focus of all programming revolves around service to the business and advancement of its goals and objectives. Unlike archival collections at academic institutions, government repositories, and other specialized research centers, outside access to documentation generally is restricted. The archivist serves as the monitor of research activities, balancing the pursuits of the scholar against the company's interest. While corporate archivists strive to open significant segments of their collection for legitimate research topics, many of the records remain closed. In the final analysis, the archivist's loyalty must be to the employer that subsidizes departmental operations.[9]

The types of records preserved in corporations tend to reflect the character of the organization itself. The basics of a good archival collection will include executive correspondence files, minutes of board meetings, records of major committee decisions, and summary financial data, but other elements will vary considerably, directly reflecting business operations. Companies with a strong advertising and marketing orientation generally find their collections weighted in that direction. More audio-visual materials, artifacts, ephemera, product samples, pamphlets, and sales aids of all descriptions find their way into these repositories. Financial institutions, such as insurance companies and banks, face a voluminous assemblage of claims, accounts, and correspondence relating to individual and corporate records, while engineering and high technology firms must consider the preservation of oversized drawings, detailed technical reports, and project files that characterize these businesses. Keeping these unique elements in mind, the archivist strives to develop a collection that represents the totality of the institution.

In most businesses, the archival holdings will represent less than 1 percent of all company records. Consequently, the appraisal criteria used to select this documentation must be based on a clear understanding of the company's history and its information needs. In this one area, historical training has its most immediate and long-term impact. The records classed as historical will determine the shape of future historical analysis of the company and will impose limitations on internal research capabilities. In reaching a decision on preservation, the archivist must always weigh the potential historical value against the cost involved in record keeping and the potential risks inherent with the files themselves. In a litigious age, subpoenas and discovery proceedings can convert a valuable corporate resource into a dangerous adversarial weapon. In some cases the concerns of staff attorneys for certain classes of records can preclude them from archival review, even extending to critical executive-level documents.

A delicate balance exists between the archivist concerned with preservation and the lawyer concerned with potential court action. The more documents that exist in a corporate collection, the higher the risk that materials may ultimately be used by opposing interests. As a result, in many businesses today, records management programs, acting on directives to decrease documentation as rapidly as possible, have assumed the major responsibility for handling the voluminous flow of records. Additionally, telecommunications and computer technologies have further reduced the need for paper records, eliminating even more potential record candidates for archival retention.

In this difficult environment, the corporate archivist must master the fine art of salesmanship and then must meet exacting performance

Figure 3. Historical photographs are a key element in most corporate collections. This is the Bookkeeping Department of the Chase Manhattan Bank, New York City, June 1919. *Photograph courtesy of Chase Manhattan Bank Archives.*

standards in providing needed data in a timely fashion. For the program to succeed, management must recognize the informational value of the assembled collection and must have confidence in the ability of the archivist to balance the needs of research against the interests of the corporation. With management support, the archivist can assemble holdings that represent the corporation in its historical totality. Without that support, the collection's contents will primarily consist of ephemeral items that have little relationship to the decision-making process and the development of the business.

Those factors that are most compelling for retention include age, scarcity, research potential, cost effectiveness, and critical importance. The higher a record scores when evaluated against these criteria, the better are its chances for inclusion in a collection. In many cases the archivist will use sampling techniques in reviewing large record groups such as personnel records or financial reports, while at other times bulky files can be converted to microfilm. The desirable objective is to assemble a collection that is representative and functional.[10]

In 1982 the Society of American Archivists issued a set of guidelines

Figure 4. Research area at the archives of Sears, Roebuck and Company. *Photograph courtesy of Sears Archives.*

for business archives that were intended to outline a set of "desirable objectives" for companies to meet. Included among them were a written statement of goals and objectives, strong administrative support, independent budgetary administration, adequate space and equipment, and the employment of at least one full-time archivist. The recommendations further suggested that a master's degree in history together with archival experience could qualify candidates to function in a business setting.[11] While doctorates, dual master's degrees, and archival institute certificates often will enhance employment opportunities for candidates seeking academic appointments, corporate employers place much greater weight on the experience factor in making hiring decisions. Most business archivists in administrative positions today had previous work experience in other archival programs. In turn, they tend to hire experienced staff who have already proven their abilities in the archival workplace.

A 1982 survey of the archival profession as a whole revealed that the profession was generally young and well educated. A mere 18 percent possessed only the bachelor's degree, while another 15 percent held dual master's degrees, and 16 percent had achieved their doctorates. More than 50 percent of the archivists were under forty, and 67 percent were under fifty.[12]

While most business archives function with small staffs, two to three

Figure 5. Records processing area of Deere and Company archives. *Photograph courtesy of Deere and Company Archives.*

people, their compensation levels are near the top of the profession, and this arena offers more opportunities for women than traditional archival outlets. In 1982 the average salary for an archivist was $21,400 compared with a mean salary of $24,540 for business archivists, second only to their colleagues in government service. Even more revealing was the fact that of sixty-seven business archivists responding to the survey, forty-one were females and twenty-six were males.[13]

In the most recent survey of business archives conducted by the Business Archives Committee of the Society of American Archivists, 141 businesses reported that they held archives. More significantly, eighteen new programs have been established in this decade with projections for a total of fifty-four new programs by 1990.[14] Additionally, over two hundred representatives of businesses have attended workshops on business archives sponsored by the Society of American Archivists over the last seven years. All of these signs are encouraging in a period when budgetary constraints are limiting historical programs in many other areas. Still, these optimistic signs must be tempered with the harsh realization that history in the corporate environment must pay its own way. The only utility for history lies in its pragmatic business applications.

NOTES

1. Meyer Fishbein, "Business Archives," *Encyclopedia of Library and Information Science*, vol. 3 (New York: Marcel Dekker, 1968), 517–26.
2. David R. Smith, "A Historical Look at Business Archives," *American Archivist* 45 (1982): 273–78. See also Helen L. Davidson, "A Tentative Survey of Business Archives," *American Archivist* 24 (1961): 323–27.
3. Laurence Vail Coleman, *Company Museums* (Washington, D.C.: American Association of Museums, 1943).
4. Robert W. Lovett, "The Status of Business Archives," *American Archivist* 32 (1969): 247–50; Gary P. Saretzky, "North American Business Archives: Results of a Survey," *American Archivist* 40 (1977): 413–20; and *Directory of Business Archives in the United States and Canada* (Chicago: Society of American Archivists, 1980).
5. Margaret Price, "Corporate Historians: A Rare But Growing Breed," *Industry Week* (23 March 1981): 87–90; and Robert Levy, "Inside Industry's Archives," *Dun's Review* (May 1982): 72–76.
6. Betsy Bauer, "Companies Save Past for Future," *USA Today*, 20 March 1984, sec. B, pp. 1–2.
7. For additional discussions of the role of strategic planning in archives, see George David Smith and Laurence E. Steadman, "Present Value of Corporate History," *Harvard Business Review* 59 (November-December 1981): 164–73; and Gilbert Tauber, "Making Corporate History a Planning Resource," *Planning Review* (September 1983): 14–19.
8. James Monteleone, "Your Bank's Archives May be Valuable," *The Bankers Magazine* 166 (January-February 1983): 69–74; and "Companies Digging Up Their Past," *Management Review* 71 (1 January 1982): 32–33.
9. For a fuller discussion of this issue, see Edie Hedlin, "Access: The Company vs. the Scholar," *Georgia Archives* 8 (1979): 1–8; and Anne Van Camp, "Access Policies for Corporate Archives," *American Archivist* 45 (1982): 296–98.
10. For a discussion of appraisal practices, see David L. Lewis, "Appraisal Criteria for Retention and Disposal of Business Records," *American Archivist* 32 (1969): 21–24.
11. Linda Edgerly, "Business Archives Guidelines," *American Archivist* 45 (1982): 267–69.
12. David Bearman, "1982 Survey of the Archival Profession," *American Archivist* 46 (1983): 233–41.
13. *SAA Newsletter*, November 1982, 1–2.
14. Unpublished survey data provided to the author by Linda Edgerly, Gary Saretzky, and Karen Benedict, compilers of the data.
    Note: See "The Business World" section of Ted Ligibel's bibliographical essay entitled "Utilizing Library Resources," an appendix to this book, for an introduction to the basic sources used to research business history or current business conditions.

Ruth Ann Overbeck has both her B.A. and M.A. from the University of Texas at Austin. Her first job after leaving UT was with the architectural firm of Page, Sutherland, and Page. She has lived in Washington, D.C., since 1970. In 1975, she founded Washington Perspectives, Inc., a for-profit public history firm, and is known throughout the mid-Atlantic region for her expertise in historic preservation and land use.

HISTORY AS A BUSINESS

Ruth Ann Overbeck

Public history, applied history, entrepreneurial history, all are terms which have been coined relatively recently. They do not, however, describe an altogether new process. For as long as most historians can recall, at least a few academically trained members of the profession have produced history in one form or another for clients outside academia or government agencies. The movie industry, for example, began utilizing history consultants years ago. Newspapers and magazines also have a track record of publishing, for pay, articles written by prominent historians and certainly the advent of television spawned an entirely new media for authorities in the field of history to conquer. If you're dubious, sample the credits on Public Broadcasting System telecasts.

Employment opportunities for the professional historian seeking a position outside the spheres of education and government have multiplied several fold in the past twenty-five years. Not only has there been a proliferation of media opportunities, increased interest in urban planning and historic preservation has provided two other major areas in which historians can carve out private sector careers. In addition to the traditional one-person consulting services and employment by organizations whose primary foci are not history, historians are pursuing new avenues.

Among the new avenues is entrepreneurial history; in other words, private sector business relationships formalized as sole proprietorships, partnerships, or corporations which are organized for the express purpose of generating history as a marketable product. Why use the term entrepreneurial history rather than contract or public history? "Public historian" in the city where I own my business almost automatically conjures up the impression that such a historian works for free, i.e., a public servant. Contract history? Well, contracts don't just arrive. We actively seek opportunities that establish business relationships and at least several firms, including mine, generate some projects on speculation.

The process is self-defining not only to me but to other owners of history businesses as well. At the 1985 meeting of the Southwestern Oral History Association, two panelists for the session "Family History and Oral History as a Business" used the term to describe their businesses. When queried after their presentation, they and a third panelist stated that they are both entrepreneurs and oral historians, ergo they own entrepreneurial history firms. Whether the result is a family's oral history, an architectural history of a commercial building, or an analysis of historic land treaties between the United States government and a tribe of American Indians, when a for-profit history firm establishes a business agreement with a client, we are dealing with entrepreneurial history.

During the past fifteen years or so, the institutions and faculties responsible for the education of historians have begun to come to grips with the fact that there are those of us with sound scholarly credentials who choose to work in these private sector nontraditional capacities. With that recognition has come some formal academic training geared to history students who intend to practice their profession in the nonacademic world.

It is not a preparation that I or many of my pioneering colleagues had. In some instances we have been quite fortunate, despite all odds. Others' early attempts resembled efforts at powered flight before the era of the Wright brothers. In spite of imaginative packaging and even extensive public relations at times, many history firms never got off the ground. Some flew only until their first grant monies ran out or until completion of a few initial contracts, but proved unable to stay airborne. Then, there are those of us who have not only survived, but have thrived for at least a decade or more. We are proof, if you will, that history is a viable commercial endeavor.

Who are the entrepreneurial historians and how many of us are there? No one knows. A directory of us published in 1981 was obsolete almost as it rolled off the press and has long been out of print. In 1985, the National Council on Public History surveyed its members attending the annual conference for their occupational affiliation. Even when results of such surveys are compiled, they are incomplete. Not all of us are members and not all members respond. Suffice it to say that entrepreneurial historians number, at a minimum, in the hundreds and most of us maintain an informal network with at least a few of our colleagues and former professors.

The fields of history which we represent are as catholic as history itself. Among the areas of concentration covered by firms I know personally are the history of: the American Indians, architecture and landscape architecture, interior design, land use, transportation, public utilities, and American social and urban history. Many of these firms additionally offer place, event, or person-specific expertise, such as in-depth knowledge about Albert Gallatin, the Red River Valley, and the development of the National Road.

Our clientele is equally diversified. Purchasers of history encompass the government bureaucracy, including executive and legislative branches of national and state governments; religious and philanthropic organizations; lobbying groups; industrialists and commercial establishments; hospitals, museums, and tour organizers; both pro- and anti-historic preservationists; and yes, the average citizen. The gamut of applications to which our products are put is equally wide-ranging. Attorneys hire us as expert witnesses, entrepreneurs underwrite searches for relevant material culture to set the theme of their latest enterprise, and cities retain us to help establish historic enclaves that will bolster their sagging economies.

ASSESSING THE RISKS AND OPTIONS

Do I recommend that historians become entrepreneurs? Yes and no. I'm doing what I love to do. It's not necessarily easy nor does my career allow my life to be one with a great degree of predictability. Indeed, there is virtually nothing routine about my professional life, a fact which frequently spills over into my private life as well. For those historians who do want to explore becoming part of the entrepreneurial group, I submit several basic questions for their consideration.

My first question is perhaps the most soul-searching one the potential entrepreneurial historian will have to answer. It is to define one's perception of history as a profession. At the end of one of my lectures to a public history graduate seminar, a student asked, "How is what you do different from selling used cars?" With a laugh, I acknowledged that while I'd never made that particular analogy of my career, in actuality it is selling a product.

I have no delusions that I will produce the next Turner Thesis, or lead the way to a redefinition of American history along Marxist lines. What I am doing is providing the general public with quality historical research and history-related projects applicable to the everyday world. The student, incidentally, later opted out of the public history program because her goal was tied strictly to becoming a professor of history in the most traditional meaning of the term, a choice she feels far more comfortable defending.

One's comfort index will have to be the primary guide throughout the whole process of being a historian involved in the free enterprise system. Thus, the index is a corollary area for careful self-examination. Numerous academically attached historians belittle entrepreneurial history as a career. Even historians employed by that most public of agencies, the federal government, are divided in their opinions of the appropriateness of entrepreneurial "public" or "applied" history as a profession. In 1982, some emotionally charged comments arose at the federal historians' conference in Washington, D.C. They followed presentations by entrepreneurial historians, several of whom are acknowledged leaders in their areas of expertise.

The tenor of the antagonists seemed to focus on the lack of institutional control over the businessperson historian, implying that "authority" and "credibility" as a historian stem from strong bonds of affiliation with "acceptable" establishments. To listen to the opponents talk, most historians have little or no chance to present accurate finely crafted history without the watchdog of peer review looming in the next office. This is a concept that I wholeheartedly dismiss, in large measure because both academia's tenure system and the U.S. civil service can cushion even the careless historian. Neither do they necessarily guarantee quality within their ranks. No entrepreneurial historian has such protection and often must be in a position to guarantee accuracy and quality, even to the point of testifying in court or before official review bodies. Each of us, moreover, is subject to the severe criticism of the marketplace as well as that of our fellow historians.

Before making a decision about entering the business world as a historian, envision skepticism at best and possibly an expression of outright disdain from one's peers in academia mixed with a sense of disbelief from most representatives of the world of business. If the idea of being a historian whose place is only tangential to the academic, institutional, or governmental world still has a strong appeal, then entrepreneurial history may be a possibility.

Although those government historians hostile to the concept of entrepreneurial history did not challenge specifically the "ethics" of entrepreneurial history, that may well be at the root of many persons' reluctance to embrace the field wholeheartedly. The question of ethical conduct is one which we all face every day and one on which we depend. In the business and professional world, we most often think of lawyers, doctors, scientists, politicans, and perhaps manufacturers as being in vulnerable positions. Entrepreneurial historians also find themselves at risk. While every professional historian must address the ethics of the craft, the historian in the business world particularly is subject to the charge of "being bought." Ethical considerations are inherent both in the use to which projects they generate are put and the findings which are expected by the client, or purchaser, if you will.

For the historian in the private sector, the historical process is more than an intellectual inquiry and presentation of the findings for the sole sake of expanding available knowledge on a given subject. As an end product, the businessperson-historian's report may be one, or even the sole, determining factor in decisions based on a complex aggregate of facts and opinions. If the research and analysis of U.S. treaties with the Indians is being sponsored by a major mineral exploration company, an entire tribe's accessibility to its land may hang in the balance. The other side of the coin may be the future of the defense of a nation. Yet a third factor, that of corporate profits, both of the history firm and its clients, may rest on the credibility and accuracy of the report. That very profit factor for the historian's client may be negated by a historically accurate report. One's self-respect and one's ability to gather and analyze historical data accurately despite pressure must be inextricably bound to a strong ethical code to survive in the world of entrepreneurial history.

Granted, identification of ethically problematic projects or clients can be difficult. Whenever possible, the history entrepreneur should maintain the posture of having a "need to know" the client's real purpose for a project. It is mutually unfair to the historian and the client for a project to have a stated purpose, that of the preparation of an alleged gift of the history of a piece of real estate, for instance, when in actuality that history is going to be utilized by the client to support development plans for a shopping mall. The historian should have the option to refuse to work on projects whose end results are contrary to the historian's ethics. Likewise, the client has the right not to engage the services of a historian who can not participate wholeheartedly in a contract.

In addition, the historian and the client must have an understanding about the historian's right to control the integrity of the history aspects of the project. If, for example, the product is to be a corporate history book or exhibit which will be produced in conjunction with a salmon cannery's seventy-fifth anniversary celebration, is the client willing to allow an accurate depiction of the company's handling of an unsuccessful attempt to unionize the workers? Are you, the entrepreneur, willing to keep your own pro- or anti-union sympathies and emotions in check as you research, write, and illustrate that portion of the text?

If the historian is fortunate, the client will bring up sensitive areas during pre-contract discussions or at contract negotiations. If not, and the historian is aware of the potential problem, the onus rests on his or her shoulders to raise the issue. Just as the historian needs the freedom to pursue a controversial or unpleasant aspect of history, the client needs assurance that the research will be equally thorough for all sides of the issue and that the analysis will treat the subject accurately and fairly. The time to come to a mutually satisfactory decision on control or censorship is before the ink is on the contract, not after.

What does the entrepreneurial historian do when in the midst of what seemed a perfectly viable, comfortable project unexpected problematic information surfaces? Several options are open. The fairest to all concerned, perhaps, is to preplan for such an occurrence by providing for periodic client updates. If material of a truly sensitive nature which could be damaging to living individuals emerges, such as an adoption or an illegitimacy which has been kept secret for a quarter of a century, the client may wish to terminate the project rather than risk the consequences. Contracts should provide for such termination with fair compensation for the historian. The historian, on the other hand, has an obligation to respect the client's wishes that the sensitive material remain secret, if that is the decision. While this type of information may be more likely to emerge during biographical or family history research, do not assume those are the only instances in which it will occur. Revelation of a corporate coverup which occurred some years in the past may hurt unknowing participants who are still alive, leaving unscathed the dead and buried instigators. Again, a resolution will have to be worked out with the client. Can both the innocent be protected and the story be told with historical accuracy?

One last consideration for the potential entrepreneur of history is the amount of nonhistory time the marketing of history is likely to demand. In numerous discussions with history faculties, I have learned that many of the most productive academic historians are expected to juggle the morass of paper work necessary to keep grant monies available, to hire and fire colleagues, to contribute to the development of departmental or institutional policies, ad nauseam. While the number of professional hours spent on nonhistory functions may be equivalent, the entrepreneurial historian will be spending those hours outside the realm of academia, with such assorted individuals as remote from the field of history as CPAs and advertising agency personnel. If the idea of devoting a significant portion, estimated to be one-third, of your career to the details of participating in the world of business does not seem appealing, entrepreneurial history is not for you.

Finding a bridge from theorizing about entrepreneurial history to its implementation is a step which a surprising number of historians are now taking during their formal education. Approximately eighty institutions of higher learning offer some academic course work designed specifically for public history. Certainly in schools with a substantial public history curriculum numerous opportunities exist for a trial run as a private contractor in the business of history. Just as one might want to test drive a Trans-Am or Porsche before deciding if it's too hot a car to handle, participating in an entrepreneurial project when one has relatively little to lose is an excellent idea. I didn't know public history would ever exist as a recognized field of study or endeavor when I was at the University of Texas in the 1960s. Still, I gained some entrepreneurial experience, researching projects for pay and writing short history articles. Looking back, I realize these experiences played an important part in subsequent career decisions.

"You're getting a degree in history and you're not going to teach?" My questioners' incredulous looks kept reminding me of the world's opinion of a suitable occupation for historians. As graduation approached, I didn't know exactly how I would utilize my academic training. I did know I wanted to be a historian and I sensed that the workaday world would have a place for me if I could just find it. Never in my wildest imaginings, however, did I think I would create my own history firm.

That occurred several years after graduate school. By that time I had worked as the research editor of the hospital planning division of a major architectural firm, a position which required a lot of "applied" history, as well as on several private consulting research and writing contracts. I had developed strong skills in demographic analysis, alternative use planning for old buildings, the organization of written and visual documentation for essentially promotional purposes, and had honed my historical research and writing abilities.

I also had discovered that I have several business-oriented skills. One is being able to sell people on ideas. Another is the ability to talk to—teach, if you will—people in both formal and informal learning situations. Yet another is putting together effective teams of problem solvers

from disparate disciplines. Barbara J. Howe's essay, "Historic Preservation: An Interdisciplinary Field," elsewhere in this book, provides a case
study of the utilization of some skills and processes useful to the
entrepreneurial historian.

When I finally decided in 1975 to establish a private enterprise history
firm, I was unaware of being at the leading edge of the "public" or
"applied" history movement. I simply made a commitment to myself to
try out my idea, one which was predicated on my track record of
previous contracts and my assumption that the American Bicentennial
would spur an upswing in the general public's interest in history. My
base of operations was and still is Washington, D.C.

For the person who has faced the philosophical and ethical issues
already raised in this essay and is still interested, what comes next for the
entrepreneur in history? To establish a sound business base in any
profession, a person must have a marketable idea. History, demonstra-
bly, is marketable. More importantly, is your particular expertise in
history marketable outside of academia? Have you identified the focal
point on which you will found your efforts? Will you offer only historical
research service, or are your writing and editing skills proficient enough
to offer as well? Will you advise a client on potential relevant projects,
then design the approach, do the necessary research, and present a
finished "product"? Is your field of history truly relevant to the
community, in the broadest sense, that you want to serve?

In my instance, I had strong groundings in local and oral history as
well as the larger issues of land use, transportation, population mobility,
and publishing. I also knew that the potential market was extremely
diversified in its interests and needs. In my prior work experience, I
gained significant expertise in locating and using many of the federal-
level historial records collections, including ones not frequently accessed
by historians. I decided to offer clients several levels of historical
services: basic research to supplement or fill in gaps of work they are
doing; a complete research package to be "applied" by the client; and
full service, taking a project from conception to completion.

Projects the firm has undertaken and the uses to which they have been
put have covered a far broader range than I ever anticipated. We have
created walking tour and architectural history brochures; histories of
corporate headquarters and houses; identified and ranked the names of
historic taverns and located their extant material culture for the owners
of a chic new restaurant; consulted on the rehabilitation or demolition of
numerous historic properties, including testifying as expert witnesses
before zoning and preservation review boards; selected archival materials to be used in a black history research project, designed code books
for gathering statistical data from those materials, trained the coders,
and advised on the statistical methodology to analyze the data; provided
documentation for a video script about a massive slave escape attempt;
and located cockpit instrumentation specifications for a World War I
fighter plane and data about experimental concrete ships the United
States used in World War II, both for a professional model builder.

After ten years as an entrepreneurial historian I still find an exciting justification for being in the history business.

ORGANIZING YOUR BUSINESS

Suppose you have now decided that you want to market your services as the expert in the history of the salmon fishing industry in the United States and that you will be able to find sufficient buyers willing to pay prices which will enable you to earn a living. That initial decision is only the beginning of the process. What has to follow falls in the sphere of the business world and you are going to need to do a number of things almost simultaneously if you do not want to make a career just of getting ready to open for business.

Be realistic. Can you truly afford to go into business for yourself? Or with someone else? If the latter, with whom? Full or part time? Do you have a lifestyle that allows bleak financial periods? Do you have adequate health care protection, insurance, and financial reserves to tide you over in between contracts? Learn everything you can about the financial risks involved in the establishment of a small business. Equally important, learn how to minimize those risks. Avail yourself of any support groups for new or small businesses. Read as much as you can on the subject of entrepreneurship. When projecting how long you may have to survive before your business becomes a success, remember that even the IRS gives a new business five full years before it either must show a profit or be considered a hobby.

Early in this decision-making process, choose the personal name you are going to use professionally. Entrepreneurial history is an unusual enough business in and of itself for you to be stymied by a nickname that does not sound serious enough. The more involved your history business is likely to be with the corporate world, the more important your professional image is to your success.

If you are female, decide on the name you will use "forever." None of us likes to think of divorce or death, but they are the facts of life, so be prepared. You will find your name published in articles, remembered by previous clients, and listed on membership rosters in professional associations. Your cohorts who become tenured professors will thereby form long-term professional relationships which are somewhat analogous to a marathon while your professional relationships will more closely resemble a series of fifty-yard dashes. Stability in something as basic as your name is important. Few prospective or repeat clients will make the effort to track you down through a series of name changes. Remember that no man has to change his name when his marital status changes, regardless of cause.

What about the format of your business? The options are numerous and each has its own set of constraints. Many other decisions will hinge on your choice between a sole proprietorship, a limited partnership, or a corporation. Each has different tax implications, legal obligations, and restrictions. Most public history firms about which I have information have been organized with two or more persons sharing top management responsibilities as well as capital risks. I, on the other hand, am the founder and president of my company with nonhistorians on my board of directors. No one way works for everyone. If you don't know the difference between the various types of organizations, formulate what you think would be ideal work arrangements.

Next, shop for two of your most valuable allies, an attorney and a tax specialist to help you through the maze of setting up the kind of business structure that suits your needs. As you will have to pay substantial hourly charges for their expertise, be certain you are well prepared BEFORE you begin spending your money.

Ask business people or professionals whose integrity you respect for their recommendations. Even if the business person helps by arranging a lunch or coffee meeting, don't expect to get much free information or advice. Rather, this is an opportunity for you to size up your prospective advisor, to see if you want to establish a more formal business relationship or meet for a full-fledged consultation. It is also the time to find out what information you should be prepared to give during the first appointment.

Once you phone your potential attorney or tax specialist, briefly state the nature of business you want to discuss at the first full meeting. Above all, ask for the estimated fee(s) you will be charged and when payment will be due. If you cannot meet the financial terms of your first choice, don't despair. The United States contains an abundance of professionals in the legal and tax fields. In general, remember that you (the history entrepreneur) will be far more unique as a professional than most of the people you are likely to meet.

Your attorney will ask, "What name do you want to use for your business?" You may keep it simple by using your personal name, followed by "Inc." or "Consultant." On the other hand, you may choose something more specifically history, subject, or place oriented. Test two or three of your favorites on other professionals in your location. I found, in the Washington of the mid-1970s, that use of one's personal name plus "Consultant" implied that one was "between jobs," something I had no intention of implying. In addition, virtually no one believed that a history firm could succeed. If it did, it was assumed that its novelty would soon wear off and the firm would collapse. To fight those preconceived ideas, I chose "Washington Perspectives, Inc.," as the name which would give me both the solidity and flexibility I wanted.

Also be prepared to answer, "What is your business address?" By this time you should have an idea of where you want to locate the office. Options again are endless. I chose a home office and after a decade, it is still the firm's headquarters. There are several reasons why I made this choice. Initially, I was concerned about costs. I had perfectly viable space for a full office and out-of-office storage in my residence and was already accustomed to doing contract work in a home office. A final factor in our location is the firm's strong emphasis on research. We spend a great deal of time in archival and other data repositories.

Appointments with clients pose no problem as by far the majority of both clients and prospects request meetings for their convenience at their office, home, or construction site. Again, no one way works for everyone. There are history firms with offices in historic buildings, in uptown commercial space, and even located next door to the firm's biggest client, a department of the United States government. Whatever your initial decision, try to choose a location that will suffice for at least a year. Not only is an image of stability important, but time and money spent on unnecessary moves are a drain.

With business name and address in hand, your first stop will be the bank. Seasoned business or professional friends can give good advice on which one to choose and may open a door or two. Commercial bank accounts are not the same as personal ones. Look your most stable, businesslike self when you open your account. If at all possible, go to one of the vice-presidents rather than a "new accounts" clerk. Your banker can be an ally, neutral, or an enemy. You want someone at the bank who can expedite a credit reference or short-term loan to tide you over when a client's check is ten days late because of a postal strike. I cannot stress enough that most of the people with whom you come in contact are going to think your business, and therefore you as well, are somewhat "unusual," to put it nicely. Remember, the more credible you are to the business community, especially bankers, the more likely you are to succeed.

You will need to make other business arrangments as well. Business cards and stationery are crucial. Select the best graphics designer you can afford and, above all, use good quality paper. The small amount of money you save buying cheap stationery can cost you bundles in the long run. Your letterhead will speak volumes about the quality of your service to the potential client who is awarding a competitive contract without having met the prospective contractor.

Your office environment and the way you staff it also need careful attention. Nothing needs to be fancy, but typewriters or word processors must produce professional looking results; filing and storage space must be adequate, organized, and accessible. If you can utilize a computer, by all means do so. A telephone answering machine, answering service, or secretary, which suits your needs and your pocketbook? Whichever you choose, do have reliable service or equipment as it is your link to the outside world.

How does one go about getting clients and contracts? By letting everyone, and I do mean everyone, know that the XYZ History Company is open for business. In casual conversations, at parties or wedding receptions, bringing up the fact that you are an entrepreneurial historian should be good for at least three to five minutes of ice-breaking conversation. More formally, send press releases to your university alumni magazine, your college classmates, your mother, as well as all the other relatives, the local Chamber of Commerce, all the historical societies in your area, the president of the garden club, and especially the news media.

Learn to handle media representatives carefully. You can be misquoted, misinterpreted, or even vilified in the press, so be alert to the ramifications of any information you release, especially if you are working on politically or socially sensitive issues. Never expect a media person to heed your request that, "This is off the record." If you do not want to go public with the information, do not tell it. On the other hand, every time your name or the name of your history firm is put before the public, there is the possibility that a contract will be generated, so do not automatically shun the media either.

Whether dealing with the press or employees, your business manners must be warm, but firm enough to cope with even the most boorish prospective client. By business manners, I mean exactly that, the manners you utilize in business situations. For example, if you are not a hand shaker, learn to be. I have met very few historians, male or female, who are good at the art. The banker, attorney, real estate developer, government official, or corporate officer with whom the entrepreneurial historian will be working has the ritual down to a fine point. So should you.

In the area of client-contractor relations, I developed a policy very early on that client information is as privileged or secure with us as it would be with a lawyer. WPI gets involved in numerous aspects of land use planning and development. One of the firm's specialities relates to the preservation and rehabilitation of historic buildings and neighborhoods. As such, we have prior knowledge of developers' target areas long before they become available to the public. We frequently are hired as early in a project as the scouting stage, a time when an entire real estate transaction could be stopped by information going beyond the inner circle of the development team.

Contract negotiation is another area of business manners, so to speak, and one which is often difficult. Few people know the time and expertise quality historical research and analysis can entail. Many of them therefore are reluctant to pay what seems a rather high fee for someone "to sit and read books and papers," as one of our clients stated. Once you have set your fee schedules to cover the costs of being in business and providing income, you will need to stick to them. Bargain if you must, but always try to get something substantial in return for a lower fee. On one of our earliest contracts, to research and design a self-conducted walking tour booklet commissioned by the United States Congress, we offered a fee plus contract with the plus being the inclusion of the firm's credit line on the booklet, a virtually unheard of constraint on a congressional contract. Almost a decade later, we are still receiving calls generated from the initial 500,000 copies printed of that booklet, a fact worth more than the additional money we would have received.

When negotiating a contract, make certain everyone understands what product is to be delivered, what the fee will be, when and how it is to be paid. During a late-December crisis related to the proposed removal of the third pilot from long-haul passenger aircraft, we were asked to undertake a rapid turnaround documentation search. The client, a lobbying group, wanted us to search for reliable statistics on any increased accident rate which resulted from the deletion, some fifteen years earlier, of firemen from train engine crews. We agreed on an hourly rate and the number of hours to be spent, everyone shook hands, and we began the research.

We exhausted the indexed published sources as well as Department of Transportation and ICC records; lots of rhetoric before the removal; nothing significant after the fact. Calls to the headquarters of the International Brotherhood of Locomotive Engineers and the firemen's counterpart yielded nothing concrete although the B of LE counsel's office could give us an explanation. First, virtually no statistics existed on the causes of accidents under the old system, whether by crew negligence, equipment failure, or outside forces such as cattle on the tracks. Because much of the railroad industry had been in the midst of a dramatic technological change simultaneously with the personnel system change, statistics comparing accident rates before and after the removal of the firemen would essentially be meaningless even had the earlier data base existed.

We wrote up our findings, including the information from the B of LE attorney's office and submitted our bill. Because we had not located the desired statistics, our client balked at paying our fee. We ultimately did get paid, but we now use caution on such contracts. "Yes, we will research," we tell our clients, "and if there's something to find within these sources and the time and financial constraints of the contract, we will find it. There is, however, no guarantee that what you are looking for exists."

Whatever restrictions you and your clients agree on verbally should be committed to writing before any work proceeds. When the contract is small, a letter from the client authorizing work on the project for a given sum may be sufficient. Clients with whom we have not worked before or those whom we know to be slow payers are asked to enclose a partial payment. For larger projects, use a standard contract drafted by an attorney, preferably yours. Whenever a client prefers to initiate a different form of contract, have the document reviewed by your counsel before signing.

In the case of competitive bidding for a contract, be certain you try to assess accurately whether or not you have a real chance to get the contract before you spend long hours preparing the proposal. Some history firms, and other types of businesses as well, try to avoid bidding on government projects. The rationale is that unless one is the "sole source" the government has, the likelihood of getting the contract is absolutely minimal to nonexistent and time could be spent more productively than chasing the golden pot of public money. Others do quite well going after such contracts. Whatever you decide, you must make sufficient money to offset the time spent not only in seeking contracts, but in performing other strictly administrative chores. It is a very fine business line to walk, but excessive paperwork can be the death knell of a young business.

Is the relatively young business of entrepreneurial history truly a long-range viable career for the historian or are there too many death knells lurking? I, for one, tend to be conservative in my estimates of the potential market. A soft economy can produce real hardships as can a change in the social climate. One history firm specializing in land use projects for the oil industry has had boom and bust times that reflect the ups and downs of the industry itself. Firms relying heavily on marketing the history of minority groups have learned the hard way that a slight shift in the prevailing political winds can blow away a goodly portion of their business.

I do think there will always be room for a substantial number of broad spectrum entrepreneurial history firms. Their long-term success, however, will be like that of any other business. It will be based on quality products and services provided by better than average professionals who operate in a well-managed environment. If you choose to participate and are prepared to be one of the best, welcome.

SUGGESTED READING

Publications pertinent to the practice and craft of entrepreneurial history are scant indeed, a sure sign of the newness of the field. The broad range quarterly publication *The Public Historian* (University of California Press, 1978 to present) contains articles of both specific and peripheral interest as does the National Council on Public History's quarterly *Newsletter*. See, especially, the Winter 1984–85 and Summer 1985 *Newsletters* for the report of the organization's Ethics Committee (Winter) and the council's "Ethical Guidelines for the Historian" (draft, Winter; final, Summer). *The Craft of Public History* (Westport, Conn.: Greenwood Press, 1983), edited by David F. Trask and Robert W. Pomeroy III, is an introduction and basic guide to the literature of public history. Again, it draws from the full spectrum of the public history palette, but does include some general and specific chapters relevant to entrepreneurial history such as "Training" and "Business Management." From time to time, locally focused magazines and newspapers run articles about history businesses or the entrepreneurs themselves. Both the Washington *Post* (7 March 1983 and again in 1984) and *Washington Woman* (Summer 1985) have featured articles about "house history" creators and an entrepreneurial historian. To locate articles such as these, consult public and newspaper libraries.

CONCLUSION

HISTORY EVERYWHERE

Even a cursory reading of the essays in this book should convince any reader that public history is everywhere. This is precisely the conclusion reached by Heather Huyck based upon her experience as a public historian and on her observation of the wide range of activities presented in these essays. Indeed, this observation seems so appropriate that it could well serve as an alternate or subtitle for the book. One finds in these essays public historians in unexpected places, bringing a sense of history to an amazing spectrum of people and institutions. We must hasten to add that not all public history positions are represented in this book, nor have we dared to predict from the book what will develop in the future.

It is intended that this book serve not only as a text for a growing number of courses in public history, but also as a reference for more specialized courses such as those in historic preservation, historical editing, and archival management. We also feel it could usefully be combined with more specialized readings from the publications of organizations such as the National Council on Public History, American Association for State and Local History, Association for Documentary Editing, American Association of Museums, or Oral History Association. The journals of these organizations are able to cover current developments in their fields in ways that books cannot. Many references to aspects of public history may also be found in *The Craft of Public History*, edited by Robert W. Pomeroy III and David Trask for the National Council on Public History (Westport, Conn.: Greenwood Press, 1983). In addition to formal courses in colleges and universities, *Public History: An Introduction* lends itself for use in workshops and short courses and to self-study by those wishing to know more about this endeavor.

As an introduction, this book is not intended to be the final word on the subject, but rather to engage the reader in further enquiry, and it may inspire a few to join the ranks. We hope that interested readers and public history students and teachers will also take the opportunity to visit historic sites, museums, and agencies discussed in the book, talk to public historians about their work, become involved in a variety of projects themselves to explore their interests in the field, and experience the missionary zeal that the authors in this book feel to bring history to the public through their work. One of the most compelling and characteristic features of public history is using teaching techniques that are not traditional to the history classroom, and we encourage these wholeheartedly. Future public historians who try their hands at compiling oral history, designing museum exhibits, developing preservation plans, or writing public policy statements will find the comments of our authors all the more relevant as they draw on the authors' experiences and grow through their own successes and frustrations. *Public History: An Introduction* can serve as a source of ideas for individuals who wish to become involved in public history in this way.

To aid the pilgrim's progress through the world of public history, specialized bibliographic material is found at the end of most essays and in Ted J. Ligibel's "Utilizing Library Resources" (Appendix A). An extensive Directory of Resources and Organizations has also been prepared as a guide or reference (Appendix B).

Public historians, under a variety of names, have been active for decades, each developing expertise in particular areas and becoming active in the professional organizations most appropriate to their specialties. Since the mid-1970s, these public historians have begun to band together, across specialized disciplines such as archival management and museology, and, increasingly, with historians in the academy, to concentrate on mutual concerns of the history profession as a whole. The education of future public historians, the relationship between historians inside and outside the academy, the effort to ensure federal support for programs such as the National Endowment for the Humanities and the National Historical Publications and Records Commission, together with other topics of mutual concern, have helped forge links among many historians. We see this book as one link in that chain.

APPENDIX A

Ted Ligibel served as survey and research director for the Landmarks Committee of the Maumee Valley [Ohio] Historical Society in 1974, in charge of the Vistula Historic Survey. In 1976 he became Historic Preservation Officer for Northwest Ohio under a joint program of the Department of the Interior, the Ohio Historical Society, and the Landmarks Committee of the MVHS, affiliating this program with Bowling Green State University in 1978. Mr. Ligibel is the former head of historical acquisitions and photographs for the Local History and Genealogy Department of the Toledo–Lucas County Public Library. A frequent lecturer and tour guide, he has authored several articles on area history, neighborhoods, and architecture and is a past chairman of the Landmarks Committee. He holds a bachelor's degree from the University of Toledo and a master's in American Studies from Bowling Green State University. He is co-author of the award-winning regional architecture book, Lights Along the River.

Currently, Mr. Ligibel is research associate in historic resources planning for the University of Toledo's Urban Affairs Center.

UTILIZING LIBRARY RESOURCES: A BIBLIOGRAPHIC ESSAY

Ted J. Ligibel

PREFACE

This essay was compiled through the generous cooperation of the department heads and staff of the Toledo–Lucas County Public Library, whom the author gratefully acknowledges. Like most survey format works, it does not pretend to be absolutely comprehensive; it does hope to be directional and practically useful. The overriding reason for this essay was to give students an idea of the types of informational sources available in many libraries, sources that provide a historical perspective for most subject classifications.

"We cannot say 'the past is past' without surrendering the future."
—Winston Churchill

INTRODUCTION

There was another revolution in 1976—a revolution not of government, but rather in the way Americans approached their heritage. Suddenly, our nation was officially 200 years old, and although historians already had thoroughly researched, analyzed, and published volumes of excellent material, there was a need for new interpretations of a heritage that had now "come-of-age." Historians of all varieties from academic to architectural to corporate renewed their zeal in the serious pursuit of American history. Perhaps the major outcome of this "bicentennial rebirth" was the realization that American history happened everywhere. It surely happened in the East, the South and the Southwest, but it also occured in Toledo, Ohio, in Rushville, Illinois, and in Kit Carson County, Colorado. In many areas, a new consciousness, with new needs and questions arose—who built that Italian Renaissance-inspired residence and why?; how long has the Sparks Corporation been in business and who founded it?' when were those patent numbers issued?; what medical instruments were introduced in response to World War I?; where did my grandparents come from and when?' what impact did a certain artist, performer, or architect have on an area or the nation?; how can black, Indian, Hispanic, and other Americans of ethnic descent trace their ancestry?

Increasingly, these and thousands of similar questions are being asked, not only by historians but by growing numbers of a curious public as well. Professionals and amateurs alike turn to libraries for the answers, and with rewarding results. In every department of the library—be it Social Science, Business, Science/Technology, Fine/ Performing Arts, History/Biography, Local History/Genealogy, or Literature—lie the books and periodicals and pamphlets and indexes and bibliographies and reports, and more recently the clippings, oral histories, manuscripts, and photographs, both primary and secondary in nature, that provide the resources necessary to gain the required data.

Similarly, the role of libraries has grown to meet the expanding needs of historians and other researchers. Material which heretofore had been underutilized became more popular, more collectible, and more acceptable as a source for interpreting history. Oral histories, photographs, architectural drawings and surveys, family histories, diaries, and local newspapers began to be used heavily as a way of cross-referencing with other sources, in many cases, as a starting point for research. Librarians in turn have had to broaden their fields of interest and expertise in order to be of service to their patrons. As a result many libraries have established or expanded local history, biography, and genealogy sections and have added staff with history backgrounds to existing departments such as business, technology, or social science.

The use of libraries as a mainstay in the quest for historical data of course is not a new endeavor, but it is an endeavor which has been, and will continue to be, reassessed and redefined. The use of a library is a foundation of historians' research and probably needs little elaboration. What is needed, I think, in light of the increased emphasis on historical perspective, is a review of library resources that can provide that perspective. This essay will serve therefore as a practical guide to some of these resources—both common and underutilized. It will review the major subject divisions, discuss their resources, and suggest ways in which their holdings can be utilized. In addition, special attention will be given to the field of genealogy, detailing sources to meet the tremendous growth of interest in family history, spurred by the publication of Alex Haley's celebrated novel *Roots* in 1976.

BASIC TOOLS

Virtually every subject area has one or two fundamental sources that are used most frequently. Readers' guides and indexes, such as the *Readers' Guide to Periodical Literature* (New York: H. W. Wilson Co, 1905–) or *The New York Times Index* (New York: New York Times Co., 1851–) may be well known, but it is worth reiterating their value in conducting nation-wide or even international research. Other basic sources which can be utilized to gather material include *Poole's Index to Periodical Literature* (Boston: Peter Smith, 1908–) by William Frederick Poole or the *Cumulative Author Index for Poole's Index to Periodical Literature* (Ann Arbor: Pierian Press, 1971) compiled and edited by C. Edward Wall. *Poole's Index* provides access to periodicals available from 1802 to 1906 and, with supplements, is a seven-volume work; Wall's *Cumulative Author Index* covers the period 1802–1906 as well.

The several "union lists," for example the *Union List of Serials in Libraries of the United States and Canada* (New York: H. W. Wilson Co., 1943; Washington, D.C.: H. W. Wilson, 1964) or *American Newspapers, 1821–1936; A Union List of Files Available in the United States and Canada* (New York: Kraus International Publications, 1967) or the *National Union Catalog of Manuscript Collections* (Hamden, Conn., 1962–) can lead the historian to the source of a certain periodical, paper, or primary account. *The Dictionary of American Biography* (New York: Charles Scribner's Sons, 1946, 1974) or the *New England Historical & Genealogical Register* (Boston: New England Historic, Genealogical Society, 1847–) are consulted by many history disciples for information about specific individuals or families. The several "Moody's Manuals," covering finance, government, industry, and utilities, are a mainstay for business/industrial historians, as is the *Applied Science and Technology Index* (New York: H. W. Wilson Co., 1913–) for researchers in technical areas. In the fine and performing arts categories, there are art, architecture, and music indexes, some dating to the late 1920s. In literature, the *Author Biographies Master Index* (Detroit: Gale Research Co., 1978) is a standard source.

Researchers should also be aware of the On-Line Computer Library Center (OCLC) Interlibrary Loan Subsystem. Through the OCLC network of libraries across the United States and in several foreign countries, this library-to-library on-line communication system can help locate any publication that is catalogued onto the system. Once the work is located, it then can be requested by the potential user and sent to any participating library. OCLC was begun as the Ohio College Library

Center in 1967 and is now a not-for-profit corporation with access to 2,100 libraries worldwide.

The following sections, divided by subject area, outline specific sources.

THE REALM OF SOCIAL SCIENCE

Perhaps no other department within a library offers such a diversified catalog of fields as social science. Religion, politics, government, law, philosophy, education, and the human sciences all fall within this broad realm of study. As a result, historians of many varieties will find themselves in the social sciences department for a variety of reasons. If, for example, you had to determine the origin of a small religious sect, J. Gordon Melton's two-volume *The Encyclopedia of American Religions* (Wilmington: McGrath Publishing Co., 1978) would be a logical starting point; *The Yearbook of American and Canadian Churches* (Nashville, Tenn.: Abingdon Press, 1974) may help to determine if the group is still extant and how many members it includes. There are also several encyclopedias of religions covering Catholicism, Judaism, and the Mennonites, for example.

A number of key sources covering politics, government, and law are available in the social science category. The *Introduction to United States Public Documents* (Littleton, Colo.: Libraries Unlimited, 1978) by Joseph Morehead is a broad-ranging source covering documents from the beginnings of this country to the late 1970s; it can be particularly helpful if you are not sure where to begin. *The Congressional Quarterly* and its yearly compendium *The Congressional Quarterly Almanac* (Washington, D.C.: Government Printing Office, 1945–) cover in detail the workings of each session of Congress going back to the end of World War II.

Congress and the Nation (Washington, D.C.: Government Printing Office, 1965–80), a five-set series, provides a comprehensive review of politics and the government from the end of World War II to 1980. If population or demographic information is needed, two important resources are *The City and County Data Book* by the U.S. Department of Commerce Bureau of the Census (Washington, D.C.: Government Printing Office, 1983) and *Population Information in Nineteenth-Century Census Volumes* (Phoenix: Oryx Press, 1983) by Suzanne Schulze. This latter work interprets the federal census from 1790 to 1890. More current census information, as well as a wealth of statistical data covering most subject categories and including the 1900 to 1970 censuses, can be obtained in the bicentennial edition of *Historical Statistics of the United States: Colonial Times to 1970* (Washington, D.C.: Government Printing Office, 1975) published in two parts by the U.S. Department of Commerce.

Certain libraries serve as "depository libraries," that is they act as depositories for all major government publications. There is one depository for each congressional and senatorial district. Depository libraries generally are found within the existing major library for an area and generally maintain their depository status for extended periods. The documents' dispersal and availability are handled by the Library Programs Service of the Superintendent of Documents, United States Government Printing Office. *The Monthly Catalog of United States Government Publications* (Washington, D.C.: Government Printing Office, 1895–) began in 1895 and is arranged according to the issuing agency and then by author, subject, title, and series/report. Access to this catalog is facilitated by the *Cumulative Subject Index to the Monthly Catalog of United States Government Publications, 1900–1971* (Washington, D.C.: Research Publications, 1973) which was compiled in fifteen volumes by William Buchanan and Edna Kavely.

Educational historians will want to refer to *Education in the United States: A Documentary History* (New York: Random House, 1974) edited by Sol Cohen into a five-volume set. It begins with the roots of education in Renaissance Europe and covers virtually all levels, movements, and issues into the 1970s. On a topical level the *Education Index* (New York: H. W. Wilson Co., 1932–) begun in 1929 serves as an author/subject index to approximately 220 periodicals, bulletins, reports, yearbooks, and government material pertinent to the field of education.

If you still cannot find the needed references, the *Social Science Index* (New York: H. W. Wilson Co., 1974–) may be able to locate what the specific indexes did not contain. It began in 1974 as a separate index to 263 periodicals, but was preceded by the *Social Sciences and Humanities Index* (New York: H. W. Wilson Co., 1965–1974) and the *International Index to Periodicals* (New York, 1916–1964). A separate *Humanities Index* (New York: H. W. Wilson Co., 1974–) also has continued since 1974. Similarly, the *Public Affairs Information Service* (PAIS) bulletin, begun in 1915 by the Public Affairs Information Service in New York City (Pierian Press), is a broad-coverage index of subjects relating to public issues and policy. Over 600 periodicals currently are indexed covering literature in the social sciences, political science, economics, sociology, international law, and public administration. Public policy-oriented publications for education, business, social work, and medicine are also listed. PAIS is published biweekly with quarterly and annual cumulations. Two recent indexes are helpful for specific research in political science and sociology: *The Combined Retrospective Index Set to Journals in Political Science, 1886–1974* (Washington, D.C.: Research Publications, 1977) and the *Combined Retrospective Index to Journals in Sociology, 1895–1975* (Washington, D.C.: Research Publications, 1977); both are multivolume sets and each has indexes for over 100,000 articles from hundreds of English-language journals. The volumes are arranged into ninety-five subject categories and then computer-sorted for easy access. Each set has a comprehensive author index as well. *The World Almanac and Encyclopedia* (New York: World Almanac, 1898–) or *Facts on File Yearbook: The Indexed Record World Events* (New York: Facts on File, 1942–) are both landmark compendiums of useful, and obscure, information that often can secure a date or describe an event which cannot be found elsewhere. *Facts on File*, incidentally, is updated weekly. Similar to a "union list," *Newspapers in Microform United States, 1948–1972* (Washington, D.C.: Library of Congress, 1973), printed by the Library of Congress, is arranged by state and is a natural complement to *American Newspapers: 1821–1963: A Union List of Files Available in the United States and Canada* (New York: Kraus International Publications, 1967) edited by Winifred Gregory.

THE SCIENTIFIC-TECHNICAL SIDE

One of the most frequently used sources for historians dealing with science and technology is *Applied Science and Technology Index* (New York: H. W. Wilson Co., 1958–) which actually began as *Industrial Arts Index* (New York: H. W. Wilson Co., 1913–1957). It indexes articles in approximately 350 technical journals. Likewise, the *Engineering Index* (New York: Macmillan Information, 1884–) lists articles covering all phases of engineering and construction, including, for example, civil and mechanical engineering, electrical mechanics, naval architecture, fluids and hydraulics, cement construction, and many other subject headings. *Engineering Index* dates back to 1884 and currently is available on-line as a computerized data base.

Another useful guide is *Index Medicus* (New York, Boston, Washington, D.C., 1879–) published by the National Library of Medicine. It can trace its ancestry to 1879 when it was first issued as a government document entitled *Index Catalogue of the Library of the Surgeon General's Office*; currently indexed are 3,600 medical journals worldwide. It also has been known as the *Current List of Medical Literature* (1945–1959) and, since 1960, as *Index Medicus*; it still is issued as a government publication.

The *Biological and Agricultural Index* (New York: H. W. Wilson Co., 1964–) surveys over 100 journals relating to the broad spectrums of biology and agriculture. Begun in 1915 as *Agricultural Index* (New York: H. W. Wilson Co., 1916–1964), it was renamed in 1964 to reflect a wider scope in coverage.

A general survey of technological developments can be found in *A History of Technology* (Oxford: Clarendon Press, 1978) edited by Trevor I. Williams which was published in seven volumes and covers the period from c. 1750 to c. 1950; volumes one to five were edited by Charles Singer et al. and published from 1954 to 1958. *The Scientific American* (New York: Scientific American, Inc., 1845–) also can be useful as it was first published in 1845 and has several cumulative indexes.

Researching patents is another aspect of technical study that may be conducted in libraries, although only about fifty libraries in the nation currently serve as patent depository libraries. *The Official Gazette of the United States Patent and Trademark Office* (Washington, D.C.: Government Printing Office, 1872–) has been published weekly by the Patent and Trademark Office since 1872, replacing the earlier *Annual Report of the Commissioner of Patents* (Washington, D.C.: Government Printing Office,

1837–1871). The *Gazette* is arranged by patent number and provides a claim as well as a short abstract and a selected drawing of the patents issued each day. The *Index of Patents*, which dates to the first U.S.-issued patent in 1790, is published annually by the Patent and Trademark Office and is organized according to patentee and patent classification. More recently, an on-line computer access to patent data has been developed by the Patent and Trademark Office. Known as CASSIS (Classification and Search Support Information System), it is a direct link to the files of the office and can provide immediate access to patents both by number and by classification. Only patent depository libraries have the CASSIS system.

THE BUSINESS WORLD

A staggering number of resources are available for use in the business of business. Areas covered include business and industry, banking and finance, government and municipal incorporations, stocks, taxes, and public utilities. As with other subject divisions, the business profession has its own serial guide, *Business Periodicals Index* (New York: H. W. Wilson Co., 1958–) which indexes approximately 250 periodicals. It now numbers twenty-seven volumes and is available in microform. A recent reference work which provides a good overview of available literature is Lorna Daniells's *Business Information Sources* (Berkeley, Calif.: University of California Press, 1976). It can help to locate sources and basic information on companies, industries, organizations, or individuals and is arranged by topic including statistics, investments, economic trends, management, marketing, personnel, and related subjects. Although Daniells's book is more recent, it does give access to many sources which offer historical perspectives.

The number of older sources for business-related material is fewer than in other areas, but among the earliest are the several manuals published by Moody's Investor Service (now a company of the Dun and Bradstreet Corporation). These include the *Bank and Finance Manual*, the *Municipal and Government Manual*, the *International Manual*, the *Industrial Manual*, the *Public Utility Manual*, the *Transportation Manual*, and the *OTC Industrial Manual*. Several of the manuals were begun in the 1920s. The *Industrial Manual* was the first to be published (1920); the *International Manual* is the most recent (1981). All the manuals are published in New York by Moody's.

Each manual is arranged alphabetically by the individual name of the specific entity. A capsule history or profile of each is given, along with products or services provided; names of officers, directors, and board members; financial statements; and where appropriate, a list of subsidiary companies. The Moody's manuals are published as a weekly, sometimes daily, series and are republished as bound volumes, logically rearranged, at the end of the year. This year-end volume has a name index covering the entire year.

While Moody's can be consulted on a yearly basis going back at least

sixty years, there are several other publications helpful when researching now defunct businesses or corporations. *The Scudder and Fisher*
manuals, as they are popularly known, offer information on businesses
whose stock has become worthless or whose charter has been forfeited.
The Marvyn Scudder Manual of Extinct or Obsolete Companies (New York,
1926–1937) becomes the *Robert D. Fisher Manual of Valuable and Worthless
Securities* (New York, 1938–) in 1938. In all there are fifteen volumes,
the most recent having been published in 1984. These volumes
are alphabetically arranged by name of company and list the state in
which the company existed and occasionally additional historical data
and the date of its cessation. Another similar issue, published by the
Financial Stock Guide Service, entitled *Directory of Obsolete Securities*
(Jersey City, N.J.: Financial Information, Inc., 1970) can serve as an
adjunct to the Scudder-Fisher volumes. Also, Prentice-Hall's *Capital
Adjustments* (Englewood Cliffs, N.J.: Prentice Hall, 1980) provides a
summary of business mergers, splits, and economic changes; it is a sort
of capsule financial history in a two-volume set, i.e., up to 1969 and
1970–1979; it is continually updated. This work lists fewer companies
than the others but gives more information about those it does cover.

The various publications of the Conference Board, a private fact-
finding organization founded in 1916 to research and publish studies on
business economics and management, can be very helpful and are made
available especially to libraries. They currently publish thirteen regular
series as well as several irregular bulletins and reports; an annual
cumulative index also is prepared. Formerly known as the National
Industrial Conference Board, since 1970 it has been known simply as the
Conference Board.

Predicast's F and S Index (Cleveland: Predicast's, Inc., 1968–) is a
source which monthly indexes 2,000 business trade journals and government publications, covering many of those not covered by *Business
Periodicals Index*. Begun by librarians dissatisfied with existing indexing,
and originally known as *F and S Index* (Detroit and Cleveland: Funk and
Scott Publishing Co., 1960–1967), *Predicast's* separately issues volumes
covering United States, European, and international publications. Each
volume is divided into sections: one listed by SIC number (Standard
Industrial Classification Code) which is arranged by universally applied
business/industrial categories; the other listed alphabetically by name of
company. Both sections provide concise "one sentence abstracts" of
individual articles so reseachers can determine which article best meets
their needs. The *F and S Index* is updated weekly, monthly, and quarterly
with an annual cumulative edition. It also offers thirteen data bases for
computer searching. This publication began indexing American journals in 1960.

If stock quotations need to be perused, Standard and Poor's *ISL Daily
Stock Price Index* (Palo Alto, Calif., and New York: Standard and Poor,
1962–) can be utilized. Although its perspective is fairly recent,
coverage has been continuous for the New York Stock Exchange since
1961, for the American Stock Exchange since 1962, and for "over the

counter" stocks since 1968. For earlier prices, the *Wall Street Journal* (New York, 1899–) can be used.

In the realm of government-related material, several publications often are helpful to researchers. These include Department of Commerce issues of the *Census of Business* (Washington, D.C.: Government Printing Office, 1934–), the *United States Industrial Outlook* (Washington, D.C.: Government Printing Office, 1960–) and for tax-related cases, the *Internal Revenue Code* (Washington, D.C.: Government Printing Office, 1939, 1954). The Commerce Clearing House, a private group, publishes serials including: *U.S. Tax Cases* (Chicago: Commerce Clearing House, 1913–) which covers federal court and landmark state court decisions, the *Tax Court Reporter* (Chicago: Commerce Clearing House, 1924–) and *Tax Court Memorandum Decisions* (Chicago: Commerce Clearing House, 1942–) which report on decisions made by the Tax Court and on memorandum decisions the Tax Court does not review due to similarity to a prior case. Each series has an index and is available in microform. The *Census of Business* actually began in 1929 as a complement to the federal population census and was taken also in 1933, 1935, 1939 (as part of the 1940 census), in 1948, 1954, and 1958; since 1958 it has been taken in five-year intervals. The *Census of Business* issues separate publications covering retail trade, wholesale trade, manufacturing, service industries, mineral industries, and construction industries. It provides retrospective and current industrial and sales statistics as well as noting trends in industrial development or decline. The *United States Industrial Outlook*, prepared since 1960 by the Department of Commerce, is category-oriented, using SIC numbers, and provides a yearly overview of domestic industries with statistics, trend synopses, and forecasts.

The *Internal Revenue Code*, first published in 1939 with major revisions in 1954, can be referenced through the *Internal Revenue Bulletin* (Washington, D.C.: Government Printing Office, 1922–) prepared by the Department of the Treasury. The *Bulletin*, which has appeared weekly with an annual cumulation since 1922, is the official publication of the IRS and announces rulings, procedures, decisions, Executive Orders, legislation, and other tax-related issues. The *Code* and *Bulletin* most likely will be found at a library which serves as a government depository.

LITERALLY SPEAKING

Reference sources for literary historians often include three major publications that are index and encyclopedia oriented. The *Essay and General Literature Index* (New York: H. W. Wilson Co., 1934) covers from 1900 and is now contained in nine volumes. It indexes essays and articles that have appeared in various anthologies and has author and subject indexes for easy access. *Author Biographies Master Index* (Detroit: Gale Research Co., 1978) is a two-volume work, with one supplement to date, which surveys author information from such standard reference books as *American Authors, 1600–1900* (New York: H. W. Wilson Co, 1938),

Contemporary Authors (Detroit: Gale Research Co., 1962–), and *Twentieth-Century Authors* (New York: H. W. Wilson Co., 1955). William Benet's *Reader's Encyclopedia* (New York: T. Y. Crowell, 1965) provides capsule entries covering authors, characters, and sites of literary history significance.

Other useful books more general in scope include the *Cambridge History of English Literature* (New York: Cambridge University Press, 1907–1933), a landmark fifteen-volume set edited by Sir Adolphus William Ward in 1932, which is a series of essays covering the major movements and people in English literature, and Robert Spiller et al.'s *Literary History of the United States* (New York: Macmillan, 1974). Edited by Spiller et al. to trace important trends in American literature, it also includes author bibliographies that serve as valuable compendiums of an author's work.

To research book reviews, the *Book Review Digest* (New York: H. W. Wilson Co., 1905–), now numbering fifty volumes, contains short synopses of book reviews found in nearly 100 periodicals, both literary and general in nature. There is a cumulated author/title index covering the years 1905 to 1974 (four volumes) as well as several subject/title indexes.

One of the most frequently used bibliographic references, *The Reader's Advisor* (New York: R. R. Bowker Co., 1921–), in three volumes, is promoted as "A Layman's Guide to Literature" and selects the "best" sources in American and British fiction, poetry, essays, reference, drama, bibliography, literary biography, and world literature (in English translation). Likewise, Altick and Wright's *Selective Bibliography for the Study of English and American Literature* (New York: Macmillan, 1971) is a concise text which surveys and simplifies literary bibliography.

Lastly, the *Oxford English Dictionary* (Oxford: Oxford University Press, 1933–), although considered a standard reference in many fields, appropriately deserves mention in any literary survey. It is the most authoritative work on the English language and provides, in twelve volumes and four supplements to date, the derivation, usage, and applications of all aspects of the language.

THE ARTS

The broad spectrum of the arts, covering in this essay the fine and performing arts, as well as architecture, antiques, and film, is a highly specialized area. Many of the references are oriented toward specific aspects of the several arts, for example ballads, ballet, windsor chairs, or Frank Lloyd Wright homes. There are, however, a number of more general sources which will aid in gaining access to the specifics. As in the other categories these include indexes, encyclopedias, and dictionaries.

There are three periodical indexes which are basic to research in the arts. The *Art Index* (New York: H. W. Wilson Co., 1924–) currently in thirty-one volumes, is an author-subject format that includes the fields of archeology, architecture, art, history, city planning, crafts, graphic art, industrial and interior design, landscape architecture, museology, photography, and film on a world-wide basis. *Art Index* currently indexes nearly 200 journals. The *Architectural Index* (Sausalito, Calif. and Boulder, Colo.: Architectural Index, 1951–) is comparatively new and now covers eleven major periodicals. Similarly, the *Music Index* (Detroit: Information Coordinators, Inc., 1950–) was initiated in 1949 and reviews approximately 300 serials for inclusion; it is international in its coverage.

Several specific sources to guide arts research include the *Benezit Dictionnaire Des Peintres, Sculpteurs, Dessinateurs et Graveurs* (Paris: Librarie Gründ, 1976) (Dictionary of Painters, Sculptors, Designers and Engravers). Although the ten-volume work is written in French, it is considered a standard source. It is arranged alphabetically by artist's name and is international in scope. The work dates to 1911, when it was initiated by Emmanuel Charles Benezit in Paris; it was revised and republished twice before the latest (1976) edition. The *Index to Artistic Biography* (Metuchen, N.J.: Scarecrow Press, Inc., 1973) by Patricia Pate Havlice is a three-part set (two 1973 volumes plus a 1981 supplement) that reviews sixty-four works in ten languages in search of artist's biographies. Such standard references as *Who's Who in American Art* (New York: R. R. Bowker Co., 1935–) are indexed in an alphabetical arrangement.

Two recent books are good sources for research on women and black artists. *Women Artists: An Historical, Contemporary and Feminist Bibliography* by Donna G. Bachmann and Sherry Piland (Metuchen, N. J., and London: Scarecrow Press, Inc., 1978) is a comprehensive reference which is divided into several sections. The sections list general works concerning women artists, works about individual artists beginning roughly with the fifteenth century, and publications on specific artistic categories such as painting, sculpture, or needlework. Lenwood G. Davis and Janet L. Sims have prepared *Black Artists in the United States: An Annotated Bibliography of Books, Articles, and Dissertations on Black Artists, 1779–1979* (Westport, Conn: Greenwood Press, 1979). This book successfully shows "that there is sufficient evidence to prove that Black artists have a long history of artistic contribution to American society." It too is divided into sections as indicated in the full title, and it has a section on black artworks in the National Archives and an extensive index.

The world of music also is represented by standard reference sources. One of the most important is the *New Grove Dictionary of Music and Musicians* (London: Macmillan Publishing, Ltd, 1980) edited by Stanley Sadie. It was first published by Sir George Grove in 1878 and has been revised and reprinted several times. The 1980 revision, in twenty volumes, greatly expanded its scope and added many more American artists. International in breadth, it is categorized by name and subject. *The Complete Encyclopedia of Popular Music and Jazz* (New Rochelle, N.Y.: Arlington House, 1974) is divided into biographies (mostly American) in volumes two and three; a year-by-year chronology of popular songs, musicals, recordings, etc. (volume one); and an index and awards listing (volume four).

Architectural researchers and historians may want to begin with Sir Banister Fletcher's *A History of Architecture* (New York: Charles Scribner, 1975), now in its eighteenth edition. It is the basic guide to architecture world-wide from Ancient Egypt to the twentieth century and includes a bibliographic section as well as an index. Standard works with current terminology detailing the architecture of this country include Marcus Whiffen's *American Architecture: 1607–1976* (Cambridge, Mass.: MIT Press, 1981) with Fred Koeper, which describes periods, trends, individual architects, and building types, and *American Architecture Since 1780: A Guide to the Styles* (Cambridge, Mass.: MIT Press, 1969) which is strictly a stylistic guide with style histories and individual illustrated examples. There are many other good illustrated field guides and surveys available, as well as several pocket-sized works. Two of the best of this latter type include John J.-G. Blumenson's *Identifying American Architecture: A Pictorial Guide to Styles and Terms, 1600–1945* (Nashville: American Association for State and Local History, 1981) and the John C. Popplier, S. Allen Chambers, Jr., and Nancy B. Schwartz, *What Style Is It?*, 2nd ed. (Washington, D.C.: Preservation Press, 1983). The most recent and one of the most comprehensive guides to American domestic architecture is Virginia and Lee McAlester's *A Field Guide to American Houses* (New York: Alfred A. Knopf, 1984). Not only does this book discuss landmark examples of residential styles, but it also provides photographs and explanations of the vernacular and folk types found throughout the country. It is a "field guide" in the true sense and, as the publisher claims, "enables you to identify, and place in their historic and architectural contexts, the houses you see in your neighborhood or in your travels . . . houses built for American families (rich, poor, and in-between), in city and countryside, from the seventeenth century to the present."

Like the other arts those pursuing research on antiques will find highly specialized offerings of printed and visual research material. For this reason, I suggest consulting *Antiques and Collectibles: A Bibliography of Works in English, 16th century to 1976* (Metuchen, N.J.: Scarecrow Press, Inc., 1978) by Linda Campbell Franklin. Broad in its coverage, this bibliography includes all ranges of antiques from, but not limited to, industrial, religious, domestic, and medical pieces. Several sources are provided for each category; additional access is provided via an author and subject index.

Perhaps the most respected specific work is the finely illustrated *Furniture Treasury* (New York: Macmillan, 1978) by Wallace Nutting. Produced in three volumes (in two books, however), Volumes one and two survey "All periods of American Furniture with Some Foreign Examples in America: also American Hardware and Household Utensils." First published by Nutting in 1928, these volumes are now in their fifteenth printing. Volume three of *Furniture Treasury* (New York, 1977) is a "Record of Designers, Details of Designs and Structure with Lists of

Clock Makers in America, and a Glossary of Furniture Terms . . . "; this volume originated in 1933 and is in its fourteenth separate printing. *American Furniture Craftsmen Working Prior to 1920: An Annotated Bibliography*, compiled by Charles J. Semowich (Westport, Conn.: and London: Greenwood Press, 1984) is a landmark compendium published as part of the "Art Reference Collection" series. It features extensive lists of references divided into individual craftsmen, groups of craftsmen, general works, and trade catalogs as well as periodicals and manuscript collections. The index offers three categorized divisions: a craftsman-biographical index, an author-title index, and a subject index.

The world of the "silver screen" and television is represented in the arts family as well. There are many guides to films, but one of the most useful is *The New York Times Films Reviews* (New York: Times Books, 1913–) which covers the years 1913–1980 in twelve volumes. The volumes are arranged chronologically and have indexes by show title and actor/actress; entries give dates, credits, and the specific reference to the paper in which the review appeared. Similarly, *The Complete Encyclopedia of Television Programs: 1947–1979* (South Brunswick, N.J.: A. S. Barnes, 1979) by Vincent Terrace is an all-encompassing two-volume work which is divided by program title and has a name index for cross-referencing.

HISTORY AND BIOGRAPHY

It may seem redundant to include this section in an essay which is designed to be used by people already in or interested in the discipline of history. There are, however, some basic sources which merit mention as important research tools. Also, history and biography are allied with genealogy and local history, and this section will serve as a natural prelude to the final section.

Historians are aware of the importance of using original source material in their research, but it often is difficult to ascertain the location of a certain resource. One important reference which helps to overcome this problem is the Encyclopedia Britannica's *Annals of America: Fourteen Ninety-Three to Nineteen Seventy-Three*, ed. Mortimer Adler (Chicago: Encyclopedian Britannica Educational Corp., 1976–). This twenty-three volume work defines the development of the United States from 1493 to 1973 through a chronological listing of events, laws, speeches, documents, reports, etc., and gives the original source of each entry. Included in the volumes are maps, tables, and illustrations that reinforce the text. A similar reference which also is arranged chronologically is *Documents of American History* (New York: Prentice-Hall, 1974) in two volumes, divided by the year 1898. This resource lists important documents relating to the origin and growth of the nation, beginning with "Privileges and Prerogatives Granted to Columbus" (1492) and ending with the landmark "Miller vs. California" (1973) obscenity case. Formerly edited by Henry Steele Commager, it is now in its ninth edition and is edited by A. Commager. It provides the full text of most documents. Scribner's *Dictionary of American History* (New York, 1976) can be useful for ready-reference as it is an alphabetical subject format in seven volumes. It has a separate index (volume seven) which is keyed to subjects, locations, and individual names. Its depth is broad, as coverage begins with American prehistory.

Military history is an aspect of historical research that offers the ability to use more readily available government source material. Virtually every major military confrontation was the subject of a government report, and many states have their own reports as well. The earlier conflicts, i.e., the Revolutionary War or War of 1812, tend to be abstracted into specific reports, like the *Index of Revolutionary War Pension Applications* (Washington, D.C.: Government Printing Office, 1966) (from the National Archives) or *Naval Records of the American Revolution: 1775–1788* (Washington, D.C.: Government Printing Office, 1906) (from the Library of Congress) or the *Roster of Ohio Soldiers in the War of 1812* (Columbus, Ohio: Adjutant General of Ohio, 1916) (from War Department records). Individual states often kept their own militia records prior to the large-scale organization of the military before the Civil War. Records for the Civil War and later wars are virtual compendiums of the entire conflict and include such titles as *The War of the Rebellion: A Compilation of the Official Records of the Union and Confederate Armies* (Washington, D.C.: Government Printing Office, 1880–1901) or the *Official Records of the Union and Confederate Navies of the War of the Rebellion* (Washington, D.C.: Government Printing Office, 1894–1922); both are multiple volume sets published by the U.S. War Department.

Confederate records are fewer in number as many official documents were burned during the war, but there is a "General Index" to *The War of the Rebellion* (Washington, D.C.: Government Printing Office, 1901) by subject and name, published by the War Department. Fredericks Dyer's *A Compendium of the War of the Rebellion* (Des Moines, Iowa: Dyer Publishing Co., 1908) is a massive 1,800-page work, privately published. It focuses on the Army and was compiled mostly from official federal and state (Adjutant General) records and registers. Divided into three sections—organization of military divisions, record of military actions, and regimental histories—it is a frequently used reference source with a subject and name index organized by state.

A plethora of regimental histories, spurred by the broad appeal of the Civil War and by the popularity of such groups as the GAR (Grand Army of the Republic), can be found in libraries throughout the country. Ohio, like many other states, has its own record of the war compiled by the Ohio Roster Commission into twelve volumes and entitled *Official Roster of the Soldiers of the State of Ohio in the War of the Rebellion: 1861–1865* (Cincinnati, Akron, Norwalk, Ohio: Ohio Roster Commission, 1866–1895). It has a separate microfilm name index. A useful guide to state publications about the war is the *Bibliography of State Participation in the Civil War: 1861–1866* (Washington, D.C.: Government Printing Office, 1913) which was published by the War Department and lists for each state the known published accounts, diaries, regimental histories, etc.

There are published rosters and/or historical overviews for the Spanish-American War and World Wars I and II, including Samuel Eliot Morison's *History of United States Naval Operations in World War II* (Boston, 1960) and the *United States Army in World War II* (Washington, D.C.: Government Printing Office, 1947–), both published in multivolume sets.

Individual veteran's records can be requested directly from the National Archives using a NATF Form 80. This form is used to order copies of pension applications, bounty-land warrants, and military service records for service prior to World War I. To obtain later service records, researchers can write to the National Personnel Records Center (Military Records) in St. Louis, Missouri. Several private societies, such as the National Society of the Daughters of the American Revolution (DAR), the National Society of the United States Daughters of 1812, or the Colonial Dames of America, publish their own material which can be helpful when researching early military service. The DAR's *Index of the Rolls of Honor (Ancestor's Index) in the Lineage Books of the National Society of the Daughters of the American Revolution, 1916 to 1940*, 4 vols. (Baltimore: Genealogy Publishers, 1980) for example can be used to trace an individual who served in the Revolutionary War and who is listed in one of their over 160 *Lineage Books* (Harrisburg, Pa., and Washington, D.C.: National Society of the Daughters of the American Revolution, 1895–1939). The several *DAR Patriot Index* (Washington, D.C., 1967–1980) volumes serve as regular updates to newly accepted and proven patriots. More information on the DAR *Lineage Books* will be given in the genealogical section as DAR material is often housed in the genealogy division of a library.

A huge selection of biographies is available in a wide range of formats. In fact, there is so much biographical material available that researchers are urged to consult the several indexes to biographies. The largest index in this field is Gale Research Co.'s *Biography and Genealogy Master Index* (Detroit: Gale Research Co., 1980) which in eight volumes provides over 3,200,000 names abstracted from more than 350 current and retrospective biographical dictionaries. The *Master Index* is alphabetical in plan and gives source citations only—not actual biographies. It covers virtually all the biographical dictionaries including the several dozen *Who's Who* and *Who Was Who* publications.

Research in American biography can be facilitated through the use of the *Dictionary of American Biography* (New York: Charles Scribner's Sons, 1928–). Originally published in twenty volumes by the American Council of Learned Societies between the years 1928 and 1936, there are now seven supplements covering the years 1935–1965. Actual biographies are offered alphabetically; entries are posthumous. The *National Cyclopedia of American Biography* (Clifton, N.J., and New York: Jacob T. White & Co., 1893–) also provides biographical sketches. It currently consists of seventy-six volumes.

Ethnic group research should be prefaced by perusal of the *Harvard Encyclopedia of American Ethnic Groups* (Cambridge, Mass.: Harvard University Press, 1980), a landmark work that is arranged like a dictionary, alphabetically by name of the group. It also includes essays on various aspects of ethnicity, as well as maps and tables. Other useful sources include, for example on American Indians, the Smithsonian Institution's two-part *Handbook of American Indians North of Mexico* (Washington, D.C.: Scholarly Press, Inc., 1907, 1910) (Bureau of American Ethnology, Bulletin 30) or the more recent Smithsonian publication, the *Handbook of North American Indians* (Washington, D.C., 1978–). This series is being published in separate volumes and to date features individual works on Indians of the Sub-arctic, California, the Southwest, and the Northwest. Biographical sketches of notable American blacks are available in Mary Spradling's *In Black and White* (Detroit: Gale Research Co., 1980), a two-volume set that lists many people not found in other sources.

If historical geography and travel research are necessary, the *Travelers Reading Guides: Bibliography of Background Books, Novels, Travel Literature and Articles* (Bayport, N.Y.: Freelance Pub., Inc., 1981) might be useful. Edited by Maggy Simony and published in three volumes, volume two covers North America and is arranged according to country and state or province. Historical atlases should not be overlooked when engaging in historical geographic studies. Such works as the *Atlas of American History* (New York: Charles Scribner's Sons, 1978) edited by Kenneth T. Jackson, and offering a variety of historical and socioeconomic maps from roughly 1492 to 1977, or Gary E. Moulton, ed. *Atlas of the Lewis and Clark Expedition* (Lincoln, Neb.: University of Nebraska Press, 1983) or *A Battlefield Atlas of the Civil War* (Annapolis, Md.: Nautical & Aviation Pub. Co. of America, 1983) by Craig L. Symonds are prime examples of the types of atlases that are available. Generally, the more specific atlases are the most useful. An enjoyable and often very helpful work on American travel is the "American Guide Series" produced as part of the Federal Writers Project of the Works Progress Administration in the 1930s and 1940s. There is a guide to each state, except Hawaii, which takes the user on a geographical, cultural, architectural, and historical tour of the United States. Several of these guides recently have been republished and are interesting barometers of both rural and urban change.

GENEALOGY AND LOCAL HISTORY

What the Bicentennial did for local history and historic preservation, the publication and television serialization of Alex Haley's novel *Roots* (Garden City, N.J.: Doubleday, 1976) did for genealogy and family history. The popularization of these areas of historical research tremendously increased the demands on local history and genealogy departments. Local history is a microcosm of the entire library on a provincial level. Virtually every category previously delineated in this essay as a separate subject area is represented in a good local history department.

In the case of the Toledo-Lucas County Public Library and other libraries as well, the local history and genealogy departments are housed together.

Local history and genealogy offer the researcher the opportunity to conduct primary level research. Manuscript collections and federal census returns are examples of available primary sources. Most local history and genealogy departments specialize in certain collection areas: labor history; the papers of a noted leader, scholar, or politician; historic photographs; or census returns for a specified area, for example. Some are noted for a single outstanding holding, others are renowned for their genealogical or manuscript collections. Some public libraries, in addition to government depositories, may serve as regional depositories, where government records, newspapers, and other local documents are collected, housed, and usually microfilmed. Regional depositories often produce their own finding aids or utilize previously issued guides such as the "Historic Records Surveys" conducted by the Works Progress Administration during the 1930s.

Due to the great interest in genealogical and ancestral research, prior knowledge of the many facets of such study can be invaluable. There are several introductory works which should serve as entrees to research, accuracy, and citation. These include *Genealogical Research: Methods and Sources* (Washington, D.C.: American Society of Genealogists, 1983) in two volumes and Noel C. Stevenson's *Genealogical Evidence: A Guide to the Standard of Proof* (Laguna Hills, Calif.: Aegean Park Press, 1979) which details the need for ways to provide documentation of genealogy research. One of the best guides that delineates the general framework of such research is Gilbert Harry Doane and James B. Bell's *Searching for Your Ancestors* (Minneapolis: University of Minnesota Press, 1980) published as a fifth edition. Two recent books serve as manuals for publishing ancestral documentation: Donald R. Barnes' *Write it Right: A Manual for Writing Family Histories and Genealogies* (Ocala, Fla.: Lyon Press, 1983) and *Cite Your Sources: A Manual for Documenting Family Histories and Genealogical Records* (New Orleans: Polyanthos, Inc., 1980), by Richard S. Lackey.

Genealogy has become more than just the casual study of one's family. Professional genealogists are hired on a world-wide basis to find answers to a variety of questions. In addition to the frequently asked family origin queries, genealogists have been asked to find heirs to wills, to prove that a known individual is indeed entitled to a certain trust, or to determine the extent of Indian ancestry to quality for educational benefits. Various types of claims can only be settled by documented ancestral relationships. Similarly, the Church of Jesus Christ of Latter-day Saints (Mormons) requires that family lineage be completed for religious purposes. Incidentally, the Mormons have perhaps the largest collection of genealogical data of any private organization, having microfilmed millions of birth, baptismal, marriage, and related records around the world. If there is a branch Mormon church in your area, and it has what is referred to as a "stake library," you may be able to do ancestral research without going to Salt Lake City.

Genealogists often are found in libraries where large local history and genealogical collections are held, as genealogy generally becomes an intensely local pursuit, once the location of a certain family is determined. As with other library departments, there are a few broad index-type sources which can be utilized to locate individuals and families. In addition to the earlier mentioned *Biography and Genealogy Master Index*, a landmark work is the double-series, multivolume *American Genealogical-Biographical Index* (Middletown, Conn: Godfrey Memorial Library, 1952–). The second series, which is being revised currently, is projected to provide references for over twelve million names. Hundreds of sources, including official Revolutionary War rosters and the entire 1790 census, have been indexed by individual names, many of which cannot be found in any other index. The *New York Times* has published an *Obituaries Index* (New York: N.Y. Times, 1970) to the *Times* covering the years 1858 to 1968, and there is a twenty-two volume *Personal Name Index to the New York Times Index* (Succasunna, N.J. and Verdi, Nev.: Roxbury Data Interface, 1976–) for 1851 to 1974, compiled by Byron and Valerie Falk, with one supplement, published in 1984, covering A–F surnames from 1975 to 1979.

On a local/regional level, many libraries have compiled their own name and obituary indexes, either in card file or book form, using local newspapers, county/city histories, and historical/genealogical periodicals as a base. Another local source, particularly in urban centers, is the city directory. Most cities have local directories which often date to the mid or late nineteenth century, although some of the oldest cities have directories dating to the late eighteenth and early nineteenth centuries. Directories serve as a local index to persons living in that city and can provide employment, filial, and local information; beware, however, of inaccurate spellings in the earlier directories.

One of the earliest genealogy periodical indexing projects was Donald Lines Jacobus's *Index to Genealogical Periodicals* (New Haven, Conn.: By the Author, 1932–1953) which was begun in 1932 as a name and place index to leading genealogical serials and covered the years 1858 to 1952. Jacobus was updated with a volume for the years 1953–1957 and followed in 1962 by the *Genealogical Periodical Annual Index* (Bladensburg and Bowie, Md.: Heritage Books, Inc., 1963–) which indexes nearly 160 English-language periodicals and has had several editors.

Most genealogical resources are however relatively specific in nature, such as the 135-volume *New England Historical and Genealogical Register* (Boston: New England Historic, Genealogical Society, 1847–) which is the oldest such ancestral publication or the *New York Genealogical and Biographical Record* (New York: New York Genealogical and Biographical Society, 1870–) which began in 1869; both have indexes and are published currently. There are hundreds of guides or keys to family research for specific areas such as *Genealogical Research in New England*

(Baltimore: Genealogical Publishing Co., 1984) which was edited by Ralph J. Crandall and details for New Hampshire, Vermont, Maine, Massachusetts, Connecticut, and Rhode Island ways in which to conduct ancestral research, or the *Guide to Genealogical and Historical Research in Pennsylvania* (Hollidaysburg, Pa.: Hoenstine Rental Library, 1978) by Floyd G. Hoenstine. Most states in fact have some finding aids which can be invaluable guides to conducting research in a particular state. Monthly or quarterly serials that provide articles about historical events, places, and people are published in many states and include periodicals such as the *New York Historical Society Quarterly* (New York: New York Historical Society, 1917–), the *Register of the Kentucky Historical Society* (Frankfort, Ky., 1903–), or the *Wisconsin Magazine of History* (Madison, Wis.: State Historical Society of Wisconsin, 1917–).

There are also dozens of county histories for each state, most published privately, that detail the complete history of a county from its creation to the time of the book's publication. The largest of these were published near the 1900s and often are entitled "Portrait and Biographical Record of . . . County." County atlases, which feature maps showing land ownership as well as village plats, line drawings, and often biographies, are also excellent resources.

Many ancestral societies are found throughout the nation, some as part of a local historical society and others as independent groups; most regularly publish monographs or magazines. Examples of this type of publication include the *National Genealogical Society Quarterly* (Washington, D.C.: National Genealogical Society, 1912–), the *Connecticut Nutmegger* (Glastonbury, Conn., 1968–) of the Connecticut Society of Genealogists, Inc., *Michigana* (Grand Rapids, Mich. 1954–) by the Western Michigan Genealogical Society or, one of the best known, the *Mayflower Descendant* (Boston, 1899–1937) begun by the Massachusetts Society of Mayflower Descendants.

In addition, private individuals are publishing personal family histories in great numbers. Many of these are amateur in nature; others are highly professional. Some printing houses even specialize in publishing family histories or republishing county histories and atlases. Genealogical groups throughout the country are indexing courthouse records, cemetery records, vital statistics, etc., and making them available in printed form. These indexes can be a boon to both the amateur and professional researcher who are working at a local, regional, or state level.

Perhaps the best known private ancestral society is the Daughters of the American Revolution, mentioned previously in the "History and Biography" section. The DAR's publications can be extremely useful if a Revolutionary War patriot is among a family's ancestors. If, using their *Patriot Index* or "Rolls of Honor" books, a DAR-accepted patriot can be located, material relating to that person can be obtained through the *Lineage Book* which gives short biographical and family details under the number and name of the accepted "daughter." Another such index is the *Mayflower Ancestral Index* (Plymouth, Mass., 1981) published by the

Genealogical Society of Mayflower Descendants. It offers over 45,000 Mayflower Lineage papers categorized by line of descent number and is arranged alphabetically.

Church registers can be useful and many have been indexed and published, some as part of the Works Progress Administration's Historic Records Survey. A helpful guide to church records is E. Kay Kirkham's *A Survey of American Church Records* (Logan, Utah: Everton Publishers, Inc., 1978) which gives bibliographic and denominational information by state, discussing both major and minor groups.

Genealogical research via government sources often leads to primary references such as federal census or passenger arrival records. Libraries specializing in genealogy are likely to have portions of the federal census, which began in 1790 and has been taken every ten years since. Microfilm reels of the 1790 to 1910 censuses are available either at a library, through interlibrary loan, or through the private carrier hired by the National Archives to rent the microfilm to participating institutions. Most libraries only purchase census films for their region or state due to the costs involved with the purchase of the numerous reels for each state and year. There are a few libraries, such as the Allen County Public Library in Fort Wayne, Indiana, which do carry the entire census for the nation. Before the 1880 census, printed indexes that list heads-of-households and persons of another surname in the same house are available for most states. Starting with the 1880 census and for the 1900 and 1910 censuses, however, the government produced a phonetic index, called Soundex or Miracode, which phonetically groups similar heads-of-household surnames together and gives exact census sheet location. The Soundex and/or Miracode indexes are available on microfilm for many states. It should be noted here that most of the 1890 census was lost in a fire; thus, only a few returns are available.

Passenger arrival records are another type of primary source material that can be utilized. A federal form, NATF Form 81, is available to request passenger arrival information from the National Archives for most East and Gulf Coast ports for the early nineteenth century onward. Pacific Coast records, if extant, are not held by the National Archives, and no records for nineteenth-century Canadian or Mexican immigration were kept. Generally, the more specific the request for National Archives records, the more likely information will be found; this is particularly pertinent in the case of the port of New York, as no overall index exists for the years 1847–1896. Worth consulting before beginning arrival research is P. William Filby's *Passenger and Immigration Lists Bibliography: 1538–1900* (Detroit: Gale Research Co., 1981) which serves as an annotated guide to over 1,000 published U.S. and Canadian arrival lists. Among the sources cited is Filby and Mary Meyer's *Passenger and Immigration Lists Index* (Detroit: Gale Research Co., 1980–), a four-volume, multiple supplement set that attempts "to merge into one, all known, published, passenger lists," and which contains over 500,000 names.

Naturalization or citizenship papers which can provide pertinent origin information may be available from the federal, state, or municipal court that issued the naturalization. The National Archives, however, does have copies of citizenship records of Massachusetts, New Hampshire, Rhode Island, and Maine for the years 1789 to 1906. A few compendiums, such as Filby's *Philadelphia Naturalization Records* (Detroit: Gale Research Co., 1982), covering 1789 to 1880, are available, but others are local in nature and not widely published.

If research leads to the National Archives, peruse the *Guide to Genealogical Research in the National Archives* (Washington, D.C.: Government Printing Office, 1982) published by the National Archives. It is an excellent guide to the genealogical holdings of the government and explains the availability of population/immigration, military, ethnic group, land, court, and map records in the archives. As an allied service, the National Archives has published several "catalogs" of its microfilm publications, including *Immigrant and Passenger Arrivals* (Washington, D.C.: Government Printing Office, 1983), *Genealogical and Biographical Research* (Washington, D.C.: Government Printing Office, 1983), *Black Studies* (Washington, D.C.: Government Printing Office, 1984), and *American Indians* (Washington, D.C.: Government Printing Office, 1984).

Ethnic genealogy traditionally has been difficult to research, but in recent years there has been great interest shown in ethnic ancestry, notably among America's black and Indian populations. Works such as Charles L. Blockson's *Black Genealogy* (Englewood Cliffs, N.J.: Prentice-Hall, 1977) and *Black Genesis* (Detroit: Gale Research Co., 1978) by James Rose and Alice Eicholz discuss migratory patterns, slavery, and an overview of American black history, as well as providing directories of sources for black ancestral research in the United States, Canada, the West Indies, and Africa. An important resource for American Indian research is E. Kay Kirkham's *Our Native Americans and Their Records of Genealogical Value* (Logan, Utah: Everton Publishers, Inc.) which is in two volumes published in 1980 and 1984. The recently published *Ethnic Genealogy: A Research Guide* (Westport, Conn.: Greenwood Press, 1983), edited by Jessie C. Smith, draws together sources for black, Asian-American, Hispanic-American, and American Indian genealogical study.

Postlude

This essay has presented a sampling of the resources available in many libraries throughout the nation. There are literally thousands of other sources that can be utilized as well. Libraries are a very foundation of research and scholarship, a foundation that is broadening its scope every day. Active use of libraries will broaden even further that scope, so use the library; it is there just waiting to be utilized.

APPENDIX B

DIRECTORY OF RESOURCES AND ORGANIZATIONS

The following list includes some of the major resources and organizations available to those interested in further exploring various aspects of public history. It is not intended to be a definitive list, and interested individuals should contact the organizations below for further information on their programs and publications.

General Information:

American Association for State and Local History
172 Second Avenue, North—Suite 102
Nashville, Tennessee 37201
(615) 383-5991
Publishes *History News* bimonthly magazine, *History News Dispatch* (which includes employment information), books, technical leaflets, and a directory of historical societies and agencies; produces independent-study courses, audio-visual instructional materials, seminars and workshops, and an annual meeting; offers awards, an internship, small research grants, a consultant service for museums, a technical information subscription program, and the National Information Center for Local Government Records (NICLOG).

American Historical Association
400 A Street, S.E.
Washington, D.C. 20003
(202) 544-2422
Publishes *American Historical Review* quarterly journal and *Perspectives* newsletter, which includes employment information; sponsors annual conference; placement service at annual conference.

National Center for the Study of History, Inc.
Drawer 730
Germantown, Maryland 20874
Publishes chart entitled "Careers for Graduates in History" that is cosponsored by American Association for State and Local History, American Historical Association, Association of American Colleges, National Coordinating Committee for the Promotion of History, National Council for Preservation Education, National Council on Public History, North Carolina Institute of Applied History, Oral History Association, Organization of American Historians, Pennsylvania Historical and Museum Commission, Phi Alpha Theta, and the Society for History in the Federal Government.

National Coordinating Committee for the Promotion of History
400 A Street, S.E.
Washington, D.C. 20003
(202) 544-2422
Coordinates state committees for the promotion of history; lobbies for
issues of importance to historians in Congress; acts as clearinghouse
for those interested in promoting all aspects of history.

National Council on Public History
Department of History
West Virginia University
Morgantown, West Virginia 26506
(304) 293-2421
Publishes *The Public Historian* quarterly journal, quarterly *Newsletter*;
published *The Craft of Public History* bibliography; maintains list of
schools with public history programs; sponsors annual conference;
distributes "History Goes Public" slide-tape show; maintains syllabus
exchange for public history courses.

Organization of American Historians
112 North Bryan Street
Bloomington, Indiana 47401
(812) 335-7311
Publishes quarterly *Journal of American History* and quarterly *OAH
Newsletter*; sponsors annual conference; publishes series of booklets on
aspects of public history; placement service at annual meeting.

Phi Alpha Theta
2333 Liberty Street
Allentown, Pennsylvania 18104
(215) 433-4140
History honorary, with membership open to undergraduate and
graduate students; publishes *The Historian*; sponsors biannual conference.

Society for the History of Technology
Smithsonian Institution
National Museum of American History—Room 5707
Washington, D.C. 20560
(202) 357-1963
Publishes *Technology and Culture* quarterly journal, which includes
frequent museum reviews; has Technology Museums Special Interest
Group that publishes *Artifactory* newsletter on museum exhibits re-
lated to the history of technology.

Archival Management:

American Association for State and Local History
(see above)
Publishes on archival management and operates National Information Center for Local Government Records (NICLOG), a promotional program to work with several archival and records-management associations to promote better care of local government records.

Association of Record Managers and Administrators, Inc. (ARMA)
4200 Somerset Drive—Suite 215
Prairie Village, Kansas 66208
(913) 341-3808
National professional society for records managers; sponsors national and regional conferences and seminars on various aspects of records management; publishes newsletter and the quarterly journal *Records Management Quarterly*. While the strong focus of its publications centers on the science of managing records and information, the journal carries articles on a regular basis that have a direct relationship to archival holdings.

Library of Congress Manuscripts Division
Washington, D.C. 20540
(202) 287-5000
Major repository for manuscripts collections.

National Association of State Archives and Records Administrators
Executive Secretariat
New York State Archives
Room 10A75, Cultural Education Center
Albany, New York 12230
(518) 473-8037
Coordinates work of state archivists and records administrators; primarily concerned with strengthening management of state government records, but also interested in improving local government records programs; publishes *Clearinghouse: News and Reports on Government Records* quarterly newsletter; published *State Archives and Records Management Terminology, Measurement, and Reporting Standards*; sponsors annual meeting.

Society of American Archivists
600 South Federal Street—Suite 504
Chicago, Illinois 60605
(312) 922-0140
Publishes *American Archivist*, *SAA Newsletter*, and employment bulletin; publishes in area of archival management; sponsors annual conference and workshops; has placement service.

Contact SAA or archivists at major repositories in your area for information on regional, state, or local archival organizations.

National Archives and Records Administration
Eighth and Pennsylvania Avenue, N.W.
Washington, D.C. 20408
(202) 523-3218
Major national archives; sponsors training programs and publications program.

Federal Archives and Records Centers are located in Waltham, Massachusetts; Bayonne, New Jersey; Philadelphia, Pennsylvania; East Point, Georgia; Chicago, Illinois; Kansas City, Missouri; Fort Worth, Texas; Denver, Colorado; Languna Niguel, California; San Bruno, California; Seattle, Washington; and Suitland, Maryland. Contact the National Archives or the closest records center for further information.

Office of Presidential Libraries
Washington, D.C. 20408
(202) 523-3212
Contact office for information on the libraries and archival holdings for presidents Herbert Hoover, Franklin D. Roosevelt, Harry S. Truman, Dwight D. Eisenhower, John F. Kennedy, Lyndon B. Johnson, Richard Nixon, Gerald Ford, and James Carter. The presidential library for Rutherford B. Hayes is maintained by a private foundation in Fremont, Ohio. Each of these libraries preserves the papers of the president and key members of his administration; museums accompany the established libraries (for all but Nixon and Carter).

Contact the SAA, college history departments, or the state historical society for information on other archival repositories in the area. These could include the state archives, city or county archives, regional collections at museums and universities, and regional repositories for the state archives. The SAA can also provide information on specialized repositories, such as those for women's history or labor history.

Oral History:

American Association for State and Local History
(see above)
Leading publisher of oral history "how-to-do-it" material

Oral History Association
P.O. Box 13734 NTSU Station
Denton, Texas 76203
(817) 387-1021
Publishes annual *Oral History Review* and quarterly *Oral History Asso-*

ciation Newsletter, in addition to *Evaluation Guidelines*, directories, bibliographies, and reports of earlier meetings; sponsors annual national workshop and colloquium.

Contact OHA for information on state or regional oral history organizations.

Editing:

Association for Documentary Editing
(No permanent address yet; contact through National Historical Publications and Records Commission)
　　Publishes journal/newsletter entitled *Documentary Editing*; sponsors annual conference; maintains placement service.

Conference of Historical Journals
c/o Raymond Grew
Department of History
The University of Michigan
Ann Arbor, Michigan 48109
　　For editors of historical journals to discuss common concerns.

National Historical Publications and Records Commission
National Archives Building
Washington, D.C. 20408
　　(202) 523-5384
　　Major federal agency funding documentary editing projects; also gives grants to state and local governments, historical societies, archives, libraries, and associations for the preservation, arrangement, and description of historical records, and for a broad range of archival training and development programs; sponsors publications related to archives and historical editing.

Librarianship:

American Library Association
50 East Huron Street
Chicago, Illinois 60611
　　(312) 944-6780
　　Publishes monthly *American Libraries* journal and specialized newsletters for various aspects of library work; sponsors annual conference that includes job placement service; sponsors midwinter conference.

Contact your local library for information on state library association, which may sponsor conferences and publications.

Library of Congress
Washington, D.C. 20540
   (202) 287-5000
   Major national library; has publications program.

Office of Presidential Libraries
(see above)

Historic Preservation:

Advisory Council on Historic Preservation
1100 Pennsylvania Avenue, N.W.
Washington, D.C. 20004
   (202) 254-3967
   Major federal agency to review procedures of federally funded,
   licensed, or assisted projects in historic preservation.

American Association for State and Local History
(see above)
   Educational programs include a twenty-kit series of historic house
   conservation audio-visual programs plus a seminar series on which
   AASLH is collaborating with the National Trust for Historic Preservation (see address below).

American Institute of Architects
1735 New York Avenue, N.W.
Washington, D.C. 20006
   (202) 626-7300
   Publishes *ARCHITECTURE: The AIA Journal*; maintains library and
   archives.

Association for Preservation Technology
P.O. Box 2487, Station D
Ottawa, Ontario KIP 5W6, Canada
   (613) 238-1972
   Publishes *APT Bulletin* journal and *Communique* newsletter; holds
   annual conference.

Historic American Buildings Survey
U.S. Department of the Interior
Washington, D.C. 20013-7127
   (202) 343-9606
   Sponsors HABS recording projects for historic buildings; results of
   surveys filed at Library of Congress.

Historic American Engineering Record
U.S. Department of the Interior
Washington, D.C. 20013-7127

(202) 343-3171
Sponsors HAER recording projects for structures related to engineer-
ing and transportation history; results of surveys filed at Library of
Congress.

National Conference of State Historic Preservation Officers
Hall of the States—Suite 332
440 North Capitol Street, N.W.
Washington, D.C. 20001
    (202) 624-5465
    National coordinating group for State Historic Preservation Officers.

National Council for Preservation Education
P.O. Box 23
Middle Tennessee State University
Murfreesboro, Tennessee 37132
    (615) 898-2544
    Sponsors meetings for those interested in preservation education;
    meets annually with National Trust for Historic Preservation; pub-
    lishes directory of preservation education programs.

National Register of Historic Places
Interagency Resources Division
National Park Service
U.S. Department of the Interior
Washington, D.C. 20240
    (202) 343-9536
    Maintains National Register of Historic Places and advises on techni-
    cal aspects of historic preservation; publishes *Preservation Briefs* series;
    Department of the Interior also publishes *CRM Bulletin* on cultural
    resources management issues.

National Trust for Historic Preservation
1785 Massachusetts Avenue, N.W.
Washington, D.C. 20036
    (202) 673-4000
    Publishes *Historic Preservation* bimonthly magazine and monthly *Pres-
    ervation News*, in addition to books on preservation; sponsors annual
    conference; sponsors National Main Street Center focusing on down-
    town revitalization; advises on all aspects of historic preservation;
    maintains historic properties around country. Contact the National
    Trust for information on regional offices in Philadelphia, Pennsylva-
    nia; Chicago, Illinois; Boston, Massachusetts; Charleston, South Caro-
    lina; Denver, Colorado; Fort Worth, Texas; and San Francisco,
    California.

Preservation Action
1700 Connecticut Avenue, N.W.—Suite 400
Washington, D.C. 20009
(202) 659-0915
Major lobbying group for historic preservation; publishes *Alert* newsletter; holds annual meeting; also meets in conjunction with National
Trust for Historic Preservation annual meeting.

Society of Architectural Historians
1700 Walnut Street—Suite 716
Philadelphia, Pennsylvania 19103
(215) 735-0224
Publishes quarterly *Journal of the Society of Architectural Historians* and
bimonthly *Newsletter*; publishes directory of schools offering architectural history programs; sponsors annual conference and tours.

State Historic Preservation Offices (SHPO)
Required by law in each state; handle federal survey and planning
funds and advise on all aspects of historic preservation, particularly
the federal programs; are involved in all issues requiring review of
federally funded, licensed, or assisted projects; handle part of review
process for investment tax credits. Contact National Trust for Historic Preservation, governor's office, state history division, or state
historical society for information on your state.

State-wide Nonprofit Historic Preservation Organizations
Located in many states; nonprofit organizations to promote preservation education, conduct surveys, publish on preservation issues, etc.
Contact your SHPO for information on the organization in your state.
The state-wide organization or SHPO should also be able to tell you
about any municipal or county-level nonprofit preservation organizations.

City or County Landmarks or Historic District Commissions
Responsible for designating and controlling local landmarks and
historic districts. Municipal or county officials should be able to help
you identify these groups in your community.

Note: See Maddex, Diane, ed. *The Brown Book: A Directory of Preservation
Information* (Washington, D.C.: The Preservation Press, 1983) for further information on preservation resources and organizations around
the country. Maddex has also edited *All About Buildings: The Whole
Preservation Catalog* (Washington, D.C.: The Preservation Press, 1985)
which is a rich compendium of preservation information.

Archeology:

American Anthropological Association
1703 New Hampshire Avenue, N.W.
Washington, D.C. 20009
  (202) 232-8800
  Major national organization for those in anthropology, including archeology; publishes *American Anthropologist* quarterly journal and *Anthropology Newsletter*; has placement service at annual meeting; major source of employment information.

Society for American Archaeology
1511 K Street, N.W.—Suite 716
Washington, D.C. 20005
  (202) 232-8800
  Major national organization for those interested in prehistoric archeology; publishes *American Antiquity* quarterly journal and *Bulletin* newsletter, which includes employment information; publishes SAA *Papers* and *Memoirs* series; sponsors annual meeting, which includes placement service.

Society for Historical Archaeology
P.O. Box 241
Glassboro, New Jersey 08028
  Publishes semiannual *Historical Archaeology* journal and quarterly *Newsletter*; sponsors annual meeting; placement service at annual meeting.

Society for Industrial Archaeology
Smithsonian Institution
National Museum of American History
Room 5020
Washington, D.C. 20560
  (202) 357-2058
  Publishes *IA, the Journal of the Society for Industrial Archaeology*, newsletter; sponsors annual conference, field trips.

Society of Professional Archeologists
The Museum
Michigan State University
East Lansing, Michigan 48824
  (517) 355-3485
  Publishes *SOPA News* newsletter and *Directory of Certified Professional Archeologists*; annual meeting held in conjunction with Society of American Archaeology meetings; purpose is to ensure that archeological work is done by qualified people, so membership is open only to certified archeologists, although one can be certified without being a member of SOPA.

Contact SHPO office, SAA, or local college or university department of anthropology for information on local and state archeology organizations.

Historic Site Interpretation:

Association for Living Historical Farms and Agricultural Museums
Smithsonian Institution
National Museum of American History
Room 5035
Washington, D.C. 20560
(202) 357-2095
Major international organization for those working with living historical farms, agricultural museums, and outdoor history and folklike museums; publishes *Bulletin* (including employment notices), *Proceedings* of annual meeting, Replica Source List; sponsors annual meeting; information available on regional organizations in United States and Canada.

American Association for State and Local History
(see above)

State Historical Societies
Programs vary by state, but many state historical societies administer historic sites, operate museums, provide consultant services for local groups, and publish a journal and newsletter. These are usually located in the state capital and may be designated as a state history commission or archives and history commission. For example, the Ohio Historical Society receives state funding and serves as the state archives, while it is run as a nonprofit organization with membership services. In Pennsylvania, the Historical and Museum Commission serves as the official state history agency while the Historical Society of Pennsylvania operates its own private facilities in Philadelphia. In West Virginia, the Department of Culture and History operates the state museum and archives, while the West Virginia Historical Society is a small nonprofit organization without permanent facilities.

Museums:

American Association for State and Local History
(see above)

American Association of Museums
1055 Thomas Jefferson Street, N.W.—Suite 428
Washington, D.C. 20007
(202) 338-5300
Publishes *Museum News* journal, *Aviso* newsletter (including employment information), and other publications; distributes directory of

museums studies programs in the United States and abroad that is published by the Smithsonian Institution; sponsors annual conference. Contact AAM for addresses for the six regional AAM conferences: Northeast, New England, Southeast, Midwest, Mountain-Plains, and Western.

Institute of Museum Services
1100 Pennsylvania Avenue, N.W.
Room 510
Washington, D.C. 20506
(202) 786-0539
Independent government agency that provides funding for museum services; publishes guide to museum education programs.

National Institute for the Conservation of Cultural Property
c/o Arts & Industries Building
Room 2225
Smithsonian Institution
Washington, D.C. 20560
(202) 357-2295
Serves as national forum for conservation in United States and clearinghouse for information; voting membership is by institution; has published series of titles on conservation issues, including 1982 pamphlet on *Careers in Conservation of Cultural Property.*

Smithsonian Institution
Washington, D.C. 20560
(202) 357-1300
Nation's museum complex, including the National Museum of American History, National Portrait Gallery, Air and Space Museum, Museum of Natural History, Hirschorn Sculpture Gallery, etc.; has Smithsonian Associates Program; sponsors publications.

State Historical Societies
Major state historical societies or state history commissions have a state museum, usually located in the capital.

Contact AAM or the state museum for information on state and local museum associations.

Public Projects:

National Endowment for the Arts
1100 Pennsylvania Avenue, N.W.
Washington, D.C. 20506
(202) 682-5400
Federal funding agency to support the arts, including museum exhibits.

National Endowment for the Humanities
1100 Pennsylvania Avenue, N.W.
Washington, D.C. 20506
(202) 786-0438
Federal funding agency to support the humanities.

Contact your state humanities council or foundation for information on funding projects aimed at the general public. State arts councils may be able to provide additional support. Your state historical society or state museum can probably put you in touch with these organizations. The National Endowment for the Arts and National Endowment for the Humanities can provide information on other sources of funding.

Historical Societies and Other Learned Societies:

American Association for State and Local History
(see above)

State Historical Societies
(see above)

Government:

American Planning Association
1313 East Sixtieth Street
Chicago, Illinois 60637
(312) 955-9100
Membership open to anyone interested in planning; publishes monthly *Planning* newsletter and quarterly *Journal*; maintains mail order bookstore; American Institute of Certified Planners, professional institute of APA, provides only national certification of planners and sponsors Planners Training Service workshops, seminars, conferences; *JobMart* and Planners Referral Service provide employment information; Planning Advisory Service provides *PAS Reports* on matters of current interest; are divisions of APA dealing with various aspects of planning that have own programs and publications; also chapter membership available.

The International City Management Association
1120 G Street, N.W.
Washington, D.C. 20005
(202) 626-4600
Provides ICMA Network to share information among city managers; publishes *ICMA Newsletter* and monthly *Public Management* magazine, as well as training books and directories of members and recognized local governments; sponsors annual conference, seminars, and training programs.

National Conference of State Historic Preservation Officers
(see above)

National League of Cities
1301 Pennsylvania Avenue, N.W.
Washington, D.C. 20004
  (202) 626-3000
  Publishes *Nation's Cities Weekly*, briefing papers, handbooks, and other
  items of interest to those involved in city government; sponsors
  annual Congress of Cities convention to discuss urban issues; sponsors annual Congressional-City Conference to focus on legislative
  issues and federal budget; services to member cities also include
  policy analysis and development, legal representation, Municipal
  Reference Service, training and technical assistance programs.

Society for History in the Federal Government
Box 14139, Ben Franklin Station
Washington, D.C. 20044
  Publishes *Directory of Federal Historical Programs and Activities* with
  AHA and National Coordinating Committee for the Promotion of
  History and *The Federalist* newsletter; sponsors annual meeting and
  other conferences; serves as network to link historians in federal
  government around the country; very interested in the documentary
  heritage of the United States and working with scholars, National
  Archives, and federal agencies to protect this heritage.

Consult the *Directory of Federal Historical Programs and Activities* for
information on history programs in various cabinet agencies such as
Agriculture, Defense, Energy, Labor, and State, as well as further
information on programs in the National Archives, Smithsonian Institution, National Park Service, etc. For example, the Army, Air Force,
Navy, and Marines all have their own history programs that may include
providing in-house research, writing institutional histories, and managing museums. The Department of State publishes the *Foreign Relations*
series.

Public Works:

Public Works Historical Society
1313 East Sixtieth Street
Chicago, Illinois 60637
  (312) 667-2200
  Publishes quarterly *Public Works Historical Society Newsletter, A History of
  Public Works in the U.S., 1776–1976, Public Works History in the United
  States: A Guide to the Literature*, and oral histories; works closely with
  American Public Works Association.

National Park Service:

U.S. Department of the Interior
National Park Service
Washington, D.C. 20240
   (202) 343-7220
   Contact NPS for information on its regional offices in Anchorage,
   Alaska; Philadelphia, Pennsylvania; Omaha, Nebraska; Washington,
   D.C.; Boston, Massachusetts; Seattle, Washington; Denver, Colorado;
   Dunwoody, Georgia; Santa Fe, New Mexico; and San Francisco,
   California.

Chief Historian
National Park Service
Division of History
Washington, D.C. 20240
   (202) 343-8163

Harpers Ferry Center
National Park Service
Harpers Ferry, West Virginia 25425
   (304) 535-6371
   Interpretive design center, conservation center, publications center
   for National Park Service.

Denver Service Center
National Park Service
755 Parfet Street
Denver, Colorado 80225
   (303) 234-4504
   Center for environmental review studies, historical research for NPS.

Public Policy:

There are no specialized groups focused specifically on history and
public policy concerns.

Business:

Business Archives Section
Society of American Archivists
c/o Edward Rider, Chairperson
Proctor and Gamble Company
Box 599
Cincinnati, Ohio 45201
   A committee of the SAA; group formally meets at the annual
   convention of the society; subcommittees undertake research projects
   in areas of interest to the group and produce reports relating to
   various aspects of business archives operations; publishes semiannual
   newsletter.

Morison, Samuel Eliot, 297
Moses, Nancy, 266
Mosher, Frederick C., 343
Moss-Bennett Bill. *See* Historical
    and Archeological Data
    Preservation Act
Mount Vernon Ladies
    Association, 120, 122
museums: career opportunities
    in, 246-48; corporate, 428;
    federal, 218-19;
    interdisciplinary nature of
    work in, 227-28; local
    historical, 241-50; open
    air, in Britain, 177;
    outdoor, 229-39; state,
    329-30. *See also*
    Smithsonian Institution
Museum Stores Association, 259
Mystic Seaport Museum, 121, 235

Napier, 299
National Aeronautics and Space
    Administration, 303
National Archives and Records
    Administration, 38, 39,
    483
National Archives and Records
    Service, 71, 115, 296
National Association of State
    Archives and Records
    Administrators, 259, 482.
    See also archives; records
    management
National Center for the Study of
    History, 480
National Conference of State
    Historic Preservation
    Officers, 486, 492
National Coordinating
    Committee for the
    Promotion of History
    (NCC), 16, 481
National Council for Preservation
    Education, 259, 486
National Council on Public
    History (NCPH), 16, 258,
    259, 481

National Endowment for the Arts
    (NEA), 490
National Endowment for the
    Humanities (NEH), 266,
    267, 268, 273, 491
National Environmental Policy
    Act (NEPA), 139-40, 147
National Forest Management Act
    (NFMA), 148
National Historical Publications
    and Records Commission
    (NHPRC), 27, 72, 79, 92,
    303, 484. *See also* editing
National Historic Landmarks
    Program, 138-39. *See also*
    Historic Sites Act of 1935
National Historic Preservation
    Act of 1966, 122, 131, 132,
    133-35, 139, 140, 147, 148,
    178, 364, 387. *See also*
    cultural resources
    management; historic
    preservation; National
    Historic Preservation Act
    of 1966 as amended;
    National Park Service
National Historic Preservation
    Act of 1966 as amended,
    137, 147, 178, 381. *See also*
    cultural resources
    management; historic
    preservation; National
    Historic Preservation Act
    of 1966
National Institute for the
    Conservation of Cultural
    Property, 490
National League of Cities, 492
National Museum of American
    History. *See* Smithsonian
    Institution
National Park Service (NPS), 304,
    358-74, 375-99, 493;
    administrative histories,
    370, 385; Branch of
    Historic Sites and
    Buildings, 360; creation of,
    133, 359, 375-76; cultural

DATE			

© THE BAKER & TAYLOR CO.